Dictionary of
Insurance Terms

Dictionary of Insurance Terms

Fifth Edition

Harvey W. Rubin, Ph.D., CLU, CPCU
Kilpatrick Life Insurance Company
Endowed Chair
Professor of Finance
Louisiana State University–Shreveport
Shreveport, Louisiana

BARRON'S

Library of Congress Control No. 2008925400

ISBN-13: 978-0-7641-3884-3
ISBN-10: 0-7641-3884-7

PRINTED IN CHINA

9 8 7 6 5 4 3 2 1

CONTENTS

PREFACE

Insurance is a financial instrument—nothing more, nothing less—that plays a critical role in both personal and business financial planning.

On the personal level, the money an individual spends for insurance over a lifetime surpasses all other types of expenditures—including the purchase of a home. Any doubt concerning this statement can be dispelled by adding up the premium payments made yearly for life insurance, health insurance, pension plan, social security, individual retirement account or Keogh Plan, automobile insurance, homeowners or tenants insurance, professional liability insurance, and umbrella liability insurance. Yet, the individual makes these expenditures usually without adequate knowledge of the insurance product purchased.

Essentially the same situation exists in the business world. Contributions paid into various insurance coverages in most instances exceed other business operating expenses. Employee benefit plan contributions alone have been estimated to range between 30–45 cents for each dollar of salary paid to an employee. When added to the cost of other business related insurance expenditures such as workers compensation, buy-sell insurance funded agreements, key person insurance, business property coverage, business liability insurance, and other business specialty insurances coverages, the total cost can be overwhelming. And, astonishingly, the business insurance purchase decision is also frequently made without sufficient basic knowledge of the various insurance products available.

Thus, one function of Barron's *Dictionary of Insurance Terms* is to serve as a reference source for individuals making personal and business insurance planning decisions. The Dictionary provides concise definitions and examples of those terms most likely to confront the insurance consumer on all levels. The insurance field is rapidly changing. More new insurance products have reached the marketplace in the last few years than in all previous years combined. The Dictionary contains definitions and illustrative examples of these "state of the art" offerings as well as of the traditional products. Cross references allow the reader to research variations of the terms to be defined and other relevant definitions.

Another reason for the existence of Barron's *Dictionary of Insurance Terms* is to provide a reference source for practitioners who require succinct, technically accurate answers to insurance and risk management terminology questions. Professionals in the field will find the Dictionary to be a readily accessible reference source for virtually all terms that are used in the everyday conduct of business. The spectrum of insurance activities that is covered ranges from the home office underwriting of the risk to the actual marketing and distribution of the insurance product to protect the risk.

The insurance agent may even find the Dictionary to be useful in marketing and servicing insurance products. Many clients have numerous questions concerning the characteristics of the various insurance products on the market, both new and traditional. The Dictionary can be used as a supplement to the sales literature to answer these questions as well as inquiries about servicing. Fast, accurate responses to these questions can sometimes mean the difference between closing and not closing a sale.

ACKNOWLEDGMENTS

The author would like to acknowledge the many contributions made by others. Barron's editor, Darrell Buono, has been invaluable in bringing the manuscript to its final form. The author's wife, Cheryl, has made the presentation of the manuscript possible through her commitment to typing and correcting the author's many errors along the way. Finally, the author wishes to thank his ever-expanding family for continuing to be an inspiration.

Harvey W. Rubin

HOW TO USE THIS BOOK EFFECTIVELY

Alphabetization: All entries are alphabetized by letter rather than by word, so that multiple-word terms are treated as single words. For example, **AGE SETBACK** follows **AGENT OF RECORD**, and **ALL RISKS** follows **ALLOCATION OF ASSETS**. In some cases (such as **NAIC** acts and regulations), abbreviations appear as entries in the main text, in addition to appearing in the back of the book in the separate listing of Abbreviations and Acronyms. This occurs when the short form, rather than the formal name, predominates in the common usage of the field. For example, **NAIC** is commonly used in speaking of the "National Association of Insurance Commissioners"; thus, the entry is at **NAIC**. Numbers in entry titles and the ampersand are alphabetized as if they were spelled out.

Many words have distinctly different meanings, depending upon the context in which they are used. The various meanings of a term are listed by numerical or functional subheading. Readers must determine the context that is relevant to their purpose.

Abbreviations and Acronyms: A separate list of abbreviations and acronyms follows the Dictionary.

Cross-References: To add to your understanding of a term, related or contrasting terms are sometimes cross-referenced. The cross-referenced term will appear in SMALL CAPITALS either in the body of the entry (or subentry) or at the end. These terms will be printed in SMALL CAPITALS only the first time they appear in the text. Where an entry is fully defined by another term, a reference rather than a definition is provided—for example: **PRODUCER** *see* AGENT.

Italics: Italic type is generally used to highlight the fact that a word or phrase has a special meaning to the trade. Italics are also used for the titles of publications.

Parentheses: Parentheses are used in entry titles for two reasons. The first is to indicate that another term has a meaning identical or very closely related to that of the entry word; for example, **BENEFITS OF BUSINESS LIFE AND HEALTH INSURANCE (KEY PERSON INSURANCE)**. The second reason is to indicate that an abbreviation is used with about the same frequency as the term itself; for example, **FEDERAL TRADE COMMISSION (FTC)**.

Special Definitions: Organizations and associations that play an active role in the field are included in the Dictionary along with a brief statement of their mission.

A

ABANDONMENT AND SALVAGE legal status giving an insurance company all rights to an insured's property. The ABANDONMENT CLAUSE is usually found in MARINE INSURANCE and not in other property insurance policies such as the HOMEOWNERS INSURANCE POLICY and the SPECIAL MULTIPERIL INSURANCE (SMP) policy. An insured may wish to abandon the hull of a ship if the cost of protecting it exceeds its value. The insured must notify the insurance company of its intent to abandon property but the company is under no obligation to accept the abandoned property.

ABANDONMENT CLAUSE in marine insurance, clause giving an insured the right to abandon lost or damaged property and still claim full settlement from an insurer (subject to certain restrictions). Two types of losses are provided for under abandonment clauses.
  1. *Actual total loss*—property so badly damaged it is unrepairable or unrecoverable; causes include fire, sinking, windstorm damage, and mysterious disappearance. For example, until the 1980s the *Titanic,* which sank off Newfoundland in 1912, was deemed to be unrecoverable and the Commercial Union Insurance Company had paid its owners for their loss due to sinking. Owners of ships that mysteriously disappeared in the Bermuda Triangle have been able to collect insurance proceeds. Disappearance of pleasure craft due to drug pirates has resulted in indemnification of owners through insurance proceeds.
  2. *Constructive total loss*– property so badly damaged that the cost of its rehabilitation would be more than its restored value. For example, a ship and/or its cargo is damaged to such a degree that the cost of repair would exceed its restored value. The insured can abandon the property if (a) repair costs are greater than 50% of the value of the property after it has been repaired and (b) the insurance company agrees to the insured's intent to abandon.

ABSOLUTE ASSIGNMENT *see* ASSIGNMENT CLAUSE.

ABSOLUTE BENEFICIARY *see* BENEFICIARY; BENEFICIARY CLAUSE.

ABSOLUTE LIABILITY liability without fault; also known as *liability without regard to fault* or STRICT LIABILITY. Absolute liability is imposed in various states when actions of an individual or business are deemed contrary to public policy, even though an action may not have been intentional or negligent. For example, in product liability, manufacturers and retailers have been held strictly liable for products that have caused injuries and have been shown to be defective, even though the manufacturer or retailer was not proven to be at fault or negligent. In many states the owner of an animal is held strictly liable for injuries it may cause, even though it does not have a past history of violence.

ABSTRACT summary of the history of the title to REAL ESTATE.

AB TRUST type of trust that minimizes the FEDERAL ESTATE TAX through the use of the MARITAL DEDUCTION and the unified tax credit.

ABUSIVE TAX SHELTER illegal tax deduction (as determined by the Internal Revenue Service) taken under the auspices of a limited partnership. One abuse of taxes is inflating the value of purchased assets far beyond their fair market value. Once the IRS determines that tax deductions are illegal, participants in the limited partnership are subject to the payment of back taxes, interest due on the back taxes, and penalties.

ACCELERATED DEATH BENEFIT *see* ACCELERATION LIFE INSURANCE.

ACCELERATED DEPRECIATION method in which larger amounts of depreciation are taken in the beginning years of the life of an asset and smaller amounts in later years. The objective is to defer taxes legally, thereby allowing funds to be retained by a business to finance growth.

ACCELERATED OPTION life insurance POLICY PROVISION under which the POLICYHOLDER may apply the accumulated cash value, in the form of a single premium payment, to pay up the policy or to mature the policy as an endowment.

ACCELERATION LIFE INSURANCE policy under which a portion of the DEATH BENEFIT (generally 25%) becomes payable to the insured for a specified medical condition prior to death. The purpose of the accelerated death benefit is to provide funds necessary to finance medical costs to extend the life of the insured. Upon proof of a specified medical condition, the insurance company will pay 25% of the death benefit. When the insured dies, the remainder of the death benefit is paid to the BENEFICIARY, just as under a traditional life insurance policy.

ACCELERATIVE ENDOWMENT life insurance policy option under which the DIVIDENDS that have ACCRUED may be applied to mature the policy as ENDOWMENT INSURANCE.

ACCEPTANCE agreement to an offer, in contract law, thus forming a contract. For insurance contracts, the insurer usually acknowledges willingness to underwrite a risk by issuing a policy in exchange for a premium from an applicant.

ACCIDENT unexpected, unforeseen event not under the control of the insured and resulting in a loss. The insured cannot purposefully cause the loss to happen; the loss must be due to pure chance according to the odds of the laws of probability. For example, under a PERSONAL AUTOMOBILE POLICY (PAP) if an accident occurs, the insured is covered for loss due to his/her negligent act or omissions resulting in bodily injury or property damage to another party.

ACCIDENTAL DEATH AND DISMEMBERMENT INSURANCE
form of accident insurance that indemnifies or pays a stated benefit to insured or his/her beneficiary in the event of bodily injury or death due to accidental means (other than natural causes). For example, an insured's arm is severed in an accident. A predetermined schedule of payments is used to compensate the insured for this particular loss. The schedule also lists the sums payable for other parts of the body that may be lost, or for death by accident.

ACCIDENTAL DEATH BENEFIT *see* ACCIDENTAL DEATH CLAUSE; RIDERS, LIFE POLICIES.

ACCIDENTAL DEATH CLAUSE in a life insurance policy, benefit in addition to the death benefit paid to the beneficiary, should death occur due to an accident. In *double indemnity,* twice the face value of the policy will be paid to the beneficiary; in *triple indemnity,* three times the face value is payable. Accidental death caused by war, aviation except as a passenger on a regularly scheduled airline, and illegal activities is generally excluded. Time and age limits are usually applicable, as for example, the insured must die within 90 days of the accident and be age 60 or less.

ACCIDENTAL DEATH INSURANCE coverage in the event of death due to accident, usually in combination with dismemberment insurance. If death is due to accident, payment is made to the insured's beneficiary; if bodily injury is the result of an accident (such as the loss of a limb), the insured receives a specified sum. *See also* ACCIDENTAL DEATH CLAUSE.

ACCIDENTAL MEANS unexpected, unforeseen event not under the control of the insured that results in bodily injury.

ACCIDENT AND HEALTH INSURANCE coverage for accidental injury, accidental death, or sickness; also called *Accident and Sickness Insurance.* Benefits include paid hospital expenses, medical expenses, surgical expenses, and income payments. *See also* GROUP HEALTH INSURANCE; HEALTH INSURANCE.

ACCIDENT AND SICKNESS INSURANCE phrase formerly used to describe coverage for *perils* of accident and sickness. For descriptions of current terms, *see also* ACCIDENT AND HEALTH INSURANCE; DISABILITY INSURANCE; GROUP DISABILITY INSURANCE; GROUP HEALTH INSURANCE; HEALTH MAINTENANCE ORGANIZATION (HMO).

ACCIDENT FREQUENCY number of times an accident occurs. Used in predicting losses upon which premiums are based.

ACCIDENT INSURANCE coverage for bodily injury and/or death resulting from accidental means (other than natural causes). For example, an insured is critically injured in an accident. Accident insurance can provide income and/or a death benefit if death ensues.

ACCIDENT PREVENTION *see* ENGINEERING APPROACH; HUMAN APPROACH.

ACCIDENT RATE see ACCIDENT FREQUENCY.

ACCIDENT SEVERITY extent of the loss caused by accidents. Used in predicting the dollar amount of losses upon which the premiums are based.

ACCIDENT-YEAR STATISTICS record of losses and premiums received for accident coverage within a 12-month period. These statistics show the percentage of each premium received that is being paid out in claims and enables the establishment of a basic premium reflecting the pure cost of protection. The trend line generated by the record of losses is an important statistical tool for predicting future losses.

ACCOMMODATION LINE agreement by an insurance company to underwrite business submitted by an AGENT or BROKER even though that business is *substandard.* The object is to continue to attract profitable business of that agent.

ACCOUNTANTS LIABILITY INSURANCE *see* ACCOUNTANTS PROFESSIONAL LIABILITY INSURANCE.

ACCOUNTANTS PROFESSIONAL LIABILITY INSURANCE insurance for accountants covering liability lawsuits arising from their professional activities. For example, an investor bases a buying decision on the balance sheet of a company's annual statement. The figures later prove fallacious and not according to GENERALLY ACCEPTABLE ACCOUNTING PRINCIPLES (GAAP). The accountant could be found liable for his professional actions, and would be covered by this policy. However, if the accountant ran over someone or damaged property with a car, this policy would not provide coverage.

ACCOUNTANTS REPORT *see* STATEMENT OF OPINION (ACCOUNTANTS REPORT, AUDITORS REPORT).

ACCOUNT BALANCE PLAN plan that takes the form of a SUPPLEMENTAL EXECUTIVE RETIREMENT PLAN. Under this plan, the executive's employer contributes to the executive's account on a performance-tied basis. For example, if the stock price of the company rises at least 20% in a given year, the employer's contribution would be 20% of the executive's salary.

ACCOUNT CURRENT financial statement, issued by the INSURANCE COMPANY on a monthly basis to its agents, showing for each agent his or her commissions earned, premiums written, policy cancellations, and any policy endorsements.

ACCOUNTING *see* GENERALLY ACCEPTED ACCOUNTING PRINCIPLES (GAAP).

ACCOUNTS RECEIVABLE INSURANCE coverage when business records are destroyed by an insured peril and the business cannot collect money owed. The policy covers these uncollectible sums plus the expense of record reconstruction and extra collection fees. It does not insure the physical value of the records themselves such as the paper or computer disks and tapes.

ACCREDITED ADVISOR IN INSURANCE (AAI) professional designation earned after the successful completion of three national examinations given by the INSURANCE INSTITUTE OF AMERICA (IIA). Covers such areas of expertise as insurance production (insurance sales, exposure identification, legal liability, personal lines insurance, commercial lines insurance); multiple-lines insurance production; and agency operations and sales management. Program of study is recommended for individuals who have production responsibilities.

ACCRUE to accumulate. For example, under one of the dividend options of a participating life insurance policy, dividends can accumulate at interest by leaving them with the insurance company; cash values of life insurance accumulate at a given rate; employee retirement credits for pension benefits accumulate at a stipulated rate.

ACCRUED BENEFIT COST METHOD actuarial method of crediting retirement benefits earned and the costs associated with these earned retirement benefits. An increment (unit) of benefit is credited for each year of recognized service that an employee has earned. Then the present value of these benefits (including the employee's life expectancy) is calculated and assigned to the year earned. The benefit earned by the employee can take the form of a flat dollar amount or a percentage of compensation. For example, this may work out to 1½% of an employee's compensation being credited to the employee's account for each year of recognized service.

ACCRUED INTEREST interest earned but not yet paid for a period of time that has elapsed since the last interest payment.

ACCUMULATED AMOUNT amount to which the original investment sums build at a stipulated interest rate.

ACCUMULATED VALUE total of the number of ACCUMULATION UNITS times the ACCUMULATION UNIT VALUE for a VARIABLE ANNUITY. Similar procedure is followed in the calculation of the current market value of a mutual fund found by multiplying the number of accumulation units times its net asset value.

ACCUMULATION BENEFITS accrual or addition to life insurance benefits. *See also* ACCRUE.

ACCUMULATION PERIOD time frame during which an ANNUITANT makes premium payments to an insurance company. The obligations of the company to the annuitant during this period depend on whether a PURE ANNUITY or REFUND ANNUITY is involved. Many factors enter an annuity purchase, but some experts suggest a pure annuity to minimize cost and if there are no dependents. In other circumstances a refund annuity might be considered. *See also* ANNUITY.

ACCUMULATION UNIT measure of policyholder interest in a VARI-ABLE ANNUITY policy prior to the ANNUITY DATE. This measure is similar to a unit in a mutual fund.

ACCUMULATION UNIT VALUE worth of each ACCUMULATION UNIT at the end of each VALUATION PERIOD for a VARIABLE ANNUITY. This value is similar to that of the NET ASSET VALUE for a mutual fund.

ACQUISITION COST expense of soliciting and placing new insurance business on a company's books. It includes agent's commissions, underwriting expenses, medical and credit report fees, and marketing support services. Because of competition, significant efforts are made by insurance companies to lower acquisition costs. Traditional captive agent companies have often turned to brokerage as additional distribution or sole distribution channels for this reason.

ACTIVELY MANAGED FUND type of MUTUAL FUND in which the managers of that fund select specific securities in order to reach a predetermined objective.

ACTIVE PORTFOLIO MANAGEMENT selection of individual securities in such a manner as to outperform indexes and/or the general market or specific segment of that market.

ACTIVE RETENTION *see* SELF INSURANCE.

ACTIVITIES OF DAILY LIVING *see* LONG-TERM CARE (LTC).

ACT OF GOD natural occurrence beyond human control or influence. Such acts of nature include hurricanes, earthquakes, and floods.

ACTS performance of a deed or function. Certain acts are prohibited from coverage in insurance. For example, if the insured commits a felony, the insured's beneficiary cannot collect under the accidental death provision of a life insurance policy. Intentional destruction of an insured's property by the insured or someone hired by an insured to destroy the property is a prohibited act under property insurance, and an insurance policy will not indemnify the insured for losses incurred.

ACTUAL AUTHORITY (EXPRESS AUTHORITY) specific powers granted by the principal (the insurance company) to the AGENT in the contract.

ACTUAL CASH VALUE cost of replacing damaged or destroyed property with comparable new property, minus depreciation and obsolescence. For example, a 10-year-old living room sofa will not be replaced at current full value because of a decade of depreciation. The actual cash value clause is common in property insurance contracts. In some instances artistic or antique property may appreciate over time. To receive full coverage such items must be specifically scheduled in a policy.

ACTUAL LOSS RATIO *see* LOSS RATIO.

ACTUAL TOTAL LOSS *see* TOTAL LOSS.

ACTUARIAL *see* ACTUARIAL SCIENCE; ACTUARY.

ACTUARIAL ADJUSTMENT modification in premiums, reserves, and other values to reflect actual loss experience and expenses and expected benefits to be paid.

ACTUARIAL BOARD FOR COUNSELING AND DISCIPLINE group charged with investigation complaints made against actuaries for alleged violation(s) of the Code of Professional Conduct.

ACTUARIAL CONSULTANT independent advisor to insurance companies, corporations, federal, state, and local governments, and labor unions on actuarial matters. These include evaluation of the liabilities of small insurance companies, estimates of pension plan liabilities and the design of such plans, appearance as an expert witness giving testimony concerning lost income due to an accident, and the design of information systems. *See also* ACTUARIAL SCIENCE; ACTUARY.

ACTUARIAL COST ASSUMPTIONS *see* ACTUARIAL ADJUSTMENT; ACTUARIAL COST METHODS; ACTUARIAL EQUITY; ACTUARIAL EQUIVALENT; ACTUARIAL GAINS AND LOSSES; ACTUARIAL RATE; ACTUARIAL SCIENCE.

ACTUARIAL COST METHODS system for calculating the relationship between a pension plan's present cost and its present future benefits. This relationship shows the extent to which a pension plan's benefits are funded. The objective is to identify on a year-by-year basis the cost of benefits accrued for the particular year. To illustrate, a relationship of 1.0 shows that there is 100% funding available for the pension plan's benefits.

ACTUARIAL EQUITY calculation of the PREMIUM based on such factors as the APPLICANT'S age, sex, health record, family history, and type of insurance plan applied for.

ACTUARIAL EQUIVALENT mathematical determination based on the expectation of loss and the benefits to be paid in such an eventuality. The premium charged will vary directly with the probability of loss.

ACTUARIAL GAINS AND LOSSES experience as it relates to the annual costs associated with a pension plan. In calculating premiums due under a pension plan, basic assumptions must be made concerning future loss experience and expenses. Actual loss experience can prove to be better or worse than envisioned. If the experience is better, the result is an *actuarial gain.* If the experience is worse, the result is an *actuarial loss.*

ACTUARIAL RATE rate based on historical loss experience, from which future loss experience is predicted. *See also* ACTUARIAL EQUIVALENT; ACTUARIAL SCIENCE; RATE MAKING.

ACTUARIAL SCIENCE branch of knowledge dealing with the mathematics of insurance, including probabilities. It is used in ensuring that risks are carefully evaluated, that adequate premiums are charged for risks underwritten, and that adequate provision is made for future payments of benefits.

ACTUARY mathematician in the insurance field. Actuaries conduct various statistical studies; construct MORBIDITY and MORTALITY TABLES; calculate premiums, reserves, and dividends for participating policies; develop products; construct annual reports in compliance with numerous regulatory requirements; and in many companies oversee the general financial function. The successful actuary has a strong general business background as well as mathematical ability. Professional actuarial associations provide actuarial qualification examinations.

ACTUARY, ENROLLED individual who has met professional standards of the Internal Revenue Service and the Department of Labor for signing the actuarial reports required by the Employee Retirement Security Act of 1974—Title II. An enrolled actuary may certify annually that benefit cost and funding requirements of a pension plan have been calculated according to accepted actuarial principles as a best estimate of expected experience of the pension plan.

ACV *see* ACTUAL CASH VALUE.

ADDENDUM addition to a written policy. *See also* ENDORSEMENT; RIDER.

ADDITIONAL CAR automobile purchased or leased by the insured or the insured's spouse that is in addition to the insured or the insured spouse's present car as covered under the PERSONAL AUTOMOBILE POLICY (PAP). In order for this car to be insured, the car must be a private passenger car and the insurance company must insure all of the insured and insured spouse's other private passenger cars. If it is a pickup or van with less than 10,000 lb. gross vehicle weight and not used in business or farming, the insurance company also must insure all the other cars owned by the insured or the insured's spouse for that car to be covered. *See also* REPLACEMENT CAR.

ADDITIONAL DEATH BENEFIT extra layer of life insurance coverage. This term is often applied to double indemnity. For example, some life insurance policies provide a death benefit of a multiple of the face value if the insured dies between certain ages when dependent children may still be living at home. *See also* ACCIDENTAL DEATH CLAUSE.

ADDITIONAL DEPOSIT PRIVILEGE clause in some CURRENT ASSUMPTION WHOLE LIFE INSURANCE policies such as UNIVERSAL LIFE INSURANCE that allows unscheduled premiums to be paid at any time prior to the policy's maturity date, provided there is no outstanding loan. If there is a loan, additional deposits will be first applied against the loan. Most policies have a minimum that will be accepted as an additional deposit, such as $1000.

ADDITIONAL INSURED individual added to a life insurance policy other than the insured named in the policy. For example, an insured father can have a dependent son and daughter added to the policy as additional insureds. In many instances, adding an additional insured to an existing policy is less expensive than purchasing a separate policy for that insured.

In property and liability insurance: another person, firm, or other entity enjoying the same protection as the named insured.

ADDITIONAL INTEREST *see* ADDITIONAL INSURED.

ADDITIONAL LIVING EXPENSE INSURANCE coverage under a *Homeowners, Condominium, and Renters* policy, that reimburses costs of residing in a temporary location until the insured's home can be made whole again. It usually provides living expenses of from 10–20% of the structural coverage on the home.

ADDITIONAL LIVING EXPENSE LOSS *see* ADDITIONAL LIVING EXPENSE INSURANCE.

ADD-ON PLAN plan that provides for payment of a claim by the insurance company with the claimant retaining the right to sue the responsible party for NEGLIGENCE.

ADD TO CASH VALUE OPTION new DIVIDEND OPTION under which the POLICYOWNER allows the dividends from the PARTICIPATING policy to be applied for the purposes of accumulating CASH VALUES.

ADEQUACY *see* RATE MAKING.

ADEQUACY, LIFE INSURANCE *see* HUMAN LIFE VALUE APPROACH (EVOIL); NEEDS APPROACH.

ADHESION INSURANCE CONTRACT agreement prepared by an insurance company and offered to prospective insureds on a take-it-or-leave-it basis. If the contracts are misinterpreted by insureds, courts have ruled in their favor since the insureds had no input into the contract. All insurance contracts have been deemed by courts to be contracts of adhesion.

AD INFINITUM continuing on an indefinite basis.

ADJACENT that which adjoins. Most property insurance policies such as the HOMEOWNERS INSURANCE POLICY provide structural coverage on an adjacent building on the same basis as the primary building.

ADJOINING *see* ADJACENT.

ADJUSTABLE LIFE INSURANCE coverage under which the face value, premiums, and plan of insurance can be changed at the discretion of the *policyowner* in the following manner, without additional policies being issued:
  1. *face value* can be increased or decreased (to increase coverage, the insured must furnish evidence of insurability). The resultant size

of the cash value will depend on the amount of face value and premium.

    2. *premiums* and length of time they are to be paid can be increased or decreased. Unscheduled premiums can be paid on a lump sum basis. Premiums paid on an adjusted basis can either lengthen or shorten the time the protection element will be in force, as well as lengthen or shorten the period for making premium payments. For example, assume that John, who is 28, buys a $100,000 adjustable term life policy to age 65 with an annual premium of $1250. As his career prospers, he finds at age 32 that he can double the annual premium payment to $2500. This increase may change the original term amount to a fully paid-up life policy at age 65. With time, John might experience economic hardship and have to decrease his annual payment by two thirds. This could result in changing the paid-up-at-65 policy back to a term policy to age 65. Thus, at any time the policy can be either *ordinary life* or *term. See also* UNIVERSAL LIFE INSURANCE.

ADJUSTABLE PREMIUM premium that can vary up or down. Some life insurance policies permit the company to change the premiums after the policy is in force, depending on mortality experience, expenses, and investment returns. If profits are sufficient, premiums can be reduced; if not, they can be raised to specific maximums.

ADJUSTABLE RATE MORTGAGE (ARM) mortgage agreement that provides initial monthly payments of a relatively low amount (compared with a fixed rate mortgage). This initial amount is subject to periodic changes based on a stipulated index. Index usually used is the change in the rates of United States Treasury bills. Homebuyers considering an ARM should compare ARMs offered by the various lending institutions in the following manner: (1) first-year rates; (2) how the interest rate is calculated in future years; (3) what the one-year and lifetime caps are on the maximum rate; and (4) rules for conversion to a fixed rate mortgage.

ADJUSTED LIABILITIES statutory liabilities minus the INTEREST MAINTENANCE RESERVE minus the ASSET VALUATION RESERVE.

ADJUSTED NET WORTH value of an insurance company or other company that consists of capital and surplus and an estimated value for business on the company's books.

ADJUSTED PREMIUM premium that equals the NET LEVEL PREMIUM plus the modification of the NET LEVEL PREMIUM to reflect the cost associated with paying for the first year initial acquisition expenses. The modification is derived by dividing the first year initial acquisition expenses by the present value of a LIFE ANNUITY DUE (thereby amortizing these expenses over the premium paying period). This is the premium used to generate a minimum CASH SURRENDER VALUE required by the NONFORFEITURE PROVISION.

ADJUSTED PREMIUM METHOD method of calculating the life insurance policy's cash surrender value (CSV) not contingent upon the calculation of the policy's RESERVE such that the CSV will approximate the ASSET SHARE VALUE of the policy as required by the STANDARD NON-FORFEITURE LAW. According to this method of determining the CSV, the following steps are taken: (1) arriving at the first year expense allowance; (2) arriving at the ADJUSTED PREMIUM; and (3) substituting the adjusted premium for the NET LEVEL PREMIUM used in the equation for arriving at the PROSPECTIVE RESERVE.

ADJUSTED SURPLUS statutory surplus plus the INTEREST MAINTE-NANCE RESERVE plus the ASSET VALUATION RESERVE.

ADJUSTED UNDERWRITING PROFIT *see* UNDERWRITING GAIN (LOSS).

ADJUSTER individual employed by a property and casualty insurance company to settle on its behalf claims brought by insureds. The adjuster evaluates the merits of each claim and makes recommendations to the insurance company. *See also* INDEPENDENT ADJUSTER.

ADJUSTER, AVERAGE *see* AVERAGE ADJUSTER.

ADJUSTER, INDEPENDENT *see* INDEPENDENT ADJUSTER.

ADJUSTER, PUBLIC *see* PUBLIC ADJUSTER.

ADJUSTER, STAFF employee of an insurance company who assesses insurance coverage for property claimed to be damaged and determines the insurance proceeds that might be payable for the claim. A *fee adjuster* works for himself and does claims adjustments on a fee basis.

ADJUSTMENT BUREAU company organized with the business objective of providing claims adjustment services to insurance companies that do not have an internal claims department. *See also* ADJUSTER, STAFF.

ADJUSTMENT INCOME income payable to a surviving spouse or other beneficiary upon the death of the primary wage earner to bridge the gap until the beneficiary is self-sufficient. For example, income can be provided for a limited period of time until a widow can regain emotional stability, receive career guidance, as well as training, to establish a permanent career if necessary. The need for adjustment income is a significant consideration in deciding how much life insurance to purchase.

ADJUSTMENT PROVISION provision in an Adjustable Life Insurance policy that permits the structure of the policy to be changed by: (1) increasing or decreasing the premium; (2) increasing or decreasing the FACE AMOUNT; (3) lengthening or shortening the period of protection; and (4) lengthening or shortening the period of premium payments.

ADMINISTERING AGENCY employer using a self-administered insurance plan; or an insurer that administers a group employee benefit plan. In an employer administered plan, the employer maintains all required administrative records based on demographic and other information from the employer's monthly reports.

ADMINISTRATION performance of management functions associated with administering an EMPLOYEE BENEFIT INSURANCE PLAN, to include actuarial services, booklet and contract plan designing, billing, accounting, and establishing evidence of insurability for the plan participants. *See also* ADMINISTERING AGENCY; ADMINISTRATIVE CHARGE; ADMINISTRATIVE SERVICES ONLY (ASO).

ADMINISTRATION BOND coverage that guarantees that the executor or administrator of an estate will conduct his or her duties according to the provisions of the will and the legal requirements of the jurisdiction. If dishonest acts by the executor or administrator result in financial loss to the estate, the bond will act as an INDEMNITOR to the estate. This bond is posted by the executor or administrator of the estate.

ADMINISTRATIVE CHARGE billing by an ADMINISTERING AGENCY for expenses associated with administering a group employee benefit plan.

ADMINISTRATIVE EXPENSES costs associated with the general administration of the insurance organization to include such items as utilities, rent, salaries, postage, furniture, and housekeeping charges.

ADMINISTRATIVE LAW law created by government regulatory agencies, such as the office of the COMMISSIONER OF INSURANCE, through decisions, orders, regulations, and rules. For example, RATE MAKING hearings conducted by the insurance commissioner are common. Based on the findings of the hearings, rate increases may or may not be granted.

ADMINISTRATIVE SERVICES ONLY (ASO) services provided in an employee benefit plan such as a PENSION PLAN. An employer provides the clerical staff to operate the plan, in effect acting as custodian. The trustee provides direction for investment of the plan's funds, usually in a self-directed investment account. Trustee plans are gaining in popularity as both the employer and employees seek more control over pension funds investments. In a self-insured property or liability plan the group may have an ASO contract with an insurance company or a third-party administrator to handle claims processing and administration.

ADMINISTRATOR court-appointed person to manage the estate of a deceased individual who declared no EXECUTOR or EXECUTRIX. This person so appointed acts in a FIDUCIARY capacity with regard to that estate.

ADMIRALTY LIABILITY maritime acts resulting in a LIABILITY circumstance falling under COMMON LAW and statutory law. *See also* JONES ACT (MERCHANT MARINE ACT).

ADMIRALTY PROCEEDING conducting of maritime suits involving OCEAN MARINE INSURANCE policy claims before an admiralty court.

ADMITTED ASSETS assets permitted by state law to be included in an insurance company's ANNUAL STATEMENT. These assets are an important factor when regulators measure insurance company solvency. They include mortgages, stocks, bonds, and real estate. Historically, a large part of admitted assets consisted of long term mortgages, but with the advent of CURRENT ASSUMPTION WHOLE LIFE INSURANCE policies, short term financial instruments can be used to make up a large part of admitted assets.

ADMITTED COMPANY life insurance company or property and casualty insurance company licensed by a particular state to conduct business there. The company is subject to the state insurance code governing such aspects as company reserves and advertising. If an insurance company is not licensed by a given state or if its license is terminated, the company can no longer conduct insurance business in that state.

ADMITTED INSURANCE insurance purchased from an insurance company that has been licensed in the state in which the policy is purchased. This insurance is purchased through an agent or broker who are licensed by that particular state, and, that state regulates the marketing of the insurance and the policy forms used.

AD VALOREM property taxes assessed according to the value of that property.

ADVANCED FUNDED PENSION PLAN retirement plan in which money is currently allocated to fund an employees' pension. *See also* ALLOCATED FUNDING INSTRUMENT; UNALLOCATED FUNDING INSTRUMENT.

ADVANCED LIFE UNDERWRITING process of analyzing complex personal and business cases according to tax and estate planning requirements to determine life insurance needs. The family life agent or underwriter normally does not become involved in complex business or personal cases, but draws on the expertise of the advanced life underwriter when needed.

ADVANCE FUNDING payment of premiums before their due date. In pension plans, premium payments are allocated to the payment of future benefits prior to benefits becoming payable. *See also* ADVANCED FUNDED PENSION PLAN.

ADVANCE PAYMENTS payments made to the insured by the insurance company before the settlement date. For example, a claim is scheduled to be settled on June 1, 2008, but the insurance company pays the claimant prior to that date.

ADVANCE PREMIUM premium paid before the due date. For example, a premium is due on July 1, 2008, but the insured actually makes the premium payment on January 1, 2008, receiving a premium discount.

ADVANCE PREMIUM MUTUAL *see* DIVIDEND OPTION; MUTUAL INSURANCE COMPANY; PARTICIPATING INSURANCE.

ADVERSE FINANCIAL SELECTION process in which the POLICY-HOLDER surrenders the policy when: (1) cash proceeds can be invested elsewhere at a higher return than that being earned on the CASH VALUE within the policy; and (2) economic recession or depression exists and the cash is required to meet other financial obligations. If the policyholder exercises the CASH SURRENDER VALUE option during these economic circumstances, the company may have to sell assets at a "fire sale" and will have fewer funds to invest at advantageous rates of return.

ADVERSE SELECTION process in life insurance by which an applicant who is uninsurable, or is a greater than average risk, seeks to obtain a policy from a company at a standard premium rate. Life insurance companies carefully screen applicants for this reason, since their premiums are based on policyholders in average good health and in non-hazardous occupations.

ADVERTISERS LIABILITY INSURANCE coverage for an advertiser's negligent acts and/or omissions in advertising (both oral and written) that may result in a civil suit for libel, slander, defamation of character, or copyright infringement.

ADVERTISING, INSURANCE COMPANY highly visible form of marketing communication with the public with these objectives: (1) encourage agents and brokers to sell insurance company products, (2) predispose customers to be receptive to sales calls, (3) enhance an insurance company's public image, (4) support introduction of new products, and (5) influence public and legislative opinions on issues of importance to the insurance industry. *Product advertising* describes particular products and why they would be beneficial. *Institutional advertising* describes the financial strength and the stability of a company. Depending on target market and size, company advertising may be national, local, or cooperative (a joint venture using both company and agency dollars).

ADVISORY COMMITTEE group that advises on employee benefit plans as to amount of benefits to be paid, how benefits are to be financed, and how employees are to qualify for benefits (VESTING *requirements*). An advisory committee only suggests; it does not have line authority.

AFFILIATED COMPANIES associated insurers that are under common stock ownership or interlocking directorates. Such an arrangement makes it easier to exchange insurance products for sale to the consumer, reduces duplication of efforts, and lowers product research and development costs.

AFFIRMATIVE WARRANTY *see* WARRANTY.

AGE CHANGE date, in insurance, on which a person becomes one year older. Depending on the insurance company, premiums in life and health insurance manuals are figured to the age-nearest-birthday or age-last-birthday.

AGE DISCRIMINATION IN EMPLOYMENT ACT (ADEA) act that prohibits employers from requiring employees to retire at age 70. Also, the act prohibits EMPLOYEE BENEFIT PLANS from discriminating against employees in the 40 to 70 age group as to contributions or benefits.

AGE LIMITS maximum age of an applicant or insured beyond which an insurance company will not initially underwrite a risk or continue to insure it. For example, under some forms of RENEWABLE TERM LIFE INSURANCE, coverage will not be renewed beyond age 60.

AGENCY individuals under common management whose goal is to sell and service insurance. Office may be managed by a GENERAL AGENT or *branch manager. See also* CAPTIVE INSURANCE COMPANY; INDEPENDENT AGENCY SYSTEM.

AGENCY AGREEMENT written document containing instructions on managing one's assets during one's lifetime. The document may be revoked (unless made irrevocable at creation), terminated, or amended at any time by the creator of the agreement provided that person is competent to make the decision. The power the agent has to make decisions for the creator of the agreement may be broad or narrow. The agent is prohibited from disclosing information about the assets held under agreement to anyone without the creator's permission. The power of an agent to act under the agency agreement terminates if the creator becomes incompetent unless the creator has signed a durable power of attorney. Upon the death of the creator, the agency agreement terminates, which requires that all of the assets under the agreement must be probated before they can be distributed to the creator's beneficiaries.

AGENCY BY ESTOPPEL *see* ESTOPPEL.

AGENCY BY RATIFICATION confirmation by an insurance company of the acts of its AGENT, regardless of whether or not these acts were committed within the limit of authority granted the agent by the company. By so ratifying the agent's acts, the company becomes responsible for consequences arising from these acts. For example, if the insurance company, with full knowledge of the agent's misdeeds in soliciting the application and the premium from the PROSPECT, accepts the premium for the policy from the agent, this acceptance constitutes ratification of the act of the agent.

AGENCY CONTRACT (AGENCY AGREEMENT) rules of conduct and commissions paid to agents. For example, under the rules of conduct agents may be required to submit all of their business to only that agency. The contract also lists commission schedules.

AGENCY MANAGER individual in charge of an insurance company agency. The manager is an employee of the company and is usually compensated on a salary-and-bonus basis, the latter relating to premium volume production of all the agents in the agency. He or she is responsible for hiring and training agents.

AGENCY PLANT insurance company's total number of agents.

AGENCY SYSTEM *see* AGENT; INDEPENDENT AGENCY SYSTEM.

AGENT individual who sells and services insurance policies in either of two classifications:

1. *Independent agent* represents at least two insurance companies and (at least in theory) services clients by searching the market for the most advantageous price for the most coverage. The agent's commission is a percentage of each premium paid and includes a fee for servicing the insured's policy. *See also* AMERICAN AGENCY SYSTEM.
2. *Direct writer* represents only one company and sells only its policies. This agent is paid on a commission basis in much the same manner as the independent agent.

AGENT COMMISSION *see* COMMISSION.

AGENT, GENERAL *see* GENERAL AGENT (GA).

AGENT, INDEPENDENT *see* INDEPENDENT AGENT.

AGENT LICENSE *see* LICENSING OF AGENTS AND BROKERS.

AGENT OF RECORD individual who has a contractual agreement with a policyowner. The agent of record has a legal right to commissions from the insurance policy.

AGENT, POLICYWRITING agent with the authority from an insurance company to prepare and to place into business an insurance policy.

AGENT, RECORDING *see* AGENT OF RECORD.

AGENT, RESIDENT *see* RESIDENT AGENT.

AGENT'S AUTHORITY authority derived from an agent's contract with an insurance company. *See also* APPARENT AGENCY (AUTHORITY).

AGENT'S BALANCE statement showing the amount of money owed the agent by the insurance company, according to the contract he or she has with the insurance company.

AGENT, SPECIAL *see* SPECIAL AGENT.

AGENT'S QUALIFICATION LAWS legislation establishing the minimum education and experience level required by the state as a prerequisite for a person to become a licensed AGENT. *See also* LICENSE; LICENSING OF AGENTS AND BROKERS.

AGENT, STATE *see* STATE AGENT.

AGE SETBACK subtraction of a number of years from a standard table of life insurance rates under the assumption that a particular group—women—outlive men and presumably will be paying premiums for a longer time. For example, a 38-year-old woman may pay the same premiums as a 35-year-old man. Age setback is a women's rights issue, with at least one state having legislated that men and women the same age must be charged the same rates for the life insurance they buy.

AGE-WEIGHTED PROFIT-SHARING PLAN plan that combines the simplicity and flexibility of the traditional PROFIT-SHARING PLAN with the best features of the DEFINED BENEFIT PLAN and the TARGET BENEFIT PLAN. By age-weighing the plan, higher contributions are permitted by the IRS for older plan participants. Under traditional profit-sharing plans, younger employees will have a larger contribution made by the employer on their behalf, but they are the least likely to be concerned with retirement and would rather have the cash.

Age-Weighted Plans offer more flexibility in making contributions. Under defined benefit plans and target benefit plans, a minimum contribution has to be made each year in contrast to the profit-sharing plan. Age-Weighted Plans, as in the case with the traditional profit-sharing plans, limit the employer's maximum deductible contribution to 15% of the participant's compensation. The maximum annual contribution of any plan participant is equal to the lesser of 25% of compensation, or $30,000. There are no minimum required annual contributions or maintenance costs to reflect fees paid for the PENSION BENEFIT GUARANTY CORPORATION (PBGC) premiums, federal, or actuarial valuations. A significantly smaller contribution made on behalf of a younger employee will ultimately equal a significantly larger contribution on behalf of an older employee. Because of the effect of COMPOUND INTEREST, the contribution on behalf of the younger employee will purchase the same retirement benefit as the contribution on behalf of the older employee.

AGGREGATE ANNUAL DEDUCTIBLE deductible that applies for the year. For example, a business pays for the first $40,000 of losses incurred during the year and the insurance company pays for all losses above that amount up to the LIMIT OF RECOVERY stated in the policy.

AGGREGATE DOLLAR LIMIT *see* AGGREGATE LIMIT.

AGGREGATE EXCESS CONTRACT policy in which an insurer agrees to pay property or liability losses (generally 80–100%) in excess of a specific amount paid on all losses during a POLICY YEAR.

AGGREGATE EXCESS OF LOSS RETENTION *see* EXCESS OF LOSS REINSURANCE; STOP LOSS REINSURANCE.

AGGREGATE INDEMNITY total limit of coverage under all policies applicable to the covered loss for which an insured can be indemnified. For example, if two health insurance policies are in force on the same person, the total limit of coverage is that provided by the *primary* policy in combination with the *secondary* policy. *See also* AGGREGATE LIMIT PRIMARY INSURANCE AMOUNT; SECONDARY PLAN.

AGGREGATE LEVEL COST METHOD actuarial method of calculating benefits and their costs for all the employees as a group rather than for each individual employee. The costs of the benefits are measured in the form of a percentage of the total payroll for the employee group.

AGGREGATE LIMIT maximum dollar amount of coverage in force under a health insurance policy, a property damage policy, or a liability policy. This maximum can be on an occurrence basis, or for the life of the policy. The following are examples.

1. HEALTH INSURANCE. The insured was billed $107,000 for a serious illness, but the aggregate limit of the policy was $100,000 for the life of the policy, so the most that the insured could be reimbursed is $100,000. The insured would have to pay $7000. Any medical expenses arising from future illness would now have to be paid by the insured.

2. LIABILITY INSURANCE. The insured is at fault in an automobile accident (single occurrence) causing injury to four individuals of $100,000, $150,000, $85,000 and $115,000, respectively, a total of $450,000. The aggregate limit of the policy is $400,000. The insured would have to pay the remaining $50,000.

AGGREGATE MORTALITY TABLE type of mortality table that is based on combined statistics from both the ULTIMATE MORTALITY TABLE and the AGGREGATE MORTALITY TABLE. It shows total statistics for the probability of living and dying throughout the entire life cycle.

AGGREGATE PRODUCTS LIABILITY LIMIT maximum sum of money that the insurance company will pay, during the time interval that the PRODUCT LIABILITY INSURANCE coverage is in effect, for all product liability-related claims arising that are covered under the policy.

AGGREGATE STOP LOSS INSURANCE coverage that goes into effect when an employer who has SELF INSURANCE has its total group health insurance claims attain a certain level, which is usually 125% of its annual projected group health claims costs.

AGREED AMOUNT CLAUSE in PROPERTY INSURANCE, a stipulated agreement between the insurance company and the insured that the amount of insurance coverage under the policy is sufficient to be in compliance with the COINSURANCE requirement.

AGREED AMOUNT FORM *see* AGREED AMOUNT CLAUSE.

AGREEMENT *see* INSURING AGREEMENT.

AGRICULTURAL EQUIPMENT INSURANCE property damage coverage for mobile agricultural equipment and machinery, including harness, saddles, blankets, and liveries. Perils insured are fire, lightning, vandalism, malicious mischief, and removal. Additional perils can be added at extra charge. Excluded from coverage are crops, aircraft, watercraft, feed, hay, and grass. (Crops, aircraft, and watercraft can be covered under other types of insurance policies.)

AIA *see* AMERICAN INSURANCE ASSOCIATION (AIA).

AIAF Associate in Insurance Accounting and Finance.

AIC Associate in Claims.

AIM Associate in Management.

AIR CARGO INSURANCE coverage for an air carrier's legal liability for damage, destruction, or other loss of a customer's property while being shipped. Coverage is on an ALL RISKS basis subject to specific perils excluded in the policy. Air cargo insurance is a form of MARINE INSURANCE, which at one time only covered goods in transit over waterways. Today, goods in transit can be insured regardless of the means of transportation.

AIRCRAFT HULL INSURANCE coverage on an ALL RISKS basis whether the airplane is on the ground or in the air; also called *hull aircraft insurance.* Exclusions, although none are standard, include illegal use of an aircraft; using an aircraft for purposes other than that described in the policy; wear and tear; piloting the aircraft by someone not named in the policy; operating an aircraft outside stipulated geographical boundaries; and damage or destruction of an aircraft resulting from war, riots, strikes, and civil commotions, mechanical breakdown loss, structural failure loss, and conversion. The hull value includes instruments, radios, autopilots, wings, engines, and other equipment attached to or carried on the plane as described in the policy.

AIRCRAFT LIABILITY INSURANCE coverage for the insured in the event that the insured's negligent acts and/or omissions result in losses in connection with the use, ownership, or maintenance of aircraft. Liability coverage can be provided for bodily injury and/or property damage to passengers and also to individuals who are not passengers. MEDICAL PAYMENTS INSURANCE may be included on an optional basis. *See also* AVIATION INSURANCE.

AIRPORT LIABILITY COVERAGE insurance for owners and operators of private, municipal, or commercial airports, as well as fixed-base operators, against claims resulting from injuries to members of the general public or physical damage to the property of members of the general public, provided that these individuals are on the premises of the airport or its related facilities. The policy may include any or all of the following coverages: (1) PREMISES AND OPERATIONS LIABILITY INSURANCE; (2) PERSONAL INJURY; (3) PREMISES MEDICAL PAYMENTS INSURANCE; and (4) contractual. The policy can be tailored to meet the particular requirements of the INSURED.

ALASKA TRUST ACT enacted on April 1, 1997; provides protection against creditors for IRREVOCABLE TRUSTS provided that the trust has a GRANTOR who is a discretionary beneficiary. In order for the statute of the Alaska Trust to be applicable, the following requirements must be met:
   1. At least one if the trustees must reside in Alaska or have his or her principal place of business in Alaska.

   2. A percentage of the assets of the trust is required to be on deposit in a checking account, brokerage account, or other similar account.

   3. The records of the trust must be physically located in Alaska and a percentage of the administration of the trust must take place in Alaska.

ALCM Associate in Loss Control Management.

ALCOHOLIC BEVERAGE CONTROL LAWS *see* DRAM SHOP LAW.

ALCOHOLIC BEVERAGE LIABILITY INSURANCE *see* DRAM SHOP LIABILITY INSURANCE.

ALEATORY CONTRACT contract that may or may not provide more in benefits than premiums paid. For example, with only one premium payment on a property policy an insured can receive hundreds of thousands of dollars should the protected entity be destroyed. On the other hand, an insurance company can collect more in premiums than it ever pays out in benefits, as in a fire insurance policy under which the protected property is either damaged or destroyed. Most insurance contracts are aleatory in nature.

ALIEN INSURER insurance company formed according to the legal requirements of a foreign country. In order for an alien insurer to be able to carry on general operations and sell its products in a particular state in the United States, it must conform to that state's rules and regulations governing insurance companies.

ALIMONY SUBSTITUTION TRUST agreement in which spouse X (the spouse who is mandated by the court to make alimony and/or child support payments to spouse Y) must put assets (the principal) in a TRUST, from which the payments are made to spouse Y. Under this trust, the payments made from the income generated by the principal is taxable income to spouse Y, but any sums paid from the corpus of the principal is not taxable income to spouse Y. Spouse X does not receive a tax deduction for payments made from the trust's corpus of principal, nor does spouse X pay income taxes on the income generated by the principal in the trust.

ALLIANCE OF AMERICAN INSURERS (AAI) membership organization, based in Chicago, Illinois, consisting principally of property and casualty insurance companies. Its objectives are to influence the public and the legislators on matters concerning the property and casualty insurance industry, to publish materials, and to conduct research and various educational programs for member companies.

ALLIED LINES property insurance closely associated with fire insurance and usually purchased in conjunction with a *Standard Fire Policy.* Allied lines include DATA PROCESSING INSURANCE, DEMOLITION INSURANCE, EARTHQUAKE INSURANCE, INCREASED COST OF CONSTRUCTION CLAUSE, RADIOACTIVE CONTAMINATION INSURANCE, SPRINKLER

LEAKAGE INSURANCE, STANDING TIMBER INSURANCE, VANDALISM AND MALICIOUS MISCHIEF INSURANCE, WATER DAMAGE INSURANCE.

ALL LINES INSURANCE combination of coverages from property, liability, health, and life insurance into a single insurance policy from one insurance company. *See also* MULTIPLE LINE INSURANCE.

ALLOCATED BENEFITS payments in a DEFINED BENEFIT PLAN. Benefits are allocated to the pension plan participants as premiums are received by the insurance company. Since the benefits purchased are paid up, the employee is guaranteed a pension at retirement, even if the firm goes out of business.

ALLOCATED FUNDING INSTRUMENT insurance or annuity contract used in pension plans to purchase increments of retirement benefits through contributions for each employee paid into a fund. Benefits are guaranteed to employees at retirement; the insurance company is legally obligated to pay all benefits for which it has received premiums. Pension plans, in which no funds are available to purchase benefits prior to retirement involve UNALLOCATED FUNDING INSTRUMENTS (benefits were not purchased at the time premium payments were made).

ALLOCATION OF PLAN ASSETS *see* ALLOCATION OF PLAN ASSETS ON TERMINATION.

ALLOCATION OF PLAN ASSETS ON TERMINATION distribution of assets if a pension plan is terminated. The allocation is made by either (1) refunding all of an employee's contributions, plus interest, or (2) establishment of classes of employees and their beneficiaries according to entitlement to benefits.

ALLOWED ASSETS *see* ADMITTED ASSETS.

ALL RISK INSURANCE now referred to as OPEN PERILS/OPEN COVERAGE.

ALTERNATIVE DISPUTE RESOLUTION (ADR) many different, unofficial, and voluntary nonlitigation processes employed by insurance companies to resolve contractual disputes with their insureds. Examples would include nonbinding arbitration, simple negotiations between the insurance company and its insured, and mediation by a neutral third party. The objective of this type of dispute resolution is to avoid the substantial expenses that protracted litigation would generate.

ALTERNATIVE MINIMUM COST METHOD means of funding permitted under the EMPLOYEE RETIREMENT INCOME SECURITY ACT OF 1974 (ERISA). The administrator of a pension plan can comply with required minimum funding standards by electing an alternative cost method under which the normal cost is the lesser of the normal cost (1) according to the actuarial cost method of the plan, or (2) according to the accrued benefit cost method without benefit projections.

ALTERNATIVE RISK FINANCING arrangement by which the insured agrees to incur a given degree of variability in the ultimate total costs associated with financing its losses.

ALTERNATIVE RISK FINANCING FACILITIES provide mainstream coverage to their members that include corporations, public entities, and professionals. These facilities were originally established and capitalized by organizations and individuals with common requirements for insurance who could not obtain coverage on the commercial markets; could not obtain coverage at an acceptable price; could not effectively act as a CAPTIVE INSURANCE COMPANY; or could not act as a SELF-INSURER. Coverages written include property insurance, WORKERS COMPENSATION INSURANCE, DIRECTORS AND OFFICERS LIABILITY INSURANCE, MEDICAL MALPRACTICE LIABILITY INSURANCE, and primary and excess liability insurance. Insureds include a broad range of organizations and individuals: medical personnel, banks, manufacturers, public entities, nonprofit entities, contractors, and transportation companies and systems. The major portion of the facilities is domiciled in Bermuda.

AMBIGUITY language in the insurance policy that can be considered unclear or subject to different interpretations. Under these circumstances, the courts have generally ruled in favor of insured individuals and against insurance companies since insurance policies are deemed to be contracts of adhesion, and also that insurance companies have sufficient legal talent at their disposal to make policy language clear.

AMENDMENT provisions added to an original insurance policy that alter or modify benefits and coverages of the contract. For example, a HOMEOWNERS INSURANCE POLICY can be endorsed to cover a secondary dwelling; perils can be added for coverage. *See also* ENDORSEMENT; RIDER.

AMERICAN ACADEMY OF ACTUARIES professional association that sets standards of performance for those engaged in actuarial functions. Members are entitled to use the professional designation MAAA (Member, American Academy of Actuaries). The U.S. Department of Labor and the Internal Revenue Service requires that documents filed with these governmental agencies be signed by a member of the American Academy of Actuaries attesting to the validity of actuarial calculations concerning benefits to be paid and their funding. The academy is located in Chicago, Illinois.

AMERICAN AGENCY SYSTEM marketing of insurance through independent agents; also called *independent agency system.* Independent agents usually represent several insurance companies and try to insure the risk according to availability of coverage and most favorable price. Independent agents are paid a commission in the form of a percentage of the premiums generated by the policy sold. They own all the records of the policies sold and have the right to solicit renewals. They are not restricted to maintaining business with just one company and can transfer the business upon renewal to another company.

AMERICAN ANNUITY TABLE, 1955 historical MORTALITY TABLE used to calculate PREMIUM rates for DEFERRED ANNUITIES and OPTIONAL MODES OF SETTLEMENT for LIFE INSURANCE policies. This table was subsequently replaced by the 1983 Table-a (mortality table for annuity rates for males).

AMERICAN COLLEGE (Formerly the American College of Life Underwriters) accrediting body for the CLU (Chartered Life Underwriter) and the ChFC (Chartered Financial Consultant) designations. Provides undergraduate, graduate and continuing education in life insurance and financial services courses on both a residence and correspondence basis. Courses include life insurance, pensions, economics, finance, investments, business evaluations, tax planning, and estate planning. The college, which also confers the Master of Science in Financial Services degree, is located in Bryn Mawr, Pennsylvania.

AMERICAN COUNCIL OF LIFE INSURANCE association of life insurance companies focusing on legislation and public relations that may affect the life insurance business on federal, state, and local levels. Membership is composed of both stock and mutual life insurance companies. The council lobbies to voice the views of the life insurance business in order to influence public opinion and legislation. It also acts as a control source of information on the life insurance business for the public. Located in Washington, D.C.

AMERICAN EXPERIENCE TABLE chart published in 1868 by Sheppard Homans, an actuary with the Mutual Life Insurance Company of New York, based on insured lives from 1843 to 1858. Historically, it was widely used for life insurance premium and reserve calculations. It was replaced by the C.S.O. Table. *See also* COMMISSIONERS STANDARD ORDINARY MORTALITY TABLE (CSO).

AMERICAN INSTITUTE FOR PROPERTY AND LIABILITY UNDERWRITERS accrediting body for the CPCU (Chartered Property and Casualty Underwriter) designation. The institute provides undergraduate and continuing education in property and casualty insurance courses on a correspondence basis. Courses include risk management and insurance, commercial property risk management and insurance, commercial liability risk management and insurance, personal risk management and insurance, insurance company operations, legal environment of insurance, management, accounting, finance, and economics. Located in Malvern, Pennsylvania.

AMERICAN INSURANCE ASSOCIATION (AIA) membership organization of property and liability insurance companies. The association promotes the economic, legislative, and public standing of its members through its attention to accounting procedures, catastrophe and pollution problems, auto insurance reform, and other activities. Located in New York City, New York.

AMERICAN JOBS CREATION ACT OF 2004 legislation that stipulates the amount of income, gift tax, or estate tax that may be taken as a deduction for the fair market value of a donated property.

AMERICAN LIFE CONVENTION *see* AMERICAN COUNCIL OF LIFE INSURANCE.

AMERICAN LLOYD'S *see* LLOYD'S ASSOCIATION.

AMERICAN MUTUAL INSURANCE ALLIANCE *see* ALLIANCE OF AMERICAN INSURERS (AAI).

AMERICAN RISK AND INSURANCE ASSOCIATION membership organization of companies, academics, and individuals in the insurance business whose interest is to further education and research in insurance and risk management. The association publishes *The Journal of Risk and Insurance,* which is devoted to scholarly articles on insurance, risk management, and allied fields of study.

AMERICANS WITH DISABILITIES ACT (ADA) act that prevents employers from rejecting disabled job applicants on the grounds that hiring such an applicant would result in higher employee health care cost. Additionally, if the job applicant has a disabled spouse, child, or other dependent, regardless of whether or not the job applicant is also disabled, the employer cannot reject the job applicant on those grounds. Thus, the employer cannot exclude disabled employees and their dependents from its health plan on the ground that providing such coverage would increase the cost of health care. Title I of the act became effective for all employers with 25 or more employees on July 26, 1992.

A disability is defined by the ADA as: "A physical or mental impairment which substantially limits one or more major life activities; or a record of such impairment; or being regarded as having such an impairment." Title I mandates that: "All personnel actions must be unrelated to either the existence or consequence of disability to include recruitment and selection of employees; compensation of employees; training and all terms, conditions, and privileges of employment. If there are any conflicts with state laws, ADA takes precedence."

AMIM Associate in Marine Insurance Management.

AMORTIZATION the systematic liquidation of a sum owed. A payment is charged at specific time intervals which will reduce the outstanding debt to zero at the end of a given period of time.

AMORTIZATION SCHEDULE method of paying a sum due whose value has been discounted, according to a predetermined schedule. Each periodic payment includes part of the principal and interest due thereon.

AMORTIZED VALUE *see* AMORTIZATION; AMORTIZATION SCHEDULE.

AMOUNT AT RISK

1. difference between the face value of a permanent life insurance policy and its accrued cash value. The pure cost of protection is based on this difference. For example, if the face value of a life insurance policy is $100,000 and the cash value is $80,000 then the net amount at risk is $20,000. From the Internal Revenue Service perspective, a corridor of protection or net amount of risk must be apparent in a life insurance policy if the policy is to retain its tax advantaged treatment.
2. in property and liability insurance, the lesser of the policy limit or the maximum possible loss to the insured.

AMOUNT FOR WHICH LOSS SETTLED *see* LOSS SETTLEMENT AMOUNT.

AMOUNT OF INSURANCE TO VALUE   proportion of the sum insured to the total property value. *See also* COINSURANCE.

AMOUNT SUBJECT *see* MAXIMUM PROBABLE LOSS (MPL).

ANALYSIS *see* ANALYSIS OF PROPERTY AND CASUALTY POLICY; RISK CLASSIFICATION.

ANALYSIS OF PROPERTY AND CASUALTY POLICY determination of (1) property covered, property excluded; (2) perils covered, perils excluded; (3) location covered, location excluded; (4) time period the policy is in force; (5) persons covered, persons excluded; (6) policy limits; and (7) coinsurance requirements.

ANALYTIC SYSTEM *see* DEAN ANALYTIC SCHEDULE.

ANCILLARY BENEFITS health insurance coverage for miscellaneous medical expenses associated with a hospital stay. Benefits provided in individual and group health insurance include ambulance service to and from a hospital, drugs, blood, surgical dressings, operating room, medicines, bandages, X-rays, diagnostic tests, and anesthetics. Ancillary benefits are expressed as a multiplier of the daily hospital benefits (10, 15, or 20 times).

ANCILLARY CHARGES *see* ANCILLARY BENEFITS.

ANIMAL HEALTH INSURANCE *see* LIVESTOCK MORTALITY (LIFE) INSURANCE; LIVESTOCK TRANSIT INSURANCE.

ANIMAL LIFE INSURANCE *see* LIVESTOCK INSURANCE.

ANNIVERSARY *see* POLICY ANNIVERSARY.

ANNUAL AGGREGATE LIMIT pre-determined dollar amount up to which an insurance policy will cover an insured each year, regardless of the number of claims submitted or defense costs associated with these claims. For example, if the policy limit was established at $1,000,000, the insurance company would pay only up to $1,000,000 regardless of the number of claims during a particular year.

ANNUAL CONVENTION BLANK *see* ANNUAL STATEMENT.

ANNUAL EXPECTED DOLLAR LOSS over a long period of time, the AVERAGE loss an individual, individuals, or an organization can expect to incur from a particular EXPOSURE.

ANNUAL INSURANCE POLICY *see* ANNUAL POLICY.

ANNUAL PERCENTAGE RATE (APR) annual rate of interest charged by the lender and paid by the borrower.

ANNUAL POLICY contract remaining in force for up to 12 months unless canceled earlier. After 12 months the policy can either be renewed or not renewed by the insurance company or the insured. The policy need not be paid for on an annual basis.

ANNUAL PREMIUM ANNUITY series of premium payments made to purchase an ANNUITY. This is the same method of purchase used for LEVEL PREMIUM INSURANCE.

ANNUAL RENEWAL AGREEMENT agreement in which the insurer promises to renew the policy provided certain conditions have been met by the insured.

ANNUAL REPORT statement of the financial condition of the insurance company, as well as significant events during the year in which the company has been involved and/or that have affected the company. This statement is furnished to the stockholders (if a STOCK INSURANCE COMPANY) or POLICYHOLDERS (if a MUTUAL INSURANCE COMPANY).

ANNUAL RESET WITH MONTHLY AVERAGING comparison of index value on a starting date with that of the index 12 month average in an EQUITY INDEXED ANNUITY.

ANNUAL STATEMENT report that an insurance company must file annually with the State Insurance Commissioner in each state in which it does business. The statement shows the current status of reserves, expenses, assets, total liabilities, investment portfolio, and employees earning over $40,000 per year. It provides information needed to assure that an insurance company has adequate reserves, and that assets are available to meet all benefit payments for which the company has received premiums. The form used is agreed upon by the National Association of Insurance Commissioners (NAIC). This form is also known as *Annual Convention Blank*.

ANNUALIZED accounting method of establishing data on an annual basis.

ANNUITANT person who receives an income benefit from an ANNUITY for life or for a specified period.

ANNUITY contract sold by insurance companies that pays a monthly (or quarterly, semiannual, or annual) income benefit for the life of a person (the ANNUITANT), for the lives of two or more persons, or for a specified period of time. The annuitant can never outlive the income from the annuity. While the basic purpose of life insurance is to provide an income for a beneficiary at the death of the insured, the annuity is intended to provide an income for life for the annuitant. There are variations in both the way that payments are made by a buyer during the ACCUMULATION PERIOD, and in the way payments are made to the annuitant during the LIQUIDATION PERIOD.

An annuity may be bought by means of installments, with benefits scheduled to begin at a specified age such as 65; or, it may be bought by means of a single lump sum, with benefits scheduled to begin immediately or at a later date. No physical examination is required. For variations in methods of payment, *see* CASH REFUND ANNUITY; FIXED DOLLAR ANNUITY; INSTALLMENT REFUND ANNUITY; JOINT-LIFE AND SURVIVORSHIP ANNUITY; JOINT LIFE ANNUITY; LIFE ANNUITY CERTAIN; PURE ANNUITY; VARIABLE DOLLAR ANNUITY.

ANNUITY ANALYSIS includes rate of return, how long the annuity's interest rate is guaranteed, loads (front, middle and back), financial ranking of the insurance company offering the annuity, the monthly income factor per $1000 of cash value on deposit. For example, for the last item, if the monthly income factor is $6.18 per $1000 of cash value on deposit and the size of the cash value on account is $100,000, a male annuitant would receive a monthly income benefit of $618 at age 65.

ANNUITY, CASH REFUND *see* CASH REFUND ANNUITY.

ANNUITY, CD product that guarantees the initial interest rate for funds on deposit for the length of the maturity, whether it is for a period of 1, 3, 5, 10, or 15 years. At maturity, the POLICYHOLDER has two choices: (1) withdraw the funds without having to pay a SURRENDER CHARGE (it is important to note that taxes must be paid on the interest earned and there is a 10% penalty on the earnings if the policyholder is less than age 59½); or (2) roll the funds over into another annuity for a limited number of years or a product of longer duration. In contrast to certificates of deposit (CDs), interest earned through this ANNUITY accumulates on a tax-deferred basis. This type of annuity provides liquidity, preserves principal, and stipulates a fixed rate of return.

ANNUITY CERTAIN *see* LIFE ANNUITY CERTAIN.

ANNUITY CONSIDERATION single payment or periodic payments that are made to purchase an annuity.

ANNUITY DATE date of the initial annuity payment.

ANNUITY, DEFERRED *see* DEFERRED ANNUITY.

ANNUITY DUE annuity under which payments are made in the beginning of each period (month, quarter, or year).

ANNUITY FORMS *see* ANNUITY, ANNUITY DUE; LIFE ANNUITY CERTAIN; CASH REFUND ANNUITY; INSTALLMENT REFUND ANNUITY; VARIABLE DOLLAR ANNUITY.

ANNUITY, GROUP *see* GROUP ANNUITY.

ANNUITY, INSTALLMENT REFUND *see* INSTALLMENT REFUND ANNUITY.

ANNUITY, JOINT LIFE *see* JOINT LIFE ANNUITY.

ANNUITY, JOINT LIFE AND SURVIVORSHIP *see* JOINT LIFE AND SURVIVORSHIP ANNUITY.

ANNUITY PAYMENT OPTION series of payments made on either a FIXED DOLLAR ANNUITY basis or VARIABLE DOLLAR ANNUITY basis.

ANNUITY RENT periodic payments to an ANNUITANT.

ANNUITY, RETIREMENT *see* ANNUITY; GROUP DEFERRED ANNUITY; GROUP DEPOSIT ADMINISTRATION ANNUITY; GROUP IMMEDIATE PARTICIPATION GUARANTEED (IPG) CONTRACT ANNUITY; PENSION PLAN FUNDING.

ANNUITY, REVERSIONARY *see* SURVIVORSHIP ANNUITY.

ANNUITY, SURVIVORSHIP *see* SURVIVORSHIP ANNUITY.

ANNUITY TABLE, 1949 table that replaced the STANDARD ANNUITY TABLE, 1937. It reflected the fact that more people were living longer in its statistics. This table was subsequently replaced by the INDIVIDUAL ANNUITY TABLE, 1971 and, to some extent, the AMERICAN ANNUITY TABLE, 1955.

ANNUITY TABLES chart showing for a group of people (1) the number living at the beginning of a designated year and (2) the number dying during that year. Yearly probabilities are used in calculating premium payments for future income payments to annuitants.

ANNUITY, TAX DEFERRED *see* TAX DEFERRED ANNUITY.

ANNUITY UNIT share of a VARIABLE DOLLAR ANNUITY paid to an ANNUITANT as an income payment.

ANTICOERCION LAW section of the "Unfair Trade Practices Code" of most states that declares the use of coercion to be in violation of the state code. *See also* UNFAIR TRADE PRACTICE.

ANTIFREEZE provision of the 1987 Tax Act that excludes life insurance owned by a third party or an irrevocable trust from FEDERAL ESTATE TAXES. Life insurance, as well as the deceased's personal residence, was exempted because neither is considered to be an "enterprise" as defined by the Internal Revenue Service (IRS). The IRS defines an enterprise as "any arrangement, relationship, or activity that has significant business or investment aspects."

ANTIREBATE LAW statute that makes it illegal in most states for an agent to rebate (return) any portion of his COMMISSION as an inducement for an applicant to purchase insurance from him.

ANTISELECTION *see* ADVERSE SELECTION.

ANY OCCUPATION FOR WHICH REASONABLY SUITED *see* DISABILITY INCOME INSURANCE.

ANY WILLING PROVIDER designation established by STATUTORY REQUIREMENTS making it mandatory for health care networks to include any health care provider that accepts the network's fees, rules, and regulations.

APP *see* APPLICATION.

APPARENT AGENCY (AUTHORITY) situation wherein the agent's conduct causes a client or prospective insured reasonably to believe that the agent has the authority to sell an insurance policy and contract on behalf of the insurance company. For example, if an agent continues to use insurance company documents, such as its application forms, rate manuals, stationery, and emblems on the door, the client has every reason to believe that the agent does in fact continue to represent the insurance company.

APPARENT AUTHORITY *see* APPARENT AGENCY (AUTHORITY).

APPARENT AUTHORITY (PERCEIVED AUTHORITY) specific powers that a prospective insured believes the insurance company has granted to its AGENT. For example, if the insurance company has furnished the agent a rate book, application forms, stationery with the company logo, and sales literature, the prospective insured has reason to believe that an agency relationship exists between the insurance company and the agent. According to the doctrine of ESTOPPEL, the insurance company is prohibited from denying the relationship.

APPEAL BOND guarantee of payment of the original judgment of a court. When a judgment is appealed, a bond is usually required to guarantee that if the appeal is unsuccessful, funds would be available to pay the original judgment as well as costs of the appeal. This serves to discourage an individual from appealing merely to stall for time or for frivolous reasons.

APPLETON RULE regulation named after a former Superintendent of Insurance of New York State, and instituted in the early 1900s. It requires every insurer admitted to New York to comply with the New York Insurance Code and even in other states where that insurer does business. This rule has had a nationwide impact on the insurance industry. New York State is known for its leadership role in insurance regulation. Thus, if an insurance company is admitted to conduct business in New York, it is a sign that it has met exacting requirements.

APPLICANT prospective insured who completes and signs a written form containing personal statements about himself/herself. *See also* APPLICATION.

APPLICATION written statements on a form by a prospective insured about himself, including assets and other personal information. These statements and additional information, such as a medical report, are used by an insurance company to decide whether or not to insure the risk. Falsification or nondisclosure of information may give the insurance company grounds for rescinding a policy that has been issued. Statements in the application are also used to decide on an applicant's underwriting classification and premium rates.

APPOINTED ACTUARY ACTUARY, appointed by the life insurance company, required by the NATIONAL ASSOCIATION OF INSURANCE COMMISSIONERS (NAIC) under the NAIC: STANDARD VALUATION LAW to provide an opinion as to the compliance of the insurance company's statutory statement with the law and the level of assets needed to support the statement of liabilities of the insurance company. In essence, this actuary is responsible for documenting the adequacy of the liability reserves according to the RESERVE LIABILITIES REGULATION as established by the NAIC.

APPOINTMENT act by a company that authorizes an AGENT to act on its behalf.

APPOINTMENT OF TRUSTEES FOR TERMINATED PLAN plan initiated by the PENSION BENEFIT GUARANTY CORPORATION (PBGC) upon the involuntary termination of a pension plan. With the concurrence of the United States District Court, the PBGC appoints a trustee(s) to administer the terminated plan. The trustee(s) safeguards the remaining assets of the pension plan, protects the assets from being further depicted, limits further increases in liabilities, and in general acts as protector of the benefits for the pension plan's participants.

APPOINTMENT PAPERS documents completed by the AGENT to effect authorization to act on behalf of the company.

APPORTIONMENT division of a loss among insurance policies in the proportion that each policy bears to the total coverage applicable to the loss. For example, assume Policies A, B, C, and D have $50,000, $60,000, $70,000 and $80,000 of insurance in force, respectively: a total of $260,000 of coverage. Under the apportionment clause found in many property insurance policies, Policy A's percentage of any loss is 19.23%, Policy B's is 21.43%, Policy C's is 26.92%, and Policy D's is 30.77%.

APPORTIONMENT CLAUSE clause in a PROPERTY INSURANCE policy that requires the insurance coverage in that policy to be allocated in the proportion that it bears to the total insurance coverage in force from all policies covering that particular property. *See also* APPORTIONMENT.

APPRAISAL valuation of property for damage resulting from an insured peril or for establishing the base amount of insurance coverage to be purchased. If an insured and an insurance company cannot agree on the amount of an insurer's liability for a property loss, the policy may specify that, upon written request, the dispute is submitted to appraisal. Usually, each party selects an appraiser and the two appraisers select a disinterested umpire. Disagreements by the appraisers go to the umpire, whose decisions typically are binding.

APPRAISAL CLAUSE clause in a PROPERTY INSURANCE policy that stipulates that either the insurer or the insured has the right to demand an APPRAISAL in order to determine the monetary damage or loss to an insured property.

APPROVAL acceptance of an application for an insurance policy by the insurance company, indicated by the signature of an officer of the company on the policy. The officer, who must have signature authority, is usually the president or the secretary of the company. The agent who sells the policy normally does not have signature authority to approve the policy.

APPROVAL CONDITIONAL PREMIUM RECEIPT insurance policy in force only after the insurance company approves the APPLICATION. Today, most companies use the INSURABILITY CONDITIONAL PREMIUM RECEIPT.

APPROVED ROOF roof used in construction that is composed of fire resistive materials such as slate as approved by the UNDERWRITERS LABORATORIES INC. (UL).

APPURTENANT STRUCTURES coverage for additional buildings on the same property as the principal insured building. Most property insurance contracts such as the HOMEOWNERS INSURANCE POLICY cover appurtenant structures. For example, under the homeowners policy a separate garage on an insured's premise would be covered up to 10% of the home's structure amount.

ARBITRATION *see* ARBITRATION CLAUSE.

ARBITRATION CLAUSE provision in a property insurance policy to the effect that in the event the insured and insurer cannot agree on the amount of a claim settlement, each appoints an appraiser. The appraisers select a disinterested umpire. When at least two of the three, appraisers and umpire, agree on the settlement amount, it is binding on both the insured and the insurer.

ARIA *see* AMERICAN RISK AND INSURANCE ASSOCIATION.

ARM Associate in Risk Management.

ARMORED CAR AND MESSENGER INSURANCE coverage during the transfer of securities and monies, precious metals, and other specified types of valuables by armored guard services. Policies are specifically designed to fit an insured's requirements. Standard coverage is available on an ALL RISKS basis, excluding perils of war, nuclear disaster, and dishonest acts of shipper and/or consignee.

ARMSTRONG INVESTIGATION inquiry conducted by a committee of the legislature of the State of New York in 1905 that looked at abuses of life insurance companies operating in the state. This study led to stricter supervision by New York and other state insurance departments. For example, many of the policies sold at that time contained language that made the receipt of benefits very difficult to obtain. As a result of the investigation, standard provisions were introduced into life insurance policies. While actual language is not dictated word for word by state regulatory authorities, a policy must provide minimum benefits (such as nonforfeiture provisions) expressed in acceptable language.

ARP Associate in Research and Planning.

ARREARS insurance policy under which premiums are past due but the GRACE PERIOD has not expired.

ARSON actual or attempted malicious and deliberate burning of a physical asset owned by another party. Coverage against arson is provided under property insurance, but only if the insured has not committed the arson. The property insurance business has long worked to discourage arson and to prosecute arsonists.

A-SHARE ANNUITY type of ANNUITY where sales charges are taken out up front. As the assets increase, this change is reduced. *See also* MUTUAL FUND CLASS A SHARES.

ASO *see* ADMINISTRATIVE SERVICES ONLY.

ASSAILING THIEVES individuals other than the crew of a ship who forcefully steal the ship and/or its cargo. This event is an INSURED PERIL under OCEAN MARINE INSURANCE.

ASSAULT threatening act, physical and/or verbal, which causes a person to reasonably fear for life or safety. For example, if a boxing champion said he was going to hit someone, this would probably cause a reasonably prudent person to fear serious bodily injury. An insured's liability for assault is excluded from all standard liability policies such as the SPECIAL MULTIPERIL INSURANCE (SMP) and the HOMEOWNERS INSURANCE POLICY.

ASSESSABLE INSURANCE coverage in which an initial premium is charged, with the stipulation that an additional premium can be charged later if the loss experience of the insurance company warrants it; that is, if losses exceed premium income. *See also* ASSESSMENT COMPANY.

ASSESSABLE MUTUAL assessment mutual company that operates on a statewide basis or in more than one state. Assessable or assessment mutuals operate by taking a cash deposit, or premium, from members in exchange for insurance protection. If the company's losses and expenses exceed these deposits, the company can assess members for additional monies to cover losses. These companies are commonly used by a group of local farmers or merchants in a small geographical area. Some states have specific laws governing these mutuals. For example, they might be limited to a certain type of business or have a maximum dollar limit for each risk.

ASSESSED VALUE monetary worth of real or personal property as a basis for its taxation. This value, established by a government agency, is rarely used as a means to determine indemnification of an insured for property damage or destruction. *See also* INDEMNITY; REPLACEMENT COST LESS PHYSICAL DEPRECIATION AND OBSOLESCENCE.

ASSESSMENT COMPANY insurance company that has the authority to assess or charge its policyholders for losses that the company is incurring. This company is sometimes called *stipulated premium company* or *assessment association.* These companies were relatively common in the 1800s and early 1900s but have since become rare. Most insurance companies cannot assess policyholders for losses. *See also* ASSESSMENT INSURANCE; ASSESSMENT PERIOD.

ASSESSMENT INSURANCE contract under which an assessment insurance company can charge policyowners additional sums if the company's loss experience is worse than had been loaded for in the premium. This insurance is sometimes called *stipulated premium* and *natural premium* insurance. *See also* ASSESSMENT COMPANY; ASSESSMENT PERIOD.

ASSESSMENT PERIOD time during which an assessment life insurance company has the right to assess policyholders if losses are worse than anticipated in the premium charged. *See also* ASSESSMENT COMPANY; ASSESSMENT INSURANCE.

ASSESSMENT PLAN see ASSESSMENT COMPANY; ASSESSMENT INSURANCE; ASSESSMENT PERIOD.

ASSET entity with exchange or commercial value, such as the book value of property owned by an insurance company as listed on its balance sheet.

ASSET ADEQUACY TESTED RESERVE required RESERVE to satisfy all life insurance policy obligations and expenses according to the APPOINTED ACTUARY's best estimate assumptions. Numerous interest rate scenarios are tested and based on the projections. The amount of asset adequacy tested reserve is established.

ASSET ALLOCATION long-term investment plan strategy under which all of the investor's investable assets are divided into predetermined proportions among several different types of securities. In theory, since these investments are placed into different classifications, each classification is subject to a different market cycle; therefore, the value of all investments should not incur a steep decline at the same time. Thus, such a portfolio approach should always have winners. Some specialized VARIABLE DOLLAR ANNUITIES offer such an approach.

ASSET DEPRECIATION RISK one of four types of risks affecting the life insurance company as identified by the SOCIETY OF ACTUARIES. This risk is associated with losses that the life insurance company may incur as the result of default on the payment of interest (dividends) or principal on bonds, mortgages, general real estate investments, and stocks, as well as the loss in value of these investments resulting from a loss in their MARKET VALUE. *See also* GENERAL BUSINESS RISK; INTEREST RATE CHANGE RISK; PRICING INADEQUACY RISK.

ASSET QUALITY RISK *see* ASSET DEPRECIATION RISK.

ASSETS AND VALUATION actuarial evaluation of the assets of a pension plan according to the fair market value of the assets.

ASSET SHARE VALUE policyholder's equity share of the life insurance company's assets. The share is based on the policyholder's contribution to assets (the company's gross premiums minus cost of insurance, expenses and dividends for the classification to which the policy belongs). This computation is derived from the actual experience of the insurance company instead of the assumptions initially used in calculating premiums and reserves. The actual experience may or may not deviate significantly from the expected experience.

ASSET SUFFICIENCY OR INSUFFICIENCY computation of the ASSET SHARE VALUE, *surrender value,* and *reserve* and the comparison of the three computations in order to judge the adequacy and equity of the tentative GROSS PREMIUM scale to be utilized.

ASSET TRANSFER direct payment to a new custodian for a retirement plan. This payment is not a taxable event since it is not a distribution. The payment must be between like plans; for example, one INDIVIDUAL RETIREMENT ACCOUNT (IRA) to another Individual Retirement Account.

ASSET VALUATION excess or deficit of gross premium above the pure cost of insurance and expenses. The result becomes the valuation of the asset share of the policyholder at the end of a given year. The valuation of the asset share reflects the policyowner's share of the asset of the insurance company.

ASSET VALUATION RESERVE (AVR) explicit liability RESERVE, required by the NATIONAL ASSOCIATION OF INSURANCE COMMISSIONERS (NAIC), established for all invested asset classes. Specific reserves are established for real estate and mortgages. In essence, the purpose of this reserve is to provide a back-up sum for potential equity and credit losses. To accomplish this objective, reserves are maintained for stocks, bonds, real estate, mortgages, and similar types of invested assets. Realized and unrealized equity and credit capital gains and losses are credited to or debited against this reserve. Amount of reserves required to be maintained for each invested asset is determined by ACTUARIAL formula.

ASSIGNED CLAIMS *see* AUTOMOBILE ASSIGNED RISK INSURANCE PLAN.

ASSIGNED RISK *see* AUTOMOBILE ASSIGNED RISK INSURANCE PLAN.

ASSIGNED RISK PLAN *see* AUTOMOBILE ASSIGNED RISK INSURANCE PLAN.

ASSIGNEE *see* COLLATERAL CREDITOR (ASSIGNEE).

ASSIGNMENT transfer of rights under an insurance policy to another person or business. For example, to secure a debt, it is not uncommon for the policyowner to transfer to the creditor his rights to borrow on the cash value. Life insurance policies are freely assignable to secure loans and notes (property and casualty insurance policies are not). Creditors such as banks often have printed assignment forms on hand at the time of making loans.

ASSIGNMENT CLAUSE, LIFE INSURANCE feature in a life insurance policy allowing a policyowner to freely assign (give, sell) a policy to another or institution. For example, in order to secure a loan, a bank asks to be assigned the policy. If the insured dies before repayment of the loan, the bank would receive a portion of the death benefit that equals the outstanding loan, the remainder of the death benefit being payable to the insured's beneficiary. The fact that life insurance is freely assignable makes it a useful financial instrument through which to secure a loan. The insurance company does not guarantee the validity of the assignment.

ASSIGNOR person who transfers rights under an insurance or mortgage contract.

ASSISTIVE TECHNOLOGY items, equipment, or systems used to increase, improve, or maintain the capabilities of people with disabilities. These devices range from simple, such as penholders or cup holders, to complex, such as computer voice communication or robots. This technology is playing an increasing role in WORKERS COMPENSATION BENEFITS in returning insured workers to their jobs.

ASSOCIATION *see* POOL; SYNDICATE.

ASSOCIATION CAPTIVE insurance company established by a trade group or other association to provide selected types of PRIMARY INSURANCE and/or LIABILITY INSURANCE for members of the association and access to REINSURANCE markets. For example, the American Newspaper Publishers Association has established an association captive to provide LIBEL INSURANCE for member newspapers, and the American Bankers Association sponsors a captive that provides DIRECTORS AND OFFICERS LIABILITY INSURANCE for member banks.

ASSOCIATION GROUP bona fide organization that purchases insurance on a group basis on behalf of members. However, a group cannot be formed for the purpose of purchasing insurance since adverse selection would take place. Group selling permits economies of scale to operate, so that the cost of insurance to a member is appreciably less than an individual policy. The insurance company/agent is able to benefit through individual sales to the group's members. *See also* ADVERSE SELECTION.

ASSOCIATION GROUP INSURANCE *see* ASSOCIATION GROUP.

ASSOCIATION OF GOVERNMENTAL RISK POOLS (AGRIP) association formed to address the requirements of government risk pools. Web site is *http://www.agrip.org.*

ASSOCIATION OF INSURANCE AND RISK MANAGERS IN INDUSTRY AND COMMERCE (AIRMIC) primarily a British association whose membership includes risk managers and insurance buyers, with the emphasis on risk management.

ASSUME to accept by a REINSURER, part or all of a RISK transferred to it by a primary INSURER or another reinsurer. *See also* CEDE; REINSURANCE.

ASSUMED INTEREST RATE/ASSUMED INVESTMENT RETURN (AIR) percentage return appropriated by the insurer for an IMMEDIATE VARIABLE ANNUITY when the insurer calculates the initial income payment to the ANNUITANT. If the variable annuity's underlying portfolio has a net return greater than or less than the AIR, the income payments will increase or decrease accordingly.

ASSUMED LIABILITY *see* CONTRACTUAL LIABILITY.

ASSUMED LOSS RATIO projected percentage of the EARNED PREMIUMS that will be required by the insurance company to pay for the INCURRED LOSSES plus the LOSS ADJUSTMENT EXPENSE.

ASSUMPTION acceptance by a REINSURER of part or all of a RISK that has been transferred to it by a primary INSURER or another reinsurer. *See also* CEDE; REINSURANCE.

ASSUMPTION CERTIFICATE *see* CUT-THROUGH ENDORSEMENT (ASSUMPTION OF RISK).

ASSUMPTION OF RISK technique of risk management (better known as *retention* or SELF INSURANCE) under which an individual or business firm assumes expected losses that are not catastrophic losses through the purchase of insurance. For example, a business firm assumes the risk of its employees being absent because of minor illness, but buys disability insurance to cover absences due to extended illness. Also refers to (1) situations where insureds place themselves in situations that they realize pose a danger, and (2) the acceptance of risks by an insurance company.

ASSUMPTION OF RISK RULE *see* ASSUMPTION OF RISK.

ASSUMPTION REINSURANCE form of insurance whereby the buyer (REINSURER) assumes the entire obligation of the CEDENT company, effected through the transfer of the policies from the cedent to the books of the reinsurer. Several thousand policies are transferred annually among insurance companies. Generally, life, health, and investment type policies such as annuities are the policies most likely to be transferred since they are of longer duration and in many instances cannot be canceled by the insurance company.

ASSUMPTIONS circumstances taken for granted. For example, in calculating annuity values, a particular interest rate is assumed. This assumption is critical to CURRENT ASSUMPTION WHOLE LIFE INSURANCE policies since projections of future cash values ultimately being realized are determined by the validity of the underlying assumptions.

ASSURANCE *see* INSURANCE.

ASSURED *see* INSURED.

ASSURER *see* INSURER.

ASYMMETRIC RISK EXPOSURE gain when the underlying asset that moves in one direction is significantly different from the loss when the underlying asset moves in the opposite direction; for example, when gains and losses associated with purchasing a call option on a stock are significantly different. Under a call option, when a stock price goes down, the loss incurred is limited to the purchase price of the option. If the stock price goes up, the purchaser of the call gains in proportion to the rise in the stock's value.

ATOMIC ENERGY COMMISSION *see* NUCLEAR REGULATORY COMMISSION.

ATOMIC ENERGY REINSURANCE *see* MUTUAL ATOMIC ENERGY REINSURANCE POOL.

ATTACHMENT addition to a basic insurance policy to further explain coverages, add or exclude perils and locations covered, and add or delete positions covered. For example, an endorsement to the *Standard Fire Policy* might add coverage for vandalism and malicious mischief. This form has largely been replaced by an ENDORSEMENT or RIDER.

ATTACHMENT POINT critical point in the total amount of claims paid above which the EXCESS INSURANCE policy pays a percentage (generally 80-100%) of the claims for any POLICY YEAR EXPERIENCE.

ATTAINED AGE insured's age at a particular point in time. For example, many TERM LIFE INSURANCE policies allow an insured to convert to permanent insurance without a physical examination at the insured's then attained age. Upon conversion, the premium usually rises substantially to reflect the insured's age and diminished life expectancy. Since later in life rates become prohibitive, many insureds do not make an attained age conversion. *See also* ORIGINAL AGE.

ATTAINED AGE CONVERSION *see* ATTAINED AGE.

ATTENDING PHYSICIAN STATEMENT document providing additional medical information on an APPLICANT. This statement is requested by the insurance company when the medical examination and/or application points to medical conditions that require greater explanations.

ATTESTATION CLAUSE clause listed after the general provisions of the insurance policy that requires the officers of the insurance company to sign their names in order for the contract to be completed. Most insurance policies list the printed signatures of the officers of the insurance company and only the authorized representative of the company will actually sign the contract prior to its delivery to the POLICYOWNER.

ATTORNEY-IN-FACT *see* RECIPROCAL EXCHANGE.

ATTORNEYS PROFESSIONAL LIABILITY INSURANCE *see* LAWYERS LIABILITY INSURANCE.

ATTRACTIVE NUISANCE property that is inherently dangerous and particularly enticing to children. For example a swimming pool has a strong attraction to children and could lead to a liability judgment against the pool's owner. The owner must take all necessary steps to prevent accidents, such as building an adequate fence around the pool.

AU Associate in Underwriting.

AUDIT premium in WORKERS COMPENSATION INSURANCE policies and several business property and liability policies, review of the payroll of a business firm in order to determine the premium for coverage. Premiums in workers compensation are based on units of payroll and adjusted at the end of the policy period to reflect the actual exposure. *See also* DEPOSIT PREMIUM.

AUDITORS REPORT *see* STATEMENT OF OPINION (ACCOUNTANTS REPORT, AUDITORS REPORT).

AUTHORITY TO TERMINATE PLAN means of ending a pension plan only for reasons of business necessity, following IRS regulations. If the IRS determines that the plan was terminated for other reasons, employee and employer contributions become taxable. Reasons acceptable to the IRS include bankruptcy, insolvency, and the inability of a business to continue to make its contributions because of adverse financial conditions.

AUTHORIZATION maximum amount of insurance coverage that an underwriter will write on a particular class of property or risk exposure.

AUTHORIZED CONTROL LEVEL RISK-BASED CAPITAL insurance company's theoretical capital amount and surplus that it should maintain.

AUTHORIZED INSURER insurance company that is *licensed* by a state to market and service particular *lines of insurance* in that state.

AUTO COVERAGE policy for a land motor vehicle, trailer, or semi-trailer that uses a public road under the BUSINESS AUTO COVERAGE FORM and the PERSONAL AUTOMOBILE POLICY (PAP) excepting mobile equipment. Under the liability sections of these policies, mobile equipment that is being carried or towed by the INSURED vehicle is also covered.

AUTO-ENROLL RETIREMENT PLAN company retirement plan in which employees are automatically enrolled into as provided under the PENSION PROTECTION ACT OF 2006. If employees do not select how their contributions will be allocated, these contributions will be automatically placed in money market and/or lifecycle MUTUAL FUNDS.

AUTOMATIC BUILDERS RISK FORM *see* BUILDERS RISKS FORMS.

AUTOMATIC COST OF LIVING ADJUSTMENT *see* COST OF LIVING ADJUSTMENT.

AUTOMATIC COVERAGE policy that comes into existence or adjusts the amount of coverage to provide protection for newly acquired or increasing values of an insured's real or personal property.

AUTOMATIC INCREASE IN BENEFIT PROVISION clause in a DISABILITY INCOME INSURANCE POLICY that will adjust the amount of the monthly income payment upwards according to a stipulated annual percentage for a given number of consecutive years. The annual premium payment will also increase on an ATTAINED AGE basis and reflect the increase in the cost of the increasing benefit.

AUTOMATIC INCREASE IN BENEFITS optional provision in a DISABILITY INCOME policy that allows the POLICYOWNER to increase the monthly income sum at an approximate rate of 6%.

AUTOMATIC INCREASE IN INSURANCE ENDORSEMENT *see* INFLATION ENDORSEMENT.

AUTOMATIC NONPROPORTIONAL REINSURANCE automatic protection for an INSURER against losses that exceed a predetermined loss limit. This reinsurance may be subdivided into three primary types: EXCESS OF LOSS, CATASTROPHE LOSS, and *stop loss. See also* REINSURANCE.

AUTOMATIC PREMIUM LOAN PROVISION life insurance policy clause. If at the end of the GRACE PERIOD the premium due has not been paid, a policy loan will automatically be made from the policy's cash value to pay the premium. The primary purpose is to prevent unintentional lapse of the policy. Funds in the cash value must at least be equal to the loan amount plus one year's interest. Many experts recommend this provision because under some circumstances the premium may go unpaid because of illness, vacations, or inadvertence.

AUTOMATIC PROPORTIONAL REINSURANCE form of coverage in which an insurer automatically reinsures individual risks with its reinsurer. The insurer must transfer (cede) the risks to its reinsurer and its reinsurer must accept this transfer (cession). Losses and premiums are shared; the reinsurer shares them in the same proportion as it does that total policy limits of the risks. The insurer receives from the reinsurer a transfer commission reflecting the so-called equity in the unearned premium reserve of the insurer. This provides for acquisition expenses, premium taxes, and the insurer's cost of servicing the business. Automatic proportional reinsurance may be subdivided into two primary types: *quota share* and *surplus*. *See also* REINSURANCE.

AUTOMATIC REINSTATEMENT CLAUSE provision in a property or liability policy stating that after a loss has been paid, the total original limits of the policy are once again in effect. For example, assume a loss of $40,000 has been paid under a $100,000 property damage coverage HOMEOWNERS INSURANCE POLICY. After payment of the loss, the original $100,000 is reinstated.

AUTOMATIC REINSURANCE automatic reinsuring of individual risks by an insurer with a reinsurer. The insurer must transfer the risks to its reinsurer and its reinsurer must accept this transfer. *See also* REINSURANCE.

AUTOMATIC SPRINKLER CLAUSE *see* SPRINKLER LEAKAGE INSURANCE; SPRINKLER LEAKAGE LEGAL LIABILITY INSURANCE.

AUTOMATIC SPRINKLER SYSTEM *see* SPRINKLER LEAKAGE INSURANCE; SPRINKLER LEAKAGE LEGAL LIABILITY INSURANCE.

AUTOMATIC TREATY *see* AUTOMATIC NONPROPORTIONAL REINSURANCE; AUTOMATIC PROPORTIONAL REINSURANCE; AUTOMATIC REINSURANCE.

AUTOMOBILE ASSIGNED RISK INSURANCE PLAN coverage in which individuals who cannot obtain conventional automobile liability insurance, usually because of adverse driving records, are placed in a residual insurance market. Insurance companies are assigned to write insurance for them, at higher prices, in proportion to the premiums written in a particular state. These plans protect motorists who suffer injury or property damage through the negligence of bad drivers who otherwise would not have insurance.

AUTOMOBILE, BOAT, AND AIRCRAFT INSURANCE coverage for motorized vehicles, each of which requires separate policies for property damage and liability exposures. Motorized vehicles are not covered under a HOMEOWNERS INSURANCE POLICY for property damage and/or bodily injury liability situations when operated away from an insured's premises.

AUTOMOBILE COLLISION *see* COLLISION INSURANCE.

AUTOMOBILE COMPREHENSIVE *see* COMPREHENSIVE INSURANCE.

AUTOMOBILE FLEET *see* FLEET POLICY.

AUTOMOBILE INSURANCE *see* BUSINESS AUTOMOBILE POLICY (BAP); PERSONAL AUTOMOBILE POLICY (PAP).

AUTOMOBILE INSURANCE PLAN *see* AUTOMOBILE ASSIGNED RISK INSURANCE PLAN.

AUTOMOBILE LIABILITY INSURANCE coverage if an insured is legally liable for bodily injury or property damage caused by an automobile. The PERSONAL AUTOMOBILE POLICY (PAP) and the BUSINESS AUTOMOBILE POLICY (BAP) cover the judgment awarded (up to the limits of the policy) and the court cost and legal defense fees. Experts advise against driving an automobile without automobile liability insurance as a matter of common sense, and because state laws require such a policy or evidence of financial responsibility. Passengers in automobiles should assure themselves that drivers are covered by this insurance.

AUTOMOBILE PHYSICAL DAMAGE INSURANCE coverage in the event an insured's automobile is damaged, destroyed, or lost through fire, theft, vandalism, malicious mischief, collision, or windstorm. There are two kinds of property damage coverage—COLLISION INSURANCE and COMPREHENSIVE INSURANCE. *See also* BUSINESS AUTOMOBILE POLICY (BAP); PERSONAL AUTOMOBILE POLICY (PAP).

AUTOMOBILE REINSURANCE FACILITY *see* AUTOMOBILE ASSIGNED RISK INSURANCE PLAN.

AUTOMOBILE SHARED MARKET *see* AUTOMOBILE ASSIGNED RISK INSURANCE PLAN.

AUTOMOBILE THEFT *see* COMPREHENSIVE INSURANCE.

AVERAGE arithmetic mean; the sum of a series of numbers divided by the number of numbers comprising the sum. For example, given the following series of numbers: 1, 4, 5, 6, 8, 9 and 10, the arithmetic mean, or average,

$$= \frac{1 + 4 + 5 + 6 + 8 + 9 + 10}{7}$$

$$= 6.143$$

The arithmetic mean is the EXPECTED LOSS that the insurance company prepares itself to pay, as reflected in the BASIC PREMIUM.

AVERAGE ADJUSTER individual employed by an OCEAN MARINE INSURANCE company to settle on its behalf ocean marine-related claims brought by its insureds. The adjuster evaluates the merits of each claim and makes recommendations to the insurance company.

AVERAGE CLAUSE *see* COINSURANCE; PRO RATA DISTRIBUTION CLAUSE.

AVERAGE EARNINGS CLAUSE (RATIO OF EARNINGS TO THE AMOUNT OF INSURANCE) provision that allows the insurer to reduce the monthly disability income payments if either the insured's total monthly income benefits from all sources exceed current total monthly earnings or average monthly earnings within two years of the first disability income payment.

AVERAGE, GENERAL *see* GENERAL AVERAGE.

AVERAGE INDEXED MONTHLY EARNINGS (AIME) method of calculating the PRIMARY INSURANCE AMOUNT (PIA) for Social Security benefits. Employees' covered monthly earnings are adjusted to reflect changes in the national average annual earnings. Benefits should rise in proportion to increases in national average annual earnings.

AVERAGE LOSS CLAUSE *see* PRO RATA DISTRIBUTION CLAUSE.

AVERAGE MONTHLY EARNINGS (AME) *see* AVERAGE MONTHLY WAGE (AMW).

AVERAGE MONTHLY WAGE (AMW) figure used in calculating a worker's PRIMARY INSURANCE AMOUNT (PIA) to determine Social Security benefits in the following manner:
1. calculate the number of years between the worker's twenty-first birthday and the year prior to the worker reaching age 62 (a maximum of 40 years).
2. exclude the five lowest years of earnings, thereby selecting the 35 highest years (420 months) of earnings.
3. divide the total of the 35 highest years of earnings by 420 months to calculate the Average Monthly Wage.

A Social Security Administration table shows the PIA for the Average Monthly Wage calculated in Step 3. The PIA is then increased to reflect the COST-OF-LIVING ADJUSTMENT (COLA) to determine the actual benefit.

AVERAGE NET COST *see* INTEREST ADJUSTED COST.

AVERAGE, PARTICULAR *see* PARTICULAR AVERAGE.

AVERAGE RATE applicable rate, in property insurance, of each location multiplied by the value of the real and/or personal property at that location, all of which is divided by the total value of all real and/or personal property at all locations multiplied by their respective rates.

AVERAGE SEMIPRIVATE RATE in HEALTH INSURANCE, the applicable average rate charged for a semiprivate room in the geographical area in which the charge is incurred.

AVERAGE WEEKLY WAGE wage rate used as the basis for calculating benefits under WORKERS COMPENSATION INSURANCE. *See also* WORKERS COMPENSATION BENEFITS.

AVIATION ACCIDENT INSURANCE life insurance policy (individual or employee group basis) providing protection for a passenger on a regularly scheduled airline. *See also* AVIATION TRIP LIFE INSURANCE.

AVIATION EXCLUSION common exclusion in life and ACCIDENTAL DEATH INSURANCE (double indemnity) policies, indicating that coverage does not apply unless an insured is a passenger on a regularly scheduled airline. For example, if an insured is killed while a passenger in a private plane crash, the aviation exclusion would apply, and the insured's beneficiary would not receive a death payment.

AVIATION HAZARD additional HAZARD associated with aeronautics other than that of being a passenger on a regularly scheduled airline. An extra premium is charged, and/or there are usually exclusions applied to certain benefits associated with this hazard. For example, pilots of small private planes are subject to this hazard.

AVIATION INSURANCE combination of PROPERTY INSURANCE on the hull of an airplane and LIABILITY INSURANCE in the following manner.
   1. *property coverage*— provided on an ALL RISKS basis or on a specified perils basis for the hull, autopilots, instruments, radios, and any other equipment in the airplane as described in the policy.
   2. *liability coverage*—provided in the event that the insured's negligent acts and/or omissions result in bodily injury and/or property damage to passengers and individuals who are not passengers.

AVIATION TRIP LIFE INSURANCE term life insurance, usually purchased at an airport by an airplane passenger. It provides a death payment to the passenger's beneficiary in the event of a fatal accident on one or more specified flights. The term of coverage is from the time that the passenger enters the airplane until the time that he leaves. Ground transportation to and from the airport may also be covered. With the advent of hijacking and terrorism, this coverage is becoming more widely purchased.

AVOIDANCE technique of risk management. It ensures that an individual or business does not incur any liability relating to a given activity by avoiding the activity in question. For example, a business that does not own computer equipment cannot incur financial loss due to the destruction of the computer by fire. However, in the real world, the risk control technique of avoidance is rarely practical. A more realistic approach is self-insurance or commercial insurance.

B

BACKDATING calculation of insurance premiums based on an age less than the current age of the insured.

BACK LOAD expenses taken out when benefits are paid. For example, a specific dollar amount is subtracted from a monthly income payment for company expenses.

BACKUP WITHHOLDING RATE effective January 4, 1994, the backup withholding rate on dividends, interest, and gross proceeds distributions increased from 20% to 31%. Backup withholding applies in the following situations: (1) if a United States citizen or resident, United States corporation, partnership, trust, estate, or other entity fails to certify their Taxpayer Identification Number (TIN) on Form W-9 (Request for Taxpayer Identification Number and Certification), or fails to provide documentation of their exemption from these rules; (2) if a taxpayer receives notification from the Internal Revenue Service (IRS) of a missing or invalid TIN and fails to certify the TIN by providing the payor with the required documentation; (3) if the taxpayer is notified by the IRS that the taxpayer is not subject to backup withholding because of underreporting of interest or dividends on the tax return and is not notified that it no longer applies.

BAGGAGE INSURANCE *see* TOURIST BAGGAGE INSURANCE.

BAIL BOND monetary guarantee that an individual released from jail will be present in court at the appointed time. If the individual is not present in court at that time, the monetary value of the bond is forfeited to the court (jumping bail). *Personal automobile policies* commonly cover fees for an insured's bail bond.

BAILEE individual who has temporary rightful possession of another's property. The bailee often furnishes a receipt in exchange for the bailor's property. For example, a dry cleaner has temporary custody of a suit to be cleaned and must exercise proper care to safeguard it against physical loss. If the property is damaged, the bailee's insurance policy often becomes the primary coverage and must indemnify the loss.

BAILEE'S CUSTOMERS INSURANCE coverage for legal liability resulting from damage or destruction of the bailor's property while under the bailee's temporary care, custody, and control. Includes property on or in transit to and from the bailee's premises. Perils covered include fire, lightning, theft, burglary, robbery, windstorm, explosion, collision, flood, sprinkler leakage, earthquake, strike, and damage or destruction in the course of transportation by a common carrier. The insurance is in effect when the bailee issues a receipt to the bailor for the item. Coverage excludes property belonging to the insured bailee and loss due to vermin and insects. For example, a suit to be cleaned is under the temporary control of the bailee (cleaner). The bailor (owner) expects the suit to be returned in good condition. If the suit is stolen from the cleaner, the insurance would cover the loss.

BAILMENT transfer of property from a bailor to a bailee; for example, transferring a suit to be cleaned from the bailor (owner) to the bailee (cleaners). *See also* BAILEE; BAILOR.

BAILOR individual who retains title to property that is being transferred on a temporary basis to the care, custody, and/or control of another. *See also* BAILEE.

BAIL-OUT PROVISION clause found in an ANNUITY contract that enables the owner of that contract to withdraw his or her money without surrender penalties, if the annual interest rate is lowered below a certain predetermined minimum.

BALANCED FUND investments in both EQUITIES (common stocks) and debt instruments (bonds) with the goal of maximizing return by reducing risk through the investment in a broad range of the market.

BALANCED PORTFOLIO investments in a broad range of assets from the most conservative to the riskiest.

BALANCE SHEET accounting statement showing the financial condition of a company at a particular date. Listed on the statement are the company's assets and liabilities, and capital and surplus.

BALANCE SHEET RESERVES amount expressed as a liability on the insurance company's balance sheet for benefits owed to policyowners. These reserves must be maintained according to strict actuarial formulas as they serve to guarantee that all benefit payments for which the insurance company has received premiums will be made.

BAND SYSTEM system of classifying FACE AMOUNT of policies according to size within a given range. The premium rate per $1,000 of face amount varies on a declining basis. As the face amount increases, the premium rate per $1,000 of face amount decreases.

BANK BURGLARY AND ROBBERY INSURANCE coverage on the bank's premises for burglary of monies, securities, and other properties from within the bank's safe(s); robbery of monies and securities; loss of monies and securities as the result of vandalism or malicious mischief; general damage due to vandalism and malicious mischief resulting from burglary and/or robbery.

BANKERS BLANKET BOND coverage for a bank in the event of loss due to dishonest acts of its employees or individuals external to the bank. For example, if a teller goes to Mexico with the bank's money, the bank would be indemnified for its loss.

BANKING ACT OF 1933 *see* GLASS-STEAGALL ACT.

BANK LOAN PLAN *see* FINANCED INSURANCE (MINIMUM DEPOSIT INSURANCE); FINANCED PREMIUM.

BANKRUPTCY liquidation, reorganization, or transfer of a business's assets to its creditors according to a prescribed legal structure.

BANK TRUST CUSTODIAL ACCOUNT type of INDIVIDUAL RETIREMENT ACCOUNT (IRA) allowed by the EMPLOYEE RETIREMENT INCOME SECURITY ACT OF 1974 (ERISA), in which contributions are paid into the bank's interest-bearing financial instruments or a SELF-DIRECTED ACCOUNT.

BARE WALL INSURANCE *see* CONDOMINIUM INSURANCE.

BARGAIN SALE charitable planning strategy in which a donor sells an asset to the charity for an amount less than its fair market value. Internal Revenue Service regulations require that the tax basis for the property be established on a pro rata schedule between the sale portion and the gift portion. The donor has a taxable gain on the sale portion.

BARRATRY violation of duty in marine insurance, such as acts of the master and crew of a ship that result in damage to the vessel including purposefully running it aground, diverting it from its true course of travel, stealing of its cargo, and abandoning the vessel.

BASELINE DATA statistics (such as health data from physical examination of employees or other insureds) used as a benchmark from which deviations and comparisons of expected losses, as well as future actual losses, are measured.

BASE PREMIUM a CEDING COMPANY'S premium to which the *reinsurance premium* factor is used to produce the reinsurance premium.

BASIC BENEFITS, BASIC HOSPITAL PLAN minimum payments provided under a health insurance policy. *See also* GROUP HEALTH INSURANCE; HEALTH INSURANCE.

BASIC HEALTH INSURANCE POLICY *see* HEALTH INSURANCE.

BASIC LIMIT minimum amount of coverage for which a company will write a LIABILITY INSURANCE policy.

BASIC LIMITS OF LIABILITY required minimum amounts of coverage that an insurance company will underwrite. For example, for auto liability coverage the minimum that many companies will write is $100,000. Most liability suits are not below this range.

BASIC MORTALITY TABLE MORTALITY TABLE that is a picture of the actual living and/or dying of the population (the universe) upon which the mortality table is based. No additions or subtractions are made to these statistics to show a greater or lesser probability of living or dying than is actually expected to occur.

BASIC PREMIUM premium applied in WORKERS COMPENSATION INSURANCE and in life insurance. In the latter, it is the portion of a premium that is loaded to reflect an insured's expectation of loss, administrative expenses associated with putting the policy on the company's books, and the agent's commission.

BASIC RATE *see* MANUAL RATE.

BASIC TIME FRAME time period, for a life insurance policy, in which losses occur. This period must be determined to project the FREQUENCY and *severity* of future loss experience.

BASIS POINT unit used to measure movements in interest rates. It is the equivalent to one one-hundredth of 1%. One hundred basis points equals 1%.

BASIS RISK type of FINANCIAL REINSURANCE risk that reflects the possibility that the movements in the values of the hedge do not precisely track the loss expectancy of the CEDING COMPANY.

BATTERY unlawful application of force to another's person; physical striking of another without permission.

BAUD RATE number of bits a MODEM can receive or send per second.

BEAR MARKET market in which sellers dominate trading and force financial asset prices down.

BENCH ERROR mistake made during the manufacturing process of a product that results in an inherent defect in the product. This mistake is covered under PRODUCTS AND COMPLETED OPERATIONS INSURANCE.

BENCHMARKING management tool through which a plan for evaluation, measurement, and improvement is implemented. The insurance entity can use this tool to analyze market trends, measure sales performance, measure market penetration, and measure product performance.

BENCHMARK SURPLUS additional amount of SURPLUS from an additional amount of CAPITAL necessary to act as a supplement to the cash flow in the event unforeseen contingencies occur that disrupt or impair the cash flow necessary for the insurance company to make future benefit payments for which it has received the premiums.

BENEFICIARY designation by the owner of a life insurance policy indicating to whom the proceeds are to be paid upon the insured's death or when an endowment matures. Anyone can be named a beneficiary (relative, non-relative, pet, charity, corporation, trustee, partnership). A *primary beneficiary* is the first-named beneficiary, who must survive the death of the insured in order to collect the proceeds. A *contingent* or *secondary beneficiary* will receive the proceeds if the primary beneficiary does not survive the insured. A *revocable beneficiary* (primary or secondary) can be changed by the policyowner at any time. An *irrevocable beneficiary* (primary or secondary) can be changed by the policyowner only with the written permission of that beneficiary. Naming an irrevocable beneficiary removes the policy from the estate of the insured, who thereby gives up incidences of ownership for estate tax purposes.

If a beneficiary is convicted of murdering the insured, the beneficiary cannot collect the death benefit. The insured's estate would receive the benefit.

BENEFICIARY CLAUSE provision in a life insurance policy that permits the policyowner to name anyone as primary and secondary beneficiaries. The policyowner may change the beneficiaries at any time by simply writing the insurance company and sending the policy for endorsement if that is requested. *See also* BENEFICIARY.

BENEFICIARY OF TRUST person for whom the trust was created and who receives the benefits thereof. In many instances a trust is established to prevent the careless exhaustion of an estate. For example, the establishment of a trust for the benefit of a child seeks to guarantee that the parent's estate will not be carelessly diminished.

BENEFIT monetary sum paid or payable to a recipient for which the insurance company has received the premiums.

BENEFIT ALLOCATION METHOD method of funding a PENSION PLAN under which a single premium payment is made to fund a single unit of benefit for one year of recognized service with the employer. For example, if the employee earned an $85 unit of benefit for year X of recognized service to begin at age 60, a SINGLE PREMIUM DEFERRED ANNUITY would be purchased for that employee's account. Each year this procedure would be repeated as additional single premium deferred annuities would be purchased for each year of recognized service. At the time of retirement, the annuities so purchased would be combined to provide a monthly income benefit for the employee.

BENEFIT/COST RATIO *see* COST-BENEFIT ANALYSIS.

BENEFIT FORMULA procedure in employee benefit plans to calculate life insurance and retirement benefits to which an employee is entitled. *See also* DEFINED BENEFIT PLAN; DEFINED CONTRIBUTION PENSION (MONEY PURCHASE PLAN); GROUP LIFE INSURANCE.

BENEFIT PERIOD in HEALTH INSURANCE, the number of days for which benefits are paid to the NAMED INSURED and his or her dependents. For example, the number of days that benefits are calculated for a calendar year consist of the days beginning on January 1 and ending on December 31 of each year.

BENEFITS OF BUSINESS LIFE AND HEALTH INSURANCE (KEY PERSON INSURANCE) life insurance and long-term disability income insurance on major employees, with benefits payable to the business. Key person insurance has these advantages: (1) enhances the ability of the business to continue operations; (2) fosters smooth sale of a going business between an estate and a purchaser by providing funds to buy out the interest of a deceased key person; (3) encourages key employees to stay on the job; (4) attracts new key employees; (5) provides funds for expenses of hiring and training of a replacement key employee; (6) provides a line of credit (A permanent life insurance policy has cash values that are available for loans at advantageous rates.); (7) policy proceeds, which are income free, are payable even if the key person is no longer in the employ of the business at the time of death; however, the business must continue to make the premium payments after the key person leaves the employment; (8) a life insurance policy can be surrendered for its cash value or sold to the insured key person; thus, the business will usually at least receive the return of premiums; (9) long-term disability income insurance on a key person also provides funds for salary continuation to the disabled key person. (For temporary disability, the business might prefer to self insure because the expense of premiums for this coverage is generally excessive when compared with the potential income benefits.)

BENEFIT TRIGGERS conditions that must be met before insurance benefits become payable.

BEQUEST property left by WILL by one person to another person.

BETA measurement of a particular stock's volatility as compared with that of the overall market as measured by the STANDARD & POOR'S 500 STOCK PRICE INDEX (S&P 500). The standard or the norm is a beta of 1.0. For example, if a stock has a beta of 1.0, it tracks the market in tandem. A beta of 1.5 indicates the stock is 50% more volatile than the market. A beta of 0.6 means the stock is 40% less volatile than the market.

BETTERMENT INSURANCE *see* IMPROVEMENTS AND BETTERMENTS INSURANCE.

BI *see* BODILY INJURY; BUSINESS INTERRUPTION.

BID price an investor is willing to pay for a financial asset.

BID AND ASK PRICE highest price investor is willing to pay for a stock or mutual fund unit and lowest price a seller of a stock or mutual fund is willing to accept.

BID BOND bond required of a contractor submitting the lowest bid on a project. If the contractor then refuses to undertake the project, the bid bond assures that the developer will be paid the difference between the lowest bid and next lowest bid. The bid bond encourages contractors to make serious bids and live up to their obligations.

BILATERAL CONTRACT contract under which there is an exchange of a promise for a promise. An INSURANCE POLICY is deemed to be a UNILATERAL CONTRACT.

BILL OF LADING document used in the transportation of goods that must be presented when a claim is made for a loss incurred. This document establishes the fact that the goods were under the care, custody, or control of the shipper at the time the loss occurred.

BINDER temporary insurance contract providing coverage until a permanent policy is issued. In property and casualty insurance, some agents have authority to bind the insurance company to cover until a policy can be issued. For example, the purchaser of an automobile can call the agent, who can then bind the insurance company to temporary coverage.

BINDING AUTHORITY *see* BINDER.

BINDING RECEIPT evidence of a temporary contract obliging a property insurance company to provide coverage as long as the premium accompanies the application. A property insurance agent can *bind* a company to cover a specific risk. Some agents are authorized to give an *oral binder,* which is generally followed with a written binder. For life and health insurance, *see also* CONDITIONAL RECEIPT.

BINOMIAL DISTRIBUTION statistical function that displays the probability of determining a stated number of successes in a series of trials in which the probability of success is the same in each trial. In insurance, the binomial distribution is used to analyze certain future events. Some chance events have only two possible outcomes; the probability of occurrence $p = 1 - q$ and the probability of nonoccurrence $q = 1 - p$. (Note that $p + q = 1$; that is to say, the probability of success plus the probability of failure is always equal to 1.) The probability of exactly x *outcomes (x successes)* in n *independent repetitions* is given by the function

$$f(x) = \left(\frac{n}{x}\right) p^x q^{n-x}$$

where: $x = 0, 1, 2, \ldots, n$

For example, if a fair coin is tossed in the air a total of six times, the *probability* of getting exactly five heads is:

$$f(5) = \left(\frac{6}{5}\right)\left(\frac{1}{2}\right)^5\left(\frac{1}{2}\right) = \frac{6}{64}$$

BIRTH RATE number of people born as a percentage of the total population in any given period of time.

BLACK LIST STATES states that preclude the placement of SURPLUS LINES with particular insurance companies.

BLACKOUT PERIOD time interval between the date benefits end under Social Security and the date these benefits resume. For example, survivor benefits are paid only as long as the parent (if less than age 60) cares for a child less than age 16. Once that child reaches age 16, the surviving parent must wait until age 60 before survivor benefits resume.

BLANKET BOND coverage for an employer in the event of dishonesty of any employee. *See also* FIDELITY BOND.

BLANKET CONTRACT policy covering an insured's property at several different locations. This coverage is used by business firms that have several locations and may move property from location to location.

BLANKET COVERAGE *see* BLANKET BOND; BLANKET CONTRACT; BLANKET CRIME POLICY; BLANKET INSURANCE; BLANKET MEDICAL EXPENSE INSURANCE; BLANKET POSITION BOND.

BLANKET CRIME ENDORSEMENT *see* BLANKET CRIME POLICY.

BLANKET CRIME POLICY coverage usually provided as part of the SPECIAL MULTIPERIL INSURANCE (SMP) policy, generally replaced by the COMMERCIAL PACKAGE POLICY, through the attachment of the *Blanket Crime Endorsement.* Perils covered include dishonesty of a business's employees; loss of money both while inside as well as outside a business's premises; lost money orders; forgery due to the acts of a depositor; and counterfeit paper currency. Since this crime policy is so comprehensive it is said to provide the insured with a *blanket of coverage.* This policy has largely been replaced by the COMMERCIAL CRIME COVERAGE FORM.

BLANKET FIDELITY BOND *see* BLANKET BOND.

BLANKET FLOATER *see* FLOATER.

BLANKET FORM *see* BLANKET INSURANCE.

BLANKET HONESTY BOND *see* COMMERCIAL BLANKET BOND.

BLANKET INSURANCE single policy on the insured's property for (1) two or more different kinds of property in the same location; (2) same kind of property in two or more locations; (3) two or more different kinds of property in two or more different locations. Blanket coverage is ideal for such businesses as chain stores, all of whose property is covered with no specific limit on each particular property regardless of its location (thereby enabling the business to shift merchandise from store to store). This insurance can (but need not) be written on an ALL RISKS basis subject to exclusions of war, nuclear disaster, and wear and tear.

BLANKET LIMIT maximum amount of insurance coverage that an insurance company will underwrite in a particular geographic area.

BLANKET MEDICAL EXPENSE INSURANCE health insurance policy providing coverage for an insured's medical expenses except those that are specifically excluded. This may be the most advantageous medical expense policy for an insured because unless a specific medical expense is excluded it is automatically covered.

BLANKET POSITION BOND covers all employees of a business on a blanket basis with the maximum limit of coverage applied separately to each employee guilty of a crime. *See also* COMMERCIAL BLANKET BOND, FIDELITY BOND.

BLANKET RATE premium charged (and applied on a uniform basis) for property insurance covering properties at multiple locations. This rate is used under a BLANKET INSURANCE policy instead of using a specific rate for each location or type of property.

BLENDED/INTEGRATED INSURANCE PROGRAM insurance programs that combine FINITE RISK INSURANCE, REINSURANCE, and traditional insurance as an alternative to SELF INSURANCE. These programs are long-term in duration. The objective is to incorporate the advantages of a finite risk insurance program (management of cash flow, smoothing of income and profit sharing) with the advantages of transferring the risk through traditional insurance.

BLENDING combination of a TERM LIFE INSURANCE policy and an ORDINARY LIFE INSURANCE policy.

BLOCK LIMITS total amount of insurance that an insurer will write on any specific city block. Such a limit will reduce the insurer's exposure to a potential catastrophic occurrence, such as a hurricane, tornado, or fire, which could destroy the entire block.

BLOCK OF POLICIES total number of INSURANCE POLICIES underwritten and issued by the INSURANCE COMPANY that uses the same policy forms and rates.

BLOCK POLICY coverage on an ALL RISKS basis for goods in transit, bailment, and while on the premises of others. *See also* JEWELERS BLOCK INSURANCE POLICY.

BLUE CROSS independent, nonprofit, membership hospital plan. Benefits provided include coverage for hospitalization expenses subject to certain restrictions: for example, semiprivate room only. A member hospital agrees to a predetermined schedule for specified medical services. The hospital sends the bills directly to the Blue Cross plan for reimbursement. Also covered are outpatient services, and supplementary or extended care such as nursing home care, as described in the contract.

BLUE SHIELD independent, nonprofit, membership medical-surgical plan. Benefits cover expenses associated with medical and surgical procedures. The physician and/or surgeon bills the Blue Shield plan directly rather than the patient, who is responsible for any difference between the scheduled rates and the doctor's fees.

BOARD INSURER *see* BUREAU INSURER.

BOAT OWNERS PACKAGE POLICY type of OCEAN MARINE INSURANCE that is a combination of property, liability, and medical expense insurance in one policy.

BOBTAIL LIABILITY INSURANCE coverage of a common carrier for liability on trucks that have delivered their cargo and are on the way back to the terminal. The company that hires the truck assumes liability while the truck is loaded, but after delivery, that firm's liability ends. The carrier can be protected by bobtail liability coverage for the return trip.

BODILY INJURY physical damage to one's person. The purpose of liability (casualty) insurance is to cover bodily injury to a third party resulting from the negligent or intentional acts and omissions of an insured.

BODILY INJURY LIABILITY INSURANCE *see* LIABILITY INSURANCE.

BOILER AND MACHINERY INSURANCE now referred to as EQUIPMENT BREAKDOWN INSURANCE.

BOND form of suretyship. For example, fidelity bonds reimburse an employer for financial loss resulting from dishonest acts of employees. *See also* BLANKET POSITION BOND; COMMERCIAL BLANKET BOND; CONTRACT BOND; FIDELITY BOND; INDIVIDUAL FIDELITY BOND; JUDICIAL BOND; NAME SCHEDULE BOND.

BOND, BAIL *see* BAIL BOND.

BOND, BANKERS BLANKET *see* BANKERS BLANKET BOND.

BOND, BID *see* BID BOND.

BOND, BLANKET *see* BLANKET POSITION BOND.

BOND, CATASTROPHE type of corporate bond in which the bondholder is required to forgo all or some of the principal and/or interest on the issue if a particular catastrophe results in losses exceeding a predetermined RETENTION level.

BOND, COMPLETION *see* COMPLETION BOND.

BOND, CONTRACT *see* CONTRACT BOND.

BOND, COURT *see* JUDICIAL BOND.

BOND DEDICATION layering of a bond portfolio where bonds are sold whose yield to maturity are low and bonds are bought whose yield to maturity are high in order that reserve requirements are met for future benefit payments by the insurance company.

BOND, FIDELITY *see* FIDELITY BOND.

BOND, FIDUCIARY *see* JUDICIAL BOND.

BOND (FINANCIAL) corporate or government security that pays interest and obligates the corporation or government agency to pay that interest at the end of specific time intervals, and to pay the principal at maturity of the security.

BOND, FORGERY *see* DEPOSITORS FORGERY INSURANCE.

BOND, LICENSE *see* LICENSE BOND.

BOND, MAINTENANCE *see* MAINTENANCE BOND.

BOND, PENALTY *see* PENALTY.

BOND, PERFORMANCE *see* CONTRACT BOND.

BOND, PERMIT *see* PERMIT BOND.

BOND, POSITION *see* FIDELITY BOND.

BOND, PUBLIC OFFICIAL *see* PUBLIC OFFICIAL BOND.

BOND, SCHEDULE *see* NAME POSITION BOND; NAME SCHEDULE BOND.

BOND, SURETY *see* SURETY BOND.

BONUS RATE extra percent of interest credited to an ANNUITY during the first year that it is in force. This extra amount is above the interest rate to be credited beginning with the second year and the remaining years that the annuity is in force. The extra rate is paid in the first year as an effort to attract new ANNUITANTS.

BOOK OF BUSINESS total amount of insurance on an insurer's books at a particular time. *See also* NET RETAINED LINES.

BOOK VALUE cost of the assets listed on the accounting records of the company. These assets include the following: real estate (to include any adjustments for depreciation), transportation equipment (to include any adjustments for depreciation), policy loans (limited to the unpaid principal balance plus any unamortized premiums minus any accrued discounts), mortgage loans (limited to the unpaid principal balance plus any unamortized premiums minus any accrued discounts), cash, and joint ventures. Not listed at book value are securities.

BOOK VALUE PER COMMON SHARE value of a share of common stock, derived by dividing the total common stockholders' equity at the end of a period of time by the total number of shares outstanding at the end of the same period of time.

BOOK VALUE PER SHARE total shareholders' equity divided by total common shares outstanding.

BOOT property or money received as additional consideration in regard to a tax-free exchange of property. If the POLICYHOLDER receives money in an otherwise nontaxable life insurance policy exchange, the money received will be taxable income to the policyholder. Likewise, if the loan on an old policy is canceled by the insurer when that policy is exchanged for a new policy, the loan amount so canceled becomes taxable income to the policyholder. *See also* MINIMUM DEPOSIT RESCUE; TAX-FREE EXCHANGE OF INSURANCE PRODUCTS.

BORDEREAU form of reinsurance that shows loss history and premium history with respect to specific risks. The CEDING COMPANY provides its REINSURER with that information. This information is used by the *reinsurance company* in establishing the reinsurance premium rates. *See also* REINSURANCE.

BORDERLINE RISK prospective insurance applicant who has questionable UNDERWRITING characteristics.

BORROWING AUTHORITY OF PENSION BENEFIT GUARANTY CORPORATION (PBGC) authorization to borrow from the U.S. Treasury by the issuance of notes to the Treasury. The Secretary of the Treasury must approve the notes and their interest rates. The PBGC must be self supporting through the premium it charges for various plans and thus its notes carry the same obligations of any notes, in that they are expected to be repaid.

BOSTON PLAN agreement named after the city of Boston under which insurance companies insure real property in lower socioeconomic neighborhoods if property owners correct any hazards found upon inspection.

BOTH-TO-BLAME CLAUSE in OCEAN MARINE INSURANCE, provision stipulating that upon the collision of two or more ships, when all ships are at fault, all owners and shippers having monetary interests in the voyage of the ships involved must share in all losses in proportion to the monetary values of their interests prior to the occurrence of the collision. This clause supercedes all other provisions for the allocation of losses among owners and shippers in ocean marine policies.

BOTTOMRY method of transferring pure risks that is perhaps the seed of the modern day insurance policy. Ancient Greece held to the concept that a loan on a ship was canceled if the ship failed to return to its port. This concept was adopted by Lloyd's of London in the 1600s when insuring England's merchants for goods shipped to the colonies. The formation of property and casualty insurance companies worldwide began by insuring the transport of merchandise over bodies of water.

BPPCF *see* BUSINESS AND PERSONAL PROPERTY COVERAGE FORM (BPPCF).

BRANCH MANAGER *see* AGENCY MANAGER.

BRANCH OFFICE local business headquarters of an insurance company that markets and services its products and lines of insurance. *See also* MANAGER.

BREACH OF CONTRACT failure of a party (not having a legal excuse) to perform in accordance with a promise made. An INSURANCE POLICY consists of legally enforceable promises made by the INSURANCE COMPANY (INSURER) only. No such promises are made by the INSURED. This is the reason why the insurance policy is a UNILATERAL CONTRACT.

BREAK IN SERVICE feature of pension plans whereby an employee whose service has been interrupted can have that period credited toward retirement.

BREEDER'S INSURANCE POLICY   *see* LIVE ANIMAL INSURANCE; LIVESTOCK FLOATER; LIVESTOCK INSURANCE; LIVESTOCK MORTALITY (LIFE) INSURANCE; LIVESTOCK TRANSIT INSURANCE.

BRIDGE INSURANCE coverage for damage or destruction to an insured bridge. Insures on an ALL RISKS basis subject to exclusions of war, wear and tear, inherent defect, and nuclear damages. Coverage is purchased by state and local governing bodies to limit exposures to the expense of an immediate tax increase to rebuild a damaged or destroyed bridge.

BRIDGE INSURANCE FOR BRIDGES UNDER CONSTRUC-TION provides coverage during the construction of a bridge in the event of fire, lightning, collision, flood, rising water, windstorm, ice, explosion, and earthquake. This coverage is essential, since the value of destroyed labor and materials could bankrupt a contractor without insurance protection.

BROAD EVIDENCE RULE rule that stipulates how to calculate the ACTUAL CASH VALUE of property that has been damaged, destroyed, or stolen. The thesis of this rule is that whatever evidence that can be produced of the true value of the property is admissible; the factual insurable value of the property can be ascertained by whatever measures provide the most accurate picture of that property's real value. Thus, this is a method of determining the true insurable worth of a structure according to any measure that will provide the most accurate analysis of that property's value. This method is becoming more widely accepted as a means of measuring actual cash value.

BROAD FORM INSURANCE coverage for numerous perils such as that found in the BROAD FORM PERSONAL THEFT INSURANCE.

BROAD FORM PERSONAL THEFT INSURANCE coverage on an ALL RISKS basis for loss due to theft or mysterious disappearance of personal property; damage to premises and property within resulting from theft; and vandalism and malicious mischief to the interior of the premises as well as to other property of an insured that is away from the insured's premises. Sublimits are in effect on specialty property that is particularly susceptible to theft, such as money, securities, paintings, coins, and jewelry. This insurance is most often found in Part I Coverage C of the HOMEOWNERS INSURANCE POLICY and is expressed as a percentage of the home's structure.

BROAD FORM PROPERTY DAMAGE ENDORSEMENT attachment to a general liability policy thereby eliminating the exclusion of property under the care, custody, and/or control of an insured. Without this endorsement there would be no coverage under the GENERAL LIA-

BILITY INSURANCE policy in the event of damage or destruction of property under the care, custody, and control of the insured.

BROAD FORM STOREKEEPERS INSURANCE coverage usually provided as part of the STOREKEEPERS BURGLARY AND ROBBERY INSURANCE in the event merchandise, fixtures, equipment, and furniture are lost due to theft and burglary.

BROAD NAMED PERILS *see* BUSINESS AND PERSONAL PROPERTY COVERAGE FORM (BPPCF)—basic form; broad form.

BROKER insurance salesperson who searches the marketplace in the interest of clients, not insurance companies. *See also* AGENT, BROKERAGE DEPARTMENT.

BROKERAGE insurance coverage sold by a BROKER as contrasted with insurance coverage sold by an AGENT. *See also* BROKERAGE FEE.

BROKERAGE BUSINESS insurance coverage placed by a BROKER with an insurance company. *See also* BROKERAGE DEPARTMENT.

BROKERAGE DEPARTMENT section of an insurance company that sells through brokers. Some brokerage departments are self-contained in that they have their own underwriting and marketing staffs. Brokerage departments have come into their own in recent times as even captive agent insurance companies have sought additional distribution channels that may be less expensive than the captive agent field force. *See also* BROKER; CAPTIVE AGENT.

BROKERAGE FEE commission paid to a broker for selling an insurance company's products. This fee may or may not include an expense allowance depending on the amount of business the broker places with the company.

BROKERAGE GENERAL AGENT independent contractor of the insurance company who has the authority to appoint BROKERS on behalf of the insurance company. This supervisor has the objective and the responsibility to sell the insurance company's products to the appointed brokers who in turn sell these products to the general public.

BROKER-AGENT independent insurance salesperson who represents particular insurers but may also function as a broker by searching the entire insurance market to place an applicant's coverage to maximize protection and minimize cost. This person is licensed as an agent and broker.

BROKERAGE SUPERVISOR employee of the insurance company who has the authority to appoint BROKERS on behalf of the insurance company. This supervisor has the objective and responsibility to sell the insurance company's products to the appointed brokers who in turn sell these products to the general public.

BROKER/DEALER business involved in buying and selling securities and mutual funds.

BROKER OF RECORD *see* AGENT OF RECORD.

BROWSER software program that can be utilized for viewing pages (web sites) on the WORLD WIDE WEB of the INTERNET.

BUDGET DEFICIT circumstance resulting when government expenditures exceed government income. To finance this difference, the United States Treasury will auction Treasury bills, notes, and bonds. In order to attract investors such as insurance companies, the Treasury will pay higher interest rates on the new issues, resulting in a decline in bond (already issued) prices and the increase in their rates.

BUILD to construct.

BUILDERS RISK COVERAGE FORM *see* BUILDERS RISKS FORMS.

BUILDERS RISK HULL INSURANCE property coverage for a builder of ships until possession passes to the owners. Protects against pre-launch and post-launch perils. Coverage can be purchased on an ALL RISKS basis subject to the exclusions of war, nuclear disaster, and inherent defects. The builder buys either insurance that covers the startup value of the property, to be adjusted upward to reflect additional construction *(Reporting Form);* or insurance to cover the completed value of the property *(Completed Form).*

BUILDERS RISK INSURANCE *see* BUILDERS RISKS FORMS.

BUILDERS RISKS FORMS types of contracts that insure building contractors for damage to property under construction. The *completed value form* requires a 100% coinsurance because insurance carried must equal the completed value of the structure. The *reporting form* allows coverage to be carried according to the stage of completion of the structure. Perils insured against are fire, lightning, vandalism, malicious mischief, riot and civil commotion, smoke, sprinkler leakage, water damage, windstorm, and hail.

BUILDING AND PERSONAL PROPERTY COVERAGE FORM *see* BUSINESS AND PERSONAL PROPERTY COVERAGE FORM (BPPCF).

BULLET GUARANTEED INVESTMENT CONTRACT (BGIC) type of GUARANTEED INVESTMENT CONTRACT (GIC) under which a single payment is made into an account of an insurance company where it will remain for a stipulated number of years. Both the principal of the account and the interest rate are guaranteed by the insurance company. At an agreed upon future date, both principal and interest are returned to the payor (usually a DEFINED BENEFIT PLAN).

BULL MARKET market in which buyers dominate trading and force financial asset prices up.

BUMBERSHOOT POLICY liability insurance coverage, primarily for shipyards for ocean marine risks, provided in much the same manner as UMBRELLA LIABILITY INSURANCE for nonmarine risks. Coverages may be provided in addition to liability include PROTECTION AND INDEMNITY INSURANCE (P&I), LONGSHOREMEN AND HARBOR WORKERS ACT LIABILITY, collision, and salvage expenses.

BUREAU INSURER insurance company that is a member of a RATING BUREAU. The insurer usually joins such an organization when its statistical experience in a given *line of insurance* is not sufficient for it to accurately predict loss experience for that line.

BUREAU OF LABOR STATISTICS *see* LABOR STATISTICS, BUREAU OF.

BUREAU RATE *see* RATING BUREAU.

BURGLARY forced entry into premises. Coverage is provided under various property insurance contracts such as HOMEOWNERS and SPECIAL MULTIPERIL INSURANCE (SMP).

BURGLARY INSURANCE coverage against loss as the result of a burglary. Found as part of the COMMERCIAL PACKAGE POLICY that has generally replaced the SPECIAL MULTIPERIL INSURANCE (SMP) policy and the MERCANTILE OPEN STOCK BURGLARY INSURANCE policy. Covers loss of merchandise, furniture, equipment, fixtures due to force and violence to the exterior of a business's premises in order to gain entry, and damage to the premises of the business as the result of the burglary. There is a coinsurance requirement that ranges from 40 to 80%.

BURGLARY/THEFT INSURANCE *see* BURGLARY INSURANCE.

BURIAL INSURANCE small face amount life insurance policy. *See also* FUNERAL INSURANCE.

BURNING COST RATIO (PURE LOSS COST) ratio of excess losses to premium income. Excess losses are those that a reinsurer is responsible for if its coverage is in effect during the period under consideration. The premium income used for EXCESS OF LOSS and CATASTROPHE LOSS reinsurance is the gross premium less the expense of reinsurance. The premium income used for STOP LOSS REINSURANCE is the earned premium income. The excess losses are defined as the incurred losses in excess of the cedent's retention up to the limits specified in the reinsurance contract. *See also* REINSURANCE.

BURNING RATIO
1. actual fire losses divided by the total value of the property exposed to the PERIL of fire.
2. actual losses resulting from fire divided by the total fire amount of IN-FORCE BUSINESS.
See also BURNING COST RATIO (PURE LOSS COST).

BUSINESS in insurance, volume of premiums written. Also describes commercial activities with the profit motive as the goal of the organization. Commercial insurance companies are organized with the profit motive as the normal business objective.

BUSINESS AND PERSONAL PROPERTY COVERAGE FORM (BPPCF) provision for coverage for buildings and personal property within the SIMPLIFIED COMMERCIAL LINES PORTFOLIO POLICY (SCLP). The buildings and personal property coverage may be classified in three ways:

1. *Owned buildings*—these buildings are listed and described in the DECLARATIONS SECTION of the policy. Also covered is anything that has become a permanent part of the buildings, to include additions, fixtures, extensions, and machinery and equipment.
2. *Owned business personal property*—property covered is the business personal property that is owned by the insured and is common in the occupancy usage by the insured.
3. *Nonowned business personal property*—properties covered are improvements and betterments (alterations made by the insured to a building that he or she is leasing and that cannot be removed upon the termination of the lease), and personal property of someone other than the insured that is under the care, custody, or control of the insured.

    Extensions of coverage are available under the BPPCF to include:

1. *outdoor property*—trees, shrubs, and plants; signs; radio and television antennas; and fences. There is an overall limit of $1000 and a sublimit of $250 for each tree, shrub, or plant.
2. *valuable papers and records*—cost of replacing or restoring information lost because of the damage or destruction of valuable papers and records. There is a $1000 limit of coverage.
3. *personal effects and property of others*—personal effects of the named insured, employees, and others that are under the care, custody, or control of the insured.
4. *business personal property on location at premises newly acquired*—10% of the owned business personal property coverage is applicable, subject to $100,000 limit for each building. Thirty days after the acquisition of property, coverage terminates.
5. *newly acquired buildings or additions*—25% of the owned building coverage is applicable, subject to $250,000 limit for each building. Within 30 days, newly acquired buildings or additions must be reported by the insured.
6. *off-premises property*—property on a temporary location (other than a vehicle) not owned, leased, or operated by the insured.

    PERILS insured against are available under three forms:

1. *basic form*—includes fire, lightning, windstorm, hail, explosion, vandalism, smoke, sprinkler leakage, riot or civil commotion, sinkhole collapse, volcano.

2. *broad form*—includes perils found under the basic form plus falling objects causing exterior damage that results in interior damage; weight of ice, sleet, and snow; accidental discharge of water or steam from a system or appliance containing steam or water, but not including an automatic sprinkler system; and breakage of glass; subject to a $500 maximum limit.

3. *special cause-of-loss form*—includes all direct accidental losses except those specifically excluded in the policy (such as flood, war, wear and tear, and earth movement).

ENDORSEMENTS can be added to the BPPCF to include:

1. *perils extension*—adds earthquake, volcanic eruption, and radioactive contamination.

2. *limits of recovery extension*—increase maximum dollar amounts of coverage for trees, shrubs, and plants; radio and television antennas; and outdoor signs.

3. *replacement cost endorsement*—changes basis of recovery under the BPPCF to a REPLACEMENT COST LESS PHYSICAL DEPRECIATION AND OBSOLESCENCE from an ACTUAL CASH VALUE basis.

BUSINESS AUTO COVERAGE FORM type of COMMERCIAL FORM that provides coverage for business vehicles regardless of whether they are owned, leased, hired, or borrowed. The form's coverages are divided into the following sections:

1. Section I—covers vehicles that are identified according to any one of nine symbols:
   a. Symbol #1—any vehicle
   b. Symbol #2—owned vehicle only
   c. Symbol #3—owned private passenger vehicles only
   d. Symbol #4—owned vehicles other than private passenger vehicles
   e. Symbol #5—owned vehicles subject to no-fault insurance
   f. Symbol #6—owned vehicle subject to compulsory uninsured motorists laws
   g. Symbol #7—specifically described vehicles (only those listed are covered)
   h. Symbol #8—hired vehicles only
   i. Symbol #9—non-owned vehicles only

Through the above forms, the business may select only the coverages desired, thereby minimizing its insurance costs. For example, if the business desired the most comprehensive coverage, symbol #1 would be selected.

2. Section II—liability coverage in the event the business' negligent acts and/or omissions result in bodily injury or property damage to a THIRD PARTY as the result of operating a vehicle.

3. Section III—physical damage coverage for property damage to the business' covered vehicles under three classifications:
   a. Comprehensive—pays for all physical damage to the business' vehicles regardless of cause with the exception of collision with another object or in the event the vehicle overturns.

  b. Specified causes of loss coverage—pays for physical damage to the business' vehicle only resulting from fire, lightning, explosion, theft, windstorm, hail, earthquake, flood, mischief, or vandalism; or sinking, burning, collision, or derailment of any conveyance transporting the business' vehicle.

  c. Collision—pays for physical damage to the business' vehicle resulting from contact with another object.

4. Section IV—conditions that describe the insured business and the insurance company's obligations if a loss should occur.

5. Section V—definitions discussing the critical terms in the vehicle form such as the meanings of accident, insured, vehicle, or suit.

BUSINESS AUTOMOBILE POLICY (BAP) coverage for automobiles used by a business when a liability judgment arises out of the use of the automobile, or the automobile is subject to damage or destruction. The business can select coverage for any auto in use, whether business, personal, or hired. The policy is organized as follows:

Parts I, II, and III—define terms used in the policy, such as auto, accident, insured bodily injury, property damage, territorial limits of coverage.

Part IV LIABILITY INSURANCE—in a liability judgment against the insured business and/or individual, the insurance company will pay the monetary damages up to the limit of the policy. Negligent acts and/or omissions of the insured business and/or individual must arise out of the ownership and operation of a covered auto, subject to specific exclusions.

Part V PHYSICAL DAMAGE INSURANCE—in the event of damage to an auto, the insurance company will pay under one of two categories: COMPREHENSIVE INSURANCE—damage resulting from fire, explosion, theft, vandalism, malicious mischief, windstorm, hail, earthquake, or flood; or COLLISION INSURANCE—damage resulting from colliding with another object or the overturning of the insured auto.

Part VI CONDITION—stipulate what the policyholder must do in the event of a loss, such as give notice to the insurance company; submit proof of the loss; submit to inpsection of damaged property by the company; cooperate with the company in the event of a liability suit.

The BAP has been largely replaced by the BUSINESS AUTO COVERAGE FORM.

BUSINESS CONTINUATION INSURANCE *see* BUSINESS LIFE AND HEALTH INSURANCE.

BUSINESS CRIME INSURANCE protection for the assets of a business (including merchandise for sale, real property, money and securities) in the event of robbery, burglary, larceny, forgery, and embezzlement. Coverage is provided in package policies such as SPECIAL MULTIPERIL INSURANCE (SMP) policy Section III, largely replaced by the COMMERCIAL PACKAGE POLICY, and the BUSINESS-OWNERS POLICY (BOP) Section III. Or coverage can be written under separate policies such as: BANK BURGLARY AND ROBBERY INSURANCE, COMBINATION SAFE

DEPOSITORY INSURANCE, MERCANTILE OPEN-STOCK, BURGLARY INSURANCE, MERCANTILE ROBBERY INSURANCE, MERCANTILE SAFE BURGLARY INSURANCE, MONEY AND SECURITIES BROAD FORM POLICY, OFFICE BURGLARY AND ROBBERY INSURANCE, PAYMASTER ROBBERY INSURANCE, STOREKEEPERS BURGLARY AND ROBBERY INSURANCE.

BUSINESS DAY day on which the New York Stock Exchange is open for transactions; used in calculating ACCUMULATION UNIT VALUES for variable dollar insurance products.

BUSINESS HEALTH INSURANCE *see* BUSINESS LIFE AND HEALTH INSURANCE.

BUSINESS INCOME COVERAGE FORM type of COMMERCIAL PROPERTY POLICY that provides coverage for a business' indirect losses resulting from damages to the property of the business. Coverage normally contains a COINSURANCE requirement. This form has replaced the BUSINESS INTERRUPTION INSURANCE policy. Included in this coverage for losses and expenses resulting from the interruption of normal business operations are:
1. *Business income*—loss of net business income plus continuing expenses according to one of the following options is:
   a. Option 1—loss of business income to include rental value
   b. Option 2—loss of business income to exclude rental value
   c. Option 3—loss of business income derived only from rental value
2. *Extra expense*—additional expense generated because of the direct loss to the property of the business.
3. *Civil authority*—loss of business income because a civil authority denies access to the premises of the business due to direct property losses at a location not at the premises of the business.
4. *Alterations and new buildings*—loss of business income because of direct property damage to new buildings or structures. Also covered is direct property damage to alterations or additions to existing buildings or structures, machinery, equipment, building materials, or supplies located within 100 feet of the premises of the business resulting in a loss of business income.
5. *Extended business income*—loss of business income beginning at the date the property of the business is returned to operating status and business operations actually start. This period of time is subject to a maximum of 30 days.

BUSINESS INSURANCE coverage designed to protect against loss exposures of business firms, as opposed to those of individuals. *See also* BUSINESS AUTOMOBILE POLICY (BAP); BUSINESS CRIME INSURANCE; BUSINESS INTERRUPTION INSURANCE; BUSINESS LIFE AND HEALTH INSURANCE; BUSINESSOWNERS POLICY; BUY AND SELL AGREEMENT; CLOSE CORPORATION PLAN; PARTNERSHIP LIFE AND HEALTH INSURANCE; SOLE PROPRIETOR LIFE AND HEALTH INSURANCE.

BUSINESS INTERRUPTION break in commercial activities due to the occurrence of a peril. Coverage against business interruption by various named perils can be obtained through insurance. *See also* BUSINESS INTERRUPTION INSURANCE.

BUSINESS INTERRUPTION INSURANCE indemnification for the loss of profits and the continuing fixed expenses. Business interruption insurance is available in these forms: CONTINGENT BUSINESS INTERRUPTION FORM, EXTRA EXPENSE FORM, GROSS EARNINGS FORM, PROFITS AND COMMISSIONS FORM, AND TUITION FORM. This form has been replaced on a general basis by the BUSINESS INCOME COVERAGE FORM.

BUSINESS INTERRUPTION INSURANCE, DEPENDENT *see* DEPENDENT BUSINESS INCOME FORM.

BUSINESS LIABILITY INSURANCE coverage for liability exposure resulting from the activities of a business; includes: (1) DIRECT LIABILITY—acts of the business resulting in damage or destruction of another party's property or bodily injury to that party; (2) CONTINGENT LIABILITY—although the business may not have direct liability, it may incur a secondary or contingent liability, for example through the employment of an independent contractor; (3) MEDICAL PAYMENTS TO OTHERS INSURANCE—acts of the business resulting in injury to another party, with the insurance company paying the medical expenses to that party (up to the policy limits) without regard to legal liability of the insured business. The policy has three principal sections:

1. DECLARATIONS SECTION lists the insured, policy limits, premium, time period of coverage, kind of policy, and endorsements, if any.
2. INSURING AGREEMENTS states that if any of the insured perils result in damage or destruction of another party's property or injury to that party, the company will pay (up to the limits of the policy) sums which the business becomes legally obligated to pay. (a) *Time Period of the Loss*—policy can be written either on a *claims occurrence* basis or a *claims made* basis; (b) BODILY INJURY—damage or destruction of a body to include sickness, disease, and/or resulting death (most liability insurance policies provide coverage for this definition); (c) PERSONAL INJURY—defamation of character, libel and slander, false arrest, malicious prosecution, and invasion of privacy (many liability policies can be endorsed to provide these coverages); (d) *Property Damages*—damage or destruction of real and personal property and the loss of use of this property; (e) DEFENSE COSTS— costs of defending the insured business to include investigation, defense, and the settlement of claims that are paid in addition to the limits of coverage under the policy; and (f) *Policy Limits*—the maximum that the insurance company is obligated to pay on behalf of the insured business.
3. EXCLUSIONS to avoid duplications of coverage in other policies and/or to eliminate certain kinds of coverage, including: property under the care, custody and control of the insured business; liability arising out of contractual obligations between the insured business and another party; liability associated with recall of the

insured business's products; liability associated with the insured business's pollution and contamination exposure; and liability that may arise out of conflict with state liquor regulations.

4. *Conditions* stipulate that (a) the insured, after an accident, must behave so as not to increase the severity of bodily injury and/or property damage that has just occurred; (b) the insurance company has the right to inspect the insured business's premises as well as its operations; and (c) if there is more than one policy covering a claim, each policy will pay an equal share of the loss.

BUSINESS LIFE AND HEALTH INSURANCE coverage providing funds for maintenance of a business as closely to normal as possible in the event of a loss of a key person, owner, or partner. *See also* BENEFITS OF BUSINESS LIFE AND HEALTH INSURANCE; BUY-AND-SELL AGREEMENT; CLOSE CORPORATION PLAN; PARTNERSHIP LIFE AND HEALTH INSURANCE.

BUSINESS LIFE INSURANCE *see* BUSINESS LIFE AND HEALTH INSURANCE.

BUSINESS OVERHEAD EXPENSE INSURANCE *see* BUSINESS INTERRUPTION INSURANCE.

BUSINESSOWNERS POLICY (BOP) combination property, liability, and business interruption policy. It is usually written to cover expenses of small and medium size businesses resulting from (1) damage or destruction of business's property or (2) when actions or nonactions of the business's representatives result in bodily injury or property damage to another individual(s). Businesses that qualify under this heading include office buildings three stories or under not to exceed 100,000 square feet; apartment buildings six stories or under not to exceed 60 dwelling units; any other buildings not to exceed 7500 square feet for mercantile space, occupied principally as an apartment, office, or engaging in trade or commerce. Properties that cannot be insured under this policy include banks, condominiums, bars, restaurants, automobiles, recreational vehicles, contractor functions, and manufacturing operations. *See also* BUSINESSOWNERS POLICY—SECTION I: PROPERTY COVERAGES; BUSINESSOWNERS POLICY—SECTION II: LIABILITY COVERAGES.

BUSINESSOWNERS POLICY—SECTION I: PROPERTY COVERAGES contract that details coverage for business property losses in three specific areas:

1. *Coverage A (Building).* All buildings on the site are covered with no coinsurance requirement and on a replacement cost basis to include: the buildings themselves; the owner's personal property used to maintain the building(s) and provided to tenants; permanent fixtures, equipment and machinery; improvements and betterments by tenants; removal of debris; and outdoor furniture and fixtures.

2. *Coverage B (Personal Property of the Business).* All personal property used in the business on the premises, as well as personal property of others under the care, custody and control of the owner of the building used to operate the business; and limited coverage for items temporarily away from the premises of the business as well as for property purchased and placed at a new business location.

3. *Coverage C (Loss of Income).* Reimbursement for loss of income because of inability to collect business rent; interruption of normal business functions; and extra expenses associated with resuming normal business activities as the result of the damage or destruction of business property by an insured peril. (Optionally, under Section I, coverage can be extended to insure against burglary, robbery, theft, employee dishonesty, and boiler and machinery explosion. Earthquake damage can be covered through an endorsement.)

BUSINESSOWNERS POLICY—SECTION II: LIABILITY COVERAGES coverage that protects a business, up to the policy limits, if actions or non-actions of the insured result in a legally enforceable claim for bodily injury, property damage, or personal injury. Included are coverages for: (1) nonowned automobiles used by the business in its normal operations (owned automobiles are excluded); (2) host liquor liability where the business is having a social gathering. For example, liability at an office party would be covered, since this social function is incidental to normal business activity (excluded would be operation of a liquor store on the premises of the business); (3) fire and explosion legal liability, where the insured is renting business space in a building. If a fire or explosion from business operations is proven to be of negligent origin, the insurer of the owner of the building has subrogation rights against the business; (4) products, for which completed operations coverage is provided. Excluded from Section II coverages are professional liability, owned automobiles of the business, operation of airplanes and other aircraft, Workers Compensation, liquor liability (other than that served as a host at business social functions), and off-premises operation of boats.

BUSINESS PROPERTY AND LIABILITY INSURANCE PACKAGE protection of the property of the business that is damaged or destroyed by perils such as fire, smoke, and vandalism; and/or if the actions (or nonactions) of the business' representatives result in bodily injury or property damage to other individuals. Many insurance policies provide such coverages, but the two most often used are the COMMERCIAL PACKAGE POLICY and the BUSINESSOWNERS POLICY (BOP).

BUSINESS RISK investment risk associated with the changes in the earnings capability of the company. If the earnings capability declines, the company's ability to maintain the current dividend level and to increase future dividends is diminished.

BUSINESS RISK EXCLUSION omissions from coverage found in PRODUCT LIABILITY INSURANCE. The policy does not provide coverage if the business manufactures a product that does not meet the level of performance as advertised, represented, or warranted. For example, an automobile antifreeze is advertised as being able to withstand temperatures as low as 30° below zero. An engine block containing the fluid freezes at a temperature of 10° above zero. In this instance a products liability policy would not provide coverage for the insured business.

BUSINESS STARTS INDEX statistical compilation that reports the number of new incorporated and nonincorporated businesses started during a single week. This index is published by Dun & Bradstreet.

BUSINESS TRANSACTED WITH PRODUCER CONTROLLED PROPERTY/CASUALTY INSURER ACT model act written and published by the NATIONAL ASSOCIATION OF INSURANCE COMMISSIONERS (NAIC) whose purpose it is to regulate BROKERS who control INSURANCE COMPANIES. The act permits the insurance commissioners to institute civil actions in the event they perceive broker violations (broker's conduct contributing to the insolvency of a controlled insurance company and the respective state insurance commissioner requires the broker to make restitution to that state's guarantee fund).

BUY-AND-SELL AGREEMENT approach used for sole proprietorships, partnerships, and close corporations in which the business interests of a deceased or disabled proprietor, partner, or shareholder are sold according to a predetermined formula to the remaining member(s) of the business. For example, a partnership has three principals. Upon the death of one, the two survivors have agreed to purchase, and the deceased partner's estate has agreed to sell, the interest of that partner according to a predetermined formula for valuing the partnership to the survivors. Funds for buying out the deceased partner's interest are usually provided by life insurance policies, with each partner purchasing a policy on the other partners. Each is the owner and beneficiary of the policies purchased on the other partners.

When a sole proprietor dies, usually a key employee is the buyer/successor. The sole proprietorship, partnership, and close corporation under the entity plan can buy and own life insurance policies on the proprietor, partner, or shareholder and achieve the same result as when an individual buys and owns the policies.

BUY-BACK DEDUCTIBLE DEDUCTIBLE eliminated through the payment of an additional premium, resulting in FIRST-DOLLAR COVERAGE under the policy.

BYPASS TRUST type of TRUST used to remove assets from a surviving spouse's estate, thereby excluding such assets from FEDERAL ESTATE TAX upon the death of the surviving spouse. This type of trust allows for a lifetime benefit to be available to both spouses while living, as well as to a single surviving spouse. A bypass trust permits a maximum of $1.2 million transfer to heirs of the spouses on a tax-free basis under the unified gift and estate tax credits.

C

CAFETERIA BENEFIT PLAN arrangement under which employees may choose their own employee benefit structure. For example, one employee may wish to emphasize health care and thus would select a more comprehensive health insurance plan for the allocation of the premiums, while another employee may wish to emphasize retirement and thus allocate more of the premiums to the purchase of pension benefits.

CAFETERIA PLANS *see* SECTION 125 PLANS (CAFETERIA PLANS).

CALCULABLE CHANGE OF LOSS *see* PROBABILITY.

CALENDAR YEAR ACCOUNTING INCURRED LOSSES losses paid plus positive or negative changes in the year-end loss reserves during that particular year. The total amount includes payments for any old claims as well as new claims, plus any reevaluation of claim amounts already on the books at the beginning of the year, as well as required reserves for the new claims.

CALENDAR YEAR DEDUCTIBLE after CALENDAR YEAR EXPERIENCE exceeds DEDUCTIBLE, claims payments insured receives up to the FACE AMOUNT (FACE OF POLICY).

CALENDAR YEAR EXPERIENCE paid loss experience for the period of time from January 1 to December 31 of a specified year (not necessarily the current year).

CALENDAR YEAR STATISTICS *see* CALENDAR YEAR EXPERIENCE.

CALL OPTION contract that gives the insurance company the right, not the obligation, to buy a stipulated stock or bond at a specified price (strike price) at or before the date of expiration of the contract.

CALL PREMIUM excess of the CALL OPTION over the par value of a bond.

CAMERA AND MUSICAL INSTRUMENTS DEALERS INSURANCE coverage on an ALL RISKS basis for the insured's own property as well as property of others under the insured firm's care, custody, and control. Exclusions are WEAR AND TEAR, MYSTERIOUS DISAPPEARANCE, earthquake, flood, theft from an unlocked and unattended vehicle, loss of market, and delay. For example, if a dealer's personal flute is damaged by fire, or if a customer's camera is stolen, the dealer would be covered for both occurrences up to the limits of the policy.

CAMERA FLOATER camera and related equipment coverage found in INLAND MARINE INSURANCE.

CANADIAN INSTITUTE OF ACTUARIES membership organization representing professional actuaries in all insurance fields in Canada including life and health, casualty, consulting and fraternal actuaries.

A member must reside in Canada and belong to an approved actuarial organization, including the SOCIETY OF ACTUARIES (SA).

CANCEL termination of a policy. Contract may be terminated by an insured or insurer as stated in the policy. If the insurance company cancels a policy, any unearned premiums must be returned. If an insured cancels the policy, an amount less than the unearned premiums is returned, reflecting the insurance company's administration costs of placing the policy on its books. Usually this term is applied only in property and disability insurance.

CANCELLABLE *see* CANCEL; CANCELLATION PROVISION CLAUSE.

CANCELLATION *see* CANCELLATION PROVISION CLAUSE.

CANCELLATION, FLAT cancellation of a policy according to its effective date excluding any premium charge.

CANCELLATION, PRO RATA *see* PRO RATA CANCELLATION.

CANCELLATION PROVISION CLAUSE provision permitting an insured or an insurance company to cancel a property and casualty or a health insurance policy (circumstances vary; *see also* COMMERCIAL HEALTH INSURANCE) at any time before its expiration date. The insured must send written notice to the insurance company, which then refunds the excess of the premium paid above the customary short rates for the expired term. If the insurance company cancels, it sends written notice to the insured of cancellation and refunds the unearned portion of the premium.

CANCELLATION, SHORT RATE *see* SHORT RATE CANCELLATION.

CAP *see* COINSURANCE.

CAPACITY maximum that an insurance company can underwrite. The limits of coverage that a property and casualty company can underwrite are determined by its retained earnings and invested capital. REINSURANCE is a method of increasing the insurance company's capacity, in that a portion of the unearned premium reserve maintenance requirement can be relieved. Commissions earned are ceded, underwriting results are stabilized, and financing of the expansion of the insurer's capacity can take place.

CAPACITY OF PARTIES legal capability of those involved in mutual assent of making a contract, including an insurance contract. Those who have been deemed to be incompetent to make a valid contract include intoxicated and insane persons, and enemy aliens. Minors can enter into a contract, but it is voidable at the option of the minor. For example, if an agent sells an insurance policy to a minor, and the insurance company agrees to underwrite it, the policy can be voided at any time the minor wishes both before and after the minor reaches the age of majority. The insurance company cannot void the contract.

CAPITAL equity of shareholders of a stock insurance company. The company's capital and SURPLUS are measured by the difference between its assets minus its liabilities. This value protects the interests of the company's policyowners in the event it develops financial problems; the policyowners' benefits are thus protected by the insurance company's capital. Shareholders' interest is second to that of policyowners.

CAPITAL ASSET PRICING MODEL (CAPM) pricing model that shows the relationship between an asset's expected return and its BETA.

CAPITAL GAINS excess of the sales price of an asset over its book value. Listed as part of the *Annual Report* in the summary of the surplus account and/or in the Summary of Operations.

CAPITAL STOCK INSURANCE COMPANY company that has a capital fund established by contributions from its stockholders in addition to its SURPLUS ACCOUNTS and RESERVE ACCOUNTS.

CAPITAL STRUCTURE combination of EQUITIES and debt of an insurance company.

CAPITAL SURPLUS PAID-IN SURPLUS, revaluation surplus, and donated surplus. This surplus includes all sources of surplus with the exception of EARNED SURPLUS.

CAPITATED CONTRACT health plan that pays a flat fee for each patient it covers.

CAPITATION FEE fixed annual payment to a medical care facility and/or physician for each member of a MANAGED CARE ORGANIZATION (MCO) regardless of type or frequency of health care benefit.

CAPITATION PAYMENTS payments made on a monthly basis by users of the medical services of HEALTH MAINTENANCE ORGANIZATIONS (HMOs). After this payment is calculated for a future period of time, usually one year, the payment will remain fixed for that period, regardless of the frequency of use of the HMO's services.

CAPTIVE AGENT representative of a single insurer or fleet of insurers who is obliged to submit business only to that company, or at the very minimum, give that company first refusal rights on a sale. In exchange, that insurer usually provides its captive agents with an allowance for office expenses as well as an extensive list of employee benefits such as pensions, life insurance, health insurance, and credit unions.

CAPTIVE INSURANCE COMPANIES ASSOCIATION (CICA) trade association located in New York City, consisting of approximately 200 CAPTIVE INSURANCE COMPANIES. The objective of the association is to further the common interests of its members.

CAPTIVE INSURANCE COMPANY company formed to insure the risks of its parent corporation. Reasons for forming a captive insurance company include:

1. Instances when insurance cannot be purchased from commercial insurance companies for a business risk. In many instances companies within an industry form a joint captive insurance company for that reason.

2. Premiums paid to a captive insurance company are deductible as a business expense for tax purposes according to the Internal Revenue Service. However, sums set aside in a self insurance program are not deductible as a business expense.

3. Insurance can be obtained through the international reinsurance market at a more favorable premium, with higher limits of coverage.

4. Investment returns can be obtained directly on its invested capital. However, competent personnel to manage and staff the company could be excessively expensive; and further, a catastrophic occurrence or series of occurrences could bankrupt the company.

CARE, CUSTODY, AND CONTROL phrase in most liability insurance policies that eliminates from coverage damage or destruction to property under the care, custody, and control of an insured. Such coverage is excluded from liability policies because the insured either has some ownership interest in such property (better covered through property not liability insurance) or is a bailor of the property (and can better cover this bailment exposure through an appropriate bailee policy).

CARGO INSURANCE shipper's policies covering one cargo exposure or all cargo exposures by sea on ALL RISKS basis. Exclusions include war, nuclear disaster, wear and tear, dampness, mold, losses due to delay of shipment, and loss of market for the cargo. *One Cargo Exposure (Single Risk Cargo Policy)* covers a single shipment of goods and/or a single trip. *All Cargo Exposure (Open Cargo Policy)* covers all shipments of goods and/or all trips generally used by most shippers that require automatic coverage for all of its shipments, subject to 30 days' notice of cancellation.

CARGO LIABILITY INSURANCE *see* CARGO INSURANCE.

CARGO MARINE INSURANCE *see* CARGO INSURANCE.

CARPENTER PLAN (SPREAD LOSS COVER, SPREAD LOSS REINSURANCE) form of excess of loss reinsurance under which each year's REINSURANCE premium is determined by the amount of the *cedent's* excess losses for a given period of time, usually three or five years. Upon renewal, the first year's initial rate is based on the total of three or five years of previous experience, a form of RETROSPECTIVE RATING. The Carpenter Plan is particularly relevant to economic conditions in the way it handles the factor of inflation.

CARRIER insurance company that actually underwrites and issues the insurance policy. The term is used because the insurance company assumes or carries the risk for policyowners. The agent usually has a *primary carrier (*the insurance company to which most of the business is submitted) and *secondary carriers* (to which lesser amounts are submitted). The primary carrier provides the agent with commission schedules, expense allowance, and the availability of markets for the agent's business.

CARVE-OUT COB *see* NON-DUPLICATION COORDINATION-OF-BENEFITS (CARVE-OUT COB).

CAS *see* CASUALTY ACTUARIAL SOCIETY (CAS).

CASH ACCUMULATION METHOD procedure used to compare the costs of life insurance policies by having equal DEATH BENEFITS of the policies held constant and accumulating the differences in the premiums paid among the policies at a given interest rate over a stipulated period of time. At the end of that time period, that policy with the largest accumulated value in the difference of the premiums paid is the best cost effective policy.

CASH-BALANCE PLAN hybrid PENSION PLAN that provides for the employer to contribute annually a hypothetical percentage, usually 4 to 5%, of the employee's salary to a hypothetical account. This employee's account is then credited with a hypothetical annual interest rate generally tied to the 30-year United States Treasury rate. If the employee should change employment, the account balance can be transferred to an INDIVIDUAL RETIREMENT ACCOUNT (IRA), subject to certain restrictions peculiar to each employer. For example, some employers restrict the withdrawal of a terminating employee to an amount no greater than the employee's one-year salary with the account's balance to be paid out as a monthly income benefit. When the employee retires at age 65 most of these plans have a five-year VESTING requirement.

CASH FLOW PLANS method of payment of an insurance premium that allows an insured to regulate the amount and frequency of the premium payments in accordance with cash flow over a stipulated period of time. This enables the insured to maintain control over the funds for a longer period of time and thus reap benefits from their earnings.

CASH FLOW SURPLUS the SURPLUS resulting from an additional amount of CAPITAL necessary to act as a supplement to the reserves in the event of unforeseen contingencies that would impair the insurance company's ability to make future benefit payments for which it has received the premiums.

CASH FLOW UNDERWRITING pricing of the insurance product below the necessary premium rate to reflect the costs of expected losses. The thesis of this pricing strategy is to obtain large sums of money to invest and earning a greater return on the investment than the costs associated with the underpricing of the insurance product.

CASH OUT OF VESTED BENEFITS money withdrawn by an employee from benefits owned. When an employee exercises this right, future benefits purchased by the employer on behalf of the employee are usually forfeited.

CASH REFUND ANNUITY (LUMP SUM REFUND ANNUITY) if the annuitant dies before receiving total income at least equal to the premiums paid, the beneficiary receives the difference in a lump sum. If the annuitant lives after the income paid equals the premiums paid, the insurance company continues to make income payments to the annuitant for life. *See also* ANNUITY.

CASH SURRENDER VALUE money the policyowner is entitled to receive from the insurance company upon surrendering a life insurance policy with cash value. The sum is the cash value stated in the policy minus a surrender charge and any outstanding loans and interest thereon.

CASH VALUE *see* CASH SURRENDER VALUE.

CASH VALUE LIFE INSURANCE policy that generates a savings element. Cash values are critical to a permanent life insurance policy. The size of a cash value buildup differs substantially from company to company. In many instances there is no correlation between the size of the cash value and premiums paid; in some cases there is an inverse relationship. Everything that the policyowner wishes to do with this policy while living is determined by the size of the cash value. For example, at some future time, a policyowner may wish to convert the cash value to a monthly retirement income. Its size will depend on (1) the amount of the cash value and (2) the attained age of the policy owner. *See also* ANNUITY; NONFORFEITURE BENEFIT (OPTION).

CASH WITHDRAWALS removal of money from an individual life insurance policy or an employee benefit plan. A cash withdrawal from a life insurance policy reduces the death benefit by the amount of the withdrawal plus interest thereon. When a cash withdrawal is made from an employee benefit such as a pension plan, the employee usually forfeits all benefits purchased on the employee's behalf by the employer. *See also* CASH VALUE LIFE INSURANCE.

CASUALTY liability or loss resulting from an ACCIDENT. Such liability or losses are covered under such policies as the following: BUSINESS AUTOMOBILE POLICY (BAP), BUSINESS PROPERTY AND LIABILITY INSURANCE PACKAGE, BUSINESSOWNERS POLICY (BOP), CASUALTY INSURANCE, COMMERCIAL GENERAL LIABILITY FORM (CGL), CONDOMINIUM INSURANCE, HOMEOWNERS INSURANCE POLICY, PERSONAL AUTOMOBILE POLICY (PAP), SIMPLIFIED COMMERCIAL LINES PORTFOLIO POLICY (SCLP), TENANTS INSURANCE, AND WORKERS COMPENSATION INSURANCE.

CASUALTY ACTUARIAL SOCIETY (CAS) accrediting body for the ACAS (Associate of the Casualty Actuarial Society) designation and the FCAS (Fellow of the Casualty Actuarial Society) designation. To earn these designations, members take a series of examinations on actuarial mathematics and related topics as they apply to the property and casualty insurance field. Passing the examinations denotes a sound background in mathematics as well as knowledge of business such as finance and economics. Located in New York City.

CASUALTY CATASTROPHE casualty losses of high severity. *See also* CASUALTY INSURANCE.

CASUALTY INSURANCE coverage primarily for the liability of an individual or organization that results from negligent acts and omissions, thereby causing bodily injury and/or property damage to a third party. However, the term is an elastic one that traditionally has included such property insurance as AVIATION INSURANCE, BOILER AND MACHINERY INSURANCE and *glass and crime insurance. See also* BUSINESS LIABILITY INSURANCE.

CATASTROPHE BOND *see* BOND; CATASTROPHE.

CATASTROPHE EQUITY PUT OPTION type of PUT OPTION utilized by the INSURER to acquire EQUITY capital by selling its stock at a specified dollar amount if losses from INSURED PERIL exceed a predetermined retention level.

CATASTROPHE EXCESS REINSURANCE *see* EXCESS OF LOSS REINSURANCE.

CATASTROPHE FUTURES financial instrument traded on the Chicago Board of Trade (CBOT). By purchasing this future, the insurance company can hedge its risk exposure against possible future catastrophic losses. The CBOT releases a report each quarter showing on a state-by-state basis the premium amount and the line of insurance that has a catastrophic exposure. Each future contract has a stated value of $25,000 multiplied by the catastrophe ratio for that particular quarter. This multiplied result forms the basis for beginning to trade the quarterly catastrophic futures contract on the CBOT. If there is a high level of catastrophes such that the actual catastrophic loss ratio is greater than the expected catastrophic loss ratio, the futures contract increases in value and the insurance company purchaser gains the difference between the initial purchase price and the quarterly ending value of the contract. Conversely, if there is a low level of catastrophes such that the actual catastrophic loss ratio is less than the expected catastrophic loss ratio, the futures contract decreases in value and the insurance company purchaser loses the difference between the initial purchase price and the quarterly ending value of the contract.

CATASTROPHE HAZARD circumstance under which there is a significant deviation of the actual aggregate losses from the expected aggregate losses. For example, a hurricane is a hazard that is catastrophic in nature, since whole units or blocks of businesses may be threatened. Catastrophic hazards often cannot or will not be insured by commercial insurance companies either because the hazard is too great or because the actuarial premium is prohibitive. Where a void exists in the marketplace, a government agency may subsidize the coverage with such programs as FEDERAL FLOOD INSURANCE and SERVICEMEN'S GROUP LIFE INSURANCE (SGLI).

CATASTROPHE INSURANCE *see* COMPREHENSIVE HEALTH INSURANCE; GROUP HEALTH INSURANCE; MAJOR MEDICAL INSURANCE.

CATASTROPHE LOSS high severity loss that does not lend itself to accurate prediction and thus should be transferred by the individual or business to an insurance company. *See also* EXPECTED LOSS; SELF INSURANCE.

CATASTROPHE REINSURANCE *see* AUTOMATIC NONPROPORTIONAL REINSURANCE; AUTOMATIC PROPORTIONAL REINSURANCE; AUTOMATIC REINSURANCE; EXCESS OF LOSS REINSURANCE; FACULTATIVE REINSURANCE; NONPROPORTIONAL REINSURANCE; PROPORTIONAL REINSURANCE; QUOTA SHARE REINSURANCE; STOP LOSS REINSURANCE; SURPLUS REINSURANCE.

CATASTROPHIC ILLNESS INSURANCE *see* DREAD DISEASE INSURANCE.

CATASTROPHIC INSURANCE FUTURES AND OPTIONS first exchange-traded RISK MANAGEMENT tool specifically developed for the insurance industry by the Chicago Board of Trade as a way for the primary insurance company to offset its underwriting exposures. *See also* FUTURES TIED TO REINSURANCE. These contracts are designed to provide the insurance company with a hedge against UNDERWRITING LOSSES resulting from catastrophic occurrences. The futures contract is an agreement to buy or sell a commodity or financial instrument at a set price on a given date. The option permits the owner to decide whether or not to exercise the option to buy or sell the commodity or financial instrument by the stipulated exercise date. The insurance option trading is based on the loss ratio concept (losses incurred over a stipulated time period divided by premiums earned over the same time period). For example, assume an insurance company buys an option on the loss ratio that will fall within the range of 50% to 70%. Should losses fall within that range, the insurance company would then exercise the option and sell the contract, thereby enabling the company to make a profit on the option. This profit could then be used by the company to offset losses. Should the loss portion not fall within the 50% to 70% range, the option would expire at zero value.

CAT SPREAD type of DERIVATIVE traded on the Chicago Board of Trade that takes the form of an option on a catastrophe futures contract using a call-option spread as the basis for the contract. The thesis of this kind of derivative is to simulate an artificial layer of EXCESS OF LOSS REINSURANCE coverage. This derivative has the origin of its value in the excess of loss reinsurance plan to be used as a mechanism for the PRIMARY INSURER hedging its risk coverage. *See also* CATASTROPHIC INSURANCE FUTURES AND OPTION; FUTURES CONTRACTS.

CAUSE OF LOSS FORM type of form that is added to a COMMERCIAL PROPERTY POLICY or COMMERCIAL PACKAGE POLICY (CPP) that lists the causes of losses that will be covered by the policy.

CAVEAT EMPTOR Latin expression meaning "let the buyer beware." The purchaser buys a product or service at his or her own risk. This principle has been modified significantly as it relates to an INSURANCE POLICY. *See also* ADHESION INSURANCE CONTRACT; FREE EXAMINATION "FREE LOOK" PERIOD.

CCC *see* CARE, CUSTODY, AND CONTROL.

CD ANNUITY *see* ANNUITY, CD.

CEDE to transfer a risk from an insurance company to a reinsurance company.

CEDENT *see* CEDING COMPANY.

CEDING COMPANY insurance company that transfers a risk to a reinsurance company.

CENTRAL GUARANTEE FUND fund from which losses are paid for the insolvent members of LLOYD'S OF LONDON. Each year, members of Lloyd's of London contribute a percentage of their premium volume to this fund to act as a reserve for losses that insolvent members are unable to pay. *See also* GUARANTY FUND (INSOLVENCY FUND).

CENTRAL LIMIT THEOREM statistical approach stating that if a series of samples is taken from a stable population, the distribution of the means (averages) of these samples will form a normal distribution whose mean approaches the population as the samples become larger.

CENTRAL LOSS FUND *see* GUARANTY FUND (INSOLVENCY FUND).

CERTAIN ANNUITY *see* LIFE CERTAIN ANNUITY.

CERTIFICATE *see* CERTIFICATE OF INSURANCE.

CERTIFICATE OF ANNUITY (COA) *see* ANNUITY, CD.

CERTIFICATE OF AUTHORITY written statement by an insurance company attesting to the powers it has vested in an agent.

CERTIFICATE OF INSURANCE document in life and health insurance issued to a member of a group insurance plan showing participation in insurance coverage. In property and liability insurance, evidence of the existence and terms of a particular policy.

CERTIFICATE OF NEED (CON) LAWS federal legislation passed in 1974 that mandated that legislators in all states that are in receipt of federal funds for health care review and approve any planned capital expenditures to be undertaken by health care institutions. Capital expenditures was defined as the purchase of major medical equipment and/or the expansion of physical facilities.

CERTIFIED EMPLOYEE BENEFIT SPECIALIST (CEBS) professional designation conferred by the International Foundation of Employee Benefit Plans and the Wharton School of the University of Pennsylvania. In addition to professional business experience in employee benefits, recipients must pass national examinations in pensions, Social Security, other retirement related plans, health insurance, economics, finance, labor relations, group insurance, and other employee benefit related plans. This program responds to the information requirements of individuals responsible for the operation of an employee benefit plan department in large and medium size businesses. (It has been estimated that for every dollar of salary an additional 40 cents is paid to cover employee benefits.)

CERTIFIED FINANCIAL PLANNER (CFP) professional designation conferred by the International Board of Standards and Practices for Certified Financial Planners. In addition to professional business experience in financial planning, recipients must pass national examinations in insurance, investments, taxation, employee benefit plans, and estate planning. This program responds to the growing need for help with personal financial planning.

CESSION *see* CEDE.

CESTUI QUE VIE person by whose life the duration of an insurance policy, estate, trust, or gift is measured. This person is generally referred as the INSURED in an insurance policy.

CHANGE IN CONDITIONS *see* DIFFERENCE IN CONDITIONS INSURANCE.

CHANGE IN OCCUPANCY OR USE CLAUSE CONDITION in which the occupancy or the purposes for which the premises are being used as described in the insurance policy change so as to result in an increased RISK. The policy is void unless prior notice is furnished to the insurance company. Once the company receives such notification, the company can either cancel the policy, or apply a surcharge to the premium to reflect this increased risk.

CHANGE OF BENEFICIARY PROVISION element of a life insurance policy permitting the policyowner to change a beneficiary as frequently as desired unless the beneficiary has been designated as irrevocable. Here the written permission of that beneficiary must be obtained in order to make a change.

CHANGE OF LOSS *see* PROBABILITY.

CHANNELING hospital insurance program that provides medical professional liability insurance coverage to nonemployed hospital physicians. The objective of this means of insurance coverage is to increase the number of patients being admitted to the hospital by tying staff physicians to that particular hospital through this insurance plan. This insurance strategy could lead to lower premiums resulting from loss control programs and joint legal liability defense programs. (The hospital and physician jointly defend against a patient's liability claim rather than each party retaining an attorney, which would increase expenses and develop an adversarial relationship between hospital and physician.) This program can be implemented through a joint hospital and physician program insuring both hospital and physician under the same insurance policy or the hospital can purchase a separate insurance policy for the physician.

CHARGEABLE describing automobile accidents that are considered to be the results of the negligent acts of the insured driver and are included in the driving record of that insured.

CHARITABLE AND GOVERNMENT IMMUNITY principle that no liability exposure can result from the performance of proprietary functions.

CHARITABLE GIFT ANNUITY donation of amount "A," made by donor X to a charity. The charity agrees to pay donor X an amount ("B") for the rest of donor X's life. Since the donation is used to fund an annuity, only a percentage of the donation can be taken as a tax-deductible gift in the year of the donation. The percentage taken is based on the Internal Revenue Service tables at the donor's age at the time of the donation. This gift is irrevocable. Since the donor is dependent on the charity to make the income payments, the donor should ascertain the financial ability of the charity to make those income payments. Thus, such an annuity permits the donor to transfer appreciated property to a charitable organization in exchange for the organization's promise to pay a continuous stream of income.

CHARITABLE GIFT LIFE INSURANCE life insurance policy given by a donor to a charity; donor only relinquishes the CASH VALUE and the cost of the PREMIUMS previously paid. The receiving charity's future value of the life insurance policy is the DEATH BENEFIT. Since the charity is the owner of the policy, it can: (1) borrow against the cash value; (2) surrender the policy for its then cash value; or (3) utilize its CONVERSION PRIVILEGES. The donor can enjoy an income tax deduction for the value of the life insurance policy contributed to a qualified charity, provided the donor does not retain any ownership rights to that policy. If the donor makes an irrevocable transfer of the life insurance policy to a qualified charity and all rights of ownership have been forfeited to the charity, the death benefit will not be included in the donor's estate, provided the donor survives for at least three years after the date of transfer.

CHARITABLE INDIVIDUAL RETIREMENT ACCOUNT (IRA) ROLLOVER provision of PENSION PROTECTION ACT OF 2006 under which a donor who is at least 70½ may transfer up to $100,000 to a qualified charity without creating a taxable event. The total charitable rollover is deductible in the year of the rollover.

The transaction does not appear on the tax return because it is not included in the taxpayer's gross income, charitable contribution, and thus taxable income. Each spouse may have an INDIVIDUAL RETIREMENT ACCOUNT (IRA) and may make a combined rollover contribution of $200,000 to a qualified single charity.

CHARITABLE LEAD TRUST trust in which a charity receives income from a donated asset for a specified number of years that it is held in that trust. After the specified period concludes, the principal is transferred to the donor's beneficiaries. This vehicle is used to keep wealth in the family by significantly reducing the costs of transfer to beneficiaries. The charity has the use of the income earned by that money, but the charity does not have use of the principal. This distribution is a taxable gift.

CHARITABLE REMAINDER ANNUITY TRUST special type of CHARITABLE REMAINDER TRUST (CRT) under which a designated beneficiary (cannot be a charitable beneficiary) receives an annual fixed income. The grantor of the trust is allowed an income tax deduction of the amount of the present value of the charity's remainder interest as of the date the asset(s) is contributed to the trust. If trust income proves to be inadequate to meet the required payments to the beneficiary, the selling-off of a portion of the trust's principal or capital gains earned by the trust may be used to make up the difference. Any excess amount of income generated by the trust above that required to pay the beneficiary is reinvested into the trust. Once this trust has been created, additional assets cannot be transferred into the trust.

CHARITABLE REMAINDER TRUST (CRT) TRUST to which a donor transfers assets and that distributes income to finance a predetermined situation. After the trust expires, any remaining assets are donated to the qualified charity that was previously designated as the remainder beneficiary (BENEFICIARY OF TRUST). In the year of transfer, the donor receives a tax deduction for the future value of the assets that were transferred to the trust. Thus, under this type of trust, the donor (person who creates the trust) simply makes an irrevocable transfer of an asset(s) to a trustee. According to the trust agreement, the trustee must: (1) invest the asset contributed to the trust; (2) pay a predetermined annual income to the donor and/or another designated beneficiary for life or stipulated number of years; and (3) distribute the asset(s) to the charity, either when the donor dies or when a specific designated income beneficiary dies.

CHARITABLE REMAINDER UNITRUST trust under which the beneficiary (cannot be a charitable beneficiary) receives a fixed percentage (not less than 5% of the trust's annual value) of the net fair market value of the trust on an annual basis. The annual income paid to the beneficiary must be either for life or for 20 or fewer years. The yearly payment will increase or decrease as the value of the trust assets increases or decreases. Additional contributions may be paid into the trust after it has been created.

CHARITABLE REVERSE SPLIT DOLLAR (CRSD) financial technique for providing term death coverage for an entity. With this procedure: (1) an individual purchases an ORDINARY LIFE INSURANCE POLICY and completes an agreement with the entity for a reverse SPLIT DOLLAR LIFE INSURANCE arrangement; (2) an individual endorses a policy's death benefit to the entity; (3) an entity assigns its interest in the policy to the charity; (4) an entity makes unrestricted gifts of cash to the charity in the form of premium payments according to the split dollar agreement; (5) an entity receives a charitable income tax deduction for gifts of cash (premium payments); (6) the POLICYOWNER (INSURED) is then entitled to make a tax-free withdrawal of all or a portion of the CASH VALUE, or take out a POLICY LOAN.

CHARITABLE SPLIT DOLLAR INSURANCE PLAN arrangement that provides for the reduction of estate taxes and the payment of tax-deductible life insurance premiums. The procedure is for a donor to present a charity with a gift of a sum of money that is tax deductible to the donor. The charity then transfers this gift in the form of a premium payment on an ORDINARY LIFE INSURANCE policy on the donor's life (the INSURED). The beneficiaries under the policy are the charity and the donor's heirs. Upon the death of the donor, the charity and the donor's heirs share in the DEATH BENEFIT from the policy. The donor's heirs also receive the cash value accrued on a tax-deferred basis within the policy.

CHARTERED FINANCIAL CONSULTANT (ChFC) professional designation awarded by the American College. In addition to professional business experience in financial planning, recipients are required to pass national examinations in insurance, investments, taxation, employee benefit plans, estate planning, accounting, and management. This program responds to the growing need for help in personal financial planning.

CHARTERED LIFE UNDERWRITER (CLU) professional designation conferred by the American College. In addition to professional business experience in insurance planning and related areas, recipients must pass national examinations in insurance, investments, taxation, employee benefit plans, estate planning, accounting, management, and economics. This program responds to a need by individuals for technically proficient help in planning their life insurance.

CHARTERED PROPERTY AND CASUALTY UNDERWRITER (CPCU) professional designation earned after the successful completion of 10 national examinations given by the American Institute for Property and Liability Underwriters. Covers such areas of expertise as insurance, risk management, economics, finance, management, accounting, and law. Three years of work experience are also required in the insurance business or a related area.

CHERRY PICK practice of selling those securities whose price has increased and retaining those securities whose price has declined. The securities that have declined are listed at their amortized value on the balance sheet resulting in a more positive profit picture for the insurance company than is warranted.

CHOICE NO-FAULT PLAN automobile owner's election to be covered under a state's no-fault law or TORT LIABILITY system (purchase of automobile liability insurance).

CHRONICALLY ILL INDIVIDUAL designation that requires certification by a physician, registered nurse, or licensed social worker that the person lacks a specific capacity to function and/or cognitive ability.

CHRONOLOGICAL STABILIZATION PLAN *see* RETROSPECTIVE RATING.

CICA *see* CAPTIVE INSURANCE COMPANIES ASSOCIATION (CICA).

CIVIL ACTION remedy imposed by a court of law, usually in the form of a monetary award, as compensation to the insured party for the CIVIL WRONG incurred. A civil action is initiated by the injured party (the plaintiff) against the party causing the damages (the defendant). The STATUTE OF LIMITATIONS applies to these actions. *See also* CIVIL DAMAGES.

CIVIL DAMAGES sums payable to the winning plaintiff by the losing defendant in a court of law; can take any or all of these forms: *general, punitive,* and *special.*

CIVILIAN HEALTH AND MEDICAL PROGRAM OF THE UNI-FORMED SERVICES (CHAMPUS) provision of health insurance benefits to families of active duty, retired, and deceased members of the military. Coverage is limited to necessary medical care and services. Excluded from coverage are active duty military personnel and anyone who is not immediate family (generally spouses and children).

CIVIL LIABILITY negligent acts and/or omissions, other than breach of contract, normally independent of moral obligations for which a remedy can be provided in a court of law. For example, a person injured in someone's home can bring suit under civil liability law.

CIVIL RIGHTS ACT OF 1964 act that prohibits employers from discriminating against employees in EMPLOYEE BENEFIT PLANS, regarding contributions or benefits based on race or gender.

CIVIL WRONG an act or violation that consists of two wrongs:
1. TORT—negligent act or omission by one or more parties against the person or property or another party or parties. LIABILITY INSURANCE is designated to cover an insured for unintentional tort.
2. Breach or violation of the provisions of a CONTRACT. *See also* CIVIL LIABILITY.

CLAIM request by an insured for indemnification by an insurance company for loss incurred from an insured peril.

CLAIM ADJUSTER *see* ADJUSTER.

CLAIM AGAINST EMPLOYERS NET WORTH claim by the PENSION BENEFIT GUARANTY CORPORATION (PBGC) against an employer for reimbursement of the PBGC's loss (for a terminated plan) up to 30% of the net worth of the employer. If this amount is not paid, the PBGC may place a lien on all of the assets of the employer.

CLAIM AGENT person who has been authorized by the insurance company to pay a loss(es) incurred by the INSURED.

CLAIMANT one who submits a claim for an incurred loss.

CLAIM DEPARTMENT section of an insurance company that evaluates claims for their subsequent payment.

CLAIM EXPENSE cost incurred in adjusting a claim. Claim-adjustment expenses include such items as attorneys' fees and investigation expenses (e.g., witness interviews). The claim settlement dollar amount awarded to the injured party is not considered a claim expense item.

CLAIM, OBLIGATION TO PAY clause in liability insurance policies stating that the insurance company has a legally enforceable obligation to pay all claims and defend all suits (even if groundless) up to the policy limits on behalf of the insured for which the insured becomes legally obligated to pay.

CLAIM PROVISION clause in an insurance policy that describes the administration and submission of claims procedure.

CLAIM REPORT report furnished by the ADJUSTER to the INSURANCE COMPANY (INSURER) that documents the amount of payment the insurer is legally obligated to pay to or on behalf of the INSURED under the terms of the POLICY. This report includes the following items:
1. Is there an INSURABLE INTEREST—did the person who submitted the claim have expectation of a monetary loss?
2. Is there a coverable cause of loss—was the source of the loss an INSURED PERIL?
3. Is the property covered—was the damaged or destroyed property insured?
4. What is the location of the loss—was the occurrence of the insured peril within the geographical scope of the policy?
5. What is the date of the loss—did the loss occur while the policy was in effect?
6. What are the applicable EXCLUSIONS—was the loss caused by a peril specifically excluded by the policy?
7. What are the applicable CONDITION(S) and WARRANTY(S)—were the condition(s) and warranty(s) under the policy complied with by the insured?

8. What is the SALVAGE value of the damaged property—is there a portion of the damaged property that can be salvaged and how does the value of the salvageable property affect the total dollar amount of the loss?

9. What is the status of any OTHER INSURANCE in force—are there any other insurance policies in force carried by the CLAIMANT covering the loss?

10. What is the status of SUBROGATION—are there any third parties responsible for a covered loss against which the insurer can take legal action?

11. Was there any MISREPRESENTATION (FALSE PRETENSE) and CONCEALMENT involved—did the insured falsify or withhold material facts from the insurer?

12. What is the status of the availability of documentation—are there photographs available of the damaged or destroyed insured property? Does the insured have receipts or other pertinent records relating to the damaged or destroyed insured property?

CLAIMS AND LOSS CONTROL *see* ENGINEERING APPROACH; HUMAN APPROACH.

CLAIMS DEPARTMENT section of the INSURANCE COMPANY that administers CLAIMS for the losses incurred by the INSURED.

CLAIMS MADE *see* CLAIMS MADE BASIS LIABILITY COVERAGE.

CLAIMS MADE BASIS LIABILITY COVERAGE method of determining whether or not coverage is available for a specific claim. If a claim is made during the time period when a liability policy is in effect, an insurance company is responsible for its payment, up to the limits of the policy, regardless of when the event causing the claim occurred. Experts often advise that it is extremely important, when purchasing a property and casualty policy, to determine if claims are paid on a claims made basis or a *claims occurrence* basis.

CLAIMS MADE FORM *see* CLAIMS MADE BASIS LIABILITY COVERAGE.

CLAIMS OCCURRENCE BASIS LIABILITY COVERAGE method of determining whether or not coverage is available for a specific claim. If a claim arises out of an event during the period when a policy is in force, the insurance company is responsible for its payment, up to the limits of the policy, regardless of when the business submits the claim. Experts often suggest that it is extremely important, when purchasing a property and casualty insurance policy, to determine if claims are paid on a *claims made* basis or on a claims occurrence basis.

CLAIMS OCCURRENCE FORM *see* CLAIMS OCCURRENCE BASIS LIABILITY COVERAGE.

CLAIMS REPRESENTATIVE *see* ADJUSTER.

CLAIMS RESERVE monetary fund established to pay for claims that the insurance company is aware of (claims incurred or future claims) but that the insurance company has not yet settled. This reserve is critical since it is an accurate indication of a company's liabilities. This reserve does not take into account INCURRED BUT NOT REPORTED LOSSES (IBNR).

CLASH REINSURANCE type of EXCESS OF LOSS REINSURANCE in which the insurance company (CEDENT) is reinsured in the event there is a casualty loss resulting in at least two INSUREDS generating losses from the single casualty occurrence.

CLASS group of insureds with the same characteristics, established for rate-making purposes. For example, all wood-frame houses within 200 feet of a fire plug in the same geographical area would have similar probabilities of incurring a total loss. *See also* RATE MAKING.

CLASSIFICATION *see* CLASS.

CLASSIFIED INSURANCE *see* SUBSTANDARD HEALTH INSURANCE; SUBSTANDARD LIFE INSURANCE.

CLASS PREMIUM RATE *see* CLASS RATE.

CLASS RATE rate applied to risks with similar characteristics or to a specified class of risk.

CLAUSE in an insurance policy, sentences and paragraphs describing various coverages, exclusions, duties of the insured, locations covered, and conditions that suspend or terminate coverage.

CLAUSES ADDED TO A LIFE INSURANCE POLICY provisions, usually requiring an additional premium, that are appended to an insurance contract. These include WAIVER OF PREMIUM (WP), DISABILITY INCOME (DI), ACCIDENTAL DEATH CLAUSE, and *policy purchase option (PPO)*. The young family with children may wish to consider these clauses since the breadwinner is seven to nine times more likely to become disabled than to die at a young age.

CLEANUP FUND component of necessary coverage determined by the "needs approach" to life insurance for a family. It is intended to cover last-minute expenses as well as those that surface after the death of an insured, such as burial costs, probate charges, and medical bills.

CLEAR-SPACE CLAUSE in PROPERTY INSURANCE policies, a clause that requires that a particular insured property be a specified distance from like insured or noninsured property. For example, stored dynamite should be at least 100 yards from an insured building.

CLIENT person who engages an AGENT or BROKER for advice and possible purchase of insurance.

CLIFFORD TRUST up to 1986, arrangement to provide a personal trust while the settlor is still alive. The income is paid to named children, who enjoy lower income taxes. After 10 years and a day, the property reverts to the original owner. The Internal Revenue Service had ruled that the income from the property in trust is not income to the original owner. The Clifford Trust was eliminated under the TAX REFORM ACT OF 1986.

CLIFF VESTING *see* TEN YEAR VESTING (CLIFF VESTING).

CLOSE end of a sales presentation designed to prompt the PROSPECT to purchase the insurance product.

CLOSE CORPORATION PLAN prior arrangement for surviving stock-holders to purchase shares of a deceased stockholder according to a pre-determined formula for setting the value of the corporation. Often, the best source for its funding is a life insurance policy in either of these forms: (1) *Individual Stock Purchase Plan (Cross Purchase Plan),* much like the *partnership cross purchase* plan. Each stockholder buys, owns, and pays the premium for insurance equal to his/her share of the agreed purchase price for the stock of the other stockholders. (2) *Corporation Stock Purchase Plan (Stock Redemption Plan),* similar to the *partnership entity plan* is a better choice if the number of stockholders is large. The corporation purchases and pays the premiums on the amount of insurance needed to purchase the decreased stockholder's interest at the price set by the predetermined formula. These premiums are not tax deductible as a business expense, but the death benefits are not subject to income tax. Life insurance owned by the corporation is listed as an asset on the corporation's balance sheet. Ownership of life insurance on the stockholders thus increases the corporation's net worth, and if per-manent insurance is purchased, its cash value would be available for loans in the event of business emergencies.

CLOSED-END INVESTMENT COMPANY type of investment com-pany that buys and sells its own shares on the stock exchanges. There are a limited number of shares available. The purchase of shares must be from an entity that already owns the shares.

CLOSING COSTS costs associated with the purchase of property to include attorneys' fees, title recording fees, discount points, and TITLE INSURANCE.

CLU *see* CHARTERED LIFE UNDERWRITER (CLU).

CODICIL amendment to a WILL that adds or modifies clauses in that will, such as adding an additional BENEFICIARY or piece of property.

CODING placement of verbal descriptive information into numerical form for the purposes of analysis.

COINSURANCE in PROPERTY INSURANCE, when the insurance policy contains this clause, coinsurance defines the amount of each loss that the company pays according to the following relationship:

$$\frac{\text{Amount of Insurance Carried}}{\text{Amount of Insurance Required}} \times \frac{\text{Amount}}{\text{of Loss}} = \frac{\text{Insurance Company}}{\text{Payment}}$$

Where:

Amount of Insurance Required = Value of Property Insured × Coinsurance Clause Percentage Amount of Insurance Required

Example:

Value of building = $100,000

Coinsurance Clause Percentage Amount of Insurance Required = 80%

Amount of Fire Damage to the Building = $60,000

Amount of Insurance Carried = $75,000

The insurance company would be required to pay $56,250 of the $60,000 loss:

$$\frac{\$75,000}{\$100,000 \times 80\%} \times \$60,000 = \$56,250$$

Note that the indemnification of the insured for a property loss can never exceed (1) the dollar amount of the actual loss; (2) the dollar limits of the insurance policy; (3) the dollar amount determined by the coinsurance relationship. The lesser of the above three amounts will always apply.

In commercial health insurance, when the insured and the insurer share in a specific ratio of the covered medical expenses, coinsurance is the insured's share of covered losses. For example, in some policies the insurer pays 75–80% of the covered medical expenses and the insured pays the remainder. In other policies, after the insured pays a DEDUCTIBLE amount, the insurer pays 75–80% of the covered medical expenses above the deductible and the insured pays the remainder until a maximum dollar amount is reached (for example, $5000). The insurer pays 100% of covered medical expenses over this dollar amount up to the limits of the policy.

COINSURANCE CAP provision found in a HEALTH INSURANCE CONTRACT. It places an annual limit on the maximum dollar amount of COINSURANCE the INSURED must renumerate.

COINSURANCE CLAUSE *see* COINSURANCE.

COINSURANCE FORMULA *see* COINSURANCE.

COINSURANCE LIMIT in a MERCANTILE OPEN-STOCK BURGLARY INSURANCE policy, the dollar amount of coverage as required by the COINSURANCE clause. This dollar amount is the MAXIMUM PROBABLE LOSS (MPL) of merchandise that the insurer estimates could result from a single burglary. The indemnification of the insured merchant cannot exceed the lesser of this coinsurance limit or the COINSURANCE PERCENTAGE of the total dollar value of the merchandise that has been insured.

COINSURANCE PENALTY reduction in the amount that the insured receives from the insurer, after having incurred a property loss, because the insurer failed to carry the amount of coverage required by the COINSURANCE clause. *See also* COINSURANCE REQUIREMENT.

COINSURANCE PERCENTAGE in many PROPERTY INSURANCE policies, a requirement that the insured carry insurance as a percentage of the total monetary value of the insured property. If this percentage is not carried, the insured is subject to the COINSURANCE PENALTY. *See also* COINSURANCE; COINSURANCE REQUIREMENT.

COINSURANCE PLAN OF REINSURANCE type of PROPORTIONAL REINSURANCE under which the CEDING COMPANY (PRIMARY INSURER) CEDES a portion of the FACE AMOUNT of the life insurance policy it has underwritten to its REINSURER. The reinsurer, in the event of the death of the insured, is obligated to pay its PRO RATA share (thus the alternate name PRO RATA REINSURANCE) of the DEATH BENEFIT to the ceding company that in turn must pay the full death benefit to the insured's BENEFICIARY. Under this plan, the reinsurer is also obligated to pay its pro rata share of all settlement options under the life insurance policy to include the CASH SURRENDER VALUE. The reinsurer receives from the ceding company a pro rata share of the GROSS PREMIUMS paid on the policy to the ceding company. In return, the ceding company receives a ceding commission (to cover its expenses incurred in marketing, underwriting, and distributing the life insurance policy) from the reinsurer.

COINSURANCE REQUIREMENT amount of insurance that the insured must carry in order to be indemnified for the total dollar amount of the actual loss. If this requirement is met by the insured, the COINSURANCE PENALTY will not go into effect. The amount of insurance required is usually expressed as a percentage of the value of the property insured at the time the loss is incurred; however, the amount may also be expressed as a flat dollar amount. *See also* COINSURANCE; COINSURANCE PERCENTAGE.

COINSURER party that shares in the loss under an insurance policy or policies. *See also* COINSURANCE; COINSURANCE LIMIT; COINSURANCE PENALTY; COINSURANCE PERCENTAGE; COINSURANCE REQUIREMENT.

COLD CALL (COLD CANVASSING) call on a prospective insurance buyer without a prior appointment. Many salespeople find this exercise the most threatening in their career development. Some observers attribute the substantial failure rate among new agents to their repugnance to cold calls.

COLD CANVASSING *see* COLD CALL (COLD CANVASSING).

COLLATERAL ASSIGNMENT designation of a policy's death benefit or its cash surrender value to a creditor as security for a loan. If the loan is not repaid, the creditor receives the policy proceeds up to the balance of the outstanding loan, and the beneficiary receives the remainder. Because life insurance is freely assignable it is readily acceptable to lending institutions as security. Also, the lender is certain to receive the money should death strike the borrower before the loan can be repaid.

COLLATERAL BOND BOND that provides additional security for a loan.

COLLATERAL BORROWER individual who assigns rights to a benefit. For example, a life insurance policy may be assigned as security for a loan made by the borrower. The policy protects the COLLATERAL CREDITOR (ASSIGNEE) if the borrower does not pay the loan when due. If a loan remains unpaid at the death of an insured, the loan balance is subtracted from the death benefit and paid to the creditor, with the balance going to the insured's beneficiary. On the other hand, if the insured (the borrower) does not pay the loan when due, the creditor can withdraw the amount due from the cash value of the policy. When a loan is repaid, the assignment ends and the policyowner is again vested with all rights to the policy.

COLLATERAL CREDITOR (ASSIGNEE) individual to whom rights to a benefit are assigned. A life insurance policy is assigned by the COLLATERAL BORROWER (assignor) to the collateral creditor (assignee) as security for a loan. *See also* COLLATERAL BORROWER.

COLLATERALIZED MORTGAGE OBLIGATIONS (CMOs) bonds that are secured by mortgage securities classified as either interest only or principal only strips (separate trading of registered interest and principal of securities). Insurance companies find CMOs desirable because of their predictable cash flow patterns.

COLLATERAL SOURCE RULE judicial rule of evidence under which no reduction in damages awarded by a court is allowed for bodily injury, sickness, illness, or accident merely because the plaintiff has other financial sources paying benefits such as HEALTH INSURANCE and DISABILITY INCOME INSURANCE.

COLLECTION BOOK record a debit (or other) agent makes for premiums collected, time period for which the policy is paid, and the week of collection or date the premium was paid. In essence, the debit agent, through the collection book, becomes a bookkeeper as well as a salesperson, since at the end of each week the agent has to balance the debit book, which in some instances is time consuming. *See also* DEBIT AGENT.

COLLECTION COMMISSION commission paid to an agent as a percentage of the premiums he or she collects on DEBT INSURANCE (HOME SERVICE INSURANCE, INDUSTRIAL INSURANCE).

COLLECTION EXPENSE INSURANCE *see* ACCOUNTS RECEIVABLE INSURANCE.

COLLECTION FEE fee paid to an agent as compensation for his or her collecting premiums for DEBIT INSURANCE (HOME SERVICE INSURANCE, INDUSTRIAL INSURANCE).

COLLECTIVE MERCHANDISING OF INSURANCE *see* MASS MERCHANDISING.

COLLEGE OF INSURANCE four-year institution of higher learning. The degree programs include insurance, risk management, actuarial science, and financial services. Became the School of Risk Management, Insurance, and Actuarial Science after its merger in 2001 with St. John's University.

COLLEGE RETIREMENT EQUITIES FUND (CREF) entity maintained by the Teachers Insurance Annuity Association. The fund essentially serves college faculties and staff, who pay premiums through salary deductions toward a tax-sheltered retirement variable annuity.

COLLISION physical contact of an automobile with another inanimate object resulting in damage to the insured car. Insurance coverage is available to provide protection against this occurrence. *See also* PERSONAL AUTOMOBILE POLICY (PAP).

COLLISION DAMAGE WAIVER special property damage coverage purchased by an individual renting an automobile under which the rental company waives any right to recover property damage to the automobile from that individual, regardless of who is at fault. A significant fee is paid by the individual to the rental company for this waiver for coverage that may already be provided by a PERSONAL AUTOMOBILE POLICY (PAP).

COLLISION INSURANCE in automobile insurance, coverage providing protection in the event of physical damage to the insured's own automobile (other than that covered under COMPREHENSIVE INSURANCE) resulting from COLLISION with another inanimate object. *See also* PERSONAL AUTOMOBILE POLICY (PAP).

COLLUSION agreement between two or more individuals to commit fraud. For example, an insured hires someone to burn down this house in order to collect the insurance proceeds.

COMBINATION AGENCY life insurance company AGENCY that sells ORDINARY LIFE INSURANCE and INDUSTRIAL LIFE INSURANCE.

COMBINATION AGENT representative of an insurance company who sells ordinary and industrial life insurance policies. In an effort to move their field forces into the ordinary life business, many industrial companies have systematically trained their agents to sell ordinary life policies.

COMBINATION COMPANY life insurance company whose agents sell ORDINARY LIFE INSURANCE and INDUSTRIAL LIFE INSURANCE.

COMBINATION POLICY (PLAN)
1. a contract in life insurance that includes elements of whole life and term insurance.
2. in pensions, a combined life insurance policy and a side (auxiliary) fund to enhance the amount of a future pension.
3. in automobile insurance, different coverages using policies of two or more insurance companies (rare).

COMBINATION SAFE DEPOSITORY INSURANCE covers property damage and theft coverage in two areas not subject to a coinsurance requirement or a deductible.
Coverage A. If the bank becomes liable for loss to a customer's property while that property is: (1) on the bank's premises in safe deposit boxes in the vault; or (2) being deposited into or taken out of the safe deposit boxes.
Coverage B. Loss to the bank customer's property due to burglary or robbery, whether actual or attempted, even if the bank is not held liable.

COMBINED RATIO in insurance, combination of the LOSS RATIO and the EXPENSE RATIO:

1. Loss Ratio = $\dfrac{\text{Incurred Losses + Loss Adjustment Expense}}{\text{Earned Premiums}}$

2. Expenses Ratio = $\dfrac{\text{Incurred Expenses}}{\text{Written Premiums}}$

The combined ratio is important to an insurance company since it indicates whether or not the company is earning a profit on the business it is writing, *not* taking into account investment returns on the premiums received. The property and casualty insurance business sometimes goes through cycles. During the 1980s, for instance, it was not unusual to have a combined ratio of over 120%. Obviously, the difference has to be made up from the company's surplus, which in some instances even put the major companies under severe financial strain.

COMBINED SINGLE LIMIT bodily injury liability and property damage liability expressed as a single sum of coverage.

COMMENCEMENT OF COVERAGE date at which insurance protection begins.

COMMERCIAL BLANKET BOND coverage of the employer for all employees on a *blanket* basis, with the maximum limit of coverage applied to any one loss without regard for the number of employees involved. Both *commercial* and *position blanket bonds* work the same way if only one employee causes the loss, or if the guilty employee(s) cannot be identified. For example, five identifiable employees as a team steal $50,000. A $10,000 BLANKET POSITION BOND would cover the loss in full. A $50,000 commercial blanket bond would be required to repay the insured business for the same loss.

COMMERCIAL CREDIT INSURANCE coverage for an insured firm if its business debtors fail to pay their obligations. The insured firm can be a manufacturer or a service organization but it cannot sell its products or service on a retail level to be covered under commercial credit insurance. Under this form of insurance, the insured firm assumes the expected loss up to the retention amount and the insurance company pays the excess losses above that amount, up to the limits of the credit insurance policy.

COMMERCIAL CRIME COVERAGE FORM type of commercial insurance that provides coverage for the business under the following policy forms:

1. *Form A*—employee dishonesty involving money, securities, and other properties and may be written on a BLANKET INSURANCE or SCHEDULED POLICY basis.
2. *Form B*—forgery or alteration involving outgoing checks, drafts, promissory notes, and other similar financial instruments.
3. *Form C*—theft, disappearance, and destruction of money and securities.
4. *Form D*—robbery and safe burglary (property excluding money and securities) involving losses inside or outside the premises of the insured business.
5. *Form E*—premises burglary involving property (excepting money and securities) inside the premises of the insured business.
6. *Form F*—computer fraud involving money, securities, and property other than money and securities.
7. *Form G*—extortion involving money, securities, and property that does not include money and securities.
8. *Form H*—premises theft and robbery outside premises other than money and securities.
9. *Form I*—lessees of safe deposit boxes involving theft, disappearance, or destruction of securities or property other than money and securities while in a vault or during the deposit or withdrawal from a safe deposit box on the premises of the insured.
10. *Form J*—securities deposited with others involving theft, disappearance, or destruction of securities that are on the inside of the premises of a custodian (party to which the insured has transferred the securities), or while the securities are outside the premises of the custodian in the possession of an employee of the custodian, or while the securities have been deposited by the custodian into a depository.
11. *Form K*—liability for guest's property in a safe deposit box involving property damage or loss.
12. *Form L*—liability for guest's property while on the premises of the business or in the possession of the business involving loss or damage to that property.
13. *Form M*—safe depository liability involving loss, damage, or destruction to the customer's property while on the premises of

the business in a safe deposit box, in a vault, or while being transferred to and from safe deposit boxes or vaults. The legal liability of the business for the customer's loss has to be established.

14. *Form N*—safe depository direct loss involving loss, damage, or destruction of the customer's property while on the premises of the business in a safe deposit box, in a vault, or while being transferred to and from safe deposit boxes or vaults. The legal liability of the business for the customer's loss does not have to be established.

15. *Form O*—public employees' dishonesty for loss involving money, securities, or property that does not include money and securities. This form is usually written to provide coverages for public entities such as schools and universities.

16. *Form P*—public employees' dishonesty for employee involving money, securities, or property that does not include money and securities. This form is usually written to provide coverages for public entities such as cities, public utilities, and public hospitals.

17. *Form Q*—robbery and safe burglary of money and securities when in the custody of the custodian inside the premises, or when in the custody of a messenger outside the premises.

18. *Form R*—money orders and counterfeit paper currency involving their acceptance in good faith by the business in exchange for money, services, or merchandise.

The above 18 coverage forms can be combined in various ways to produce numerous plans of insurance. For example, STOREKEEPERS BURGLARY AND ROBBERY INSURANCE would combine forms D, E, and Q. OFFICE BURGLARY AND ROBBERY INSURANCE would combine forms D, H, and Q.

COMMERCIAL FORGERY POLICY coverage for an insured who unknowingly accepts forged checks. Coverage can be found under the SPECIAL MULTIPERIL INSURANCE (SMP) policy (SECTION III CRIME COVERAGE INSURING AGREEMENT 5—DEPOSITORS FORGERY).

COMMERCIAL FORMS insurance policies covering various business risks.

COMMERCIAL GENERAL LIABILITY FORM (CGL) liability coverage section of a SIMPLIFIED COMMERCIAL LINES PORTFOLIO POLICY (SCLP). Provides for separate limits of coverage for general liability, fire legal liability, products and completed operations liability, advertising and personal liability, and medical payments. An AGGREGATE LIMIT of liability is in force for the general liability, fire legal liability, advertising and personal liability, and medical payments claims. When total claims for all of these areas exceed a given annual aggregate limit of liability, the policy limits are said to be exhausted and no more claims for that year will be paid under the policy. There is also an aggregate limit of liability in force for products and completed operations liability claims. This form has replaced the COMPREHENSIVE GENERAL LIABILITY INSURANCE (CGL) form.

COMMERCIAL HEALTH INSURANCE coverage that provides two types of benefits, DISABILITY INCOME (DI) and *medical expenses.* Sold by insurance companies whose business objective is the profit motive (as distinct from Blue Cross/Blue Shield) it can be classified by its RENEWAL PROVISION, and types of *benefits provided.*

1. *Renewal Provisions:* (a) Optionally renewable. The insurance company has the option to renew the policy at the end of the term period (one year, six months, three months, or one month). If the company renews the policy, it has the option to adjust the premium up or down; limit the types of perils insured against; and limit some or all of the benefits. (b) Nonrenewable for stated reasons only. When the insured reaches a certain age or when all similar policies are not renewed, the policy is said to be nonrenewable for the reasons stated. (c) Noncancellable. The insurance company must renew the policy and cannot change any of the provisions of the policy nor raise the premium while the policy is in force. (d) Guaranteed renewable. The company must renew the policy but the company has the option to adopt a new rate structure for the future renewal premiums.

2. *Benefits Provided:* (a) Disability income for total and partial disability subject to a maximum dollar amount and maximum length of time. Limitations include: pre-existing injury or condition; elimination period beginning with the first day of disability during which no benefits are paid; probationary period during which no benefits are paid for a sickness contracted or beginning during the first 15, 20, 25, or 30 days that the policy is in force; a recurrent disability such that before the current disability will be deemed to be a new disability, the insured must have returned to full time continuous employment for at least six months. (b) medical expense benefits for hospital charges for room, board, nursing, use of the operating room, physicians and surgeons fees; and miscellaneous medical expenses for laboratory tests, drugs, medicines, X-rays, anesthetics, artificial limbs, therapeutics, and ambulance service to and from the hospital.

COMMERCIAL INSURANCE insurance sold by privately formed insurance companies with the objective of making a profit.

COMMERCIAL INSURANCE COMPANY privately formed insurance company whose objective is to make a profit.

COMMERCIAL LINES insurance coverages for businesses, commercial institutions, and professional organizations, as contrasted with PERSONAL INSURANCE. *See also* BUSINESS AUTOMOBILE POLICY (BAP): BUSINESS CRIME INSURANCE; BUSINESS INCOME COVERAGE FORM; BUSINESS LIFE AND HEALTH INSURANCE; BUSINESSOWNERS POLICY (BOP); BUY-AND-SELL AGREEMENT; CLOSE CORPORATION PLAN; COMMERCIAL GENERAL LIABILITY FORM (CGL); PARTNERSHIP LIFE AND HEALTH INSURANCE; SIMPLIFIED COMMERCIAL LINES PORTFOLIO POLICY (SCLP); SOLE PROPRIETOR LIFE AND HEALTH INSURANCE.

COMMERCIAL MULTIPLE PERIL POLICY *see* COMMERCIAL PACKAGE POLICY (CPP)

COMMERCIAL PACKAGE POLICY (CPP) insurance policy that is COMMERCIAL LINES in orientation and is composed of two or more of the following coverages: COMMERCIAL PROPERTY, BUSINESS CRIME, BUSINESS AUTOMOBILE, BOILER AND MACHINERY, COMMERCIAL GENERAL LIABILITY (CGL), INLAND MARINE INSURANCE, and FARMOWNERS and RANCHOWNERS INSURANCE.

COMMERCIAL POLICY *see* COMMERCIAL HEALTH INSURANCE.

COMMERCIAL PROPERTY FLOATER means of providing insurance protection for the property of a business that is not at a fixed location.

COMMERCIAL PROPERTY FORM ENDORSEMENT to the STANDARD FIRE POLICY increasing the insurance protection to an ALL RISKS basis.

COMMERCIAL PROPERTY POLICY coverage for business risks including goods in transit, fire, burglary, and theft. A common example is the COMMERCIAL PACKAGE POLICY (CPP).

COMMERCIAL UMBRELLA INSURANCE *see* UMBRELLA LIABILITY INSURANCE.

COMMINGLED TRUST FUND pooling of assets of two or more pension funds under common portfolio management.

COMMISSION fee paid to an insurance salesperson as a percentage of the premium generated by a sold insurance policy.

COMMISSION, CONTINGENT COMMISSION that is paid based on how profitable a particular type of business proves to be that is written by an AGENT.

COMMISSIONER OF INSURANCE (INSURANCE COMMISSIONER, SUPERINTENDENT OF INSURANCE) top state regulator of the insurance business who is either elected to office or appointed by a state to safeguard the interests of policyowners.

COMMISSIONERS ANNUITY RESERVE VALUATION METHOD (CARVM) term for statutory reserves for annuities that can be calculated using various methods but at the minimum, the reserve must be at least equal to the CARVM. The CARVM equals the greatest present value of future guaranteed benefits to include NONFORFEITURE BENEFITS in excess of future required premiums. Not included in this calculation are expenses and policy lapses.

COMMISSIONERS STANDARD INDUSTRIAL MORTALITY TABLE (CSI) table used in calculating various nonforfeiture values for industrial life insurance policies. These tables give the minimum values that must be generated to the policyowner. The insured's life expectancy, according to the Commissioners Standard Industrial Mortality Table, is shorter than the life expectancy given in ordinary life tables such as the COMMISSIONERS STANDARD ORDINARY MORTALITY TABLE (CSO). Thus the Industrial Mortality Table's premiums are relatively higher than those based on the CSO Table. This is because the life expectancy of purchasers of industrial policies tends on average to be less than that of people who buy ordinary life policies.

COMMISSIONERS STANDARD ORDINARY MORTALITY TABLE (CSO) table used in calculating minimum nonforfeiture values and policy reserves for ordinary life insurance policies. These tables, which give minimum values that must be guaranteed to policyowners as approved by the NATIONAL ASSOCIATION OF INSURANCE COMMISSIONERS (NAIC), depict the number of people dying each year out of the original population, not as individuals, but in age groups.

COMMISSIONERS STANDARD ORDINARY TABLE (CSO) 2001 table that replaces the COMMISSIONERS STANDARD ORDINARY MORTALITY TABLE 1980 as the standard mortality table for nonforfeiture and valuation calculations.

COMMISSIONERS VALUES specific values of securities computed annually by the NATIONAL ASSOCIATION OF INSURANCE COMMISSIONERS (NAIC) as guidelines and procedures for insurance companies in listing of their securities in their annual statements. Values are the same for all insurers. This gives insurance commissioners a basis for valuing securities and ensuring that a company has sufficient assets to back up the reserve requirements.

COMMISSION OF AUTHORITY powers of an AGENT delegated by an insurance company and shown in the form of a document.

COMMITMENT insurance company's promise to insure particular risks.

COMMODITY FUTURES specified contracts of commodities such as pork bellies, wheat, soybeans, gold, silver, and cattle purchased for future delivery at a given price and date.

COMMON CARRIER transportation firm that must carry any customer's goods if the customer is willing to pay. Common carriers include trucking companies, bus lines, and airlines. *See also* INLAND MARINE INSURANCE.

COMMON DISASTER CLAUSE (SURVIVORSHIP CLAUSE) wording in life insurance policies to determine the order of deaths when the insured and the beneficiary die in the same accident. For example, if the insured is deemed to have died first, the proceeds are payable to a named contingent beneficiary. Otherwise, the proceeds are payable to the insured's estate and are subject to probate and other legal fees.

COMMON LAW legal system in the United States, Great Britain, and other countries. Inherited from England, it is based on case decisions acting as the precedent, not on written law. *See also* STATUTORY LIABILITY.

COMMON LAW DEFENSES arguments composed of ASSUMPTION OF RISK, CONTRIBUTORY NEGLIGENCE, and FELLOW SERVANT RULE.

COMMON POLICY DECLARATIONS *see* DECLARATION; DECLARATIONS SECTION.

COMMON STOCK INVESTMENTS allocation of monetary resources to equities.

COMMON STOCKS *see* EQUITIES.

COMMON TRUST FUND *see* COMMINGLED TRUST FUND.

COMMUNITY PROPERTY all property acquired after marriage, deemed to be the result of the joint efforts of both spouses (regardless of whether or not only one spouse has earned income). Each spouse is entitled to one half of the property. Community property states are Arizona, California, Hawaii, Idaho, Louisiana, New Mexico, Oklahoma, Texas, and Washington.

COMMUTATION in LIFE INSURANCE, the exchange of a series of installment payments, as the result of an INSTALLMENT SETTLEMENT, for a LUMP SUM DISTRIBUTION.

COMMUTATION RIGHT right of a BENEFICIARY of a LIFE INSURANCE POLICY to exchange the future installments due that beneficiary for a LUMP SUM DISTRIBUTION.

COMMUTATIVE CONTRACT type of two-party contract in which there is an equal exchange of something of value.

COMMUTE *see* COMMUTATION RIGHT.

COMMUTED VALUE *see* COMMUTATION RIGHT.

COMPANY ORGANIZATION *see* INSURANCE COMPANY ORGANIZATION.

COMPARATIVE INTEREST RATE METHOD *see* LINTON YIELD METHOD.

COMPARATIVE NEGLIGENCE in some states, principle of tort law providing that in the event of an accident each party's negligence is based on that party's contribution to the accident. For example, if in an auto accident both parties fail to obey the yield sign, their negligence would be equal, and neither would collect legal damages from the other.

COMPENSATING BALANCES PLAN premium paid by an insured business to an insurance company from which the company subtracts charges for the cost of putting a policy on its books, premium taxes, and profit. The remainder of the premium is deposited in the insured business's bank account from which the insured business can make withdrawals.

COMPENSATORY DAMAGES *see* LIABILITY, CIVIL DAMAGES AWARDED.

COMPETENCE capacity of parties to an insurance contract to understand the meanings of their action in order for the contract to be valid.

COMPETITIVE STATE FUND *see* MONOPOLISTIC STATE FUND.

COMPLETED OPERATIONS INSURANCE coverage for a contractor's liability for injuries or property damage suffered by third parties as the result of the contractor completing an operation. The contractor must take reasonable care in rendering a project safe and free from all reasonable hazards. *See also* COMMERCIAL GENERAL LIABILITY FORM (CGL).

COMPLETION BOND protection for a mortgagee guaranteeing that the mortgagor will complete construction. The mortgagee (such as a savings and loan association) lends money to the mortgagor (the owner of the project) in order to pay the contractor who is actually physically building the project. Upon completion, the project then serves to secure the loan. Should the project not be completed, the mortgagee is protected through the completion bond.

COMPOUND INTEREST accumulation of interest yearly or more frequently, including interest paid on interest.

COMPOUND PROBABILITY theory that the PROBABILITY that two independent events will occur is equal to the probability that one independent event will occur times the probability that a second INDEPENDENT EVENT will occur. For example, on a single toss of two dimes (each dime having a head and a tail), the probability that both will land on their tails is equal to $\frac{1}{4}$ ($\frac{1}{2} \times \frac{1}{2}$).

COMPOUND VALUE FUTURE VALUE of an ASSET for at least one time period.

COMPREHENSIVE AUTOMOBILE LIABILITY INSURANCE *see* AUTOMOBILE LIABILITY INSURANCE; COMPREHENSIVE INSURANCE.

COMPREHENSIVE CRIME ENDORSEMENT attachment to a COMMERCIAL PACKAGE POLICY to cover counterfeit currency, depositor's forgery, employee dishonesty, and the loss of money, money orders, and securities by the insured business. *See also* COMMERCIAL PACKAGE POLICY for a listing of actual coverages available.

COMPREHENSIVE ENVIRONMENTAL RESPONSE, COMPENSATION, AND LIABILITY ACT OF 1980 (CERCLA) act that makes the liability cost for cleanup joint and several. Even if a party is only partially responsible for losses inflicted, that party may be liable for the payment of the total cost involved in the cleanup. This liability is retroactive without stipulation as to time limit.

COMPREHENSIVE GENERAL LIABILITY INSURANCE (CGL) coverage against all liability exposures of a business unless specifically excluded. Coverage includes products, completed operations, premises and operations, elevators, and independent contractors. This form has been replaced by the COMMERCIAL GENERAL LIABILITY FORM (CGL).

Products coverage insures when a liability suit is brought against the manufacturer and/or distributor of a product because of someone incurring bodily injury or property damage through use of the product. (The manufacturer of the product must use all reasonable means to make certain that the product is free from any inherent defect.)

Completed operations coverage insures for bodily injury or property damage incurred because of a defect in a completed project of the insured.

Premises and operations coverage insures for bodily injury incurred on the premises of the insured, and/or as the result of the insured's business operations.

Elevator coverage insures for bodily injury incurred in an elevator or escalator on the insured's premises.

Independent contractors coverage insures for bodily injury incurred as the result of negligent acts and omissions of an independent contractor employed by the insured.

COMPREHENSIVE GLASS INSURANCE coverage on an ALL RISKS basis for glass breakage, subject to exclusions of war and fire. Thus, if a vandal throws a brick through a window of an insured's establishment, the coverage would apply.

COMPREHENSIVE HEALTH INSURANCE complete coverage for hospital and physician charges subject to deductibles and coinsurance. This coverage combines basic medical expense policy and major medical policy. *See also* GROUP HEALTH INSURANCE; HEALTH MAINTENANCE ORGANIZATION (HMO).

COMPREHENSIVE INSURANCE coverage in automobile insurance providing protection in the event of physical damage (other than COLLISION) or theft of the insured car. For example, fire damage to an insured car would be covered under the comprehensive section of the PERSONAL AUTOMOBILE POLICY (PAP).

COMPREHENSIVE LIABILITY INSURANCE policy providing businesses with coverage for negligence based civil liability in: (1) Bodily injury and property damage liability, on an occurrence basis, resulting from the ownership, use, and/or maintenance of the premises, completed operations and products. (2) Bodily injury and property damage liability for operation of an elevator. (3) Medical expenses resulting from bodily injury incurred by a member of the general public through the use of the premises or involvement in the operations. Medical expense reimbursement of the business is without regard to fault of the business.

COMPREHENSIVE MAJOR MEDICAL INSURANCE *see* GROUP HEALTH INSURANCE; HEALTH INSURANCE; HEALTH MAINTENANCE ORGANIZATION (HMO).

COMPREHENSIVE MEDICARE SUPPLEMENT insurance policy designed to provide coverage for the DEDUCTIBLE amount and the COINSURANCE amount required to be paid by the MEDICARE recipient. Some of these policies will also continue to provide coverage for hospital and nursing home expenses for a substantial amount or an unlimited amount per period of confinement after Medicare benefits have been exhausted. *See also* MEDIGAP INSURANCE.

COMPREHENSIVE PERSONAL LIABILITY INSURANCE coverage such as HOMEOWNERS INSURANCE POLICY—SECTION II on an ALL RISKS basis for personal acts and omissions by the insured and residents of the insured's household. Included are sports activities, pet activities, and miscellaneous events such as someone tripping in an insured's cemetery plot.

COMPREHENSIVE POLICY combination of several coverages to protect the insured. For example, the COMPREHENSIVE HEALTH INSURANCE policy combines the *basic hospital plan* with MAJOR MEDICAL INSURANCE to cover medical expenses (room, board, surgical, and physician expenses) and miscellaneous expenses (surgical dressings, drugs, ambulance services, blood, and operating room). Many policies have a maximum lifetime limit of $1 million for the insured and for each member of the insured's family who is a dependent resident of the insured's household. The COMPREHENSIVE PERSONAL LIABILITY INSURANCE policy covers the insured for just about any negligent act or omission that results in property damage or bodily injury to another party, subject to the exclusions of automotive liability and professional liability. The SPECIAL MULTIPERIL INSURANCE (SMP) policy provides the businessowner with comprehensive property damage coverage on an ALL RISKS basis.

COMPREHENSIVE THEFT, DISAPPEARANCE, AND DESTRUCTION INSURANCE *see* THEFT, DISAPPEARANCE, AND DESTRUCTION POLICY (FORM C).

COMPREHENSIVE "3-D" POLICY *see* DISHONESTY, DISAPPEARANCE, AND DESTRUCTION POLICY (3-D POLICY).

COMPULSORY AUTOMOBILE LIABILITY INSURANCE *see* COMPULSORY INSURANCE.

COMPULSORY INSURANCE coverage required by the laws of a particular state. For example, many states stipulate minimum amounts of automobile liability insurance that must be carried. *See also* FINANCIAL RESPONSIBILITY LAW.

COMPULSORY RETIREMENT AGE mandatory age of retirement.

COMPUTER FRAUD INSURANCE type of CRIME INSURANCE that provides coverage in the event of the fraudulent transfer of insured property from the insured's premises to a premise not belonging to the insured. For example, a thief gives directions to the insured's computer to illegally transfer funds to the thief's bank account.

CONCEALMENT intention to withhold or secrete information. If an insured withholds information on a material fact, about which the insurance company has no knowledge, the company has grounds to void the contract. For example, the insured neglects to tell the company that, within a week of the policy issue date, the manufacture of gunpowder in the insured business's building will commence. If an explosion related to the gunpowder then occurs in the building the company has legal grounds for not paying for the property damage.

CONCURRENCY circumstance in which at least two insurance policies provide identical coverage for the same risk. *See also* DOUBLE RECOVERY.

CONCURRENT CAUSATION loss caused by two or more perils. A certain amount of controversy exists when one of the perils is insured and the other peril is excluded from coverage. Some courts are beginning to find that even if only one of the perils is insured against, the policy providing the coverage for that peril must pay the damages.

CONCURRENT INSURANCE *see* CONCURRENCY.

CONDITION action(s) that the insured must take, or continue to take, for the insurance policy to remain in force and the insurance company to process a claim. For example, the insured must pay the premiums when due, notify the insurance company as soon as possible in the case of an accident, and cooperate with the company in defense of the insured in case of a liability suit.

CONDITIONAL terms specifying obligations of an insured to keep a policy in force. For example, an insured must pay the premiums due; in life insurance, if death occurs, the beneficiary or the insured's estate must submit proof of death; if there is a property loss, the insured must submit proof of loss.

CONDITIONAL BINDING RECEIPT *see* BINDING RECEIPT; CONDITIONAL RECEIPT.

CONDITIONAL INSURANCE *see* CONDITIONAL SALES FLOATER.

CONDITIONALLY RENEWABLE *see* COMMERCIAL HEALTH INSURANCE.

CONDITIONAL RECEIPT evidence of a temporary contract obliging a life or health insurance company to provide coverage as long as a premium accompanies an acceptable application. This gives the company time to process the application and to issue or refuse a policy, as the case may be. If the applicant were to die before a policy is issued, the company will pay the death benefit if the policy would have been issued. For example, Mr. A applies for $100,000 of life insurance but is killed by an automobile before the policy is issued. The company finds that it would have issued the policy, and therefore pays $100,000 to the beneficiary. *See also* BINDING RECEIPT.

CONDITIONAL RENEWABLE HEALTH INSURANCE automatic right of an insured to renew a policy until a given date or age except under stated conditions. It is extremely important for the purchaser to review the conditions for renewal in order to make sure of their acceptability.

CONDITIONAL SALES FLOATER coverage for the seller of property on an installment or conditional sales contract if it is damaged or destroyed. For example, a television set is sold on an installment basis but is destroyed by a customer. The seller would be indemnified for the loss.

CONDITIONAL VESTING *see* VESTING, CONDITIONAL.

CONDITION PRECEDENT contractual obligation that requires one party to the contract to fulfill its obligation before another party to the contract is required to fulfill its contractual obligation. For example, under the HOMEOWNERS INSURANCE POLICY, in the event the insured suffers a property loss, that insured must provide the insurer with immediate notice of the loss as well as an inventory of the damaged property within 60 days of the occurrence of the loss.

CONDITIONS FOR QUALIFICATION rights and duties of an insured as a prerequisite for collecting benefits. For example, in the event of property damage, the insured may be required to submit proof of loss to the insurance company.

CONDITION SUBSEQUENT termination of a contractual obligation for immediate performance. For example, under the HOMEOWNERS INSURANCE POLICY, if the INSURER refuses to pay a claim, the INSURED (if not satisfied with the reason) must bring suit against the insured within one year of having incurred the loss or he/she will forgo forever the right to sue the insurer.

CONDOMINIUM INSURANCE coverage under the *Homeowners Form-4 (HO-4)* for the insured's personal property and loss of use against fire and/or lightning; vandalism and/or malicious mischief; windstorm and/or hail; explosion, riot and/or civil commotion; vehicles; aircraft; smoke; falling objects; weight of ice, sleet, and/or snow; volcanic eruption; damage from artificially generated electricity; freezing of plumbing, heating, air conditioning or sprinkler system or household appliances; accidental tearing apart, cracking, burning, or bulging of a steam or hot water heating system, air conditioning system, or an automatic fire protective sprinkler system.

CONFIDENCE LEVEL percentage of confidence in a finding. For example, if an insurance company's total LOSS RESERVES should be $10,000,000 in order to attain an 80% confidence level that enough money will be available to pay anticipated claims, then, in 8 times out of 10, after all claims have been settled the total claims paid out will be less than $10,000,000. Conversely, in 2 times out of 10 the total claims paid out will be greater than $10,000,000. In another example, a 70% confidence level of one's house burning would mean that the house would burn approximately once every 3.33 years $[1 \div (1-0.70) = 3.33]$.

CONFINING CONDITION term describing illness, sickness, or disability incurred by the insured such that the insured is restricted to his or her home, a hospital, or a nursing home. Many HEALTH INSURANCE policies provide benefits only if the insured is restricted in such a manner.

CONFLAGRATION fire that spreads substantial destruction.

CONFUSION OF GOODS peril that occurs when personal property of two or more people is mixed to such an extent that any one owner can no longer identify his or her property.

CONSEQUENTIAL DAMAGE ENDORSEMENT *see* BUSINESS INTERRUPTION INSURANCE; CONSEQUENTIAL LOSS.

CONSEQUENTIAL LOSS value of loss resulting from loss of use of property. For example, a fire damages the structure of business premises and the business loses customer income until it can reopen. The loss in income—the consequential loss—can be covered under BUSINESS INTERRUPTION INSURANCE. Basic property insurance policies, such as the *fire policy,* do not cover the consequential or indirect loss.

CONSERVATION effort to keep life insurance policies from *lapsing.* Many life insurance companies have conservation officers who contact lapsing *policyowners* explaining the benefits of keeping their policies in force. Often, the AGENT OF RECORD is notified of policies in danger or in process of lapsing so that the agent may also contact the policyowner.

CONSERVATOR court-appointed or COMMISSIONER OF INSURANCE-appointed custodian to manage the affairs of an insurance company whose management is deemed unable to manage that company in a proper fashion. Usually such a company faces INSOLVENCY prior to the appointment of the conservator.

CONSIDERATION
1. under contract law, anything of value exchanged for a promise or for performance that is needed to make an instrument binding on the contracting parties.
2. adherence to all provisions of an insurance policy by an insured; for example, the insured agrees to make all premium payments when due in order to maintain a policy in full force.
3. payment for an annuity. *See also* INSURANCE CONTRACT, LIFE; INSURANCE CONTRACT, PROPERTY AND CASUALTY.

CONSIGNMENT INSURANCE coverage for items that are on consignment, including exhibits, goods up for auction, and goods awaiting someone's approval. The stipulation for coverage is that these items cannot be under the care, custody, and control of the owner.

CONSOLIDATED CAPTIVE consolidation of a noninsurance parent company with its wholly owned subsidiary, thereby creating, allowable under current tax law, a consolidated balance sheet. This consolidation of balance sheets permits the offsetting of UNDERWRITING LOSSES with taxable income of a noninsurance subsidiary.

CONSORTIUM UNDERWRITING method of underwriting by which one or a group of LLOYD'S UNDERWRITERS write business on behalf of a number of Lloyd's syndicates and other insurance companies. Among the benefits of underwriting in this manner are that potential earnings could equal the SYNDICATE'S expenses and stabilize the planning of staff as well as other general overhead requirements.

CONSTRUCTION BOND *see* BID BOND; COMPLETION BOND; LABOR AND MATERIAL BOND; MAINTENANCE BOND; SURETY BOND.

CONSTRUCTION INSURANCE property coverage for damage or destruction of structures in the course of construction. For example, the standing frame of a house destroyed by fire would be covered. *See also* BUILDER'S RISK PROPERTY INSURANCE.

CONSTRUCTIVE RECEIPT specific date determined by the Internal Revenue Service on which a beneficiary has received a death benefit from an insurance company, an ANNUITANT has received an income benefit, or a retiree has received a retirement benefit.

CONSTRUCTIVE TOTAL LOSS partial loss of such significance that the cost of restoring damaged property would exceed its value after restoration. For example, an automobile is so badly damaged by fire that fixing it would cost more than the restored vehicle would be worth.

CONSULTANT in insurance, independent advisor who specializes in pension and profit sharing plans. Usually a licensed insurance agent.

CONSUMER CONFIDENCE INDEX measurement of how people feel about prevailing economic conditions, employment outlook, and personal finances. This index is based on statistics gathered from questionnaires mailed by the Conference Board to a nationwide representative sample of 5000 households, with a response rate of 70%.

CONSUMER CREDIT PROTECTION ACT 1968 federal legislation that makes it mandatory for lenders to disclose to credit applicants the annual interest percentage rate (APR) and any finance charge.

CONSUMER PRICE INDEX (CPI) measurement of the rate of inflation according to a weighted market basket of goods and services that includes such items as transportation costs, health care costs, housing costs, and food costs. These statistics are released monthly by the United States Bureau of Labor Statistics.

CONSUMER PRODUCTS SAFETY ACT OF 1972 act that established mandatory notification by manufacturers of products and the distributors of these products to the Consumer Product Safety Commission in the event they become aware of a faulty product, or part of that product, that could result in bodily injury and/or property damage.

CONSUMER PROTECTION ACT *see* CONSUMER CREDIT PROTECTION ACT.

CONTENTS
1. in PERSONAL PROPERTY insurance, coverage is for personal property items that are movable, that is, not attached to the building's structure (the home), such as television sets, radios, clothes, household goods. Not included under the coverage are animals, automobiles, and boats.
2. in COMMERCIAL PROPERTY insurance, coverage is for the business's personal property items that are movable, that is, not attached to the building's structure such as inventory, machinery, equipment, furniture, and fixtures. Not included under the coverage are animals, automobiles, boats, and crops.

CONTENTS RATE premium rate charged on the property within a building, but not on the building structure.

CONTESTABLE CLAUSE *see* INCONTESTABLE CLAUSE.

CONTIGUOUS adjoining.

CONTINGENCIES unexpected claims occurring above the expected claims for which a CONTINGENCY RESERVE is maintained.

CONTINGENCY event that may or may not occur in a given time period. For example, whether a specific person will die, or a particular house will burn this year is a contingency.

CONTINGENCY RESERVE percentage of total surplus retained, in insurance company operations, that serves as a reserve to cover unexpected losses as well as to cover the shortfall if the earned surplus in a particular year is not adequate to maintain a company's announced dividend scale for participating policies.

CONTINGENCY SURPLUS *see* CONTINGENCY RESERVE.

CONTINGENT ANNUITANT *see* BENEFICIARY.

CONTINGENT ANNUITY contract providing income payments beginning when the named contingency occurs. For example, upon the death of one spouse (the contingency), a surviving spouse will begin to receive monthly income payments.

CONTINGENT BENEFICIARY *see* BENEFICIARY.

CONTINGENT BUSINESS INCOME COVERAGE FORM coverage for loss in the net earnings of a business if a supplier business, subcontractor, key customer, or manufacturer doing business with the insured business cannot continue to operate because of damage or destruction. For example, a specialty hot dog stand noted for its great buns cannot sell its product if the bakery supplier of hot dog buns burns down. In instances where a business is heavily dependent on its suppliers or subcontractors, interruption of the flow of material from the supplier usually results in a substantial loss to the business.

CONTINGENT BUSINESS INCOME COVERAGE INSURANCE *see* CONTINGENT BUSINESS INCOME COVERAGE FORM.

CONTINGENT FEE amount paid by the attorney of the plaintiff in a liability suit. Usually the attorney receives as a fee from 30 to 50% of the case settlement or reward.

CONTINGENT LIABILITY (VICARIOUS LIABILITY) liability incurred by a business for acts other than those of its own employees. This particular situation may arise when an independent contractor is hired. The business can be held liable for negligent acts of the contractor to the extent that its representatives give directions or exercise control over the contractor's employees.

CONTINGENT LIABILITY INSURANCE coverage for contingent liability exposure. *See also* CONTINGENT LIABILITY.

CONTINGENT TRANSIT INSURANCE coverage if an insured cannot collect on property damage or destruction losses from the hired transporter. For example, a truck transporting furniture of the insured is involved in an accident and the furniture is damaged. The truck owner refuses to compensate the insured for damages; the recourse of the insured is to collect from the insurance company.

CONTINUANCE TABLE table used in health insurance premium rate calculations that depicts the probability that a claim will continue by time and amount.

CONTINUING CARE RETIREMENT COMMUNITY retirement center with a focus on group living arrangements for senior citizens. The center has separate apartments for each resident as well as an onsite nursing facility. Generally, these centers are quite expensive; they require monthly fees as well as a one-time payment (entrance fee). The monthly fee entitles the inhabitant to an apartment, one to three meals a day (depending on the facility), maid service (in some facilities), medical service (if needed), and nursing home care (also, if needed).

CONTINUITY OF COVERAGE CLAUSE included in or attached to a FIDELITY BOND designed to pay the losses that would have been paid under another specific bond had that specific bond's period of discovery not expired.

CONTINUOUS PREMIUM WHOLE LIFE *see* ORDINARY LIFE INSURANCE.

CONTRACT in insurance, agreement between an insurer and an insured under which the insurer has a legally enforceable obligation to make all benefit payments for which it has received premiums.

CONTRACT ANNIVERSARY *see* POLICY ANNIVERSARY.

CONTRACT BOND a guarantee of the performance of a contractor. In general, contract bonds are used to guarantee that the contractor will perform according to the specifications of the construction contract. If the contractor fails to perform according to contract, the insurance company is responsible to the insured for payment, up to the limit of the bond, which is usually for an amount equal to the cost of the construction project. The insurance company then has recourse against the contractor for reimbursement. *See also* BID BOND; PAYMENT BOND; PERFORMANCE BOND.

CONTRACT CARRIER transportation firm that carries only select customers' goods and is not obligated to carry any particular customer's goods even if that customer is willing to pay. Contrast with COMMON CARRIER.

CONTRACT DATE date of issue of the policy.

CONTRACT HOLDER in insurance, individual with rightful possession of an insurance policy, usually the *policyowner.*

CONTRACT INCEPTION AND TIME OF LOSS *see* CLAIMS MADE BASIS; CLAIMS OCCURRENCE BASIS LIABILITY COVERAGE.

CONTRACT OF ADHESION *see* ADHESION INSURANCE CONTRACT.

CONTRACT OF INDEMNITY property and liability insurance contracts that restore the insured to his/her original financial condition after suffering a loss. The insured cannot profit by the loss; otherwise an unscrupulous homeowner, for example, could buy several fire insurance policies, set fire to the house, and collect on all the policies.

CONTRACT OF INSURANCE *see* CONTRACT; HEALTH INSURANCE CONTRACT; INSURANCE CONTRACT, GENERAL; INSURANCE CONTRACT, LIFE; INSURANCE CONTRACT, PROPERTY AND CASUALTY.

CONTRACT OF UTMOST GOOD FAITH *see* UBERRIMAE FIDEI CONTRACT.

CONTRACTORS EQUIPMENT FLOATER form of marine insurance that covers mobile equipment of a contractor, including road building machinery, steam shovels, hoists, and derricks used on the job by builders of structures, roads, bridges, dams, tunnels, and mines. Coverage is provided on a specified peril or an ALL RISKS basis, subject to exclusions of wear and tear, work, and nuclear disaster.

CONTRACTORS EQUIPMENT INSURANCE *see* CONTRACTORS EQUIPMENT FLOATER.

CONTRACTORS PREMIUM ADJUSTMENT PROGRAM part of the WORKERS COMPENSATION INSURANCE program that provides for a reduction in the premium paid by the employer of high hourly wage construction employees.

CONTRACT OWNER *see* CONTRACT HOLDER.

CONTRACTUAL LIABILITY liability incurred by a party through entering into a written contract. *See also* CIVIL LIABILITY; CIVIL WRONG.

CONTRIBUTE-TO-LOSS STATUTE law in some states that permits an insurance company to deny payment of a claim resulting from an insured loss because of breach of warranty or misrepresentation, provided that the breach of warranty or misrepresentation made a material contribution to the loss.

CONTRIBUTING INSURANCE *see* CONTRIBUTION.

CONTRIBUTING PROPERTIES COVERAGE *see* CONTINGENT BUSINESS INCOME COVERAGE FORM.

CONTRIBUTING PROPERTY BUSINESS INCOME COVERAGE FORM that covers an insured business in the event that a manufacturer's operations are interrupted or suspended, thereby resulting in a monetary loss because a supplier of the insured has had his facility damaged or destroyed by an insured peril. *See also* CONTINGENT BUSINESS INCOME COVERAGE FORM.

CONTRIBUTION principle of equity in property, casualty, and health insurance. When two or more policies apply to the loss, each policy pays its part of the loss, unless its terms provide otherwise. For example, if two policies each insure a risk for $100,000 and there is a $50,000 loss, then each policy (depending on coinsurance requirements) will pay $25,000. In employee benefits, payment made by an employee.

CONTRIBUTION BY EQUAL SHARES type of OTHER INSURANCE CLAUSE that requires all insurance policies involved in the settlement of a CLAIM to pay their equal share until that share equals the lowest limit of liability under the policy or until the total amount of the claim has been paid.

CONTRIBUTION CLAUSE clause, generally found in BUSINESS INTERRUPTION INSURANCE, that establishes the same indemnification basis as the COINSURANCE clause.

CONTRIBUTION PRINCIPLE rule that concerns the distribution of the aggregate SURPLUS among the policies in the same proportion as each respective policy has contributed to the surplus.

CONTRIBUTORY employee benefit plans under which both the employee and the employer pay part of the premium. Contribution ratios vary. For example, an employer contributes two dollars for every dollar contributed by the employee up to 6% of the employee's salary.

CONTRIBUTORY NEGLIGENCE principle of law recognizing that injured persons may have contributed to their own injury. For example, by not observing the "Don't Walk" sign at a crosswalk, pedestrians may cause accidents in which they are injured.

CONVENTIONAL MORTGAGE mortgage loan made by a lender that is not insured by the VETERANS ADMINISTRATION (VA) or the FEDERAL HOUSING ADMINISTRATION (FHA).

CONVENTION BLANK *see* ANNUAL STATEMENT.

CONVENTION EXAMINATION audit of the *convention blank* (NAIC Statement Blank) every third year as to (1) all of the financial activities of a company; (2) company claim practices; and (3) general policyowner relations.

CONVENTION VALUES monetary sums attached to an insurance company's assets, as listed on the ANNUAL STATEMENT.

CONVERGENCE combination of the insurance and CAPITAL markets through the issuing of event- or RISK-based securities in tandem with insurance policies. The result is HEDGING through FINANCIAL RISK MANAGEMENT instead of utilizing DERIVATIVES.

CONVERGENCE PRODUCT type of hybrid financial instrument that features a combination of insurance, investments, and banking products.

CONVERSION
1. tort against another person's property, designed to detain or dispose of it in a wrongful manner. For example, wrongful selling of another person's automobile without permission would qualify as an act of conversion.
2. in group life and health insurance, a provision that allows a certificate holder to convert group coverage to an individual policy under specified conditions.

CONVERSION FACTOR FOR EMPLOYEE CONTRIBUTIONS inverse of the actuarial present value of a life annuity, taking the employee's life expectancy into account, to commence income payments at the NORMAL RETIREMENT AGE of the employee. It is used in a DEFINED BENEFIT PLAN to determine the amount of accrued benefits that result from the employee's contributions.

CONVERSION PRIVILEGE right of a certificate holder to convert group life or group health insurance to an individual policy without a physical examination to furnish evidence of insurability. Usually this must be done within 31 days of termination of employment. Under group life insurance, conversion is made at the employee's attained age rate, which can be prohibitively costly in later years. Many term life insurance policies can be converted to a whole life policy at the insured's attained age, with no physical examination required.

CONVERTIBLE *see* CONVERTIBLE TERM LIFE INSURANCE.

CONVERTIBLE BOND bond that can be exchanged for a common stock of the same company according to the terms specified when the bond was issued.

CONVERTIBLE TERM LIFE INSURANCE coverage that can be converted into permanent insurance regardless of an insured's physical condition and without a medical examination. The individual cannot be denied coverage or charged an additional premium for any health problems.

COOPERATIVE INSURANCE *see* SOCIAL INSURANCE.

COOPERATIVE INSURER mutual insurance association that issues insurance to its members on a nonprofit basis. Examples of such associations include fraternal societies, unions, and employee membership groups.

COORDINATION OF BENEFITS arrangement in health insurance to discourage multiple payment for the same claim under two or more policies. When two or more group health insurance plans cover the insured and dependents, one plan becomes the *primary* plan and the other plan(s) the *secondary* plan(s). For example, two working spouses have health insurance at their respective places of employment. If one spouse becomes ill, his/her policy at work would become the primary plan. Medical expenses not covered under the primary plan would be covered under the secondary plan of the other spouse. *See also* COINSURANCE.

COPAYMENT partial payment of medical service expenses required in group health insurance, in addition to the membership fee. For example, for each visit of a physician a member may be required to pay $5, regardless of the expense of the services rendered. Or, for each prescription for drugs and medicines, the member may have to pay a flat $2 regardless of the actual cost.

CORPORATE AND CRIMINAL FRAUD ACCOUNTABILITY ACT OF 2002; WHITE COLLAR CRIME PENALTY ENHANCEMENT ACT OF 2002; CORPORATE FRAUD ACCOUNTABILITY ACT OF 2002 legislation found in the SECURITIES AND EXCHANGE COMMISSION (SEC) Titles VIII, IX, and XI of the SARBANES-OXLEY ACT OF 2002. These acts affect the shredding or destruction of documents that are not securities related and the nondischarging of fraudulent acts in bankruptcy in connection with the purchase or sale of any publicly or nonpublicly traded securities. It also prohibits through an obstruction of justice statute the retaliation against informants regardless of the source and application of the information provided.

CORPORATE-OWNED LIFE INSURANCE insurance on the life of the employee, paid for by the company, with the company being the beneficiary under the policy. This insurance vehicle is being used more and more to fund postretirement employee plans, in which the cash values are listed as assets on the company's balance sheet.

CORPORATION STOCK PURCHASE PLAN *see* CLOSE CORPORATION PLAN.

CORRIDOR the space created between the total death benefit and the cash value of a UNIVERSAL LIFE INSURANCE policy. An automatic increase in the death benefit results when the CASH VALUE approaches the initial face amount under Option A. If this space did not exist, the universal life insurance policy would not qualify as a life insurance policy under the definition of life insurance by the Internal Revenue Code (IRC) and would cease to reap the favorable tax treatment afforded life insurance policies by the IRC.

CORRIDOR DEDUCTIBLE type of major medical deductible amount that acts as a corridor between benefits under a basic health insurance plan and benefits under a major medical insurance plan. After benefits are paid under the basic plan, a fixed dollar per-loss deductible amount often is required of the insured (benefits paid under the basic plan do not apply towards this deductible) before major medical benefits are paid.

COST *see* PREMIUM, PURE PREMIUM RATING METHOD.

COST ALLOCATION METHOD method of funding a pension plan through: (1) an individual level cost basis, where future benefits for the employee are estimated and contributions are made periodically while the employee is working to fund these future benefits; or (2) an aggregate level cost basis, where future benefits for all current employees are estimated and aggregate contributions are made periodically while the current employees are working to fund these future benefits.

COST-BENEFIT ANALYSIS comparison of the cost of a solution and the economic benefits that would accrue if the solution is put into effect. This analysis is a prerequisite to the installation of an employee benefit plan. Questions to be answered include: (1) will the cost result in greater loyalty of employees? (2) will the cost result in greater productivity; and (3) will the benefits encourage employees to participate in their cost?

COST CONTAINMENT PROVISION in many HEALTH INSURANCE and DENTAL INSURANCE policies, stipulation that, if the estimated cost of a recommended plan of treatment exceeds a specified sum, the insured must submit the plan of treatment to the insurance company for review and predetermination of benefits before service begins. Usually, however, predetermination of benefits is not necessary for emergency treatment.

COST OF INSURANCE value or cost of the actual net protection, in life insurance, in any year (face amount less reserve) according to the yearly renewal term rate used by an insurance company. *See also* INTEREST ADJUSTED COST.

COST-OF-LIVING ADJUSTMENT (COLA) automatic adjustment applied to Social Security retirement payments when the consumer price index increases at a rate of at least 3%, the first quarter of one year to the first quarter of the next year. *See also* RIDERS, LIFE POLICIES.

COST-OF-LIVING INCREASE *see* COST-OF-LIVING ADJUSTMENT (COLA); COST-OF-LIVING RIDER.

COST-OF-LIVING PLAN plan providing benefits that are adjusted according to variations in a specified index of prices. For example, some pension plans adjust retirement benefits yearly according to the rise in the Consumer Price Index (CPI).

COST-OF-LIVING RIDER usually term insurance for one year added to a basic life insurance policy. In effect, this increases or decreases the face amount of the basic policy to reflect cost-of-living changes as measured by the Consumer Price Index (CPI). This rider can also be used in conjunction with a disability income policy in which the income benefit is adjusted to reflect fluctuations in the CPI.

COST OF LOSS *see* EXPECTED LOSS.

COST OF PROTECTION *see* COST OF INSURANCE; PREMIUM; PURE PREMIUM RATING METHOD.

COST OF RISK (COR) quantitative measurement of the total costs (losses, risk control costs, risk financing costs, and administration costs) associated with the RISK MANAGEMENT function, as compared to a business's sales, assets, and number of employees. The purpose of such a comparison is to determine whether the total costs of the risk management function are increasing, decreasing, or remaining constant as a function of the business's economic activity. After the quantitative measurement has been derived, a comparison can be made between the COR of that business and the CORs of its peer groups. In addition, COR will allow the business to focus on the areas of operation that will have the greatest long-term effects on its total risk management function costs.

COST PLUS insured plan under which the insurance company agrees to provide the insured with a series of benefits on a benefits-paid basis plus administrative services on a stipulated-fee basis. This plan enables the POLICYHOLDER to control more of its own cash flow than it can under traditional insurance plans. While this plan is similar to the ADMINISTRATIVE SERVICES ONLY (ASO) plan, it is dissimilar in that it is an insured plan.

COST TO REPAIR BASIS actual cost to repair damaged INSURED property not necessarily using predetermined materials of the same value.

COTTON INSURANCE coverage for property damage by a covered peril to insured cotton during the time period from its weighing in at the gin until its delivery to the buyer. Written either on a *specified peril* basis or on an ALL RISKS basis. The purpose of cotton insurance is much the same as the purchase of insurance by a merchant to protect business inventory prior to its sale, since in many instances the primary asset is the inventory.

COUNTERSIGNATURE licensed AGENT'S signature on an insurance policy.

COUNTERSIGNATURE LAW state law that requires that an insurance policy issued by an insurance company in a particular state be signed by an AGENT of the company holding a LICENSE in that state.

COUPON fixed or stated amount of interest paid by a security expressed as a percent of the par value of the security. The longer the length of time until maturity, the higher the coupon rate to reflect the greater risk associated with a longer loan period. The higher the creditworthiness of the borrower, the lower the coupon rate. For example, United States Treasury issues have a low coupon rate because the United States has a long history of political and economic stability.

COUPON POLICY *nonparticipating life insurance* (also called a *guaranteed dividend* or *guaranteed investment policy*) sold by a stock life insurance company, usually as a 20-payment policy with coupons attached. The *policyowner* can cash in each coupon (which is actually one of a series of pure endowments) for a stipulated sum at the time of paying the annual premium.

COUPON RATE rate obtained by dividing the annual COUPON by the FACE VALUE of a bond.

COURT BOND *see* JUDICIAL BOND.

COVER to place insurance in force on an individual. individuals, or an organization. *See also* CONTRACT; COVERAGE, INDIVIDUAL; COVERAGE, LOCATION; COVERAGE OF HAZARD; COVERAGE, PERIL; COVERAGE, PROPERTY; COVERED EXPENSES.

COVERAGE protection under an insurance policy. In property insurance, coverage lists perils insured against, properties covered, locations covered, individuals insured, and the limits of indemnification. In life insurance, living and death benefits.

COVERAGE, INDIVIDUAL *see* INDIVIDUAL INSURANCE.

COVERAGE, LOCATION *see* PROPERTY INSURANCE, COVERAGE.

COVERAGE OF HAZARD *see* HAZARD INCREASE RESULTING IN SUSPENSION OR EXCLUSION OF COVERAGE.

COVERAGE PART section of the INSURANCE POLICY that lists all of the provisions that are applicable to the insurance coverage provided under that section. This section is attached to the policy JACKET (which lists the provisions common to all the insurance coverages) to form the insurance policy.

COVERAGE, PERIL *see* ALL RISKS; PROPERTY INSURANCE, COVERAGE.

COVERAGE, PROPERTY *see* PROPERTY INSURANCE, COVERAGE.

COVERED *see* COVERAGE.

COVERED AUTOMOBILE (1) vehicle in DECLARATIONS SECTION; (2) vehicle temporarily used as substitute for vehicle in declarations section; (3) vehicle within 30 days of purchase.

COVERED EXPENSES
1. in health insurance, reimbursement for an insured's medically related expenses, including room and board, surgery, medicines, anesthetics, ambulance service to and from a hospital, operating room expenses, X-ray, and fluoroscope.
2. in business interruption insurance, reimbursement of an insured for loss if a business cannot operate, including payroll expense and taxes.
3. in extra expense insurance, reimbursement of an insured for extra expenditures made to keep a business operating even under emergency conditions.

COVERED EXPENSES, PRO RATA DISTRIBUTION CLAUSE *see* DOUBLE RECOVERY; PRO RATA DISTRIBUTION CLAUSE.

COVERED LOCATION, PROPERTY INSURANCE *see* PROPERTY INSURANCE, COVERAGE.

COVERED LOSSES *see* LOSS.

COVERED PERSON, PROPERTY INSURANCE *see* PROPERTY INSURANCE, COVERAGE.

COVER NOTE statement made by AGENT or BROKER in written form attesting to the INSURED that the insurance policy is in effect. This statement is prepared by the agent or broker, unlike the BINDER, which is prepared by the INSURANCE COMPANY (INSURER).

CPCU *see* CHARTERED PROPERTY AND CASUALTY UNDERWRITER (CPCU).

CPL *see* COMPREHENSIVE GENERAL LIABILITY INSURANCE (CGL).

CREDIBILITY OF LOSS EXPERIENCE *see* LOSS DEVELOPMENT.

CREDIT CARD FORGERY *see* CREDIT CARD INSURANCE.

CREDIT CARD INSURANCE coverage under a HOMEOWNERS INSURANCE POLICY in the event that a credit card is fraudulently used or altered. Fraud includes theft and the unauthorized use of a credit card.

CREDIT HEALTH INSURANCE coverage issued to a creditor on the life of a debtor so that if the debtor becomes disabled, the insurance policy pays the balance of the debt to the creditor.

CREDIT INSURANCE *see* CREDIT HEALTH INSURANCE; CREDIT LIFE INSURANCE (CREDITOR LIFE INSURANCE).

CREDIT INVESTIGATION *see* RETAIL CREDIT REPORT.

CREDIT LIFE INSURANCE (CREDITOR LIFE INSURANCE) insurance issued to a creditor (lender) to cover the life of a debtor (borrower) for an outstanding loan. If the debtor dies prior to repayment of the debt, the policy will pay off the balance of the amount outstanding. Credit life insurance is sold on a group or individual basis, and usually is purchased to cover small loans of short duration. When issued under a group policy, a certificate is issued to the debtor, the master policy being issued by the creditor. The face value of a credit life insurance policy decreases in proportion to the reduction in the loan amount until both equal zero.

CREDITOR LIFE INSURANCE *see* CREDIT LIFE INSURANCE (CREDITOR LIFE INSURANCE).

CREDITOR RIGHTS IN LIFE INSURANCE *see* LIFE INSURANCE, CREDITOR RIGHTS.

CREDIT, PENSION PLAN value of benefit or contribution allocated to an employee under a pension plan; method of determining benefits due a retired employee. Each private pension plan establishes rules for awarding credits to employees, taking into account age, amount of time with the employer, number of days worked per year, breaks in service, maximum salary, and position in the company. For an employee who joined a firm before the plan was put in place, the company computes *past service credit,* crediting work done prior to establishment of the plan. Ultimately, credits determine the level of pension income the employee receives upon retiring.

CREDIT RECEIVABLE RISK risk that PREMIUMS and REINSURANCE, as well as other receivable instruments, will not be collected.

CREDIT REPORT *see* RETAIL CREDIT REPORT.

CREDIT RISK possibility that a borrower will not be able to service the debt (pay the interest on the borrowed funds) or make the principal payments when due. The greater this type of risk, the greater the yield.

CREDIT SHELTER TRUST vehicle through which the FEDERAL ESTATE TAX credit is protected from estate tax payment. The procedure is to leave the federal estate tax credit to the shelter trust with the trust established for the benefit of one's spouse (spouse receives the income from the trust and the assets of the trust are held for the benefit of the spouse). The assets of the trust are not subject to federal estate tax upon the death of the spouse since the assets are not in the spouse's estate at that time.

CRIME INSURANCE coverage for the perils of burglary, theft, and robbery. *See also* BURGLARY INSURANCE; BUSINESS INSURANCE; HOME-OWNERS INSURANCE POLICY; PERSONAL AUTOMOBILE POLICY (PAP); SIM-

PLIFIED COMMERCIAL LINES PORTFOLIO POLICY (SCLP); COMMERCIAL
PACKAGE POLICY (CPP).

CRIMINAL LIABILITY crime against the state for which an officer of
the state can bring legal action. Society is harmed by an individual
breaking the laws of the state. Usually there is no statue of limitations
for criminal liability. Property and casualty insurance is not designed
to provide coverage for the criminal acts of an insured individual.

CRITICAL ILLNESS INSURANCE insurance policy that pays a FACE
AMOUNT/ LUMP SUM if the INSURED is diagnosed with a specified critical
illness. This sum is paid directly to the insured regardless of any other
sources of income (job-related and non-job-related), expenses incurred
(medical and nonmedical), and any other factors. Generally, critical
illnesses include stroke, heart attack, cancer that is life threatening,
paralysis, deafness, organ transplant requirement, blindness, and kidney failure. Some policies pay a percentage of the face amount, for
example 15 to 30%, if a less serious illness occurs or medical procedure such as a coronary bypass must be performed. The illness does
not have to result in the disability of the insured (total or partial); the
insured still receives the face amount payment. This type of insurance
can be purchased as a separate policy or as a rider to a LIFE INSURANCE
or DISABILITY INCOME policy. The face amount is not paid if the insured
dies within 30 days of being diagnosed with the covered illness and
there is usually a WAITING PERIOD before the coverage is in force. This
coverage may be purchased on both a personal and business basis.

**CRITICAL REVIEW OF THE U.S. ACTUARIAL PROFESSION
(CRUSAP)** report discussing the future of the ACTUARIAL SCIENCE profession. The report defines the actuarial profession, sets forth a policy
of inclusion and encourages actuaries to become involved in the public arena.

CROP INSURANCE coverage for crops in the event of loss or damage
by insured perils including hail, fire, and lightning. Prior to the passage
of the Federal Crop Insurance Act in 1938 it was virtually impossible
to obtain insurance protection against crop damage. Today coverage is
available from the Federal Crop Insurance Corporation as well as from
private sources. Exclusions from coverage include the perils of war
and nuclear disaster.

CROSS LIABILITY LIABILITY incurred by one INSURED as the result of
his or her damaging another insured when both insureds are covered
under the same LIABILITY INSURANCE policy. Each insured must be
treated as a separate entity under a cross-liability clause in a liability
insurance policy.

CROSS PURCHASE PLAN *see* PARTNERSHIP LIFE AND HEALTH INSURANCE.

CRUDE DEATH RATE total deaths as a percentage of total population
for a stipulated period of time.

CRUMMEY TRUST unfunded trust that acts as the owner of a life insurance policy. The trust receives a donor's cash payments on a periodic basis, from which the beneficiary of the trust has a specified period in which to make a cash withdrawal. If this is not done, the cash paid by the donor is used to pay the premiums due on the life insurance policy. Under this circumstance the IRS deems that a gift of present value interest by the donor has been made. It is important that a gift of present value interest be established because such a gift in trust will enable the donor to contribute up to $10,000 ($20,000 if two donors such as husband and wife contribute) in premium payments and enjoy the gift tax exclusion. When the donor dies, the life insurance policy in trust is effectively removed from the donor's estate.

CSL *see* COMBINED SINGLE LIMIT.

CSO TABLE *see* COMMISSIONERS STANDARD ORDINARY MORTALITY TABLE (CSO).

CUMULATIVE INJURIES sum total of an employee's job-related injuries resulting in disabilities over the working career. For example, exposure to radiation over many years on the job would have a compounding injury effect resulting in ultimate disability.

CUMULATIVE LIABILITY
Reinsurance: total of the limits of liability of all reinsurance policies that a reinsurer has outstanding on a single risk. The total of all such limits includes all *ceding* contracts from all insurers representing all lines of coverage for the single risk.
Liability insurance: total of the limits of liability of all policies that an insurer has outstanding on a single risk. Examples are the HOMEOWNERS INSURANCE POLICY, PERSONAL AUTOMOBILE POLICY (PAP), and *personal umbrella liability policy.*

CUMULATIVE TRAUMA injury that continues after a wound from physical or psychic entry. (The latter is a wound that makes a lasting impression on the mind, especially upon the subconscious mind; for example, a three-year-old child could be traumatized by seeing father abuse mother.) Trauma results in other injuries of a continuing nature and is usually covered under health insurance policies.

CUMULATIVE TRAUMA DISORDERS injuries that afflict the tendons, bones, muscles, and nerves of the back, hands, arm, shoulders, and neck. These are the fastest growing areas of workers compensation claims. The symptoms of these injuries range from swelling and deformity to intense pain and numbness.

CUMULATIVE TREND METHOD approach to derive trend lines that can be applied to rating insured losses. Other methods require substantial preliminary operations to solve systems of equations of several unknowns. The cumulative method reduces the probability of mistakes because a relatively simple computation is required to prepare a set of data for the BURNING COST RATIO.

CURE *see* REST CURE.

CURRENCY RISK situation where the United States dollar rises in value in comparison with other foreign currencies resulting in the decrease in the value of the foreign securities. This is due to the fact that the principal and income payments on the foreign securities are based on that particular foreign currency and thus must be converted into United States dollars. When that particular foreign currency is weak, and the United States dollar is strong, fewer dollars will be received upon conversion.

CURRENT ASSUMPTIONS basis for calculating life insurance premiums and benefits using current interest and mortality rates, rather than historic rates. Current assumptions are critical to interest-sensitive products such as *Universal Life*. When interest rates are high, benefits projections (such as cash values) are high. When interest rates are low, these projections are not as alluring. The thesis of current-assumption life insurance products is that policyowner earnings should reflect current market conditions.

CURRENT ASSUMPTION WHOLE LIFE INSURANCE variation of ORDINARY LIFE INSURANCE under which current mortality experience and investment earnings are credited to the insurance policy either through the cash value account and/or the premium structure (in a stock company) or the dividend structure (in a mutual company). Regardless of whether a company is stock or mutual, the policy has these characteristics:
1. premiums are subject to change based on the experience (mortality, expenses, investment) of the company. The *policyowner* does not exercise any control over the changes.
2. a policyowner can use the cash value to make loans just as with traditional ordinary life insurance.
3. a minimum amount of cash value is guaranteed, just as with traditional ordinary life insurance.
4. the death benefit does not fluctuate.

CURRENT DISBURSEMENT payment of premiums and benefits as they come due. In pension plans, known as the "pay as you go basis." The plan depends on new employees coming into the work force so that their contributions can help pay for the benefits of the retiring employees. If the company is not experiencing growth and is in fact part of a matured or even a dying industry, there may not be enough on hand to pay benefits of retiring employees.

CURRENT INCOME average earned monthly income of the insured wage earner after regular earned income has been interrupted or terminated because of illness, sickness, or accident. This income amount is important to the calculation of the MONTHLY INDEMNITY benefit and the LOSS OF INCOME amount under the DISABILITY INCOME INSURANCE policy.

CURRENTLY INSURED under SOCIAL SECURITY, workers who have at least six quarters of earnings of adequate amount to qualify for credit of the last 13 quarters prior to the worker's death. If this is the case, SURVIVOR BENEFITS will be paid by Social Security to the dependents of the deceased worker. *See also* QUARTERS OF COVERAGE.

CURRENT YIELD the closing price of the bond divided by the COUPON of the bond.

CURTESY INTEREST husband's interest in his wife's property upon her death. A husband has an INSURABLE INTEREST in that property and can purchase a property and casualty insurance policy to cover the EXPOSURES on it. *See also* DOWER INTEREST.

CUSTODIAL ACCOUNT account established to manage the assets of a minor. This account is under the auspices of a custodian (either an individual or an institution). The GIFT TAX exclusion would apply on any annual gifts to a minor.

CUSTODIAL CARE assistance provided to a person in performing the basic daily necessities of life, such as dressing, eating, using a toilet, walking, bathing, and getting in and out of bed. This type of care does not require hospitalization for the treatment of a disease, illness, accident, or injury. Its cost may or may not be covered by health insurance.

CUSTOMARY AND REASONABLE CHARGE term referring to the most common charge, in HEALTH INSURANCE, for a service.

CUSTOMER RELATIONSHIP MANAGEMENT (CRM) agreement that permits an insurance company to target a single potential client by combining data on that potential client from several other databases.

CUT-OFF CLAUSE in a REINSURANCE policy that excludes the reinsurer's liability for losses occurring after a stipulated date.

CUT RATE PREMIUM rate charged by the INSURANCE COMPANY (INSURER), which is below the standard rate.

CUT-THROUGH ENDORSEMENT (ASSUMPTION OF RISK) guarantee by a reinsurance company that payment for losses incurred by a third party will be made even though that third party has no contractual arrangement with the reinsurance company.

D

DAILY FORM (REPORT) shortened report showing pertinent insurance policy information, copies of which are distributed in the insurance company's HOME OFFICE and BRANCH OFFICES, as well as to AGENTS and BROKERS.

DAMAGES sum the insurance company is legally obligated to pay an insured for losses incurred.

DAMAGE TO OWN AUTOMOBILE optional coverage that can be added to the PERSONAL AUTOMOBILE POLICY (PAP) providing coverage for damage, destruction, and/or theft of the insured automobile.

DAMAGE TO PROPERTY OF OTHERS *see* HOMEOWNERS INSURANCE POLICY—SECTION II (LIABILITY COVERAGE).

D&O *see* DIRECTORS AND OFFICERS LIABILITY INSURANCE.

DATA PROCESSING INSURANCE coverage on data processing equipment, data processing media (such as magnetic tapes, disks), and extra expense involved in returning to usual business conditions. The data processing equipment is usually written as ALL RISKS on a specifically scheduled basis. The data processing media is usually written on an ALL RISKS basis. No COINSURANCE is required for the data processing media and the extra expense coverage.

DATE OF INCEPTION OF THE INSURANCE POLICY *see* EFFECTIVE DATE.

DATE OF ISSUE date when an insurance company issues a policy. This date may be different from the date the insurance becomes effective.

DATE OF PLAN TERMINATION stipulation of the exact time when the PENSION BENEFIT GUARANTY CORPORATION assumes the legal liabilities for an insured pension plan that is being terminated. *See also* PENSION BENEFIT GUARANTY CORPORATION (PBGC).

DATE OF RECORD entitlement date on which stockholders receive dividends.

DATE OF SUBSCRIPTION OF THE POLICY specific time at which the INSURANCE POLICY coverage begins and ends.

DAY ORDER buy or sell order for security that expires at the end of the trading date on which it was entered if not executed.

DAYS OF GRACE *see* GRACE PERIOD.

DDD *see* DIRECTORS AND OFFICERS LIABILITY INSURANCE.

DEALERS INSURANCE coverage on an ALL RISKS basis, subject to listed exclusions, for personal property of the insured dealer that is used in normal business activities. Goods that have been sold on an installment basis contract upon leaving the care, custody, and control of the insured dealer; furniture and fixtures used in the business activities of the insured dealer; money; securities; and items that are in the process of being manufactured are generally excluded from coverage.

DEAN ANALYTIC SCHEDULE rating method for commercial fire insurance according to a predetermined schedule. Published by A. F. Dean in 1902, this method was the first comprehensive qualitative analysis procedure to take into consideration the numerous physical factors impacting the fire exposure. No longer widely used, because most companies have developed their own schedules or use schedules advocated by the INSURANCE SERVICES OFFICE (ISO).

DEATH termination of life. A death certificate is required by a life insurance company for a beneficiary to receive the death payment.

DEATH BENEFIT amount payable, as stated in a life insurance policy, upon the death of the insured. This is the face value of the policy plus any riders, less any outstanding loans and the interest accrued thereon.

DEATH BENEFIT ONLY LIFE INSURANCE PLAN *see* KEY EMPLOYEES, INSURANCE PLANS FOR.

DEATH CLAIM proof of death of the INSURED form filed with the INSURANCE COMPANY establishing the rights of the BENEFICIARY to the DEATH BENEFIT.

DEATH PLANNING estimate of the funds necessary to maintain the life-style of a family after the death of the wage earner. *See also* HUMAN LIFE VALUE APPROACH (ECONOMIC VALUE OF AN INDIVIDUAL LIFE).

DEATH RATE *see* MORTALITY RATE.

DEBENTURE unsecured bond. The only protection for the lender is the credit and reputation of the borrower. The method of evaluating the quality of debentures is to analyze the earning power, overall status, and outlook of the borrowing corporation.

DEBENTURE, SUBORDINATED very junior issues of debt, according to explicit statements in the indenture, which rank after other unsecured debt.

DEBIT in insurance, DEBIT AGENTS list of total premiums to be collected. This also applies to the geographical area in which an agent collects the premiums.

DEBIT AGENT (HOME SERVICE AGENT) insurance company representative who sells debit life insurance (industrial life insurance). This agent is usually more of a collector of small premium payments on a weekly, biweekly, or monthly basis than a salesperson.

DEBIT INSURANCE (HOME SERVICE INSURANCE, INDUSTRIAL INSURANCE) life insurance on which a premium is collected on a weekly, bi-weekly, or monthly basis, usually at the home of a policyholder. The face value of the policy is usually $1000 or less. *See also* DEBIT; DEBIT AGENT.

DEBIT LIFE INSURANCE *see* DEBIT INSURANCE.

DEBIT SYSTEM *see* DEBIT INSURANCE.

DEBRIS REMOVAL CLAUSE in property insurance, contract section providing for reimbursement for removal of debris resulting from an insured peril. The amount of reimbursement under the HOMEOWNERS INSURANCE POLICY ranges from 5–10% of the face value.

DEBT CANCELLATION CONTRACT two-party agreement between borrower and lender that cancels the outstanding debt upon the occurrence of a specified event.

DEBT PROTECTION PRODUCT two-party agreement between borrower and lender that restructures debt upon the occurrence of a specified event. These are not regulated as insurance products. The lender receives a monetary sum and agrees to modify, cancel, or suspend the terms of a loan agreement if a specific event occurs. For example, the agreement would go into effect in the event of the death, disability, or unemployment of the borrower.

DEBT SUSPENSION CONTRACT (DEBT DEFERMENT CONTRACT) two-party agreement between borrower and lender that freezes the balance of a loan and cancels all interest accrued to date upon the occurrence of a specified event.

DECEDENT dead INSURED.

DECEPTIVE PRACTICE CONCEALMENT of the actual fact. For example, an insurance agent tells a prospective insured that a policy provides a particular benefit when in actual fact this benefit is not in the written language of the policy. *See also* TWISTING.

DECLARATION statement that the insured makes (declares) about loss exposures in an application for a policy. For example, in a personal automobile policy the applicant states his/her name, address, occupation, type of automobile, expected mileage per year, etc. Based on this information, the insurance company decides which underwriting classification in which to place the risk; applicable premium rate; maximum limits of coverage; and any special conditions to govern the insured's behavior that is to be attached to the policy.

DECLARATIONS SECTION in property and casualty insurance, contract section containing such information as name, description, and location of insured property; name and address of the insured; period a policy is in force; premiums payable; and amount of coverage.

DECLINATION rejection by an insurance company of an application for a policy.

DECREASING TERM LIFE INSURANCE coverage in which the face amount of a life insurance policy declines by a stipulated amount over a period of time. For example, the initial face amount of a $100,000 decreasing term policy decreases by $10,000 each year, until after 10 years the face value equals zero. The premium does not decrease.

DEDUCTIBILITY OF EMPLOYER CONTRIBUTIONS contributions (under qualified employee benefit plans, such as pensions and health insurance) made by an employer on behalf of employees, deducted as a business expense for tax purposes. Employer contributions are not considered current taxable income to the employee. Thus, significant tax advantages are available to both an employer and an employee.

DEDUCTIBLE amount of loss that insured pays in a claim; includes the following types:
1. *Absolute dollar amount.* Amount the insured must pay before the company will pay, up to the limits of the policy. The higher the absolute dollar amount, the lower the premium.
2. *Time period amount* (ELIMINATION PERIOD/*Waiting period*). Length of time the insured must wait before any benefit payments are made by the insurance company. In disability income policies it is common to have a waiting period of 30 days during which no income benefits are paid to the insured. The longer this time period, the lower the premium.
   The consumer would be well advised to select the highest deductible (by dollar amount and/or time period) that he/she can afford. First dollar coverages are very costly. A high deductible allows the insured to self-insure expected losses—those of high frequency and low severity.

DEDUCTIBLE, AGGREGATE ANNUAL *see* AGGREGATE ANNUAL DEDUCTIBLE.

DEDUCTIBLE, BUY-BACK *see* BUY-BACK DEDUCTIBLE.

DEDUCTIBLE CLAUSE provision in insurance policies that states the DEDUCTIBLE. *See also* COINSURANCE; LOSS SETTLEMENT AMOUNT; SETTLEMENT OPTIONS, PROPERTY AND CASUALTY INSURANCE.

DEDUCTIBLE, CORRIDOR *see* CORRIDOR DEDUCTIBLE.

DEDUCTIBLE, DISAPPEARING *see* DISAPPEARING DEDUCTIBLE.

DEDUCTIBLE, FRANCHISE *see* FRANCHISE DEDUCTIBLE.

DEDUCTIBLE IRA limited to federal income taxpayers who are not covered by a retirement plan at employment. *See also* INDIVIDUAL RETIREMENT ACCOUNT (IRA).

DEDUCTIBLE, PERCENTAGE-OF-LOSS *see* PERCENTAGE-OF-LOSS DEDUCTIBLE.

DEDUCTIBLE, PERIOD *see* DISABILITY INCOME INSURANCE (ELIMINATION PERIOD).

DEDUCTIBLE, SPLIT *see* SPLIT DEDUCTIBLE.

DEDUCTIVE REASONING observance of an event occurring on a repeated basis that leads one to believe that a certain PROBABILITY is attached to the occurrence of that event. For example, if there are a red ball and a blue ball in a bag, and each color ball is drawn one-half of the time, we come to believe that each color ball has a one-half probability of being drawn at any one time.

DEFAMATION OF CHARACTER oral or written statement that results in injuring the good name or reputation of another, causing that individual to be held in disrepute.

DEFEASANCE procedure that moves up the maturity date of the municipal bond to its call date. The call date permits the issuer of the bond to redeem the bond at any time after a stipulated minimum number of years have passed at a given price.

DEFENDANT one of two parties in a negligence lawsuit (the other party being the PLAINTIFF) from whom the plaintiff seeks releases because of bodily injury and or property damage incurred as the result of the defendant's allegedly negligent acts.

DEFENDANT BOND type of COURT BOND filed on behalf of the defendant and used to release assets to him or her that have been attached pending a court decision. *See also* APPEAL BOND; BAIL BOND; INJUNCTION BOND; JUDICIAL BOND.

DEFENSE AGAINST UNINTENTIONAL TORT *see* TORT, DEFENSE AGAINST UNINTENTIONAL.

DEFENSE CLAUSE *see* DEMOLITION CLAUSE.

DEFENSE COSTS expense of defending a lawsuit. To mount a legal defense against civil or criminal liability, a defendant faces expenses for lawyers, investigation, fact gathering, bonds, and court costs. Of critical importance in purchasing liability insurance is not only the limits of coverage under the policy but also the obligation of the insurance company to defend the insured against suits, even if a suit is without foundation. Because legal defense costs can be extremely high, the consumer should consider liability insurance that pays all defense costs in addition to the policy limits.

DEFENSE OF SUIT AGAINST INSURED clause in a liability insurance policy under which an insurance company agrees to defend an insured even if a lawsuit is without foundation. The costs of defending the insured are covered, in addition to the limits of coverage under the policy. For example, if the limits of coverage under a policy is $1,000,000 and defense costs are $120,000, the $120,000 costs are in addition to the $1,000,000 of coverage. This is critical, since defense costs can be quite high.

DEFENSE RESEARCH INSTITUTE (DRI) organization of trial attorneys who specialize in the representation of defendants who become subject to TORT actions. Generally, these tort actions involve bodily injury or personal injury claims against the defendant.

DEFENSIVE MEDICINE extensive medical procedures conducted by physicians in order to document the patient's file in the event of a negligence liability suit.

DEFERRED ANNUITY annuity that can be paid either with a single premium or a series of installments. For example, an annuitant pays a single premium of $100,000 on June 1 of the current year and is scheduled to receive a monthly income of $1300 at a specified later date. Or, the annuitant pays $50 a month to the insurance company, starting June 1, 2008, and ending June 1, 2027, and begins receiving a monthly income of $1300, beginning July 1, 2027. *See also* ANNUITY.

DEFERRED BENEFITS AND PAYMENTS *see* DEFERRED CONTRIBUTION PLAN, DEFERRED RETIREMENT CREDIT.

DEFERRED COMPENSATION PLAN means of supplementing an executive's retirement benefits by deferring a portion of his or her current earnings. Deferring income in this manner encourages the loyalty of executives. To qualify for a tax advantage, the IRS requires a written agreement between an executive and the employer stating the specified period of deferral of income. An election by an executive to defer income must be irrevocable and must be made prior to performing the service for which income deferral is sought.

DEFERRED CONTRIBUTION PLAN arrangement in which an unused deduction (credit carryover) to a profit sharing plan can be added to an employer's future contribution on a tax deductible basis. It occurs when the employer's contribution to a profit sharing plan is less than the annual 15% of employee compensation allowed by the Federal Tax Code.

DEFERRED DIVIDENDS end of a defined time period that dividends become payable to the POLICYHOLDER.

DEFERRED GROUP ANNUITY retirement income payments for an employee that begin after a stipulated future time period, and continue for life. (A beneficiary of a deceased annuitant may receive further income, depending on whether the contract is a PURE ANNUITY or REFUND ANNUITY). Each year, contributions are used to buy a paid-up single premium deferred annuity. These increments, added together, provide income payments at retirement.

DEFERRED PREMIUM life insurance premium that is not currently due. Future payments are made on a frequency basis other than annual.

DEFERRED PROFIT-SHARING portion of company profits allocated by an employer, in good years, to an employee's trust. Contributions on behalf of each employee are expressed as a percentage of salary with 5% being common practice. If the profit sharing plan is a *qualified* plan according to the IRS, employer contributions are tax deductible as a business expense. These contributions are not currently taxable to the employee; benefits are taxed at the time of distribution.

DEFERRED RETIREMENT retirement taken after the normal retirement age. For example, if the normal retirement age is 65 or 70 an employee may continue to work beyond those ages. Normally the election of deferred retirement does not increase the monthly retirement income when the employee actually retires.

DEFERRED VESTING *see* VESTING, DEFERRED.

DEFICIENCY RESERVE addition to reserves of a life insurance company required by various states because the VALUATION PREMIUM is greater than the GROSS PREMIUM. Without a deficiency reserve, the normal reserve by itself would be less than the actual reserve required.

DEFICIT REDUCTION ACT OF 2005 legislation that allows states to charge unlimited premiums as well as COPAYMENTS (not to exceed 20% of the costs) of the provided medical benefits under MEDICAID for families that have income in excess of 150% of the poverty level. To receive benefits, all assets in excess of $2000 must be divested. Equity of $500,000 or less in the home is excludable. There is a five-year look-back period for assets that are transferred for less than their fair market value.

DEFICIT REDUCTION CONTRIBUTION contribution whose purpose is to increase funding of underfunded PENSION PLANS. It is part of the calculation that is made to arrive at the plan's minimum funding requirement. Usually a pension plan requires such a contribution when the assets of the plan become less than 80 to 90% of the current liabilities of the plan.

DEFINED BENEFIT PLAN retirement plan under which benefits are fixed in advance by formula, and contributions vary. The defined benefit plan can be expressed in either of two ways:
   1. *Fixed Dollars:* (a) *Unit benefit* approach—a *discrete* unit of benefit is credited for each year of service recognized by the employer. The unit is either a flat dollar amount or (more often) a percentage of compensation—usually 1½–2½%. Total years of service are multiplied by this percentage. For example, if total years of service is 30 and the percentage is 1½, 45% would be applied to either the career average earnings or final average earnings (highest three of five consecutive years of earnings). If the average of the highest five consecutive years of earnings is $100,000, the yearly retirement benefit would be $45,000. (b) *Level Percentage of Compensation—*

After a minimum number of years of service (usually 20) and a minimum age (usually 50), all employees will receive the same percentage of earnings as a retirement benefit, regardless of income, position in the company, or years of service. For example, each employee who is at least 50 years of age, with at least 20 years of service receives 20% of compensation. This plan is more common than the flat amount approach described below. (c) *Flat Amount*— After having attained a minimum number of years of service (usually 20) and a minimum age (usually 50), all employees will receive the same absolute dollar amount as a retirement benefit, regardless of income, position in the company, or years of service. For example, each employee who is at least 50 years of age, with at least 20 years of service receives $8000 a year in retirement benefits.

2. *Variable Dollars:* (a) Cost-of-Living Plan—benefits are modified according to changes in a predetermined price index—usually, the Consumer Price Index (CPI). For example, when the CPI increases by at least 3% benefits are increased by that percentage. (b) Equity Annuity Plan—premiums are paid into a variable annuity plan to purchase accumulation units. At retirement, the accumulation units are converted to *retirement* units whose values fluctuate according to the common stock portfolio in which the premiums were invested.

DEFINED BENEFIT/401(k) combination of a traditional DEFINED BENEFIT PLAN and a DEFINED CONTRIBUTION PENSION PLAN or SECTION 401(K) PLAN that becomes effective in 2010. This plan can provide benefits based on either a traditional defined benefit formula or a cash balance formula. Under the defined benefit formula, employees must have credited to their account at least 1% of their final average salary (subject to no more than the highest five years average earnings) for each year of service up to 20 years. Under the cash balance formula, employees must have credited to their account various percentages of compensation based on the employee's age at the beginning of each plan's year as follows: younger than age 30, 2% of earnings; ages 30–39, 4% of compensation; ages 40–49, 6% of compensation; age 50 and older, 8% of compensation. For the 401(k) portion of the plan, if the employee does not select to be enrolled, that employee is automatically enrolled at a rate of 4% of compensation with a mandatory employer contribution of 2% of compensation. These contributions, both employee and employer, must be on a nonforfeitable basis. The FIDUCIARY for the 401(k) part of the plan is relieved from liability for default investments to include a third-party managed account, a balanced mutual fund, and a lifecycle mutual fund.

DEFINED CONTRIBUTION HEALTH INSURANCE combination of a high-deductible insurance policy with a savings account. The savings account's contributions are on a pre-tax basis, and health care expenses are withdrawn from the account on a tax-free basis. The plan enables employees to select from a range of health care plans to fit their own particular requirements.

DEFINED CONTRIBUTION PENSION PLAN (MONEY PURCHASE PLAN) retirement plan under which contributions are fixed in advance by formula, and benefits vary. These plans are often used by organizations that must know what the cost of employee benefits will be in the years ahead. For example, nonprofit organizations such as charities need to project future pension expenses that will not rise above a preset limit. This enables budgets to be established that provide guidelines for their solicitation of funds.

DEFINITE LOSS *see* REQUIREMENTS OF INSURABLE RISK.

DEFINITIONS essential parts of insurance policies that explain the meanings of important words and phrases found in those policies.

DEGREE OF CARE minimum of care owed by one party for the physical safety of another. Liability suits are brought because of negligent acts and omissions resulting from failures to exercise due care.

DEGREE OF RISK amount of uncertainty in a given situation. Probability that actual experience will be different from what is expected.

DELAY CLAUSE in CASH VALUE LIFE INSURANCE policies, provision that allows the insurance company to refuse the POLICYHOLDER a loan on the cash value for a period of time, usually up to 6 months, from the request date. The only exception is for premium payments due on the policy.

DELAYED PAYMENT CLAUSE life insurance policy provision stating that after the death of an insured, the proceeds from a policy are not immediately paid to the primary beneficiary; instead, they are delayed for a specified time period. This usually occurs in *common disaster* situations.

DELIVERY physical handing of an insurance policy to the insured. Sales training emphasizes the importance of delivery of a policy by the agent. This develops a caring attitude on the part of the agent and reinforces the insured's belief that he or she made the right decision in purchasing the policy.

DELIVERY RECEIPT signed receipt by POLICYOWNER acknowledging that policyowner is in possession of the policy.

DEMOLITION CLAUSE in PROPERTY INSURANCE policies, provision that excludes the insurance company's liability for indemnification of the insured for the insured's expenses incurred in the demolition of undamaged property.

DEMOLITION INSURANCE coverage that will indemnify the insured for the expenses, up to the limits of the policy, if a building is damaged by a peril such as fire, and zoning requirements and/or building codes mandate that the building be demolished.

DEMURRAGE compensation payable to the owner of a ship detained for reasons beyond his or her control who incurs a loss of earnings because of the delay. Detainment can be caused by a delay in the loading or unloading of the ship.

DEMUTUALIZATION (STOCKING A MUTUAL) conversion of form of ownership from a MUTUAL INSURANCE COMPANY to a STOCK INSURANCE COMPANY. Interest in demutualization of life insurance companies surged in the early 1980s among many large mutual companies because they felt they needed new sources of capital to compete in the financial services revolution.

DENTAL EXPENSE INSURANCE insurance that usually follows the format of COMPREHENSIVE HEALTH INSURANCE plans in that there is a COINSURANCE requirement of usually 75 to 80%, and a limit on benefits for any one person per calendar year. In many instances, there is no deductible for annual preventive oral examinations. Orthodontia benefits are usually provided separately.

DENTAL INSURANCE coverage for dental services under a group or individual policy.

DEPARTMENT STORE INSURANCE FLOATER coverage for items of property being delivered to a customer. The means of transportation covered include such common carriers as aircraft, railroads, trucks, express carrier, and other variations, as well as the department store's trucks and other delivery vehicles. Coverage can be purchased on an ALL RISKS basis subject to excluded perils such as war and nuclear disaster. Coverage applies on a *blanket* basis meaning that all locations of points of delivery are covered.

DEPENDENT a person who relies on another for economic support. For insurance purposes, the following may be included: (1) the insured's legal spouse; (2) any unmarried children younger than a specified age who are dependent upon the insured for support (age requirements vary from plan to plan); (3) unmarried children between specified years of age who are dependent upon the insured for support, and who are full-time students in an educational institution (age requirements vary).

A dependent child cannot be covered under more than one insured employee's plan. For example, if the husband and wife are both insured employees of different companies, coordination of benefits would determine which plan is *primary* and which plan is *secondary*. In some states, the father's plan is primary; in other states, the *birthday rule* would be used: the parent with the earlier birthday would have the primary plan.

DEPENDENT ADMINISTRATION COVERAGE *see* DEPENDENT; DEPENDENT COVERAGE.

DEPENDENT CARE ACCOUNT type of FLEXIBLE SPENDING ACCOUNT. *See also* FLEXIBLE SPENDING ACCOUNT—HEALTH CARE/DEPENDENT CARE EXPENSES.

DEPENDENT CARE FLEXIBLE SPENDING ACCOUNT account that is similar in form to the HEALTH PLAN FLEXIBLE SPENDING ACCOUNT (FSA) with contributions to this account used to reimburse employees who are parents for expenses at a children's day care center or home child care. Employees can also be reimbursed for expenses associated with caring for an elderly parent.

DEPENDENT COVERAGE coverage under life and health insurance policies for dependents of a named insured to include a spouse and unmarried children under a specified age. Under some life insurance policies an insured's spouse and dependent children, unmarried and under age 21, can be added at favorable rates. Health insurance policies cover the same dependent individuals at a far cheaper rate than the cost of separate policies for them.

DEPENDENT PROPERTIES BUSINESS INCOME FORM form that provides insurance coverage for the insured in the event the damage or destruction of non-owned property reduces or terminates the insured's earnings. For example, if the insured manufactures plastic airplane kits, and the supplier of the plastic for making the airplanes has a catastrophic fire at its plant, the manufacturer would not be able to continue to produce the kits in the necessary volume. Thus, the manufacturer would be indemnified by the insurance company for its lost earnings.

DEPOSIT ADMINISTRATION GROUP ANNUITY *see* PENSION PLAN FUNDING: GROUP DEPOSIT ADMINISTRATION ANNUITY.

DEPOSIT ADMINISTRATION PLAN unallocated funding instrument for pension plans under which premiums are placed on deposit, and are not currently allocated to the purchase of benefits for the employee. At retirement, an immediate retirement annuity is purchased for the employee. The amount of monthly income depends on the investment results of the funds left on deposit. Many insurance companies guarantee a minimum rate of return on funds left on deposit.

DEPOSITORS FORGERY INSURANCE coverage provided for individuals or businesses for loss due to forgery or alteration of such financial instruments as notes, checks, drafts, and promissory notes.

DEPOSIT PREMIUM premium required by an insurance company for plans subject to premium adjustment. The initial provisional premium is paid to put a commercial property or liability insurance policy into force. The final premium is determined at the end of the policy period, based on an insured's actual exposures and loss experience.

DEPOSIT TERM LIFE INSURANCE policy in which a premium (the deposit) is paid in the first policy year, in addition to the regular term insurance premiums required. The deposit is left to accumulate at interest for a specific number of years, e.g., 10. Thereafter, the *policyowner* can receive the deposit plus interest or may renew the policy without the INSURED having to furnish EVIDENCE OF INSURABILITY. This procedure can be repeated every 10 years, in some instances up to age 100. A deposit term policy can be converted to ORDINARY LIFE, or DECREASING TERM LIFE INSURANCE without evidence of insurability. However, if the policyowner cancels the policy prior to the initial 10 years, the deposit and any interest is forfeited. If the insured dies before the policy is converted, the deposit plus the interest is added to the death benefit.

DEPRECIATION actual or accounting recognition of the decrease in the value of a hard asset (property) over a period of time, according to a predetermined schedule such as *straight line depreciation.*

DEPRECIATION INSURANCE *see* REPLACEMENT COST LESS PHYSICAL DEPRECIATION AND OBSOLESCENCE.

DERIVATIVES securities that derive their value from other financial instruments that are used by the insurance company to hedge its bets on which direction the market is moving. For example, cattle futures are a simple derivative in that the cattle futures contract increases or decreases in value as future prices change for cows on the hoof. When insurance companies use derivatives, they are more likely to use them in association with currency and interest rate transactions as a means of protecting themselves against adverse moves in interest rates or foreign currency exchanges. This instrument provides a mechanism for hedging against the interest rate risks that are inherent within insurance products by pricing in that risk in advance and protecting against future negative occurrences.

DEVIATED RATE rates used by a property and casualty insurance company that are different from that suggested by a RATING BUREAU. An insurance company may use deviated rates because it feels they are more indicative of the company's experience.

DEVIATING INSURANCE COMPANY insurance company whose premium rates are usually below that of other insurance companies and the RATING BUREAU.

DEVIATION *see* DEVIATED RATE.

DEVIATION POLICY INSURANCE POLICY that differs from the STANDARD FORM.

DIAGNOSIS RELATED GROUP method of determining reimbursement from medical insurance according to diagnosis on a prospective basis. It originated with the MEDICARE program.

DIC *see* DIFFERENCE IN CONDITIONS INSURANCE.

DIFFERENCE IN CONDITIONS INSURANCE coverage for a physical structure, machinery, inventory, and merchandise within the structure in the event of earthquakes, flood collapses, and subsidence strikes. Even though coverage is on an ALL RISKS basis, important perils are excluded such as fire, vandalism, sprinkler leakage, employee dishonesty, boiler and machinery losses, and mysterious disappearance, since it is assumed that the insured business already has coverage for these perils under a business property insurance policy.

DIFFERENCE IN CONDITIONS LIABILITY POLICY (DICLP) coverage for the liability exposures of directors and officers of an organization where there is a gap in the protection under the standard DIRECTORS AND OFFICERS LIABILITY INSURANCE policy. Under this DICLP, (1) any liability claims against the organization do not diminish the limits of coverage; (2) the policy goes into effect if the organization is unable to indemnify and/or defend the officers and directors; (3) the policy goes into effect if the standard directors and officer liability policy denies coverage; (4) protection is provided against fines levied under section 308 of the SARBANES-OXLEY ACT; (5) the policy can be written as PRIMARY INSURANCE or as EXCESS INSURANCE.

DIP-DOWN CLAUSE provision in an UMBRELLA LIABILITY INSURANCE policy under which the policy will pay those losses that come within the retention limits of the primary policy, but the primary policy cannot pay because its aggregate limits have no further capacity.

DIRECT COVER AUTOMATIC NONPROPORTIONAL REINSURANCE treaty or AUTOMATIC PROPORTIONAL REINSURANCE treaty that provides coverage for losses upon which claims are made while the treaty is in force, without regard to when these losses actually occurred. *See also* CLAIMS MADE BASIS LIABILITY COVERAGE; CLAIMS OCCURRENCE BASIS LIABILITY COVERAGE.

DIRECT LIABILITY legal obligation of an individual or business because of negligent acts or omissions resulting in bodily injury and/or property damage or destruction to another party. There are no intervening circumstances.

DIRECT LOSS property loss in which the insured peril is the *proximate cause* (an unbroken chain of events) of the damage or destruction. Most basic property insurance policies (such as the *standard fire policy)* insure against only direct loss and not INDIRECT LOSS or CONSEQUENTIAL LOSS. For example, a fire within the wall structure of a house causes the drapes to catch fire, which in turn fans flames onto the furniture—a direct loss. An indirect loss would be inconvenience of the inhabitants, who would not be able to sleep in their home, thus causing a drop in their efficiency at work.

DIRECTORS AND OFFICERS LIABILITY INSURANCE coverage when a director or officer of a company commits a negligent act or omission, or misstatement or misleading statement, and a successful libel suit is brought against the company as a result. Usually a large deductible is required. The policy provides coverage for directors' and officers' liability exposure if they are sued as individuals. Coverage is also provided for the costs of defense such as legal fees and other court costs.

DIRECT PLACEMENT security sold by the issuer of the security directly to the purchasing financial institution without the inclusion of the investment banker in this process. Insurance companies are frequent purchasers of securities in this way. Only the largest firms with the highest credit ratings are able to issue these types of securities. The issuer avoids the uncertainty of the market through these private negotiations.

DIRECT PROPERTY EXPOSURES circumstance in which there is a PROBABILITY loss to PERSONAL PROPERTY or REAL PROPERTY resulting from property damage, destruction, or disappearance. *See also* COMMERCIAL PROPERTY FLOATER; COMMERCIAL PROPERTY FORM; HOMEOWNERS INSURANCE POLICY; PERSONAL ARTICLES INSURANCE; PERSONAL EFFECTS INSURANCE; PERSONAL PROPERTY FLOATER; COMMERCIAL PACKAGE POLICY (CPP).

DIRECT RECOGNITION immediate taking-into-account of present interest rates, mortality experience, and expenses in premiums currently charged. This is critical to the formulation of CURRENT ASSUMPTION WHOLE LIFE INSURANCE products. *See also* UNIVERSAL LIFE INSURANCE.

DIRECT REGISTRATION SYSTEM system in which shareholders are not issued physical stock certificates; instead, they are sent a statement that shows the number of shares registered in the shareholder's name on the insurance company's books (on direct deposit with the company).

DIRECT RESPONSE MARKETING (DIRECT SELLING SYSTEM) method of selling insurance directly to insureds through a company's own employees, through the mail, or at airport booths. The company uses this method of distribution rather than independent or captive agents for effectiveness and efficiency.

DIRECT ROLLOVER ELIGIBLE ROLLOVER DISTRIBUTION that is paid directly from an employee's EMPLOYEE BENEFIT INSURANCE PLAN to the employee's INDIVIDUAL RETIREMENT ACCOUNT (IRA) or to another plan maintained by the employer that accepts rollovers. Under such a rollover, the employee is not taxed on any part of the distribution until it is withdrawn from the IRA or the employer-maintained plan. The employee can open an IRA to receive the distribution. If an employee is employed by a new employer who maintains an employee benefit insurance plan that accepts rollovers, the distribution can be placed directly into that plan. If the new employer does not accept rollovers, the employee can place the distribution into an IRA.

DIRECT SELLING *see* DIRECT RESPONSE MARKETING (DIRECT SELLING SYSTEM).

DIRECT SELLING SYSTEM *see* DIRECT RESPONSE MARKETING.

DIRECT WRITER
1. property insurer that distributes its products through a *direct selling system.* Traditionally, insurers often were known as direct writers if they used either a direct selling system or an *exclusive agency system* for distribution. Increasingly, the term applies only to those using a direct selling system.
2. reinsurer that deals directly with a CEDING COMPANY, without using a REINSURANCE BROKER.

DIRECT WRITING AGENT *see* CAPTIVE AGENT.

DIRECT WRITTEN PREMIUM total premiums received by a PROPERTY AND LIABILITY insurance company without any adjustments for the ceding of any portion of these premiums to the REINSURER.

DISABILITY physiological or psychological condition that prevents an insured from performing normal job functions.

DISABILITY BENEFIT income paid under a disability policy that is not covered under WORKERS COMPENSATION BENEFITS. It is usually expressed as a percentage of the insured's income prior to the disability, but there may be a limit on the amount and duration of benefits. The most advantageous policy pays a monthly disability income benefit for as long as the insured is unable to perform suitable job functions determined by experience, education, and training.

DISABILITY BENEFIT, COMMERCIAL HEALTH INSURANCE *see* DISABILITY BENEFIT.

DISABILITY BUY-OUT INSURANCE buy-sell agreements found in partnerships, sole proprietorships, and close corporations. Either the business entity or the surviving members of the business agree to buy out the interest of a disabled member according to a predetermined formula funded through insurance. Disability buy-out insurance can be more important to a business than death buy-out insurance because the chances of becoming disabled are 7 to 10 times greater than death, depending on the age of the individual. The mechanisms available for the disability buyout are the same as those found under BUSINESS LIFE AND HEALTH INSURANCE. *See also* PARTNERSHIP LIFE AND HEALTH INSURANCE.

DISABILITY CLAUSE PROVISION found in a LIFE INSURANCE POLICY that provides that certain benefits will be paid in the event the insured becomes totally and permanently disabled from an accident incurred or sickness contacted. *See also* WAIVER OF PREMIUM (WP).

DISABILITY INCOME (DI) life insurance payment issued after the insured has been disabled for at least six months. One percent of the face value of the policy is paid the insured as a monthly income benefit and premiums are waived for the duration of the disability. A DISABILITY INCOME RIDER can be attached to an ordinary life insurance policy to provide this disability income benefit at extra charge. The insured can have a WAVIER OF PREMIUM benefit without a disability income benefit, but cannot have the disability income benefit without the waiver of premiums benefit.

DISABILITY INCOME INSURANCE health insurance that provides income payments to the insured wage earner when income is interrupted or terminated because of illness, sickness, or accident. Definitions under this insurance include:

1. *Total and Partial Disability*—reduction in benefits if the insured is found to be partially disabled instead of totally disabled.

2. *Amount of Benefits*—many policies stipulate that all sources of disability income cannot exceed 50% to 80% of the insured's earnings prior to the disability, subject to a maximum absolute dollar amount.

3. *Duration of Benefits*—length of time benefits will be paid. Some policies will pay benefits for one or two years, whereupon the insured must agree to be retrained for other work. Other policies pay benefits as long as the insured is unable to do the job for which he or she is suited by training, education, and experience (often up to age 65, when retirement programs take over). Some policies pay lifetime benefits.

4. ELIMINATION PERIOD *(Waiting Period)*—period beginning with the first day of disability, during which no payments are made to the insured. The longer this period, the lower the premiums.

5. *Physician's Care*—the insured must be regularly attended by a legally qualified physician because it is necessary to assess changes in severity of disability.

6. PREEXISTING CONDITION—if an insured has a preexisting injury, sickness, or illness, most policies will not pay income benefits either for the duration of the policy or until a period of time (usually from six months to one year) has elapsed.

7. *Recurrent Disability*—most policies will not pay income benefits to an insured who is experiencing a recurrent disability unless the recurrent disability is deemed a new disability. Some more progressive policies define a recurrent disability as a new disability if there has been a break of at least six months between the first disability and the current disability, and the insured has returned to work during that break.

8. RESIDUAL DISABILITY—many policies pay for the unused portion of the total disability period, limited to age 65.

DISABILITY INCOME RECORD SYSTEM (DIRS) service under the auspices of the MEDICAL INFORMATION BUREAU (MIB) that provides the insurance company with nonmedical information concerning the APPLICANT for DISABILITY INCOME INSURANCE. The purpose of this system is to warn the insurance company in the event the applicant tries to purchase excessive amounts of disability income insurance from various companies. The member insurance company is required to report to the DIRS an applicant for disability income insurance in amounts of at least $300 per month to be paid to the disabled insured for at least 12 months. The DIRS then stores this information in its computer files, from which it is retrievable by any member company.

DISABILITY INCOME RIDER addition to a life insurance policy stating that when an insured becomes disabled for at least six months, premiums due are waived. Depending on the rider, the insured may begin to receive a monthly income (usually 1% of the face value of the policy), or only the premium may be waived. The length of time that income payments will continue depends on the definition of disability in the policy. During the time that premiums are waived, the life insurance policy stays in force, so that if the insured dies, the beneficiary receives the face value of the policy. Cash values continue to build, and if the policy is participating, dividends continue to be paid. *See also* DISABILITY INCOME (DI); DISABILITY INCOME INSURANCE.

DISABILITY INSURANCE *see* DISABILITY BENEFIT; DISABILITY BUY-OUT INSURANCE; DISABILITY INCOME (DI); DISABILITY INCOME INSURANCE; DISABILITY INCOME RIDER; PARTNERSHIP LIFE AND HEALTH INSURANCE.

DISABILITY INSURANCE, CONDITIONS *see* DISABILITY BENEFIT; DISABILITY INCOME INSURANCE.

DISABILITY, LONG-TERM *see* LONG-TERM DISABILITY INCOME INSURANCE.

DISABILITY OF PARTNER BUY AND SELL INSURANCE *see* PARTNERSHIP LIFE AND HEALTH INSURANCE.

DISABILITY, PARTIAL inability of the INSURED to perform one or more of the important daily duties of that insured's occupation. The income payment to the insured is reduced from that of TOTAL DISABILITY.

DISABILITY, PERMANENT PARTIAL *see* DISABILITY INCOME INSURANCE; PERMANENT PARTIAL DISABILITY.

DISABILITY, PERMANENT TOTAL *see* DISABILITY INCOME INSURANCE; PERMANENT TOTAL DISABILITY.

DISABILITY REDUCING TERM POLICY policy that reduces the disability income benefit in tandem with the reduction in the outstanding debt. *See also* DECREASING TERM LIFE INSURANCE.

DISABILITY, SHORT-TERM *see* DISABILITY INCOME INSURANCE.

DISABILITY, TEMPORARY PARTIAL *see* DISABILITY INCOME INSURANCE; TEMPORARY DISABILITY BENEFITS.

DISABILITY, TEMPORARY TOTAL *see* DISABILITY INCOME INSURANCE; TEMPORARY DISABILITY BENEFITS.

DISABILITY, TOTAL inability of the INSURED to perform any and all important daily duties of that insured's occupation.

DISAPPEARING DEDUCTIBLE in property insurance, amount that an insured does not have to pay when a loss exceeds a predetermined sum; here the insurance company pays more than 100% of the loss, so that the deductible amount specified in a contract "vanishes." For example, if a deductible amount is $100, an insurance company may pay 125% of the losses exceeding $100, 150% of the losses exceeding $200, and if the losses exceed $300, the company pays the total amount of the loss (so that the insured does not assume any deductible for losses over $300). In another application an insured pays 125% of all losses over $100, the deductible disappears for any loss of $500 or more. *See also* DEDUCTIBLE.

DISASTER CLAUSE *see* COMMON DISASTER CLAUSE (SURVIVORSHIP CLAUSE).

DISCLAIMER statement issued by the INSURANCE COMPANY denying a claim under the INSURANCE POLICY on the grounds that a CONDITION or POLICY PROVISION has been breached.

DISCONTINUANCE termination of coverage in insurance.

DISCONTINUANCE OF CONTRIBUTIONS termination of premium payments by an employer on behalf of an employee to an employee benefit plan. *See also* GROUP DISABILITY INSURANCE; GROUP HEALTH INSURANCE; GROUP LIFE INSURANCE; GROUP PAID-UP LIFE INSURANCE; GROUP PERMANENT LIFE INSURANCE; GROUP TERM LIFE INSURANCE; PENSION PLAN; PENSION PLAN FUNDING INSTRUMENTS.

DISCONTINUANCE OF PLAN termination of a plan. Under federal tax law, a plan can only be terminated for reasons of business necessity. Otherwise, prior employer tax deductible contributions under the plan are disallowed.

DISCOUNTED PREMIUM lump sum premium paid in advance instead of the frequency of premium payments stipulated in the INSURANCE POLICY. This lump sum premium payment will be less than the PRESENT VALUE of the single premium payments.

DISCOUNT POINT *see* POINT.

DISCOUNT RATE rate charged by the Federal Reserve to commercial banks for overnight loans made by these banks. If the Federal Reserve decreases the discount rate, other rates will decline as well. Conversely, if the Federal Reserve increases the discount rate, other rates will also rise.

DISCOUNT VALUE present value of a future sum of money to be paid at a stipulated future date.

DISCOVERY PERIOD clause in a BOND that permits a principal who was formerly insured by the bond to report a loss to the surety company that occurred while the bond was in force. The period of time for reporting after the bond terminates is usually limited to one year.

DISCRETE UNIT *see* DEFINED BENEFIT PLAN.

DISCRETIONARY AUTHORITY legal power of the commissioner of Internal Revenue to approve any classification of employees that does not discriminate in favor of a prohibited group. Such approval is necessary before a retirement plan can be a *qualified pension plan* and thus subject to tax benefits.

DISCRIMINATION failure of an insurance company to offer similar insurance coverages at comparable premium rates to all individuals or groups with the same UNDERWRITING characteristics. Such discriminatory practices are prohibited by state and federal law.

DISEASE illness or sickness such as cancer, poliomyelitis, leukemia, diphtheria, smallpox, scarlet fever, tetanus, spinal meningitis, encephalitis, tularemia, hydrophobia, and sickle cell anemia, all of which are covered in health insurance policies as specified.

DISHONESTY, DISAPPEARANCE, AND DESTRUCTION POLICY (3-D POLICY) type of CRIME INSURANCE that provides the business with coverages for employee dishonesty, loss (both inside and outside the business's premises), depositor forgery, and counterfeit paper currency and money orders.

DISINTERMEDIATION flow of funds out of one financial instrument, whose interest rates are low, into another financial instrument, whose interest rates are higher. In the early 1980s, insurance companies experienced disintermediation as whole life policies were surrendered for their cash values and these sums were then transferred to higher interest-paying noninsurance products. Because of this situation, INTEREST SENSITIVE POLICIES were developed by INSURANCE COMPANIES.

DISMEMBERMENT BENEFIT income paid under health insurance for loss of use of various parts of the body due to an accident. A schedule of benefits available in a policy lists payments for each part of the body that is dismembered.

DISMEMBERMENT INSURANCE *see* ACCIDENTAL DEATH AND DISMEMBERMENT INSURANCE.

DISQUALIFIED PERSON individual prohibited under the EMPLOYEE RETIREMENT INCOME SECURITY ACT OF 1974 (ERISA) from conducting transactions with a trust plan. The prohibition is intended to prevent a conflict of interest between the prohibited person with a vested interest in the trust plan and the trust plan itself. Prohibited individuals include employer, trust plan participant, trustee of the plan, and fiduciary of the trust plan.

DISQUALIFIED PERSON (TAX-EXEMPT ORGANIZATION) person deemed to be an insider (according to SECTION 4958 OF THE INTERNAL REVENUE CODE) in a tax-exempt organization who, during the last five-year period ending as of the date of the transaction, exercised substantial influence over the decision-making process of that organization.

DISTRIBUTION BY LIVING HAND *see* ESTATE PLANNING; ESTATE PLANNING DISTRIBUTION.

DISTRIBUTION CLAUSE *see* PRO RATA DISTRIBUTION CLAUSE.

DISTRIBUTION OF PROPERTY AT DEATH OF OWNER *see* ESTATE PLANNING; ESTATE PLANNING DISTRIBUTION.

DIVERSIFICATION RISK distribution included by type of coverage, by kind of risk, and by geographical location.

DIVIDED COVER insurance coverage purchased on the same item from two or more insurance companies.

DIVIDEND sum returned to a policyowner by an insurance company under a participating policy. Dividends are not deemed as taxable distributions, as the Internal Revenue Service interprets them as a refund of a portion of the premium paid. There are several ways in which the policyowner may use dividends. *See also* DIVIDEND OPTION.

DIVIDEND ACCUMULATION option under a participating life insurance policy in which dividends are left on deposit with the company to accumulate at a specified interest rate. If this option is chosen, it is important to determine the interest rate. Interest on dividends left on deposit is taxable.

DIVIDEND ADDITION option in a participating policy under which dividends are used to purchase fully paid-up units of whole life insurance. This option deserves careful consideration by young families since it allows the purchase of extra life insurance without having to take a physical examination. Paid-up additions generate dividends and cash values that in turn will generate additional dividends and cash values.

DIVIDEND ILLUSTRATION picture of future DIVIDENDS that the insurance company expects to be allocated to a specific BLOCK OF POLICIES. The accuracy of this picture depends on the actual future mortality, investment, and expense experience being the same as that of the projected dividends. One way to judge the validity of the projected dividends is to ascertain the dividends that the company has actually paid out in the past and the dividends that it is currently paying out. Although this is not a guarantee of future payments, it can be a strong indication of future payouts.

DIVIDEND OPTION methods of handling policyholder dividends. In a participating life insurance policy, dividends are paid to the policyowner according to which of the following options is selected: (1) applied to reduce premiums; (2) paid in cash; (3) purchase increments of paid-up life insurance; (4) left on deposit with the insurance company to accumulate at interest; or (5) purchase extended term life insurance for one year in the amount a dividend can buy (Fifth Dividend Option). Some health and property insurance policies have dividend options.

DIVIDEND RATIO relationship of POLICYOWNER DIVIDENDS to EARNED PREMIUMS.

DIVIDENDS ACTUALLY PAID historical record of DIVIDENDS paid.

DIVIDEND SCALE DIVIDENDS paid historically, currently, and projected. *See also* DIVIDEND ILLUSTRATION.

DIVISIBLE CONTRACT CLAUSE in PROPERTY INSURANCE contracts, provision that states that the violation of one or more contract condition(s) at a particular location that is insured will not void coverage at other insured locations.

DIVISIBLE SURPLUS proportion of an insurance company's total surplus at the end of each year's operation that is distributed to policyowners of participating life insurance policies.

DOC *see* DRIVE OTHER CAR INSURANCE.

DOCTRINE OF LAST CLEAR CHANCE *see* LAST CLEAR CHANCE.

DOLLAR COST AVERAGING strategy of regularly investing a fixed amount of dollars into a VARIABLE DOLLAR ANNUITY over a substantial period of time regardless of the ACCUMULATION UNIT VALUE. The investment will be made when the unit value is low, high, or moderate, permitting the average cost per unit to be significantly below the high point in the market. Thus, the investor will not be confronted with "Buying High" and "Selling Low."

DOLLAR THRESHOLD *see* THRESHOLD LEVEL.

DOMESTIC INSURER insurance company incorporated according to the laws of the state in which a risk is located and the policy issued. The insurance company is *domiciled* in that state.

DOMICILE state in which an insurance company has its principal legal residence; where an individual resides in a fixed permanent home.

DOMINO THEORY OF ACCIDENT CAUSATION theory developed in 1931 by *H. W. Heinrich;* states that an accident is only one of a series of factors, each of which depends on a previous factor in the following manner:
1. accident causes an injury.
2. individual's negligent act or omission, or a faulty machine, causes an accident.
3. personal shortcomings cause negligent acts or omissions.
4. hereditary and environment cause personal shortcomings. *See also* HEINRICH, H. W.

DONOR individual or organization that transfers PROPERTY to a TRUST.

DONOR ADVISED FUND type of charitable giving through a qualified public charity where the donor recommends how contributions are granted to charitable organizations.

DO-OVER PROVISION guarantee that gives plan participants the right to elect not to participate in the automatic enrollment and to receive amounts withheld from their earnings provided request is made within 90 days of enrollment. The withdrawal amounts must be 100% of the earnings withheld plus any amount earned. There is no early withdrawal penalty paid. The withdrawal sums are included in the participant's earnings for the distribution year.

DOUBLE INDEMNITY *see* ACCIDENTAL DEATH CLAUSE.

DOUBLE-PROTECTION POLICY life insurance contract that combines TERM LIFE INSURANCE with WHOLE LIFE INSURANCE. The term portion of the contract expires after a stipulated time period. If the insured dies during this stipulated period, both the term portion and the whole life portion of the contract will pay. If the insured dies after the stipulated time period, only the whole life portion of the contract will pay.

DOUBLE RECOVERY payments in excess of the value of the loss—a prohibited practice. When an insured has more than one policy covering a risk, the full value cannot be collected from each policy if a loss occurs. The most that can be collected is each policy's pro rata share of the loss. For example, a home is insured under two policies of $100,000 each. If there is a fire loss of $100,000, the most that can be collected from each policy is $50,000.

DOWER INTEREST wife's interest in her husband's property upon his death. The wife has an INSURABLE INTEREST in that property and can purchase a property and casualty insurance policy to cover the EXPOSURES faced by it. *See also* COURTESY INTEREST.

DOWNSTREAM HOLDING COMPANY holding company established by a MUTUAL INSURANCE COMPANY. The mutual insurance company has 100% ownership of the holding company.

DRAM SHOP EXCLUSION excluded coverage in LIABILITY INSURANCE policies for claims resulting from the serving or distribution of alcoholic beverages. *See also* DRAM SHOP LAW; DRAM SHOP LIABILITY INSURANCE.

DRAM SHOP LAW liquor liability legislation in 20 states under which a dispenser of alcoholic beverages is held responsible for bodily injury and/or property damage caused by its customers to a third party. Insurance coverage is available, but at a high premium rate. *See also* DRAM SHOP LIABILITY INSURANCE; LIQUOR LIABILITY LAWS.

DRAM SHOP LIABILITY INSURANCE coverage for dispensers of alcoholic beverages against suits arising out of bodily injury and/or property damage caused by its customers to a third party. Establishments covered include bars, restaurants, hotels, motels, or wherever the alcoholic beverages are dispensed. These establishments are excluded from coverage under GENERAL LIABILITY INSURANCE.

DREAD DISEASE INSURANCE health insurance coverage only for a specified catastrophic disease such as cancer. It is important to ascertain the waiting period required, maximum benefits and maximum length of time they are payable, and the exact definition of the disease covered. Individual and group health insurance usually cover all diseases, including dread diseases.

DRIVE OTHER CAR INSURANCE (DOC) endorsement to an automobile insurance policy that protects an insured in either or both of two circumstances when driving a nonowned car:
1. *business endorsement*—if the insured's negligent acts or omissions result in bodily injury or property damage to a third party while the insured is driving a nonowned car for business activities.
2. *personal endorsement*—if the insured's negligent acts or omissions result in bodily injury or property damage to a third party while the insured is driving a nonowned car for nonbusiness activities.

DRIVING WHILE INTOXICATED (DWI) term for operating an automobile while under the influence of alcoholic beverages so as to be unable to drive safely. An insurance company can suspend auto coverage under a PERSONAL AUTOMOBILE POLICY (PAP).

DROP DOWN in REINSURANCE contracts, clause that requires the REINSURER to provide coverage if an underlying carrier is unable to fulfill its obligations under the policy CEDED to the reinsurer.

DRUG FORMULARIES recommendation of medications that should be prescribed for certain ailments. They can be classified as follows: (1) open or voluntary—recommends a list of drugs to physicians that is supposed to be the most cost-effective for a certain ailment; (2) closed—dictates which drugs will be covered by a benefit plan.

DRUGGISTS LIABILITY INSURANCE coverage in the event that, while practicing the profession of druggist, an act or omission is committed resulting in bodily injury, personal injury, and/or property damage to a customer. Also covered is liability arising through the use of products on or off of the business's premises. For example, a child is born after a druggist negligently places sugar tablets instead of birth control pills in a container for a customer. The druggist may have to provide funds necessary to sustain the child until the age of majority.

DUAL CAPACITY DOCTRINE rule of law under which a defendant who has two or more relationships with a plaintiff may be liable under any of these relationships. For example, an employer may be liable in two ways to an employee who incurs bodily injury on the job as the result of using a product or service produced by that employer: first, as the employer of the injured employee, and second, as the producer of the product or service that caused injury to the employee. The injured employee may then either collect benefits for job-related injuries under *workers compensation* or sue the employer as the producer of the defective product or service. For example, if an employee injures an arm at work while operating a machine with a defective blade that the employer manufactures, the employee can receive benefits under workers compensation or sue the employer as the manufacturer of the defective blade.

DUAL LIFE STOCK COMPANY stock life insurance company that sells PARTICIPATING INSURANCE and NONPARTICIPATING INSURANCE.

DUE CARE/DUE DILIGENCE assurance by the agent that the recommended insurance plan for the client is suitable for that client's specific needs. This assurance is derived from a careful analysis by the agent of the insurance company's financial strength, the accuracy of the policy illustrations, and the treatment of its previous and current policyowners.

DUPLICATION OF BENEFITS coverage in health insurance by two or more policies for the same insured loss. In such a circumstance, each policy pays its proportionate share of the loss, or one policy becomes *primary* and the other policy *secondary. See also* COORDINATION OF BENEFITS.

DUPLICATION OF EXPOSURE UNITS *see* SEGREGATION OF EXPOSURE UNITS.

DURABLE POWER OF ATTORNEY authority to act on behalf of an individual that terminates upon its revocation or death of that individual.

DURATION AVERAGING disciplined approach to managing an INSURANCE COMPANY'S bond portfolio duration. When interest rates rise, the average maturity and duration of the bond portfolio is lengthened, resulting in the portfolio becoming more aggressively positioned to take advantage of the falling bond prices. Conversely, when interest rates fall, the average maturity and duration of the bond portfolio is shortened, resulting in the portfolio becoming more defensively positioned to take advantage of the rising bond prices.

DURATION OF BENEFITS *see* DISABILITY INCOME INSURANCE.

DUTIES OF AN INSURED IN THE EVENT OF LOSS UNDER PROPERTY AND CASUALTY POLICY *see* PROPERTY AND CASUALTY INSURANCE PROVISIONS.

DUTIES OF INSURED *see* INSURANCE CONTRACT, LIFE; INSURANCE CONTRACT, PROPERTY AND CASUALTY.

DWELLING private residence in DECLARATIONS SECTION to include attached structures. *See also* DWELLING, BUILDINGS, AND CONTENTS INSURANCE (DB&C); DWELLING INSURANCE POLICY PROGRAM.

DWELLING, BUILDINGS, AND CONTENTS INSURANCE (DB&C) coverage when residential property does not qualify according to the minimum requirements of a homeowner's policy, or because of a requirement for the insured to select several different kinds of coverage and limits on this protection. DB&C insurance coverages can be selected from the following forms and attached to the Standard Fire Policy:

1. *Basic/Regular/General Form*—Coverage for property damage to a building used as a dwelling, as well as its contents. (Contents coverage is not restricted to the building or dwelling; coverage can be applied to contents of buildings such as hotels, that do not qualify as dwellings under the DB&C). The property coverage for the building includes items attached to the building such as equipment and fixtures, built-ins, furnace, air conditioner, hot water heater, and lighting fixtures. An optional extension of the dwelling coverage of up to 10% can be applied to private structures on the premises such as a garage. Contents coverage on household and personal goods within the dwelling can be extended to off-premises household and personal contents for up to 10%. Perils insured for both dwelling and contents are fire, lightning, and removal of the property from the premises to further protect it from damage from the perils. For an additional charge, vandalism and malicious mischief can also be insured against.

2. *Broad Form*—Includes the basic coverages plus the additional perils of burglary; falling objects; weight of snow and/or ice; accidental discharge, leakage, or overflow of water or steam from an air conditioning, heating, and/or plumbing mechanism and/or household appliance; glass breakage; damage resulting from water or freezing of plumbing and/or heating mechanisms; and structural problems leading to the collapse of the building. Damage from insured perils resulting in additional living expenses is also provided.

3. *Special Form*—Coverage on an ALL RISKS basis for only the structure of a dwelling, with no coverage for its contents.

DWELLING COVERAGE *see* DWELLING, BUILDINGS, AND CONTENTS INSURANCE (DB&C).

DWELLING FORM *see* DWELLING, BUILDINGS, AND CONTENTS INSURANCE (DB&C).

DWELLING INSURANCE POLICY PROGRAM coverage for a dwelling's structure; appurtenant structures on the premises; personal contents and household items within the dwelling; and 10% of the coverage applicable to such personal contents and household items away from the premises, for example at a hotel. Additional living expenses are covered because of the damage of an insured peril to the dwelling and/or its contents, and loss of rental value of the dwelling and/or its contents.

DYNAMIC changing state of the economy associated with changes in human wants and desires such that losses or gains occur. Dynamic changes are not insurable.

DYNAMIC FINANCIAL ANALYSIS procedure for examining the total financial position of the insurance company over future time periods under various changing scenarios of uncertainty involving interest rates, mortality rates, and equity rates of return.

DYNAMIC RISK *see* DYNAMIC.

DYNAMO CLAUSE *see* ELECTRICAL EXEMPTION CLAUSE.

DYNASTY TRUST TRUST in which ASSETS are controlled through several generations and makes use of generation-skipping tax exemption.

E

E&O *see* ERRORS AND OMISSIONS LIABILITY INSURANCE.

EARLY DISTRIBUTIONS FROM SECTION 401(a), 403(a), 403(b) RETIREMENT PLAN plan in which funds are withdrawn or income begins before the plan participant reaches age 59½. An extra 10% early distribution tax on the taxable amount may have to be paid unless any one of the following conditions exist: (1) distribution because the participant is disabled; (2) participant is separated from job after the attainment of at least age 55 and the distribution is received at that time; (3) participant terminates job and begins to receive annuity income consisting of a series of substantially equal payments at regular intervals (at least on an annual basis) over the lifetime, or life expectancy, or joint life expectancies of the participant and the participant's beneficiary; and (4) participant incurs medical expenses of at least 7½% of adjusted gross income. If the participant dies before reaching age 59½, the beneficiary(s) will not be subject to the payment of the 10% early distribution tax.

The availability of cash withdrawals and annuity income based on funds contributed as well as earnings on those funds under salary reduction plans beginning January 1, 1989 is restricted by the Internal Revenue Code. Such withdrawals and receipt of income can only be made if the plan participant is at least age 59½, terminates employment, becomes disabled, or dies.

EARLY INTERVENTION PROGRAM routine screening of short-term disability claims in order to evaluate rehabilitation progress of injured/sick insureds according to predetermined benchmarks.

EARLY RETIREMENT term in pensions; leaving a job before normal retirement age, subject to minimum requirements of age and years of service. There usually is a reduction in the monthly retirement benefit.

EARNED PREMIUM portion of a premium paid by an insured that has been allocated to the insurance company's loss experience, expenses, and profit year to date.

EARNED RIGHT basic feature of the SOCIAL SECURITY ACT under which benefits paid are associated with the employee's earnings that have been taxed during the employment period.

EARNED SURPLUS *see* RETAINED EARNINGS.

EARNINGS ENHANCEMENT BENEFIT (EEB) provision attached to a VARIABLE DOLLAR ANNUITY that will pay the BENEFICIARY an additional sum of money upon the death of the owner of the annuity. This EEB is a type of VARIABLE ANNUITY GUARANTEED MINIMUM DEATH BENEFIT (GMDB) that will pay this additional death benefit as a percentage of the variable annuity's gain. Since the earnings on annuities are taxed as ordinary income, this extra death benefit will help the beneficiary in this tax.

EARNINGS INSURANCE see GROSS EARNINGS FORM.

EARNINGS MULTIPLE APPROACH benefit found in GROUP LIFE INSURANCE—DEATH BENEFIT structure in which the insured employee's BENEFICIARY usually receives 1 to 2½ times the employee's yearly earnings upon the death of the employee.

EARNINGS TEST provision found in OLD AGE, SURVIVORS, DISABILITY, AND HEALTH INSURANCE (OASDHI) that provides for a reduction in the recipients' monthly income should their net earned income exceed a specified amount.

EARTHQUAKE INSURANCE coverage that can be purchased as an endorsement to many property policies such as the *Standard Fire Policy* or as a separate policy. Coverage is for direct damage resulting from earthquake or volcanic eruption. If there is a lapse of at least 72 hours between earthquake shocks, then each loss by a given earthquake is subject to a new claim. Excluded are losses resulting from fire, explosion, flood, or tidal wave.

EASEMENT right of one party to use land owned by another party. For example, an electric utility can obtain an easement through court action to place its power lines across someone's property, even if the owner is unwilling to give permission.

ECONOMIC BENEFIT *see* SPLIT DOLLAR LIFE INSURANCE.

ECONOMIC GROWTH AND TAX RELIEF RECONCILIATION ACT (EGTRRA) OF 2001 legislation that increased contribution limits and deductions to qualified retirement plans to include the increase from 15 to 25% of the employee's earnings for the amount of the employer's deductible contribution. Participants have portability of benefits in that they are permitted under the Act to roll over balances among the various retirement plans, including the SECTION 401(K) PLAN (SALARY REDUCTION PLAN); SECTION 457 DEFERRED COMPENSATION PLAN; INDIVIDUAL RETIREMENT ACCOUNT (IRA); and SECTION 403(B) PLAN.

ECONOMIC LOSS total estimated cost incurred by a person or persons, a family, or a business resulting from the death or disability of a wage earner (KEY EMPLOYEE), damage or destruction of property, and/or a liability suit (negligent acts or omissions by a person result in property damage or bodily injury to a THIRD PARTY). Factors included in the total cost are loss of earnings, medical expenses, funeral expenses, property damage restoration expenses, and legal expenses. *See also* ECONOMIC OR USE VALUE; HUMAN LIFE VALUE APPROACH (ECONOMIC VALUE OF AN INDIVIDUAL LIFE) (EVOIL); SPLIT DOLLAR LIFE INSURANCE.

ECONOMIC OR USE VALUE property valued according to its earnings potential. However, property insurance contracts generally

indemnify an insured on a REPLACEMENT COST LESS PHYSICAL DEPRECI-
ATION AND OBSOLESCENCE BASIS.

ECONOMIC VALUE OF AN INDIVIDUAL LIFE (EVOIL) *see*
HUMAN LIFE VALUE APPROACH.

EDUCATIONAL FUND factor considered in determining amount of
life insurance to purchase in order that funds will be available to pay
for a child's education expenses in the event of the premature death of
the wage earner. *See also* NEEDS APPROACH.

EDUCATION INDIVIDUAL RETIREMENT ACCOUNT (IRA)
type of INDIVIDUAL RETIREMENT ACCOUNT (IRA) in which an annual sum
of money can be paid into a fund on a nondeductible basis to cover
higher education expenses (tuition, books, supplies, and various fees).
The recipient must be younger than age 18. The accumulation and distribution of funds for higher education expenses are on a tax-free
basis. If the distributions are not used for higher education expenses,
they are taxed at an ordinary income tax basis plus a 10% surcharge.
If the recipient does not attend college or if there are any excess funds
remaining after recipient attains age 30, these funds can be rolled over
into another recipient's IRA (if younger than age 30 and a family
member) without a surcharge.

EEL *see* EMERGENCY EXPOSURE LIMIT (EEL).

EFFECTIVE ANNUAL RATE rate of interest equated to an annual
COMPOUND VALUE.

EFFECTIVE DATE date at which an insurance policy goes into force.
See also DATE OF ISSUE.

EFFECTIVE FEDERAL INCOME TAX RATE ratio of insurance
company's federal income taxes to pretax net income.

EFFECTIVE TIME *see* DATE OF ISSUE; EFFECTIVE DATE.

EGRESS exit, act of leaving or going out.

ELECTIVE DEFERRAL an employee's not-currently-taxed contributions to a RETIREMENT PLAN.

**ELECTRICAL (ELECTRICAL APPARATUS) EXEMPTION
CLAUSE** common element in property insurance that excludes electrical damage or destruction of an appliance unless the damage is
caused by a resultant fire.

ELECTRONIC DATA INTERCHANGE (EDI) method used to
reduce WORKERS COMPENSATION INSURANCE costs by using a single
database system to electronically link claims administration, medical
claim costs, RISK MANAGEMENT, and vendor services. EDI can reduce
errors in claims handling thereby making the process more efficient.
Also, EDI permits the comprehensive gathering of demographic
claims data pinpointing the factors that affect the risk.

ELEMENTS OF AN INSURANCE CONTRACT *see* ANALYSIS OF PROPERTY AND CASUALTY POLICY; INSURANCE CONTRACT, GENERAL; INSURANCE CONTRACT, HEALTH; INSURANCE CONTRACT, LIFE; INSURANCE CONTRACT, PROPERTY AND CASUALTY.

ELEVATOR COLLISION INSURANCE liability coverage for damage or destruction of a structure, elevator, and/or personal property due to the collision of an elevator.

ELEVATOR LIABILITY INSURANCE coverage for suits brought by a plaintiff as the result of bodily injury incurred while using an elevator on the insured's premises.

ELIGIBLE EXPENSES *see* GROUP HEALTH INSURANCE.

ELIGIBLE RETIREMENT PLAN plan under which an employee may make a ROLLOVER contribution. If that contribution is from a QUALIFIED TRUST, the employee may make rollover contributions to an employer's qualified trust, INDIVIDUAL RETIREMENT ACCOUNT (IRA), or an ANNUITY.

ELIGIBLE ROLLOVER DISTRIBUTIONS payments from an employee's EMPLOYEE BENEFIT INSURANCE PLAN that can be rolled over to an INDIVIDUAL RETIREMENT ACCOUNT (IRA) or to another plan maintained by the employer that accepts rollovers.

ELIGIBILITY PERIOD length of time in life and health insurance in which an employee can apply for and pay the first premium without having to show evidence of insurability (take a physical examination). The period is usually the first 30 days of employment. After expiration of the eligibility period, an employee may have to take a physical or provide medical history information to qualify for coverage. If the employee does not pass the physical, coverage can be denied under a group plan or the employee can be charged a much higher premium rate than the group rate. This is why it is extremely important for a new employee to apply for group life and health insurance during the eligibility period.

ELIGIBILITY REQUIREMENTS conditions found in employee benefit plans such as pensions, under which minimum requirements, such as 20 years of service, must be met by an employee to qualify for benefits.

ELIMINATION PERIOD form of deductible usually found in disability income insurance; for example, no benefits may be payable for a length of time beginning with the first day of illness. Subsequently, benefits are usually paid only for costs incurred after the end of the elimination period. The longer the elimination period in a policy, the lower the premium.

EMBEZZLEMENT theft of another's property by a person entrusted with that property. Coverage can be found under various bonding arrangements. *See also* FIDELITY BOND.

EMERGENCY EXPOSURE LIMIT (EEL) maximum amount of a toxic agent to which an individual can be exposed for a very brief (emergency) period of time and still maintain physical safety. *See also* THRESHOLD LEVEL.

EMERGENCY FUND factor considered in determining amount of life insurance to purchase in order that funds will be available to pay the emergency expenses following the death of a family member. *See also* NEEDS APPROACH.

EMPIRICAL CONSIDERATION LOADING to the BURNING COST RATIO for a reinsurer's expenses, profit, and to build a reserve to meet unusually large claims.

EMPIRICAL PROBABILITY mathematical relationship resulting from experimentation. For example, the PROBABILITY DISTRIBUTION for the possible number of heads from four tosses of a fair coin having both a head and a tail can be calculated from experimentation and observation by allowing for the accumulation of empirical data.

EMPIRICAL RATE CALCULATION adjustment of the BURNING COST RATIO for the increase in number and size of losses (losses likely in excess of that used in the unadjusted burning cost rate), INCURRED BUT NOT REPORTED LOSSES (IBNR), inflation, expenses, profits, and contingencies.

EMPLOYEE AS AN INSURED *see* BUSINESS LIABILITY INSURANCE; BUSINESSOWNERS POLICY (BOP).

EMPLOYEE ASSISTANCE PROGRAMS (EAPs) programs that deal with troublesome personal and family problems such as alcohol and drug abuse, marital problems, workplace violence, compulsive gambling, child care, legal problems, and care of elderly relatives.

EMPLOYEE BENEFIT INSURANCE PLAN provision by an employer for the economic and social welfare of employees. Generally include: (1) pension plans for retirement; (2) group life insurance for death; (3) group health insurance for illness and accident; (4) group disability income insurance for loss of income due to illness and accident; and (5) accidental death and dismemberment. Dental insurance, eyeglass insurance, and legal expense insurance may be included. These plans are established for the reasons of morale, to reduce turnover, and for tax benefits (contributions are usually deductible as business expenses to employers and not currently taxable income to employees).

EMPLOYEE CONTRIBUTIONS workers' premiums in a contributory employee benefit plan.

EMPLOYEE DEATH BENEFITS *see* EMPLOYEE BENEFIT INSURANCE PLAN.

EMPLOYEE DISHONESTY *see* FIDELITY BOND.

EMPLOYEE FRIENDLY BENEFITS employee benefit plan that provides such benefits as long-term care insurance, dependent care spending amounts, sabbaticals, and parental leave.

EMPLOYEE HEALTH BENEFITS *see* EMPLOYEE BENEFIT INSURANCE PLAN.

EMPLOYEE RETIREMENT INCOME SECURITY ACT OF 1974 (ERISA) law that established rules and regulations to govern private pension plans, including vesting requirements, funding mechanisms, and general plan design and descriptions. For example, three ways of vesting were established: full vesting after 10 years of service (Cliff Vesting); FIVE TO FIFTEEN YEAR RULE (at least 25% of benefits vest at end of 5 years of service, 5% each year during the next 5 years, and 10% each year during the next 5 years); and Rule of 45 (when employee's age and years of service add up to 45), 50% of the benefits must be vested with 10% additional vesting each year thereafter.

Under the TAX REFORM ACT OF 1986, vesting requirements were changed to 100% vesting after 5 years of service or 20% vesting after 3 years of service, 40% at the end of 4 years of service, 60% at the end of 5 years of service, 80% at the end of 6 years of service and 100% at the end of 7 years of service. (These vesting requirements were effective as of January 1, 1989.) With the passage of the PENSION PROTECTION ACT OF 2006, employer nonelective contributions as well as employer matching contributions must vest according to either the minimum three-year cliff or six-year graded vesting schedule: year 1 = 0% vested, year 2 = 20% vested, year 3 = 40% vested, year 4 = 60% vested, year 5 = 80% vested, year 6 = 100% vested.

EMPLOYEE RETIREMENT INCOME SECURITY ACT OF 1974 (ERISA) BOND federal law requiring that all PENSION PLAN trustees and anyone else who handles pension funds must obtain a FIDELITY BOND. This bond covers the plan in the event of embezzlement and theft. It is important to note that this bond does not provide coverage in the event poor investment choices result in losses. The insurance company as well as the amount of the bond must be stated in FORM 5500 filed annually with the Internal Revenue Service. The amount of the bond must be at least 10% of the pension plan's assets or $1000, whichever is the greatest amount.

EMPLOYEE SAVINGS PLAN type of RETIREMENT PLAN in which both the employee and the employer contributes. *See also* PAYROLL DEDUCTION INSURANCE.

EMPLOYEE STOCK OWNERSHIP PLAN (ESOP) TRUST type of benefit in which an employee obtains shares of stock in the company, the amount normally determined by the employee's level of compensation. ESOP acts as a leverage tool through which the business is able to obtain a source of capital. The procedure is for a lender (usually a bank) to lend money to the ESOP. The ESOP then takes the borrowed money to buy stock from the company's treasury. In the meantime, the ESOP has signed a note with the lender for the borrowed funds with the stock pledged as collateral for the loan, and the business has guaranteed repayment if the ESOP fails to do so. The stock held in the ESOP is allocated to each employee as the business pays its contributions into the ESOP. The ESOP uses the company's contributions to repay the loan and the interest thereon. The contributions per employee that the company makes into the ESOP are tax deductible, and they are not taxable to the employee until the benefits are received.

EMPLOYER CREDITS in a pension plan that an employer is required to make against future contributions (other than a cash basis as required by the IRS). Such credits may arise when an employee leaves an employer prior to being fully *vested,* or works beyond normal retirement age.

EMPLOYERS CONTINGENT ESCROWING OF ASSETS LIA-BILITY *see* EMPLOYERS CONTINGENT NET WORTH LIABILITY DETERMINATION.

EMPLOYERS CONTINGENT INSURANCE COVERAGE LIABILITY coverage mandated by the EMPLOYEE RETIREMENT INCOME SECURITY ACT OF 1974 (ERISA) under which employers are required to purchase insurance to cover their contingent liability for unfunded employee pension benefits in the event a pension plan is terminated. This requirement is enforced by the PENSION BENEFIT GUARANTY CORPORATION (PBGC).

EMPLOYERS CONTINGENT LIABILITY *see* EMPLOYERS CONTINGENT INSURANCE COVERAGE LIABILITY; EMPLOYERS CONTINGENT LIEN AGAINST ASSETS LIABILITY.

EMPLOYERS CONTINGENT LIEN AGAINST ASSETS LIABILITY claim (lien) of the PENSION BENEFIT GUARANTY CORPORATION (PBGC) against an employer's assets upon termination of a pension plan for the amount of an employee's unfunded benefits.

EMPLOYERS CONTINGENT NET WORTH LIABILITY DETERMINATION requirement upon termination of a pension plan; an employer must reimburse the PENSION BENEFIT GUARANTY CORPORATION (PBGC) for any loss that the PBGC incurs as the result of paying employee benefits that were the responsibility of the employer. The law requires reimbursement of up to 30% of the plan's net worth without regard to any contingent liability. This net worth is increased by escrowing or transferring any assets by the employer in contemplation of the plan's termination.

EMPLOYERS INSURANCE *see* BUSINESS AUTOMOBILE POLICY (BAP); BUSINESS CRIME INSURANCE; BUSINESS INCOME COVERAGE FORM; BUSINESS LIFE AND HEALTH INSURANCE; BUSINESS PROPERTY AND LIABILITY INSURANCE PACKAGE; BUSINESSOWNERS POLICY (BOP).

EMPLOYERS LEGAL OBLIGATION TO FUND pension plan format. After deciding how much to contribute, the employer can suspend, reduce, or discontinue contributions during the first 10 years only for reasons of business necessity; otherwise the employer will face a substantial IRS tax penalty. If a plan is terminated or if contributions to the plan are discontinued, the employer is only liable for benefit payments for which contributions were previously made.

EMPLOYERS LIABILITY COVERAGE *see* WORKERS COMPENSATION, COVERAGE B.

EMPLOYERS NET WORTH *see* EMPLOYERS CONTINGENT NET WORTH LIABILITY DETERMINATION.

EMPLOYERS NONOWNERSHIP LIABILITY INSURANCE coverage for the employer in the event of a TORT committed by an employee in the use of his or her own car while conducting business on behalf of the employer.

EMPLOYMENT COST INDEX measurement of the changes in labor costs for money wages and salaries and noncash fringe benefits in nonfarm private industry and state and local governments for employees. The statistics are provided on a quarterly basis by the United States Bureau of Labor Statistics.

EMPLOYMENT PRACTICES LIABILITY COVERAGE plan that provides protection in the event of legal actions resulting from charges of harassment, discrimination, wrongful termination of employment, defamation, and invasion of privacy.

ENCUMBRANCE claim, such as a worker's lien, to property under the care, custody, and control of another. This situation occurs when a worker is not paid for labor provided. For example, a carpenter unable to collect payment for installing wood finishings seeks an encumbrance on the owner's property.

ENDORSEMENT written agreement attached to a policy to add or subtract insurance coverages. Once attached, the endorsement takes precedence over the original provisions of the policy. For example, under a homeowners policy an inflation guard endorsement is used so that property damage limits are increased automatically to reflect an increase in the cost of construction in the community. Vandalism and malicious mischief can be added to the *Standard Fire Policy* through an endorsement.

ENDORSEMENT SPLIT DOLLAR LIFE INSURANCE type of SPLIT DOLLAR LIFE INSURANCE where the employer is the policyowner. The employer owns the total CASH SURRENDER VALUE. The employer's share of the DEATH BENEFIT equals the cash value of the policy. These cash values can also be used to fund a SALARY CONTINUATION PLAN on the employee's retirement.

ENDOWMENT ANNUITY INSURANCE INSURANCE POLICY that combines the elements of a DEFERRED ANNUITY with the elements of DECREASING TERM LIFE INSURANCE. This policy was originally designed to act as a funding instrument for PENSION PLANS but is rarely used today.

ENDOWMENT INSURANCE life insurance under which an insured receives the face value of a policy if the individual survives the endowment period. If the insured does not survive, a beneficiary receives the face value of the policy. An endowment policy is the most expensive type of life insurance.

ENERGY-RELEASE THEORY (OF ACCIDENT CAUSATION) method, developed in 1970 by Dr. William Haddon, Jr., of classifying and preventing damage caused by accidents. The thesis is that accidents are caused by the transfer of energy with such force that bodily injury and property damage result. According to Dr. Haddon, strategies can interrupt or suppress the chain of accident-causing events. These strategies revolve around (1) control and prevention of buildup of energy that is inherently injurious; (2) creation of an environment that is not conducive to injurious buildup of energy; and (3) production of counteractive measures to injurious buildup of energy.

ENGINEERING APPROACH approach in loss prevention placing emphasis on physical features of the workplace as a potential cause of injuries. For example, if a product is inherently dangerous in design or during manufacture, an insurance company may assign an engineer to analyze the situation and recommend changes that could improve safety and lower insurance premiums.

ENHANCED ORDINARY LIFE modified PARTICIPATING level coverage permanent life insurance policy under which the dividends are credited to the policy, thereby reducing the premiums below that usually charged for an ordinary life insurance policy. The structure of the policy is such that the dividends are used to purchase increments of PAID-UP ADDITIONS of permanent life insurance. As the FACE AMOUNT (FACE OF POLICY) is reduced (usually after 2, 3, or 4 years that the policy is issued), the accumulated paid-up additions are generally sufficient to make up the difference between the reduced face amount of insurance and the initial face amount of insurance purchased. The purpose of this approach is to maintain the DEATH BENEFIT at a level at least equal to the original amount of insurance purchased. Most of these policies guarantee that the death benefit will not fall below the original amount of insurance purchased, regardless of the fact that the dividends prove to be inadequate to purchase sufficient amounts of paid-up additions.

Another approach to the structuring of this product is to stipulate that the face amount of the policy is equal to 50 to 90% of the death benefit. The difference between the face amount and the death benefit is comprised of paid-up additions of permanent insurance and term insurance purchased by the dividends. This procedure will guarantee that the payable death benefit will not fall below that initially purchased. As time goes on, the aggregate paid-up additions should be sufficient so that it is no longer required that term insurance be purchased.

ENROLLED ACTUARY *see* ACTUARY, ENROLLED.

ENROLLMENT CARD document used to sign up employees for plans such as salary savings, life insurance, or other employee benefits.

ENTERPRISE RISK summation of all risks to which a business is subject include PURE RISK; SPECULATIVE RISK; DYNAMIC RISK; STATIC RISK; BUSINESS RISK; INTEREST RATE RISK; POLITICAL RISK; PARTICULAR RISK; FUNDAMENTAL RISK; and PURCHASING POWER RISK. *See also* FINANCIAL RISK MANAGEMENT.

ENTERPRISE RISK MANAGEMENT complete RISK MANAGEMENT program that analyzes the company's PURE RISK; SPECULATIVE RISK; DYNAMIC RISK; STATIC RISK; BUSINESS RISK; INTEREST RATE RISK; PARTIC- ULAR RISK; FUNDAMENTAL RISK; POLITICAL RISK; and PURCHASING POWER RISK.

ENTIRE CONTRACT CLAUSE feature of life and health insurance policies that stipulates that the policy represents the whole agreement between the insurance company and the insured, and that there are no other outstanding agreements.

ENTITY PLAN *see* PARTNERSHIP LIFE AND HEALTH INSURANCE.

ENURE CLAUSE in an INSURANCE POLICY stipulating that the benefits under the policy will accrue to the right of the INSURED. For example, if the insured leaves a violin at a repair shop and that violin, which is insured under the HOMEOWNERS INSURANCE POLICY, is stolen, the insurance company will pay the benefits to the insured and not to the repair shop.

ENVIRONMENTAL IMPAIRMENT LIABILITY negligent acts and/or omissions by the individual(s) and the organization(s) resulting in damage to the environment. For example, pollution of the environ- ment suits against manufacturers are quite common today. The pollu- tion risk is an excluded uninsurable risk under most liability policies; however, insurance coverage in some instances is becoming available under ENVIRONMENTAL IMPAIRMENT LIABILITY (EIL) INSURANCE policies.

ENVIRONMENTAL IMPAIRMENT LIABILITY (EIL) INSUR- ANCE coverage in the event that negligent acts and/or omissions by individual(s) and organization(s) result in damage to the environment and a liability suit against these parties.

ENVIROSOURCES search engine site that emphasizes the fields of envi- ronmental risk management, environmental engineering, environmental planning, physical and biological sciences, and various environmental issues of public interest. Web site is *http://www.envirosource.com.*

EQUAL SHARES type of APPORTIONMENT CLAUSE in which insurance companies share equally in the claim up to their own policy limit.

EQUIPMENT BREAKDOWN INSURANCE covers losses resulting from the malfunction of boilers and machinery pressure, mechanical and electrical equipment. Most property insurance policies exclude these losses, which is why a separate EQUIPMENT BREAKDOWN POLICY or a COMMERCIAL PACKAGE POLICY is needed. The insurance covers business property, other property involved, and legal fees, if any. Formerly referenced as BOILER AND MACHINERY INSURANCE.

EQUIPMENT DEALERS INSURANCE coverage on ALL RISKS basis for such items as binders, reapers, harvesters, plows, tractors, pneumatic tools and compressors, bulldozers, and road scrapers. Excluded from coverage are wear and tear, loss due to delay, loss of market, consequential loss such as loss of income because of damage to the equipment, and mechanical breakdown. Property excluded includes aircraft, water craft, motor vehicles, and property sold on an installment contract basis after it has left the care, custody, and control of the insured dealer.

EQUIPMENT FLOATERS INSURANCE coverage for property that moves from location to location from the perils of fire, lightning, explosion, windstorm, earthquake, collapse of bridges, flood, collision under one of the following forms: AGRICULTURAL EQUIPMENT INSURANCE; CONTRACTORS EQUIPMENT FLOATER; LIVESTOCK INSURANCE; PHYSICIANS AND SURGEONS EQUIPMENT INSURANCE.

EQUITIES representation of ownership rights such as stocks.

EQUITY fairness (as an objective of insurance pricing). Premium rates are set according to expectation of loss among a classification of policyowners. The premise is that all insureds with the same characteristics should have the same expectation of loss and should be listed under the same underwriting classification. For example, in life insurance, individuals with a good personal health history, family health history, a job with no special hazards, and who are of good character, should be classified as standard risks and thereby pay standard rates.

EQUITY AMONG POLICYOWNERS grouping of applicants for life insurance according to expected mortality, so as to produce an underwriting classification in which the spread between health of the worst and best applicant is not so great as to skew the distribution curve.

EQUITY ANNUITIES *see* VARIABLE DOLLAR ANNUITY.

EQUITY INDEXED ANNUITY modifications of the SINGLE PREMIUM DEFFERED ANNUITY, which usually guarantees at a minimum a return of a stipulated amount (usually at least 90% of the single premium accumulated at the annual rate of 3 or 4%). Additional interest can be earned that is linked to an increasing specified stock index. Thus, this insurance product guarantees the principal of the investment (single premium), while at the same time providing the opportunity for increasing values tied to the equities market. Under the STANDARD NONFORFEITURE LAW, there must be guaranteed at the minimum 90% of the single premium accumulated at a rate of at least 3% interest per year. The index most often used as a link to this product is the S&P 500. Should the equity index increase, the invested single premium could be credited with a percentage of that increase, typically ranging from 50 to 100% of that increase. These contracts have terms ranging from one to fifteen years and at the end of the term, the owner/ANNUITANT can start a new term or transfer the CASH VALUE to another product. Should the contract be terminated before the end of a term, frequently the owner/annuitant forfeits all index gains and will receive only the minimum return guaranteed.

EQUITY INDEXED UNIVERSAL LIFE INSURANCE insurance in which most of the premium (generally 80 to 90%) is invested in traditional fixed income securities. The remainder of the premium is invested in call option contracts tied to a stipulated stock index. In those instances where there is an increase in the market, exercising of the option contracts takes place and a given percentage of the gain is then credited to the policy. Conversely, should the market decline, the option contracts are said to expire worthlessly and the policy is credited with the minimum guaranteed rate. This type of policy may be suitable for that person who has an interest in purchasing a VARIABLE LIFE INSURANCE policy but is not at ease in participating in the equities market. This type of person could have the best of both worlds: the potential high returns of the equities market without the risk to the initial investment (principal).

EQUITY, POLICYOWNERS *see* POLICYOWNERS EQUITY.

EQUITY SPLIT DOLLAR LIFE INSURANCE *see* SPLIT DOLLAR LIFE INSURANCE.

ERGONOMICS RISK MANAGEMENT control device used to minimize accidents and injuries to employees resulting from an unsafe working environment. For example, potential CUMULATIVE TRAUMA DISORDERS losses may be lowered by using office furniture that reduces the physical and mental stress resulting from repetitive motions, such as constantly reading a computer screen.

ERISA *see* EMPLOYEE RETIREMENT INCOME SECURITY ACT OF 1974 (ERISA).

ERRORS AND OMISSIONS LIABILITY INSURANCE policies generally available to the various professions that require protection for negligent acts and/or omissions resulting in bodily injury, personal injury, and/or property damage liability to a client. For example, insurance agents are constantly exposed to the claim that inadequate or improper coverage was recommended, resulting in the client suffering a loss of indemnification. If sustained, the agent (or the carrier) would have to make good the claim of the client without the adequate insurance coverage.

ESCROW ACCOUNT funds that the lender collects monthly to pay the monthly MORTGAGE INSURANCE premiums, HOMEOWNERS INSURANCE POLICY premiums, and yearly property taxes.

ESTATE sum total of the ASSETS owned by an individual.

ESTATE EQUALIZATION technique of ESTATE PLANNING under which an estate is divided into two parts and taxed at a lower rate rather than remaining as a whole and taxed at a higher rate. This division may be necessary because of the progressive nature of the FEDERAL ESTATE TAX.

ESTATE PLANNING procedure for accumulating, conserving, and distributing personal wealth. In essence, estate planning focuses on enhancement of the value of an estate and its conservation. At the death of an owner, estate planning seeks to transfer the estate to the heir(s) with a minimum loss in taxes and other expenses. Depending on the size and nature of an estate, the expertise of one or more of these specialists may be useful: lawyer, accountant, life insurance agent, banker, or a qualified financial or estate planner.

ESTATE PLANNING, DEATH PLANNING *see* ESTATE PLANNING; ESTATE PLANNING DISTRIBUTION.

ESTATE PLANNING DISTRIBUTION plan that involves distribution of property by living hand and distribution of property after the death of its owner. Distribution by living hand can take the form of an outright gift, a grant of limited property interest, or a gift in trust. Distribution at death can be accomplished through a will or, if there is no will, as directed by state law. Common terms include:

Beneficiary of Trust person who receives the benefits of the trust.

Life Estate property that can be used in any manner that pleases the donee during his/her life. Upon the death of the donee, the property reverts to the donor or the donor's estate.

Living Trust property distributed by living individuals.

Personal Trust one in which an owner of property gives it to another person to safeguard, hold, and use for the benefit of a third party.

Power of Appointment owner of a property grants the right to another person to decide who should receive title to the property.

Tenancy donee has the right to use property and to receive income it generates for a limited time, whereupon the property reverts to the owner.

Testamentary Trust property disposed at the death of the trustor, who has previously described what property is to be placed in the trust, how it is to be managed, and who is to be the trustee. The trustor can change the provisions of the trust by a will. But at the death of the trustor, the testamentary trust becomes irrevocable.

Trustee person to whom a trustor transfers property. The trustee is obligated to safeguard, manage, and use the property in accordance with the terms and conditions of the trust.

Trustor individual who puts his/her thoughts in writing concerning the terms of the trust and the process of transferring the property to the trustee.

ESTATE PLANNING, LIFE PLANNING *see* ESTATE PLANNING; ESTATE PLANNING DISTRIBUTION.

ESTATE SETTLEMENT COSTS expenses connected with resolving an estate to include medical expenditures, funeral expenditures, probate expenditures, estate taxes, legal fees, and other administrative expenditures.

ESTATE SHRINKAGE decline in an estate's value, when the estate owner dies, because of death-related expenses to include estate taxes, estate administration costs, funeral expenses, and outstanding estate debts. Through proper ESTATE PLANNING, this shrinkage can be minimized.

ESTATE TAX *see* FEDERAL ESTATE TAX.

ESTATE TRANSFERS conveying of assets from the donor to the beneficiary as a means of minimizing the legal tax obligation of the estate of the donor and avoiding PROBATE.

ESTIMATED PREMIUM method of premium payment under which a temporary premium is charged based on projected loss experience. At the end of the year this premium is adjusted to reflect the actual loss experience. *See also* RETROSPECTIVE RATING.

ESTOPPEL stop or bar, such that one party makes a statement upon which a second party has every reason to rely, thereby preventing the first party from denying the validity of that statement. For example, the misleading actions of an agent of the insurance company result in the insured being estopped from having to perform according to the provisions of the contract.

EVIDENCE CLAUSE clause requiring an insured to cooperate with an insurance company by producing all evidence requested in settlement of a claim. The company may have difficulty settling a claim without the proper examination and documentation of evidence.

EVIDENCE OF INSURABILITY documentation of physical fitness by an applicant for insurance. Usually this takes the form of a medical examination. Group plans (life, health, disability) require such evidence if the 30-day eligibility period expires before the employee has applied for coverage. *See also* ELIGIBILITY PERIOD.

EXAMINATION *see* CONVENTION EXAMINATION; MEDICAL EXAMINATION.

EXAMINED BUSINESS life or health insurance policy written on an applicant who has passed a MEDICAL EXAMINATION and signed the APPLICATION but has not paid the premium due.

EXAMINER

Life and Health: physician appointed by an insurance company to examine applicants for insurance. *See also* EXAMINED BUSINESS.

Regulatory: representative of the COMMISSIONER OF INSURANCE who conducts an audit of the insurance company's records. *See also* CONVENTION EXAMINATION.

EXCEPTED PERIOD *see* ELIMINATION PERIOD; PROBATIONARY PERIOD.

EXCEPTION *see* EXCLUSIONS; EXCLUSIONS, BUSINESS LIABILITY INSURANCE; EXCLUSIONS FROM MEDICAL BENEFITS EXEMPTION; EXCLUSIONS, HOMEOWNERS INSURANCE; EXCLUSIONS, PROPERTY AND CASUALTY INSURANCE.

EXCESS BENEFIT TRANSACTION transaction by a tax-exempt organization with a person from inside the organization (DISQUALIFIED PERSON) that provides an economic benefit to that person that is in excess of the value of the consideration received. Compensation that is deemed to be unreasonable comprises an excess benefit and is subject to a penalty excise tax under SECTION 4958 OF THE INTERNAL REVENUE CODE.

EXCESS INSURANCE layer of property, liability, or health coverage above or in excess of the primary amount or layer of insurance. For example, the primary coverage is $100,000 and the excess insurance is $1 million. After the losses exceed $100,000, the excess insurance will pay for the losses up to a total of $1 million.

EXCESS INTEREST amount credited to the cash value of an insured's life insurance policy above the minimum interest rate it guarantees. This payment is of extreme importance to a policyowner since it will directly affect the size of the cash value. *See also* CASH VALUE LIFE INSURANCE.

EXCESS INTEREST WHOLE LIFE INSURANCE type of insurance under which it is assumed that the interest earned will exceed the interest rate guaranteed. Excess interest is credited to the policyowner in the following manner:
1. in a mutual company—paid to policyowners through the policy dividend structure.
2. in a stock company—paid to policyowners through their cash values or future premiums due. *See also* CURRENT ASSUMPTION WHOLE LIFE INSURANCE.

EXCESS LIMIT in a LIABILITY INSURANCE policy, limit above the minimum amount of coverage for which the policy can be written according to company or legal restrictions. *See also* EXCESS INSURANCE.

EXCESS LINE BROKER (SURPLUS LINE BROKER) insurance salesperson who is licensed to place coverage with an insurance company that is not licensed to do business in the state of domicile of the broker. The excess line coverage must be unavailable from a company licensed in the broker's state.

EXCESS LOSS COVER *see* EXCESS OF LOSS REINSURANCE.

EXCESS MAJOR MEDICAL INSURANCE type of policy that pays only after limits of the MAJOR MEDICAL INSURANCE policy have been exhausted.

EXCESS (NONPROPORTIONAL) REINSURANCE *see* EXCESS OF LOSS REINSURANCE.

EXCESS OF LOSS REINSURANCE method whereby an insurer pays the amount of each claim for each risk up to a limit determined in advance and the reinsurer pays the amount of the claim above that limit up to a specific sum. For example, assume that an insurer issues automobile liability policies of $150,000 on any one risk and retains the first $50,000 of any risk. The insurer purchases excess loss reinsurance for $100,000 in excess of $50,000 on any one risk. The insurer pays the first $50,000 of all losses, and the reinsurer pays any excess amount up to a maximum of $100,000.

EXCESS OF TIME REINSURANCE term used in the reinsuring of DISABILITY INCOME INSURANCE policies in that, after an extended period of time expires (in addition to the ELIMINATION PERIOD found in the disability income policy), the REINSURER usually reimburses the CEDING COMPANY for approximately 70 to 80% of the monthly disability income payment that the ceding company is required to pay the POLICYHOLDER.

EXCESS PER RISK REINSURANCE *see* EXCESS OF LOSS REINSURANCE.

EXCESS POLICY policy that pays benefits only when coverage under other applicable insurance policies has become exhausted. For example, the *personal umbrella liability* policy pays after the liability limits in the homeowners insurance policy have been exceeded.

EXCESS-SURPLUS LINES *see* SURPLUS LINES (EXCESS-SURPLUS LINES).

EXCHANGE *see* NEW YORK INSURANCE EXCHANGE.

EXCHANGE RATE relationship of the value of one country's currency expressed in terms of the value of another country's currency.

EXCLUDED PERIL *see* EXCLUSIONS; EXCLUSIONS, BUSINESS LIABILITY INSURANCE; EXCLUSIONS FROM MEDICAL BENEFITS EXEMPTION; EXCLUSIONS, HOMEOWNERS INSURANCE; EXCLUSIONS, MEDICAL BENEFITS; EXCLUSIONS, PROPERTY AND CASUALTY INSURANCE.

EXCLUDED PERIOD *see* PROBATIONARY PERIOD.

EXCLUDED PROPERTY *see* EXCLUSIONS, BUSINESS LIABILITY INSURANCE; EXCLUSIONS, PROPERTY AND CASUALTY INSURANCE.

EXCLUSION RATIO *see* TAX DEFERRED ANNUITY.

EXCLUSION RIDER ENDORSEMENT attached to an insurance policy that eliminates coverage for certain specified PERILS.

EXCLUSIONS provision in an insurance policy that indicates what is denied coverage. For example, common exclusions are: hazards deemed so catastrophic in nature that they are uninsurable, such as war; wear and tear, since they are expected through the use of a product; property covered by other insurance, in order to eliminate duplication that would profit the insured; liability arising out of contracts; and liability arising out of Workers Compensation laws. Exclusions are also listed in a BOILER AND MACHINERY INSURANCE policy, BUSINESS AUTOMOBILE POLICY, BUSINESS INCOME COVERAGE FORM, HOMEOWNERS INSURANCE POLICY, *Liability Policy,* and COMMERCIAL PACKAGE POLICY.

EXCLUSIONS, BUSINESS LIABILITY INSURANCE provision used to avoid duplication of coverage in other policies; to eliminate coverage for property under the care, custody, and control of an insured business; as well as to avoid liability arising out of contractual obligations between the insured business and another party; liability associated with recall of the insured business's products; liability associated with the insured business's pollution and contamination exposure; and liability that may arise if the insured business is found to be in conflict with state liquor regulations.

EXCLUSIONS FROM MEDICAL BENEFITS EXEMPTION found under the "Exceptions and Exclusions Section for All Medical Benefits" in many health insurance policies that exclude:
1. complications arising from elective, nontherapeutic voluntary abortion.
2. necessary cosmetic surgery for the immediate repair of a nonoccupational disease, illness, accident, or injury.
3. custom-built orthopedic shoes, wedges, or arch supports.
4. speech therapy ordered by a physician to restore partial or complete loss of speech resulting from stroke, cancer, radiation laryngitis, or cerebral palsy.
5. services, supplies, or treatment in connection with or related to endogenous obesity or obesity resulting from external causes that the physician certifies is associated with a serious or life-threatening disorder.

EXCLUSIONS FROM MEDICAL BENEFITS GROUP HEALTH INSURANCE *see* EXCLUSIONS, MEDICAL BENEFITS; EXCLUSIONS FROM MEDICAL BENEFITS EXEMPTION.

EXCLUSIONS, HOMEOWNERS INSURANCE provision that excludes from coverage under *Form No. 3*: flood damage, except if the flood causes a fire, explosion, or theft; water damage from the backup of sewers; earthquake, except if the earthquake causes a fire explosion, theft, or glass breakage; war; nuclear exposure (hazard); wear and tear;

vandalism and malicious mischief, or glass breakage if the house has been vacant for more than 30 consecutive days before the day of the loss.

EXCLUSIONS, MEDICAL BENEFITS limiting provision. Exclusions listed in group health plans include: benefits under Workers Compensation; certain dental procedures; convalescent or rest cures; medical expenses resulting from the insured person and/or covered dependents committing a felony or misdemeanor; cosmetic surgery, unless required immediately because of non-occupational disease, illness, accident, injury, or congenital anomaly in an insured newborn infant; expenses incurred by a member of a HEALTH MAINTENANCE ORGANIZATION (HMO) or other prepaid medical plan; expenses associated with intentional self-inflicted injuries or attempt at suicide; unreasonable charges for services or supplies; convenience items such as telephone and television.

EXCLUSIONS OF POLICY *see* EXCLUSION.

EXCLUSIONS, PROPERTY AND CASUALTY INSURANCE denial of coverage for various perils (such as war, flood); hazards (storing dynamite in the home, thereby increasing the chance of loss); property (such as pets); and locations. These are excluded because they are uninsurable by nature in that the loss frequency and severity do not lend themselves to accurate predictions, the premium rates chargeable would be prohibitive, and in some instances coverages are found in other policies.

EXCLUSIVE AGENCY SYSTEM *see* CAPTIVE AGENT.

EXCLUSIVE AGENT *see* CAPTIVE AGENT.

EXCLUSIVE PROVIDER ORGANIZATION (EPO) organization that is part of a PREFERRED PROVIDER ORGANIZATION (PPO) in which enrollees select an EPO provider to act as their primary care physician and serve as the gatekeeper. This gatekeeper approves the maximum level of benefits to which the enrollee is entitled. Characteristics of the EPO include emphasis placed on quality of care, utilization of the primary physician, and specified financial structure with the providers on a fee-for-service basis.

EXCLUSIVE REMEDY a procedure in which the employer has ABSOLUTE LIABILITY for the injuries incurred by the employee and the employee does not have the right to sue the employer for those injuries suffered. (For job related injuries under WORKERS COMPENSATION INSURANCE, the sole source of funds for the injured employee is the WORKERS COMPENSATION BENEFITS.)

EXCULPATORY PROVISION clause in legal contracts that excuses a given party to the contract from liability for unintentional negligent acts and/or omissions.

EXECUTOR fiduciary named in a will to settle an estate of a deceased person. The executor must act as a reasonably prudent man in safeguarding that property in his care, custody, and control. Insurance coverages are available for executors. *See also* FIDELITY BOND.

EXECUTOR FUND monies held by the EXECUTOR to pay the deceased's estate expenses to include outstanding debts, FEDERAL ESTATE TAX, and INHERITANCE TAX.

EXECUTRIX woman executor. *See also* EXECUTOR.

EXEMPLARY DAMAGES *see* LIABILITY, CIVIL DAMAGES AWARDED.

EXEMPTION size of estate passing free from estate and gift of taxes. The exempted amount as of January 1, 2008, is $2,000,000.

EX GRATIA PAYMENT "from favor" payment by an insurance company to an insured even though the company has no legal liability. The company makes such a payment for goodwill purposes.

EXHAUSTIVE resulting when all possible outcomes from all the events being studied have been considered.

EXHIBITION INSURANCE coverage provided on an ALL RISKS basis for an exhibitor whose product, while being displayed at a public exhibition, is damaged or destroyed by a peril that is not specifically excluded in the policy.

EXPECTATION OF LIFE *see* LIFE EXPECTANCY.

EXPECTATION OF LOSS *see* EXPECTED LOSS.

EXPECTED EXPENSE RATIO relationship between expected incurred insurance-related costs (not including claims) and expected written premiums. *See also* EXPENSE RATIO; MANUAL RATE; RATE MAKING.

EXPECTED EXPENSES anticipated insurance-related costs, not including claims-related costs.

EXPECTED LOSS probability of loss upon which a basic premium rate is calculated.

EXPECTED LOSS RATIO proportion of a premium allocated to pay losses, which is equivalent to (1.00 — EXPENSE RATIO).

EXPECTED MORBIDITY expectation of illness or injury. The probability of such occurrence is shown by a MORBIDITY TABLE, which is important in determining the premiums for health insurance policies.

EXPECTED MORTALITY expectation of death. The probability of its occurrence is shown by a MORTALITY TABLE, which is important in determining the premiums for life insurance policies.

EXPECTED VALUE sum of money to be received by an insured in the event a given loss occurs.

EXPEDITING EXPENSES payment by an insurance company to a damaged or destroyed business to hasten its return to normal business operations. For example, if a kitchen of a restaurant is damaged by fire, the insurance company may be willing to pay overtime wages to enable the restaurant to return to normal operations as soon as possible.

EXPENSE cost of doing business, not including pure *expectation of loss. See also* EXPENSE LOADING.

EXPENSE ALLOWANCE payment to an insurance agent in addition to commissions. Expense allowances, that differ from company to company, vary with the amount of business agents place with that company and the need of the company to attract future business.

EXPENSE CONSTANT flat dollar amount that is added to the PURE PREMIUM for an insured risk that is smaller than that of the lowest EXPERIENCE RATING band. This dollar amount serves the purpose of generating enough additional premium dollar to cover the cost of issuing and servicing an insurance policy on a risk whose size does not readily allow it to be experience rated.

EXPENSE LIABILITIES expenses and taxes incurred by the insurance company resulting from the normal business activities of the company before the due date of the ANNUAL STATEMENT.

EXPENSE INCURRED *see* INCURRED EXPENSE.

EXPENSE LIMITATION ceiling on expense reimbursement allowance, as stated in New York insurance law, that an insurance company licensed in New York State can give its agents. This is one reason why a company that is admitted (licensed) in all states but New York may have a sister company doing business only in New York State. If an insurance company is not admitted in New York State, it can allocate greater expense allowances and commissions to agents, thereby attracting more of their business.

EXPENSE LOADING amount added to the basic premium (expectation of loss) to cover an insurance company's expenses. These expenses include agent commissions, premium taxes, costs of putting a policy on the books, marketing support costs, and contingencies. CURRENT ASSUMPTIONS products, in order to be competitive, must emphasize low expense loadings. Companies that sell these products make special efforts to control expenses.

EXPENSE RATIO formula used by insurance companies to relate income and expenses:

$$\text{Expense Ratio} = \frac{\text{Incurred Insurance} - \text{Related Expenses}}{\text{Written Premiums}}$$

This ratio is of critical importance to the insurance company since it reflects the percentage of the premiums income that goes for expenses; that is, how much it costs the company to acquire the premiums, a key element in today's competitive marketplace.

EXPENSE REIMBURSEMENT ALLOWANCE *see* EXPENSE ALLOWANCE.

EXPENSE RESERVE insurance company's liability for incurred but unpaid expenses. *See also* INCURRED BUT NOT REPORTED LOSSES (IBNR).

EXPENSE RISK measure of the sensitivity of the insurance company's liability for the resultant higher expense rates than charged for in the premium.

EXPENSES OF REPLACEMENT *see* VALUABLE PAPERS (RECORDS) INSURANCE.

EXPENSES PAID funds paid by an INSURANCE COMPANY associated with the normal costs of doing business other than the costs of claims payments.

EXPERIENCE record of losses, whether or not insured. This record is used in predicting future losses and in developing premium rates based on *expectation of insured losses.*

EXPERIENCE ACCOUNT loss experience of a given insured.

EXPERIENCED MORBIDITY actual morbidity experience of an insured group as compared to the EXPECTED MORBIDITY for that group.

EXPERIENCED MORTALITY actual mortality experience of an insured group as compared to the EXPECTED MORTALITY for that group.

EXPERIENCE MODIFICATION adjustment of premiums resulting from the use of EXPERIENCE RATINGS. Experience rating plans take the form of *retrospective plans* or *prospective plans.* Under retrospective plans, premiums are modified after the fact. That is, once the policy period ends, premiums are adjusted to reflect actual loss experience of an insured. In contrast, under prospective plans, an insured's past experience (usually for the immediate preceding three years) is used to determine the premium for the current year of coverage.

EXPERIENCE, POLICY YEAR *see* POLICY YEAR EXPERIENCE.

EXPERIENCE RATING statistical procedure used to calculate a premium rate based on the loss experience of an insured group. Applied in group insurance, it is the opposite of manual rates. Here the premiums paid are related to actual claims and expense experience expected for that specific group. In PROSPECTIVE RATING, the past three years loss experience of the insured is the basis for the premium calculation for the current year of coverage. In RETROSPECTIVE RATING, the current premium rate for the current period of time is modified at the close of that period to reflect actual loss experience. The premium actually paid then can be adjusted, subject to a pre-agreed minimum and maximum rate.

EXPERIENCE REFUND return of a percentage of premium paid by a business firm if its loss record is better than the amount loaded into the basic premium. *See also* EXPERIENCE MODIFICATION.

EXPIRATION termination date of coverage as indicated on the insurance policy. *See also* EXPIRATION FILE.

EXPIRATION CARD *see* EXPIRATION FILE.

EXPIRATION DATE *see* EXPIRATION.

EXPIRATION FILE agents' records showing when clients' policies expire.

EXPIRATION NOTICE written notice to an insured showing date of termination of an insurance policy.

EXPIRY point in time when a TERM LIFE INSURANCE policy terminates its coverage.

EXPLOSION, COLLAPSE, AND UNDERGROUND EXCLUSION inherent danger resulting from certain construction procedures that are excluded from general business liability policies. Coverage for this exclusion can be acquired at an extra premium through an ENDORSEMENT to the various business liability policies.

EXPLOSION INSURANCE *see* EXTENDED COVERAGE ENDORSEMENT.

EXPORT-IMPORT BANK partnership between an agency of the U.S. government and the Foreign Credit Insurance Association (50 commercial insurance companies, both stock and mutual). Insures that businesses are indemnified for losses resulting from uncollectible accounts for goods sold in foreign markets. Additional perils covered are war, insurrection, confiscation, and/or currency devaluation. This coverage encourages American businesses to sell their products in foreign markets.

EXPORTING type of SURPLUS LINES in which an EXCESS LINES BROKER places insurance with an approved but NONADMITTED INSURER. The state publishes an export list identifying the types of insurance that an ADMITTED COMPANY does not write and thus may be transferred to surplus lines insurance companies.

EXPOSURE possibility of loss. The most cost efficient way to purchase insurance is to insure an unexpected loss with a low probability of occurrence. Insuring a loss with a high probability of occurrence means swapping dollars with an insurance company, since the premium charged would reflect the expected probability of loss. Expense and profit loadings would also be added by the insurer. *See also* SELF INSURANCE.

EXPOSURE UNIT used in PREMIUM calculations to measure a unit of RISK.

EXPRESSED WARRANTY *see* WARRANTY.

EXPROPRIATION INSURANCE coverage against foreign country expropriation underwritten by the OVERSEAS PRIVATE INVESTMENT CORPORATION (OPIC) for U.S.-owned companies investing in given developing countries.

EXTENDED COVERAGE ENDORSEMENT added to an INSURANCE POL-ICY or a CLAUSE found in an insurance policy that will provide additional coverage for RISKS to be insured other than those covered under the basic policy's PROVISIONS.

EXTENDED COVERAGE ENDORSEMENT extension of coverage available under the *Standard Fire Policy.* The standard policy only covers the perils of fire and lightning. The endorsement covers riot, riot attending a strike, civil commotion, smoke, aircraft and vehicle damage, windstorm, hail, and explosion.

EXTENDED NON-OWNED COVERAGE extension of coverage in the liability section of the PERSONAL AUTOMOBILE POLICY (PAP) and the BUSINESS AUTOMOBILE POLICY (BAP) to an INSURED who frequently drives non-owned automobiles.

EXTENDED PERIOD OF INDEMNITY type of INDEMNITY provision that permits the INSURED to seek compensation for a loss up to five years after its occurrence even though no claim was made during the POLICY PERIOD.

EXTENDED PERIOD OF INDEMNITY ENDORSEMENT type of ENDORSEMENT that compensates the insured for loss of income until the normal cash flow resumes.

EXTENDED REPLACEMENT COVERAGE type of HOMEOWNER INSURANCE POLICY—SECTION I (PROPERTY COVERAGE) that will pay the FACE AMOUNT (FACE OF POLICY) plus an additional 20 to 25% to repair or replace the home with one of like kind and quality regardless of the original cost.

EXTENDED REPORTING PERIOD INSURANCE (ERPI) policy underwritten on either a monoline primary insurance or monoline EXCESS INSURANCE basis that will allow the purchaser to increase the limits of liability coverage above that of policies already purchased as well as fill gaps in liability coverages. These policies usually provide liability protection on a worldwide basis to include coverage for bodily injury, property damage, products-completed operations, premises and operations, and personal injury. The period for claims reporting can be on a fixed or unlimited basis. Legal defense expenses and other supplementary expenses can be included within the policy limits or can be in addition to the policy limits. An endorsement can be added to provide coverage for known circumstances, thereby permitting the purchaser to retroactively add additional limits of coverage for current evolving liability situations. In addition, this policy can provide coverage for residual liability exposures by focusing on a particular risk.

EXTENDED TERM INSURANCE nonforfeiture option that uses the cash value of an ordinary life policy as a single premium to purchase term life insurance in the amount of the original policy. The length of the term policy depends on (1) the size of the cash value and (2) the attained age of the insured.

EXTORTION INSURANCE coverage in the event of threats to injure an insured or damage or destroy his property.

EXTRA DIVIDEND DIVIDEND paid in addition to the regular dividend on a PARTICIPATING INSURANCE policy.

EXTRA EXPENSE INSURANCE form that covers exposures associated with efforts to operate a business that is damaged by a peril such as fire. For example, a special electrical generator may have to be purchased in the event of a long-range loss of electricity if the business is to continue to operate.

EXTRA PERCENTAGE TABLES form of substandard ratings that shows additions to standard premiums to reflect physical impairments of applicants for life or health insurance. The additions reflect the greater probability of mortality or morbidity. *See also* SUBSTANDARD HEALTH INSURANCE; SUBSTANDARD LIFE INSURANCE.

EXTRA PREMIUM addition to reflect exposures with a greater probability of loss than standard exposures. For example, insuring a munitions factory obviously requires a premium greater than that required for insuring an accounting office.

EXTRATERRITORIALITY provision in WORKERS COMPENSATION INSURANCE under which an employee who incurs an injury in another state, and elects to come under the law of his home state, will retain coverage under the workers compensation policy.

F

401 (k) PLAN *see* SECTION 401 (K) PLAN (SALARY REDUCTION PLAN).

403 (b) PLAN *see* SECTION 403 (B) PLAN.

FACE first page of an insurance policy.

FACE AMOUNT (FACE OF POLICY) sum of insurance provided by a policy at death or maturity.

FACE OF POLICY *see* FACE AMOUNT (FACE OF POLICY).

FACE VALUE *see* PAR VALUE.

FACILITY OF PAYMENT CLAUSE element usually found in industrial life insurance policies under which the insurance company upon the death of the insured under certain conditions is allowed to choose the beneficiary if the beneficiary named in the policy is a minor or deceased. For example, the funeral home may receive a death benefit if the beneficiary is not alive.

FACILITY PLAN *see* AUTOMOBILE ASSIGNED RISK INSURANCE PLAN.

FACTORY INSURANCE ASSOCIATION (FIA) association of stock property insurance companies, formed to provide engineering services for member companies. These companies generally insure highly protected risks (risks characterized by a high degree of care taken for safety and potential loss reduction).

FACTORY MUTUAL organization of a group of insurers composed of mutual property and casualty insurance companies, a subsidiary stock insurance company, and a subsidiary safety engineering company. Their objective is to provide insurance and safety engineering services for large manufacturing companies, substantial housing projects, public institutions, and educational institutions. Coverage includes the perils of fire, explosion, windstorm, riot, civil commotion, sprinkler leakage, malicious mischief, damage to vehicles, and damage to aircraft. Field offices staffed by salaried personnel deal directly with insureds; there is no agency field force.

FACTUAL EXPECTATION strong expectation of an occurrence resulting in a monetary interest that gives rise to an insurable interest. For example, a daughter has a strong expectation of wearing her mother's wedding gown and thus has an insurable interest in the gown even though the gown is still the property of her mother.

FACULTATIVE REINSURANCE term under which the REINSURER exercises its faculty or prerogative to insure a risk or reject a risk from a CEDING COMPANY.

FACULTATIVE OBLIGATORY TREATY hybrid between FACULTATIVE REINSURANCE and *treaty reinsurance* where the CEDING COMPANY may elect to assign certain risks that the reinsurer is obligated to accept.

FACULTATIVE REINSURANCE individual risk offered by an insurer for acceptance or rejection by a reinsurer. Both parties are free to act in their own best interests regardless of any prior contractual arrangements. With proportional facultative reinsurance, the reinsurer assumes a proportional share of premiums and losses. On a nonproportional basis, the reinsurer is liable only for losses which exceed the insurer's retention level; premiums vary with loss expectation.

FAILURE MODE AND EFFECT ANALYSIS analytical procedure to predict the failure rate of a system still in the design stage.

FAILURE TO PERFORM EXCLUSION coverage that is excluded under COMMERCIAL GENERAL LIABILITY INSURANCE (COMPREHENSIVE GENERAL LIABILITY INSURANCE) for the loss of use of undamaged tangible real or personal property as the result of failure of the performance of a product or service as warranted or represented by the insured.

FAIR ACCESS TO INSURANCE REQUIREMENTS (FAIR) PLAN insurance that grew out of the urban demonstrations and riots of the 1960s. Because of the deteriorated social and economic circumstances in these areas, it became impossible for many business owners and homeowners to purchase property insurance. As a result, the federal government established the FAIR plans based on the stop loss reinsurance method. If a business owner or homeowner cannot purchase property insurance through conventional means, application can be made through an agent who represents an insurance company participating in the FAIR plan. If the property is acceptable to the company, insurance will be provided. If the property is deficient, improvements are suggested, and upon compliance the policy is issued.

FAIR CREDIT REPORTING ACT federal legislation giving an insurance applicant the right to contact a reporting organization doing a credit check and be advised of information contained in the applicant's file showing the reason for rejection for insurance.

FAIR PLAN *see* FAIR ACCESS TO INSURANCE REQUIREMENTS (FAIR) PLAN.

FAIR RENTAL VALUE *see* RENT INSURANCE.

FALLEN BUILDING CLAUSE section in some property insurance contracts that eliminates further coverage for buildings after they have collapsed from causes other than fire or explosion. For example, fire coverage would not be applicable to buildings that collapse because of inherent defects.

FALSE IMPRISONMENT tort of wrongful physical confinement of an individual. This is not restricted to physical confinement but includes any unjustified limitation of another's freedom of movement. If an individual is intimidated into responding to an order, the courts have interpreted this as false imprisonment.

FALSE PRETENSE *see* MISREPRESENTATION.

FAMILY AUTOMOBILE INSURANCE POLICY *see* PERSONAL AUTOMOBILE POLICY (PAP).

FAMILY CONSIDERATIONS factors influencing the amount of life insurance to purchase, such as marketable skills of spouse, age of children, savings, investments, number of future working years' expectancy, amount of bills and notes outstanding, and funds necessary to maintain the family's customary life-style should the wage earner die. *See also* LIFE INSURANCE.

FAMILY COVERAGE insurance coverage for the NAMED INSURED and his or her eligible dependents.

FAMILY EXPENSE INSURANCE type of health insurance under which an insured's coverage extends to all family members if they are residents of the insured's household. Insures all medical expenses (except those excluded), among them room and board, surgical and physician costs, drugs and medicines, blood, ambulance service to and from the hospital, X-rays, and floor nursing. *See also* INSURANCE.

FAMILY HISTORY background information used in life and health insurance underwriting to ascertain the probability of hereditary disease. The purpose is to determine if the disease is of such a nature that the life expectancy of an applicant will be adversely affected, and if so, to what degree.

FAMILY INCOME POLICY contract combining whole life and decreasing term insurance. A monthly income is paid to a beneficiary if an insured dies during a specific period. At the end of that period, the full face amount of the policy is also paid to the beneficiary. It is designed to provide income for a household while the children are still young. If an insured dies after the specified period, only the face amount of the policy is paid. For example, the face value of a family income policy is $100,000 and the specified period is 20 years. If the insured dies 10 years into the specified period, the beneficiary receives a monthly income of 1% of the face amount ($1000) for the remaining 10 years. At the end of the 10 years, the beneficiary also receives $100,000. If the insured dies after the 20-year specified period, the beneficiary receives $100,000, which is the face amount. *See also* FAMILY INCOME RIDER; FAMILY MAINTENANCE POLICY.

FAMILY INCOME RIDER attachment of decreasing term life insurance to an ordinary life policy to provide monthly income to a beneficiary if death occurs during a specified period. If the insured dies after the specified period, only the face value is paid to the beneficiary since the decreasing term insurance has expired. *See also* FAMILY INCOME POLICY.

FAMILY LIMITED PARTNERSHIP partnership in which family members hold all interest in the partnership. This partnership is treated as a cash flow through stand-alone entity. All sums of income and credits, as well as deductions, flow through the partnership to the partners on a pro rata basis. The partners report their pro rata share on their individual personal income tax returns.

FAMILY MAINTENANCE POLICY combination of whole life and level term that provides income to a beneficiary for a selected period of time (e.g., 20 years) if an insured dies during that period. At the end of the income-paying period the beneficiary also receives the entire face amount of the policy. If an insured dies after the end of the selected period, the beneficiary receives only the face value of the policy. The remainder of the benefits are the same as under the FAMILY INCOME POLICY. See also FAMILY INCOME RIDER.

FAMILY MEDICAL LEAVE ACT (FMLA) legislation that requires an employer who has more than 50 employees for each 12-month period of time to provide: (1) each employee with at least 12 weeks of unpaid or paid leave; (2) medical care treatment leave upon the development of serious health problems by the employee; (3) medical care treatment leave upon the development of serious health problems by the spouse, parent, or child; (4) employee leave for child birth, adoption, or placement in a foster home; (5) employee reinstatement of same coverage after the return to work.

FAMILY POLICY contract providing whole life insurance on the father and term insurance on the mother and all children, including newborns after reaching a stated age, usually 15 days. Children, upon reaching the age of majority, have the right to convert their insurance to a permanent policy up to the amount of term coverage without having to show evidence of insurability (take a physical examination). The premium is the same regardless of the number of children covered.

FAMILY PROTECTION AUTOMOBILE INSURANCE COVER-AGE see UNINSURED MOTORIST COVERAGE.

FAMILY PROTECTION ENDORSEMENT see UNDERINSURED MOTORIST ENDORSEMENT; UNINSURED MOTORIST COVERAGE.

FARMERS COMPREHENSIVE PERSONAL LIABILITY INSUR-ANCE provides the same coverage as a COMPREHENSIVE PERSONAL LIABILITY INSURANCE policy, plus coverage to exposures that are peculiar to farms, such as farm business operations, farm employees engaged in farm business activities, and liability arising out of selling farm products.

FARMOWNERS AND RANCHOWNERS INSURANCE package coverage for a dwelling and its contents, barns, stables, and other land structures as well as liability coverage. By means of a number of special forms that follow the format of the HOMEOWNERS INSURANCE POLICY, this insurance protects a number of named perils and liabilities.

FASB 113 Financial Accounting Standards Board.

FASB 115 Financial Accounting Standards Board.

FAULT TREE ANALYSIS diagram of cause and effect relationships, showing the possible outcomes if a particular course of action is taken or continued. This method of analysis, which is founded in the testing of aerospace materials, has increasingly been applied to safety engineering accident cause and prevention.

FAULTY INSTALLATION coverage in the event of property damage or destruction resulting from wrongful installation of equipment.

FAYOL, HENRI French industrialist whose thesis is that all business activities revolve around six areas: *technical* (production), *commercial* (buying and selling), *financing* (capital employment), *accounting* (financial record keeping), *managerial* (planning, organizing, directing, coordinating, controlling), and *security* (protection of property against loss and the physical safety of individuals). Fayol's view of security has become the RISK MANAGEMENT of modern business.

FCAS *see* FELLOW, CASUALTY ACTUARIAL SOCIETY.

FC&S *see* FREE-OF-CAPTURE-AND-SEIZURE CLAUSE.

FCIC *see* FEDERAL CROP INSURANCE.

FDIC *see* FEDERAL DEPOSIT INSURANCE CORPORATION.

FEDERAL CRIME INSURANCE protection under the auspices of the federal government where such insurance cannot be purchased by a homeowner, business owner, or tenant at affordable community rates. A homeowner's or tenant's personal property is covered for burglary and/or robbery, and premises for damage due to burglary and robbery. A business owner's fixtures, furniture, equipment, merchandise, money, and securities due are covered for burglary and/or robbery. *See also* FEDERAL INSURANCE ADMINISTRATION.

FEDERAL CROP INSURANCE protection against natural disasters that may strike crops. Coverage on ALL RISKS basis began in 1948 under the auspices of the U.S. Department of Agriculture. Premiums reflect actual losses incurred by farmers. The objective is to level out farmers' income that otherwise would be adversely affected by natural disasters striking their crops. *See also* FEDERAL INSURANCE ADMINISTRATION.

FEDERAL DEPOSIT INSURANCE CORPORATION (FDIC) agency formed as the result of bank failures in the 1930s to insure the deposits of customers of member banks. The FDIC, an agency of the federal government, is self-supporting in that it receives fees from the member banks at the rate of .5% of the bank's deposits and the income from reserves that have been invested. Each account is insured up to $100,000.

FEDERAL EMPLOYEES GROUP LIFE INSURANCE (FEGLI) plan administered through a primary private life insurer and reinsured through other private life insurers, providing a death benefit equal to: (1) one year's salary for active employees at least age 45 until they reach age 65; and (2) two years' salary for active employees age 35 and under. The death benefit is graduated for federal employees age 36 through 44. After retirement, the full death benefit remains in force until the retired employee reaches age 65, whereupon the death benefit is reduced by 2% per month until it levels off at 25% of the employee preretirement annual salary. The federal government pays approximately one-third of the monthly premium, and the employee pays the remainder.

FEDERAL EMPLOYERS LIABILITY ACT (FELA) federal law comparable to state workers compensation statutes setting out liability of railroads for work-related injuries or death of their employees. Railroad employees are not covered by *workers compensation* laws. Under normal tort law, the injured party must prove he or she did nothing to contribute to the negligence or the risk. But under the terms of the federal act, railroad employees must only show that negligence on the part of the employer contributed to the injury. Therefore, this law gives railroads responsibility for on-the-job injuries to employees. But the railroads are not protected by the theory that workers compensation should be the only responsibility of employers for their employees, or by the prescribed schedule of benefits.

FEDERAL ESTATE TAX federal tax imposed on the estate of a decedent according to the value of that estate. The first step in the computation of the federal estate tax owed is to determine the value of the decedent's gross estate. This determination can be made by adding the following values of assets owned by the decedent at the time of death:
1. property owned outright.
2. gratuitous lifetime transfers, but with the stipulation that the decedent retained the income or control over the income.
3. gratuitous lifetime transfers subject to the recipient's surviving the decedent.
4. gratuitous lifetime transfers subject to the decedent's retaining the right to revoke, amend, or alter the gift.
5. annuities purchased by the decedent that are payable for the lifetime of the named survivor as well as the annuitant.
6. property jointly held in such a manner that another party receives the decedent's interest in that property at the decedent's death because of that party's survivorship.
7. life insurance in which the decedent retained incidents of ownership.
8. life insurance that was payable to the decedent's estate.

    The second step in the computation of the federal estate tax owed is to subtract allowable deductions (including bequests to charities, bequests to the surviving spouse, funeral expenses, and other administration expenses) from the gross estate. This results in the taxable estate. Adjustable taxable gifts are then added to the taxable estate, resulting in the computational tax base. From the table below, the appropriate tax rate is then applied to the computational tax base, resulting in the tentative (certain credits may still be subtracted) federal estate tax.

Note that the tax schedule is applicable to the taxable estate only after the adjustment for settlement costs, administrative expenses, and the unified estate and gift tax credit.

It is important to note that there is an unlimited marital deduction (the estate of the decedent passes to the spouse free of federal estate taxes) and that all federal estate taxes are eliminated on estates having a computational tax base of $2,000,000 or less in 2007. The unified credit (estate exemption amount) will be increased from the current $2,000,000 in the year 2007 according to the following schedule:

Year	Estate Exemption Amount	Minimum Estate Tax Rate
2008	$2,000,000	45%
2009	$3,500,000	45%
2010	No Tax	Not Applicable
2011	$1,000,000	55% (if repeal is not reenacted)

In 2010, estate taxes are scheduled to be repealed. If legislation is not enacted to extend this repeal to the years 2011 and beyond, estate tax exemption and rates revert back to those in existence in 2001.

To conform with the unlimited marital deduction in estates, tax-free gifts between spouses are allowed in unlimited amounts.

FEDERAL FLOOD INSURANCE coverage made available to residents of a community on a subsidized and nonsubsidized premium rate basis once the governing body of the community qualifies that community for coverage under the National Flood Insurance Act. Residents include business and nonbusiness operations with coverage written on structures and their contents. Coverage is purchased through licensed agents. Prior to passage of the Housing and Urban Development Act of 1968, of which the National Flood Insurance Act is a part, it was virtually impossible to obtain flood insurance coverage on an industrial building, residential building, retailing building, or a single family dwelling.

FEDERAL FLOOD INSURANCE: UPTON-JONES AMENDMENT amendment that modifies the FEDERAL FLOOD INSURANCE program by providing relocation and acquisition coverage for structures in imminent danger from an encroaching shoreline. This amendment enables the Federal Flood Insurance Program to pay up to 40% of the policy to property owners who relocate structures in imminent danger and up to 110% of the policy to property owners who demolish those structures and remove the debris. A prerequisite for the property owner to receive these funds is for the property structures to be declared uninhabitable by the local permit authority and to be subject to erosion or to be within the geographical boundaries of an erosion zone that has been included in a program approved by the state. Under the Federal Flood Insurance Program, coverage is available for homes, apartments, businesses, and condominiums for: (1) structural damage; (2) damage and/or destruction of floor surfaces; (3) clean-up expenses for flood-related debris; (4) damage and/or destruction of the furnace, air conditioning, and water heater; (5) contents to include furniture, clothing, jewelry, and collectibles. The amount of flood coverage limits available is

1. One- to four-family structure—$250,000
2. One- to four-family home contents—$100,000
3. Other residential structures—$250,000
4. Other residential contents—$100,000
5. Business structure—$500,000
6. Business contents—$500,000
7. Rental contents—$100,000

FEDERAL GOVERNMENT INSURANCE (FTC) *see* FEDERAL CRIME INSURANCE; FEDERAL CROP INSURANCE; FEDERAL DEPOSIT INSURANCE CORPORATION (FDIC); FEDERAL FLOOD INSURANCE; FEDERAL SAVINGS AND LOAN INSURANCE CORPORATION (FSLIC); SOCIAL INSURANCE.

FEDERAL HOUSING ADMINISTRATION (FHA) agency of the United States Government that insures primarily residential mortgage loans against default. The agency also establishes underwriting and construction standards.

FEDERAL IDENTITY THEFT AND ASSUMPTION DETERRENCE ACT OF 1998 law that makes it a federal felony to use another person's identity in an unlawful act as defined by federal, state, or local laws.

FEDERAL INSURANCE ADMINISTRATION government agency whose function is to administer the FEDERAL FLOOD INSURANCE PROGRAM, the FEDERAL CRIME INSURANCE program, and the FAIR ACCESS TO INSURANCE REQUIREMENT (FAIR) PLAN.

FEDERAL INSURANCE CONTRIBUTIONS ACT (FICA) legislation that consists of both Social Security and Medicare taxes charged to finance the OLD AGE, SURVIVORS, DISABILITY, AND HEALTH INSURANCE (OASDHI) plan. Both employer and employee share in the cost, making contributions on an equal basis. The employer and the employee share in the cost, making contributions on an equal basis. The employer pays the tax on its payroll, and the employee pays the tax on wages earned. In 2008, the maximum wage base became $102,000 with the maximum tax being 6.2% for Social Security. There is a tax of 1.45% for Medicare not subject to a maximum wage base. The combined total is 7.65% for the employee. The employer matches at the same rate for a total employer/employee contribution of 15.3%.

FEDERAL NUCLEAR REGULATORY COMMISSION *see* NUCLEAR REGULATORY COMMISSION.

FEDERAL OFFICIALS BOND coverage for the federal government in the event of loss due to dishonest acts of federal government employees.

FEDERAL RULES OF CIVIL PROCEDURE (FRCP) rules governing all legal proceedings requiring insurance companies to identify, locate, and produce electronic documents as requested by plaintiffs or defendants in the event of a legal proceeding. Companies are required to clearly define the informational procedures employed as requested by opposing counsel. The company must retain the integrity of the data and avoid the inadvertent damaging or flawing of the data. In order to achieve this objective, a single systematic protocol must be established to reflect total depository data that are readily available in a special format.

FEDERAL SAVINGS AND LOAN INSURANCE CORPORATION (FSLIC) agency of the federal government formed as the result of bankruptcies of savings and loan associations during the 1930s. Insures deposits of customers up to $100,000 for each account. In 1986, 1987, 1988, 1989, and 1990, when numerous savings and loan associations failed or nearly failed, FSLIC backed up their deposits and prevented runs. Abolished in 1989 by the FINANCIAL INSTITUTIONS REFORM, RECOVERY, AND ENFORCEMENT ACT OF 1989 (FIRREA), which passed responsibility for savings and loan deposit insurance to the FEDERAL DEPOSIT INSURANCE ADMINISTRATION (FDIC).

FEDERAL TAXATION *see* ANNUITY; TAX-FREE INCOME; TAXATION, INSURANCE COMPANIES; TAXATION, INTEREST ON DIVIDENDS; TAXATION, PARTICIPATING DIVIDENDS; TAXATION, PROCEEDS; TAX BENEFITS OF LIFE INSURANCE.

FEDERAL TRADE COMMISSION (FTC) government agency, under the MCCARRAN-FERGUSON ACT (PUBLIC LAW 15), that has no authority over insurance matters to the extent the states regulate insurance to the satisfaction of Congress. However, this does not prevent the FTC from conducting investigations into the insurance industry. For example, in 1970 the Congress charged the FTC with the responsibility of enforcing the FAIR CREDIT REPORTING ACT, which requires an insurance company to notify an insurance applicant of an impending INSPECTION REPORT and to release information so collected to the applicant upon request. If the report results in the applicant's rejection for insurance, he must be notified of the adverse report and his right to its contents. Perhaps the best known FTC investigation involved its study "Life Insurance Cost Disclosure," that was extremely critical of industry cost disclosure practices.

FEDERAL UNEMPLOYMENT INSURANCE TAX tax assessed by the states as a payroll tax on employers to pay for UNEMPLOYMENT COMPENSATION.

FEE FOR SERVICE PLAN traditional insurance plan under which the patient can select the physician and hospital of his or her choice. The patient is responsible for paying the CO-PAYMENT and the DEDUCTIBLE and the insurance company pays the excess up to the policy's limit.

FEE SIMPLE ESTATE form of common law ownership of real property that permits disposition of property by its holder in any manner desired. Both the holder and the holder's heirs have use of property in perpetuity and have an insurable interest in the property.

FELLOW, CASUALTY ACTUARIAL SOCIETY (FCAS) designation earned by passing 10 national examinations on subjects including mathematics of property and casualty insurance, actuarial science, insurance, accounting, and finance. Examinations and course materials are prepared and administered by the Casualty Actuarial Society.

FELLOW, LIFE MANAGEMENT INSTITUTE (FLMI) professional management designation earned by passing 10 national examinations on life and health insurance subjects including insurance, finance, marketing, law, information systems, accounting, management, and employee benefits. Examinations and course materials are prepared and administered by the Life Office Management Association.

FELLOW OF THE INSTITUTE OF ACTUARIES *see* CANADIAN INSTITUTE OF ACTUARIES.

FELLOW SERVANT RULE formerly an employer's defense under which an injured employee had to bring a cause for action against the fellow employee causing the injury, not the employer. Workers Compensation laws have nullified the rule for job-related injuries. *See also* WORKERS COMPENSATION, COVERAGE B.

FELLOW, SOCIETY OF ACTUARIES (FSA) designation earned by passing 10 national examinations on subjects including mathematics of life and health insurance, actuarial science, insurance, accounting, finance, and employee benefits. Examinations and course materials are prepared and administered by the Society of Actuaries.

FIA *see* FEDERAL INSURANCE ADMINISTRATION.

FICTITIOUS GROUP assembly of people formed only for obtaining GROUP INSURANCE. Such a group is uninsurable and violates underwriting principles concerning group insurance.

FIDELITY AND SURETY CATASTROPHE INSURANCE mechanism used by a fidelity and surety insurance company to spread its liability through REINSURANCE by issuing a *surplus treaty* as a first layer of coverage, thereby enabling a *cedent* to limit its liability on the business written, while at the same time utilizing the flexibility that the surplus method offers. The reinsurance *catastrophe cover* provides a second layer of coverage. Reinsurance covers are used by the insurance company to:

1. avoid accumulation of liability on individual principles. Warehouse bonds are an example of such accumulations, because they are required in great number and they result in large aggregate amounts.
2. achieve a balance among the various types of bonds that the insurer assumes.
3. reduce violent fluctuations in experiencing high loss ratios on many classes of bonds.

FIDELITY BOND coverage that guarantees that the insurance company will pay the insured business or individual for money or other property lost because of dishonest acts of its bonded employees, either named or by positions. The bond covers all dishonest acts, such as larceny, theft, embezzlement, forgery, misappropriation, wrongful abstraction, or willful misapplication, whether employees act alone or as a team. Businesses often bond their employees not only because the insurance will pay for the losses, but also because the bonding company may prevent losses by uncovering dishonesty in the work history of a new employee. Since a fidelity bond makes up only a part of protection against theft, other crime insurance is mandatory. Employee dishonesty insurance is usually bought through an individual Fidelity Bond, BLANKET POSITION BOND, COMMERCIAL BLANKET BOND, or a NAME SCHEDULE BOND.

FIDELITY EXCLUSION provision of liability insurance that excludes coverage for dishonest acts of an insured.

FIDUCIARY holding of property, or otherwise acting on behalf of another in trust. The fiduciary must exercise due care in safeguarding property left under personal care, custody, and control. Insurance coverage is available for this exposure. *See also* JUDICIAL BOND.

FIDUCIARY ASPECT OF INSURANCE status in which an insurance company holds funds of its insureds (the payment of premiums) in trust, and through an INSURING AGREEMENT promises to make all benefit payments for which it has received premiums.

FIDUCIARY BOND *see* JUDICIAL BOND.

FIDUCIARY LIABILITY INSURANCE coverage for administrators of employee benefit plans. The perils insured against are errors and omissions and negligence in the administration of the plan's funds.

FIELD FORCE agents, managers, and office personnel serving in the branches of an insurance company.

FIELD UNDERWRITING judgment decision by the insurance agent concerning whether or not to submit an application. The decision is based on the agent's familiarity with the insurance company's UNDERWRITING requirements for STANDARD RISK and SUBSTANDARD RISK.

FILE-AND-USE RATING LAWS use of new rate structures by an insurance company without first obtaining approval of a State Insurance Department.

FILE AND USE STATE *see* RATING BUREAU.

FILIAL RESPONSIBILITY LAWS legislation enacted in over 30 states that enables a nursing home to apply for a reimbursement from the children for the costs of medical benefits given to a resident.

FILING INSURANCE COMPANY BUREAU INSURER that files its statistical and underwriting experience with a RATING BUREAU.

FINAL AVERAGE method of calculating retirement benefits under pension plans, by averaging the highest three or five years of earnings (usually the final five years).

FINAL EXPENSE FUND amount of life insurance required to purchase burial, probate, medical, and other costs associated with death.

FINAL INSURANCE (MINIMUM DEPOSIT INSURANCE) premiums paid out of funds borrowed from the cash value of a life insurance policy.

FINANCED INSURANCE *see* FINAL INSURANCE (MINIMUM DEPOSIT INSURANCE).

FINANCED PREMIUM premiums paid with funds that are not borrowed from life insurance. It is important to ascertain the finance charges and the costs/benefits of such a transaction.

FINANCIAL CONSIDERATIONS investment and savings position of an insured used in determining the amount of life insurance to purchase. The amount of investment and savings is subtracted from the total insurance requirement.

FINANCIAL INSURANCE structured product designed to meet specific needs of the insured that may involve any of the following funding arrangements: (1) loss portfolio transfers in which the self-insurer transfers the reserves that it had established for its known losses to the insurance company; by concluding such a transfer, the self-insurer can use the capital it had previously set aside for loss reserves; (2) retrospective transfers in which a self-insurer has losses for which inadequate insurance coverage exists and now these companies require additional insurance coverages so that the limits can be raised to an adequate amount; and (3) prospective loss transfers in which a self-insurer has a requirement to fund in advance its future losses, thereby removing its liability for loss reserves from its balance sheet. The premium paid by the self-insurer to the insurance company reflects the self-insurer's expectation of loss.

Under the three funding approaches, the self-insurer must have adequate loss experience so that the LAW OF LARGE NUMBERS will be able to operate; that is, so that the credibility of the prediction will approach one and the standard deviation of the actual losses (X) from the expected losses (X) will approach zero. This statistical base is important because the self-insurer's loss experience is not combined with another self-insurer's loss experience to form an overall statistical bank from which to develop premiums for a specific category of self-insurers.

This specifically designed structured product enables the self-insurer to eliminate its liability for maintaining loss reserves. Also, this product enables the self-insurer to protect itself against adverse future loss experience resulting in earnings per share not being affected by unexpected losses.

FINANCIAL MODERNIZATION ACT OF 1999 law that permits financial institutions (insurance companies, banks, brokerage houses) to compete for the consumer's dollar when purchasing insurance, stocks, bonds, mutual funds, and other financial instruments.

FINANCIAL PLANNING acquisition and employment of ASSETS in order to maximize the return on these assets through: (1) establishment of FINANCIAL PLANNING OBJECTIVES; (2) development of financial plans by which these objectives are to be achieved; (3) establishment of a budget by which funds can be allocated to the purchase of the financial assets; and (4) review and, if necessary, revision of the financial plan to make sure acceptable progress is being made toward the achievement of the objectives.

FINANCIAL PLANNING OBJECTIVES goals of the financial planning process as follows:
1. *Standard of Living*—Maslow's basic needs satisfied such as food, water, clothing, shelter, and nice-to-have discretionary items, such as automobiles, vacations, entertainment.
2. *Savings*—emergency funds for sudden and unexpected events, such as extra living expenses because of a fire at one's home.
3. *Protection*—DISABILITY INCOME INSURANCE; HEALTH INSURANCE; LIFE INSURANCE; PROPERTY AND LIABILITY INSURANCE (all forms designed to offer coverage against the uncertainty of a financial loss due to the PURE RISK).
4. *Investment*—Accumulation of wealth through the return on assets deployed leading to financial independence.
5. *Estate Planning*—distribution of the invested assets held for the purpose of the accumulation of wealth in a tax efficient and effective manner.

FINANCIAL REINSURANCE transaction of REINSURANCE under which there is a limit on the total liability of the REINSURER and future investment income is a recognized component of the underwriting process. This financial instrument incorporates the time value of money into the CEDING process such that the CEDENT can reinsure its liabilities at a premium rate less than the true rate for the liabilities transferred (difference in the two rates to be made up by the investment income generated during the years the reinsurance contract remains in force). Financial reinsurance can be used effectively in several situations:

1. *surplus relief* (QUOTA SHARE REINSURANCE)—CEDING COMPANY transfers a percentage of its book of business to the reinsurer (the reinsurer will limit its total liability under any one contract).

2. *portfolio transfers*—ceding company transfers reserves on known losses to the reinsurer in exchange for premiums equal to the present value of the future claims experience.

3. *retrospective aggregates*—ceding company transfers reserves on known losses as well as INCURRED BUT NOT REPORTED LOSSES (IBNR).

4. *prospective aggregates*—ceding company pays a premium on a PROSPECTIVE RATING basis to the reinsurer. In exchange, the reinsurer is obligated to pay future losses incurred by the cedent. If these future losses are less than expected, the cedent will receive the UNDERWRITING GAIN. Any gains from investments and fees will be retained by the reinsurer. Through this mechanism, in essence, the cedent gains current capacity for writing additional business by borrowing against income to be received in the future.

5. *catastrophe protection*—coverage against shock losses is provided by spreading the payment of such losses over several years.

FINANCIAL REPORTING recording and presentation of financial statements, such as the ANNUAL STATEMENT, by the insurance company. Financial reporting statements are used by the State Insurance Commissioner in regulating the adequacy of company reserves for benefit liabilities, assets availability, and worth.

FINANCIAL RESPONSIBILITY CLAUSE provision in automobile insurance, such as the PERSONAL AUTOMOBILE POLICY (PAP), stating that a particular policy furnishes adequate coverage, the minimum of which is at least equal to that required by the financial responsibility laws in the state in which the insured is driving.

FINANCIAL RESPONSIBILITY LAW law requiring the operator of an automobile to show financial ability to pay for automobile-related losses. In many states evidence usually takes the form of a minimum amount of automobile liability insurance.

FINANCIAL RISK *see* FINANCIAL RISK MANAGEMENT.

FINANCIAL RISK MANAGEMENT management of investment risks associated with BUSINESS RISK, INTEREST RATE RISK, POLITICAL RISK, and PURCHASING POWER RISK. Usually fixed income financial instruments, such as fixed dollar life insurance, fixed dollar annuities, and bonds, are most susceptible to business, purchasing power, interest rate, and political risks. Variable dollar life insurance, variable dollar annuities, and common stocks are most subject to business, market, and political risks.

FINANCIAL STATEMENT balance sheet and profit and loss statement of an insurance company. This statement is used by State Insurance Commissioners to regulate an insurance company according to reserve requirements, assets, and other liabilities.

FINANCIAL STRUCTURE *see* ANNUAL STATEMENT, FINANCIAL STATEMENT.

FINANCING securement of funds from outside sources such as by borrowing or by attracting equity control. Use of leverage to improve the profitability of a business. Achievement of an investment return on the borrowed funds at a higher rate than the interest being paid for the use of the funds.

FINDER'S FEE monetary sum paid to an intermediary who acts as the contact between the lender (an insurance company) and the borrower.

FINE ART DEALERS INSURANCE coverage for works of art, antiques, and similar articles of value on ALL RISKS basis, subject to exclusion of wear and tear, war, breakage, repairing, infidelity of the insured's employees, and mysterious disappearance. Fine Arts Insurance Policies are written on a scheduled basis with damaged or destroyed items being indemnified on a valued basis. The same type of coverage for fine arts is available through a *Fine Arts Endorsement* for a SPECIAL MULTIPERIL INSURANCE (SMP) policy.

FINE ARTS AND ANTIQUES INSURANCE coverage for paintings, pictures, etchings, tapestries, art glass windows, antique furniture, coin collections, and stamp collections owned by individuals and businesses. These works are not covered if owned by dealers or auction firms. Protection is on an ALL RISKS basis subject to exclusions of damage from ordinary breakage, wear and tear, war, and nuclear disaster. Each item must be specifically listed and valued in the policy.

FINITE RISK INSURANCE type of insurance that provides a single aggregate limit of coverage within the insurance policy terms, thereby limiting the insurance company's liability for a RISK transferred to it. The insurance coverage is tailored to the requirements of the INSURED company to reflect the insured's actual coverage needs. If the insured's losses are favorable, the insured receives the return of a portion of the premium paid. The insured's premium costs are based on the insured's own loss experience, rather than the overall loss experience of a pool of similar insureds. In essence, through this type of insurance, the insured pays for exposure to loss and if there is not a substantial loss, the insured receives the return of a portion of the premium paid in. This insurance mechanism is ideal for insureds who exhibit a frequency distribution of high severity loss or an unusual loss frequency. *See also* FINANCIAL REINSURANCE.

FINITE RISK REINSURANCE contracts of REINSURANCE in which expected income from investments is a major component of the UNDERWRITING process. Also, the ultimate liability of the reinsurer is limited. The reinsurer cannot cancel these contracts, but the CEDING COMPANY may exchange this contract for another contract.

FIRE intense combustion resulting in a flame or glow. In order for the fire PERIL to be covered under PROPERTY INSURANCE, the fire must be a HOSTILE FIRE, not a FRIENDLY FIRE.

FIRE CATASTROPHE REINSURANCE means used by a *direct fire underwriter* to protect against accumulation for a fire account, as well as against extremely large fire account liability. For example, heavy liabilities under individual risks can be analyzed by the initial fire underwriter to determine the number of separate fire risks involved. The reinsurance method applied to the risks is a QUOTA SHARE or *surplus* share treaty with the use of a FACULTATIVE REINSURANCE cover if necessary. Under this method, the reinsurer assumes the liability of a proportionate share of the risks in exchange for a proportionate share of the premiums. An extremely large number of losses under individual risks caused by a single event, commonly referred to as a conflagration hazard, arises when different risks may be affected by one fire. An example would be widespread damage to many adjacent private houses. While the loss for each individual risk would be small, the aggregate would be so large that it would affect the stability of the fire insurance company. Catastrophe reinsurance would protect any SURPLUS REINSURANCE and EXCESS OF LOSS REINSURANCE up to a stated amount.

FIRE DEPARTMENT SERVICE CLAUSE in PROPERTY INSURANCE policies, provision that states that the INSURED will receive INDEMNITY for expenses incurred as a result of acts by the fire department taken to save or reduce damage to the insured's property. For example, if the insured has a house outside the fire district, the fire department might charge a fee for responding to a fire call.

FIRE DIVISION separation of a building into distinct separate parts by FIRE WALL or open air spaces between buildings to minimize the probability of a fire spreading horizontally or vertically.

FIRE DOOR partition of noncombustible material in a wall of similar material, designed when closed to slow the spread of fire from one side of the wall to the other. The NATIONAL FIRE PROTECTION ASSOCIATION rates the doors according to the number of hours they can be expected to withstand fire before burning through.

FIRE EXTINGUISHER instrument that uses noncombustible substances such as carbon dioxide to deprive a fire of oxygen, thereby extinguishing it.

FIRE, FRIENDLY *see* FRIENDLY FIRE.

FIRE, HOSTILE *see* HOSTILE FIRE.

FIRE INSURANCE—STANDARD FIRE POLICY policy known as the 165-line policy because of the standard form used in most states. The policy is not complete, and additional forms and endorsements are added so that it can cover numerous direct and indirect risks. The Standard Fire Policy is *Section I*—property coverage of most package policies such as the HOMEOWNERS and SPECIAL MULTIPERIL. It provides the foundation for property insurance coverages regardless of the form in which they appear. The Standard Fire Policy has four sections:

1. DECLARATIONS—description and location of property, insured amount, name of insured.
2. INSURING AGREEMENTS—premium amount, obligations of the insured, actions the insured must take in the event of loss and resultant claim.
3. *Conditions*—describes that which suspends or restricts the coverage, such as an increase in the hazard with the knowledge of the insured.
4. EXCLUSIONS—perils not covered under the policy, such as enemy attack, including action taken by military force in resisting actual or immediately impending enemy attack.

Forms that can be added to a Standard Fire Policy include DWELLING BUILDINGS AND CONTENTS *Basic Form; Dwelling, Buildings and Contents Broad Form;* GENERAL PROPERTY FORM. Since the Standard Fire Policy insures only against fire and lightning, the EXTENDED COVERAGE ENDORSEMENT can cover the additional perils of windstorm, hail, riot, civil commotion, vehicle and aircraft damage to the insured property, explosion, and smoke damage. A VANDALISM AND MALICIOUS MISCHIEF ENDORSEMENT can also be added.

FIRE LEGAL LIABILITY INSURANCE coverage for property loss liability as the result of negligent acts and/or omissions of the insured that allows a spreading fire to damage others' property. Negligent acts and omissions can result in fire legal liability. For example, an insured through negligence allows a fire to spread to a neighbor's property. The neighbor then brings suit against the insured for negligence. In another example, a tenant occupying another party's property through negligence causes serious fire damage to the property.

FIRE LOAD amount of combustible matter present that can act as a fuel to feed a HOSTILE FIRE.

FIRE MAP detail showing distribution of property coverages written by an insurance company. Illustrates a potential danger of concentration of insured risks.

FIRE MARK historic insignia representing evidence of coverage placed on property insured by a particular insurance company. If the property on fire did not have the company's fire mark, its private fire department would not fight the fire.

FIRE MARK SOCIETY sales honor group of property and casualty insurance agents created by the National Association of Professional Insurance Agents.

FIREPROOF use of engineering approved fire resistive construction materials exclusively within a structure. *See also* FIRE RESISTIVE CONSTRUCTION.

FIRE PROTECTION *see* FIRE RESISTIVE CONSTRUCTION; FIRE WALL; FIREPROOF.

FIRE RESISTIVE CONSTRUCTION use of engineering-approved masonry or fire resistive materials for exterior walls, floors, and roofs to reduce the severity of a potential fire and lower premium rates.

FIRE WALL structure separating parts of a building in order to contain the spread of fire. Fire walls reduce the severity of a potential fire and lower premium rates.

FIRST-DOLLAR COVERAGE insurance policy under which payment is made for a loss not subject to any DEDUCTIBLE or under which payment is made up to the limits of the policy, and then an EXCESS INSURANCE policy takes effect. For example, a HOMEOWNERS INSURANCE POLICY—SECTION II (LIABILITY COVERAGE) would pay up to its limits for an insured loss, whereupon an UMBRELLA LIABILITY INSURANCE policy would go into effect.

FIRST LOSS RETENTION (DEDUCTIBLE) *see* EXCESS OF LOSS REINSURANCE.

FIRST PARTY INSURANCE coverage for the insured's personal and real property and the insured's own person. Contrast with THIRD PARTY.

FIRST POLICY YEAR year in which an annually renewable INSURANCE POLICY was first issued. *See also* EFFECTIVE DATE; DATE OF ISSUE.

FIRST SURPLUS REINSURANCE *see* SURPLUS LINES; SURPLUS REINSURANCE.

FIRST SURPLUS TREATY *see* SURPLUS REINSURANCE.

FIRST-TO-DIE INSURANCE *see* JOINT LIFE INSURANCE.

FIRST-TO-DIE LIFE INSURANCE *see* JOINT LIFE INSURANCE.

FIRST YEAR COMMISSION percentage of first year's premium paid to compensate an insurance agent. This is known as the *"First Years"* to show how much new business the agent is generating, compared with RENEWAL COMMISSIONS generated by previous business.

FIRST YEAR EXPENSES costs associated with the selling of a new insurance policy to a POLICYHOLDER. The costs include the acquisition commission as a percentage of the first year's premium, underwriting charges, and the issuing of the policy charges.

FISCAL POLICY government policy of pumping money into the economy by spending or taking money out of the economy by taxing.

FIVE PERCENT RULE coinsurance requirement such that if a loss is less than $10,000 and also less than 5% of the total of insurance to cover a loss, then the insurance company will not require that the property not damaged by the peril be inventoried or appraised.

FIVE PERCENT WAIVER CLAUSE *see* FIVE PERCENT RULE.

FIVE TO FIFTEEN YEAR RULE VESTING provision of the EMPLOYEE RETIREMENT INCOME SECURITY ACT OF 1974 (ERISA) under which vesting must accrue at not less than the following rates:

Years of Service	Vesting
0 to less than 5	0
at least 5	25%
6 to 10	5% increase per year
11 to 15	10% increase per year

At the end of 15 years, 100% vesting has been achieved. The TAX REFORM ACT OF 1986 eliminated this option of vesting beginning January 1, 1989. With the passage of the PENSION PROTECTION ACT OF 2006, employer nonselective contributions as well as employer matching contributions must VEST on either the minimum three-year Cliff or six-year GRADED VESTING sechedule (Year 1 = 0% vested; Year 2 = 20% vested; Year 3 = 40% vested; Year 4 = 60% vested; Year 5 = 80% vested; Year 6 = 100% vested).

FIVE-YEAR VESTING (CLIFF VESTING) method of VESTING under the TAX REFORM ACT OF 1986 that requires an employee to have five years of service with an employer to be vested. An employee who leaves an employer prior to that time does not receive retirement benefits from that job. *See also* TEN-YEAR VESTING (CLIFF VESTING). With the passage of the PENSION PROTECTION ACT OF 2006, employer nonelective contributions as well as employer matching contributions must VEST according to either the minimum three-year Cliff or six-year GRADED VESTING schedule (Year 1 = 0% vested; Year 2 = 20% vested; Year 3 = 40% vested; Year 4 = 60% vested; Year 5 = 80% vested; Year 6 = 100% vested).

FIXED-AMOUNT SETTLEMENT OPTION choice of beneficiary in which the death benefit of a life insurance policy is retained by the company to be paid as a series of installments of fixed dollar amounts per installment until the death benefit and interest are exhausted. Any excess interest earned above the minimum guaranteed is applied to extend the time period for making the payments. This option emphasizes dollar amount per installment as opposed to length of time installments are to be paid. *See also* LIFE INSURANCE; OPTIONAL MODES OF SETTLEMENT.

FIXED ANNUITY *see* FIXED DOLLAR ANNUITY.

FIXED BENEFITS payment to a beneficiary that does not vary; for example, a fixed monthly retirement income benefit of $800 paid to a retired employee.

FIXED DOLLAR ANNUITY ANNUITY that guarantees that a specific sum of money will be paid in the future, usually as monthly income, to an annuitant. For example, a $1000-a-month income benefit will be paid as long as the annuitant lives; the dollar amount will not fluctuate regardless of adverse changes in the insurance company's mortality experience, investment return, and expenses.

FIXED DOLLAR INVESTMENTS financial instruments whose principal and income are established in advance according to contractual terms set forth in the financial instrument's document. Examples of such investments include savings accounts, certificates of deposit, ORDINARY LIFE INSURANCE, and the ANNUITY.

FIXED INCOME financial instrument such as a FIXED DOLLAR ANNUITY or BOND that pays a minimum periodic income at a minimum guaranteed rate of interest.

FIXED INCOME FINANCIAL INSTRUMENT coverage that pays a fixed dollar amount of interest at regular intervals.

FIXED-PERIOD OPTION SETTLEMENT beneficiary's choice, in a life insurance policy or annuity, for receiving income payments for a given period of time. The number of payments are fixed by the payee; the benefit amount is determined by the death proceeds. For example, an income benefit of $1000 per month is paid for a period of 48 months, whereupon all income payments cease.

FIXED PERIOD PAYOUT income paid for a specified number of years from an ANNUITY.

FIXED PREMIUM payment for coverage that remains throughout the same premium-paying period.

FLAT AMOUNT *see* DEFINED BENEFIT PLAN.

FLAT CANCELLATION cancellation of an insurance policy on the date that policy becomes effective. This type of cancellation does not require any fees to be paid to the insurance company.

FLAT COMMISSION compensation to an agent in the same absolute dollar amount, regardless of the type of insurance policy sold. Contrast with GRADED COMMISSION.

FLAT DEDUCTIBLE *see* DEDUCTIBLE.

FLAT EXTRA PREMIUM certain fixed payment made in addition to the regularly scheduled premium.

FLAT MATERNITY BENEFIT stated fixed payment for maternity costs regardless of the actual costs.

FLAT RATE (FLAT SCHEDULE) rate not subsequently adjusted. The rate stays in effect regardless of an insured's subsequent loss record.

FLAT RATE METHOD type of asset allocation model that calculates the future value of assets at a constant rate.

FLAT SCHEDULE *see* FLAT RATE (FLAT SCHEDULE).

FLEET OF COMPANIES several insurance companies under common ownership and, often, common management.

FLEET POLICY numerous automotive vehicles covered under a common insurance policy.

FLEXIBLE BENEFIT PLAN employee benefit plan that allows the employee to choose among several different benefits offered by the employer. In essence, the employee is provided with the opportunity to make a trade-off by trading one benefit for another that best meets the employee's needs at a particular point in time. Contributions paid into the plan, whether on a CONTRIBUTORY or NONCONTRIBUTORY basis, can be allocated to satisfy the needs of a particular employee rather than those of the employees as a whole. The result should be a balance between the employee's primary needs and the benefit/cost constraints. Among the personal choices that the employee can make are health care plans (choices in types and amount of coverages). WELLNESS PROGRAM plans, child-care benefits, and LONG-TERM CARE (LTC) PLANS.

FLEXIBLE ENHANCED ORDINARY LIFE modified ENHANCED ORDINARY LIFE in which there is a combination of dividends purchasing PAID-UP ADDITIONS, TERM LIFE INSURANCE, and ORDINARY LIFE INSURANCE. The structure of this product is such that a minimum FACE AMOUNT of ordinary life insurance must be maintained, but the POLICYOWNER is not limited in the amount of term life insurance that may be added. Since the ordinary life and term life product mix can vary, the premium rate per $1000 will also vary. (Life insurance is sold in units of $1000 and rated in terms of $1000 units.) There is, however, a minimum rate per $1000 that must be paid. At any time after issue, the policyowner may increase or decrease the amount of term life insurance as well as increase or decrease the amount of extra premiums paid into the policy. These extra premiums will purchase paid-up additions. *See also* ENHANCED ORDINARY LIFE.

FLEXIBLE FUNDING arrangement whereby the insured pays the insurance company a relatively small monthly premium payment. In exchange for this premium payment, the insurance company processes and pays claims from a fund owned and maintained by the insured. Should the claims exceed a stipulated limit, the insurance company pays the excess amount of claims.

FLEXIBLE INDEX EQUITY ANNUITY type of equity indexed annuity that provides policy owner the right to select how interest will be credited to the policy. For example, one month the owner may elect to have 100% of the premium allocated to the S&P 500 Index, the next month to a fixed rate, and the third month to the Nasdaq Composite Index.

FLEXIBLE PORTFOLIO ACCOUNTS accounts in which assets are allocated across the spectrum of equity, debt, and money market instruments. They are the most popular equity investment in VARIABLE ANNUITIES and VARIABLE LIFE INSURANCE.

FLEXIBLE PREMIUM one in which the amount and frequency of payment may fluctuate. *See also* FLEXIBLE PREMIUM ANNUITY; FLEXIBLE PREMIUM LIFE INSURANCE; FLEXIBLE PREMIUM VARIABLE LIFE; UNIVERSAL LIFE INSURANCE; UNIVERSAL VARIABLE LIFE INSURANCE.

FLEXIBLE PREMIUM ANNUITY annuity with no fixed schedule for payment of premiums. For example, premiums can be paid for 10 straight months, then not paid for the next 10 months, then paid every other month, or any combination thereof.

FLEXIBLE PREMIUM DEFERRED ANNUITY (FPDA) contract sold by an insurance company under which the premium payment frequency (monthly, quarterly, semiannually, yearly) may vary and the amount of each premium payment (usually subject to a minimum of $100) may vary. This contract pays a monthly (or quarterly, semiannual, or annual) income benefit for the life of a person (the ANNUITANT), for the lives of two or more persons, or for a specified period of time. These income payments are scheduled to begin at a specified later date. The annuitant can never outlive the income from the annuity. While the basic purpose of life insurance is to provide an income for a beneficiary at the death of the insured, the annuity is intended to provide an income for life for the annuitant. *See also* ANNUITY; CASH REFUND ANNUITY; FIXED DOLLAR ANNUITY; INSTALLMENT REFUND ANNUITY; JOINT-LIFE AND SURVIVORSHIP ANNUITY; JOINT LIFE ANNUITY; LIFE ANNUITY CERTAIN; PURE ANNUITY; VARIABLE DOLLAR ANNUITY.

FLEXIBLE PREMIUM LIFE INSURANCE policy that has an initial premium with flexible premiums thereafter. Within limits, a policyowner can select both the future amount and frequency of premiums, or can stop and start premium payments at his or her discretion. Lump sum premium payments can be deposited, subject only to federal tax code restrictions.

FLEXIBLE PREMIUM VARIABLE LIFE insurance that combines features of FLEXIBLE PREMIUM LIFE INSURANCE and UNIVERSAL LIFE INSURANCE into one policy in the following manner:
1. *Premiums*—after the required minimum initial premium payment, premiums are flexible. The policyowner can select both their future amount and frequency, with certain restrictions that depend on the design of the policy. The policyowner can stop and start the premiums at his or her discretion, and a lump sum premium can be made at any time subject only to federal tax restrictions.
2. *Variable*—the death benefit may increase or decrease subject to the performance of an investment account of equities in which the premiums are placed. However, a minimum death benefit is guaranteed—the initial face value of the policy. Cash values fluctuate according to the performance of this investment account.

FLEXIBLE RATING LAWS types of FILE AND USE RATING LAWS that allow an INSURANCE COMPANY (INSURER) to charge a PREMIUM if it does not exceed a maximum or minimum percentage of the premium previously charged.

FLEXIBLE SPENDING ACCOUNT—HEALTH CARE/DEPENDENT CARE EXPENSES plan established by the employer that permits the employee to defer pretax earnings into a specifically designated account. From this account, the employee may withdraw funds to pay unreimbursed medical expenses and/or qualified child-care expenses. Generally, there is a cap set by the employer that limits the maximum amount the employee can pay into this account. In addition, there is a $5000 limit set by the federal government for the child-care expenses account. Any unused funds remaining in this account at year's end are forfeited by the employee.

FLEXIBLE SPENDING ACCOUNT LIFE INSURANCE account established by the insurance company specifically for beneficiaries of a life insurance policy where the beneficiary has the choice of leaving the death benefit on deposit in the account earning interest or writing checks on the deposited amount.

FLMI *see* FELLOW, LIFE MANAGEMENT INSTITUTE (FLMI).

FLOAT funds set aside by an insurance company to pay INCURRED LOSSES which have not yet been paid.

FLOATER coverage for property which moves from location to location either on a scheduled or unscheduled basis. If the floater covers scheduled property, coverage is listed for each item. If a floater covers unscheduled property, all property is covered for the same limits of insurance. *See also* PERSONAL ARTICLES INSURANCE; PERSONAL PROPERTY FLOATER.

FLOOD INSURANCE *see* FEDERAL FLOOD INSURANCE.

FLOOR OF PROTECTION provision that provides basic limit of income needed by the INSURED to pay for the necessities of life.

FLOOR PLAN INSURANCE coverage for a lender who has accepted property on the floor of a merchant as security for a loan. If the merchandise is damaged or destroyed, the lender is indemnified. The policy is on an ALL RISKS basis.

FLOW-THROUGH COST (NO LOAD INSURANCE) net cost of insurance with no markup to cover an intermediary's profit or expenses. An intermediary, such as a broker, sells an insurance product net; that is, there is no loading for his own cost of soliciting business or his profit margin.

FOLLOWING FORM written form which has precisely the same terms as the other PROPERTY INSURANCE policies covering a particular property.

FOLLOWING THE FORTUNES REINSURANCE CLAUSE that stipulates that the REINSURER will be subject to the same fate as the CEDING COMPANY. *See also* AUTOMATIC NONPROPORTIONAL REINSURANCE; AUTOMATIC PROPORTIONAL REINSURANCE; AUTOMATIC REINSURANCE; EXCESS OF LOSS REINSURANCE; FACULTATIVE REINSURANCE; NONPROPORTIONAL REINSURANCE; PROPORTIONAL REINSURANCE; QUOTA SHARE REINSURANCE; STOP LOSS REINSURANCE; SURPLUS REINSURANCE.

FOREIGN CARRIER *see* ALIEN INSURER; FOREIGN INSURER.

FOREIGN COMPANY *see* ALIEN INSURER; FOREIGN INSURER.

FOREIGN CREDIT INSURANCE ASSOCIATION *see* EXPORT-IMPORT BANK.

FOREIGN INSURER insurance company whose domicile is in a state other than the one in which the company is writing business.

FORFEITURE relinquishment of rights in an insurance policy or pension plan. For example, by withdrawing contributions to a pension plan, an employee forfeits future retirement benefits under that plan.

FORFEITURE OF VESTED BENEFITS relinquishment of rights to benefits when an employee withdraws previous contributions to a plan. An employee who had not withdrawn these contributions would have been entitled to full benefits at normal retirement age or to a reduced benefit at early retirement, whether or not he or she is in the service of the employer at that time.

FORGERY BOND *see* DEPOSITORS FORGERY INSURANCE.

FORGERY INSURANCE insurance with two types of policies available: DEPOSITORS FORGERY INSURANCE; FORGERY AND ALTERATION, FORM B.

FORM attachment to an insurance policy to complete its coverage. For example, the *Standard Fire Policy* must have certain forms attached for it to provide the coverage desired.

FORM NO. 1 (BASIC OR STANDARD), HOMEOWNERS INSURANCE POLICY *see* HOMEOWNERS INSURANCE POLICY—SECTION I (PROPERTY COVERAGE).

FORM NO. 2 (BROAD), HOMEOWNERS INSURANCE POLICY *see* HOMEOWNERS INSURANCE POLICY—SECTION I (PROPERTY COVERAGE).

FORM NO. 3 (SPECIAL), HOMEOWNERS INSURANCE POLICY *see* HOMEOWNERS INSURANCE POLICY—SECTION I (PROPERTY COVERAGE).

FORM NO. 4 (CONTENTS BROAD FORM), HOMEOWNERS INSURANCE POLICY *see* HOMEOWNERS INSURANCE POLICY—SECTION I (PROPERTY COVERAGE).

FORM NO. 6 (CONDOMINIUM UNIT OWNER'S FORM), HOMEOWNERS INSURANCE POLICY *see* HOMEOWNERS INSURANCE POLICY—SECTION I (PROPERTY COVERAGE).

FORM 5500 form that reports the status and activity of retirement plans to the Internal Revenue Service (IRS). The IRS uses this form to determine whether a retirement plan is in compliance with all requirements. Form 5500 must be filed with the IRS by the last day of the seventh month following the plan's year-end.

FORTUITOUS EVENT *see* FORTUITOUS LOSS.

FORTUITOUS LOSS loss occurring by accident or chance, not by anyone's intention. Insurance policies provide coverage against losses that occur only on a chance basis, where the insured cannot control the loss; thus the insured should not be able to burn down his or her own home and collect. Insurance is not provided against a certainty such as wear and tear. Life insurance will not pay a death benefit if the insured commits suicide within the first two years that the policy is in force. Even though death is a certainty, the insured cannot buy a policy with the intention of suicide within the first two years.

FORWARD COMMITMENT RISK RISK incurred by the insurance company after it makes the commitment to make the loan at some future time and the borrower may not accept the loan at that time.

FORWARD CONTRACT arrangement between the buyer and the seller in which there is a mutual agreement to buy or sell a security at a given price at a stipulated future date. These contracts are effected on a private placement or over-the-counter basis.

FPA *see* FREE OF PARTICULAR AVERAGE (FPA).

FRACTIONAL PREMIUM annual premium expressed on a proportionate basis such as monthly, quarterly, or semiannually.

FRANCHISE CLAUSE CLAUSE found in a MARINE INSURANCE policy that states that the policy will not pay any CLAIMS less than a given amount but will pay claims in excess of that amount. The purpose of this clause is to eliminate the costs associated with processing small claims because their costs could easily exceed the actual amount of the claim. This is a form of deductible insurance.

FRANCHISE DEDUCTIBLE stipulation that no claim will be paid until a loss exceeds a flat dollar amount or a given percentage of the amount of insurance in force. After the loss exceeds this dollar amount or percentage amount, the insurance company pays 100% of the claim loss.

FRANCHISE INSURANCE (WHOLESALE INSURANCE) coverage for small groups that cannot meet the underwriting standards of *true group* insurance. Even though the franchise insurance covers an entire group, individual policies are written on each insured person, each having the right to different coverage than other members. Usually sold to employer groups.

FRATERNAL LIFE INSURANCE group coverage for members of a fraternal association, usually on a nonprofit basis.

FRAUD dishonest act. Coverage for loss by fraud (not liability for committing fraud) is provided under the various bonds and crime insurance policies. *See also* FIDELITY BOND.

FRAUD BOND *see* BOND; BLANKET POSITION BOND; COMMERCIAL BLANKET BOND; CONTRACT BOND; FIDELITY BOND; JUDICIAL BOND; NAME SCHEDULE BOND.

FRAUDULENT CLAIM demand without foundation, such as a claim submitted to an insurance company by an insured who caused a loss, or for a loss that never occurred.

FRAUDULENT MISREPRESENTATION dishonest statement to induce an insurance company to write coverage on an applicant. If the company knew the truth, it would not accept the applicant. Fraudulent misrepresentation gives a property and casualty company grounds to terminate a policy at any time. A life insurance company, on the other hand, can terminate a policy on the grounds of fraudulent misrepresentation only during its first two years; after that, the INCONTESTABLE CLAUSE takes effect.

FREE ALONGSIDE SHIP (FAS) term meaning that an exporter of goods that are damaged or destroyed during international shipment relinquishes responsibility for the damage or destruction once the goods leave the point of origination.

FREE EXAMINATION "FREE LOOK" PERIOD right, in most states, of an insured to have 10 days in which to examine an insurance policy, and if not satisfied, to return it to the company for a full refund of the initial premium.

FREE LOOK PERIOD *see* FREE EXAMINATION "FREE LOOK" PERIOD.

FREE-OF-CAPTURE-AND-SEIZURE CLAUSE exclusion of coverage in marine insurance if damage or destruction of property results from war, capture, or seizure.

FREE OF PARTICULAR AVERAGE (FPA) marine insurance contract clause that limits an insurance company's liability. The company agrees to pay only losses that exceed a percentage or flat dollar amount; partial (below this percentage or amount) losses are not paid. In essence, the principle is like the DEDUCTIBLE feature of other policies.

FREE ON BOARD (FOB) term meaning that an exporter of goods that are damaged or destroyed during international shipment relinquishes responsibility for the damage or destruction once the goods reach the point of destination.

FREE TRADE ZONE geographical area in which commerce can be conducted without tariffs being applied. The concept was adopted in insurance through the use of a REINSURANCE FACILITY for buying and selling of insurance coverages without a premium tax being applied.

FREEZING OF SUPPLEMENTAL LIABILITY procedure whereby there is no amortization of the employer's liability for the supplemental cost of an employee's future benefits to be paid at retirement. *See also* INDIVIDUAL LEVEL COST METHOD WITH SUPPLEMENTAL LIABILITY.

FREIGHT INSURANCE coverage for goods during shipment on a common carrier. *See also* CARGO INSURANCE.

FREQUENCY number of times a loss occurs.

FREQUENCY AND DISTRIBUTION OF LOSSES number of times losses occur, and their severity. These statistics measure expectation of loss, and are critical in establishing a basic premium or the pure cost of protection that is based on expectation of loss.

FRIENDLY FIRE kindling intentionally set in a fireplace, stove, furnace, or other containment that has not spread beyond it. Property insurance does not protect against damage from a friendly fire. For example, smoke damage to the inside of a fireplace is not covered because the fire is in its normal habitat; to insure it would be insuring against a certainty. Insurance is designed to provide coverage against the fortuitous loss. *See also* HOSTILE FIRE.

FRONT END LOADED TERM *see* DEPOSIT TERM LIFE INSURANCE.

FRONTING COMPANY *see* FRONTING.

FRONTING (FRONTING COMPANY) procedure under which the CEDING COMPANY (the primary or fronting company) cedes the risk it has underwritten to its *reinsurer* with the ceding company retaining none or a very small portion of that risk for its own account. *See also* REINSURANCE.

FRONT LOADING expenses added to the beginning of a premium payment period. For example, an annuity with a 10% front load would include $10 of expenses for each $100 premium paid.

FROZEN KEOGH PLAN plan to which contributions are not being made, but which has not been formally terminated. The freezing of a KEOGH PLAN (HR-10) may occur in the following circumstances:
1. self-employed person stops contributing to the plan.
2. personal corporation is dissolved and stops contributing to the plan even though the employee of the personal corporation may continue in the same occupation.
3. self-employed person under the original plan may form a partnership or incorporate, necessitating the freezing of the original plan and the establishment of a new plan.

Owners of a frozen plan must make sure the plan continues to conform to current regulations and continue to file annually FORM 5500. Annual administrative costs may be saved by terminating the frozen plan and rolling over its assets into a currently active qualified plan.

FSA *see* FELLOW, SOCIETY OF ACTUARIES (FSA).

FSLIC *see* FEDERAL SAVINGS AND LOAN CORPORATION (FSLIC).

FTZ *see* FREE TRADE ZONE.

FULL COVERAGE all insured losses paid in full.

FULL-PAID ADDITIONS *see* DIVIDEND ADDITION.

FULL PRELIMINARY TERM RESERVE PLAN method of valuing a reserve under which a life insurance policy, from an actual point of view, combines one-year term insurance and a one-year deferred plan. Here the net premium is sufficient only to pay first-year death claims. For example, a 10-pay life insurance policy issued at age 30 would be viewed actuarially, for full preliminary term reserve plan purposes, as one-year term insurance at age 30 plus a nine-pay policy issued at age 30 but deferred to age 31.

FULL PRELIMINARY TERM RESERVE VALUATION mathematical combination of one-year term insurance and one-year deferred permanent insurance such that no reserve has to be set up for the first year the policy is in force and allowance is made for adjustment in future reserves to reflect this one-year lag.

FULL REPORTING CLAUSE provision in commercial property coverage under which an insured must report the value of an insured property at periodic intervals in order to preserve coverage up to values reported. In essence, this clause requires the insured to maintain total insurance to the value of the property, or 100% coinsurance. If the insured maintains less than the 100% requirement and a loss takes place, only a portion of that loss will be paid. *See also* COINSURANCE.

FULL VALUATION RESERVE method of valuing a reserve under which no reserve is established for a life insurance policy at the end of the first policy year, but reserves are established at the end of the second policy year. This approach enables the company to have more funds available during the first policy year to pay the expenses associated with selling the policy. *See also* FULL PRELIMINARY TERM RESERVE PLAN.

FULL VALUE LOSS RESERVES undiscounted LOSS RESERVES that must be maintained by property and casualty insurance companies in an adequate amount to provide for the payment of the settlement value of the outstanding claims of the companies. These reserves cannot be reduced by the expected return from any investment considerations.

FULL VESTING entitlement to pension benefits without a reduction, even though an employee is no longer in the service of an employer at retirement. For example, under the TEN YEAR VESTING rule, an employee who has worked 10 years for an employer is automatically credited with future retirement benefits. *See also* VESTING, CONDITIONAL.

FULLY INSURED STATUS provision in Social Security: to receive retirement monthly income, a participant must have earned income on which Social Security taxes were paid for at least 10 years or 40 quarters.

FULLY PAID POLICY limited pay whole life policy under which all premium payments have been made. For example, a 20 pay policy is completely paid for after 20 payments; no future premiums have to be made, and the policy remains in full force for the life of the insured.

FUNCTIONAL REPLACEMENT COST type of replacement cost that provides funds actually required to replace or repair damaged or destroyed property with functionally equivalent property or material. In some instances, replacement materials may be less expensive than the original materials. This type of replacement cost is used for damaged or destroyed collectibles.

FUNDAMENTAL basic requirements of an employee benefit insurance plan such as minimum age and years of service with an employer.

FUNDAMENTAL RISK type of RISK that affects large numbers of people and/or capital. The individual is said not to be able to control its occurrences or non-occurrences. The risk may be economic, such as interest rate change, or natural, such as a hurricane, in cause and effect.

FUNDED COVER transaction in which the CEDING COMPANY pays a premium and is guaranteed certain future payments to fund future losses. If losses are less than was expected, the ceding company receives a profit commission. Conversely, if catastrophic losses are occurring at a faster rate than the investment return earned on the premium, the ceding company will not receive its full recovery on its reinsurance. *See also* FINANCIAL REINSURANCE.

FUNDED PENSION PLAN plan in which funds are currently allocated to purchase retirement benefits. An employee is thus assured of receiving retirement payments, even if the employer is no longer in business at the time the employee retires. *See also* ALLOCATED FUNDING INSTRUMENT.

FUNDED RETIREMENT PLAN *see* FUNDED PENSION PLAN.

FUNDED TRUST *see* LIFE INSURANCE TRUST.

FUNDING allocation of funds in a retirement plan. *See also* ALLOCATED FUNDING INSTRUMENT.

FUNDING AGENCY individual or organization that provides the mechanism in which financial assets are accumulated for the purpose of paying accrued pension benefits. *See also* ACCRUED BENEFIT COST METHOD; PENSION PLAN FUNDING, GROUP DEPOSIT ADMINISTRATION ANNUITY; PENSION PLAN FUNDING, GROUP IMMEDIATE PARTICIPATING GUARANTEE (IPG) CONTRACT ANNUITY; PENSION PLAN FUNDING, GROUP PERMANENT CONTRACT; PENSION PLAN FUNDING, INDIVIDUAL CONTRACT PENSION PLAN.

FUNDING AGREEMENT private placement investment contract sold by insurance companies. This product has no registration requirement and pays the investor a higher rate of return than commercial paper. Frequently associated with this product are PUT OPTIONS that permit the investor to terminate the contract provided 7, 30, 90, or 180 days' notification is given.

FUNDING COVER refers to the insured or reinsured paying premiums into an account at a commercial bank that will be used to pay for future or past losses. Portions of the premiums not required to pay for these losses are refunded to the POLICYOWNER or CEDING COMPANY.

FUNDING INSTRUMENT/FUNDING MEDIA/FUNDING VEHICLE legal contract, such as an insurance policy, annuity or pension plan, containing ACTUARIAL EQUIVALENT considerations for the proper rate structure so that premium payments will be adequate to provide for future benefit payments.

FUNDING STANDARD ACCOUNT approach in pension plan funding under which a separate account is maintained for comparing actual contributions to the plan with the minimum contributions required to meet future employee benefit liabilities. This account acts as a reservoir in that it can store excess contributions above the minimum required. It also allows excess contributions to accumulate at interest and then applies these accrued contributions to reduce the minimum required future contributions.

FUNDS PAID IN ADVANCE TO COVER EXPENSES *see* RAIN INSURANCE.

FUND TRANSFER FRAUD INSURANCE type of CRIME INSURANCE that provides coverage in the event a financial institution fraudulently receives instructions to transfer funds from the customer's account to another person or organization.

FUNERAL INSURANCE modest life insurance coverage to pay burial expenses upon the death of an insured.

FUR AND JEWELRY FLOATER coverage on an ALL RISKS basis for loss or damage to fur and jewelry at any location. Furs and jewelry must be scheduled in order to be covered.

FURRIER'S BLOCK INSURANCE coverage for furs owned by a furrier, or a customer's furs in the care, custody, and control of the furrier. Coverage is on an ALL RISKS basis except those specifically excluded:

wear and tear; war; delay; loss of market; flood; earthquake; loss or damage while furs are being worn by the insured or his or her representatives; loss resulting from infidelity of any person under the care, custody, and control of the insured; damage or destruction of the furs after they leave the care, custody, and control of the insured that has been sold under an installment contract; and mysterious disappearance.

FURRIERS CUSTOMERS POLICY coverage on an ALL RISKS basis for fur garments belonging to customers of a furrier. *See also* FURRIERS BLOCK INSURANCE.

FURS INSURANCE coverage on fur coats as well as other clothes that have fur trim. Protection is provided at any location on an ALL RISKS basis subject to the exclusions of wear and tear, war, and nuclear disaster. Each item must be specifically listed in the policy.

FUTURE BUY-OUT EXPENSE OPTION option clause in a DISABILITY BUY-OUT INSURANCE POLICY that permits the owner of the policy to increase the limits of coverage for the expenses associated with the buy-out process. Usually, the limits can be increased only on the dates stipulated in this option clause.

FUTURE INSURABILITY GUARANTEE/FUTURE INCREASE OPTION option clause in a DISABILITY INCOME POLICY that the insured can exercise that would permit the insured the right to purchase additional limits of coverage regardless of the insured's physical condition. These additional purchases are limited by the insured's age and a maximum dollar amount, as well as twice the total monthly disability income from all insurance companies that the insured has in force, at which time the lesser of these two amounts would apply. This option may be exercised by the insured annually, usually until age 55.

FUTURES CONTRACTS DERIVATIVE representing a legal obligation to carry out a transaction that has been prearranged according to a stipulated price and date in the future. There are numerous types of financial instruments through which the value of this obligation may be established to include commodities, currencies, market indexes, interest rates, stocks, and bonds.

FUTURE SERVICE BENEFITS retirement payments to be credited for future years of service with an employer.

FUTURES TIED TO REINSURANCE futures contracts based on automobile and health REINSURANCE policies to be traded on the Commodity Future Exchange of the Chicago Board of Trade. The purpose is to allow insurance companies in the United States and abroad to use these futures contracts to hedge against losses on automobile and health policies that the companies underwrite. At the expiration point of the 3-month-long futures contract, certificates of reinsurance (showing evidence of the existence and terms of a particular policy or policies) are issued to the remaining contract holders. After all the claims have been paid, the reinsurance certificates are redeemed for an amount equal to the net earned premium. *See also* AUTOMATIC NON-PROPORTIONAL REINSURANCE; AUTOMATIC PROPORTIONAL REINSURANCE; AUTOMATIC REINSURANCE; EXCESS OF LOSS REINSURANCE; FACULTATIVE REINSURANCE; FINANCIAL REINSURANCE; NONPROPORTIONAL REINSUR-ANCE; PROPORTIONAL REINSURANCE; QUOTA SHARE REINSURANCE; STOP LOSS REINSURANCE; SURPLUS REINSURANCE.

FUTURE VALUE amount a sum of money today is worth at a specified future date because of the effect of compound interest.

FUTURISM methodology in which a range of plausible alternatives is suggested concerning future scenarios. The scenarios describe possi-bilities rather than predictions.

G

GAMBLING RISK-creating device as compared with INSURANCE, which is a risk-reducing or -eliminating device. This is a form of speculative risk.

GAMBLING INSURANCE *see* WAGERING AND INSURANCE.

GARAGE INSURANCE coverage for bodily injury, property damage or destruction, for which the insured garage and/or its representatives become legally liable resulting from the operation of the garage. For example, negligent repair to a customer's automobile brakes cause them to fail, thereby injuring the driver. The garage faces a liability suit for perhaps three types of damages: special, general, and punitive.

GATEKEEPER primary care physician. This physician is normally associated with a HEALTH MAINTENANCE ORGANIZATION (HMO) whose job is preventive health care and making sure only needed medical procedures are provided.

GENERAL ACCOUNT GUARANTEED INVESTMENTS CONTRACT (GIC) type of GUARANTEED INVESTMENTS CONTRACT in which funds for the contract are put in the insurance company's general account.

GENERAL ADJUSTMENT BUREAU (GAB) national agency supported by property insurance companies. The bureau is used by companies that do not have their own claims adjusters.

GENERAL AGENCY SYSTEM means of distribution that uses general agents rather than branch offices to sell life and health insurance. *See also* GENERAL AGENT (GA).

GENERAL AGENT (GA) individual responsible for insurance agency operation in a particular area, including sale of life and health insurance, servicing policies already sold, recruiting and training agents, and providing administrative support. General agents are compensated on a commission basis and usually pay all expenses of administering their agencies.

GENERAL AGENTS AND MANAGERS CONFERENCE (GAMC) association of general agents and managers affiliated with the NATIONAL ASSOCIATION FOR LIFE UNDERWRITING (NALU). Their objective is to seek solutions to common managerial problems. GAMC provides a forum for the exchange of ideas and gives awards for outstanding performance by members.

GENERAL AVERAGE expenses and damages incurred as the result of damage to a ship and its cargo and/or of taking direct action to prevent initial or further damage to the ship and its cargo. These expenses and damages are paid by those with an interest in the ship and its cargo in proportion to their values exposed to the common danger. Contrast with PARTICULAR AVERAGE.

GENERAL CHARACTERISTICS attributes of a particular employee benefit plan. For example, a general characteristic of group life insurance is that the whole group is underwritten, not individual members.

GENERAL CONSIDERATIONS *see* GENERAL CHARACTERISTICS.

GENERAL DAMAGES *see* LIABILITY, CIVIL DAMAGES AWARDED.

GENERAL INSURANCE *see* PROPERTY AND LIABILITY INSURANCE.

GENERAL LIABILITY INSURANCE coverage for an insured when negligent acts and/or omissions result in bodily injury and/or property damage on the premises of a business, when someone is injured as the result of using the product manufactured or distributed by a business, or when someone is injured in the general operation of a business.

GENERALLY ACCEPTED ACCOUNTING PRINCIPLES (GAAP) type of accounting method, in life insurance, designed to match revenues and expenses of an insurer according to principles designed by the FINANCIAL ACCOUNTING STANDARDS BOARD and the *Audit Guide for Stock Life Insurance Companies* published by the American Institute of CPAs. For example, under GAAP, acquisition expenses (costs of placing insurance on a company's books such as administrative expenses and agent commissions) are recognized in the same proportion that premium income is recognized over the premium paying period, with losses subtracted from premium and investment income as they occur.

GENERAL OPERATING EXPENSE costs incurred by an insurance company other than agent commissions and taxes; that is, mainly the administrative expense of running a company.

GENERAL PARTNER part of a LIMITED PARTNERSHIP such that this partner has unlimited legal responsibility for the debts and liabilities of the partnership.

GENERAL PROPERTY FORM attachment to a property business insurance policy providing coverage for a business structure and any additions and/or extensions; merchandise and other stock and inventory within the structure (not including animals, pets, watercraft, outdoor trees, shrubs, and plants, outdoor signs, fences, and swimming pools); personal property of the insured while in the insured structure and within 100 feet of the premises; and personal property of a third party under the safekeeping of the insured in the insured structure and within 100 feet of the premises. The General Property Form Provides coverage in three ways:

1. *Specific*—an amount of insurance is provided on a specified piece of property.
2. *Schedule*—an amount of insurance is provided on several specified pieces of property listed in the policy.

3. *Blanket*—an amount of insurance is provided on several different kinds of property, several different locations, or a combination of several different kinds of property at several different locations.

GENERATION SKIPPING TRANSFER TAXES provision under the Internal Revenue Code, Chapter 13, that specifies a transfer tax of 55% of the gift to a person at least two generations younger than the transferor (person who gives the gift). This tax is imposed in addition to any estate taxes or regular gift taxes.

GEOGRAPHICAL LIMITATION *see* TERRITORIAL LIMITS.

GIFT transfer of property without payment.

GIFT ANNUITY type of an ANNUITY in which a donor transfers funds to a charitable organization, and in turn the donor receives fixed income payments for life. These payments may continue for the life of a second individual under a JOINT LIFE AND SURVIVORSHIP ANNUITY as well. Such an annuity allows for an immediate income tax charitable deduction, a percentage of the income payment received not subject to ordinary income tax (exclusion ratio), and funds transferred to create the annuity not included in the taxable estate of the grantor.

GIFT IN TRUST value or property given by an individual to a *trustee* who holds and administers it for the benefit of the donee (recipient of the gift). For example, a father entrusts a life insurance policy with all ownership rights to a trustee. The trustee owns the policy, collects the proceeds, and administers the proceeds for the benefit of the donee son. *See also* ESTATE PLANNING DISTRIBUTION.

GIFT OUTRIGHT value or property given by an individual directly to a donee (recipient of the gift), for example, when a father gives a life insurance policy with all ownership rights to his son. *See also* ESTATE PLANNING DISTRIBUTION.

GIFT TAX tax, under federal and state laws, on transfer of property made without payment or other value in exchange.

GIFT TAX EXCLUSION amount, not in excess of $12,000 per year, given to each of an unlimited number of donees free of FEDERAL ESTATE TAX and GIFT TAX. Each individual can give up to $12,000 to any one donee, or up to $12,000 each to an unlimited number of donees, provided the gift has no conditions attached. A gift completed in this manner will not reduce the donor's MARITAL DEDUCTION.

Wealth can be transferred on a significant basis free from federal estate tax by careful planning providing the donor is comfortable giving away acquired wealth while still alive. A word of caution: If the gift is in the form of a check, the Internal Revenue requires that the check be paid and cleared by the donor's bank before the gift can be considered complete. Thus, if the check is given in December, but does not clear the donor's bank until January, the gift would be deemed to have been given in the new year and the old year's gift allowance will have been wasted.

G.I. INSURANCE *see* GOVERNMENT LIFE INSURANCE.

GLASS INSURANCE *see* COMPREHENSIVE GLASS INSURANCE.

GLASS-STEAGALL ACT (BANKING ACT OF 1933) legislation excluding commercial banks that are members of the Federal Reserve System from most types of investment banking activities. The coauthor of the Act, Senator Carter Glass of Virginia, believed that commercial banks should restrict their activities to involvement in short-term loans to coincide with the nature of their primary classification of liabilities, demand deposits. Today, many in the banking field view these constraints as particularly burdensome because of increased competition from other financial institutions for customers' savings and investment dollars.

GOLFERS EQUIPMENT INSURANCE coverage for golf clubs and golf equipment on an ALL RISKS basis subject to exclusions of wear and tear, war, and nuclear disaster. Location of coverage is a clubhouse locker or any other building used in golf activities. For example, if a golfer's clubs were in the locker in the clubhouse and they were stolen, the golfer would be indemnified. There is usually no coinsurance requirement, and coverage is provided on a replacement cost basis.

GOOD SAMARITAN COVERAGE *see* HOMEOWNERS INSURANCE POLICY—SECTION II (LIABILITY COVERAGE).

GOOD STUDENT DISCOUNT reduction in automobile insurance rate for a student with a good academic record. Some statistical studies suggest that good students have fewer automobile accidents.

GOODWILL monetary value of the reputation of a business. Goodwill is an intangible asset and thus may be difficult to measure.

GOVERNMENT INSURANCE coverage under the auspices of a federal or state agency that can be either mandatory or elective. *See also* SOCIAL INSURANCE.

GOVERNMENT LIFE INSURANCE coverage for present and past U.S. uniformed services members under one of these programs:
1. *United States Government Life Insurance (USGLI)*—established in 1919 to provide RENEWABLE TERM LIFE INSURANCE up to $10,000. This program is no longer available.
2. *National Service Life Insurance (NSLI)*—established in 1940 to take the place of USGLI; terminated in 1950. Today NSLI exists for amounts ranging from $1000 to $10,000 under five-year renewable term and permanent forms of life insurance. The latter policies have the same *nonforfeiture benefits* and OPTIONAL MODES OF SETTLEMENT as COMMERCIAL FORMS of life insurance.
3. SERVICEMEN'S GROUP LIFE INSURANCE (SGLI)—established in 1965 to cover active members of the U.S. uniformed forces; purchased through *commercial insurance companies* on a group basis at a government subsidized rate. Each service person pays a premium

that reflects nonmilitary mortality expectation and administrative expenses. The federal government subsidizes the premium by paying for any extra mortality and administrative expenses associated with the military exposure. Upon discharge, a SGLI policy can be converted, regardless of physical condition, to a five-year nonrenewable Veterans Group Life Policy (VGLI), and then can be converted (after five years)—again regardless of health—to an individual life policy with any of the participating commercial life insurance companies.

   4. VETERANS GROUP LIFE INSURANCE (VGLI)—nonrenewable convertible five-year term insurance to which SGLI is converted at the time a service person is discharged. It has no cash or loan value, disability benefits, paid-up benefits, or extended term benefits. It can be converted to an individual policy with a participating company.

GOVERNMENT MONEY MUTUAL FUNDS investments made in a variety of securities issued by government agencies.

GRACE PERIOD period after the date the premium is due during which the premium can be paid with no interest charged, the policy remaining in force. This period is for 30 or 31 days. If the insured dies during this period, the beneficiary would receive the full face amount of the policy minus the premium owed. Thus the use of the grace period allows the financial technique of leveraging.

GRADED *see* GRADED COMMISSION; GRADED DEATH BENEFIT; GRADED PREMIUM, WHOLE LIFE INSURANCE.

GRADED COMMISSION compensation that varies with the class and type of insurance sold. Many insurance companies offer varying commissions according to the volume of business an agent places with the company.

GRADED DEATH BENEFIT death payment that increases with the age of an insured. Graded benefits may increase gradually and then level off, or may increase sharply before becoming level. This type of coverage is most common in juvenile life insurance.

GRADED POLICY insurance for which premiums are charged according to the size of the FACE AMOUNT of the policy, so that the greater the face amount, the lower the cost per $1000 unit of insurance.

GRADED PREMIUM, WHOLE LIFE INSURANCE coverage under which initial premiums are less than normal for the first few years, then gradually increase for the next several years until they become level for the duration of the policy.

GRADED VESTING VESTING, DEFERRED or VESTING, IMMEDIATE under which the accrued benefits of the employee increase on a percentage basis (according to years of service and/or attained age) until 100% VESTING is achieved.

GRADUATED LIFE TABLE MORTALITY TABLE that reflects irregularities from age to age due to chance fluctuations in the sequence of the rates of mortality. The rates of death as reflected by the mortality table in its most idealized form (the "perfect world" approach) should proceed smoothly from age bracket to subsequent age bracket. Irregularities may result from:
1. statistical fluctuations due to an insufficiently large data base.
2. use of statistics that are not homogeneous.
3. statistics of one particular mortality study not representing other mortality studies.
4. mortality statistics for later policy years too scanty to yield reliable information, and too heavily weighted towards the earlier policy years.

GRADUATED MORTALITY TABLE *see* GRADUATED LIFE TABLE.

GRADUATION statistical procedure applied to the data that comprises a MORTALITY TABLE. It is designed to smooth out the irregularities in that data believed to not be truly indicative of the population from which the sample data has been taken.

GRAMM-LEACH BLILEY FINANCIAL SERVICES MODERNIZATION ACT OF 1999 (GLBA) legislation that allows insurance companies, securities firms, and banks to merge and/or affiliate within financial holding companies and to expand their financial activities to include the issuance and distribution of ANNUITIES and indemnification for death, disability, and damage. State insurance regulators maintain control over insurance-related activities conducted by a bank. In effect, GLBA repeals the provisions in the GLASS-STEAGALL ACT (BANKING ACT OF 1933) that restricted banks from selling insurance products in communities with more than 5000 people. Banks or other institutions acting as depositories must disclose that neither they nor the FDIC guarantee an INSURANCE POLICY or ANNUITY.

GRANT OF LIMITED PROPERTY INTEREST *see* ESTATE PLANNING DISTRIBUTION.

GRANTOR individual who creates a TRUST and generally places his or her assets in it.

GRANTOR RETAINED ANNUITY TRUST (GRAT) irrevocable TRUST into which the GRANTOR places assets and receives in turn a fixed amount of income from a fixed ANNUITY (amount of income stipulated at the time the trust is established) for either a given number of years, or for the lesser of a given number of years, or until the grantor's death. When the term of the trust expires, assets in the trust to include any appreciation are distributed to the named remainder beneficiary(s). If the assets in the trust fail to generate sufficient income to make the required annuity payments, the principal of the asset on deposit in the trust must be liquidated in an amount needed to meet the required income payments. This principal could diminish dramatically by the time it is transferred to the remainder beneficiary(s). If the grantor is alive when the trust terminates, the assets and their appreciation within the trust are not included in the grantor's estate.

GRANTOR-RETAINED INCOME TRUST (GRIT) irrevocable TRUST into which the GRANTOR places assets and retains the income from or the use of these assets for a stipulated period of time. At the termination of this time period, the principal (assets) of the trust is transferred to the grantor's noncharitable BENEFICIARY. The noncharitable beneficiary may include individual(s) such as a grandchild, niece, nephew, son, or daughter. Should the grantor survive the stipulated period of time, he or she will incur substantial savings in estate and gift taxes. In order for these savings in taxes to occur, the following requirements must be met by the grantor:

1. income to the grantor must be the sole result of the income generated by assets held in the trust.
2. any income generated by the assets held in the trust can be paid only to the grantor of the trust.
3. neither the grantor nor the spouse of the grantor can act as a trustee of the trust.
4. any income retained by the grantor must be for a period of time not to exceed 10 years.

   Should the grantor die before the stipulated period of time the trust expires, the value of the assets of the trust are included in the grantor's estate for FEDERAL ESTATE TAX purposes, even though the assets are not physically transferred to the estate of the grantor. *See also* SUPERGRIT.

GRANTOR RETAINED TRUST TRUST under which grantor retains income from the ASSETS that have been transferred to the trust. This trust permits the avoidance of probate, protects the assets from creditors, and leads to the savings of substantial taxes. *See also* GRANTOR-RETAINED INCOME TRUST (GRIT); SUPERGRIT.

GRANTOR RETAINED UNITRUST (GRUT) irrevocable TRUST into which the GRANTOR places assets and receives in turn a variable amount of income from a VARIABLE ANNUITY (amount of income will vary yearly depending upon the increase or decrease in the value of the assets on deposit in the trust) for either a given number of years, or for the lesser of a given number of years, or until the grantor's death. When the term of the trust expires, assets in the trust to include any appreciation are distributed to the named remainder beneficiary(s). If the grantor is alive when the trust terminates, the assets and their appreciation within the trust are not included in the grantor's estate.

GRID METHOD type of asset allocation model that distributes investments according to the age and risk tolerance level of an investor.

GROSS *see* GROSS EARNINGS FORM; GROSS INCOME; GROSS PREMIUM.

GROSS DOMESTIC PRODUCT (GDP) measurement of the nominal value of all goods and services produced in a one year period. This production includes that by United States-owned companies as well as by production plants located in the United States and owned by foreign companies. As GDP increases, there is a tendency for company profits and interest rates to rise as well. Conversely, as GDP decreases, there is a tendency for company profits and interest rates to also decline. These figures are published on a quarterly basis by the United States Department of Commerce.

GROSS EARNINGS FORM coverage for loss in the gross earnings of the business (minus expenses that cease while the business is inoperative) as the result of the interruption of normal business activities caused by damage to the premises by an insured peril. Noncontinuing expenses include light, gas, and advertising for which there is no contractual obligation. Coverage can be obtained on either a 50, 60, 70, or 80% coinsurance basis. Selection of the coinsurance percentage is dependent upon the length of time business is expected not to operate in the worst of circumstances.

GROSS ESTATE sum total of all assets owned by the decedent to include personal property, real property, and trust property.

GROSS INCOME total income before adjustment for deduction as applied to tax calculation for both the individual and the firm.

GROSS LINE total limit on the amount of coverage an INSURER will underwrite on an individual RISK. The amount underwritten includes the amount to be CEDED through a REINSURANCE agreement.

GROSS NATIONAL PRODUCT (GNP) total value of all goods and services produced by companies located in the United States as well as that produced by United States companies whose production facilities are outside the United States.

GROSS NEGLIGENCE reckless action without regard to life, limb, and/or property; for example, driving 100 miles per hour on a road or highway.

GROSS PREMIUM
General: net premium, plus operating and miscellaneous expenses, and agent's commissions.
Life insurance: premium before dividends are subtracted.

GROUP ACCIDENT AND HEALTH INSURANCE *see* GROUP DISABILITY INSURANCE; GROUP HEALTH INSURANCE; GROUP INSURANCE.

GROUP ANNUITY contract providing a monthly income benefit to members of a group of employees. A group annuity has the same characteristics as an individual annuity, except that it is underwritten on a group basis. *See also* ANNUITY.

GROUP ANNUITY TABLE, 1951 first historical MORTALITY TABLE used for the calculation of PREMIUM rates for GROUP ANNUITIES. This table was subsequently replaced by the GROUP ANNUITY TABLE, 1971.

GROUP ANNUITY TABLE, 1971 historical MORTALITY TABLE that replaced the GROUP ANNUITY TABLE, 1951, whose statistics at that time were more current than the replaced table. This table was subsequently replaced by the 1983 GAM table (mortality table used to calculate male annuity rates on a group basis).

GROUP CERTIFICATE summary certificate of benefits issued to an employee in lieu of a policy. The master contract remains with the employer. For example, in group life insurance, an employee receives only a summary certificate of benefits, while the master contract remains with the employer.

GROUP CONTRACT *see* GROUP INSURANCE.

GROUP CREDIT INSURANCE coverage issued to a creditor on the lives of debtors for outstanding loans. If a debtor dies before repayment, the policy pays the remainder of the loan to the creditor. The contract covers an entire group of debtors rather than each debtor separately.

GROUP CREDITOR INSURANCE *see* CREDIT LIFE INSURANCE (CREDITOR LIFE INSURANCE); GROUP CREDIT INSURANCE.

GROUP DEFERRED ANNUITY contract for retirements benefits in which an entire group of employees is underwritten, as opposed to a single annuity for each employee. Each premium pays for an increment of a paid-up annuity; thus a group deferred annuity is a series of single premium paid-up annuities. It may be considered an ALLOCATED FUNDING INSTRUMENT for purchasing retirement benefits. Single premium paid-up annuities that have already been purchased guarantee that an employee will receive retirement income whether or not the employer remains in business at the time he or she retires.

GROUP DEPOSIT ADMINISTRATION ANNUITY *see* PENSION PLAN FUNDING.

GROUP DISABILITY INSURANCE coverage of an employee group whose members receive a monthly disability income benefit, subject to a maximum amount, if illness or accident prevents a member from performing the normal functions of his or her job. Benefits are usually limited to a stated length of time, and the maximum monthly income benefit is usually no more than 50-60% of earnings prior to the disability, or a flat dollar amount, whichever is less.

GROUP HEALTH INSURANCE coverage underwritten on members of a natural group, such as employees of a particular business, union, association, or employer group. Each employee is entitled to benefits for hospital room and board, surgeon and physician fees, and miscellaneous medical expenses. There is a DEDUCTIBLE and a COINSURANCE requirement each employee must pay. Characteristics of group health insurance include:

1. TRUE GROUP PLAN—one in which all employees must be accepted for coverage regardless of physical condition. (For example, coverage cannot be denied because of a pre-existing condition such as cancer.) Usually an employee must apply and pay the first premium within the first 30 days of employment or he or she forfeits the right to automatic coverage (a form of GUARANTEED INSURABILITY). Individuals are covered under a MASTER CONTRACT, each receiving a certificate denoting coverage.

2. *Schedule of Benefits*—describes what the insured and his or her covered dependent(s) is entitled to in the event of disease, illness, or injury. After the insured or the covered dependent has satisfied the DEDUCTIBLE (defined as the first portion of all of the eligible expenses that occur during a calendar year of coverage), the insurance company pays a given percentage (usually 80%) until a total sum *(stop loss),* usually $5000, is reached for the calendar year. After the total sum has been reached, the insurance company pays 100% of the total eligible expenses until the end of the calendar year subject to a maximum lifetime amount. *See also* DEPENDENT.

3. *Eligible Expenses*—include hospital bills, surgery, doctor's services, private nursing, medicines, and X-rays. Payment allowed for these and other expenses are spelled out in the policy. For example, the hospital's daily charge for room and board is subject to a specified maximum.

4. *Exclusions from Provisions of Medical Benefits*—many exclusions occur in group health plans, including benefits under Workers Compensation; certain mouth conditions; convalescent or rest cures; expenses incurred by a member of a HEALTH MAINTENANCE ORGANIZATION (HMO) or other prepaid medical plan; expenses associated with intentional self-inflicted injuries or attempt at suicide.

5. COORDINATION OF BENEFITS—when there are two or more group health insurance plans covering the insured, one plan becomes the *Primary Plan* and the other plan(s) becomes the *Secondary Plan(s).* *The Primary Plan is* required to pay benefits due the insured and/or covered dependents before any other plan pays benefits. When a claim is made, the primary plan must pay the claim without regard to the benefits provided under any other plan. The secondary plan pays the difference between the total claim amount and the amount that the primary plan has paid, up to total allowable expenses.

GROUP IMMEDIATE PARTICIPATION GUARANTEED ANNU-ITY *see* PENSION PLAN FUNDING; GROUP IMMEDIATE PARTICIPATION GUARANTEED (IPG) CONTRACT ANNUITY.

GROUP INSURANCE single policy under which individuals in a natural group (such as employees of a business firm) and their dependents are covered. *See also* GROUP ANNUITY; GROUP CERTIFICATE; GROUP CREDIT INSURANCE; GROUP DEFERRED ANNUITY; GROUP DISABILITY INSURANCE; GROUP HEALTH INSURANCE; GROUP LIFE INSURANCE; GROUP PAID-

UP LIFE INSURANCE; GROUP PERMANENT LIFE INSURANCE; GROUP TERM LIFE INSURANCE; PENSION PLAN FUNDING; GROUP DEPOSIT ADMINISTRATION ANNUITY.

GROUP LIFE INSURANCE basic employee benefit under which an employer buys a master policy and issues certificates to employees denoting participation in the plan. Group life is also available through unions and associations. It is usually issued as yearly renewable term insurance, although some plans provide permanent insurance. Employers may pay all the cost or share it with employees. Characteristics include:

1. *Group Underwriting*—an entire group of employees is underwritten, unlike individual life insurance whereunder only the individual is underwritten.
2. *Guaranteed Issue*—every employee must be accepted; an employee cannot be denied coverage because of a pre-existing illness, sickness, or injury.
3. *Conversion at Termination of Employment*—regardless of whether termination is because of severance, disability, or retirement, the employee has the automatic right to convert to an individual life policy without evidence of insurability or taking a physical examination. Conversion must be within 30 days of termination. The premium upon conversion is based on the employee's age at the time (ATTAINED AGE).
4. DISABILITY BENEFIT—available in many policies to an employee less than 60 years of age who can no longer work because of the disability. The benefit takes the form of waiver of premium, and the employee is covered for as long as the disability continues. The beneficiary will receive the death benefit even though the employee may not have been in the service of the employer for a long time.
5. DEATH BENEFIT Structure or Schedule—is usually based on an employee's earnings. The benefit is a multiple of the employee's earnings, normally 1 to 2½ times the employee's yearly earnings. In many companies, if the employee dies while on company business, 6 times the yearly earnings are paid as a death benefit. For example, a $50,000 a year employee dies in an accident while traveling on company time; the beneficiary would receive $300,000. But if the same employee dies in his sleep at home, the beneficiary would receive $100,000 (assuming that the normal death benefit is twice annual earnings).

GROUP LONG-TERM DISABILITY POLICY group insurance contract under which a periodic (usually monthly) disability income benefit is paid to the insured as long as he or she remains disabled.

GROUP OF COMPANIES *see* FLEET OF COMPANIES.

GROUP ORDINARY INSURANCE *see* GROUP PERMANENT LIFE INSURANCE.

GROUP PAID-UP LIFE INSURANCE combination of two basic plans: (1) accumulating units of paid-up permanent life insurance, and (2) decreasing units of group term life insurance. The premium paid each month consists of the (a) employee's contribution and (b) employer's contribution. The employee's portion purchases increments of paid-up insurance, and the employer's portion purchases group decreasing term. The employer's contribution is tax deductible as a business expense, and these contributions are not taxable income to the employee. (However, if the employer purchases increments of paid-up units of permanent insurance, these contributions are taxable income to the employee on a current basis.) Paid-up units purchased by an employee are vested and thus can be taken as a paid-up life benefit regardless of the reason for termination of employment. The paid-up benefit will always remain in force; no further premium payments are required.

GROUP PERMANENT *see* GROUP PERMANENT LIFE INSURANCE.

GROUP PERMANENT LIFE INSURANCE coverage following the same structure as *group term,* the significant difference being that premiums go toward the purchase of permanent insurance instead of term insurance. The employee has a vested interest in the increments of paid-up insurance purchased. Because of the tax consequences to the employee, group permanent insurance usually is applied to fund retirement plans such as pensions instead of providing life insurance coverage. If the employer purchased permanent insurance on the employee's behalf, the contributions would become taxable income to the employee on a current basis. Group life insurance is *experience rated,* in that the loss experience of the entire group determines the premium rate applied to each employee.

GROUP PRACTICE HEALTH MAINTENANCE ORGANIZA-TION (HMO) HEALTH MAINTENANCE ORGANIZATION that restricts to a relatively small amount the number of medical providers from which an HMO member may seek services. Usually, HMO members may select the primary care physician of their choice from this number. After rendering services to the HMO member, the physician charges the HMO a predetermined fee. Frequently, this select group of medical providers are exclusively in the employment of this particular HMO.

GROUP TERM LIFE INSURANCE one-year coverage that is renewable at the end of each year. Since the group plan is subject to EXPERIENCE RATING, the premium rate upon renewal is based on such factors as the loss record (death) of the group and range of employee ages. All employees are insured with term life insurance. Realistically, coverage is temporary because on termination of employment, the employee usually does not convert group term to individual permanent insurance because the conversion is at a higher attained age rate. *See also* ATTAINED AGE.

GROUP UNDERWRITING process of forming a large group of homogeneous lives that in order to allow the LAW OF LARGE NUMBERS to operate, thereby projecting a probable rate of mortality or morbidity whose creditability approaches one, and standard deviation approaches zero. Since no evidence of insurability has to be submitted on an individual basis, the objective of this type of UNDERWRITING is to minimize ADVERSE SELECTION by any member of that group. In an effort to achieve this minimization, certain underwriting rules apply: (1) the group must be formed for reasons other than obtaining insurance, or people who have a particular disease would join together for the sole purpose of buying insurance; (2) a constant flow of young people into the group and outflow of older people out of the group is required so that, statistically, the average person (standard health) will continue to be insured; (3) the insurance benefits should automatically be determined by some type of formula on behalf of the members, or only those members who are in poor health would select the higher limits of coverage; and (4) close to total participation of all eligible employees should be achieved.

GROUP UNIVERSAL LIFE INSURANCE policy similar to that of an individual UNIVERSAL LIFE INSURANCE policy except that the coverage is provided (up to a limit) without the requirement of the submission of EVIDENCE OF INSURABILITY.

GROWTH OF ASSETS rate of increase in asset value.

GUARANTEE COST NONPARTICIPATING LIFE INSURANCE policy whose premiums, cash value, and face amount are guaranteed (all values are fixed and do not fluctuate according to the loss experience, expenses, and investment returns of the insurance company). The advantage of this policy to the POLICYOWNER is that, when the company experiences adverse conditions, they are not passed on to the policyowner. Likewise, the disadvantage of this policy to the policyowner is that the policyowner does not reap the benefits when the company experiences good conditions.

GUARANTEED COST PREMIUM premium charged for an insurance policy whose coverage does not vary according to the insured loss experience. The premium is calculated either on a specified rating basis or on a prospective basis (fixed or adjustable).

GUARANTEED COST (TRADITIONAL) INSURANCE PROGRAM arrangement under which the insured pays a fixed premium to the insurance company in exchange for the total transfer of the risk to that company.

GUARANTEED DEFINED CONTRIBUTION PLAN guaranteed minimum rate of return under a DEFINED CONTRIBUTION PENSION PLAN (MONEY PURCHASE PLAN). Typically, the employer who sponsors the plan and makes up the difference between the minimum guarantee and the rate actually earned provides the guarantee. To affect this guarantee, some plans permit the participants to purchase a FIXED DOLLAR ANNUITY or an EQUITY INDEXED ANNUITY. *See also* GUARANTEED INVESTMENT CONTRACT (GIC).

GUARANTEED FOR LIFE WITHDRAWAL BENEFIT provision found in VARIABLE DOLLAR ANNUITIES that guarantees the POLICYOWNER can make withdrawals for life (even if the account value decreases to zero) while continuing to invest in the subaccounts of the variable annuity.

GUARANTEED FULL REPLACEMENT COVERAGE type of HOMEOWNER INSURANCE POLICY—SECTION I (PROPERTY COVERAGE) that will pay the total cost to repair or replace the home with one of like kind and quality regardless of the original cost.

GUARANTEED INSURABILITY right of an insured to make additional purchases of life insurance without having to take a physical examination or show other evidence of insurability. Additions can be bought (1) at stated times; (2) upon specified policy anniversaries such as every fifth year of a policy up to a maximum age (usually 40 or 45); or (3) upon the birth of a child. Many young families should consider adding this option, since a likely time to add to a life insurance portfolio is when family obligations increase. *See also* RIDERS, LIFE POLICIES.

GUARANTEED INTEREST RATE *see* INTEREST RATES, GUARANTEED/EXCESS.

GUARANTEED INTEREST RATE FIXED ACCOUNT account in which a predetermined interest rate is paid for a predetermined period of time. For each contribution that is paid into the fixed account, a new guarantee period begins for that particular contribution.

GUARANTEED INVESTMENT CONTRACT (GIC) institutional investment sold by life insurance companies that guarantees principal and offers withdrawal flexibility. This conservative investment, which can be used with a corporate qualified plan, became one of the most popular choices in such *salary reduction plans* as the 401 (k) plan. Many of these plans offered employees three choices for depositing their pre-tax retirement dollars: a stock fund, a bond fund, and a GIC. By 1987, about 40% of employees had elected GIC investments.

GUARANTEED INVESTMENT POLICY *see* GUARANTEED INVESTMENT CONTRACT (GIC).

GUARANTEED ISSUE the right to purchase insurance without physical examination; the present and past physical condition of the applicant are not considered.

GUARANTEED MINIMUM INCOME BENEFIT (GMIB) IN VARIABLE ANNUITIES guaranteed minimum income payment to the annuitant for life regardless of the underlying portfolio performance. Usually requires that the variable annuity be in force a minimum number of years (10 years is the most common) before the guarantee goes into effect.

GUARANTEED MINIMUM WITHDRAWAL BENEFIT (GMWB) feature of VARIABLE DOLLAR ANNUITY that guarantees the POLICY-

HOLDER at a minimum the return of principal paid-in upon annuitization or withdrawal regardless of the level of the EQUITIES market.

GUARANTEED MINIMUM WITHDRAWAL BENEFIT (GMWB) IN VARIABLE ANNUITIES guaranteed minimum number of stipulated income payments to the annuitant regardless of the underlying portfolio performance. Usually requires that the variable annuity be in force a minimum number of years (10 years is the most common) before the guarantee goes into effect.

GUARANTEED PURCHASE OPTION *see* GUARANTEED INSURABILITY.

GUARANTEED RENEWABLE CONTRACT (LIFE OR HEALTH) insurance policy renewable at the option of the insured for a specified number of years or to a stated age. The insurance company cannot refuse to renew the policy and cannot change any of its provisions except the PREMIUM RATE. If the insurance company changes the premium, it must do so for the entire policyholder classification, not just for one or a few members. *See also* GUARANTEED INSURABILITY.

GUARANTEED RENEWABLE HEALTH INSURANCE *see* COMMERCIAL HEALTH INSURANCE.

GUARANTEED REPLACEMENT COST agreement by the INSURANCE COMPANY (INSURER) to replace the damaged or destroyed PROPERTY with one of like kind and quality even if the cost is greater than the policy limit. *See also* REPLACEMENT COST LESS PHYSICAL DEPRECIATION AND OBSOLESCENCE.

GUARANTEES, LACK OF *see* UNALLOCATED FUNDING INSTRUMENT.

GUARANTOR term in surety coverage. Through the issue of a surety bond, a surety company is in effect the guarantor. *See also* SURETY BOND.

GUARANTY FUND (INSOLVENCY FUND) aggregate sums, in certain states, to pay claims of insolvent insurance companies. These funds are maintained by contributions of companies operating in a particular state in proportion to their business written in the state. A guaranty fund insures the integrity of the insurance business.

GUARDIAN individual who is legally responsible for taking care of another individual(s) who is deemed to be incapable of managing his/her own affairs. For example, children under the age of majority are not assumed to be able to manage their own affairs.

GUERTIN LAWS standard State Valuation and Nonforfeiture Law approved by the NATIONAL ASSOCIATION OF INSURANCE COMMISSIONERS (NAIC) in 1942. This law is named for Alfred N. Guertin, the actuary who headed the NAIC committee that studied the need for a new mortality table to be used in calculating life insurance nonforfeiture values. In essence, application of this law guarantees that an insured is entitled to all benefits for which the life insurance company has received premiums. The insured cannot be made to forfeit the equity that has built up in a life insurance product. *See also* NONFORFEITURE BENEFITS (OPTION).

GUEST LAW legal right of a passenger in an automobile involved in an accident to bring a liability suit against the driver. It is deemed that a special standard of care is owed by an automobile driver towards the passenger. This law bars suits only for ordinary—not gross or criminal—negligence. In many states, such actions by a passenger are prohibited; in other states, intentional misconduct of the driver must be shown.

GUIDING PRINCIPLES title of a published set of rules, adhered to by member companies of major property and liability associations, that stipulate how losses should be adjusted when the same loss is covered by more than one insurance company. Particular emphasis is placed on how the cost of the losses should be apportioned among the companies under various situations.

H

HABITS behavior or character standing of an individual in a community. Some personal habits are considered in underwriting an insurance application.

HAIL INSURANCE coverage against hail damage to crops. Coverage is on a proportionate basis; that is, in the event of loss, a farmer will recover an amount based on the ratio of the damaged part of a crop to the entire crop.

HANGARKEEPERS LEGAL LIABILITY INSURANCE coverage for the owner of an airplane in circumstances where use of the owner's premises as an aircraft hangar results in bodily injury or property damage to a third party. Excluded from coverage is property under the care, custody, and control of the insured. Another application of this policy covers the operator of a hangar for liability from damage to an aircraft that the owner has placed under the operator's care, custody, and control for storage or repair.

HARD INSURANCE MARKET *see* UNDERWRITING CYCLE.

HARDSHIP existence of a financial need which permits in-service withdrawals of funds from a SECTION 401 (k) PLAN or a SECTION 403 (b) PLAN to pay tuition for postsecondary education for a participant or his or her spouse, children, or other dependents.

HAZARD circumstance that increases the likelihood or probable severity of a loss. For example, the storing of explosives in a home basement is a hazard that increases the probability of an explosion.

HAZARD INCREASE RESULTING IN SUSPENSION OR EXCLUSION OF COVERAGE provision commonly found in fire insurance contracts. If the insured knows that a hazard is increased, most property contracts permit the insurance company to suspend or terminate coverage. For example, manufacture of drugs in the home would give the insurance company the right to invoke this clause if it could show that the manufacturing process increases the probability of fire. *See also* LOSSES PAID.

HAZARD, MORAL *see* MORALE HAZARD.

HAZARD, MORALE *see* MORAL HAZARD.

HAZARD, PHYSICAL *see* HAZARD; INCREASED HAZARD.

HEAD OFFICE *see* HOME OFFICE.

HEALTH CARE POWER OF ATTORNEY legal instrument that authorizes a person to make medical decisions for another person should that person become permanently or temporarily incapable of making those decisions. This power is usually coupled with a LIVING WILL to indicate the type of health care desired if the person no longer has control of his or her faculties or is terminally ill.

HEALTH CARE VILLAGE vast insurance purchase market that permits the combination of companies and the self-employed to join together to purchase insurance coverage on a reduced cost group basis.

HEALTH CERTIFICATE statement submitted to the INSURANCE COMPANY to accompany a request for the REINSTATEMENT of an INSURANCE POLICY that has LAPSED. This statement certifies that the INSURED'S health has not materially changed during the lapsed period.

HEALTH INSURANCE three basic plans are available to cover the costs of health care: COMMERCIAL HEALTH INSURANCE, *private noncommercial* (BLUE CROSS/BLUE SHIELD), and SOCIAL INSURANCE *(Social Security)*. *See also* MEDICAID; MEDICARE; WORKERS COMPENSATION INSURANCE.

HEALTH INSURANCE ASSOCIATION OF AMERICA (HIAA) organization that seeks to educate the public on the benefits of private health insurance coverage. Its membership consists of private companies that sell health insurance. The HIAA publishes materials and lobbies federal and state legislatures in an effort to support its objective. Based in Washington, D.C.

HEALTH INSURANCE BENEFITS *see* COMMERCIAL HEALTH INSURANCE; DISABILITY INSURANCE; GROUP DISABILITY INSURANCE; GROUP HEALTH INSURANCE; HEALTH MAINTENANCE ORGANIZATION (HMO); PRIVATE NONCOMMERCIAL (BLUE CROSS/BLUE SHIELD); SOCIAL INSURANCE (SOCIAL SECURITY); SURGICAL EXPENSE INSURANCE.

HEALTH INSURANCE CONTRACT policy that pays benefits to an insured who becomes ill or injured, provided that documentation is offered to confirm the illness or injury. *See also* DISABILITY INSURANCE; GROUP DISABILITY INSURANCE; GROUP HEALTH INSURANCE; HEALTH INSURANCE; HEALTH MAINTENANCE ORGANIZATION (HMO); SURGICAL EXPENSE INSURANCE.

HEALTH INSURANCE FUTURES one-year futures contract (standardized agreement between two parties to buy or sell a commodity or financial instrument on an organized futures exchange such as the CBOT within some future time period at a present stipulated price), traded at the Chicago Board of Trade (CBOT), which would allow health insurance companies and self-insured employers to hedge their losses. The essential design of this contract is such that when actual claims exceed expected claims by amount "X," the futures contract would increase by the same amount "X." The financial instrument that forms the basis of this futures contract is an index that reflects the claims experience of ten health insurance companies. By buying futures contracts that will appreciate in the future as claims increase in the future, insurance companies and self-insured employers can profit from increasing futures prices through which they can offset their losses. Accordingly, by selling futures contracts that will decline in the future, these organizations can profit from decreasing futures prices that can be used to offset smaller cash flow. For example, if a health insurance company buys a futures contract for $40,000 and then sells it for $50,000, the company will recognize a profit of $10,000, which can be used to pay the higher than expected claims incurred. The cost effectiveness of hedging through the buying and selling of futures contracts depends on high correlations between expected claims payments and the futures contracts prices. If there is a low correlation between expected claims payments and the futures contracts prices, the less cost effective the hedge becomes. Thus, it is critical for the insurance company or the self-insured employer to establish the correlation between its block of business and the health insurance futures index.

HEALTH INSURANCE RENEWABILITY *see* HEALTH INSURANCE.

HEALTH MAINTENANCE ORGANIZATION (HMO) prepaid group health insurance plan that entitles members to services of participating physicians, hospitals, and clinics. Emphasis is on preventive medicine. Members of the HMO pay a flat periodic fee (usually deducted from each paycheck) for these medical services:

1. *HMO Managing Physician*—a new member can select an HMO physician, who is then responsible for providing all of his or her health care needs. If necessary, the managing physician makes arrangements for the member to see a specialist.
2. *HMO Copayment*—a member may be required to pay an amount in addition to required penodic payments, for example, a $5 flat fee for each visit regardless of how expensive the services may be. Or, for each prescription, to pay a flat amount of $2 regardless of the actual cost.
3. *HMO Hospital Services*—include, among others, room and board, operating room, laboratory tests, radiation, medications, and physical therapy.
4. *HMO Physicians and Surgeons Services in Hospital*—include surgeons and related medical specialists, with no copayment.
5. *HMO Outpatient Hospital Care*—members receive the same services that are provided under Inpatient Hospital Services, as authorized by the managing physician; there is no copayment.
6. *HMO Outpatient Health Services Provided at HMO Facility*—include physician services, preventive health services, diagnosis and treatment services, skilled nursing facility services, mental health and/or alcohol and drug abuse services, dental care under specific circumstances, and emergency services in and out of the HMO area. A copayment may be required.

HMO exclusions include custodial care, experimental procedures, conveniences not medically related such as television, radio, and telephones, and cosmetic care except for medically necessary reconstruction.

HEALTH MAINTENANCE ORGANIZATION (HMO) ACT OF 1973 federal legislation requiring employers with traditional health plans to also provide an HMO to its employees. The act also makes it mandatory for employers to contribute as much to the HMO as they did to their regular plan. The requirement that employers offer an HMO alternative was repealed in 1993. In 1988, the act was amended so that the employer gained greater flexibility in determining its HMO contributions.

HEALTH PLAN FLEXIBLE SPENDING ACCOUNT (FSA) central fund into which employees contribute untaxed earnings to pay for the insurance premiums and uninsured medical costs. When the employee submits evidence of unreimbursed medical expenses, the employee is then indemnified. This indemnification fund uses untaxed dollars to pay for family health care costs that are not covered by the employer's health care plan. Examples would include elective surgery, eyeglasses, orthodontia, and the deductibles and coinsurance requirements that are part of the insured medical claims. The amount that the employee contributes to this account must be spent in total during that year. If this amount or any part thereof is not spent during that year, it is forfeited in total to the employer.

HEALTH REIMBURSEMENT ARRANGEMENT (HRA) agreement that may operate in connection with SECTION 125 PLANS (CAFETERIA PLANS) and must adhere to the following restrictions: (1) account must be funded only by employer contributions; (2) account cannot be part of a salary reduction plan; (3) account must be used only to reimburse employees for their medical expenses, or expenses of their spouse, children, or other dependents; (4) account may not cover business partners or any type of partnership, Sub-Chapter S stockholders, or the self-employed; (5) employer's contributions are a tax deductible expense and are not to be considered taxable income to the employee; (6) benefits are not taxable income to the employee.

HEALTH SAVINGS ACCOUNTS (HSA) agreement that may operate in conjunction with SECTION 125 PLANS (CAFETERIA PLANS) and must adhere to the following restrictions: (1) Account may be on a contributory or noncontributory basis. Individuals can contribute to the individual deductible or $2600, whichever is the lesser amount per year. Families can contribute up to the family deductible or $5150, whichever is the lesser amount per year. (2) Contributions placed into the account can only pay for employee's future health-related expenses. (3) The plan usually does not go into effect until high deductible (for individuals, $1050; for a family, $2100, and there is no other health insurance coverage including MEDICARE and MEDICAID) has been reached in the HEALTH INSURANCE CONTRACT. (4) Benefit payments are tax free if used exclusively for medical expenses. (5) Contributions into the account accrue on a tax-deferred basis and may be used later to fund employee's retirement income or other nonmedical expenses after age 65. *See also* HEALTH PLAN FLEXIBLE SPENDING ACCOUNT (FSA).

HEDGING method of transferring RISK to permit the RISK BEARER to assume two offsetting positions at the same time so that, regardless of the outcome of an event, the risk bearer is left in a no win/no lose position. For example, in the options market, a stock owner of an underlying stock can write calls or buy puts. In the same options market, the short sellers of the underlying stock can buy calls or write puts.

HEDONIC DAMAGES in personal injury cases, damages awarded to the plaintiff for the loss of joy of living. For example, if a person's negligent act results in damage to another person's leg, the injured person claims that he/she can no longer walk his/her dog and thus has been deprived of one of the greatest joys in the injured person's life.

HEINRICH, H. W. executive of Travelers Insurance Company who developed the DOMINO THEORY OF ACCIDENT CAUSATION by studying over 75,000 industrial accidents and concluding that most accidents would be preventable if only the acquired behavior of individuals could be changed. Heinrich held that extensive programs should be conducted by industrial companies to convince employees to act safely.

HIGHLY PROTECTED RISK exposures where action has been taken to reduce the frequency and severity of loss, such as adding sprinkler systems in public buildings. These actions may result in a significant reduction in the fire insurance premium.

HIGH-PRESSURE SELLING extremely aggressive behavior by an INSURANCE AGENT to convince a PROSPECT to purchase the insurance product without due regard for the prospect's ability to pay the PREMIUMS and/or needs for the product.

HIGH RISK POOLS FOR THE MEDICALLY UNINSURABLE *see* STATE HIGH RISK POOLS FOR THE MEDICALLY UNINSURABLE.

HOBBIES OR AVOCATIONS activities of interest in underwriting an application for life insurance to determine the rate classification (premium) for the applicant. For example, a sky diver is at greater personal risk than average, and accordingly is charged a much higher premium for life insurance.

HOLD-HARMLESS AGREEMENT assumption of liability through contractual agreement by one party, thereby eliminating liability on the part of another party. An example is a railroad sidetrack agreement with a manufacturing company under which the manufacturer is held harmless for damage to railroad equipment and tracks.

HOLOGRAPHIC WILL will written totally in the handwriting of that individual whose name appears on the will. *See also* ESTATE PLANNING; ESTATE PLANNING DISTRIBUTION.

HOME BUSINESS INSURANCE added coverage through an ENDORSE-MENT for property and liability perils resulting from business operations at the insured's residence. Excluded from coverage are PROFESSIONAL LIABILITY and injuries sustained by employees.

HOME OFFICE central (main) office of an insurance company whose facilities usually include actuarial, claims, investment, legal, underwriting, agency, and marketing departments.

HOME OFFICE LIFE UNDERWRITERS ASSOCIATION (HOLUA) organization of home office underwriters of life insurance companies. HOLUA offers educational material and national examinations for home office life underwriters, the individuals who evaluate applications for insurance, decide if an applicant meets the requirements of the company for issuing insurance, and determine the rate classification into which the applicant should be placed.

HOME OFFICE UNDERWRITER *see* UNDERWRITER LAY; UNDERWRITING; UNDERWRITING CYCLE; UNDERWRITING GAIN (OR LOSS).

HOMEOWNERS FORM NO. 1 (BASIC OR STANDARD FORM) *see* HOMEOWNERS INSURANCE POLICY—SECTION I (PROPERTY COVERAGE).

HOMEOWNERS FORM NO. 2 (BROAD FORM) *see* HOMEOWNERS INSURANCE POLICY—SECTION I (PROPERTY COVERAGE).

HOMEOWNERS FORM NO. 3 (SPECIAL FORM) *see* HOMEOWNERS INSURANCE POLICY—SECTION I (PROPERTY COVERAGE).

HOMEOWNERS FORM NO. 4 (CONTENTS BROAD FORM) *see* HOMEOWNERS INSURANCE POLICY—SECTION I (PROPERTY COVERAGE).

HOMEOWNERS FORM NO. 6 (UNIT OWNERS FORM) *see* HOMEOWNERS INSURANCE POLICY—SECTION I (PROPERTY COVERAGE).

HOMEOWNERS FORM NO. 8 (MODIFIED COVERAGE FORM) *see* HOMEOWNERS INSURANCE POLICY—SECTION I (PROPERTY COVERAGE).

HOMEOWNERS INSURANCE POLICY package policy that combines (1) coverage against the insured's property being destroyed or damaged by various perils, and (2) coverage for liability exposure of the insured.

Homeowners policies cover both individuals as well as property. In addition to the insured, those covered include his or her spouse, their relatives, and any others under 21 who are residents of the insured's household.

HOMEOWNERS INSURANCE POLICY—SECTION I (PROPERTY COVERAGE) section providing protection in four areas:
1. *Coverage A (Home)*—the structure of the home (basic contract amount). Other property coverages in Section I are expressed as a percentage of Coverage A.

2. *Coverage B (Garage or Appurtenant Private Structures)*—structures not attached to or part of the home, covered up to 10% of the basic home structure.

3. *Coverage C (Contents or Personal Property)*—coverage of 40 to 50% (depending on the form selected) of the structural coverage of the home for the contents or personal property in the home; coverage of up to 10% applies to contents away from the home. For example, a home whose value is $100,000 would have coverage on the contents of $50,000 (assuming 50% contents coverage); away from home, contents coverage would be up to $5000.

4. *Coverage D (Additional Living Expenses)*—coverage if the home is damaged or destroyed and the insured must seek temporary lodging. Reimbursement is 10 to 20% of the structural coverage of the home, depending on the form selected,

All four property coverages A, B, C, and D are offered through one of the following forms:

1. *Form No. 1 (Basic or Standard)*—coverage for fire, lightning, windstorm, hail, explosion, smoke, theft, vandalism, malicious mischief, riot, civil commotion, glass breakage, vehicles, and aircraft.

2. *Form No. 2 (Broad)*—coverage for a broader spectrum of perils than under Form No. 1.

3. *Form No. 3 (Special)*—provides that Coverage A *(Home),* Coverage B *(Garage or Appurtenant Private Structures),* and Coverage C *(Contents or Personal Property)* are insured on an ALL RISKS basis. This form is sometimes called "landlords and tenants insurance" since the building and garage or appurtenant private structure and contents are covered on an all risks basis. There are a number of exclusions under Form No. 3.

4. *Form No. 4 (Contents Broad Form)*—coverage only for the contents of a dwelling (Coverage C) and additional living expense (Coverage D) as the result of the perils listed in Form No. 2. This form is called the "renters form" since it does not cover damage to the structure of an apartment building, its garages or appurtenants.

5. *Form No. 6 (Condominium Unit Owners Form)*—provides the same coverage as Form No. 4 but extends coverage for damage to additions and/or alterations that the unit owner may have made inside the unit. Coverage goes into effect as an excess amount above that insurance (if any) that the condominium association may have.

Numerous endorsements can be added to each one of the above forms to increase the limits of coverage and the properties insured. For example, specified property such as jewelry, furs, silverware, and guns can be added through a *valuable personal articles endorsement.* Also, an inflation guard endorsement (reflecting increases in the cost of construction) can be added to Coverage A, which automatically increases Coverages B, C, and D, since they are expressed as a percentage of Coverage A.

The insured is obligated to take certain actions following a loss, including: notifying the company or agent immediately; if the loss is due to theft, notifying the police immediately; if credit cards are stolen, notifying the credit card company immediately; and protecting the property from further damage.

There is usually an 80% coinsurance requirement which means that the insured must carry insurance on a replacement cost basis of at least 80%. For example, a home is worth $200,000, and a fire does $50,000 damage. If the insured carries $150,000 of insurance, only $46,875 would be covered according to the following formula:

$$\frac{\text{Amount of Insurance Carried}}{80\% \text{ Insurance to Value}} \times \text{Loss} = \text{Insured Reimbursement}$$

Replacement Cost Basis

$$\frac{\$150,000}{\$160,000} \times \$50,000 = \$46,875$$

If, however, the insured had carried an 80% insurance to a value of $160,000, then the total loss of $50,000 would have been to the following formula:

$$\frac{\$160,000}{\$160,000} \times \$50,000 = \$50,000$$

6. *Form No. 8 (Modified Coverage Form)*—provides coverage for a loss to a dwelling and other structures on the INSURED premises on a repair cost basis. This form is appropriate for long-existing dwellings and structures where the market value is less than the REPLACEMENT COST.

HOMEOWNERS INSURANCE POLICY—SECTION II (LIABILITY COVERAGE) section providing protection under three coverages:

1. *Coverage E (Personal Liability)*—coverage in the event a suit is brought against the insured because of bodily injury and/or property damage resulting from the acts or non-acts of the insured. Also covers the insured's spouse, relatives of either, and others under age 21 under the insured's care. Just about any personal act is insured. For example, if the insured lives in Shreveport, Louisiana, and hits someone with a tennis ball in a game in Hong Kong, the insured is covered against a possible lawsuit. The insurance company must also pay for the costs of defending the insured, even if a suit has no reasonable basis. Defense costs are separate and in addition to the limits of liability in the policy. For example, if the limits of the policy are $100,000 and the defense costs are $200,000, the insurance company could have to pay a total of $300,000 on behalf of the insured. Once the insurance company pays the $100,000 limit in the policy, the insurance company's obligation to defend the insured any further ends. The basic liability limits are $100,000—the minimum amount stipulated in the policy. (For a relatively few dollars these limits can be increased substantially.)

2. *Coverage F (Medical Payments to Others)*—coverage for reimbursement of reasonable medical expenses incurred (a) by the insured (and individuals as defined in Coverage E, above); and (b) for injuries sustained by a third party either on or off of the insured's premises as a result of the activities of the insured and others covered. This is called "Good Samaritan Coverage" because by providing emergency medical expenses of an injured third party, the insured does not admit liability, nor does the injured third party relinquish his or her right to bring suit against the insured by accepting the medical aid.

3. *Coverage G (Damage to Property of Others)*—as with Coverage F, the insured is reimbursed for expenses incurred up to $250 regardless of legal liability for damage to the property of a third party. The insured and covered residents of the household make payment out of a feeling of moral responsibility for the damage to the property, which may have the result of a liability suit not being brought.

HOME SERVICE AGENT *see* DEBIT AGENT (HOME SERVICE AGENT).

HOME SERVICE INDUSTRIAL INSURANCE *see* INDUSTRIAL LIFE INSURANCE.

HOME SERVICE LIFE INSURANCE *see* DEBIT INSURANCE (HOME SERVICE INSURANCE, INDUSTRIAL INSURANCE).

HOME SERVICE ORDINARY life insurance in which the *debit system* is used to collect premiums on a monthly basis. *See also* DEBIT INSURANCE (HOME SERVICE INSURANCE, INDUSTRIAL INSURANCE); ORDINARY LIFE INSURANCE.

HOMESTEAD RIGHT use of a home, and the land and buildings surrounding that home, free from the claim of creditors. This right gives rise to an INSURABLE INTEREST.

HOMOGENEITY *see* INSURABLE RISK.

HOMOGENEOUS EXPOSURES elements within a group under study that have the same characteristic(s), have the same EXPECTATION OF LOSS, are very much alike with respect to the variable under consideration, and do not show significant differences through any given time periods. Homogeneity of exposure units is extremely important to the accuracy of the prediction of future losses based on historical loss experience. For example, if an ACTUARY is going to predict the number of wood-frame houses likely to suffer a fire loss, the sample upon which the prediction is based should consist of wood-frame houses, not brick-frame houses.

HOSPICE facility that provides short periods of stay for a terminally ill person in a homelike setting for either direct care or respite. A "terminally ill" person has a life expectancy of six months or less. A hospice provides continuous care. Some health insurance plans pay benefits in full up to a maximum without a deductible for charges incurred for a terminally ill person while in a hospice care program. Also provided are bereavement benefits up to a maximum (usually $200) per family unit.

HOSPITAL CONFINEMENT INDEMNITY INSURANCE policy that pays a fixed dollar amount for each day the insured is confined to the hospital. This method of payment is in contrast with most other MEDICAL EXPENSE INSURANCE that reimburses the insured on the costs incurred.

HOSPITAL EXPENSE INSURANCE *see* GROUP HEALTH INSURANCE; HEALTH INSURANCE; HEALTH MAINTENANCE ORGANIZATION (HMO).

HOSPITAL INDEMNITY INSURANCE *see* GROUP HEALTH INSUR-ANCE; HEALTH INSURANCE; HEALTH MAINTENANCE ORGANIZATION (HMO).

HOSPITALIZATION INSURANCE *see* GROUP HEALTH INSURANCE; HEALTH INSURANCE; HEALTH MAINTENANCE ORGANIZATION (HMO).

HOSPITAL LIABILITY INSURANCE form of insurance covering (1) liability arising out of the provision or nonprovision of hospital ser-vices so as to have an action brought against the hospital for malprac-tice, error, or mistake; (2) injuring of a patient by another patient; (3) food and other items resulting in injury to the patients; (4) injury to a person treated in an ambulance; and (5) costs to defend the hospital even if the suit is groundless.

HOSPITAL MEDICAL INSURANCE *see* GROUP HEALTH INSURANCE; HEALTH INSURANCE; HEALTH MAINTENANCE ORGANIZATION (HMO).

HOSPITAL SERVICES, HMO *see* HEALTH MAINTENANCE ORGANIZA-TION (HMO).

HOSPITAL, SURGICAL, AND MEDICAL EXPENSE INSUR-ANCE *see* GROUP HEALTH INSURANCE; HEALTH INSURANCE; HEALTH MAINTENANCE ORGANIZATION (HMO).

HOSTILE FIRE unfriendly fire not confined to its normal habitat. For example, fire in the fireplace leaps onto the sofa. Property contracts protect against damage from a hostile fire, not from damage from fire in the fireplace, its normal habitat. The insurance is designed to cover FORTUITOUS LOSS, which the hostile fire is. *See also* FRIENDLY FIRE.

HOST LIABILITY exposure created by an individual acting as a host serving alcoholic beverages at no charge to persons already intoxi-cated, resulting in these intoxicated individuals causing property dam-age and/or bodily injury to third parties. *See also* DRAM SHOP LAW.

HOST LIQUOR LIABILITY *see* HOST LIABILITY.

HOUSEHOLD INVENTORY list and description of valuables, to be utilized in the event an insurance claim must be filed. Included should be: (1) a detailed explanation of possessions that are of special value, such as a piano or violin; (2) appraisals on expensive items such as jew-elry, art, furs, and antiques; (3) make and model numbers of electronic equipment and appliances. A photograph and/or videotape should be taken of the important items in the home showing their condition and quality.

HOUSING STARTS INDICATOR index that traces the construction of new single-family homes, townhouses, and multifamily apartment buildings. These statistics are published monthly by the United States Department of Commerce. Rising housing starts is one sign of a healthy economy.

HOW LONG A POLICY WILL BE IN FORCE duration of a policy. Property and casualty coverages are usually written for one year, although a personal automobile policy can be for six months. Life insurance can be written on (1) a term basis (1 year, 5 years, 20 years, to age 65), (2) whole or life basis, or (3) any combination of the two. Health insurance can be written on a multiple time period basis.

HR-10 PLAN *see* KEOGH PLAN (HR-10).

HULL MARINE INSURANCE coverage of the hull of a ship and its tackle, passenger fittings, equipment, stores, boats, and ordnance. Coverage is provided under the following types of policies: BUILDERS RISK HULL INSURANCE; NAVIGATION RISK INSURANCE, and PORT RISK INSURANCE.

HUMAN APPROACH technique of loss control and reduction of losses in insurance. Supporters of this method believe that the safety attitudes of individuals determine the safety precautions they take. The human approach seeks to convince people to *want* to be safe in order to reduce loss frequency and severity. For example, campaigns encouraging the use of seat belts help promote a safety-conscious society.

HUMAN FACTORS ENGINEERING *see* HUMAN APPROACH.

HUMAN LIFE VALUE APPROACH (ECONOMIC VALUE OF AN INDIVIDUAL LIFE) (EVOIL) quantitative measure to determine the amount of life insurance required to replace lost future earnings of a wage earner. Three steps are used in arriving at the needed sum:
1. Determine average yearly earned income devoted to a family in the future by the wage earner (AEIDF).
2. Determine future number of years wage earner is planning to work (*n*).
3. Determine the interest rate (*i*) (discount factor) to be used in calculating the present value of the average yearly earned income devoted to family.

    The calculation uses this equation:

$$\text{EVOIL} = \sum_{n=1}^{m} \text{AEIDF}\,(1 + i)^{-n}$$

where *m* = last year at work before normal retirement
      n = first remaining year of life

HURRICANE INSURANCE part of windstorm coverage, usually one of a group of property coverages that covers all kinds of winds such as storms and tornadoes. *See also* STORM INSURANCE (WINDSTORM INSURANCE).

HYBRID LONG-TERM CARE (LTC) HOME CARE PLANS combination of a reimbursement plan with a CASH BENEFIT or an ENHANCEMENT OPTION. Under the cash benefit option the policyowner can select the monthly home care benefit that will reimburse the costs related to home care or receive a lump sum amount. The lump sum amount is usually stated as a percentage of the monthly policy limit. Under the enhancement option, the policyowner can select the monthly home care benefit that will reimburse the costs related to home care or receive a lump sum amount above the policy limit to be used at the discretion of the policyowner.

I

IBNR *see* INCURRED BUT NOT REPORTED LOSSES (IBNR).

I-BONDS bonds issued by the United States Treasury that earn a fixed interest rate plus the rate of inflation. These bonds are sold at face value in denominations of $50 up to $5000 and may earn interest for up to 30 years. These bonds may be liquidated at any time after they have been in force for at least six months, but if liquidation occurs during the first five years, three months of interest must be forfeited. The interest earned is compounded twice a year and paid when the bond is redeemed. Protection against loss of principal and purchasing power while accumulating tax-deferred interest are some of the advantages of this Treasury-backed issue.

IDENTIFICATION first step in the risk management process. The objective is to determine the sources of losses. For example, the profit and loss statement of a business firm not only shows the sources of its earnings but identifies exposures that these sources face from various perils, such as worker injuries, ill-designed products, and hazardous manufacturing conditions.

IMMEDIATE ANNUITY ANNUITY that begins payments after a single premium is paid. For example, the annuitant pays a single premium of $100,000 on June 1 of the current year and begins receiving a monthly income of $1200 for life starting July 1.

IMMEDIATE NOTICE provision found in PROPERTY AND LIABILITY INSURANCE policies that mandates that the insured notify the insurance company as soon as possible following the occurrence of a covered loss under the policy.

IMMEDIATE PARTICIPATION GUARANTEE PLAN (IPG) *see* PENSION PLAN FUNDING: GROUP IMMEDIATE PARTICIPATION GUARANTEED (IPA) CONTRACT ANNUITY.

IMMEDIATE VARIABLE ANNUITY CONTRACT a contract sold by insurance companies that is bought by means of a single lump sum payment usually providing a monthly income payment for the ANNUITANT's life. The amount of the monthly income payment varies according to the performance of the underlying portfolio of investments. A stipulated rate of return (ASSUMED INTEREST RATE/ASSUMED INVESTMENT RETURN) is assumed when the insurer calculates the initial income payment to the annuitant. If the underlying portfolio produces a net return greater than or less than the stipulated rate of return, the income payments will rise or decline accordingly. *See also* ANNUITY; VARIABLE ANNUITY.

IMMEDIATE VESTING entitlement of an employee to benefits immediately upon entering a retirement plan. As benefits are earned, they are credited to the employee's account. These "portable" future benefits can be withdrawn by individuals leaving the service of the employer.

IMPAIRED RISK IMMEDIATE ANNUITIES income payments that are calculated based on the ANNUITANT'S LIFE EXPECTANCY and adjusted to reflect the annuitant's medical circumstance. For example, a person age 63 may have a medical impairment that gives him or her the same life expectancy as that of a person age 73. The income payment can be increased accordingly to reflect the shorter life expectancy.

IMPAIRED RISK (SUBSTANDARD RISK) in life and health insurance, person whose physical condition is less than standard or who has a hazardous occupation or hobby. For example, an applicant with a history of strokes is regarded as an impaired risk. Some substandard insurance companies specialize in insuring substandard risks, applying an additional premium (surcharge) to reflect the higher probability of loss from a particular impairment.

IMPAIRMENT OF CAPITAL situation where a stock insurer must invade its capital account in order to meet its obligations. Most states do not allow insurers to do this and quickly rescind their right to do business.

IMPLIED AUTHORITY *see* APPARENT AGENCY (AUTHORITY).

IMPLIED WARRANTY type of WARRANTY that is not a provision in the contract but is thought to be true by the respondents.

IMPREST ACCOUNT fund established to pay specified losses, usually the low *severity* property losses. This type of account is an excellent device in conjunction with a SELF-INSURANCE plan, in which the fund is infused with new money as it goes to zero after paying property losses.

IMPROVEMENTS AND BETTERMENTS INSURANCE tenant's modifications of leased space to fit his particular needs. Up to 10% of contents coverage inside the structure may be applied to insure against damage or destruction of improvements or betterments made by a tenant who does not carry coverage on the structure itself. For example, under the HOMEOWNERS INSURANCE POLICY, if the contents of an apartment are insured for $25,000, then $2500 would apply to cabinets that the tenant built into the kitchen.

IMPUTED ACTS *see* NEGLIGENCE, IMPUTED.

INADMITTED ASSET ASSET excluded from the FINANCIAL STATEMENTS submitted to the state INSURANCE EXAMINER because the asset has virtually no value in meeting claims in the event the INSURANCE COMPANY must be liquidated. Also called NONADMITTED ASSET.

IN-AREA EMERGENCY SERVICES provision of HEALTH MAINTENANCE ORGANIZATION (HMO) coverage. A member who is critically injured within the geographical service area of the HMO can use the nearest hospital for emergency care, rather than a more distant HMO-authorized hospital.

INCENDIARISM act of starting a fire; arson. Arson is a covered peril under a PROPERTY INSURANCE contract, provided that the owner of the property is not responsible for the arson.

INCEPTION DATE *see* EFFECTIVE DATE.

INCHMAREE CLAUSE provision of MARINE INSURANCE. It protects property damaged or destroyed as the result of the negligent acts of the crew. The name is derived from a steamer in which a pump was damaged by its crew's negligence.

INCIDENCE RATE *see* FREQUENCY AND DISTRIBUTION OF LOSSES.

INCIDENTAL CONTRACT secondary (not primary) reason for forming a contract. In group insurance, the group must be formed and maintained for reasons other than obtaining insurance. If the group were formed primarily to obtain insurance, ADVERSE SELECTION would take place.

INCIDENTAL MALPRACTICE medical malpractice that is the legal responsibility of a person or organization not in the medical profession or business. It is usually covered under a PROFESSIONAL LIABILITY INSURANCE policy.

INCIDENTS OF OWNERSHIP policyowner rights under a life insurance policy, including the right to name a new beneficiary at any time and to surrender the policy for its cash value.

INCOME all sources of cash flow, usually stated on an annual basis.

INCOME AND PRINCIPAL POLICY policy that provides an income for life to the primary BENEFICIARY upon the death of the INSURED. The FACE AMOUNT of the policy becomes payable to the secondary beneficiary upon the death of the primary beneficiary. Should the primary beneficiary die before the insured, the face amount of the policy is paid to the secondary beneficiary upon the death of the insured.

INCOME AVERAGING income averaged over a specified period of years. For example, to calculate benefits in a pension plan, it is common to average the highest three years or five years of earnings.

INCOME BENEFICIARY individual(s) entitled to receive the income generated by the TRUST.

INCOME CONTINUATION INSURANCE *see* PARTNERSHIP LIFE AND HEALTH INSURANCE.

INCOME IN RESPECT OF A DECEDENT (IRD) classification at death of all PENSION PLANS, PROFIT-SHARING PLANS, INDIVIDUAL RETIREMENT ACCOUNTS (IRAS), ANNUITIES, and installment payments to the extent to which the deceased was entitled to receive income and that income was not included in the deceased's taxable income in the year of the death. This income is ruled to be subject to income tax to the BENEFICIARY as well as ESTATE TAX to the heirs.

INCOME OPTION choice or choices the ANNUITANT has in deciding how income is to be received from an ANNUITY.

INCOME (PERSONAL) INSURANCE *see* DISABILITY INCOME INSURANCE.

INCOME POLICY proceeds from a life insurance policy paid on a monthly basis instead of in a lump sum.

INCOME REIMBURSEMENT INSURANCE *see* INCOME REPLACEMENT.

INCOME REPLACEMENT benefit in disability income insurance whereby an injured or ill wage earner receives a monthly income payment to replace a percentage of his or her lost earnings. *See also* DISABILITY INCOME INSURANCE (Amount of Benefits).

INCOME REPLACEMENT RATIO percentage of income required by a retiree to maintain a desired standard of living during the retirement years.

INCOME-SHIFTING STRATEGIES ownership of tax-free or tax-deferred investments by a child or for a child, given that these investments will not reach maturity before the child attains at least age 14. The objective is to shift investment producing current income from high-tax-bracket adults to low-tax-bracket children. Possible means of achieving this objective would be the utilization of the following investment instruments:

1. *Municipal bonds*—interest earned is not subject to federal or state taxes.
2. *Savings bonds* U.S. EE savings bonds that have a maturity date after the child attains age 14—these bonds guarantee payment of 85% of the average interest rate of U.S. Treasury notes and bonds subject to a minimum guarantee rate of 6%. These bonds must be held for at least five years for the full interest rate to apply.
3. PERMANENT LIFE INSURANCE—earnings accumulate on a tax-deferred basis with the possibility of avoiding taxes on the accrued earnings if the policy remains in force until the insured's death.
4. DEFERRED ANNUITY—this instrument offers the same tax-deferred treatment as life insurance.
5. *Growth equities*—taxes need not be paid on "paper gains;" taxes on gains are paid only after stock is sold.
6. CUSTODIAL ACCOUNT—parent retains control of the asset owned by the child until the child reaches the age of majority. The first $1000 of income in the account is taxed at the child's rate (if child is less than age 14), and any additional income is taxed at the parent's rate. When the child reaches age 14, all income in the account becomes taxable at the child's rate.

INCONTESTABLE CLAUSE section in a life insurance policy stating that after the policy is in force two years, the company cannot void it because of misrepresentation or concealment by the insured in obtaining the policy. For example, when asked on the application if there is a history of diabetes in the family, the applicant writes no, knowing that his or her father and mother both have diabetes. This does not void the policy after two years. However, if the age of the applicant had been understated—say, to obtain a lower premium—the company will recalculate the benefit according to the correct age.

INCORPORATION INTO FUNDING AGREEMENT factors taken into account concerning the instrument used in funding a pension plan. For example, an allocated funding instrument guarantees that benefits will be paid for all premium payments received. This should eliminate concerns of employees about the availability of funds to pay their benefits at retirement.

INCORPOREAL INTERESTS right to insurable interest in property such as the right of a secured creditor in the property pledged as security.

INCREASED COST ENDORSEMENT coverage for extra expenses associated with the reconstruction of a damaged or destroyed building where zoning requirements mandate more costly construction material. This endorsement is attached to property policies.

INCREASED COST OF CONSTRUCTION CLAUSE coverage if state or municipal law requires that a damaged or destroyed building must be rebuilt at an increased cost to comply with building code provisions that were not in effect when the building was originally constructed.

INCREASED HAZARD state that increases the probability of a loss. For example, storage of flammable material next to a furnace in one's home increases the hazard with the knowledge of an insured, and is grounds for suspension of a policy by an insurance company.

INCREASING LIFE INSURANCE term or whole life policy with a face value that increases over time.

INCURRED BUT NOT REPORTED LOSSES (IBNR) insured losses that have occurred but have not been reported to a PRIMARY INSURANCE company. These types of claims have a tremendous effect on a REINSURANCE treaty, which may be showing a healthy profit when in reality it is losing money. Hence, under this false security, the reinsurer will continue operating under a rating plan that is totally inadequate for the losses. This explains why a provision for incurred but not reported losses should be made in a rating plan. Also, the reinsurer must establish an adequate reserve for IBNR claims to make a correct analysis of its business. If such a reserve is not established, overly optimistic evaluation of the real loss may not be revealed for several years. A method of deriving the reserve for IBNR claims is to calculate a percentage of the *Claims Paid and Outstanding*.

INCURRED EXPENSES expenses that have or may not yet have been paid by an insurance company.

INCURRED LOSSES losses that have occurred within a stipulated time period whether paid or not.

INCURRED LOSS RATIO proportion of losses incurred to premiums earned. This ratio indicates the amount of a premium dollar that is being consumed by losses.

INDEMNIFICATION *see* INDEMNITY.

INDEMNIFY *see* INDEMNITY.

INDEMNITEE recipient of an indemnity.

INDEMNITOR provider of an indemnity payment.

INDEMNITY compensation for loss. In a property and casualty contract, the objective is to restore an insured to the same financial position after the loss that he or she was in prior to the loss. But the insured should not be able to profit by damage or destruction of property, nor should the insured be in a worse financial position after a loss.

In life insurance the situation is totally different. By the payment of a single premium, the beneficiary of an insured can be placed in a much better financial position at the death of an insured than he or she was in prior to the death. However, the payment of a predetermined amount upon the insured's death does not make a life insurance policy a contract of indemnity.

In hospital indemnity and other health insurance plans, COORDINATION OF BENEFITS is designed so that the insured cannot profit from an illness. *See also* COORDINATION OF BENEFITS.

INDEMNITY AGREEMENT policy provision designed to restore an insured to his or her original financial position after a loss. The insured should neither profit nor be put at a monetary disadvantage by incurring the loss. *See also* INSURANCE CONTRACT, GENERAL; INSURANCE CONTRACT, LIFE; INSURANCE CONTRACT, PROPERTY AND CASUALTY.

INDEMNITY BOND coverage for loss of an obligee in the event that the principal fails to perform according to standards agreed upon between the obligee and the principal.

INDEMNITY COMPANY INSURANCE COMPANY that specializes in UNDERWRITING CASUALTY INSURANCE.

INDEMNITY DISABILITY INCOME POLICY policy used to provide the funds necessary for BUY-AND-SELL AGREEMENTS whereby an income payment or a series of income payments are paid to the buyer of the disabled partner's interest contained in a PARTNERSHIP LIFE AND HEALTH INSURANCE PLAN or disabled stockholder's interest contained in a CLOSE CORPORATION PLAN to reimburse that buyer for the sum paid. If this sum to be paid the buyer by the insurance company exceeds the actual market value of the business at the time of the sale, that sum must still be paid.

INDEMNITY OR FEE-FOR-SERVICE INSURANCE coverage for the percentage of the health care costs paid by the health insurance company, which is usually 80% above the insured's deductible up to a dollar amount of approximately $5000. The company then pays 100% of the costs up to the policy limits. The insured may select a physician of his or her choice.

INDEPENDENT ADJUSTER independent contractor who adjusts claims for different insurance companies. Such services are used by insurance companies whose financial resources or volume of claims do not warrant employing their own in-house adjusters.

INDEPENDENT AGENCY SYSTEM means of selling and servicing property and casualty insurance through agents who represent different companies. The agents own the records of the policies they sell. *See also* INDEPENDENT AGENT.

INDEPENDENT AGENT contractor who represents different insurance companies and who searches the market for the best place for a client's business. The independent agent, who owns the records of policies sold, is not controlled by any one company, pays agency's expenses out of the commissions earned, and is responsible for maintaining employee benefits.

INDEPENDENT CONTRACTORS INSURANCE *see* OWNERS AND CONTRACTORS PROTECTIVE LIABILITY INSURANCE.

INDEPENDENT EVENTS events that do not have any influence on the occurrence or nonoccurrence of another event; for example, a plane crashing in Shreveport should have no influence on a plane crashing in Dallas.

INDEPENDENT INSURANCE AGENTS OF AMERICA (IIAA) association of independent agents whose objective is to further the interests of these agents through education, lobbying, and professional ethics.

INDEPENDENT INSURER insurance company that is not a member of a rating bureau or is not under common ownership or management with other companies. The insurance company is said to *stand alone. See also* INDEPENDENT AGENCY SYSTEM; INDEPENDENT AGENT.

INDEPENDENT PRACTICE ASSOCIATION (IPA) type of HEALTH MAINTENANCE ORGANIZATION (HMO) that issues contracts to independent physicians. These physicians are paid a per visit fee for seeing an HMO member or are paid an annual fixed sum. The HMO members are covered only when they use an HMO hospital or physician.

INDETERMINATE PREMIUM LIFE INSURANCE *nonparticipating life insurance* under which the first few annual premiums are smaller than would be the case under a traditional nonparticipating policy. While the maximum amount of these initial premiums is guaranteed, future premiums can be increased, but not beyond a guaranteed maximum. Adjustments to premiums reflect the insurance company's anticipated mortality experience, investment return, and expenses. If these three elements are more profitable than had been loaded for in the initial premiums, future premiums will be reduced; if less profitable, they will be increased, but not greater than the guaranteed maximum. *See also* ADJUSTABLE LIFE INSURANCE.

INDEX proxy for the performance of a given ASSET class. For example, the S&P 500 is comprised of 500 companies representing a broad range of industries. Many professional investors believe that "as goes the S&P 500, so goes the general equities market."

INDEX ANNUITY *see* EQUITY INDEXED ANNUITY.

INDEX FUND type of MUTUAL FUND that tracks a stock or bond INDEX. The fund tries to duplicate the performance of either a segment of the market or the whole market by investing in stocks or bonds that reflect that market.

INDEXED LIFE INSURANCE policy with a face value that varies according to a prescribed index of prices; otherwise benefits provided are similar to ordinary whole life. The death benefit is based on the particular index used, such as the Consumer Price Index (CPI). The policyowner has the choice of having the index applied either automatically or on an elective basis. With an *automatic index* increase, the premium remains level since it has already been loaded to reflect the automatic increase. If the policy allows for an *optional index increase,* an extra premium is charged when this option is exercised by the policyowner. Regardless of which index is selected—automatic or optional—the increased death benefit does not require another physical examination or other evidence of insurability.

INDEXED GUARANTEED INVESTMENT CONTRACT (GIC) type of GUARANTEED INVESTMENT CONTRACT in which the interest rate credited is tied to an external index such as the United States Treasury Bond Index.

INDEXED LIFE POLICIES *see* INDEXED LIFE INSURANCE.

INDEXED SECURITIES (STRUCTURED NOTES) bond DERIVATIVES of short-term duration whose principal or coupon value is determined by a market index. Market indexes that can be utilized include securities, commodity prices, and short-term bond rates.

INDEXED UNIVERSAL LIFE type of UNIVERSAL LIFE INSURANCE policy that has an underlying guaranteed minimum interest rate that is credited to the policy for the specified time period. Interest above the guaranteed minimum, based upon an external benchmark such as the S&P 500, is credited to the policy subject to the participation rate. The participation rate is the percentage of the movement in the index that will be credited to the policy subject to a cap. The cap is the maximum interest that will be credited to the policy for the specified time period, such as one year. For example, if the S&P 500 increased 15%, the participation rate is 80%, and the cap is 7%, the policy would be credited with 7%.

INDIRECT LOSS loss that is not a direct result of a peril. For example, damage to property of a business firm would be a direct loss, but the loss of business earnings because of a fire on its premises would be an indirect loss.

INDIRECT PROPERTY EXPOSURES loss of income resulting from the damage or destruction of a person's property or a business's property. For example, if a store is damaged by fire and is unable to sell its inventory to customers, a loss of income results.

INDIVIDUAL ANNUITY TABLE, 1971 historical MORTALITY TABLE that replaced the ANNUITY TABLE, 1949, used for the calculation of annuity rates with more-current mortality experience at that time. This table was subsequently replaced by the 1983 Table-a (mortality table used for the calculation of annuity rates for males).

INDIVIDUAL BALANCE SHEET statement showing assets and liabilities of an individual.

INDIVIDUAL CONTRACT PENSION PLAN *see* PENSION PLAN FUNDING; INDIVIDUAL CONTRACT PENSION PLAN.

INDIVIDUAL FIDELITY BOND bond that reimburses a business for loss caused by the dishonest act of an employee. Since crime insurance policies exclude coverage of dishonest acts of employees, it is necessary to have a fidelity bond for this protection. Fidelity bonds cover mercantile business and financial institutions. *See also* FIDELITY BOND.

INDIVIDUAL HEALTH INSURANCE POLICY HEALTH INSURANCE CONTRACT sold to an individual to provide coverage for medical expenses. Contrast with GROUP HEALTH INSURANCE.

INDIVIDUAL INCOME STATEMENT report showing sources of income and expenses of an individual.

INDIVIDUAL INSURANCE single policy under which one individual is insured. *See also* ANNUITY; BROAD FORM PERSONAL THEFT INSURANCE; COMPREHENSIVE PERSONAL LIABILITY INSURANCE; DISABILITY INCOME INSURANCE; FAMILY INCOME POLICY; FAMILY INCOME RIDER; FAMILY MAINTENANCE POLICY; FAMILY POLICY; FARMERS COMPREHENSIVE PERSONAL LIABILITY INSURANCE; HEALTH INSURANCE; HOMEOWNERS INSURANCE POLICY; INDIVIDUAL LIFE INSURANCE; LIFE AND HEALTH INSURANCE, PERSONAL AND FAMILY EXPOSURES; PERSONAL AUTOMOBILE POLICY (PAP).

INDIVIDUAL LEVEL COST METHOD means, in pension plans, by which a projection is made of benefits credited to each employee's account at retirement age. Costs are then allocated on a level basis over a specified future period of time. This cost method can be classified according to whether there is or is not a supplemental liability. *See also* INDIVIDUAL LEVEL COST METHOD SUPPLEMENTAL WITHOUT LIABILITY; INDIVIDUAL LEVEL COST METHOD WITH SUPPLEMENTAL LIABILITY.

INDIVIDUAL LEVEL COST METHOD WITHOUT SUPPLEMENTAL LIABILITY means of projecting the costs of pension plans on a level basis over a specified future period of time. The actuarial value of each employee's future benefits to be paid at retirement is determined (including past service benefits to be credited, if any), and their costs are spread equally over the remaining work experience of the employee. The equation states that the present value of future benefits equals the present value of future costs.

INDIVIDUAL LEVEL COST METHOD WITH SUPPLEMENTAL LIABILITY means of projecting the costs of pension plans on a level basis over a specified future period of time. The actuarial value of each employee's future benefits to be paid at retirement is determined (beginning with the first day an employee could have joined the pension plan, had it been in effect at that time—thereby creating a supplemental liability), and their costs are spread equally over the remaining work experience of the employee.

INDIVIDUAL LIFE INSURANCE coverage of a single life, in contrast to group life insurance, which covers many lives. *See also* ENDOWMENT INSURANCE; LIFE INSURANCE; ORDINARY LIFE INSURANCE; TERM LIFE INSURANCE.

INDIVIDUAL POLICY PENSION TRUST type of PENSION PLAN in which the employer (if NONCONTRIBUTORY plan) or the employer and employee (if CONTRIBUTORY plan) make level annual premium payments to fund the future retirement benefits, through an individual DEFERRED ANNUITY, of the employee. Also funded in this manner is a separate life insurance policy on each employee. (This policy is usually held in the trust.) *See also* PENSION PLAN FUNDING, INDIVIDUAL CONTRACT PENSION PLAN.

INDIVIDUAL PRACTICE ASSOCIATION HEALTH MAINTENANCE ORGANIZATION (HMO) HEALTH MAINTENANCE ORGANIZATION that provides medical services to the HMO members through an exclusive contract with specific physicians and hospitals. These selected physicians and hospitals provide medical services to both HMO members and non-HMO members. Generally, HMO members may select the primary care physician of their choice from the list of specific physicians. After rendering services to the HMO member, the physician is paid a predetermined fee by the HMO.

INDIVIDUAL RETIREMENT ACCOUNT (IRA) traditional fund under the TAX REFORM ACT OF 1986 into which any individual employee can contribute up to $2000 per calendar year. Under the tax law in 1986, unemployed spouses may have contributed up to $2000 even if the working spouse did not make a contribution. However, income level and eligibility for an employee pension plan determined whether or not the employee's contribution or a percentage was tax deductible. The following are the circumstances of contribution to an IRA and the tax consequences under the current law, the ECONOMIC GROWTH AND TAX RELIEF RECONCILIATION ACT OF 2001.

Income		Covered by Employee Pension Plan (Either or both spouses)	Tax Consequences of $5000 (age 50+)
Individual	*Family*		*Contribution*
No restrictions on income		No	Totally deductible
$50,000 or less	$75,000 or less	Yes	Totally deductible
Between $50,000 and $60,000	Between $75,000 and $85,000	Yes	Partially deductible
More than $60,000	More than $85,000	Yes	No deduction

In order to offset the effects of inflation, the Tax Relief Act of 2001 raises the minimum annual contribution limits to $4000 in 2007 and $5000 in 2008. After 2008, limits may be increased in increments of $500 according to the rate of inflation. Also, people older than age 50 can make additional "catch-up" contributions of $1000 per year. Thus, in 2007 the total annual contribution is $5000, and in 2008, that contribution is $6000. Equal contributions are available for the spouse.

Note that relevant employee pension plans include *401(k), 403(b), Keogh,* and DEFINED BENEFIT PLAN. (There is no requirement to have benefits vested.) IRA earnings remain tax deferred. Withdrawals prior to age 59½ are subject to a 10% penalty except for disability or death or to pay for qualified higher education expenses, a first home (there is a $10,000 lifetime limit on withdrawals for first-time home buyers), or qualified medical expenses.

INDIVIDUAL RETIREMENT ACCOUNT FUNDING INSTRU-MENTS under the EMPLOYEE RETIREMENT INCOME SECURITY ACT OF 1974 (ERISA), the INDIVIDUAL RETIREMENT ACCOUNT (BANK TRUST CUSTODIAL ACCOUNT, MUTUAL FUND CUSTODIAL ACCOUNT, SELF-DIRECTED CUSTODIAL ACCOUNT), or the INDIVIDUAL RETIREMENT ANNUITY may be utilized.

INDIVIDUAL RETIREMENT ACCOUNT PLUS (IRA PLUS) proposal, endorsed by then-President Bush and Secretary of the Treasury Nicholas Brady, which expands in a significant manner the number of individuals who could take advantage of the effect of tax-deferred compounding of savings for retirement. The plan would be available to everyone since there are no income caps, to include employees who are covered under an employer's qualified pension plan. A spouse without an earned income could also establish such an account. Contributions to this account would be made with after-tax dollars. All principal would compound on a tax-free basis, so that no taxes would be due upon distribution. As the plan is currently designed, a participant could withdraw without penalty up to 25% of his or her account to purchase a first home, to meet catastrophic medical bills, or to pay for college expenses. Contrast with INDIVIDUAL RETIREMENT ACCOUNT (IRA).

INDIVIDUAL RETIREMENT ANNUITY type of INDIVIDUAL RETIREMENT ACCOUNT (IRA) allowed by the EMPLOYEE RETIREMENT INCOME SECURITY ACT OF 1974 (ERISA) whereby contributions in the form of premium payments are made on a FIXED DOLLAR ANNUITY or VARIABLE DOLLAR ANNUITY or both.

INDIVIDUAL RISK PREMIUM MODIFICATION PLAN in group insurance, adjustment of premiums, because of reduced expenses due to economy of scale. Group life premiums are subject to negotiation and modification because of administrative savings in dealing with large numbers of people. In contrast, a single person cannot negotiate his or her premium rate because each policy is handled individually.

INDIVIDUAL STOCK PURCHASE PLAN *see* CLOSE CORPORATION PLAN.

INDIVISIBLE CONTRACT inability to divide a CASH VALUE LIFE INSURANCE policy into a savings element and a protection element because, in theory, if the POLICYOWNER withdraws a portion or all of the cash value, there is a reduction in the DEATH BENEFIT.

INDUCEMENT TO ESTABLISHMENT OF PENSION PLANS circumstances that encourage the organization of pension plans by employers. For example, employer contributions are tax deductible as business expenses and not currently taxable income to employees. Pensions also help attract employees, maintain employee loyalty, and help improve the image of a business firm in its community.

INDUCTIVE REASONING type of logic that makes the assumption that what has happened in the past will happen in the future, given the same conditions surrounding the two occurrences. In other words, "History repeats itself." In insurance, an example would involve the assumption of future wooden frame houses burning if the same conditions exist now that existed in the past when wooden frame houses burned.

INDUSTRIAL INSURANCE *see* INDUSTRIAL LIFE INSURANCE.

INDUSTRIAL INSURED one who purchases insurance, usually property and liability and not life or annuities, by utilizing his or her own employee purchaser or licensed broker/agent at a minimum annual premium of not less than six digits.

INDUSTRIAL INSURED CARRIER insurance company that sells property and casualty insurance only to INDUSTRIAL INSUREDS. These companies are separately licensed and separately capitalized to market insurance to cover the risks of industrial insureds.

INDUSTRIAL LIFE INSURANCE modest amounts of coverage sold on a DEBIT basis. The face amount is usually less than $1000. *See also* DEBIT INSURANCE (HOME SERVICE INSURANCE, INDUSTRIAL INSURANCE).

INDUSTRIAL PRODUCTION INDEX index that reflects changes in industrial output by manufacturers, mines, electric utilities, and natural gas utilities. This is a monthly index published by the Federal Reserve.

INDUSTRIAL PROPERTY POLICY PROGRAM predecessor of SPECIAL MULTIPERIL INSURANCE (SMP) policy and COMMERCIAL PACKAGE POLICY, which covered property of manufacturing installations, in at least two different locations, including machinery and equipment, and, optionally, improvements and betterments.

INEVITABLE ACCIDENT ACCIDENT that is unforeseen and unpreventable. *See also* FORTUITOUS LOSS.

INFIDELITY EXCLUSION *see* FIDELITY EXCLUSION.

INFLATION ENDORSEMENT attachment to a property insurance policy that automatically adjusts its coverage according to the construction cost index in a community. This endorsement is necessary in a property contract to maintain adequate coverage. Otherwise, it is advisable for a policyowner, at time of renewal, to adjust the limits of coverage to reflect the increased cost of construction and the market value of the property.

INFLATION FACTOR adjustment in property insurance to reflect increased construction costs. *See also* INFLATION ENDORSEMENT.

INFLATION GUARD ENDORSEMENT *see* INFLATION ENDORSEMENT.

INFLATION INDEXED BOND issues of the U.S. Treasury that provide for the adjustment of the interest rate paid according to the change in the rate of inflation.

INFLATION RISK coverage for a decrease on the purchasing power of an asset because of an increase in the cost of living.

IN-FORCE BUSINESS aggregate amount of insurance policies that are paid-up (or are being paid) that a life or health insurance company has on its books. The size of a life or health insurance company is often measured by its in-force business. In a life insurance company, the measure is expressed as a face amount of the insurer's portfolio. In a health insurance company, the measure is expressed as premium volume.

IN-FORCE REQUIREMENT need for an insurance policy to be paid up or to be paid for a minimum number of years before the insured is eligible to receive any benefits. This requirement is typically found in LONG-TERM CARE (LTC) insurance policies.

INHERENT EXPLOSION CLAUSE provision of a property insurance policy which covers conditions usually present in a particular location. For example, there is an inherent risk of explosion in a flour mill.

INHERENT VICE EXCLUSION provision of a property policy that excludes construction that is likely to suffer a loss. For example, the roofing material used may not be able to withstand a wind force of more than 15 miles per hour.

INHERITANCE TAX tax on the right to acquire ASSETS that are transferred to a BENEFICIARY at the death of the owner of those assets.

INITIAL PREMIUM premium paid at the time a policy goes into effect. With some policies, such as group health insurance, premiums are subject to adjustment at the end of the policy period to reflect loss experience. If the loss experience is good (that is, if the losses are smaller than anticipated in the premium loading), a significant premium reduction can be made at the end of the policy period, with a refund going to the policyowner. *See also* PREMIUM.

INITIAL PUBLIC OFFERING (IPO) issue of a stock by a company for the first time in the market.

INITIAL RESERVE reserve at the beginning of the POLICY YEAR that is equal to the TERMINAL RESERVE for the preceding year plus the NET LEVEL PREMIUM for the current year.

INJUNCTION BOND type of judicial bond under which a plaintiff is held liable for damages in the event of a false injunction. The objective of this bond is to protect the party who has been wrongly accused by a plaintiff and suffers financial loss.

INJURIES AND DISEASES COVERED list of injuries and diseases covered in a health insurance policy. Consumers are well advised to read and understand the definitions of injuries and diseases in a health insurance policy. *See also* HEALTH INSURANCE.

INJURY INDEPENDENT OF ALL OTHER MEANS injury covered in a health insurance policy that is isolated from any previous injury.

INLAND MARINE transit over land.

INLAND MARINE EXPOSURE *see* INLAND MARINE INSURANCE (TRANSPORTATION INSURANCE): BUSINESS RISKS.

INLAND MARINE INSURANCE BUREAU rate-making division of INSURANCE SERVICES OFFICES (ISO) for inland marine insurance coverages of member companies.

INLAND MARINE INSURANCE (TRANSPORTATION INSURANCE): BUSINESS RISKS coverage for (1) property damage or destruction of an insured's property and (2) liability exposure of an insured for damage or destruction of someone else's property under his or her care, custody, or control. The insured (shipper) needs this insurance because the carrier (who can also be the insured and purchase inland marine insurance) may be found not at fault for damage to a property; or the carrier may not have any insurance or adequate insurance.

Perils covered include fire, lightning, windstorm, flood, earthquake, landslide, theft, collision, derailment, overturn of the transporting vehicle, and collapse of bridges. Specialty coverages include: ACCOUNTS RECEIVABLE INSURANCE; AIR CARGO INSURANCE; ARMORED CAR AND MESSENGER INSURANCE; CONSIGNMENT INSURANCE; CONTINGENT TRANSIT INSURANCE; COTTON INSURANCE; DEPARTMENT STORE INSURANCE FLOATER; EQUIPMENT FLOATERS INSURANCE; INSTALLATION INSURANCE; INSTALLMENT INSURANCE; INSTRUMENTALITIES OF TRANSPORTATION INSURANCE; MOTOR TRUCK CARGO INSURANCE; PARCEL POST INSURANCE; RAILROAD ROLLING STOCK INSURANCE; REGISTERED MAIL AND EXPRESS MAIL INSURANCE; STOCK PROCESSING INSURANCE; TRIP TRANSIT INSURANCE; VALUABLE PAPERS (RECORDS) INSURANCE.

INLAND MARINE UNDERWRITERS ASSOCIATION organization of inland marine insurance underwriters.

INLAND TRANSIT INSURANCE POLICY particular type of INLAND MARINE INSURANCE.

INNKEEPERS LIABILITY liability arising out of the operation of a motel or hotel as it pertains to the physical safety of guests and their property.

INNKEEPERS LIABILITY INSURANCE coverage for negligent acts or omissions of an operator of a motel or hotel resulting in bodily injury to guests and damage or destruction of a guest's property.

IN-PATIENT resident patient of a medical installation. Previously, health insurance benefits were limited to in-patient care. Today health insurance policies provide an extensive list of out-patient benefits. *See also* GROUP HEALTH INSURANCE; HEALTH MAINTENANCE ORGANIZATION (HMO); OUTPATIENT.

INSECT EXCLUSION exclusion in property insurance eliminating coverage for damage or destruction of property due to insects.

IN-SERVICE ROLLOVER a transfer by employees of a portion of their SECTION 401(K) PLAN (SALARY REDUCTION PLAN) into an INDIVIDUAL RETIREMENT ACCOUNT (IRA).

INSIDE AND OUTSIDE PREMISES ROBBERY INSURANCE *see* INTERIOR ROBBERY POLICY, MESSENGER ROBBERY INSURANCE.

INSIDE BUILDUP increase in cash value in a LIFE INSURANCE and/or ANNUITY policy.

INSOLVENCY bankruptcy. If an insured business firm becomes bankrupt, the circumstance does not relieve an insurance company of its obligations under an insurance contract.

INSOLVENCY CLAUSE provision of a reinsurance contract that states that the reinsurance company remains liable for its predetermined share of a claim submitted by an insured, even though the primary insurance company is no longer in business.

INSOLVENCY FUND *see* GUARANTY FUND (INSOLVENCY FUND).

INSPECTION in *property* or *liability* insurance, right retained by the company to inspect the insured premises as well as its operations in order to detect inherent structural defects and other hidden hazards. Inspections also help reduce loss frequency and severity through recommended safety engineering loss prevention and reduction procedures. In WORKERS COMPENSATION INSURANCE, the insurance company must inspect the business's payroll record since premiums are based on the business's gross payroll. In LIFE INSURANCE, the company may obtain verification of statements by an applicant and other information.

INSPECTION RECEIPT form provided for an INSPECTION REPORT.

INSPECTION REPORT statement prepared by an *inspection bureau* for a life or health insurance company that summarizes information about an applicant for a policy, including financial standing, morals, physical condition, habits, and other information. This report is used by a company underwriter in evaluating an application for insurance; that is, whether the company should classify an individual as a standard risk at standard insurance rates, as a substandard risk (charged an extra rate), or as uninsurable.

INSPECTION SLIP *see* INSPECTION RECEIPT.

INSPECTOR person who has the responsibility for examining the RISK to determine whether or not to insure it.

INSTALLATION INSURANCE property coverage on a dealer's interest in equipment while it is being installed. Labor and material are protected against such perils as fire, lightning, and windstorm. For example, if an elevator was installed and it was damaged or destroyed before the buyer could take possession, the contractor would lose the cost of labor and materials if there was no installation insurance.

INSTALLMENT REFUND *see* INSTALLMENT REFUND ANNUITY.

INSTALLMENT REFUND ANNUITY ANNUITY contract. If the annuitant dies before receiving income at least equal to the premiums paid, a beneficiary receives the difference in installments. If the annuitant lives after the income paid equals the premiums paid, the insurance company continues to make income payments to the annuitant for life.

INSTALLMENT SALES FLOATER *see* CONDITIONAL SALES FLOATER.

INSTALLMENT SETTLEMENT life insurance policy DEATH BENEFIT or cash value paid out in a series of installments, rather than in a lump sum. *See also* FIXED-AMOUNT SETTLEMENT OPTION; FIXED-PERIOD OPTION SETTLEMENT; LIFE INCOME; LIFE INCOME WITH PERIOD CERTAIN.

INSTITUTE OF ACTUARIES *see* CANADIAN INSTITUTE OF ACTUARIES.

INSTITUTE OF LONDON UNDERWRITERS trade association of insurance companies that writes transportation, aviation, and marine insurance. The association began operation in the 1880s and it suggests standard clauses to be incorporated in policies written by the underwriters in London.

INSTRUMENTALITIES OF TRANSPORTATION INSURANCE coverage for entities (other than motorized vehicles) used in the transportation of property, including BRIDGE INSURANCE; BRIDGE INSURANCE FOR BRIDGES UNDER CONSTRUCTION; PIERS, WHARVES, DOCKS AND SLIPS INSURANCE; RADIO AND TELEVISION TRANSMITTING EQUIPMENT; TRANSMISSION LINES, PIPE LINES; TRAFFIC LIGHTS INSURANCE; TUNNEL INSURANCE.

INSURABILITY circumstance in which an insurance company can issue life or health insurance to an applicant based on standards set by the company.

INSURABILITY CONDITIONAL PREMIUM RECEIPT offer made by the insurance company to insure an applicant, provided the applicant is insurable according to the UNDERWRITING standards of the company, and the applicant accepts the offer by making the PREMIUM payment. If the applicant should die prior to the APPLICATION and premium reaching the HOME OFFICE, and the applicant would have qualified for INSURED status according to the underwriting standards of the company, the DEATH BENEFIT would be paid to the applicant's BENEFICIARY. Thus, the insurance policy applied for goes into effect upon the date of the CONDITIONAL RECEIPT if the applicant is later found to be insurable according to the underwriting standards of the company.

INSURABLE INTEREST expectation of a monetary loss that can be covered by insurance. Insurable interest varies according to the type of policy. These relationships give rise to insurable interest: (1) owner of the property; (2) vendor (to the extent of the unpaid balance due on the property sold to the vendee); (3) vendee; (4) bailee (to the extent of the value of the property under his or her temporary care, custody, and control); (5) bailor; (6) life estates; (7) fee simple estates; (8) mortgagee (to the extent of the unpaid balance due on the loan to which the property is pledged as security); and (9) mortgagor. *See also* INSURABLE INTEREST: LIFE INSURANCE; INSURABLE INTEREST: PROPERTY AND CASUALTY INSURANCE.

INSURABLE INTEREST LAW requirement by statutes of some states that individuals and/or organizations may only purchase new insurance policies on other individuals with whom they are directly connected.

INSURABLE INTEREST: LIFE INSURANCE

1. each individual has an unlimited insurable interest in his or her own life, and therefore can select anyone as a beneficiary.
2. parent and child, husband and wife, brother and sister have an insurable interest in each other because of blood or marriage.
3. creditor-debtor relationships give rise to an insurable interest. The creditor can be the beneficiary for the amount of the outstanding loan, with the face value decreasing in proportion to the decline in the outstanding loan amount.
4. business relationships give rise to an insurable interest. An employee may insure the life of an employer, and an employer may insure the life of an employee. *See also* BENEFITS OF BUSINESS LIFE AND HEALTH INSURANCE (KEY PERSON INSURANCE): KEY EMPLOYEE (KEY MAN); PARTNERSHIP LIFE AND HEALTH INSURANCE.

   Insurable interest must exist at the inception of the contract, not necessarily at the time of loss. For example, because a woman has an insurable interest in the life of her fiance, she purchases an insurance policy on his life. Even if the relationship is terminated, as long as she continues to pay the premiums she will be able to collect the death benefit under the policy.

INSURABLE INTEREST: PROPERTY AND CASUALTY INSURANCE

1. owner of property has an insurable interest because of the expectation of monetary loss if that property is damaged or destroyed.
2. creditor of an insured has an insurable interest in property pledged as security.

   Insurable interest has to exist both at the inception of the contract and at the time of a loss. For example, an insured can purchase a homeowners policy because of insurable interest in a home. Upon selling it, the insured no longer has an insurable interest because there is no expectation of a monetary loss should the home burn down.

INSURABLE RISK condition in which an applicant has met an insurance company's standards. Requirements include a loss that is (1) definable; (2) fortuitous; (3) one of a large number of homogeneous exposures; and (4) carries a premium reasonable in relation to a potential loss.

INSURABLE VALUE *see* INSURABLE RISK.

INSURANCE mechanism for contractually shifting burdens of a number of PURE RISKS by pooling them.

INSURANCE AGENT representative of an insurance company in soliciting and servicing policyholders. An agent's knowledge concerning an insurance transaction is said to be the knowledge of the insurance company as well. Wrongful acts of the agent are the responsibility of the company; these bind the company to the customer. Notice given by an insured to the agent is the same as notice to the company. *See also* AGENT; CAPTIVE AGENT; INDEPENDENT AGENT.

INSURANCE AGENTS AND BROKERS LIABILITY INSURANCE coverage for acts or omissions committed by an agent or broker resulting in adequate insurance in the event of a liability suit or property damage to a client.

INSURANCE AND SOCIETY phrase referring to constructive relationship, in which insurance provides society with benefits such as security, savings, encouragement of investment, and reduction in prices of goods to consumers.

INSURANCE BROKER representative of an insured, not of an insurance company. Acts of a broker are not the responsibility of the company, and notice given by an insured to a broker is not the same as notice to the company. The broker searches the insurance marketplace for a company in which to place the insured's business for the most coverage at the best price. The broker is not restricted to placing business with any one company.

INSURANCE CARRIER *see* INSURANCE COMPANY (INSURER); INSURER.

INSURANCE CHARGE *see* RETROSPECTIVE RATING.

INSURANCE COMMISSIONER *see* COMMISSIONER OF INSURANCE (INSURANCE COMMISSIONER, SUPERINTENDENT OF INSURANCE).

INSURANCE COMPANY, CHOOSING AN consideration should be given to a company's capacity to underwrite a particular risk, as indicated by its financial standing, claims philosophy, price structure, agent representation, loss prevention and reduction services, and risk analysis expertise. Information can be gained in several ways:

1. *Reputation*—a prospective insured can fairly easily learn something about an insurance company through business and professional associates (lawyer, accountant, banker), through conversations with others in the same field, and by discussions with agents and brokers.
2. *Financial capacity*—larger businesses and public libraries often have up-to-date reference books, such as *Best's Insurance Reports* (available in *Life-Health* and *Property-Casualty* editions) giving detailed analyses of hundreds of companies.
3. *State Insurance Department*—information about specific insurance companies may be available from the insurance departments located in state capitals.

INSURANCE COMPANY DEPARTMENT *see* INSURANCE COMPANY ORGANIZATION.

INSURANCE COMPANY FLEET *see* FLEET OF COMPANIES.

INSURANCE COMPANY (INSURER) organization that underwrites insurance policies. There are two principal types of insurance companies: *mutual* and *stock.* A mutual company is owned by its policyowners, who elect a board of directors that is responsible for its operation. A stock company is owned by its stockholders. In a mutual company, profits take the form of *policy dividends,* or refunds of part of premiums paid, which are distributed to policyowners. Profits in a stock company take the form of stockholders dividends, which are distributed to stockholders.

INSURANCE COMPANY ORGANIZATION structure. In general, company functions are delegated to several departments: *actuarial,* AGENCY, *claims and loss control,* INVESTMENTS, *legal,* MARKETING, and UNDERWRITING.

INSURANCE CONTRACT *see* HEALTH INSURANCE CONTRACT; INSURANCE CONTRACT, GENERAL; INSURANCE CONTRACT, LIFE; INSURANCE CONTRACT, PROPERTY AND CASUALTY.

INSURANCE CONTRACT, GENERAL legally binding unilateral agreement between an insured and an insurance company to indemnify the buyer of a contract under specified circumstances. In exchange for premium payment(s) the company covers stipulated perils. *See also* ADHESION INSURANCE CONTRACT; ALEATORY CONTRACT; APPLICATION; CAPACITY OF PARTIES; CONDITIONAL; CONSIDERATION; ENDORSEMENTS; INDEMNITY; INSURABLE INTEREST; LEGAL PURPOSE; MUTUAL ASSENT; UTMOST GOOD FAITH.

INSURANCE CONTRACT, HEALTH *see* HEALTH INSURANCE CONTRACT.

INSURANCE CONTRACT, LIFE *see* BENEFICIARY; CLAUSES ADDED TO A LIFE INSURANCE POLICY; NON-FORFEITURE PROVISION; POLICY LOAN; REPRESENTATIONS; STANDARD PROVISIONS, LIFE INSURANCE; SUICIDE CLAUSE; VALUED POLICY; WAR EXCLUSION CLAUSE.

INSURANCE CONTRACT, PROPERTY AND CASUALTY *see* CONCEALMENT; DEDUCTIBLE; DOUBLE RECOVERY; ESTOPPEL; INDEMNITY; INSURANCE TO VALUE; LARGE LOSS PRINCIPLE; MISREPRESENTATION (FALSE PRETENSE); PERSONAL CONTRACT; SMALL LOSS PRINCIPLE; STANDARD PROVISIONS; LIFE INSURANCE; SUBROGATION CLAUSE; WAIVER; WARRANTY.

INSURANCE COVERAGE *see* COVERAGE.

INSURANCE CRIME PREVENTION INSTITUTE organization of over 300 property and casualty insurance companies whose mission is to investigate fraudulent claims and bring to justice those making such claims.

INSURANCE DEPARTMENT authority that administers state laws regulating insurance and licenses insurance companies and their agents.

INSURANCE EXAMINER employee of a state insurance department who audits statements of insurance companies to determine their continued solvency.

INSURANCE EXCHANGE *see* NEW YORK INSURANCE EXCHANGE.

INSURANCE EXPENSES costs associated with FIRST-YEAR EXPENSES, CLAIMS EXPENSES, ADMINISTRATIVE EXPENSES, and RENEWAL EXPENSES.

INSURANCE FIELDS *see* SOCIAL INSURANCE.

INSURANCE FORM attachment to a property and casualty policy that makes it operative. For example, the *Standard Fire Policy* remains inoperative until a form such as the *Buildings and Contents Form* is attached.

INSURANCE FRAUD PREVENTION ACT legislation that makes insurance fraud a federal crime. This act is part of the Omnibus Crime Bill. Under the act, it is a federal crime to embezzle or misappropriate funds, money, or premiums from an insurance company, to knowingly file false financial information with regulators, to obstruct the investigation of an insurance regulator, and to work or allow such work in an insurance field after conviction of a felony involving dishonesty.

INSURANCE FUTURES futures contracts (legally binding contract that stipulates that delivery of an ASSET will be taken or delivery of an asset will be made at a future time at an agreed upon price at the current moment) on insurance lines to include CATASTROPHIC INSURANCE FUTURES, automobile insurance futures, homeowners insurance futures, and so forth, traded on the Chicago Board of Trade (CBOT). Traditionally, precious metals such as gold and silver; agriculture commodities such as cattle, corn, and soy beans; and United States Treasury issues such as bonds and bills, have all been traded on the CBOT. The aim of the transaction with these futures is to cancel the contract with a gain before the delivery of the commodity. (Who would want cattle delivered to their house?) On the other hand, the insurance futures contract concerns itself with the dollar value the market attaches to an index. In turn, this index is an expectation of how much of the premium income generated by a particular line of insurance will have to be allocated to pay off incurred losses. For example, if the automobile insurance line generates an income of $5,000,000 and the market has an expectation that 90% of that income will have to be allocated to paying off incurred losses, the market will value that futures contract at a price somewhat less than $450,000. This is because of such factors that have to be accounted for as incurred but not reported losses (IBNR).

INSURANCE GUARANTY ACT law, in several states, establishing a fund to guarantee benefits under policies issued by insurance companies that become insolvent.

INSURANCE IN FORCE *see* IN-FORCE BUSINESS.

INSURANCE INFORMATION INSTITUTE organization having as its objective the education of the general public concerning items of national concern of member property and casualty insurance companies.

INSURANCE INSTITUTE FOR HIGHWAY SAFETY organization located in Washington, D.C., whose membership consists of automobile insurers.

INSURANCE INSTITUTE FOR PROPERTY LOSS REDUCTION association of insurance companies formed to reduce deaths, injuries, and the loss of property resulting from all types of natural hazards in the United States. This institute concentrates on improving construction and building techniques in order to minimize the damage resulting from natural hazards.

INSURANCE INSTITUTE OF AMERICA (IIA) organization that develops and publishes educational material and administers national examinations in supervisory management, general insurance, claims, management, risk management, underwriting, loss control management, accredited adviser in insurance, premium auditing, research and planning, and accounting and finance.

INSURANCE MARKETPLACE STANDARDS ASSOCIATION (IMSA) voluntary market conduct compliance organization whose purpose is to protect the public interest and to enhance the insurance buyer's perception of the life insurance instrument. The member companies place the emphasis on self-regulation. Each member company is required to perform a self-assessment of its sales and marketing practices. Member companies are required to adhere to six principles of ethical market conduct that specifies compliance supervision, complaint procedures, types of sales materials, procedure for replacement and fair competition, agent selection and training, and suitability.

INSURANCE MARKETPLACE STANDARDS ASSOCIATION PRINCIPLE 6 rule that provides four requirements for monitoring the INDEPENDENT AGENT distribution system:
1. The insurance company must be involved in the training of the independent agent.
2. The insurance company must monitor the sales practices employed by the independent agent in selling its product.
3. The insurance company must have a written contract with the independent agent that describes the responsibilities of the agent as well as the limitations on the agent's authority.
4. The insurance company must perform DUE DILIGENCE on the independent agent.

INSURANCE PLANS COVERED *see* BUSINESS INSURANCE; GROUP INSURANCE; INDIVIDUAL INSURANCE.

INSURANCE PLANS FOR KEY EMPLOYEES *see* KEY EMPLOYEES, INSURANCE PLANS FOR.

INSURANCE POLICY written contract between an insured and an insurance company stating the obligations and responsibilities of each party. *See also* INSURANCE CONTRACT, LIFE; INSURANCE CONTRACT, PROPERTY AND CASUALTY.

INSURANCE POOL *see* POOL.

INSURANCE PREMIUM *see* PREMIUM.

INSURANCE RATE amount charged to an insured that reflects expectation of loss for a covered risk; and insurance company expenses and profit. *See also* PREMIUM; PURE PREMIUM RATING METHOD.

INSURANCE REGISTER *see* REGISTER.

INSURANCE REGULATION *see* STATE SUPERVISION AND REGULATION.

INSURANCE REGULATORY INFORMATION SYSTEM (IRIS) financial analysis method established by the NATIONAL ASSOCIATION OF INSURANCE COMMISSIONERS (NAIC) to detect problems of property and casualty insurance companies and life and health insurance companies according to these audit ratios:
Property and casualty insurance companies: (1) current year increase or decrease in net written premiums to net written premiums in previous year; (2) net written premiums to adjusted policyowners' surplus; (3) loss ratio for two years; (4) expense ratio for two years; (5) net investment income to average invested assets; (6) liabilities to liquid assets; (7) unpaid premiums to surplus; and (8) previous year adjusted surplus to current year adjusted surplus.
(Other property and casualty audit ratios concern measurement of the adequacy of a company's *reserve.*)
Life and health insurance companies: (1) yield on investments; (2) nonadmitted assets to assets; (3) net gain to total income; (4) investments in affiliates to capital and surplus; (5) expenses (including agents commissions) to premiums; (6) exchange in capital and surplus; and (7) surplus increase or decrease.

INSURANCE RISK coverage for exposures that exhibit a possibility of financial loss. *See also* PRICING INADEQUCY RISK.

INSURANCE SCORE rating based on prospective insured's credit score that is said to predict the probability of having a loss. In theory, there is a relationship between a high score (good credit record) and low claim FREQUENCY and low score (poor credit record) and high claim frequency.

INSURANCE SERVICES OFFICE (ISO) organization that calculates rates and develops insurance policies for its property and casualty member companies. The suggested rates are used by smaller companies where the loss experience lacks actuarial accuracy. Its rates are also used by larger companies, which modify them to fit their own loss experience.

INSURANCE SOLICITOR *see* SOLICITOR.

INSURANCE SUPERINTENDENT *see* INSURANCE COMMISSIONER.

INSURANCE TITLE *see* TITLE INSURANCE.

INSURANCE TO VALUE in property coverage, ratio of the amount of insurance to the value of an insured property. This ratio, multiplied by the amount of the loss, determines the indemnification payment. *See also* COINSURANCE.

INSURED party covered by an insurance policy. In life insurance policies there is one designated insured, the person so named; or a policy can be issued to numerous insureds on a group basis. The insured persons in property and casualty policies may also include residents of the insured's household, such as a spouse, relatives of either, and other individuals under their care, custody, and control if under age 21.

INSURED LOAN type of loan that has been insured by the Federal Housing Administration or a private mortgage insurance company.

INSURED, NAMED *see* NAMED INSURED.

INSURED PERIL source of loss that is covered under an insurance policy, such as a fire, and explosion, among others.

INSURED PREMISES real property (structure(s) attached to the land) that is occupied and/or is under the care, custody, or control of an individual, individuals, or an organization for which an insurance policy provides coverage. Within the insurance policy, the premises will be listed in the DECLARATIONS SECTION and/or further defined in the policy.

INSURED'S OBLIGATION AFTER LOSS *see* PROPERTY AND CASUALTY INSURANCE PROVISIONS.

INSURER company offering protection through the sale of an insurance policy to an insured. *See also* INSURANCE COMPANY (INSURER).

INSURER FINANCES: LIFE AND HEALTH, PROPERTY AND CASUALTY management of premium inflow and benefit outflow. *See also* ASSETS AND VALUATION; FULL PRELIMINARY TERM RESERVE PLAN; INVESTMENTS AND REGULATION PROSPECTIVE RESERVE; REINSURANCE RESERVE; RETAINED EARNINGS; UNDERWRITING GAIN (LOSS).

INSURING AGREEMENT section describing coverages under a policy. Elsewhere in the policy other sections may restrict or exclude coverages. *See also* INSURING AGREEMENT, PROPERTY AND CASUALTY POLICY.

INSURING AGREEMENT, AUTOMOBILE POLICIES *see* INSURING AGREEMENT, PROPERTY AND CASUALTY POLICY.

INSURING AGREEMENT, FIRE *see* INSURING AGREEMENT, PROPERTY AND CASUALTY POLICY.

INSURING AGREEMENT, LIABILITY *see* INSURING AGREEMENT, PROPERTY AND CASUALTY POLICY.

INSURING AGREEMENT, PROPERTY AND CASUALTY POLICY section of a policy specifying: (1) *parties to the contract* (the insurance company and the person or business to be insured); (2) terms of the policy—when it goes into force, and when it ends; (3) premiums and their due date; (4) limits of insurance; (5) types and location of property to be insured; (6) CONSIDERATION; (7) perils (what the policy protects against); and (8) assignment (and under what conditions the policy can be assigned).

INSURING AGREEMENT, WORKERS COMPENSATION AND EMPLOYERS LIABILITY *see* INSURING AGREEMENT, PROPERTY AND CASUALTY POLICY.

INSURING CLAUSE essential part of an insurance policy. It names the individual(s) covered, property and locations covered, perils covered, the time a policy goes into force, and its termination date. *See also* INSURING AGREEMENT, PROPERTY AND CASUALTY POLICY.

INTANGIBLE PERSONAL PROPERTY that which cannot be touched; having no meaning to the senses. It is represented by incorporeal rights in property (that which is evidence or represents value; for example, a copyright).

INTEGRATED DEDUCTIBLE deductible amount between a basic health insurance plan and major medical insurance.

INTEGRATED PLAN EMPLOYEE BENEFIT PLAN that includes benefits to be received from Social Security when determining the allowable benefit amount to be received by that employee or beneficiary.

INTEGRATION PERCENTAGE *see* INTEGRATION WITH SOCIAL SECURITY.

INTEGRATION WITH SOCIAL SECURITY method of reducing an employee pension according to IRS procedures:
1. *Offset method*—restricted to a DEFINED BENEFIT PLAN under which a mandatory percentage of the monthly Social Security benefit payable to a retired employee is subtracted from the monthly retirement benefit payable to the employee under a business firm's qualified retirement plan.
2. *Integration method*—used with a defined benefit plan or a *defined contribution plan* under which a basic level of compensation is established for a retired employee so that (a) for compensation above this level, the employee receives a greater retirement benefit; or (b) for compensation below this level, the employee receives a smaller retirement benefit.

INTENTIONALLY DEFECTIVE IRREVOCABLE TRUST type of IRREVOCABLE TRUST in which all of the income of the TRUST is attributable to the GRANTOR and not the trust.

INTENTIONAL TORT deliberate act or omission, including trespass, assault and battery, invasion of privacy, libel, and slander. An intentional tort is a branch of civil liability. Liability insurance can be purchased to cover libel and slander, but not the other intentional torts.

INTERCOMPANY ARBITRATION settlement of a dispute that arises when two or more insurers cover a single loss, and there is a question concerning the amount each is responsible to pay. The companies are bound by the arbitration decision.

INTERCOMPANY DATA information generated by the MEDICAL INFORMATION BUREAU (MIB) and made available to member companies concerning medical information of applicants for life and health insurance. Member companies are required to report to the MIB physical impairments of an applicant as uncovered through the underwriting process.

INTEREST money paid by one party for the use of another party's funds.

INTEREST ADJUSTED COST procedure for calculating the cost of life insurance, taking into account the TIME VALUE OF MONEY (investment return on sums placed in premium dollars had these sums been invested elsewhere). There are several ways to calculate interest adjusted cost based on time value of money. *See also* LINTON YIELD METHOD; NET PAYMENTS INDEX; SURRENDER COST INDEX.

INTEREST-ADJUSTED METHOD *see* INTEREST ADJUSTED COST.

INTEREST AND DIVIDEND TAX COMPLIANCE ACT requirement of the Internal Revenue Service that any dividend payments received are subject to a 20% withholding if the investor fails to furnish the dividend payor with the investor's correct tax identification number.

INTEREST ASSUMPTION minimum rate of return, in life insurance, guaranteed to a policyowner in calculating benefits for a life insurance policy. It is also used by an insurance company as the minimum rate of return it expects on its investments in calculating reserves.

INTEREST FREE LOANS means of borrowing at no charge by a policyowner under UNIVERSAL LIFE INSURANCE policies.

INTEREST MAINTENANCE RESERVE (IMR) liability RESERVE, establishment required by the NATIONAL ASSOCIATION OF INSURANCE COMMISSIONERS (NAIC), the purpose of which is to accumulate realized capital gains and losses resulting from fluctuations in the interest rate. These gains and losses in the IMR are amortized and shown as an adjustment to the net investment income over the remaining life of the sold assets.

INTEREST OPTION use of a life insurance policy dividend by the owner of a participating policy. Here the policy dividend is left with the insurance company to accumulate at a guaranteed minimum interest rate. Also, an interest option is a choice a beneficiary can make by leaving death proceeds with the insurance company to accumulate at interest. Interest earned under either option is subject to federal and state income taxes.

INTEREST POLICIES *see* CURRENT ASSUMPTION WHOLE LIFE INSURANCE; INTEREST SENSITIVE POLICIES; UNIVERSAL LIFE INSURANCE; UNIVERSAL VARIABLE LIFE INSURANCE.

INTEREST RATE CAP maximum amount of interest ANNUITANT can earn in an EQUITY INDEXED ANNUITY. For example, if the underlying cap on the earned interest rate is 4% and the index actually gains 12%, the annuitant will only be credited with 4%.

INTEREST RATE CHANGE RISK one of four types of risks used by the SOCIETY OF ACTUARIES (SA) to determine a life insurance company's overall risk profile when fluctuations in interest rates result in abnormal cash inflows or outflows causing positive or negative investment implications. *See also* ASSET DEPRECIATION RISK; GENERAL BUSINESS RISK; INTEREST RATE CHANGE RISK; PRICING INADEQUACY RISK.

INTEREST RATE COLLAR combination of an INTEREST RATE CAP and an INTEREST RATE FLOOR, creating a band within which interest rates can range. For example, if an interest rate band is between 6% and 10%, the insurance company does not receive or pay a continuous stream of interest payments from or to another party within this band. Above the upper limit on the maximum possible interest rate an insurance company will pay, and below the lower limit of the maximum possible interest rate an insurance company will pay, the insurance company and another party will exchange interest payments.

INTEREST RATE FLOOR lower limit on the maximum possible interest rate an insurance company will pay. If the market interest rates are below that lower limit, the insurance company pays the lower limit rate. In this way, the insurance company can hedge its interest rate exposure (risk that interest rates will rise or fall at some stipulated time), reflected by changes in the value of its assets on the balance sheets.

INTEREST RATE RISK investment risk associated with the possibility that there is a rise in the interest rates after a fixed income security has been purchased resulting in a decline in that security's price. The longer the maturity date of that security, the greater the exposure of the security's price to interest rate fluctuations. The fluctuations in interest rates can have a dramatic effect on the insurance company's bond portfolio.

INTEREST RATE SCENARIO set of yield curves in which an interest rate is specified for various maturities such as monthly, quarterly, or annually. The basis of the interest rate can be corporate bond rates, United States Treasury Issues, Commercial Mortgage Rate, or other fixed interest rate instruments. Since the assets and liabilities of pension plans and insurance companies are interest-rate sensitive, it is important to be aware of possible future interest rate movements.

INTEREST RATES, GUARANTEED/EXCESS circumstances in life insurance in which, although a minimum rate is guaranteed, a policyowner may earn additional (excess) interest, depending on the company's investment return. *See also* CURRENT ASSUMPTION.

INTEREST RATE SWAP contractual agreement between two parties in which they agree to exchange a stream of interest payments on either a fixed rate for a floating rate or a floating rate for a fixed rate. The insurance company is most likely to select a floating rate for a fixed rate because it needs to know exactly what it will be paying in future interest. In this way, the insurance company can hedge its interest rate exposure (risk that interest rates will rise or fall at some stipulated time), reflected by changes in the value of its assets on the balance sheet.

INTEREST SENSITIVE CASH FLOW ANALYSIS measurement of the response of the cash flow of an insurance company to various interest rate scenarios; for example, how rising interest rates will affect the number of life insurance policies surrendered and thus the cash flow.

INTEREST SENSITIVE POLICIES a newer generation of life insurance policies that are credited with interest currently being earned by insurance companies on these policies.

INTERGOVERNMENTAL POOLS tool of RISK MANAGEMENT used for risk financing by local governments. The technique is for many local governments to combine resources in order to SELF INSURE a particular line of business, such as general liability, automobile, and WORKERS COMPENSATION. Above the RETENTION level, there is the collective purchase of REINSURANCE for the required excess coverage.

INTERINSURANCE CLAIM SERVICE ORGANIZATION type of organization of property and casualty insurance companies whose objective is to share information on fraudulent claims, handle claims in an expeditious manner, and disseminate public information concerning safeguarding of property. Some interinsurer organizations are the AMERICAN INSURANCE ASSOCIATION (AIA) Index Bureau, INSURANCE CRIME PREVENTION INSTITUTE, NATIONAL ASSOCIATION OF INDEPENDENT INSURANCE ADJUSTERS (NAII), and NATIONAL AUTOMOBILE THEFT BUREAU.

INTERINSURANCE COMPANY CLAIMS those claims that arise when two or more property and casualty insurance companies have coverage on a loss. Which company then owes which portion of the claim must be determined. *See also* INTERCOMPANY ARBITRATION.

INTERINSURANCE EXCHANGE *see* RECIPROCAL EXCHANGE.

INTERIOR ROBBERY POLICY coverage for the inside of an insured premises of a business firm if it experiences a loss of money, securities, personal property, and damage or destruction of real or personal property due to robbery, whether successful or attempted.

INTERMEDIARY reinsurance broker for a primary company *(the reinsured)*. This broker is paid commissions by the reinsurance company, just as an agent is paid commissions by an insurance company for selling its policies.

INTERMEDIATE DISABILITY *see* DISABILITY INCOME INSURANCE; TEMPORARY DISABILITY BENEFITS.

INTERMEDIATE POLICY INSURANCE POLICY that combines the characteristics of a DEBIT INSURANCE policy with that of an ORDINARY LIFE INSURANCE policy. These policies were historically sold by the DEBIT AGENT.

INTERNAL RATE OF RETURN method used to determine the POLICYHOLDER'S return on premiums paid into a life insurance policy. This method is illustrated in two ways:
1. *Surrender of Policy Approach*—calculation of the interest rate required for the accumulated value of the total premiums paid (minus any DIVIDENDS) into the policy at a given time to equal the CASH SURRENDER VALUE of the policy at that time;
2. DEATH BENEFIT *Paid Approach*—calculation of the interest rate required for the accumulated value of the total premiums paid (minus any dividends) into the policy at a given time to equal the death benefit of the policy at that time.

INTERNAL REVENUE CODE federal statute defining the federal tax code, covering such topics as credits against tax; business-related credits; computing credit for investment in certain depreciable property; computation of taxable income; definition of gross income, adjusted gross income, and taxable income; itemized deductions; pensions, profit-sharing, and stock bonus plans; taxation of estates and trusts; taxation of life insurance companies, capital gains and losses; and other areas.

INTERNAL REVENUE CODE: RULE 72(t) portion of the federal tax code that provides participant with access to funds in a SECTION 401(K) PLAN (SALARY REDUCTION PLAN) and INDIVIDUAL RETIREMENT ACCOUNT (IRA) regardless of age, provided income distributions are made in equal periodic payments based on the participant's LIFE EXPECTANCY. Once the decision is made to begin the distribution, the decision becomes irrevocable.

INTERNAL REVENUE CODE: SECTION 303 STOCK REDEMPTION PLAN portion of the federal tax code outlining the procedure by which a corporation cancels or redeems its shares with funds paid out of earnings or profits, thus making the distribution a taxable dividend.

INTERNAL REVENUE CODE: SECTION 501(c) portion of the federal tax code that determines which organizations are exempt from federal income taxation. These are generally nonprofit corporations, funds, and foundations for education, religious, charitable, or scientific purposes; civic leagues for general social welfare; fraternal beneficial societies, orders, or associations; and others.

INTERNATIONAL EMPLOYEE BENEFIT NETWORK agreement among insurance companies through which a multinational employer is permitted to purchase employee benefits coverages for two or more of its overseas subsidiaries under a single master policy. This working arrangement (network) may be composed of several overseas independent insurance companies, may consist of a cooperative agreement between a U.S. insurance company and an overseas insurance company, or may be administered by an insurance company that has several subsidiary companies overseas. Employee benefits provided through these multinational networks include life, health, pensions, disability income, and accidental death. Such a network pools the loss experiences of a particular employer's overseas subsidiaries. If the pooled loss experience is better than that expected through the premium charged, a dividend is paid to the employer. However, if the loss experience is worse than that expected through the premium charged, three courses of action are available: (1) the adverse loss experience is charged to the employer's account with any negative balance shifted to the following loss-experience year; (2) the adverse loss experience is absorbed by the insurance companies in the network, and any negative balance is *not* shifted to the following loss-experience year; (3) the adverse loss experience is charged to the employer's account with any negative balance shifted to the following loss-experience year, and a contingency fund is established with annual contributions against which future adverse loss experiences can be charged. The pooling effect allows the employer's adverse loss experience in one country to be offset by better than expected loss experience in another country.

INTERNATIONAL INSURANCE INSURANCE transactions conducted across national boundaries. Such transactions occur when the insurance company sells insurance outside the country of the company's domicile.

INTERNATIONAL INSURANCE SEMINARS, INC. (IIS) annual meetings of insurance practitioners and academicians from throughout the world interested in exchanging ideas concerning the theory and applications of insurance. The meeting is held in a different part of the world each year.

INTERNET immense collection of networks that are interconnected on a global basis providing services to the general public. These services include the transferring of files among computers, hypertext transfer protocol (HTTP) involving the reading and interpreting of hypertext files (web pages) that contain pictures and sounds, and operating computers from distant locations. Computers use telephone lines, optical fibers, and radio transmissions to connect networks thereby forming Internets. Thus, the Internet is really a super highway along which information travels to the electronic address of its destination computer. Along the way this information may pass through computer network to computer network several times before reaching its electronic address.

1. The Internet can be used to determine life insurance needs and compare costs and types of life insurance policies by referencing the following web sites: *www.rightquote.com; www.quickquote.com;* and *www.accuquote.com*

2. Similar analysis of health and disability insurance can be found at these web sites:
   www.northcoast.com/unlimited/services_listing/greg_connors/gci.html;
   www.service.com/answers/health_insurance.html

3. For homeowners, renters, and automobile insurance, the following web sites may be referenced: *www.insure.com; www.iiaa.iix.com; www.insuremarket.com*

INTERNET SERVICE PROVIDER (ISP) company that provides access to the INTERNET through electronic communications.

INTERPLEADER legal procedure through which a court determines the rightful claimant (of two or more claimants making the same claim) against a third party. Insurance companies use interpleader if claims are made by different parties. For example, upon the death of an insured, two or more individuals (such as the widow and a former wife) may contest the beneficiary's rights. The insurance company will deposit the policy proceeds with the court until it decides on the ownership.

INTERSTATE COMMERCE COMMISSION ENDORSEMENT certificate of insurance required by law under the auspices of the Interstate Commerce Commission. The endorsement is attached to all INLAND MARINE policies issued to interstate motor carriers. The insurance company covers all damage or destruction on an ALL RISKS basis to property being transported.

INTERSTATE COMMERCE COMMISSION (ICC) federal agency that regulates commerce across state lines. The ICC does not oversee insurance, which is subject to regulation by the states according to Public Law 15, McCarran-Ferguson Act. However, insurance companies must comply with many federal laws and regulations.

INTER-VIVO TRUST trust that is established by people still alive. *See also* ESTATE PLANNING; ESTATE PLANNING DISTRIBUTION.

INTESTACY *see* INTESTATE.

INTESTATE death without a will having been drawn. Under this circumstance, the court follows state law in deciding how the estate of the deceased is to be distributed. *See also* ESTATE PLANNING; ESTATE PLANNING DISTRIBUTION.

INTESTATE DISTRIBUTION *see* ESTATE PLANNING DISTRIBUTION.

INTRASTATE CARRIER insurance company that restricts its UNDERWRITING of RISKS to one state.

IN-TRUST (ON-CONSIGNMENT) POLICIES insurance that follows an insured property. *See also* CONSIGNMENT INSURANCE.

INVERSE FLOATING RATE NOTE variable-rate bonds whose coupon and value increases as interest rates decrease.

INVERTED YIELD CURVE curve that results when yields on short-term treasury issues exceed those on long-term government debt. A widely accepted theory holds that when short-term and intermediate-term issues are higher than those on long-term issues, a recession is imminent and investors expect rates to decline further.

INVESTMENT AND VALUATION OF ASSETS *see* INVESTMENTS AND REGULATION.

INVESTMENT COMPANY ACT OF 1940 act that regulates the variable dollar insurance products (equity related) sold by insurance companies. The act includes regulations that stipulate: (1) the variable dollar insurance products must be funded through a separate account (segregated from the other investment accounts of the insurance company); (2) benefits and cash values must vary in tandem with the investment returns of this separate account; (3) mortality and expense fluctuations (above the maximum chargeable stipulated in the policy) must be borne by the insurance company; (4) maximum sales load; and (5) periodic financial reports must be sent to the POLICYOWNER.

INVESTMENT EARNINGS OF INSURANCE COMPANY investment income. Insurance companies invest part of their premiums that are not immediately needed for claims and administrative expenses. These earnings are critical to an insurance company. A property and casualty company depends on investment earnings to balance underwriting losses. A life company depends on the investment earnings to help build policy cash values.

INVESTMENT EXPENSES expenses associated with the investment of the company's assets to include such items as transaction and research costs.

INVESTMENT GENERATION METHOD DIVIDEND paid to POLICYHOLDER according to the time period in which the policy was sold and the investment return the insurance company made on that policy during that time period. *See also* THREE-FACTOR CONTRIBUTION METHOD.

INVESTMENT GRADE rating attached to a bond because it has a very low risk of default.

INVESTMENT INCOME earnings by an insurance company from dividends on its equity portfolio, rent from real estate and other property it owns, and interest on its bond holdings.

INVESTMENT IN COMMON STOCK RATIO ratio of the insurance company's investment in common stocks dividend to its ADJUSTED SURPLUS account. This ratio shows how vulnerable the company's surplus is to the stock market fluctuations.

INVESTMENT IN JUNK BONDS RATIO ratio of the company's investment in noninvestment grade bonds dividend to its ADJUSTED SURPLUS. This ratio shows how vulnerable the company's surplus is to the market fluctuations in noninvestment grade bonds. The lower this ratio, the more financially sound the insurance company.

INVESTMENT RATIO relationship of gains from investments (including realized capital gains) resulting from insurance operations to EARNED PREMIUMS.

INVESTMENT RISK possibility of a reduction in value of an insurance instrument resulting from a decrease in the value of the assets incorporated in the investment portfolio underlying the insurance instrument. This reduction can also be effected by a change in the interest rate.

INVESTMENTS money expended with the object of profit. The goal of an insurance company is to invest in assets with a rate of return greater than that to be paid out as benefits under its policies. Traditionally, life insurance companies have invested in long-term financial instruments such as mortgages. Today, under CURRENT ASSUMPTION life insurance policies, investments are in short-term financial instruments. Property and casualty insurance companies, because of the nature of their policies, favor short-term financial instruments as investments.

INVESTMENTS AND REGULATION
Life insurance:
1. *Bonds*—most state regulations permit life insurance company investments in debentures, mortgage bonds, and blue chip corporate bonds.
2. *Stocks*—(a) *preferred stock* investment is limited to 20% of the total stock of any one company, not exceeding 2% of a company's admitted assets; (b) COMMON STOCK INVESTMENT is limited to the lesser amount of 1% of the ADMITTED ASSETS or the *policyowner's surplus.*
3. *Mortgage*—investment is unlimited in first mortgages on residential, commercial, and industrial real estate.
4. *Real Estate*—investment is limited to 10% of admitted assets.
   Valuation of the assets in a typical state is accomplished in the following manner: (1) stocks or bonds in default (principal or interest) cannot be valued at greater than market value; (2) bonds not in default valued according to their purchase price adjusted to equal par at maturity; (3) preferred and common stocks of firms in good financial condition are valued according to purchase price; (4) preferred and common stocks in companies not in good financial condition are valued at market price; and (5) real estate, mortgages, and policy loans are valued at book value.

Property and casualty insurance:
1. DOMESTIC INSURERS and FOREIGN INSURERS must invest according to the minimum capitalization requirement in federal, state, or municipal bonds.

2. Company funds in excess of minimum capitalization and reserve requirements can be invested in federal, state, or municipal bonds as well as stocks or real estate. The insurance company is limited in its investment in any one firm up to no more than 10% of its admitted assets; its real estate investment can be no more than 10% of its admitted assets.

INVESTMENT YEAR METHOD OF ALLOCATING INVESTMENT INCOME procedure in which investment income is paired with each life insurance policy according to the time frame in which the premiums for that particular policy are received.

INVESTOR-RELATED LIFE INSURANCE type of life insurance policy that allows the selling of the right to death benefits by owners of the policies to investors. The seller of this right exchanges the policy for cash received from the investor.

INVITEE person who is expressly or by implication asked to visit property in the possession, care, or control of another person. The inviter has the obligation to render his or her property safe for the visit of the invitee. Liability insurance is designed to protect an insured in the event that his or her negligent acts or omissions result in bodily injury to the invitee.

IRA *see* INDIVIDUAL RETIREMENT ACCOUNT.

IRREVOCABLE something that cannot be changed. In life insurance, a beneficiary who has been named as irrevocable cannot be changed without his or her formal (written) permission.

IRREVOCABLE BENEFICIARY *see* BENEFICIARY CLAUSE.

IRREVOCABLE LIFE INSURANCE TRUST ESTATE PLANNING device used so that any life insurance policies that are owned by and paid to the TRUST will avoid ESTATE TAX upon the death of the INSURED, and, upon the death of the insured's spouse, estate taxes will be avoided as well. The requirement of this trust are: (1) it must be irrevocable; and (2) no distributions of the trust's principal or income can be made to the insured. All income generated by the trust must be accumulated and then distributed along with the trust's principal to the trust's beneficiary(s). The methods of operation of this trust could include the following forms:

1. Trustee (insured's spouse) has the right to distribute income generated by the trust as well as the principal of the trust to the insured's spouse as long as the insured lives. The trustee also has the right to borrow on the CASH VALUE of the life insurance policies on the life of the insured owned by the trust and then distribute the funds so obtained to the insured's spouse as long as the insured is alive.

2. Trustee (cannot be insured) has the right to distribute income generated by the trust and/or principal of the trust to the insured. The trustee also has the right to borrow on the cash value of the life

insurance policies on the life of the insured owned by the trust and then distribute the funds so obtained to the insured.

   3. SPLIT DOLLAR LIFE INSURANCE policy is established within the trust with the insured's spouse having ownership rights to the cash value part of the split dollar policy and the trust having ownership rights to the death benefit minus the cash value. Through this mechanism, the insured's spouse has access to the cash value while the insured is alive. Upon the death of the insured and insured's spouse, the amount of the death benefit minus the cash value will not be subject to estate tax.

IRREVOCABLE LIVING TRUST TRUST in which rights to make any changes therein are surrendered permanently by the GRANTOR. The grantor uses this type of trust to transfer assets and any potential depreciation out of his or her estate in order to avoid FEDERAL ESTATE TAX on the second estate distributions to heirs, as well as to avoid PROBATE expenses. The primary disadvantage of this type of trust is that the grantor surrenders all control over the assets and the right to change the terms of the trust. *See also* ESTATE PLANNING DISTRIBUTION; REVOCABLE LIVING TRUST.

IRREVOCABLE TRUST trust that cannot be revoked by the creator. *See also* ESTATE PLANNING DISTRIBUTION.

ISO *see* INSURANCE SERVICES OFFICE.

ISSUED BUSINESS policies that have been sold to and paid for by an insured, but not yet delivered to the insured.

ISSUE DEPARTMENT department in an INSURANCE COMPANY that prepares policies to be sent to the POLICYHOLDER, sends the policies, and keeps records of the policies that were sent.

J

JACKET outer covering containing an insurance policy; in many instances it lists provisions common to several types of policies.

JANITORS LIFE INSURANCE POLICY type of LIFE INSURANCE policy that provides coverage on the lives of relatively low-income employees. Under this type of policy, the employer purchases life insurance on the life of this employee, is the policyowner, and is the BENEFICIARY. The life insurance purchased is CASH VALUE LIFE INSURANCE. The employer may borrow the cash value. The cash values grow on a tax-advantaged basis, and when the employee or former employee dies, the employer receives the death benefit tax free. The life insurance policy stays in effect even if the employee is no longer employed. It is not necessary for the employee to consent to the life insurance coverage. The CASH SURRENDER VALUE of the policy is listed as an asset on the employer's balance sheet.

JEWELER'S BLOCK INSURANCE POLICY type of INLAND MARINE INSURANCE that provides coverage for jewels, watches, gold, silver, platinum, pearls, precious and semiprecious stones. Property can be owned by the insured jeweler, or can be customer's property in care, custody, and control of the jeweler. Coverage is on an ALL RISKS basis except specifically excluded perils such as wear and tear; war; delay; loss of market; flood; earthquake; loss or damage while jewelry is being worn by the insured or his or her representatives; loss resulting from the infidelity of any person under the care, custody, and control of the insured; damage or destruction of jewelry after it leaves the insured under an installment contract; mysterious disappearance; and shipments of jewelry not sent registered first class mail.

JEWELRY FLOATER *see* PERSONAL JEWELRY INSURANCE.

JEWELRY INSURANCE *see* PERSONAL JEWELRY INSURANCE.

JOB LOSS MORTGAGE PAYMENT INSURANCE type of insurance policy that provides coverage in the event a homeowner is unable to make the mortgage payments due to involuntarily loss of job. Eligibility for this type of coverage is restricted to individuals who have been employed in a permanent job for at least 30 hours per week for 12 consecutive weeks. There is an ELIMINATION PERIOD of 180 days beginning with the EFFECTIVE DATE of the policy. The policyowner must be involuntarily unemployed for at least 30 consecutive days and have qualified for UNEMPLOYMENT COMPENSATION. All benefit payments are made directly to the mortgage company in lieu of the homeowner making the monthly mortgage payments.

JOB RELATED INJURIES, DEATH incidents covered under WORKERS COMPENSATION BENEFITS.

JOBS AND GROWTH TAX RELIEF RECONCILIATION ACT OF 2003 legislation that provides for the acceleration of some of the tax revision under the ECONOMIC GROWTH AND TAX RELIEF RECONCILIATION ACT (EGTRRA) OF 2001. Of importance to investors, is the lowering of the maximum tax rate on capital gains from 20 to 15% and on dividends to 15%.

JOINT AND ONE-HALF ANNUITY/JOINT AND TWO-THIRDS ANNUITY modified JOINT LIFE AND SURVIVORSHIP ANNUITY under which the income payments are reduced to one-half or two-thirds of the initial income amounts upon the death of the first ANNUITANT.

JOINT AND SEVERAL LIABILITY legal obligation under which a party may be liable for the payment of the total judgment and costs that are associated with that judgment, even if that party is only partially responsible for losses inflicted, whether bodily injury and/or property damage.

JOINT AND SURVIVOR OPTION settlement choice under a life insurance policy whereby a beneficiary may elect to have the death proceeds paid in the form of a joint and survivor annuity. *See also* JOINT LIFE AND SURVIVORSHIP ANNUITY.

JOINT ANNUITANT person other than the ANNUITANT as designated by the POLICYHOLDER on whose life expectancy the annuity payment is also based.

JOINT ANNUITY *see* JOINT LIFE ANNUITY.

JOINT CONTROL estate under the legal and administrative guidance of both the *surety* and the FIDUCIARY. Any actions on the part of the estate requires the signatures of both in order to reduce the chances of fraud.

JOINT INSURANCE *see* JOINT LIFE AND SURVIVOR INSURANCE; JOINT LIFE AND SURVIVORSHIP ANNUITY; JOINT LIFE ANNUITY; JOINT LIFE INSURANCE.

JOINT LIFE AND SURVIVOR INSURANCE coverage for two or more persons with the death benefit payable at the death of the last of those insured. Premiums are significantly lower under joint life and survivor insurance than for policies that insure only one person, since the probability of having to pay a death claim is lower.

JOINT LIFE AND SURVIVORSHIP ANNUITY ANNUITY that continues income payments as long as one annuitant, out of two or more annuitants, remains alive. For example, a married couple would receive an income for as long as both spouses are alive. Thereafter, payments would continue as long as the surviving spouse is alive, usually for a smaller amount. This type of annuity is ideal for a husband and wife in that it guarantees the surviving spouse an income for life. Even with a LIFE ANNUITY CERTAIN or other type of refund annuity, it is possible for a surviving spouse to outlive the money that has been funding the annuity. *See also* ANNUITY.

JOINT LIFE ANNUITY retirement plan in which income payments continue until the death of the first of two or more annuitants. This type of annuity is not appropriate for a husband and wife since at the death of the first spouse income payments cease. The monthly benefit is greater than with other annuities since income payments cease at the first death. *See also* ANNUITY.

JOINT LIFE INSURANCE coverage of two or more persons with the death benefit payable at the first death. Premiums are significantly higher than for policies that insure one person, since the probability of having to pay a death claim is higher.

JOINT LOSS APPORTIONMENT *see* APPORTIONMENT.

JOINT PROTECTION *see* JOINT-LIFE AND SURVIVORSHIP ANNUITY; JOINT LIFE INSURANCE.

JOINT TENANCY *see* JOINT TENANTS.

JOINT TENANTS property owned by two or more parties in such a way that at the death of one, the survivors retain complete ownership of the property.

JOINT UNDERWRITER ASSOCIATION combination of several insurance companies to provide the capacity to underwrite a particular type or size of exposure. For example, liability coverage for a drug company's vaccine has been instituted as the result of several insurance companies working together to provide the required capacity due to the extra hazard.

JOINT VENTURE agreement of two or more insurance companies to provide a product or service.

JONES ACT (MERCHANT MARINE ACT) federal law passed in 1920 that allows any seaman incurring bodily injury as the result of the performance of one or more functions of the job to bring a suit for damages against the employer. The employer's exposures under the act consist of negligence, unseaworthiness of the vessel, and disability income for the injured man or woman.

JOURNAL OF RISK AND INSURANCE academic publication of the AMERICAN RISK AND INSURANCE ASSOCIATION in which articles deal with aspects of risk, insurance, and allied fields of study.

JUDGMENT decision by a court of law.

JUDGMENT BY DEFAULT decision in the absence of a plaintiff or defendant at the specified court time.

JUDGMENT RATING underwriting phrase denoting the best judgment based on the experience of an underwriter, in classifying a particular risk.

JUDICIAL BOND type of SURETY BOND that is either a *fiduciary* or a *court bond.*

1. *Fiduciary Bond*—guarantees that individuals in a position of trust will safeguard assets belonging to others placed under their control. For example, guardians appointed by a court who are authorized to pay expenses of the minor and administrators of estates who take care of a deceased's assets may require fiduciary bond.

2. *Court Bond*—guarantees concerning ligation such as: (a) APPEAL BOND, which guarantees that a judgment will be paid if an appeal is lost in a higher court; (b) *Plaintiff's Replevin Bond,* which guarantees that damages will be paid if the replevin action is wrongfully brought; (c) *Removal Bond,* which guarantees that damages will be paid if improper removal actions are taken.

JUMPING JUVENILE POLICY (JUVENILE ESTATE BUILDER) life insurance coverage on a child in which the initial face amount of the life insurance policy increases when the child reaches the age of majority, with no corresponding increase in premium.

JUVENILE ENDOWMENT POLICY life insurance on the life of a child that provides a DEATH BENEFIT to a BENEFICIARY should the child die during a stipulated time period and the maturity value of the policy at the end of that time period to the child if that child is still alive. This policy has typically been used to provide funds to finance a college education.

JUVENILE ESTATE BUILDER *see* JUMPING JUVENILE POLICY (JUVENILE ESTATE BUILDER).

JUVENILE INSURANCE life insurance on the life of a child.

K

KEETON-O'CONNELL AUTOMOBILE INSURANCE PLAN early type of no-fault automobile insurance developed by two law professors, Robert Keeton and Jeffrey O'Connell. Its basic premise is that for many accidents it is impossible to place the blame as required by the tort legal system. In this approach, each individual would be able to collect from his or her own insurance company without having to prove fault on the part of anyone.

KENNEY RATIO proposal by Roger Kenney, an insurance journalist, that in order to maintain the solvency of a property and casualty insurance company, insurance premiums written should not exceed more than twice the company's surplus and capital. This historical measure is used by regulators to determine a property and casualty company's capacity to make claim payments while maintaining its solvency.

KEOGH PLAN (HR-10) act first passed in 1962 that permits the self-employed individual to establish his or her own retirement plan. This individual can make nondeductible voluntary contributions and tax-deductible contributions subject to a maximum limit of 25% of earned income up to $45,000 for a defined contribution plan after the reduction for the contribution to the Keogh Plan. This is an equivalent rate of 20% of earned income prior to the contribution to the Keogh Plan.

KEY EMPLOYEE INSURANCE *see* BENEFITS OF BUSINESS LIFE AND HEALTH INSURANCE (KEY PERSON INSURANCE); KEY EMPLOYEE (KEY PERSON).

KEY EMPLOYEE (KEY PERSON) individual who possesses a unique ability essential to the continued success of a business firm. For example, this individual might have the technical knowledge necessary for research and development of products that keep the company at the cutting edge of its field. The death or disability of this key individual could severely handicap the company. *See also* BENEFITS OF BUSINESS LIFE AND HEALTH INSURANCE (KEY PERSON INSURANCE).

KEY EMPLOYEES, INSURANCE PLANS FOR typical NONQUALIFIED PLANS of life insurance for key employees include:

1. PERMANENT LIFE INSURANCE—dividends generated by the policy are used to pay the income tax of the key employee that results from the premiums paid by the employer on the permanent insurance policy. For federal tax purposes the employer-paid premiums are taxed as additional earned income for the employee. Under the better permanent policies, after the policy has been in force a few years the dividends should exceed the taxable premium income to the employee. The advantages of permanent insurance to the key employee include life insurance coverage for life, increasing cash values, increasing dividends selection of beneficiary, and ownership of policy.

2. TERM LIFE INSURANCE—premiums paid by the employer are considered federal taxable income to the employee. Employee selects beneficiary and owns policy. Policy probably will not remain in force after retirement because the premiums continue to increase in cost and become prohibitive.

3. SPLIT DOLLAR LIFE INSURANCE—permanent life insurance is purchased on the life of the employee. Premium payments are split between the employee and the employer. The employer has an equity interest in the cash value of the policy to the extent of the premium payment he or she has paid in. The employee has an equity interest in the cash value of the policy to the extent that the cash value exceeds the premiums paid in by the employer. Under the better permanent policies, the cash values will accumulate to a substantial sum, whereupon the employer can withdraw from the cash value an amount equal to his or her premium paid in. At this point the split dollar plan is said to terminate, and the employee has sole possession of the policy. The cash values remaining should be sufficient so that no further premium payments are required by the employee to keep the policy in force.

4. SALARY CONTINUATION PLAN—employer usually purchases permanent life insurance on the life of the employee, is the beneficiary of the policy, and owns the policy. If the employee dies before receiving all promised supplemental pension benefits, the employer will pay the remaining supplemental pension benefits to the beneficiary of the deceased employee. Funds for payments are provided from the life insurance proceeds.

5. *Death Benefit Only Life Insurance Plan*—employer usually purchases permanent life insurance on the life of the employee, is the beneficiary of the policy, and owns the policy. Premiums paid by the employer are not considered federal taxable income to the employee. Upon the death of the employee, the employer will use the life insurance proceeds to pay death benefits for several years to the employee's beneficiary. The employer receives the life insurance proceeds tax free; however, the death payments to the employee's beneficiary are federal taxable income to that beneficiary. This plan can also be utilized to supplement the employee's pension plan at retirement.

KEYNESIAN ECONOMICS theory, named after the British economist John Maynard Keynes, that deals with current consumption at the expense of saving. This theory has important implications for life insurance products and annuities since their purchase requires foregoing a portion of current consumption in favor of savings and future financial security. *See also* ANNUITY; SAVINGS ELEMENT, LIFE INSURANCE.

KEY PERSON INSURANCE *see* BENEFITS OF BUSINESS LIFE AND HEALTH INSURANCE (KEY PERSON INSURANCE).

KEY PERSON LIFE AND HEALTH INSURANCE *see* BENEFITS OF BUSINESS LIFE AND HEALTH INSURANCE (KEY PERSON INSURANCE); BUSINESS LIFE AND HEALTH INSURANCE.

KIDDIE TAX tax on a child's income at the parent's marginal tax rate (top tax bracket). *See also* UNIFORM GIFTS TO MINORS ACT.

KIDNAP INSURANCE coverage in the event an employee is kidnapped from an insured business's premises and forced to return to aid a criminal in a theft.

KIDNAP-RANSOM INSURANCE *see* RANSOM INSURANCE.

KNOCK-FOR-KNOCK AGREEMENT arrangement between two or more insurance companies under which the parties to the agreement waive their SUBROGATION rights against the other. Most such agreements are no longer in use. *See also* INTERCOMPANY ARBITRATION.

L

LABOR AND MATERIAL BOND coverage to indemnify an owner for whom work was done if the completed work is not free of worker's liens for labor and material.

LABOR MANAGEMENT RELATIONS ACT OF 1947 *see* TAFT-HARTLEY ACT.

LABOR STATISTICS, BUREAU OF federal agency that collects and analyzes numerous U.S. demographics used by government and industry. Insurance companies use the demographics to predict areas of high demand for their products, to perform market segmentation studies, and to position distribution systems.

LADDERING purchasing bond investments that mature at different time intervals.

LADDER PORTFOLIO method of investing that staggers the maturities of a group of bonds. As a bond matures, the investor can reinvest the proceeds in either short- or long-term bonds depending on the interest rate and economic environment at that time. For example, if interest rates are rising, the matured bond's proceeds can be invested in longer term, higher yielding bonds. As interest rates decline, higher interest rates would have already been locked in through the previous purchase of higher yielding bonds. As bonds continue to mature in a falling interest rate environment, the proceeds can be invested in bonds of shorter maturities, thereby having liquidity for future investment in longer maturity bonds if interest rates increase.

LAG time that has elapsed between when claims actually occurred and when claims are actually paid.

LAND OWNERSHIP, USE AND POSSESSION OF liability exposure, in insurance, associated with three classifications of individuals that may come upon an insured property:
  1. TRESPASSER—individual enters without permission. Generally the insured has no legal obligation to render his or her land safe for the trespasser, but the insured cannot create a death trap.
  2. LICENSEE—individual enters with permission, but there is no mutual profit motive involved. Generally, the insured's only obligation to the licensee is to warn of any hidden dangers of which the insured is aware.
  3. INVITEE—individual expressly or by implication is invited to enter property; there is a mutual profit motive. Generally, the insured must use reasonable care to render his property safe for the invitee's visit.

LAPSE
  1. in property and casualty insurance, termination of a policy because of failure to pay a renewal premium.

2. in life insurance, termination of a policy because of failure to pay a premium and lack of sufficient cash value to make a premium loan.

LAPSED POLICY *see* LAPSE.

LAPSE RATIO percentage of a life insurance company's policies in force at the beginning of the year that are no longer in force at the end of the year. This ratio is critical because it indicates the rate at which policies are going off the books and the resultant loss of earnings to the company.

LAPSE RISK measure of the sensitivity of the insurance company's liability to changing policy surrender distributions.

LAPSE SUPPORTED LIFE INSURANCE POLICIES policies that have their future cash values closely correlated with a high LAPSE RATIO of the insurance company's BOOK OF BUSINESS. In theory, gains resulting from these lapses will result in a greater SURPLUS ACCOUNT, thereby building the future cash values of these policies. In essence, the policy is specifically designed so that if it is surrendered, its SURRENDER VALUE would be less than its ASSET SHARE VALUE.

LARGE LOSS PRINCIPLE transfer of high severity risks through the insurance contract to protect against catastrophic occurrences. While insurance is generally not the most cost-effective means of recovery of minor losses, an insured cannot predict catastrophes and thus set aside enough money to cover losses on a mathematical basis or to self-insure. Actuarial tables are based on the large loss principle: the larger the number of exposures, the more closely losses will match the probability of loss. In essence, a large number of insureds, each paying a modest sum into an insurance plan, can protect against the relatively few catastrophes that will strike some of their numbers.

LAST CLEAR CHANCE common law rule of negligence that imposes liability on an individual who had one last opportunity to avoid an accident but did not take it. An example is a driver who could have avoided hitting another automobile by applying his brakes but did not do so. One reason for not avoiding—or even causing—an accident is a desire to collect insurance proceeds.

LAST SURVIVOR ANNUITY *see* JOINT LIFE AND SURVIVORSHIP ANNUITY.

LAST SURVIVOR INSURANCE coverage of two or more individuals with the death benefit payable at the last death. Premiums are significantly lower than for policies that insure one person, since the probability of having to pay a death claim on the second death is lower.

LATE RETIREMENT *see* DEFERRED RETIREMENT.

LAW OF LARGE NUMBERS mathematical premise stating that the greater the number of exposures, (1) the more accurate the prediction; (2) the less the deviation of the actual losses from the expected losses ($X - x$ approaches zero); and (3) the greater the credibility of the prediction (credibility approaches 1). This law forms the basis for the statistical expectation of loss upon which premium rates for insurance policies are calculated. Out of a large group of policyholders the insurance company can fairly accurately predict not by name but by number, the number of policyholders who will suffer a loss. Life insurance premiums are loaded for the expected loss plus modest deviations. For example, if a life insurance company expects (x) 10,000 of its policyholders to die in a particular year and that number or fewer actually die (X), there is no cause for concern on the part of the company's actuaries. However, if the life insurance company expects (x) 10,000 of its policyholders to die in a particular year and more than that number dies (X) there is much cause for concern by actuaries.

LAW OF MORTALITY premise that, out of a large group of people, a given number will die each year (conversely, a given number will remain alive each year) until all the people in that original group are dead. This life and death event will allow the LAW OF LARGE NUMBERS to operate effectively.

LAWYERS (ATTORNEYS PROFESSIONAL) LIABILITY INSURANCE coverage if a lawyer's professional act (or omission) results in the client inflicting bodily injury or property damage to another party, or if personal injury and/or property damage is incurred by a client who brings an action for injuries and or damages suffered. The policy also provides for defense costs, legal fees, and court costs of the defendant, even if the suit is without foundation.

LAYERING combination of several policies with each adding an additional layer or limit of coverage above the limits of the policy that comes before it. For example, Policy A adds $100,000, then Policy B adds $200,000 and then Policy C adds $300,000, for a total of $600,000. In some instances a business firm cannot obtain the total coverage it requires from a single insurance company. Thus, the business may have to buy several policies from different companies in order to acquire the total needed.

LAY UNDERWRITER home office underwriter who evaluates risk based on probability, statistics, and medical knowledge.

LEAD INSURER insurance company that puts together a consortium of insurance and reinsurance companies to provide an adequate financial base with sufficient underwriting capacity to insure large risks. Usually the lead insurer will take a large percentage of the risk for its own account.

LEASE use of another party's property in exchange for rental payment. *See also* LEASEHOLD INSURANCE; LEASEHOLD PROFIT INTEREST; LEASEHOLD VALUE INTEREST.

LEASEHOLD *see* LEASE.

LEASEHOLD INSURANCE coverage for a tenant with a favorable lease (enabling the lessee to rent premises for less than the market value). If the lease is canceled by the *lessor* because an insured peril (such as fire) strikes, the lessee is indemnified for the loss incurred. The premise is that the lessee will have to forgo earnings derived from having an advantageous lease, and should be indemnified for this incurred loss.

LEASEHOLD PROFIT INTEREST difference between the rent received by a lessee for the subletting property and the rent the lessee pays the lessor.

LEASEHOLD VALUE INTEREST difference between the rent paid by a lessee as fixed by a lease prior to destruction of property and the rent received by the lessor after that property has been restored.

LEDGER COST *see* LIFE INSURANCE COST.

LEGACY SALE utilization of life insurance to make annual gifts into a trust in order to produce the largest tax-free death benefit possible to the trust beneficiaries.

LEGAL *see* LEGAL PURPOSE; LEGAL RESERVE; LIABILITY, LEGAL.

LEGAL EXPENSE INSURANCE prepaid legal insurance coverage plan sold on a group basis. Entitles a group member to a schedule of benefits, at a stipulated premium, for adoptions, probates, divorces, and other legal services. This emerging employee benefit has had wide acceptance in some localities but limited acceptance elsewhere. After scheduled benefits have been exhausted, subsequent legal fees are usually based on the attorney's customary rate. For example, a prepaid legal insurance plan may provide only three legal consultations a year.

LEGAL LIABILITY *see* LIABILITY, LEGAL.

LEGAL LIABILITY INSURANCE POLICY *see* LIABILITY INSURANCE.

LEGAL PLAN group arrangement in which a network of attorneys provides legal services to the participants in the plan with the attorney fees being reimbursed by the provider. The attorneys who are members of the network provide their legal services at a reduced rate from their customary fee to the plan participants. Most legal plans are voluntary on the part of the employees with the employees paying their entire cost through PAYROLL DEDUCTION INSURANCE. There are two main types of group legal plans:
1. *Access plans*—participants in the plan receive legal advice for such matters as simple wills, and demand letters plus other legal advice over the telephone.
2. *Comprehensive plans*—participants in the plan receive legal advice through office and telephone consultations for such concerns as wills, trusts, bankruptcy, civil litigation, real estate transactions, and other general legal planning.

LEGAL RESERVE type of reserve that represents a liability on the LIFE INSURANCE company's balance sheet. The reserve must be established to account for the excess premiums paid on an ORDINARY LIFE INSURANCE policy in the beginning policy years, thereby guaranteeing the financial integrity of the policy for the duration. *See also* RESERVES AND THEIR COMPUTATION.

LEGATEES individuals who inherit ASSETS as the result of being named in a WILL.

LEMON AID INSURANCE property and casualty coverage that indemnifies automobile dealers if a dissatisfied customer demands a refund within the period of time allowed under the Uniform Commercial Code. This insurance is not widely sold today because of the increase in recalls of vehicles for inherent defects.

LENDER ESTATE V. COMMISSIONER legal decision wherein proceeds of a life insurance policy on which the decedent's corporation paid the premiums within three years of his or her death are not includable in the decedent's gross estate, as affirmed by the Tenth Circuit Court of Appeals.

LENDERS HOLDER-IN-DUE-COURSE INSURANCE coverage that indemnifies a third party lender if a customer refuses to repay a loan made on a faulty product and the dealer who arranged the loan refuses to correct the fault. This coverage has gained new importance as more customers are refusing to repay loans on products with inherent defects.

LENGTH OF PAYMENT provision found in DISABILITY INCOME INSURANCE that stipulates length of time benefits are paid during disability.

LEVEL uniformity. *See also* COMMERCIAL HEALTH INSURANCE, LEVEL COMMISSION; LEVEL PREMIUM INSURANCE; LEVEL TERM INSURANCE.

LEVEL COMMISSION compensation in which an insurance agent's fee for the sale of a policy is the same year after year. Most life insurance companies pay a high first year commission and lower commissions in later years. This commission structure is controversial since critics feel that it is heavily weighted towards selling a product at the expense of subsequent service.

LEVEL PERCENTAGE OF COMPENSATION *see* DEFINED BENEFIT PLAN.

LEVEL PREMIUM premium that remains unchanged over time, regardless of any change in the nature of the risk.

LEVEL PREMIUM GROUP ANNUITY type of PREMIUM PLAN under which the employer (if NONCONTRIBUTORY plan) or the employer and employee (if CONTRIBUTORY plan) make level annual premium payments to fund the future retirement benefits of the employee, through a GROUP DEFERRED ANNUITY, plus a GROUP LIFE INSURANCE policy on the employee, usually held in the trust.

LEVEL PREMIUM INSURANCE coverage in which premiums do not increase or decrease for as long as the policy remains in force. In the early years of a policy, the premiums are greater than is necessary to pay mortality costs. The excess is used to build the cash value and to provide for the increasing mortality costs later in the life of the policy.

LEVEL PREMIUM RENEWABLE TERM HEALTH INSURANCE *see* COMMERCIAL HEALTH INSURANCE.

LEVEL TERM INSURANCE coverage in which the face amount of a policy remains uniform, neither increasing nor decreasing for as long as the policy is in force.

LEVERAGE the investment of borrowed money with the goal of earning more of a return on the investment than the interest that has to be paid on the borrowed funds.

LEVERAGED BUYOUT (LBO) purchase of controlling interest in a company by an entity. The entity borrows funds to execute the purchase using the assets of the acquired company as security for the loan.

LEVERAGED SPLIT DOLLAR LIFE INSURANCE modified collateral SPLIT DOLLAR LIFE INSURANCE plan under which the employee purchases and owns a life insurance policy on the employee's own life. The employer makes the unscheduled premium payments on the policy. The employee makes a collateral assignment of the policy to the employer, which acts as security for the unscheduled premiums paid by the employer. Upon this assignment, the life insurance company that issued the policy lends the employer the amount of the unscheduled premium payment; interest paid the insurance company by the employer for the loan is tax-deductible to the employer. Part of this interest paid by the employer is credited to the cash value of the policy by the insurance company. During this period of time, the employer is also making the scheduled premium payments due on this policy (at least seven annual premium payments must be made if the policy is to retain its tax-advantaged status). The scheduled premium payments are taxed as ordinary current income to the employee. When the employee retires, the split dollar plan is terminated and all of the unscheduled premium payments made by the employer are repaid to the employer, either through loans on the cash value of the policy or through cash withdrawals from the policy. With the repaid premiums amount, the employer then repays the insurance company for the previous loans made to pay the unscheduled premium payments. The repaid loan amount is credited to the cash value of the policy by the insurance company. From the reconstituted cash values, the employee then borrows a series of annual income payments based on the employee's life expectancy. When the employee dies, the DEATH BENEFIT from the policy repays the amount owed the insurance company for the loans from the cash value made to fund the retirement income of the employee. The excess amount (if any) of the death benefit minus the policy loan repayment is paid to the BENEFICIARY(S) of the employee.

LIABILITIES: LIFE INSURANCE COMPANIES future benefits to be paid to the policyholders and beneficiaries, assigned surpluses, and miscellaneous debts. These primary liabilities take the form of reserves, which must be listed on the company's balance sheet as part of the liabilities section. The valuation of a company's reserves, which guarantee that funds will be available to meet its liabilities, is strictly regulated by the state insurance departments. Life insurance company liabilities also include cash surrender values of its policies and annuities.

LIABILITY legal obligation to perform or not perform specified act(s). In insurance the concern is with the circumstance in which (1) one party's property is damaged or destroyed, or (2) that party incurs bodily injury as the result of the negligent acts or omissions of another party. Liability insurance is designed to provide coverage for exposure on either a business or a personal basis. *See also* BUSINESS LIABILITY INSURANCE; COMPREHENSIVE PERSONAL LIABILITY INSURANCE; LIABILITY, PERSONAL EXPOSURES.

LIABILITY, ABSOLUTE *see* ABSOLUTE LIABILITY.

LIABILITY, BUSINESS EXPOSURES negligent acts or omissions that result in actual or imagined bodily injury and/or property damage to a third party, who brings suit against a business firm and its representatives.

LIABILITY, CIVIL alleged torts or breaches of contract, but not crimes. Action is brought by one individual against another at the litigant's own expense, within the statute of limitations. The losing party must pay any judgment plus court expenses. Casualty insurance provides coverage for an insured in a civil liability suit for alleged negligent acts or omissions, even if the suit is without foundation.

LIABILITY, CIVIL DAMAGES AWARDED three types of damages can be awarded to a plaintiff:
1. *Special Damages*—reimbursement for out-of-pocket expenses, including medical bills, legal charges, cost of repairing damaged or destroyed property, and loss of current and projected income.
2. *General Damages*—reimbursement for damages that do not readily lend themselves to quantitative measurement, commonly known as "pain and suffering."
3. *Punitive Damages*—reimbursement for damages due to gross negligence by a defendant.

LIABILITY CLAIM *see* CLAIMS MADE BASIS LIABILITY COVERAGE; CLAIMS OCCURRENCE BASIS LIABILITY COVERAGE.

LIABILITY, CONTINGENT *see* CONTINGENT LIABILITY (VICARIOUS LIABILITY).

LIABILITY, CONTRACTUAL *see* CONTRACTUAL LIABILITY.

LIABILITY, CRIMINAL wrong against the government or society as a whole. An individual representing the state (usually the district attorney) brings an action on behalf of the state against an individual(s) or entity who has broken a criminal (non-civil) law. Insurance is not designed to cover criminal liability; to do so would encourage criminal behavior.

LIABILITY INSURANCE coverage for all sums that the insured becomes legally obligated to pay because of bodily injury or property damage, and sometimes other wrongs to which an insurance policy applies. Personal liability policies include COMPREHENSIVE PERSONAL LIABILITY (CPL), HOMEOWNERS INSURANCE POLICY, PERSONAL AUTOMOBILE POLICY (PAP), *Personal Umbrella Liability,* and the *Uninsured Motorist Endorsement.* Business liability policies include BUSINESS AUTOMOBILE POLICY (BAP), BUSINESSOWNERS POLICY, *Completed Operations and Products Liability,* COMMERCIAL GENERAL LIABILITY INSURANCE (CGPL), *Employers Liability and Workers Compensation,* MANUFACTURERS AND CONTRACTORS LIABILITY (M&C), OWNERS, LANDLORDS AND TENANTS LIABILITY INSURANCE POLICY (OL&T), *Physicians, Surgeons and Dentists Professional Liability,* STOREKEEPERS LIABILITY INSURANCE, *Umbrella Liability Policy,* and the *Uninsured Motorists Coverage.*

LIABILITY INSURANCE, BODILY INJURY *see* LIABILITY INSURANCE.

LIABILITY INSURANCE, COMPREHENSIVE GENERAL *see* COMMERCIAL GENERAL LIABILITY INSURANCE (CGL).

LIABILITY INSURANCE, COMPREHENSIVE PERSONAL *see* COMPREHENSIVE PERSONAL LIABILITY INSURANCE; HOMEOWNERS INSURANCE POLICY; PERSONAL AUTOMOBILE POLICY (PAP); PERSONAL UMBRELLA LIABILITY; UNINSURED MOTORIST ENDORSEMENT.

LIABILITY INSURANCE, ELEVATOR *see* ELEVATOR LIABILITY INSURANCE.

LIABILITY INSURANCE, EMPLOYERS *see* BUSINESS AUTOMOBILE POLICY (BAP); BUSINESS OWNERS POLICY (BOP); BUSINESS PROPERTY AND LIABILITY INSURANCE PACKAGE; EMPLOYERS CONTINGENT INSURANCE COVERAGE; WORKERS COMPENSATION, COVERAGE B.

LIABILITY INSURANCE, OWNERS, LANDLORDS, AND TENANTS *see* OWNERS, LANDLORDS, AND TENANTS LIABILITY POLICY.

LIABILITY INSURANCE, PHYSICIANS AND SURGEONS *see* PHYSICIANS, SURGEONS, AND DENTISTS INSURANCE.

LIABILITY INSURANCE, PRODUCTS *see* PRODUCT LIABILITY INSURANCE; PRODUCT RECALL INSURANCE; PRODUCTS AND COMPLETED OPERATIONS INSURANCE.

LIABILITY INSURANCE, PROPERTY DAMAGE *see* PROPERTY DAMAGE LIABILITY INSURANCE.

LIABILITY INSURANCE, PROTECTIVE *see* OWNERS AND CONTRACTORS PROTECTIVE LIABILITY INSURANCE.

LIABILITY INSURANCE, PUBLIC *see* PUBLIC LIABILITY INSURANCE.

LIABILITY, LEGAL obligations and responsibilities subject to evaluation, interpretation, and enforcement in a court of law. Casualty insurance provides coverage for an insured against a civil legal liability suit, not criminal legal liability, intentional torts, or liability for breach of contract. *See also* LIABILITY, CIVIL; LIABILITY, CIVIL DAMAGES AWARDED.

LIABILITY: LIMITATIONS ON INSURERS exceptions to coverage. There is no obligation for an insurance company to pay a claim if:
1. the loss is not covered by a policy, or a particular person is not included in the definition of the insured.
2. the loss takes place outside the territorial coverage of the policy. For example, there is no coverage under the PERSONAL AUTOMOBILE POLICY (PAP) outside the United States and Canada.
3. the loss takes place after the policy has expired.
4. the insured involved in the loss was in violation of public law; for example, an insured's car that is damaged as the result of his transporting drugs.
5. the insured is in violation of contract law.
6. the limit of coverage under the policy is not sufficient to cover a loss.

LIABILITY LIMITS maximum amount of coverage available under a liability insurance policy. *See also* AGGREGATE LIMIT; BASIC LIMITS OF LIABILITY; BUSINESS LIABILITY INSURANCE (Insuring Agreements section); LIABILITY: LIMITATIONS ON INSURERS; LOSS.

LIABILITY, NO-FAULT INSURANCE *see* NO-FAULT AUTOMOBILE INSURANCE.

LIABILITY, PERSONAL EXPOSURES acts or omissions that result in suits against an individual and/or residents of the individual's household for actual or imagined bodily injury and/or property damage to a third party. Exposures include:
1. ownership, use, and possession of property concerning: (a) trespass—the obligation is not to render property safe for a trespasser, but one cannot create a death trap or maintain an attractive nuisance, such as a swimming pool, without proper safeguards; (b) licensee—the obligation is not to render property safe for a licensee but to provide adequate warning of any hidden dangers such as quicksand at the side of an approach road; (c) invitation—the obligation is to render the property safe for an invitee's visit. For example, if someone trips on a throw rug, the owner or occupier of the premises can be held liable.
2. ownership, use, and possession of a motorized vehicle on or off premises.
3. involvement in sports.
4. actions of pets.

LIABILITY, PROFESSIONAL liability created when an individual who offers services to the general public claims expertise in a particular area greater than the ordinary layman. Today, suits are frequently brought alleging that a professional, such as a physician, attorney, or CPA, has committed negligent acts or omissions in performing the purchased service. For some professions, such as medical specialties, it has become impossible to purchase professional liability insurance at a reasonable price. Premiums have become prohibitive because of the frequency and severity of both reasonable and unreasonable professional liability suits.

LIABILITY, PRO RATA *see* PRO RATA LIABILITY CLAUSE.

LIABILITY RISK *see* LIABILITY, BUSINESS EXPOSURES; LIABILITY, PERSONAL EXPOSURES.

LIABILITY, STRICT *see* STRICT LIABILITY.

LIABILITY, VICARIOUS *see* CONTINGENT LIABILITY (VICARIOUS LIABILITY).

LIABILITY WITHOUT REGARD TO FAULT *see* ABSOLUTE LIABILITY; STRICT LIABILITY.

LIBEL *see* TORT, INTENTIONAL.

LIBEL INSURANCE coverage for an insured in the event that he writes and publishes libelous statements and the injured party brings suit against the insured.

LIBERALIZATION CLAUSE in PROPERTY INSURANCE policy, clause that stipulates that if legislative acts or acts of the insurance commissioner's office expand the coverage of an insurance policy or endorsement forms without requiring an additional premium, then all similar insurance policies and endorsement forms will automatically have such expanded coverage.

LICENSE in insurance, legal authority obtained by an insurance company, agent, broker, or consultant that permits them to do business in a particular state. The document issued by the state shows that the company or person is in compliance with the various governing laws and thus is authorized to conduct insurance business in that jurisdiction. A license, in and of itself, is not a guarantee that a consumer will be sold the best product to fit his or her needs or that an agent will have the proper technical expertise to evaluate the products on a consumer's behalf.

LICENSE, AGENTS *see* LICENSING OF AGENTS AND BROKERS.

LICENSE BOND instrument that guarantees compliance with various city, county, and state laws that govern the issuance of a particular license to conduct business.

LICENSED CARRIER insurance company that is organized under the state laws by which the company is licensed and that is called a DOMESTIC INSURER. Also, this insurance company may be chartered and licensed in another state or country and has obtained a license to conduct business in that particular state.

LICENSEE individual permitted to enter property with the permission of the owner or the person who controls the property. There is no mutual profit motive; the licensee comes onto the property for his or her sole benefit. For example, the owner of land gives an individual permission to hunt on the property but does not charge a fee. The owner must warn the licensee of any hidden dangers on the property of which he or she is aware.

LICENSE FEE sum paid by an insurance company or other firms or individuals to designated types of business in a particular state or municipality.

LICENSING OF AGENTS AND BROKERS legal authority granting individuals the right to conduct insurance business in a particular state. In many states, agents and brokers must pass a written exam as a prerequisite to being licensed. In others, a professional designation such as the CLU or CPCU can be substituted for the examination requirement. The caliber of examinations varies from state to state. A license is usually issued for one or two year periods, and then must be renewed.

LIEN action brought by a worker or creditor for failure to receive payment for labor and material provided. Property insurance is available for individuals with an insurable interest in property against which they may bring a lien.

LIFE AND HEALTH, BUSINESS EXPOSURES loss of a key person due to death, disability, sickness, resignation, incarceration, or retirement. Because of the expertise of such an individual, there could be a loss of income, market share, research and development advantage, and line of credit by the firm. Also, there are extra expenses associated with training a replacement for a key person. Coverage for many of these exposures is available under key person life and health insurance. *See also* BUY AND SELL AGREEMENT.

LIFE AND HEALTH INSURANCE PARTNERSHIP *see* PARTNERSHIP, LIFE AND HEALTH INSURANCE.

LIFE AND HEALTH INSURANCE, PERSONAL AND FAMILY EXPOSURES personal and family loss by death, disability, sickness, old age, accident, and unemployment. All of these exposures are insurable, and coverages can be purchased under a variety of policies. In life insurance these include ADJUSTABLE LIFE, CURRENT ASSUMPTION, ENDOWMENT, FAMILY INCOME POLICIES, FAMILY MAINTENANCE POLICIES, FAMILY POLICY, LIMITED PAYMENT LIFE, TERM LIFE, UNIVERSAL LIFE, and VARIABLE LIFE. In annuities, both fixed and variable types are available;

in health insurance, medical expense and disability income coverages are available. In pensions, there are DEFINED BENEFIT and DEFINED CONTRIBUTION PENSION plans. The various Social Security benefits also provide considerable protection against personal and family exposures.

LIFE ANNUITY *see* ANNUITY.

LIFE ANNUITY CERTAIN ANNUITY guaranteeing a given number of income payments whether or not the annuitant is alive to receive them. If the annuitant is living after the guaranteed number of payments have been made, the income continues for life. If the annuitant dies within the guarantee period, the balance is paid to a beneficiary. For example, under one common contract, a life annuity certain for 10 years, income payments are guaranteed for a minimum of 10 years. If the annuitant dies after receiving two years of payments, the beneficiary would receive the remaining eight years of income. An annuitant who lives out the 10 years would receive income payments for life, but there would be none available to a beneficiary.

LIFE ANNUITY CERTAIN AND CONTINUOUS *see* LIFE ANNUITY CERTAIN.

LIFE ANNUITY DUE *see* ANNUITY DUE.

LIFE CARE ANNUITY type of annuity contract that provides guaranteed income payment of an ANNUITY plus LONG-TERM CARE (LTC). A steady stream of income payments would be paid to the ANNUITANT. Upon the disability of the annuitant, the income would be increased substantially to provide for the expenses of long-term care. Under the provisions of the PENSION PROTECTION ACT OF 2006, which becomes effective January 1, 2010, withdrawal from annuities that specifically pay tax-qualified long-term care insurance will not be subject to income tax. (Currently, benefits from qualified long-term care and ACCIDENT AND HEALTH INSURANCE are not subject to income tax.) Also provided under the act is the income tax-free exchange of a qualified annuity or life insurance policy for a long-term care policy.

LIFE CARE COMMUNITIES facilities for senior adults who pay an entrance fee to move into the facility as well as a monthly fee. The adults receive, in return, a place to live and long-term care usually for the adult's life. Questions to be asked before joining a community include:
1. Who sponsors the community?
2. What is the financial condition of the community?
3. Is the community accredited?
4. Who are the trustees?
5. Does the community provide educational and recreational opportunities?
6. May the residents of the community have visitors and pets and under what circumstances?

7. Who makes the rules for the community and to what extent are the members allowed to contribute?

8. What legal rights do the members have to the assets of the community?

LIFE ESTATE *see* ESTATE PLANNING DISTRIBUTION.

LIFE EXPECTANCY probability of one's living to a specific age according to a particular mortality table. Life expectancy is the beginning point in calculating the pure cost of life insurance and annuities and is reflected in what is known as the BASIC PREMIUM. The probability of living longer has continued to increase in the U.S., and thus the pure cost of insurance continues to decrease. This is reflected in a declining premium rate. Increasing life expectancy is critical to the cash value projection in CURRENT ASSUMPTIONS life insurance products, such as universal life insurance and variable life insurance.

LIFE EXPECTANCY TERM INSURANCE type of TERM LIFE INSURANCE policy that has a FACE AMOUNT that increases to a predetermined sum and then decreases to zero at the termination point of the policy, while at the same time generating a CASH VALUE. The number of years that the term policy will be in force is determined by the average LIFE EXPECTANCY for the age and sex classification in which the prospective insured falls.

LIFE INCOME annuity payments that continue for the life of the annuitant. *See also* ANNUITY.

LIFE INCOME POLICY policy that has many similar characteristics to that of the SURVIVORSHIP ANNUITY in that the ANNUITANT receives a predetermined monthly income benefit for life upon the death of the INSURED. The annuitant's LIFE EXPECTANCY as well as the insured's life expectancy must be taken into consideration when determining the premium; thus, the annuitant cannot be changed after having been selected. The essential difference between this policy and the survivorship annuity is that under this policy a minimum number of payments are guaranteed to be paid after the insured's death, regardless of whether or not the annuitant is alive to receive them. If the annuitant does not survive the guarantee period (PERIOD CERTAIN), a contingent annuitant will receive the remaining guaranteed monthly income payments.

LIFE INCOME WITH PERIOD CERTAIN annuity payments that continue for the life of the annuitant; should the annuitant not survive a stated period, the payments are then made to a beneficiary until the stated period ends.

LIFE INSURANCE protection against the death of an individual in the form of payment to a beneficiary—usually a family member, business, or institution. In exchange for a series of premium payments or a single premium payment, upon the death of an insured, the face value (and any additional coverage attached to a policy), minus outstanding policy loans and interest, is paid to the beneficiary. *Living benefits* may be available for the insured in the form of surrender values or income payments. *See also* ADJUSTABLE LIFE INSURANCE; ENDOWMENT INSURANCE; FAMILY INCOME POLICY; FAMILY INCOME RIDER; FAMILY MAINTENANCE INSURANCE; LIMITED PAYMENT LIFE INSURANCE; ORDINARY LIFE INSURANCE; TERM INSURANCE; UNIVERSAL LIFE INSURANCE; VARIABLE LIFE INSURANCE.

LIFE INSURANCE, ASSIGNMENT CLAUSE *see* ASSIGNMENT CLAUSE, LIFE INSURANCE.

LIFE INSURANCE, BUSINESS USES *see* BUSINESS LIFE AND HEALTH INSURANCE.

LIFE INSURANCE CONTRACT *see* INSURANCE CONTRACT, LIFE.

LIFE INSURANCE COST amount paid to an insurer. Determination of the actual cost (not the price paid) of a life insurance policy has been widely discussed for many years in life insurance and consumer circles. The *traditional* or *net cost* method (that adds a policy's premiums, and subtracts dividends, if any, and cash value) does not consider the TIME VALUE OF MONEY. The LINTON YIELD METHOD, a theoretical approach, attempted to remedy this by comparing a cash value policy with a combination of decreasing term insurance and the yield of a side fund of bonds and other investments. Other methods have been proposed. At present many states require prospective insureds to be given INTEREST-ADJUSTED COST figures that do take into consideration the time value of money. This method is not altogether practical for INTEREST SENSITIVE POLICIES, but it is generally felt that present work toward a new approach will eventually result in a useful means of comparing the costs of these policies.

LIFE INSURANCE, CREDITOR RIGHTS protection given to life insurance beneficiaries by state laws, under which the benefits of a life insurance policy usually cannot be attached by creditors of an insured and/or beneficiary. These laws are based on philosophical concerns—dating back to the founding of the U.S., and the Homestead Laws—that a widow and children should not be made to pay for the financial sins of the father.

LIFE INSURANCE, FAMILY PROTECTION *see* FAMILY INCOME POLICY; FAMILY INCOME RIDER; FAMILY MAINTENANCE POLICY; FAMILY POLICY.

LIFE INSURANCE ILLUSTRATION QUESTIONNAIRE form whose purpose it is to help the agent and the prospective policyowner judge the validity of the insurance company's policy illustrations. This questionnaire's focus is on the nonguaranteed elements of the policy and how these nonguaranteed elements compare with the company's current experience. Some of the questions this questionnaire seeks to answer include:

1. To what degree are the mortality rates in the illustration reflective of the true mortality rates that the company is currently experiencing?

2. To what degree are the interest rates in the illustration reflective of the true interest rates that the company is currently experiencing? Upon what is the interest rate to be based (new money or portfolio average)?

3. To what degree are the expense charges in the illustration reflective of the true expense charges that the company is currently experiencing? Are these expense charges significantly understated in the illustration?

4. To what degree are the persistency rates in the illustration reflective of the true persistency rates that the company is currently experiencing? Are these persistency rates significantly understated in the illustration, thereby increasing policy cash value?

LIFE INSURANCE ILLUSTRATIONS MODEL REGULATION regulation set forth by the NATIONAL ASSOCIATION OF INSURANCE COMMISSIONERS (NAIC) to govern life insurance sales illustrations. Includes the following major provisions:

1. POLICYOWNER must be provided an annual report of the policy status if illustrations were used in conjunction with selling the policy.

2. An agent must sign the illustrations with copies furnished to the insurance company and the policyowner.

3. The COMMISSIONER OF INSURANCE must be notified by the insurance company if a policy is to be sold with or without illustrations.

4. Illustrations' nonguaranteed elements cannot be more favorable than the lesser of the currently payable scale or the disciplined current scale as defined by law.

5. Specific format guidelines must be followed by the illustrations.

6. Illustrations must contain a narrative summary and a numerical table, as well as tabular details.

7. The regulation applies to all individual life, group life, and certificate life policies with the exceptions of individual and group annuities, variable life, credit life, and those life policies whose death benefits are less than $10,000.

8. The board of directors of the insurance company is required to appoint an illustration actuary who must certify on an annual basis that the illustrations meet the requirements of the regulation.

LIFE INSURANCE IN FORCE aggregate of face amount of coverage paid up, or on which premiums are still being paid, as issued by a life insurance company. This is one measure used to rank life insurance companies by size.

LIFE INSURANCE, INDUSTRIAL *see* INDUSTRIAL LIFE INSURANCE.

LIFE INSURANCE, LEGAL RESERVE *see* LEGAL RESERVE LIFE INSURANCE COMPANY.

LIFE INSURANCE: LIFE RISK *see* HUMAN LIFE VALUE APPROACH (EVOIL); NEEDS APPROACH.

LIFE INSURANCE, LIMITED PAYMENT *see* LIMITED PAYMENT LIFE INSURANCE.

LIFE INSURANCE LIMITS *see* FACE AMOUNT (FACE OF POLICY); RENEWABLE TERM LIFE INSURANCE.

LIFE INSURANCE, LIVING BENEFITS *see* LIVING BENEFITS OF LIFE INSURANCE.

LIFE INSURANCE MARKETING AND RESEARCH ASSOCIA-TION (LIMRA) organization that conducts research on distribution systems for the life and health insurance products on behalf of its member companies. Studies range from consumer attitudes towards the life insurance product to reasons for turnover of the agency field force. Headquarters in Hartford, Connecticut.

LIFE INSURANCE, ORDINARY *see* ORDINARY LIFE INSURANCE.

LIFE INSURANCE PLANNING determination of the amount of life insurance required in light of the financial strategy. *See also* HUMAN LIFE VALUE APPROACH.

LIFE INSURANCE POLICIES PROVIDING FAMILY PROTEC-TION coverage giving income benefits to surviving family member(s) if one member should die. These include the FAMILY INCOME POLICY, FAMILY INCOME RIDER, FAMILY MAINTENANCE POLICY, and the FAMILY POLICY.

LIFE INSURANCE POUR-OVER TRUST ASSETS from a WILL transfer into an established LIFE INSURANCE TRUST. Through this mechanism, assets that have been probated are transferred into a LIVING TRUST.

LIFE INSURANCE PROGRAMMING process used to determine the amount of life insurance required on the life of the prospective insured. The process involves an analysis of the prospective insured's current financial condition (income, expenses, liquid and nonliquid assets, liabilities, savings, and investments), the financial objectives of the POLICYOWNER, the development and installation of a plan designed to achieve these objectives, and the periodic monitoring of the plan to determine the extent to which the plan is achieving the objectives. *See also* ESTATE PLANNING; ESTATE PLANNING DISTRIBUTION; HUMAN LIFE VALUE APPROACH (ECONOMIC VALUE OF AN INDIVIDUAL LIFE [EVOIL]).

LIFE INSURANCE RENEWABILITY *see* RENEWABLE TERM LIFE INSURANCE.

LIFE INSURANCE RESERVES *see* FULL PRELIMINARY TERM RESERVE PLAN; PROSPECTIVE RESERVE; RETROSPECTIVE METHOD RESERVE COMPUTATION.

LIFE INSURANCE SETTLEMENT OPTIONS *see* OPTIONAL MODES OF SETTLEMENT.

LIFE INSURANCE, STRAIGHT *see* ORDINARY LIFE INSURANCE.

LIFE INSURANCE, TERM *see* TERM LIFE INSURANCE.

LIFE INSURANCE TRUST agreement establishing a trust for the named beneficiary under a life insurance policy. Upon the death of the insured, the trust has the legal obligation to pay the policy proceeds in the manner stipulated in the trust agreement.

LIFE INSURANCE, WHOLE LIFE *see* ORDINARY LIFE INSURANCE.

LIFE INSURERS CONFERENCE (LIC) organization of *home service debit* life insurance companies and combination companies. *See also* COMBINATION AGENT; DEBIT INSURANCE (HOME SERVICE INSURANCE, INDUSTRIAL INSURANCE).

LIFE MANAGEMENT INSTITUTE unit of the LIFE OFFICE MANAGEMENT ASSOCIATION (LOMA), which prepares and administers educational materials for the Fellow Life Management Institute (FLMI) Program. Upon successful completion of its examinations, the student receives the FLMI designation.

LIFE OFFICE MANAGEMENT ASSOCIATION (LOMA) organization that develops and administers educational materials and examinations for the life insurance industry. It awards the FELLOW, LIFE MANAGEMENT INSTITUTE (FLMI) designation to individuals who pass a series of 10 national life and health insurance examinations on insurance, accounting, marketing, information systems, finance, law, management, and computers.

LIFE PAID UP AT SPECIFIED AGE *see* LIMITED PAYMENT LIFE INSURANCE.

LIFE PLANNING *see* ESTATE PLANNING; ESTATE PLANNING DISTRIBUTION: HUMAN LIFE VALUE APPROACH (ECONOMIC VALUE OF AN INDIVIDUAL LIFE) (EVOIL).

LIFE REINSURANCE system whereby a life insurance company (the reinsured) reduces its possible maximum loss on either an individual life insurance policy (FACULTATIVE REINSURANCE) or a large number of life insurance policies (AUTOMATIC REINSURANCE) by giving (ceding) a portion of its liability to another insurance company (the reinsurer). *See also* REINSURANCE.

LIFE RISK FACTORS information needed for underwriting a life insurance policy, such as an applicant's age, weight, height, and build; personal and family health record; occupation; and personal habits. These factors decide into which rate classification to place the applicant since they determine to a significant degree the probability of an applicant's length of life.

LIFE SETTLEMENT agreement targeted to people older than age 65 whose life expectancies range from 2 to 12 years. The policyowner sells the ownership rights of the policy to another party in exchange for a lump sum of cash. Upon transfer, this party becomes the new owner (enjoying all the OWNERSHIP RIGHTS UNDER LIFE INSURANCE) and BENEFICIARY under the policy. *See also* VIATICAL SETTLEMENT.

LIFE TABLE *see* MORBIDITY TABLE; MORTALITY TABLE.

LIFETIME DISABILITY BENEFIT provision in some disability income policies that provides a monthly income benefit to a disabled insured for as long as he or she remains disabled according to the definition of disability in the policy. *See also* DISABILITY INCOME INSURANCE.

LIFETIME MAXIMUM provision found in HEALTH INSURANCE policies that limit the total benefit INSURERS can receive during their lifetime. Usually once a year a portion of the used benefits can be restored until the original limits are reached.

LIFETIME POLICY *see* LIFETIME DISABILITY BENEFIT.

LIFE UNDERWRITER life insurance agent.

LIFE UNDERWRITER POLITICAL ACTION COMMITTEE (LUPAC) affiliate of the NATIONAL ASSOCIATION OF LIFE UNDERWRITERS (NALU) that supports legislators in the interest of the insurance agents. One becomes a member of LUPAC through a monetary contribution.

LIFE UNDERWRITING TRAINING COUNCIL (LUTC) organization that develops and administers educational materials and examinations for life insurance agents. A significant objective of the courses is sales technique.

LIGHTNING discharge of electricity from the atmosphere, one of the perils covered in most fire insurance policies.

LIMIT, AGGREGATE *see* AGGREGATE LIMIT.

LIMIT, ANNUAL AGGREGATE *see* ANNUAL AGGREGATE LIMIT.

LIMITATIONS exceptions and limitations of coverage; that is, the maximum amount of insurance coverage available under a policy. *See also* COINSURANCE.

LIMITATIONS ON AMOUNT OF MONTHLY BENEFITS clause in some DISABILITY INCOME INSURANCE policies under which there is a maximum an insured can receive from all sources of disability income benefits. For example, the clause may stipulate that all sources of disability income cannot exceed 50% of the insured's gross earnings prior to the disability.

LIMITATIONS ON INSURERS LIABILITY *see* LIABILITY: LIMITATIONS ON INSURERS.

LIMIT, BASIC *see* BASIC LIMITS OF LIABILITY.

LIMIT, BLANKET *see* BLANKET LIMIT.

LIMIT, DIVIDED *see* SPLIT LIMIT.

LIMITED LIABILITY COMPANY (LLC) company in which shareholders limit their liability exposure to their percentage of ownership or equity interest in the company. Shareholders' personal assets are protected in the event of business-related lawsuits. The tax situation for this type of company is much like that of the partnership in that it acts as a pass-through tax entity. A tax return for a partnership is filed with the IRS for information purposes only. All income and expenses are attributed to the stockholders of the LLC. According to the LLC agreement, the stockholders can allocate income and its resultant tax liability the same way as partners in a partnership.

The LLC has advantages over the subchapter "S" corporation to include the following: (1) LLC has no restriction on number of persons who may be stockholders; "S" corporations are limited to 35 stockholders; (2) LLC may have multiple classes of stock; an "S" corporation can have only one issue of stock; and (3) LLC may own subsidiaries; an "S" corporation cannot own subsidiaries.

LIMITED PARTNERSHIP type of business organization composed usually of a GENERAL PARTNER and several limited partners. The limited partner usually just contributes assets to the partnership and has limited legal obligations and no management responsibilities. The general partner manages the partnership and has extensive legal obligations associated with that partnership.

LIMITED PAYMENT LIFE INSURANCE type of policy with premiums that are fully paid up within a stated period. For example, a 20-payment life insurance policy has 20 annual premium payments, with no further premiums to be paid.

LIMITED POLICY type of health insurance providing benefits for only a particular peril, such as cancer.

LIMITED POLLUTION LIABILITY COVERAGE FORM commercial liability insurance form providing coverage for an insured business in the event of a pollution liability suit. The insurance provides CLAIMS MADE BASIS LIABILITY COVERAGE. Excluded from coverage are cleanup costs.

LIMIT, EXCESS *see* EXCESS LIMIT.

LIMIT, LINE *see* LINE LIMIT.

LIMIT OF LIABILITY *see* LIABILITY; LIMITATIONS ON INSURERS.

LIMIT OF RECOVERY *see* COINSURANCE.

LIMIT ORDER purchase or sale of a stock at a stipulated or better than stipulated price.

LIMIT, PER ACCIDENT *see* PER ACCIDENT LIMIT.

LIMIT, PER PERSON maximum amount under a liability policy that insurance company will pay for bodily injury incurred by any one person in any one accident.

LIMIT, POLICY *see* LIMITATIONS.

LIMITS *see* LIABILITY; LIMITATIONS ON INSURERS; COINSURANCE.

LIMIT, SCHEDULED *see* SCHEDULED LIMIT.

LIMIT, SINGLE *see* SINGLE LIMIT.

LIMIT, SPECIFIC *see* SPECIFIC LIMIT.

LIMIT, STANDARD *see* BASIC LIMITS OF LIABILITY.

LIMITS UNDER MULTIPLE POLICY YEARS (LUMP) single limit insurance program remaining in force for several years as compared with traditional insurance programs where there is a series of annual limits. The LUMP insurance program is most effective in those instances where the statistical analysis shows low-frequency, short-tail (length of time elapsed between the act giving rise to the claim and when the claim is recognized or reported to the insurance company) risks that have a potential for catastrophic loss. LUMP insurance programs provide insurance coverages for such exposures as marine liability, directors and officers liability, general liability, and workers compensation.

LIMIT, VARIABLE *see* VARIABLE LIMIT.

LINE term used for a general class of insurance such as LIFE INSURANCE, PROPERTY INSURANCE, or WORKERS COMPENSATION INSURANCE.

LINE CARD record of insurance policies sold to an individual.

LINE, GROSS *see* GROSS LINE.

LINE LIMIT maximum amount of a specified type of insurance coverage, according to underwriting guidelines, that an insurance company feels it can safely underwrite on a particular exposure without having to acquire REINSURANCE for that exposure. *See also* LINE; SURPLUS LINES; SURPLUS REINSURANCE.

LINE, NET *see* NET LINE.

LINE OF BUSINESS *see* LINE; LINES OF INSURANCE, MAJOR.

LINE OF CREDIT borrowing power that a business firm or an individual has with a lending institution such as a bank.

LINES *see* SURPLUS LINES.

LINE SHEET amount of insurance coverage that an insurance company is willing to write on a given category of business.

LINES OF INSURANCE, MAJOR five primary sectors of insurance coverage. Their purposes are:

1. LIFE INSURANCE—provides income to a beneficiary in the event of the death of the insured.
2. HEALTH INSURANCE—provides two types of coverage: (a) *Medical Expense,* which indemnifies an insured for hospital, physician, and related expenses; (b) DISABILITY INCOME (DI), which provides a source of income for an insured in the event of partial or total disability. It is generally felt that this source of income should approximate at least 50% of earnings prior to a disability.
3. ANNUITY—provides monthly income to an annuitant for life.
4. PROPERTY INSURANCE—indemnifies an insured for damages or destruction of property.
5. LIABILITY INSURANCE—covers damages on behalf of an insured who becomes legally obligated to pay because of actual (or alleged) negligent acts and omissions.

LINKED BENEFIT INSURANCE combination of LONG-TERM CARE insurance with a LIFE INSURANCE policy or a retirement annuity.

LINTON YIELD METHOD interest adjusted method that measures the cost of life insurance. Named for the late distinguished actuary M. Albert Linton. This method compares a whole life policy with a combination of a decreasing term policy and a side fund. The rate of return of the side fund is called the Linton Yield, in that it brings the side fund up to an amount equal to the cash value of the whole life policy after a specified period of time.

LIQUIDATION AND REHABILITATION taking over of an insurance company's assets by the State Insurance Commissioner when examination of the annual report reveals that the company is in substantial financial difficulty. The State Insurance Commissioner will then operate the company in what is deemed to be the best interest of the policyowners, insureds, and creditors. If the State Insurance Commissioner believes it is possible to save the company, rehabilitation (reorganization of the company's structure) may be ordered; if salvage is deemed impossible, liquidation may be necessary.

LIQUIDATION CHARGE amount subtracted from an annuity or from mutual fund proceeds payable to an annuity owner or mutual fund owner to reflect expense fees described in the annuity contract or mutual fund prospectus. This charge may be viewed as a penalty for cashing in the annuity or mutual fund early. This fee is meant to discourage early withdrawal of funds and/or to enable the company to recoup its expenses associated with marketing, administering, and liquidating the product.

LIQUIDATION PERIOD time frame during which an annuitant receives income payments from the insurance company, usually on a monthly basis. The obligations of the company to the annuitant during the liquidation period depend on whether it is a *pure* or *refund* annuity. For the PURE ANNUITY, all payments cease upon the death of the annuitant. For the REFUND ANNUITY, a beneficiary is usually entitled to payments upon the death of the annuitant.

LIQUIDITY *see* LIQUIDITY OF ASSETS.

LIQUIDITY OF ASSETS financial holdings that can be converted into cash in a timely manner without the loss of principal, such as U.S. Treasury Bills. Liquidity of assets is one of the most important principles of investment strategies, especially the first layer of an investment portfolio. Life insurance is generally placed in this first layer because of its cash value. The owner has complete liquidity since it can be used as collateral for a loan a any time.

LIQUOR LIABILITY LAWS legislation that makes an establishment and/or individual selling liquor responsible for injuries caused by its customers to third parties. The best known law governing dispensation of liquor on premises is the DRAM SHOP LAW. For example, an individual is served liquor at an establishment and becomes intoxicated. On his way home he or she causes an accident, injuring another party. The injured third party can bring a liability suit against the establishment that dispensed the liquor for injuries suffered.

LIVE ANIMAL INSURANCE coverage under the COMMERCIAL PROPERTY FLOATER for loss under two forms: LIVESTOCK MORTALITY LIFE INSURANCE and LIVESTOCK FLOATER. This is really life insurance coverage for livestock.

LIVESTOCK FLOATER standard COMMERCIAL PROPERTY FLOATER form covering death or damage to livestock as the result of insured perils such as fire, lightning, explosion, smoke, wind, hail, aircraft, earthquake, theft, flood, collapse of bridges, collision, or overturn of a vehicle used in transporting the livestock from the point of destination. Some insurance companies also cover attacks by domestic or wild animals, drowning, and accidental shooting. Common exclusions include illegal acts, confiscation by the order of a government authority, loss due to quarantine, war, loss due to sleet or snow, and loss due to the acceptance by the owner of a check covered by insufficient funds.

LIVESTOCK INSURANCE coverage for designated horses and other farm animals if they are damaged or destroyed. The insurance includes registered cattle and herds, other farm livestock, and zoo animals. This type of insurance protects the farmer or rancher against the premature death of animals resulting from natural causes, fire, lightning, accidents, and acts of God, acts of individuals other than the owner or employees, and destruction for humane purposes.

LIVESTOCK MORTALITY (LIFE) INSURANCE coverage that provides a death benefit to the owner of a policy in the event of the death of insured livestock.

LIVESTOCK TRANSIT INSURANCE coverage in event of damage or destruction of animals that are being shipped.

LIVING still with life. This is a life insurance term used to describe the *living benefits* available under a life insurance policy such as a monthly retirement payment to an insured.

LIVING BENEFITS OF LIFE INSURANCE benefits provided to and obtained by those insured, while still alive. They include the ANNUITY, CASH SURRENDER VALUE, DISABILITY INCOME (DI), POLICY LOAN, and WAIVER OF PREMIUM (WP).

LIVING DEATH BENEFITS early payout of anticipated death benefits from a RIDER attached to an existing policy or from a separate policy. The purpose is to allow the terminally ill insured an additional source of finance to pay medical bills and/or nice-to-have items. There are basically two methods for paying out these benefits: (1) the policyholder gains access to the benefits when the policyholder contracts an illness that has been diagnosed as terminal with a life expectancy usually of less than two years; (2) the policyholder gains access to the benefits when the policyholder is confined to a nursing home or a long-term care facility and can be expected to remain in this facility until death. Generally, as long as the POLICYHOLDER is expected to die within 12 months of the date of the payment of the living death benefit, and that benefit is discounted only by an amount that is consistent with a life expectancy no greater than one year in duration, the beneficiary(s) is not taxed on the life insurance proceeds.

LIVING TRUST *see* ESTATE PLANNING DISTRIBUTION.

LIVING WILL legal document that permits the individual to declare his or her desires concerning the use of life-sustaining treatment to be made at the point in time when death is imminent and the individual no longer has control of his or her faculties. This type of will has the advantages of ensuring that the individual's wishes are followed to the conclusion and that a family member does not have the burden of making extremely agonizing decisions on behalf of the individual. It is the requirement of most state statutes that such a will be signed, dated, and witnessed (excluding anyone who has an interest in the estate of the individual affirming the will). Also required by most state statutes is that the will include both a statement of capacity and a statement of intent by the individual. The following states have statutes addressing the living will issue: Alabama, Arizona, Arkansas, California, Colorado, Connecticut, Delaware, Florida, Georgia, Idaho, Illinois, Indiana, Iowa, Kansas, Louisiana, Maine, Maryland, Mississippi, Missouri, Montana, Nevada, New Hampshire, New Mexico, North Carolina, Oklahoma, Oregon, South Carolina, Tennessee, Texas, Utah, Vermont, Virginia, Washington, West Virginia, Wisconsin, and Wyoming, as well as Washington, D.C. *See also* ESTATE PLANNING DISTRIBUTION.

LLOYD'S ASSOCIATION organization following the format of LLOYD'S OF LONDON.

LLOYD'S BROKER specialist whose task is to place insurance with the specialized syndicates that underwrite particular risks at LLOYD'S OF LONDON.

LLOYD'S OF LONDON insurance facility composed of many different syndicates, each specializing in a particular risk; for example, hull risks. Lloyd's provides coverage for primary jumbo risks as well as offering REINSURANCE and RETROCESSIONS. Membership in a syndicate is limited to individuals with a large personal net worth, and each member may belong to one or more syndicates depending upon his or her net worth. Although much of the publicity Lloyd's receives involves insuring exotic risks such as an actress' legs, this represents only a very small portion of its total business, most of which involves reinsurance and retrocessions.

LLOYD'S REGISTER OF SHIPPING classification of ships according to their construction material, age, physical condition, propulsion type, stress tests of structure, and owners. Marine insurance rates for a particular vessel are based on these demographics. Lloyd's register is used worldwide by government agencies and industry to track and identify vessels. In many instances the country of registration is of strategic importance if a vessel is exposed to attack, say, in the Middle East and in other danger points in the world.

LLOYD'S SYNDICATE group of underwriters with LLOYD'S OF LONDON who specialize in underwriting a particular risk such as hull insurance.

LLOYD'S UNDERWRITER individual member of one of the syndicates of LLOYD'S OF LONDON.

LOADING addition to the pure cost of insurance that reflects agent commissions, premium taxes, administrative costs associated with putting business on an insurance company's books, and contingencies.

LOAN money that is lent. In life insurance, a loan can be taken against the cash value of a life insurance policy at any time. The policyholder does not have to repay the loan until the policy matures or until the loan and any outstanding interest equals the cash value.

LOAN RECEIPT acknowledgment by the POLICYOWNER that he or she has received the POLICY LOAN requested.

LOAN VALUE amount that a policyowner can borrow from a cash value of a permanent life insurance policy.

LOCAL AGENT *see* INDEPENDENT AGENT.

LOCAL AREA NETWORKS (LANs) systems composed of personal computers linked by a file server. These computers share software as well as databases that enable the risk manager access to information in a quick and efficient manner. For example, in Workers' Compensation claims the risk manager can quickly analyze claims data and pinpoint the exact area of the company's operations that is responsible for the most severe injuries incurred by the workers.

LOCAL GOVERNMENT ENVIRONMENTAL ASSISTANCE NETWORK (LGEAN) clearinghouse and forum of information concerning the environment used by local governments. Included in the information are topics on drinking water systems, pesticide management, public safety, solid waste management, vehicle/equipment maintenance, wastewater collection and treatment, and water resources management. Web site is *http://www.lgean.org.*

LOCATION CARD insurance record showing the amount of INSURANCE coverage placed on any one location.

LOCK-IN PRINCIPLE accounting rule found under the Generally Accepted Accounting Principles (GAAP) that prohibits the insurance company from restating assumptions that it made for interest earned, expenses paid, and mortality charges for policies in force.

LOCK-IN RATE commitment that a lending institution makes to offer a loan at a stipulated interest rate at a predetermined future time, usually limited to 90 days.

LODGE SYSTEM OF INSURANCE *see* FRATERNAL LIFE INSURANCE.

LONDON INSURANCE AND REINSURANCE MARKET ASSOCIATION (LIRMA) association that represents reinsurance companies as well as insurance companies that do not market MARINE INSURANCE. LIRMA and the INSTITUTE OF LONDON UNDERWRITERS share the same facility for processing policies and claims.

LONDON INSURANCE MARKET NETWORK (LIMNET) computer system established by London trade associations for processing insurance policies. The work of LIMNET involves the notification and settlement of insurance policy claims.

LONGEVITY INSURANCE combination of an IMMEDIATE ANNUITY and a DEFERRED ANNUITY. Premiums are currently paid in, and the annuitant receives monthly income payments at some future age (usually between age 80 and 85) for the annuitant's life (the deferred part of the annuity). The amount of the future monthly benefit is calculated at the time this annuity is purchased (the immediate part of the annuity). This monthly income stream is substantially higher than that of traditional deferred annuity because (1) this product does not pay a death benefit—everything is forfeited if the annuitant is not alive at the income starting date; (2) the amount of the income payment is determined when the premium is paid, unlike the typical deferred annuity where the premium and interest earned is annuitized at the time the income payments begin. This could lead to larger income payments if the interest rates exceed the rate agreed to when the premium was paid. In essence, the product allows an individual who is at a minimum age (usually 55) to invest a lump sum at that age, thereby purchasing a future income stream (usually beginning at age 85).

LONGSHOREMEN AND HARBOR WORKERS ACT LIABILITY coverage under the Workers Compensation Act for all employees in the maritime industry who perform their function in navigable U.S. waters, including dry docks, wharves, piers, and other places for docking. Excluded are the master and crew of the ship, and any individual involved in loading, unloading, or repairing of a ship whose weight is less than 18 tons.

LONGSHOREMEN AND HARBOR WORKERS ENDORSE-MENT extension of a Workers Compensation and Employers Liability Insurance policy to cover workers who go aboard ship to perform their jobs. *See also* WORKERS COMPENSATION BENEFITS; WORKERS COMPENSATION, COVERAGE B.

LONG-TAIL LIABILITY one where an injury or other harm takes time to become known and a claim may be separated from the circumstances that caused it by as many as 25 years or more. Some examples: exposure to asbestos, which sometimes results in a lung disease called asbestosis; exposure to coal dust, which might cause black lung disease; or use of certain drugs that may cause cancer or birth defects. These long-tail liabilities became very expensive for many corporations in the 1970s and 1980s, also causing problems for insurers because it was unclear when the situation that gave rise to the claim happened and who should pay the claim. One theory, the MANIFESTATION/INJURY THEORY, states that the insurer is responsible whenever the disease is diagnosed. The other view, the OCCURRENCE/INJURY THEORY, states that the insurer must pay only when the person is injured.

LONG-TERM CARE (LTC) day-to-day care that a patient (generally older than 65) receives in a nursing facility or in his or her residence following an illness or injury, or in old age, such that the patient can no longer perform at least two of the five basic activities of daily living: walking, eating, dressing, using the bathroom, and mobility from one place to another. There are basically three types of LTC plans:
1. *Skilled nursing care* provided only by skilled medical professionals as ordered by a physician. MEDICARE will pay a limited amount of the associated cost.
2. *Intermediate care* provided only by skilled medical professionals as ordered by a physician. This care involves the occasional nursing and rehabilitative assistance required by a patient.
3. *Custodial care* provided only by skilled medical professionals as ordered by a physician. The patient requires personal assistance in order to conduct his or her basic daily living activities.

When selecting a LTC policy, some of the more important considerations include:

1. *Renewability*—policy should be a GUARANTEED RENEWABLE CONTRACT.
2. *Waiting period*—length of time before benefits are paid should not exceed 90 days.
3. *Age eligibility*—upper age limit should be at least 80.
4. *Length of time benefits are paid*—typically the range is 5 to 10 years. It would be preferable to have benefits paid for life.
5. *Inflation guard*—the benefit level should be automatically adjusted each year according to the increase in the costs charged by the long-term-care providers.
6. *Premium waiver*—after the patient has received benefits for at least 90 days, the patient is no longer required to make premium payments for as long as he or she is under long-term care.
7. *No increase of premiums with age*—premiums should be based on the age at the time of application and should never increase as a result of changes in age.
8. *No limitations for preexisting conditions*—there should be no PREEXISTING CONDITION limitations.

LONG-TERM CARE (LTC) LINKED INSURANCE combination of life insurance and an annuity contract with a LONG-TERM CARE (LTC) rider. This combination policy provides long-term care income on a nontaxable basis to the insured with an unused portion of the policy transferred to the beneficiary on a nontaxable basis upon the death of the insured.

LONG-TERM CARE RIDER *see* LIVING DEATH BENEFIT.

LONG-TERM DISABILITY INCOME INSURANCE coverage that provides monthly income payments for as long as an insured remains disabled. The insurance policy defines the nature of the disability it covers. Most policies discontinue income payments beyond age 65. *See also* DISABILITY INCOME INSURANCE.

LONG-TERM INSURANCE insurance written for a period of time greater than one year.

LOSS damage through an insured's negligent acts and/or omissions resulting in bodily injury and/or property damage to a third party; damage to an insured's property; or amount an insurance company has a legal obligation to pay.
1. a company is legally obligated to pay the least of the following amounts: (a) amount of the loss; (b) limits of coverage; (c) amount resulting from the application of the coinsurance formula, such that

$$\frac{\text{Insurance Carried}}{\text{Insurance Required}} \times \text{Amount of Loss} = \begin{matrix}\text{Amount of}\\\text{Payment to}\\\text{Insured}\end{matrix}$$

where Insurance Required = Value of Property × Coinsurance

For example, assume that the insured had a $200,000 home destroyed totally by fire; carried $150,000 in insurance coverage; and there was an 80% coinsurance requirement. Then, according to the formula

$$\frac{\$150,000}{\$200,000 \times 80\%} \times \$200,000 = \$187,500 = \begin{array}{l} \text{Amount} \\ \text{of Payment} \\ \text{to Insured} \end{array}$$

(d) amount according to the pro rata distribution clause. If there is more than one insurance policy covering the damaged or destroyed property, each policy will pay no more than its proportionate share of the loss. In the foregoing example, if the insured had two separate $200,000 policies, each would pay no more than $100,000.

2. questions regarding loss coverage include: Is the peril covered? Is the property covered? Is the person covered? Is the policy in force? Are the limits of coverage adequate? Is the location covered? Has the hazard been increased?

3. steps an insured should take: (a) send written notice immediately to the insurance company or its agent; (b) do everything reasonable to protect the property from further damage; (c) separate damaged from undamaged property; (d) provide the insurance company with a written inventory of damaged or destroyed property; (e) submit within 60 days following the loss written proof of the loss; and (f) make the damaged or destroyed property available for examination by the insurance company.

LOSS ADJUSTMENT EXPENSE cost involved in an insurance company's adjustment of losses under a policy.

LOSS AND LOSS ADJUSTMENT EXPENSE RESERVES amount of the insurance company's liabilities for claims that have not been settled. If this reserve increases significantly in relation to the company's SURPLUS, the risk is greater for potential deficiencies in the reserves; that is, the reserves could prove to be inadequate to meet future claim payments.

LOSS ASSUMPTION *see* RETENTION AND LIMITS CLAUSE; RISK MANAGEMENT; SELF INSURANCE.

LOSS AVOIDANCE *see* AVOIDANCE.

LOSS CARRYBACK ruling that, under current tax law, if an insurance company is to use a LOSS CARRYFORWARD accounting adjustment, the company must first offset a net income loss in a specified time period against a net income gain in the three preceding years.

LOSS CARRYFORWARD ruling that, under current tax law, an insurance company that has incurred a net income loss in a given year may charge that loss against its taxable income in a subsequent year. This accounting adjustment may be made provided that the insurance company first offsets its net income loss in a given period against its net income gain in the three preceding years, or thus adopts a loss carryback accounting procedure.

LOSS CLAUSE feature of property and casualty policy providing coverage without a reduction in the policy's limits after a loss is paid. For example, if the limit of coverage under a property policy is $100,000 and a loss of $50,000 is paid, the limit still remains $100,000. Thus, the total amount of coverage in force for future losses is $100,000. In the absence of a loss clause, the total limit of coverage is reduced after payment of a loss.

LOSS CONSTANT surcharge, in retrospective rating of property and liability insurance, added to the BASIC PREMIUM rate charged to reflect fixed cost of adjusting or settling losses.

LOSS CONTROL *see* ENGINEERING APPROACH; HUMAN APPROACH; RISK MANAGEMENT.

LOSS CONVERSION FACTOR measure used in the RETROSPECTIVE RATING method for WORKERS COMPENSATION INSURANCE. A factor is applied to the INCURRED LOSSES during the rating period in question in order to generate a loss adjustment expense amount to be used in claim investigation and settlement.

LOSS DEPARTMENT *see* CLAIMS DEPARTMENT.

LOSS DEVELOPMENT difference in the amount of losses between the beginning and end of a time period.

LOSS DEVELOPMENT FACTOR element used to adjust losses to reflect the INCURRED BUT NOT REPORTED CLAIM (IBNR) under the retrospective method of rating. *See also* RETROSPECTIVE RATING.

LOSS DRAFT payment of INSURANCE proceeds for a claim resulting from a loss to INSURED mortgaged property.

LOSSES reductions in the value of property due to physical damage or destruction.

LOSSES INCURRED important quantitative measure for an insurance company indicating the percentage of each premium dollar that is going to pay for losses. Based on losses incurred, appropriate reserves are established. Changes in incurred losses over several policy periods indicate the trend in the loss picture and the accuracy of the basic premium charged to reflect expected losses.

LOSSES OTHER THAN COLLISION *see* OTHER THAN COLLISION LOSS.

LOSSES OUTSTANDING losses representing claims not paid.

LOSSES PAID losses representing claims paid.

LOSS EVENT circumstance that produces the loss.

LOSS EXPECTANCY *see* EXPECTED LOSS; EXPECTED LOSS RATIO; EXPECTED MORBIDITY; EXPECTED MORTALITY; LOSS FREQUENCY METHOD.

LOSS FREQUENCY *see* FREQUENCY; FREQUENCY AND DISTRIBUTION OF LOSSES.

LOSS FREQUENCY METHOD procedure used in projecting the number of future losses within a given time frame. This prediction of future losses forms the basic premium onto which loadings are made for an insurance company's expenses, profits, and contingencies.

LOSS LOADING *see* LOADING.

LOSS MITIGATION INSURANCE coverage in the event there is a pending third-party claim against the insured, a chance that a third-party claim against the insured will arise from an occurred event, or a chance that a third-party claim against a buyer from the insured will arise after a sale.

LOSS OF INCOME insured's income prior to the disability minus the insured's income after the disability. *See also* DISABILITY INCOME INSURANCE.

LOSS OF INCOME INSURANCE coverage in property insurance for an employee's lost income if a peril such as fire damages or destroys the place of employment, causing the worker to become unemployed. For example, a fire destroys a manufacturing plant, and as a result employees are placed on indefinite leave without pay. This coverage would then go into effect. In health insurance, loss of income benefits are paid when an insured becomes disabled and cannot work.

LOSS OF TIME INSURANCE *see* LOSS OF INCOME INSURANCE.

LOSS OF USE INSURANCE coverage in the event that property is damaged or destroyed so that an insured cannot use the property for its intended purpose. For example, loss of use of a drill press because of vandalism would be covered.

LOSS PAYABLE CLAUSE coverage for a mortgagee where real or personal property, used as security for a loan, is damaged or destroyed. For example, a bank (mortgagee) lends money to an individual (mortgagor) who pledges certain valuables as security. The valuables are stolen. If the individual defaults on the loan, the bank would be indemnified under the policy for an amount up to the outstanding loan.

LOSS PORTFOLIO TRANSFER REINSURANCE type of EXCESS OF LOSS REINSURANCE in which the insurance company (CEDENT) cedes its known LOSS REVENUES to its reinsurer.

LOSS PREVENTION *see* ENGINEERING APPROACH; LOSS PREVENTION AND REDUCTION.

LOSS PREVENTION AND REDUCTION risk management control procedure that emphasizes safety management. Its purpose is to reduce the frequency and severity of potential losses. Business firms apply this procedure by posting safety signs, holding safety meetings, and providing cash awards for employees with the best safety records. *See also* ENGINEERING APPROACH; HUMAN APPROACH.

LOSS PREVENTION SERVICE *see* ENGINEERING APPROACH.

LOSS RATE frequency of losses. *See also* LOSS FREQUENCY METHOD.

LOSS RATIO relationship of incurred losses plus loss adjustment expense to earned premiums.

LOSS RATIO METHOD modification of premium rates by a stipulated uniform percentage for closely related classes of property or liability insurance policies. The objective of such modification is to more directly align the combined actual loss ratio of the classes of policies under consideration with the expected loss ratio of these classes. The resultant alignment should show no significant STANDARD DEVIATION OR VARIATION of the actual loss ratio from the expected loss ratio.

LOSS RATIO RESERVE METHOD formula for a given line of insurance used by property and casualty insurance companies to compare losses and loss adjustment expense with premiums. This shows (1) the amount of each premium dollar generated that is used to pay losses and expenses, and (2) the reserves that must be maintained to pay for those losses and expenses.

LOSS REDUCTION *see* LOSS PREVENTION AND REDUCTION.

LOSS REPORT *see* CLAIM REPORT.

LOSS RESERVES provision for known claims due but not paid, known claims not yet due, and provision for INCURRED BUT NOT REPORTED (IBNR) claims. The critical problem facing a casualty insurance company is the amount of reserves necessary for the incurred but not reported losses (IBNR) because many of these claims and their resultant settlements may not manifest themselves until several years in the future. This is known as the *tail end distribution liability. See also* FULL PRELIMINARY TERM RESERVE PLAN; PROSPECTIVE RESERVE; RESERVE LIABILITIES REGULATION; RETROSPECTIVE METHOD RESERVE COMPUTATION.

LOSS RETENTION *see* RETENTION AND LIMITS CLAUSE; RISK MANAGEMENT; SELF INSURANCE.

LOSS RUN *see* LOSS DEVELOPMENT; LOSS FREQUENCY METHOD.

LOSS SETTLEMENT *see* LOSS SETTLEMENT AMOUNT.

LOSS SETTLEMENT AMOUNT in homeowners insurance, usually an 80% coinsurance requirement, which means the insured must carry insurance on the value of a home on a replacement cost basis of at least 80%. For example, a home is worth $200,000, and a fire does $50,000 damage. If there is $150,000 of insurance, it may appear that the insured would be reimbursed for the total loss. But the homeowner would receive only $46,875 according to the following formula:

$$\frac{\text{Amount of Insurance Carried}}{80\% \text{ Insurance to Value}} \times \text{Loss} = \text{Insured Reimbursement}$$
(Replacement Cost Basis)

$$\frac{\$150,000}{\$160,000} \times \$50,000 = \$46,875$$

If, however, the insured had carried an 80% insurance to value of $160,000, then the insured would have been reimbursed for the total loss of $50,000 according to the following formula:

$$\frac{\$160,000}{\$160,000} \times \$50,000 = \$50,000$$

See also COINSURANCE; SETTLEMENT OPTIONS, PROPERTY AND CASUALTY INSURANCE.

LOSS SEVERITY *see* SEVERITY RATE.

LOSS TRENDS projections of future accidental losses based on analyses of historical loss patterns. A projected loss picture is used to determine the pure cost of protection and the resultant basic premium, contingency reserves, and whether or not the company should continue selling a given line of business, or remain in a particular geographical area. However, loss trends based on historical data may not really represent likely loss outcomes in the future.

LOSS VALUATION procedure for determining the value of a loss.

LOSS-YEAR STATISTICS *see* ACCIDENT-YEAR STATISTICS.

LOST-INSTRUMENT BOND indemnification bond under which a stock certificate holder who loses the original certificate will be issued a duplicate. The indemnity bond guarantees that if the original stock certificate is recovered, the holder will send it to the surety company.

LOST POLICY RECEIPT life insurance company form to be signed by a policyholder who wishes to surrender a policy that has been lost. The signed receipt then becomes evidence that the policy is no longer in force. This protects the insurance company if a policyholder claims that the policy was never surrendered.

LOST POLICY RELEASE *see* LOST POLICY RECEIPT.

LUMP SUM in life insurance, single payment instead of a series of installments. *See also* LUMP SUM DISTRIBUTION.

LUMP SUM DISTRIBUTION death benefit option in which a beneficiary of a life insurance policy receives the death benefit as a single sum payment instead of installments.

LUMP SUM REFUND ANNUITY *see* CASH REFUND ANNUITY (LUMP SUM REFUND ANNUITY).

M

MACHINERY MALFUNCTION (BREAKDOWN) INSURANCE
see BOILER AND MACHINERY INSURANCE.

MAIL ORDER INSURANCE insurance marketed through advertising
in such media as newspapers, magazines, television, and radio. The
mail is used to collect the application and distribute the policy. An
insurance agent is not involved in the process. *See also* DIRECT
RESPONSE MARKETING (DIRECT SELLING SYSTEM).

MAINTAINING A NUISANCE *see* ATTRACTIVE NUISANCE.

MAINTENANCE BOND legal instrument posted by a contractor or
craftsman to guarantee that completed work is free of flaws and will
perform its intended function for a specified period of time.

MAJOR MEDICAL INSURANCE coverage in excess of that provided
by a basic hospital medical insurance plan. After the limits of coverage have been exhausted under a basic plan, major medical then covers medical expenses relating to room and board; physician fees;
miscellaneous expenses such as bandages, operating room expenses,
drugs, X-ray, and fluoroscopy. There may be a lifetime limit. For
example, if the lifetime limit is $500,000 and an insured uses
$100,000 of coverage in a given year, the lifetime limit would be
reduced to $400,000. *See* also GROUP HEALTH INSURANCE: HEALTH
INSURANCE; HEALTH MAINTENANCE ORGANIZATION (HMO).

MALICIOUS MISCHIEF intentional damage or destruction of another
person or business's property. Insurance can be purchased by the owner
of the property to protect against this exposure. *See also* HOMEOWNERS
INSURANCE POLICY; PERSONAL AUTOMOBILE POLICY (PAP); COMMERCIAL
PACKAGE POLICY; VANDALISM AND MALICIOUS MISCHIEF INSURANCE.

MALINGERING effort by an individual to continue to receive disability income benefits by faking a continuing sickness or injury.

MALPRACTICE LIABILITY INSURANCE professional liability
coverage for a practitioner in a given field of expertise. Coverage
takes the form of defending the practitioner against liability suits
whether or not with foundation, and paying on behalf of the insured,
court awarded damages up to the limits of the policy. *See also* PRO-
FESSIONAL LIABILITY INSURANCE.

MANAGED CARE plan to control employer's health care cost through
the introduction of practice guidelines or protocols for health care
providers, and to improve the methods used by employers and employees to select health care providers. The goal of the plan is to create a
financial accounting system in order to manage the impact of medical
treatment on the patient's clinical response and quality of life. Once

such a system is created, the employer and the employee will be better able to judge which health provider is more effective and efficient.

MANAGED CARE ORGANIZATION (MCO) entity that offers a MANAGED CARE plan for WORKERS COMPENSATION BENEFITS that joins a provider network with the following parts: case management personnel, medical bill review personnel, internal dispute resolution vehicle, written guidelines for treatment of cases, quality assurance program, and a utilization review committee. This mechanism executes in the following manner:

1. *Case management personnel*—monitors treatment of an injured employee to make sure the employee recovers from illness and returns to work in a timely fashion.
2. *Guidelines for treatment of cases*—written criteria for determining when an illness requires medical treatment, scope of the medical treatment, and acceptable disability time periods.
3. *Internal dispute resolution vehicle*—provides written instructions for procedures to resolve conflicts in issues between health providers and fee payers regarding the size of medical fees charged, type and scope of medical treatment, and overutilization of medical facilities.
4. *Utilization review committee*—provides guidelines for inpatient hospital care, outpatient care, and physician care.

MANAGED COMPETITION government-supervised health care system with economic incentives for providers and consumers.

MANAGEMENT FEE administration charge by a manager for overseeing a portfolio of asset(s).

MANAGER *see* AGENCY MANAGER.

MANAGING PHYSICIAN, HMO *see* HEALTH MAINTENANCE ORGANIZATION (HMO).

MANDATORY SECURITIES VALUATION RESERVE (MSVR) liability RESERVE required to be maintained by the NATIONAL ASSOCIATION OF INSURANCE COMMISSIONERS (NAIC) prior to 1992 for fluctuations in the values of investments in securities. Realized and unrealized capital gains and losses involving invested securities were credited and debited respectively to the MSVR. Beginning in 1992, the MSVR was discontinued, and ending December 31, 1991, MSVR was transferred into the ASSET VALUATION RESERVE.

M&C *see* MANUFACTURERS AND CONTRACTORS LIABILITY INSURANCE.

MANIFESTATION INJURY THEORY approach that maintains injury or sickness begins when it is first detected by an obvious appearance. This argument is used in determining if liability insurance is afforded in a particular bodily injury case.

MANUAL publication stipulating underwriting rules applicable for a given line of insurance, classifications of exposures within that line of insurance, and premium rates per classification. For example, a life insurance manual shows the PREMIUM MODE factor, POLICY FEE, PREMIUMS, and values per $1000 of coverage, to include CASH VALUE, PAID-UP INSURANCE and EXTENDED TERM INSURANCE, available at the end of each policy year. *See also* MANUAL RATE.

MANUAL RATE published cost per unit of insurance, usually the standard rate charged for a standard risk. For example, one company's manual yearly rate per $1000 of life insurance for a given policy for a male age 26 is $12.02. *See also* RATE MAKING.

MANUFACTURERS AND CONTRACTORS LIABILITY INSURANCE coverage for liability exposures that result from manufacturing and/or contracting operations in process on a manufacturer's premises (all locations of ongoing operations) or, in the case of the contractor, off-premises operation at a construction site. Excluded are activities of independent contractors, damage to property by explosion, collapse, and underground property damage. Additional coverages apply to the acts of the insured's employees when constructing new structures, demolishing old structures, and changing the size and/or location of existing structures.

MANUFACTURERS OUTPUT INSURANCE coverage for personal property of a manufacturer on an ALL RISKS basis when that property is off the manufacturer's premises.

MANUFACTURING INSURANCE *see* BUSINESS INCOME COVERAGE FORM.

MANUSCRIPT INSURANCE coverage tailored to the particular requirements of an insured, when a *standard policy* cannot be used to provide coverage for real or personal property. A manuscript policy is often written on site by an agent (most often representing a large *brokerage house*) to reflect the special conditions and provisions.

MAP diagram used in property insurance to locate the geographical area in which risks reside. Maps are also used to reveal areas of high concentration of insured risks and their potential impact on an insurance company should a catastrophe occur, such as a hurricane.

MARGIN fluctuation in claims arising from ADVERSE SELECTION.

MARINE INSURANCE coverage for goods in transit and the vehicles of transportation on waterways, land, and air. *See also* INLAND MARINE INSURANCE (TRANSPORTATION INSURANCE): BUSINESS RISKS; INSTRUMENTALITIES OF TRANSPORTATION INSURANCE; NATIONWIDE MARINE DEFINITION; OCEAN MARINE INSURANCE.

MARINE INSURANCE CERTIFICATE special policy blank issued by an insured for individual shipments or other purposes under an OPEN POLICY. The open policy allows an insured to buy protection for all marine business for an indefinite period. When required to show evidence of insurance for a particular shipment, or to protect the cargo or ship of a client, the insured may issue a certificate of insurance backed by his or her own overriding open policy.

MARINE INSURANCE OFFICERS PROTECTIVE *see* OFFICERS PROTECTIVE MARINE INSURANCE.

MARITAL DEDUCTION provision in the Federal Tax Code for favorable treatment of an estate. Under the UNLIMITED MARITAL DEDUCTION no federal estate tax is imposed on qualified transfers between a husband and wife. Under the QUALIFIED TERMINABLE INTEREST PROPERTY (Q TIP) TRUST all income from assets in trust is paid at least annually for the life of the spouse. *See also* ESTATE PLANNING.

MARITAL TRUST TRUST that qualifies assets under the MARITAL DEDUCTION provision in the Federal Tax Code for favorable treatment of an estate. The surviving spouse has the full power to use the assets of the trust as well as to transfer assets to any heirs. Upon the death of the surviving spouse, any assets in the trust are subject to FEDERAL ESTATE TAX. *See also* BYPASS TRUST; ESTATE PLANNING DISTRIBUTION; GIFT IN TRUST.

MARKET ASSISTANCE PLANS (MAPs) voluntary state insurance programs that aid small businesses in acquiring insurance coverages when there are impediments to obtaining the coverage.

MARKETING creation of a demand for a company's products, its distribution, and services for customers who purchase that product. Actuarial research and development, underwriting efficiency, and claim payment promptness is of little value if no one is willing to purchase insurance products. *Agency and marketing departments* are the focus of all sales activity within an insurance company, and touch every aspect of a company by generating (1) premium income for securities, real estate, and mortgage investments; (2) sales for review by the underwriting department and their issuance by policyholder services; (3) need for data storage and retrieval by the company's data processing center; (4) legal analysis and decisions by the law department; and (5) need for corporate planning.

MARKETING REPRESENTATIVE *see* SPECIAL AGENT.

MARKET RISK investment risk associated with the psychology of the market in that emotions affect the price of a company's stock that, in most instances, has nothing to do with the current or potential earnings per share of that company.

MARKET TIMING investment strategy that advocates the transfer of amounts from one category of investment to another category according to a perception of how each of these categories of investments will perform relative to other categories of investments at a stipulated point in time. This strategy may be applied by purchasers of the VARIABLE DOLLAR ANNUITY or VARIABLE LIFE INSURANCE, both of which have provisions for the transfer of sums between stock, bond, and real estate accounts.

MARKET VALUE price a willing buyer will pay a willing seller for an asset on the open market. The value is what the last person is willing to pay for the asset. *See* MARKET VALUE V. ACTUAL CASH VALUE.

MARKET VALUE ADJUSTMENT (MVA) increase or decrease in the SURRENDER CHARGE of the LIFE INSURANCE policy or annuity contract depending on the current financial markets. The CASH VALUE is adjusted upward if the policy interest rate is greater than the current interest rate on new money and thus, if interest rates decline after the insurance policy or annuity contract purchase date, the surrender charge becomes less than that exhibited. Conversely, the cash value is adjusted downward if the policy interest rate is less than the current interest rate on new money and thus, if interest rates rise after the insurance policy or annuity contract purchase date, the surrender charge becomes greater than that exhibited.

MARKET VALUE CLAUSE provision of property insurance that establishes the amount for which an insured must be reimbursed for damaged or destroyed property according to the price a willing buyer would pay for the property purchased from a willing seller, as opposed to the ACTUAL CASH VALUE of the damaged or destroyed property. *See also* MARKET VALUE V. ACTUAL CASH VALUE.

MARKET VALUE v. ACTUAL CASH VALUE value of property as established by the price a willing buyer would pay for property purchased from a willing seller, compared with the replacement cost of damaged or destroyed property minus depreciation and obsolescence. Usually, replacement cost basis is used in property insurance to indemnify an insured for damaged or destroyed property. *See also* MARKET VALUE CLAUSE.

MASS MARKETING *see* MASS MERCHANDISING.

MASS MERCHANDISING coverage for a group of individuals under one policy. Usually, members belong to a particular company, union, or trade association. In a CONTRIBUTORY plan a lump sum premium is paid by the group to the insurance company using salary deductions.

MASS UNDERWRITING evaluation of the demographic characteristics of the entire group (such as age, sex, MORBIDITY, MORTALITY), as opposed to the evaluation of individuals in that group. *See also* MASS MERCHANDISING.

MASTER CONTRACT *see* MASTER POLICY.

MASTER POLICY single contract coverage on a group basis issued to an employer. Group members receive certificates as evidence of membership summarizing benefits provided. *See also* GROUP HEALTH INSURANCE; GROUP LIFE INSURANCE.

MASTER-SERVANT RULE assumption that an employer is liable for negligent acts or omissions of employees that result in bodily injury and/or property damage to third parties if those acts are in the course of employment.

MATCHING requiring assets and liabilities of an insurance company to go up or down together on a proportional basis. The duration of the asset and liability should be approximately the same. For example, an insurance policy of 12 months in duration should be identified with an asset that matures in 12 months. As interest rates go up, thereby requiring the insurance company to pay a higher return to its policyholders, the interest earned on investments should go up on a proportionate basis.

MATCHED SET OR PAIR INSURANCE *see* SET CLAUSE (PAIR OR SET CLAUSE).

MATERIAL BOND BOND issued to a contractor guaranteeing that the supplier (individual posting the bond) will provide all of the necessary materials for the satisfactory completion of the contracted project.

MATERIAL FACT *see* MATERIAL MISREPRESENTATION.

MATERIAL MISREPRESENTATION falsification of a material fact in such a manner that, had the insurance company known the truth, it would not have insured the risk. A material misrepresentation gives an insurance company grounds to rescind a contract. *See also* CONCEALMENT.

MATURED describing the time of payment of FACE AMOUNT (FACE OF POLICY) upon the death of the INSURED, or when the cash value in an ENDOWMENT INSURANCE policy equals the face amount.

MATURED ENDOWMENT endowment period of time, in life insurance, at which the face amount of the policy is payable to the insured.

MATURITY AT AGE 100 under ORDINARY LIFE INSURANCE, accumulated cash value equals FACE AMOUNT (FACE OF POLICY) when the INSURED reaches age 100.

MATURITY DATE time at which life insurance death proceeds or endowments are paid, either at the death of an insured or at the end of the endowment period.

MATURITY FUNDING CONTRACT type of PENSION PLAN under which a RETIREMENT ANNUITY is purchased at the time of retirement of the employee, funded by means of a single premium payment made to the insurance company.

MATURITY VALUE specified amount received by an insured at the end of an endowment period (usually the face amount of the endowment policy), or by the owner of an ordinary life policy (usually the individual insured) who lives to a given age.

MAXIMUM total amount of insurance coverage available for an INSURED.

MAXIMUM BENEFIT *see* BENEFIT FORMULA; COINSURANCE.

MAXIMUM DEDUCTIBLE CONTRIBUTION limit allowed by law on employee salary reduction plans. Many pension plans, as well as the popular *401 (k) plan,* allow employees to set aside pre-tax dollars in a company-sponsored retirement account, often matched by a company contribution. But the amount contributed by the employee is regulated by law. For example, the maximum annual contribution for the 401 (k) plan, which was $30,000 per year in 1986, was reduced to $7000 by the TAX REFORM ACT OF 1986. In 2007, under the ECONOMIC GROWTH AND TAX RELIEF RECONCILIATION ACT OF 2001, the maximum was $15,500 in salary deferral plus a "catch-up" deferral of $5000 for those age 50+.

MAXIMUM FAMILY BENEFIT *see* COORDINATION OF BENEFITS; GROUP HEALTH INSURANCE.

MAXIMUM FORESEEABLE LOSS (MFL) worst case scenario under which an estimate is made of the maximum dollar amount that can be lost if a catastrophe occurs such as a hurricane or firestorm.

MAXIMUM POSSIBLE LOSS *see* MAXIMUM FORESEEABLE LOSS (MFL).

MAXIMUM PROBABLE LOSS (MPL) estimate of maximum dollar value that can be lost under realistic situations. For example, a fire or other peril occurs, but a sprinkler system works and a fire department responds in good order.

MAXI TAIL (FULL TAIL) extended reporting period, for an unlimited length of time, during which claims may be made after a CLAIMS MADE BASIS LIABILITY COVERAGE policy has expired. *See also* INCURRED BUT NOT REPORTED LOSSES (IBNR); LONG-TAIL LIABILITY.

McCARRAN-FERGUSON ACT (PUBLIC LAW 15) 1945 federal legislation in which the Congress declared that the states may continue to regulate the insurance industry. Nevertheless, in recent years Congress has expanded the federal government's insurance activities into *flood insurance,* FEDERAL CROP INSURANCE, and *riot and civil commotion insurance. See also* SOUTH-EASTERN UNDERWRITERS ASSOCIATION (SEUA) CASE.

MEAN *see* EXPECTED LOSS.

MEAN RESERVE INITIAL RESERVE plus the TERMINAL RESERVE divided by two for any year of valuation.

MEANS TEST principle that holds that SOCIAL INSURANCE programs should be for the benefit of lower socioeconomic segments of society and not for that segment of society that does not require financial assistance.

MEASUREMENT *see* LOSS DEVELOPMENT; LOSS FREQUENCY METHOD; LOSS TRENDS.

MEDIAN statistical term indicating the central value of a frequency distribution, such that smaller and greater values than this central value occur at an equal rate. For example, given the numbers 1, 7, 10, 12, 14, 17, 19, 20, and 22, the median is 14.

MEDIATION situation in which parties agree to take part in a structured settlement negotiation through the guidance of a neutral expert. By participating in this process, the parties do not agree that they will actually settle and the mediator does not have the authority to impose such a settlement. The mediation process may be terminated at any time without cause by either party. The advantage of this process includes the claimant's ability to have quick settlements, thereby enabling the claimant to pay medical bills and to replace lost wages.

MEDICAID assistance program for the financially needy. Medicaid, also referred to as *Title XIX* of the Social Security Act, was enacted in 1965 at the same time as MEDICARE. It is a joint federal-state program that provides medical assistance for the aged, blind, and disabled, and families with dependent children who cannot pay for such assistance themselves. Benefits vary widely among the states.

MEDICAID QUALIFYING TRUST IRREVOCABLE LIVING TRUST (rights to make any changes are forfeited by the GRANTOR permanently) in which the grantor forfeits control of all assets placed in the trust. However, the grantor retains the right to all income produced by the assets in the trust, and the assets can be distributed to beneficiaries at the grantor's death. The objective of this trust is to protect the assets of the grantor against depletion to pay the costs of LONG-TERM CARE or against dissipation by the grantor's heirs during the grantor's lifetime.

MEDICAL *see* MEDICAL EXAMINATION.

MEDICAL EXAMINATION physical checkup required of applicants for life and/or health insurance to ascertain if they meet a company's underwriting standards or should be classified as substandard or uninsurable. Physicals are administered by medical personnel selected by the insurance company at its expense. Physicals may also be used to determine extent of disability for insurance purposes. *See also* MEDICAL EXAMINER.

MEDICAL EXAMINER physician who conducts physicals of applicants for life and/or health insurance. This physician is selected by the insurance company at its expense. *See also* MEDICAL EXAMINATION.

MEDICAL EXPENSE BENEFITS *see* COORDINATION OF BENEFITS; GROUP HEALTH INSURANCE; HEALTH INSURANCE CONTRACT; HEALTH MAINTENANCE ORGANIZATION (HMO); MAJOR MEDICAL INSURANCE.

MEDICAL EXPENSE INSURANCE *see* COORDINATION OF BENEFITS; GROUP HEALTH INSURANCE; HEALTH INSURANCE CONTRACT; HEALTH MAINTENANCE ORGANIZATION (HMO).

MEDICAL INFORMATION BUREAU (MIB) central computerized facility that keeps on file the health history of the applicants for life and health insurance with member MIB companies. For example, the health record of an applicant for insurance with a member MIB company in Atlanta, Georgia, is available to another member MIB company in Shreveport, Louisiana. The MIB was organized to guard against fraud by applicants.

MEDICAL PAYMENTS INSURANCE provision of liability policies and the liability sections of *package insurance* policies, such as the PERSONAL AUTOMOBILE POLICY (PAP), that pay medical expenses without regard to fault. The insured does not admit liability for bodily injury to another party, nor does an injured party forfeit the right to sue the insured.

MEDICAL PAYMENTS TO OTHERS INSURANCE *see* HOMEOWNERS INSURANCE POLICY—SECTION II (LIABILITY COVERAGE).

MEDICAL POWER OF ATTORNEY legal instrument that authorizes a person to be informed about someone's medical condition and make medical decisions on that person's behalf. *See* POWER OF ATTORNEY.

MEDICAL SAVINGS ACCOUNTS (MSAs) savings accounts that have tax advantages combined with HEALTH INSURANCE plans for the benefit of the employee. Both the employee and the employer are permitted to contribute to the MSA. The contributions can be directed to pay the deductible under the health insurance plan and/or the medical expenses not covered by the health insurance plan. Funds not spent are allowed to accumulate in the MSA on a continuous basis. When the employee reaches retirement age, the accumulated funds may be allocated to the employee's retirement income. The MSA differs from a FLEXIBLE SPENDING ACCOUNT (FSA) in one very important respect: Under an MSA, funds not used for current health care expenses belong to the employee. Under an FSA, funds not under the current health care expenses belong to the employer.

MEDICAL SPENDING ACCOUNT type of FLEXIBLE SPENDING ACCOUNT. *See also* FLEXIBLE SPENDING ACCOUNT—HEALTH CARE/DEPENDENT CARE EXPENSES.

MEDICARE program enacted in 1965 under Title XVIII of the Social Security Amendments of 1965 to provide medical benefits to those 65 and older. The program has four parts in 2007:
1. *Part A, Hospital Insurance,* contributes to the payment of inpatient hospital, skilled nursing expenses, hospice, and other ancillary expenses. The DEDUCTIBLE is $992 for 60 or less days in a benefit period. For days 61–90, the deductible is $248 per day, and for more than 90 days, the deductible is $496 per day up to the lifetime maximum days. No premium is paid if the BENEFICIARY has at least 40 quarters of Medicare covered employment.
2. *Part B, Medical Insurance,* provides coverage for medical services that Part A does not cover for a premium and subject to a deductible ($93.50 per month standard premium and a deductible of $131 per

benefit payment in 2007). Coverage includes ambulance services, ambulatory surgery center, blood, bone mass measurement, cardiovascular screenings, limited chiropractic services, clinical laboratory services, clinical trials, colorectal cancer screenings, diabetes screenings, diabetic supplies, doctor services, durable medical equipment, emergency room services, limited eyeglasses, flu shots, foot exams and treatment, glaucoma tests, hearing and balance exam, Hepatitis B shots, home health services, kidney dialysis services and supplies, mammograms, medical nutrition therapy services, outpatient mental health care, occupational therapy, outpatient hospital services, outpatient medical and surgical services and supplies, pap test and pelvic exam, one-time physical exam within the first six months, physical therapy, pneumococcal shot, practitioner services, limited prescriptions (injectable drugs), prostate cancer screenings, prosthetic/orthotic items, second surgical opinions, smoking cessation, speech-language pathology services, surgical dressings, telemedicine, tests (X-rays, MRIs, CT scans, EKGs, and other diagnostic tests), transplant services, and urgently needed care (nonmedical emergency illness or injury). The initial enrollment period for Medicare Part B begins three months before age 65 and continues for the next seven months. If enrollment is not effected in this time period, there is a waiting time until the general enrollment period from January 1 through March 31 every year. Coverage then begins the following July 1.

3. *Part C, Medicare Advantage,* provides for individuals with Part A and Part B coverage to receive all of their health care coverage through a single health care provider. *See also* MEDICARE PLUS CHOICE (MEDICARE PART C).

4. *Part D, Prescription Drug Insurance*, contributes to the payment of medication/prescription expenses as prescribed by a physician. Coverage added for drugs by joining a Medicare Prescription Drug Plan through private insurance companies. A separate monthly premium (varies by plan) is required. Each plan must cover at least two drugs in all of the classes of drugs that are the most commonly prescribed. For those people covered under Medicare A, coinsurance or copayment is required and a yearly deductible may be in force.

Retired workers qualified to receive Social Security benefits, and their dependents, also qualify for the hospital insurance portion. The program is paid for by payroll taxes on employees and covered workers. Parts B, C, and D insurance provides additional coverage on a voluntary basis for physician services. The Prescription Drug Plans are optional and can be added by paying an additional premium. Those enrolled in the program pay a monthly premium. Coverage is also available to persons younger than 65 who are disabled and have received Social Security disability benefits for 24 consecutive months.

MEDICARE ADVANTAGE federal government health insurance program in which the government pays sums to private health plans in order to provide health expense benefits to some MEDICARE participants. These plans are part of Medicare and often referred to as Part C providing coverage for Part A (hospital) and Part B (medical) for all medically necessary expenses. Usually these plans provide services through a network of physicians and hospitals requiring the participant to use a network affiliation for covered medical expenses. These plans include PREFERRED PROVIDER ORGANIZATION (PPO); HEALTH MAINTENANCE ORGANIZATION (HMO); FEE FOR SERVICE PLAN; and MEDICARE MEDICAL SAVINGS ACCOUNT.

MEDICARE GAP INSURANCE *see* MEDICARE; MEDICARE INSURANCE.

MEDICARE MEDICAL SAVINGS ACCOUNT combination of MEDICAL SAVINGS ACCOUNTS (MSA) with high-deductible HEALTH INSURANCE CONTRACTS. This combination plan is part of MEDICARE ADVANTAGE federal government insurance program. Under this MSA, the federal government pays private health plans to provide health insurance coverage for MEDICARE participants. A portion of the sum paid by the federal government on behalf of the Medicare participant goes into that participant's special savings account to pay medical expenses. All sums not used are carried forward into future years. Funds paid into the participant's account are tax-free and the investment earnings also accumulate on a tax-free basis provided expenditures are for specific medical expenses.

MEDICARE SUPPLEMENTARY INSURANCE *see* MEDIGAP INSURANCE.

MEDICARE SUPPLEMENT INSURANCE two basic kinds of policies sold by health insurance companies: (1) MEDIGAP INSURANCE (MEDICARE SUPPLEMENTARY INSURANCE); and (2) MEDICARE WRAP-AROUND INSURANCE.

MEDICARE WRAPAROUND INSURANCE insurance that acts as a supplement to MEDICARE in that it will pay the DEDUCTIBLES and COINSURANCE sums that the Medicare recipient is responsible for paying. In addition, some policies pay amounts for hospital and nursing home expenses after the Medicare limits have been reached.

MEDIGAP INSURANCE (MEDICARE SUPPLEMENTARY INSURANCE) policy designed to act as a supplement to Medicare. The supplementation is in the form of additional benefits to that provided by Medicare. The additional benefits are in the form of payment for medical expenses incurred but excluded by Medicare's deductibles, by limitations on approval medical charges, by limitations on length and type of care in nursing facilities, and by limitations imposed by various cost-sharing requirements. Most of these policies pay substantially less than 100% of the expenses not covered under Medicare. Insurance companies that sell Medigap policies are required by law to have an open enrollment period of six months for those individuals who first enroll in Medicare Part B at age 65 or older. Insurance companies can, however, exclude preexisting conditions from the data of initial coverage, but for no more than six months. Insurance companies are restricted by the National Association of Insurance Commissioners to the selling of 10 standard Medigap insurance policies. Each policy is mandated to provide a basic amount of benefits.

MEMBER person covered by insurance under a BLUE CROSS or BLUE SHIELD plan.

MEMORANDUM CLAUSE provision in *ocean marine cargo* policies to limit an insurance company's liability for partial losses; the company has liability only for losses that exceed a stipulated PERCENTAGE of the value of the cargo.

MENTAL HEALTH PARITY ACT OF 1996 act that prohibits insurance companies, group health plans, and HEALTH MAINTENANCE ORGANIZATIONS from establishing lifetime limits or annual limits on mental health coverage that are lower than the limits on medical coverage. These plans that do not have limits on medical coverage cannot establish limits for mental health coverage. Under this act, the employer is not required to offer mental health or substance abuse benefits. This act applies to those companies with at least 50 employees and became effective for the plan year beginning on or after January 1, 1998.

MERCANTILE OPEN-STOCK BURGLARY INSURANCE coverage for damage or destruction of property due to a crime, and property lost due to a burglary, whether successful or attempted. An endorsement provides coverage for robbery and theft of merchandise. Coverage is provided for merchandise, equipment, fixtures, furniture left in the open on the business premises. There is a coinsurance basis of 40 to 80%. This policy has generally been replaced by current COMMERCIAL CRIME COVERAGE FORMS.

MERCANTILE ROBBERY INSURANCE coverage available under two forms for actual or attempted robbery of money, securities or other property. Under the *First Form* the policy covers if the robbery is committed on the premises of the business. The *Second Form* covers if the robbery is committed against a messenger of the business off its premises. An endorsement can provide coverage if employees have property of the business in their custody at home, and this property is lost through robbery or burglary. This policy has generally been replaced by current COMMERCIAL CRIME COVERAGE FORMS.

MERCANTILE SAFE BURGLARY INSURANCE coverage in the event a safe of a business is forceably entered, either on or off the premises, and property is stolen from the safe. Also covered is damage to the premises during actual or attempted burglary. Premium rates can be reduced through precautions such as burglar alarms, guards, and other protective measures. There is no coinsurance or deductible requirement. This policy has generally been replaced by current COMMERCIAL CRIME COVERAGE FORMS.

MERCHANT MARINE ACT *see* JONES ACT.

MERGER, CONSOLIDATION OR REORGANIZATION OF PLAN SPONSOR change in the nature of an employer or other organization that sponsors a *qualified pension plan.* A qualified plan must guarantee vested benefits due to participants in the event of a merger, acquisition, or change in employer status. For example, the value of benefits cannot be reduced as the result of a merger.

MERIT RATE *see* MERIT RATING.

MERIT RATING system of charges to an insured that fluctuates according to the loss experience of that insured. This is a form of EXPERIENCE RATING. *See also* PROSPECTIVE RATING; RETROSPECTIVE RATING.

MESSENGER INSURANCE *see* MESSENGER ROBBERY INSURANCE.

MESSENGER ROBBERY INSURANCE coverage for an insured who is authorized to convey property such as money, securities, and other valuables, away from a business's premises.

MEXICO INSURANCE coverage through an endorsement to the PERSONAL AUTOMOBILE POLICY (PAP) to extend its protection against accidents within a 25 mile radius of the U.S. border. This coverage is excess over liability insurance with a licensed Mexican insurance company. The purchase of Mexican liability insurance is a prerequisite to the extended coverage of PAP.

MFL *see* MAXIMUM FORESEEABLE LOSS.

MIB *see* MEDICAL INFORMATION BUREAU.

MIDI TAIL automatically extended reporting period of five years, during which claims may be made after a CLAIMS MADE BASIS LIABILITY COVERAGE policy has expired, provided these claims are the result of an event that took place within 60 days of the termination of the policy. *See also* INCURRED BUT NOT REPORTED LOSSES (IBNR); LONG-TAIL LIABILITY.

MILITARY SERVICE EXCLUSION clause common to life and health insurance policies issued during wartime that exclude benefits for military service-connected perils of death, disability, illness, accident, or sickness. This clause is usually canceled with the declaration of peace.

MILLION DOLLAR ROUND TABLE (MDRT) association of life insurance agents who meet minimum life insurance sales standards predetermined each year by the organization. Membership is a primary goal of professional life insurance agents, as it denotes personal sales achievement.

MINIMUM AMOUNT POLICY *see* MINIMUM BENEFIT.

MINIMUM BENEFIT smallest face amount of life insurance that an insurance company will write on any one person.

MINIMUM CONTINUATION PREMIUM smallest PREMIUM necessary to keep the life insurance policy in force regardless of the current mortality, interest, and expense experience of the insurance company. This type of premium is usually associated with UNIVERSAL LIFE INSURANCE.

MINIMUM CONTRIBUTION *see* MINIMUM PREMIUM PLAN.

MINIMUM COVERAGE REQUIREMENT minimum number of employees and participation percentage for a PENSION PLAN. Can be a Qualified Pension Plan and thus subject to tax benefits. *See also* DISCRETIONARY AUTHORITY.

MINIMUM DEPOSIT INSURANCE *see* FINAL INSURANCE (MINIMUM DEPOSIT INSURANCE).

MINIMUM DEPOSIT RESCUE technique designed to permit the exchange of a life insurance policy that has an outstanding loan charged against it for another life insurance policy on a tax-free basis. The procedure is for the insurer to issue a new policy subject to a loan in the amount equal to the outstanding loan on the old policy. If the new policy so issued is of the form of a FLEXIBLE PREMIUM policy such as UNIVERSAL LIFE, the loan from the old policy can be replaced by the new policy assuming the loan.

MINIMUM DEPOSIT WHOLE LIFE INSURANCE ORDINARY LIFE INSURANCE that generates a first year cash value from the payment of the first year premium. Using this cash value, loans could be made to finance premiums due in the future, with the interest deductible for tax purposes under specified IRS rules. However, the 1986 Tax Code revision appears to have canceled this arrangement.

MINIMUM DISTRIBUTION REQUIREMENTS AND TAXES FROM SECTION 401(a), 403(a), 403 RETIREMENT PLAN OR IRA requirement that income payments must begin from tax-deferred saving programs by April 1 of the calendar year after the calendar year in which the plan participant becomes age 70½ or retires.

MINIMUM GROUP smallest number of individuals for which an insurance company will issue a policy. A minimum number is required because the fixed expenses of placing a policy on the books exist regardless of the size of a group.

MINIMUM PREMIUM DEPOSIT PLAN *see* MINIMUM DEPOSIT WHOLE LIFE INSURANCE.

MINIMUM PREMIUM PLAN smallest acceptable premium for which an insurance company will write a policy. This minimum charge is necessary to cover fixed expenses in placing the policy on the books.

MINIMUM STANDARDS lowest acceptable criteria that a risk must meet in order to be insurable. For example, life insurance companies require an applicant for individual (nongroup) coverages to be free of terminal illness.

MINI TAIL automatically extended reporting period of 60 days, during which claims may be made after a CLAIMS MADE BASIS LIABILITY COVERAGE policy has expired. *See also* INCURRED BUT NOT REPORTED LOSSES (IBNR); LONG-TAIL LIABILITY.

MINOR'S TRUST (2503(c)) TRUST whereby asset management is provided until a child reaches the age of majority. Upon reaching majority, the child has full use and control over the assets. The GRANTOR of the trust cannot receive any income from the assets held in the trust. All undistributed income is taxed at trust rates, which are low. The grantor, through this type of trust, is able to control the time at which the minor has access to the assets given to him or her by the grantor (who wishes to take advantage of the annual GIFT TAX exclusion). *See also* ESTATE PLANNING DISTRIBUTION; GIFT IN TRUST.

MISCELLANEOUS EXPENSES hospital charges in addition to room and board. Miscellaneous expenses are covered under a *basic hospital plan,* with the limits of coverage expressed either as a multiple of the daily hospital benefit for room and board or as a flat dollar amount. Expenses included in the coverage are X-rays, drugs, bandages, operating room expenses, and ambulance services. *See also* GROUP HEALTH INSURANCE; HEALTH INSURANCE; HEALTH MAINTENANCE ORGANIZATION (HMO).

MISCELLANEOUS VEHICLES COVERAGE endorsement to the PERSONAL AUTOMOBILE POLICY (PAP) that insures other motorized vehicles such as golf carts and motorcycles owned by a policyholder.

MISREPRESENTATION (FALSE PRETENSE) intent to defraud. An insured is required to answer truthfully all questions on the application. The insurance company can void a contract if it would not have issued a policy had it known the true facts. For example, on a PERSONAL AUTOMOBILE POLICY application, if the insured answers that the car is used only for pleasure (when in fact it is used in stock car races), the insurance company can void the policy.

MISSTATEMENT OF AGE falsification of birth date by an applicant for a life or health insurance policy. If the company discovers that the wrong age was given, the coverage will be adjusted to reflect the correct age according to the premiums paid in.

MISSTATEMENT OF AGE OR SEX CLAUSE *see* MISSTATEMENT OF AGE.

MIXED AGENCY AGENCY that sells INSURANCE POLICIES from both a STOCK INSURANCE COMPANY and a MUTUAL INSURANCE COMPANY.

MIXED INSURANCE COMPANY one that combines the two forms of ownership, stock and mutual. A STOCK INSURANCE COMPANY is owned by stockholders, whereas a MUTUAL INSURANCE COMPANY is owned by its policyholders. A mixed company is owned in part by stockholders and in part by policyholders. Most mixed companies issue *participating* and *nonparticipating* policies.

MIXED PERILS several different types of perils covered under one policy. *See also* HOMEOWNERS INSURANCE POLICY; PERSONAL AUTOMOBILE POLICY (PAP); COMMERCIAL PACKAGE POLICY (CPP).

MOBILE EQUIPMENT INSURANCE *see* CONTRACTORS EQUIPMENT FLOATER.

MOBILE HOME INSURANCE coverage similar to a HOMEOWNERS INSURANCE POLICY in that Section I covers property exposure and Section II covers liability exposure.
1. *Section I (property)* Coverage A—structural coverage of the mobile home; Coverage B—unscheduled personal property coverage; Coverage C—additions to the structure of the mobile home to include equipment; Coverage D—additional living expense.
2. *Section II (liability)* Coverage E—liability coverage for personal acts and/or omissions; Coverage F—medical payments to others.

MODE frequency of premium payment; for example annually, semiannually, quarterly, or monthly.

MODEL SURPLUS LINES LAW law that requires that all SURPLUS LINES insurance companies maintain a minimum specified amount of CAPITAL and SURPLUS; also requires that ALIEN INSURERS maintain a trust fund on location in the United States.

MODEM device that connects a computer to a telephone line. This device permits the computer to communicate with other computers through the telephone system.

MODE OF ENTRY
1. method of gaining illegal entry to perform a criminal act. If a policyholder makes a claim for loss of jewelry or rugs under a homeowners policy, or if a business owner makes a claim for damage caused by vandals, the insurer must establish how the vandal or burglar gained entry. The mode of entry is important both (a) to determine that someone did actually enter the premises and (b) to establish that the policyholder was not unduly negligent.
2. path by which a toxic substance enters the human body, such as by inhalation, injection, ingestion, or absorption.

MODIFICATION OF CONTRACT adaptation of a standard insurance contract for special needs. Standard forms do not cover all needs but they can be adapted by an underwriter, broker, or an insurance company at the request of an insured. Risk managers may request many modifications in property and casualty coverage to meet the needs they have diagnosed for their corporations. Some risk managers even write their own contracts. Many insurers write their own contracts as well rather than use forms designed by a RATING BUREAU.

MODIFICATION RATING (also known as MERIT RATING) method of setting property insurance rates by modifying or adjusting the MANUAL RATE for various classifications of risks. Modifications may be based on past or anticipated loss experience. The three types of modification rating are EXPERIENCE RATING, RETROSPECTIVE RATING, and SCHEDULE RATING.

MODIFIED CASH REFUND ANNUITY form of CASH REFUND ANNUITY used by contributory pension or employee benefit plans. When employee participants die before receiving all of their contributions in the form of retirement benefits, this type of annuity guarantees to repay the remainder of those contributions, with interest, to the beneficiaries.

MODIFIED ENDOWMENT CONTRACT type of LIFE INSURANCE policy whereby the premiums are greater than that required to pay seven annual premiums for an ORDINARY LIFE INSURANCE policy. (This is better known as the *seven-pay test*.) This test is used in an effort to eliminate the dumping of large sums of money into LIMITED PAYMENT LIFE INSURANCE in order to gain a tax advantage investment. Prior to the passage of legislation in 1988, the policy owner could make withdrawals from the CASH SURRENDER VALUE on a tax-free basis. If the policy does not pass the seven-pay test, withdrawals from the cash value are taxed as ordinary income plus a 10% surcharge.

MODIFIED LIFE INSURANCE ORDINARY LIFE INSURANCE under which premiums are calculated so that the first few years of premiums are less than normal, and subsequent premiums are higher than normal. *See also* GRADED PREMIUM, WHOLE LIFE INSURANCE.

MODIFIED PRIOR APPROVAL *see* RATING BUREAU.

MODIFIED PRIOR APPROVAL RATING form of state rating law that requires prior approval of property and casualty insurance premiums by the state insurance department for certain changes. Here, a state generally allows new rates to go into effect immediately after filing with the insurance department. However, changes in classification of risks or other substantial changes require prior insurance department approval. There are four methods of rate approval. In addition to modified prior approval, they are PRIOR APPROVAL RATING, *open competition,* and *file and use.*

MODIFIED RESERVE METHODS accounting procedures that defer the full funding of a life insurance NET LEVEL PREMIUM RESERVE to accommodate the policy ACQUISITION COST in the early years of a policy. First-year policy expenses, such as *agent commission,* MEDICAL EXAMINATION, and PREMIUM TAX, often result in little of the PREMIUM remaining for the premium reserve required under FULL VALUATION RESERVE standards. In such cases, the difference comes out of the insurer's SURPLUS ACCOUNT. To avoid this, two types of modified reserve methods are used: (1) the FULL PRELIMINARY TERM RESERVE

VALUATION method, and (2) the modified preliminary term reserve valuation method, better known as the *commissioners' reserve valuation method.* The full preliminary term method does not require any TERMINAL RESERVE at the end of the first year and in effect accounts for reserves like *term insurance* during this period. This leaves more of the premium available to cover acquisition cost and first-year claims. In subsequent years, for reserve accounting purposes, the policy is considered to have been issued one year later than its actual date on an insured who was one year older than his actual age. This results in stepping up additions to the premium reserve, eventually making up for the first year's shortfall.

The commissioners' reserve valuation method limits first-year expenses and thus the amount of deferred funding of policy reserves. Policies whose premiums fall below a certain level can be accounted for under the full preliminary term method. For policies with premiums above that level, the full preliminary term method is modified by a limitation on the amount of expenses that can be used in figuring the schedule of deferred reserve funding.

MODIFIED RESERVE STANDARDS *see* MODIFIED RESERVE METHODS.

MODUS OPERANDI method of operation.

MONETARY POLICY federal regulation of the money supply through changing commercial bank reserve requirements and interest rates, thereby stimulating the economy or deflating the economy.

MONEY AND SECURITIES BROAD FORM POLICY coverage providing protection for a business against loss from a hazard under the *On-Premises Form,* that provides ALL RISK protection against the loss of money and securities; or the *Off-Premises Form,* ALL RISK protection against loss of money and securities while they are in possession of a messenger. There is no coinsurance deductible requirement.

MONEY DAMAGES payments awarded by a court in a liability suit. Money damages can be broken down into *compensatory* and *punitive.* Compensatory damages reimburse a plaintiff for expenses incurred for such things as disability, disfigurement, and pain and suffering. Punitive damages go beyond this to punish and make an example of a defendant. In recent years, punitive damages have become increasingly common, and insurers claim that the frequency of multimillion dollar jury awards has made the business of underwriting difficult.

MONEY MARKET INVESTMENTS short-term investments, to include the following: commercial paper, interest-bearing balances with banks, federal funds sold and securities purchased under agreements to resell, trading account securities, and loans held for resale.

MONEY MARKET MUTUAL FUND fund that concentrates primarily on short-term government securities, certificates of deposit with maturities less than one year, and high-quality interest-bearing corporate debt. The fund is a pool of money from many investors from which interest is paid to these investors on the income earned by that pool of money. Income and yield fluctuate on a daily basis, but each share in the mutual fund maintains a constant value of $1, resulting in no capital gains or losses. These funds are ideal for short-term needs.

Since these funds invest in financial instruments whose maturities are very short, reinvesting is on a continuous basis. Thus, as interest rates rise or fall, the funds' yields will correspond accordingly.

MONEY PURCHASE PLAN contributions to a pension plan on a fixed basis according to a formula, with variable benefits. Contributions can be made under an ALLOCATED FUNDING INSTRUMENT (paid to an insurance company that purchases an individual ANNUITY or a group DEFERRED ANNUITY), or under an UNALLOCATED FUNDING INSTRUMENT. Individual benefits will be determined by the person's age, sex, normal retirement age, and rate schedules in effect at the time the insurance company receives the contributions. These plans are appropriate for an organization that must know its premium outlay in the years ahead. *See also* DEFINED CONTRIBUTION PLAN.

MONOLINE POLICY insurance protection written in the form of a single line policy.

MONOPOLISTIC STATE FUND state operated insurance company used in WORKERS COMPENSATION INSURANCE in some states where the risks are so great that the commercial insurance companies cannot operate at affordable rates.

MONOPOLY type of market in which a seller may sell only to one buyer.

MONTHLY DEBIT ORDINARY INSURANCE (MDO) coverage in which premiums are collected monthly on an ordinary life insurance policy. *See also* DEBIT INSURANCE (HOME SERVICE INSURANCE, INDUSTRIAL INSURANCE).

MONTHLY INDEMNITY monthly income payment provided by a DISABILITY INCOME INSURANCE policy to the insured wage earner when income has been interrupted or terminated because of illness, sickness, or accident.

MONTHLY REPORTING FORM type of INLAND MARINE insurance used to provide coverage for domesticated animals, including poultry, cattle, horses, sheep, and swine. *See also* LIVESTOCK INSURANCE; LIVESTOCK MORTALITY (LIFE) INSURANCE. For application to inventory and other fluctuating values, *see also* OPEN FORM (REPORTING FORM).

MOP *see* MANUFACTURERS OUTPUT INSURANCE.

MORALE HAZARD circumstance that increases the probability of loss because of the insured's indifferent attitude. For example, if an insured leaves the doors unlocked and the windows open when leaving home, a morale hazard is created.

MORAL HAZARD circumstance which increases the probability of loss because of an applicant's personal habits or morals; for example, if an applicant is a known criminal.

MORBIDITY frequency of illness, sickness, and diseases contracted.

MORBIDITY ASSUMPTION statistical projection of future illness, sickness, and disease.

MORBIDITY RATE relationship of the frequency of illness, sickness, and diseases contracted by individual members of a group to the entire group membership over a particular time period.

MORBIDITY TABLE number of individuals exposed to the risk of illness, sickness, and disease at each age, and the actual number of individuals who incurred an illness, sickness, and disease at each age.

MORTALITY frequency of death.

MORTALITY ADJUSTMENT additions or subtractions of a MORTALITY TABLE to reflect changing levels of mortality due to advancement in medicine, geriatrics, and sanitation. These adjustments make a mortality table more representative of probable future death experience.

MORTALITY ASSUMPTION statistical projection of future deaths.

MORTALITY CHARGES *see* MORTALITY ADJUSTMENT; MORTALITY RATE; MORTALITY TABLE.

MORTALITY RATE relationship of the frequency of deaths of individual members of a group to the entire group membership over a particular time period.

MORTALITY RISK measure of the sensitivity of the insurance company's liability for resultant higher mortality rates than charged for in the premium.

MORTALITY SAVINGS difference between the actual mortality experience and the expected mortality experience. In statistical terms, this is known as the deviation of the actual (X) from the expected (X). The MORTALITY TABLE is conservative by nature in that the table assumes more people will die than is the case. When fewer people die than was assumed by the table, the savings results.

MORTALITY TABLE chart showing rate of death at each age in terms of number of deaths per thousand.

MORTALITY TABLE WITH PROJECTION MORTALITY TABLE whose statistics have been adjusted to show expected mortality experience.

MORTGAGE purchase of real estate through borrowed funds with the real estate acting as security for the loan.

MORTGAGE COVER type of CRITICAL ILLNESS INSURANCE where benefits are correlated with the home mortgage. Benefits are paid, either in a lump sum or installments, directly to the insured upon the diagnosis of a covered critical illness. Typically, benefits are used to pay related and nonrelated medical expenses.

MORTGAGE DEFAULT RATIO insurance company's investment in mortgages that have defaulted (MORTGAGES IN DEFAULT) divided by its ADJUSTED SURPLUS account. The smaller this ratio, the more financially sound the insurance company.

MORTGAGEE CLAUSE attachment to a property insurance policy to protect the interest of the mortgagee in the mortgaged property. If the property is damaged or destroyed, the mortgagee is indemnified up to his or her stated interest in the property.

MORTGAGEE INSURANCE *see* MORTGAGEE CLAUSE.

MORTGAGE GUARANTEE INSURANCE *see* MORTGAGE INSURANCE.

MORTGAGE INSURANCE life insurance that pays the balance of a mortgage if the mortgagor (insured) dies. Coverage is usually in the form of decreasing term insurance, with the amount of coverage decreasing as the debt decreases.

MORTGAGE INSURANCE PREMIUM PREMIUM paid by the mortgagor for MORTGAGE INSURANCE to either a private mortgage insurance company or to the Federal Housing Administration.

MORTGAGE PROTECTION INSURANCE *see* MORTGAGE INSURANCE.

MORTGAGE REDEMPTION INSURANCE *see* MORTGAGE INSURANCE.

MORTGAGES IN DEFAULT total of the insurance company's mortgages whose interest has not been paid for at least three months. These are mortgages upon which the insurance company is in the process of foreclosing, and foreclosed property. *See also* MORTGAGE DEFAULT RATIO.

MORTICIANS PROFESSIONAL LIABILITY INSURANCE coverage for malpractice suits resulting from professional acts and/or omissions of morticians. *See also* PROFESSIONAL LIABILITY INSURANCE.

MOTOR TRUCK CARGO INSURANCE protection required under the Motor Carrier Act of 1935. The policy covers the motor truck carrier if it is legally liable for the damage, destruction, or other loss of the customer's property being shipped. This includes lost packages, broken contents, and stolen articles. Two types of policies are available: (1) those that list the specific trucks to be covered in which the property may be damaged or destroyed; and (2) those that cover all of the insured's trucks, with no trucks listed specifically. This coverage is on the *Gross Receipts Form,* which in essence covers all operations of a motor carrier.

MOTOR TRUCK CARGO RADIOACTIVE CONTAMINATION INSURANCE coverage for a common carrier (the insured) for damage or destruction due to radioactive contamination from commercial radioisotopes of a property in the custody of the insured or that of a connecting carrier. Transport of nuclear waste is excluded.

MOTOR VEHICLES *see* MOTOR TRUCK CARGO INSURANCE.

MOVING AVERAGE RATING METHOD procedure, in insurance, used in time series analysis to smooth out irregularities in projections of loss expectations. Irregularities to be smoothed out include: (1) loss experience that is not homogeneous, (2) loss experience from early policy years not representative of current loss experience, (3) adverse selection by policyholders, (4) changes in loss experience due to changing social values, and (5) loss experience distortion due to misleading averages.

MOVING INSURANCE (FOR A MOVING COMPANY) INLAND MARINE policy to cover liability for goods that belong to clients while in a mover's possession.

MPL *see* MAXIMUM POSSIBLE LOSS; MAXIMUM PROBABLE LOSS.

MULTICAR DISCOUNT provision reduces automobile insurance premium for two or more insured owned vehicles.

MULTIEMPLOYER PLAN pension or other employee benefit to cover employees at two or more financially unrelated companies. The companies may employ workers from the same labor union or those in the same industry. Employer contributions go into a common pool from which benefits are paid. Employees may transfer between employers in the fund and still retain their benefits. Multiemployer plans have grown rapidly in recent years as smaller employers band together to provide pension benefits to employees. *See also* MULTIEMPLOYER TRUST.

MULTIEMPLOYER TRUST one that provides group health or pension benefits for a MULTIEMPLOYER PLAN. To lower the cost, small firms band together to take advantage of the economies of large group underwriting.

MULTIPERIL POLICY *see* MULTIPLE PERIL INSURANCE.

MULTIPLE DISTRIBUTION SYSTEMS system that allows the selling of insurance products and services through MARKETING channels to include MASS MERCHANDISING; INDEPENDENT AGENCY SYSTEM; CAPTIVE AGENT; BROKER; and GENERAL AGENT (GA).

MULTIPLE EMPLOYER TRUST *see* MULTIEMPLOYER TRUST.

MULTIPLE EMPLOYER WELFARE ARRANGEMENT (MEWA) arrangement by which two or more employers form a coalition to offer a health plan to their employees. The purpose of the coalition is not to purchase health insurance. The MEWAs can be self-insured or fully insured and are subject to the regulations of each state. The objective of the MEWA is to provide a mechanism through which the small employers can have access to affordable health care for their employees through their combined purchasing power.

MULTIPLE INDEMNITY *see* ACCIDENTAL DEATH CLAUSE.

MULTIPLE LINE CONTRACT *see* MULTIPLE LINE INSURANCE.

MULTIPLE LINE INSURANCE combination of coverages from property and liability policies. *See also* HOMEOWNERS INSURANCE POLICY; PERSONAL AUTOMOBILE POLICY (PAP); COMMERCIAL PACKAGE POLICY.

MULTIPLE LINE INSURANCE COMPANY INSURANCE COMPANY that underwrites and sells more than one LINE of insurance.

MULTIPLE LINE LAW state legislation that allows insurers to offer both property and casualty insurance. At one time, U.S. insurers sold only one type of insurance, a practice that gradually became written into state law. Most significantly, New York State, where many insurers want to be licensed, allowed insurers to write only one line of insurance early in the 20th century. But in 1949 New York passed a multiple line law, and most other states followed.

MULTIPLE LOCATION FORMS type of coverage of property owned by one person at several locations, including merchandise, materials, fixtures, furniture, specified machinery, betterments, and improvements made by tenants.

MULTIPLE LOCATION POLICY *see* MULTIPLE LOCATION FORMS.

MULTIPLE LOCATION RISKS *see* MULTIPLE LOCATION FORMS.

MULTIPLE PERIL INSURANCE personal and business property insurance that combines in one policy several types of property insurance covering numerous *perils*. However, no liability insurance is provided.

MULTIPLE PROTECTION LIFE INSURANCE POLICY single LIFE INSURANCE policy combining TERM LIFE INSURANCE and ORDINARY LIFE INSURANCE. If the INSURED dies during the term period, a multiple of the FACE AMOUNT is paid to the BENEFICIARY. If the insured dies after the term period has expired, only the face amount is paid to the beneficiary. For example, if the insured dies during the first 10 years that the policy is in force, three times the face amount is paid to the beneficiary; after the 10 years expires, the single face amount is paid to the beneficiary. Thus, during the multiple protection period both term insurance and ordinary life insurance are in force; after the multiple protection period expires, only ordinary life insurance is in force.

MULTIPLE RETIREMENT AGES arrangement by which an employee can retire and receive full benefits without reduction, or reduced benefits subject to a penalty. These ages can be classified in the following manner:

1. *normal retirement*—earliest an employee can retire and receive full benefits, having reached a minimum age with a minimum number of years of service.
2. *early retirement*—earliest an employee can retire, having reached a minimum age and a minimum number of years of service, but with a penalty in the form of a reduction in benefits. The reduction is usually a percentage of benefit subtracted for each month of retirement earlier than the normal retirement age.
3. *deferred retirement*—work beyond the normal retirement age. This may or may not result in an increase of benefits.

MUNICIPAL BOND INSURANCE coverage that guarantees bondholders against default by a municipality. This form of financial guarantee was introduced in the early 1970s and became a runaway success. Municipalities embraced it because their offerings took on the credit rating of the company that wrote the insurance, rather than their own ratings. It meant that most municipal bond offerings were elevated to Triple-A, and municipalities could raise money at a lower rate of interest. For investors, it made municipal bonds less risky.

MUNICIPAL INSURANCE property and/or liability coverage for a municipality. Municipalities are responsible for maintenance of throughways as well as a myriad of public services. Liability insurance for municipalities became an issue in the insurance crunch of 1985–1986, when this coverage became difficult to find, or became overly expensive. The problem was aggravated by court decisions in negligence cases in which the doctrine of *joint and several liability* came into play. This doctrine provides that a judgment against several defendants could be collected from one if the others were unable to pay. A municipality found to have been 10% liable in a traffic accident because of the improper placement of a stop sign might end up paying 100% of the judgment if the driver who was 90% responsible had no assets. This resulted in sharply higher premiums for municipal insurance.

MUSICAL INSTRUMENTS INSURANCE coverage for musicians and other providers of musical services such as musical instrument dealers. Musical instruments, service equipment, and sheet music are insured on an ALL RISKS basis at any location, subject to exclusions of wear and tear, war, and nuclear disaster. Each item must be specifically listed in the policy.

MUTUAL ASSENT offer and acceptance upon which an agreement is based. For a contract to be legal (and thus enforceable in a court of law), an offer must be made by one party to another party, who accepts the offer. If properly negotiated, the insurance contract is deemed to be a contract of mutual assent.

MUTUAL ATOMIC ENERGY REINSURANCE POOL group of mutual insurers that provides insurance for nuclear reactors that standard property and liability policies exclude. The federal government provides supplementary coverage. *See also* NUCLEAR ENERGY LIABILITY INSURANCE.

MUTUAL BENEFIT ASSOCIATION *see* ASSESSMENT COMPANY; ASSESSMENT INSURANCE; ASSESSMENT PERIOD.

MUTUAL FUND combination of contributions of many investors whose money is used to buy stocks, bonds, commodities, options, and/or money market funds, or precious metals such as gold, or foreign securities. In theory, mutual funds offer investors professional money management and diversification into conservative investments, aggressive investments, or combinations of these. Mutual funds are sold either with a sales charge (load), no sales charge (no-load), or a moderate sales charge (low load). These funds charge a management fee as a percentage of assets under management, usually 1% per year on a downward sliding scale as the asset base increases. Many insurance companies sell mutual funds.

MUTUAL FUND 12b-1 FEE annual fee paid by fund shareowners to cover distribution and service costs.

MUTUAL FUND CLASS A SHARES front-end sales charge on purchased shares. This is a fee paid by the purchaser on the initial purchase of a fund's shares.

MUTUAL FUND CLASS B SHARES contingent sales charge on shares purchased. This is a fee paid by the purchaser if fund shares are sold within a specified period of time. Usually the fee reduces on a sliding scale basis until reaching zero at the end of the specified time period.

MUTUAL FUND INSURANCE financial guarantee policy that insures against loss of principal invested in a mutual fund.

MUTUAL INSURANCE COMPANY company owned by its *policyowners;* no stock is available for purchase on the stock exchanges. *See also* DIVIDEND OPTION, PARTICIPATING INSURANCE; STOCK INSURANCE COMPANY.

MUTUALIZATION transformation of a STOCK INSURANCE COMPANY into a MUTUAL INSURANCE COMPANY, in which the stock company buys up and retires its shares.

MUTUALIZATION OF RISK process of distributing the costs associated with losses and risks over a number of insureds.

MUTUALLY EXCLUSIVE describing an instance where the occurrence of one event precludes the occurrence of a second event; for example, if a long-distance runner dies during a track meet, the runner cannot enter future track meets.

MUTUAL MORTGAGE INSURANCE FUND fund that insures mortgages on homes for one to four families; also insures property improvement loans and loans to repair homes after a disaster. It is one of three funds operated by the Federal Housing Administration, which oversees mortgage guarantee insurance.

MYSTERIOUS DISAPPEARANCE EXCLUSION policy clause that excludes coverage for loss of property if the cause of the loss cannot be identified. Mysterious disappearance is an exclusion in a standard INLAND MARINE insurance all-risks policy. Because some theft insurance policies do not contain this exclusion, they implicitly insure against mysterious disappearance and would cover the loss of a diamond necklace, for example, even if the owner did not recall how it had been lost.

N

NAIB National Association of Insurance Brokers.

NAIC National Association of Insurance Commissioners.

NAII National Association of Independent Insurers.

NAMED INSURED person, business, or organization specified as the insured(s) in a property or liability insurance policy. In some instances, the policy provides broader coverage to persons other than those named in the policy if they have the insured's permission to use the property that is insured. For example, someone who drives a car with the permission of the owner is protected by a PERSONAL AUTOMOBILE POLICY (PAP). In other cases, if the owner of a property is not named as an insured party, his or her interests may not be protected by the policy. For example, if two persons own a home and only one is named on the HOMEOWNERS INSURANCE POLICY, the interest of the other may not be covered. *See also* OTHER INSUREDS.

NAMED NONOWNER COVERAGE insurance under the PERSONAL AUTOMOBILE POLICY (PAP) through a *named nonowner coverage endorsement* offering protection for LIABILITY, *uninsured motorists,* and *medical payments* to a named insured who does not own an automobile.

NAMED PERIL POLICY insurance contract under which covered perils are listed. Benefits for a covered loss are paid to the *policyowner.* If an unlisted peril strikes, no benefits are paid. For example, under the *standard fire policy,* fire is a particular listed peril. If an insured's home burns, he will be indemnified. *See also* ALL RISKS.

NAME POSITION BOND FIDELITY BOND that covers a business if employees in listed positions commit dishonest acts, such as stealing money. *See also* BLANKET BOND; NAME SCHEDULE BOND.

NAME SCHEDULE BOND FIDELITY BOND under which an insured employer is reimbursed for loss caused by the dishonest act of two or more employees named or listed in a schedule attached to the bond. The specific amount of coverage is listed beside the name of each employee on the schedule. Coverage is the same as that found under the individual fidelity bond. *See also* INDIVIDUAL FIDELITY BOND.

NATIONAL FLOOD INSURANCE PROGRAM coverage against flooding for personal and business property under the National Flood Act of 1968, which encourages participation by private insurers in the program through an industry flood insurance pool. Property insurance companies with assets of $1 million or more may become members, either as *risk bearers* (who may issue their own policies) or as *nonrisk bearers* (who are limited to act as fiscal agents for the pool, and hence must use a syndicate-type policy as dictated by the pool). National

Flood Insurance makes reasonable coverage available to those who could not buy it through private insurers before the 1968 act, and it encourages maximum participation extent by the private sector.

NATIONAL FLOOD INSURERS ASSOCIATION pool of private insurers that provide initial flood insurance in cooperation with the U.S. Department of Housing and Urban Development (HUD). In 1978, the association was superseded by the NATIONAL FLOOD INSURANCE PROGRAM administered by HUD.

NATIONAL HEALTH INSURANCE government health care program in several European countries that has been proposed in various forms for the U.S., to be administered by the federal government.
1. *Plan A*—would cover all U.S. residents. Comprehensive benefits, financed by a combination of payroll taxes and general revenues, would include physician services, inpatient and outpatient hospital care, home health services, and supporting services such as optometry, podiatry, devices and appliances, and dental care.
2. *Plan B*—would expand MEDICARE to cover the general population.
3. *Plan C*—would pay premiums for the needy and allow income tax credits for others to purchase private health insurance. The entire U.S. population would be covered. Individuals with no federal income tax liability would receive full payment of health insurance premiums.

NATIONWIDE DEFINITION OF MARINE INSURANCE *see* NATIONWIDE MARINE DEFINITION.

NATIONWIDE MARINE DEFINITION statement of the types of exposures classified under *marine, inland marine* or *transportation insurance* by placing them in the following categories: imports, exports, domestic shipments (goods in transit), communication vehicles (tunnels, bridges, piers, and power transmission lines), personal property floaters (stamp collections, coin collections, fine arts, paintings, musical instruments, silverware, and furs), commercial property floaters (accounts receivable, valuable papers, valuable records, and physicians' and surgeons' instruments). The definition also makes use of the following differences in condition: electronic data, property in a bailee's custody, and property for sale by a dealer (such as musical instruments, cameras, fine arts, and jewelry).

NATURAL DEATH death from other than accidental means. *See also* ACCIDENTAL DEATH CLAUSE; RIDERS, LIFE POLICIES.

NATURAL LOSSES property damage, accident, or injury resulting from vagaries of nature, including tornadoes, hurricanes, and floods.

NATURAL PREMIUM *see* PURE PREMIUM RATING METHOD.

NAVIGATION RISK INSURANCE coverage during the operation of a ship for: (1) *Property of Ship* (ship's hull, tackle, passenger fittings, equipment, stores, boats), and ordnance; (2) *Property Damage*

Liability (ship's owner and/or operator is protected if the ship collides with another, causing damage and loss of use). Excluded is liability to the owner and/or operator for damage to piers, wharves, bodily injury, or loss of coverage on the insured ship's hull and/or cargo (this coverage amount is in addition to the amount of coverage on the insured ship's hull and cargo); and (3) *Bodily Injury Liability Insurance.*

NCCI National Council on Compensation Insurance.

NECESSITIES OF LIFE basic needs, such as food, water, clothing, and shelter, that a person requires to survive. These needs are the first layer of Maslow's Hierarchy of Needs, and are the minimum that should be provided by any LIFE INSURANCE plan.

NEEDS APPROACH personal insurance method used to analyze the amount necessary to maintain a family in its customary life-style, should the primary wage earner die. This includes such considerations as:
1. immediate needs ("cleanup fund")—expenses associated with final medical treatments and burial, inheritance taxes, estate taxes, probate costs, outstanding debt.
2. continued income—while children are still in school and depend on family support.
3. continued income—for the surviving spouse after children no longer depend on family support.
4. continued income—to pay a mortgage, education expenses, emergency expenses, and miscellaneous expenses.
5. retirement fund—for the surviving spouse.
    From the sum of these expenses, subtract sources of income available to the surviving spouse (Social Security, investments, employee benefit plans such as group life insurance and pensions), to arrive at a final figure on which to base the amount of life insurance the wage earner should consider.

NEGLECT failure to exercise proper care. Many property insurance policies exclude losses that result from negligence. Neglect is also the basis for many liability suits. If an injury can be demonstrated to result from negligence on the part of a homeowner, a product manufacturer, or a municipality responsible for maintaining streets, an injured party can often collect damages.

NEGLIGENCE failure to act with the legally required degree of care for others, resulting in harm to them. *See also* TORT, UNINTENTIONAL.

NEGLIGENCE, COMPARATIVE *see* COMPARATIVE NEGLIGENCE.

NEGLIGENCE, CONTRIBUTORY *see* CONTRIBUTORY NEGLIGENCE.

NEGLIGENCE, GROSS *see* GROSS NEGLIGENCE.

NEGLIGENCE, IMPUTED type of NEGLIGENCE under which the at-fault risk can be transferred from the negligent party to another party (such as from the negligent employee to the employer).

NEGLIGENCE, PRESUMED *see* RES IPSA LOQUITOR.

NEGLIGENT LIABILITY INSURANCE POLICY *see* LIABILITY INSURANCE.

NEGLIGENT MANUFACTURE charge against a business firm in a PRODUCT LIABILITY INSURANCE lawsuit. Manufacturers have been held responsible for their products. When consumers become injured while operating a lawnmower, flying in an airplane, driving a car, or any of hundreds of other ways, they have grounds to sue the manufacturer of these products for negligence. Product liability has become one of the most rapidly growing areas of liability exposure for businesses and one of the most difficult to insure against.

NEGOTIATED CONTRIBUTION PLAN defined contribution pension plan in which employer contributions are set under a collective bargaining agreement. It usually covers the employees of a number of firms and is administered by a board of trustees on which participating employers and unions are equally represented.

NEON AND ELECTRIC SIGNS FLOATER coverage on an ALL RISKS basis through an endorsement to a business PROPERTY INSURANCE policy in which each sign is specifically scheduled, subject to the exclusions of wear and tear, and damage caused by nuclear hazard, war, and electricity.

NEON AND FLUORESCENT SIGN INSURANCE coverage through an endorsement to the *glass insurance* policy on an ALL RISKS basis, subject to the exclusions of wear and tear, and damage caused by nuclear hazard, war, and electricity.

NET AMOUNT AT RISK in life insurance, difference between the face value of a life insurance policy and its cash value (also known as "pure amount of protection").

NET ASSETS EQUATION income (premiums + investment earnings) minus disbursements (DIVIDENDS + death claims + policies surrendered for benefits + general expenses).

NET ASSET VALUE (NAV) the market value of one unit of a MUTUAL FUND. This figure is derived by adding the underlying market value of the total securities in the fund, subtracting total liabilities, and dividing the result by the number of outstanding units.

NET COST *see* LIFE INSURANCE COST.

NET COST METHOD *see* LIFE INSURANCE COST.

NET GAIN FROM OPERATIONS STATUTORY ACCOUNTING principles (SAP), as listed in the insurance company's annual financial statements filed with the insurance commissioner of each state in which it is licensed. Income that is equal to the net income is filed under GENERALLY ACCEPTED ACCOUNTING PRINCIPLES (GAAP).

NET INCOME AFTER TAXES total of OPERATING INCOME plus realized capital gains (losses) from investment and underwriting operations minus federal income taxes.

NET INCOME MAKE-UP CHARITABLE REMAINDER UNI-TRUSTS (NIMCRUTs) type of CHARITABLE REMAINDER TRUST (CRT) that pays interest income for life or for a specified term to a noncharitable beneficiary. The remainder of the interest is received by a charity. This trust pays a specified percentage of its fair market value with the beneficiary receiving only the interest and dividends earned by the trust for the current year. The trust does not pay out any unrealized income. If this payout of interest and dividends is less than the specified percentage as stated in the trust documents, the shortage is accumulated and paid to the beneficiary at some future date (the net income make-up provision goes into effect). For example, assume that the trust earns 6% in interest and 16% in UNREALIZED CAPITAL GAINS during the current year. The beneficiary receives only the 6% earned interest with the 16% in unrealized capital gains being accumulated for distribution to the beneficiary at a future date when the recognized income in the trust is sufficient to affect the payout. In those situations where the trust has no income from interest and dividends, the shortage owed to the beneficiary is accumulated for future distribution to that beneficiary.

NET INCOME WITH MAKE-UP PROVISION CHARITABLE REMAINDER UNITRUST (NIMCRUT) irrevocable trust that generates income reflecting the investment performance of the trust. Assets that reflect this fluctuating income are donated to charity. If the value of the assets in the trust increases, the result will be a corresponding increase in the income. However, if the assets decrease in value, there will be an accompanying decrease in income. A make-up provision allows the recipient to recoup the last income in those years when the investment performance is positive.

NET INCREASE amount of the increase in the BOOK OF BUSINESS of an INSURANCE COMPANY over a specified time interval. This increase is calculated as follows:

$$\text{Net Increase} = \frac{\text{New Issued Policies} + \text{Renewed Policies}}{- \text{Lapsed Policies} - \text{Cancelled Policies}}$$

NET INTEREST EARNED average interest earned by an insurer on its investments after investment expense, but before federal income tax.

NET INVESTMENT INCOME total of interest, dividends, and other earnings derived from the insurance company's invested assets minus the expenses associated with these investments. Excluded from this income are capital gains or losses as the result of the sale of assets, as well as any unrealized capital gains or losses.

NET LEVEL *see* NET LEVEL PREMIUM; NET LEVEL PREMIUM RESERVE.

NET LEVEL PREMIUM life insurance payment that is constant from year to year. The premium may be paid throughout the life of an insured or may be limited to a maximum number, such as 30 annual premiums. The premium is based only on interest and a mortality assumption and does not consider an expense assumption. *See also* GROSS PREMIUM.

NET LEVEL PREMIUM RESERVE fund that comes into existence because premiums for ordinary life insurance policies in their early years are higher than necessary for the pure cost of protection. These excess premiums, plus the interest credited, create the net level reserve. When an insured dies, the reserve comprises part of the death benefit. The net premium is calculated according to this fundamental actuarial equation: *present value of future premiums = present value of future benefits.*

This relationship holds only at the point of issue of a life insurance policy. Thereafter, future benefits will exceed future premiums because fewer premiums are left to be paid and benefits are coming closer to being due. The reserve makes up the difference between the future benefits and future premiums at any point. This reserve can be calculated on either a *prospective* or *retrospective* basis, but it is important to note that the various state minimum reserve valuation laws are stated in terms of the prospective basis. *See also* FULL PRELIMINARY TERM RESERVE PLAN; PROSPECTIVE RESERVE; RETROSPECTIVE METHOD RESERVE COMPUTATION.

NET LINE *see* NET RETAINED LINES.

NET LINE LIMIT maximum amount of INSURANCE that an INSURANCE COMPANY will issue on a particular risk exposure. This limit is used by the insurance company to avoid having to pay for a loss on the exposure in excess of that which is acceptable to the company.

NET LOSS amount of the loss absorbed by an INSURANCE COMPANY after deducting any REINSURANCE applicable to the loss, as well as SUBROGATION and ABANDONMENT AND SALVAGE rights.

NET PAYMENT METHOD OF COMPARING COSTS *see* INTEREST ADJUSTED COST; LIFE INSURANCE COST.

NET PAYMENTS INDEX table charting relative costs of a group of CASH VALUE LIFE INSURANCE policies derived by using the *net cost method* of comparing costs *(traditional net cost method of comparing costs; net payment method).* The net payments index contrasts with the interest adjusted SURRENDER COST INDEX and the INTEREST ADJUSTED COST index, which are derived by using the interest adjusted method of comparing policy costs.

NET PREMIUM *see* NET SINGLE PREMIUM.

NET PREMIUMS WRITTEN total premiums written by a CEDING COMPANY minus premiums ceded to its REINSURER.

NET PRESENT VALUE excess of an asset's market value over the asset's cost.

NET RATE *see* NET SINGLE PREMIUM.

NET RETAINED LINES amount of insurance remaining on a CEDING COMPANY'S books, net of the amount reinsured.

NET RETENTION *see* NET RETAINED LINES.

NET SINGLE PREMIUM *pure cost of protection,* or the premium covering the present value of future claims (not including loadings for the various expenses).

NET UNDERWRITING PROFIT (OR LOSS) statutory UNDERWRITING GAIN minus (or LOSS plus) POLICYHOLDER'S dividends.

NET VALUATION PREMIUM *see* VALUATION PREMIUM.

NET WORTH total assets minus liabilities. It is used by underwriters to evaluate the financial standing of applicants for surety bonds.

NET YIELD gross yield minus total costs (expenses).

NEW ACQUIRED CAR REPLACEMENT CAR or ADDITIONAL CAR as used in the PERSONAL AUTOMOBILE POLICY.

NEW FUNDS injection of fresh capital from investors or from a parent corporation that is not an insurance company.

NEW YORK INSURANCE CODE standard for insurance regulation in New York State and a model for insurance regulation elsewhere. For example, the *standard fire policy* was first adopted in New York State. Similarly, following the ARMSTRONG INVESTIGATION, the New York Insurance Code of 1906 became a model for cleaning up life insurance industry abuses. New York is widely viewed as the toughest state to get an insurance license, but because of the size of the insurance market there, many companies are willing to meet the stiff requirements.

NEW YORK INSURANCE EXCHANGE reinsurance marketplace modeled after LLOYD'S OF LONDON. Like Lloyd's, the New York Insurance Exchange is a market for hard-to-place risks and for the placement of excess or surplus lines. *See also* SURPLUS LINES (EXCESS SURPLUS LINES).

NEW YORK STANDARD FIRE POLICY contract first written in 1918 that provided the basis for modern-day property insurance, both personal and commercial. *Forms* and *endorsements* must be added to complete the policy and tailor it to cover the particular insured property. This policy is also known as the "165 Line" policy, for the number of lines in its text that covers CONCEALMENT or MISREPRESENTATION (FALSE PRETENSE), property and perils excluded; OTHER INSURANCE; cancellation due to increase in hazards; obligations to a mortgagee; pro rata contribution of a company; requirements of an insured in case of loss; conditions when a company must pay a loss incurred by an insured; and SUBROGATION. The New York Standard Fire Policy has become largely obsolete since 1980, but its provisions have been incorporated into many other property insurance policies.

NEW YORK STATE COLLEGE CHOICE TUITION SAVINGS PROGRAM (NEW YORK'S COLLEGE SAVINGS PROGRAM) vehicle that is available to anyone in the United States as a means for savings in a tax-exempt fashion for college, graduate, or professional schools or other eligible accredited business, trade, occupational, or technical schools domiciled in the United States. Under the plan, there is a deferral of federal taxes on earnings of the account until the funds are distributed for education expenses by the beneficiary of the account. The account earnings are not subject to New York state taxes either. Upon withdrawal by the beneficiary, the earnings distribution is federally taxed at the beneficiary's tax rate and not subject to New York state tax provided the distribution is used for the above-approved education expenses. Any distributions not used for the approved education expenses are taxed at the regular federal and state income tax rate, and a 10% withdrawal penalty on the earnings must be paid.

NFIA *see* NATIONAL FLOOD INSURERS ASSOCIATION.

NFPA National Fire Protection Association.

NICHE WRITERS insurance companies that seek an economic advantage, thereby increasing their returns on equity by utilizing their specialized knowledge about a given line of insurance, territory, or risk classification.

NO-FAULT AUTOMOBILE INSURANCE type of coverage in which an insured's own policy provides indemnity for bodily injury and/or property damage without regard to fault. In many instances it is difficult if not impossible to determine the original cause—such as who is at fault in a chain car collision. In states with no-fault liability insurance, an insured cannot sue for general damages until special damages including medical expenses exceed a minimum amount. This is an effort to eliminate groundless suits for general damages.

NO-FAULT LIABILITY INSURANCE *see* NO-FAULT AUTOMOBILE INSURANCE.

NO-FAULT THRESHOLD amount for which financial loss for bodily injury incurred by the plaintiff must exceed before a TORT liability action may be brought.

NO-LAPSE GUARANTEE agreement by the insurance company to keep the UNIVERSAL LIFE INSURANCE policy in force, even if the CASH VALUE becomes zero or less than zero, provided that a specified MINIMUM CONTINUATION PREMIUM is made at the required time.

NO-LAPSE VARIABLE UNIVERSAL LIFE INSURANCE policy of VARIABLE UNIVERSAL LIFE INSURANCE (VUL) under which, if the accumulation of the premiums paid at any point in time (minus policy loans, and withdrawals) equals or exceeds the minimum premiums due at that point in time, the policy is prevented from lapsing. This lapse prevention is guaranteed regardless of the underlying portfolio return or policy changes. Usually this feature is the same per option A (level death benefit) or option B (increasing death benefit) under VUL.

NO-LOAD INSURANCE *see* FLOW-THROUGH COST (NO LOAD INSURANCE).

NOMINAL INTEREST RATE interest rate credited on three-month United States Treasury bills.

NONADMITTED ASSETS assets, such as furniture and fixtures, that are not permitted by state law to be included in an insurance company's ANNUAL STATEMENT. *See also* ADMITTED ASSETS.

NONADMITTED INSURANCE policy purchased by an insured from an insurer in another state. This insurer is not licensed in the state where the insured's risk is located.

NONADMITTED INSURER company not licensed by a particular state to sell and service insurance policies within that state.

NONADMITTED REINSURANCE *see* SURPLUS LINES (EXCESS SURPLUS LINES).

NONASSESSABLE MUTUAL insurance company whose corporate charter and bylaws prevent assessment of its policyowners, regardless of how adverse its loss and expense experience may become. *See also* ASSESSMENT COMPANY.

NONASSESSABLE POLICY insurance contract under which a policy owner cannot be assessed for adverse loss and expense experience of the insurance company. *See also* ASSESSMENT INSURANCE.

NONASSIGNABLE POLICY insurance policy, particularly PROPERTY AND LIABILITY INSURANCE, which the owner cannot assign to a third party. *See also* ASSIGNMENT; ASSIGNMENT CLAUSE, LIFE INSURANCE.

NONBOARD COMPANY INSURANCE COMPANY that does not utilize the rates and policies of a RATING BUREAU.

NONCANCELLABLE DISABILITY INCOME INSURANCE type of DISABILITY INCOME INSURANCE that provides income payments to the wage earner when income is interrupted or terminated because of illness, sickness, or accident and can continue to remain in force at the option of the INSURER until some stipulated age has been reached.

NONCANCELLABLE GUARANTEED RENEWABLE POLICY health insurance that is not subject to alteration, termination, or increase in premium upon renewal.

NONCANCELLABLE HEALTH INSURANCE *see* COMMERCIAL HEALTH INSURANCE.

NONCANCELLABLE INSURANCE POLICY INSURANCE contract that cannot be cancelled by the INSURANCE COMPANY. Since the insurance policy is a UNILATERAL CONTRACT instead of a BILATERAL CONTRACT, the INSURED may cancel at will. Only the insurer makes a promise of future performance and only the insurer can be charged with breach of contract.

NONCONCURRENCY circumstance under which several insurance policies cover an insured's property against damage or destruction, but since the limits of coverage, kinds of property, and perils covered are not the same under all policies, the insured may not be fully covered in the event of a loss.

NONCONCURRENT APPORTIONMENT RULES standards used to determine claims payments in cases of overlapping property/liability insurance coverage. At one time, each type of insurance had its own rules to govern claims where more than one policy provided coverage. In 1963, several property/casualty industry groups agreed on a set of principles to be used in apportioning claims among insurers.

NONCONFINING SICKNESS sickness incurred by the insured that does not require restriction of activity to the indoors. *See also* HEALTH INSURANCE.

NONCONTRIBUTION MORTGAGE CLAUSE endorsement to *standard fire policy* to protect the interests of a mortgage lender without providing for APPORTIONMENT. A mortgage lender may choose to have his or her rights to the property protected by a MORTGAGE CLAUSE. Where an insured has more than one policy, claims are normally paid by assigning a portion of the loss among the insurance carriers under terms of the policy's PRO RATA LIABILITY CLAUSE. A *full contribution mortgage clause* provides that losses on the lender's interest would be apportioned in the same manner as the rest of the policy. But with a noncontribution mortgage clause, the lender's interest would be protected up to the policy limits with no apportionment.

NONCONTRIBUTORY EMPLOYEE BENEFIT INSURANCE PLAN under which an employer pays the entire direct cost of the plan; employees do not share in the cost, except perhaps through comparatively lower wages.

NONDEDUCTIBLE IRA contribution to INDIVIDUAL RETIREMENT ACCOUNT (IRA) regardless of coverage by a retirement plan at employment or income level. Internal investment and interest gains are tax-deferred; taxes are paid upon receiving withdrawals.

NONDEDUCTIBILITY OF EMPLOYER CONTRIBUTIONS law that payments by an employer to a NONQUALIFIED PLAN are not deductible as a business expense for federal tax purposes.

NONDISABLING INJURY injury that does not qualify either for *partial* or *total disability income* under a disability income or Workers Compensation policy.

NONDISCRIMINATION RULES rules stating that, under the TAX EQUITY AND RESPONSIBILITY ACTS OF 1982 AND 1983 (TEFRA), a plan cannot discriminate in favor of key employees regarding contributions and benefits if favorable tax treatment is to be retained. For example, the premiums the employer pays on behalf of the employee for the first $50,000 of group term life insurance are not considered taxable income to the employee if the plan does not discriminate.

NONDUPLICATION COORDINATION-OF-BENEFITS (CARVE-OUT COB) requirement that the combination of MEDICARE and the employer's plan can not be greater than the amount the employer's plan would pay without Medicare.

NONDUPLICATION OF BENEFITS *see* COORDINATION OF BENEFITS.

NONECONOMIC DAMAGES CAP statutory law that lowers the defendant's liability by restricting the monetary recovery of the plaintiff incurring a specified injury, such as pain and suffering, or by restricting the total amount of recoverable damages.

NONFORFEITABILITY
1. provision in a CASH VALUE INSURANCE policy that an insured will receive the equity in some form even if the insurance is canceled.
2. vested benefit to a retirement plan participant. It is enforceable against the plan.
    See also NONFORFEITURE BENEFIT (OPTION); NONFORFEITURE CASH SURRENDER BENEFIT; NONFORFEITURE EXTENDED TERM BENEFIT; NONFORFEITURE REDUCED PAID-UP BENEFIT.

NONFORFEITURE BENEFIT (OPTION) provision that the equity of an insured in a life insurance policy cannot be forfeited. There are four benefits a policyholder can select under the option: CASH SURRENDER VALUE, EXTENDED TERM INSURANCE, LOAN VALUE, and PAID-UP INSURANCE. If none is elected, a clause in the policy will stipulate the option that automatically goes into effect, usually extended term insurance.

NONFORFEITURE CASH SURRENDER BENEFIT amount in a cash value life insurance policy that a policyowner will receive upon surrender of the policy, minus any outstanding loan and accrued interest. A table in the policy shows the amount of cash surrender values. With some policies, the insurance company reserves the right to hold the cash surrender value for six months from time of notification, but this is rarely if ever applied today.

NONFORFEITURE EXTENDED TERM BENEFIT right of a policyholder, in life insurance with cash values, to continue full coverage for a limited period, as shown in a table in the policy, with no further premiums payable.

NONFORFEITURE FACTOR modified premium used to calculate CASH SURRENDER VALUES in excess of that required by the NAIC: STANDARD NONFORFEITURE LAW.

NONFORFEITURE PROVISION value in life insurance policies that entitle the insured to these choices:

(1) to relinquish the policy for its CASH SURRENDER VALUE. (Note that in the beginning years the cash value may be minimal because of expenses such as agent's commission, premium tax, and the cost of putting the policy on the insurance company's books.)

(2) to take *reduced paid-up insurance* instead of the cash surrender value.

(3) to take EXTENDED TERM INSURANCE for the full face amount instead of the cash surrender value.

(4) to borrow from the company, using the cash value as collateral.

Each policy provides a table illustrating the first 20 years of its guaranteed cash values.

NONFORFEITURE REDUCED PAID-UP BENEFIT right of a policyholder in life insurance with cash value to elect a smaller, fully paid-up policy, without any further premiums to pay. The amount of the paid-up policy is determined by the insured's age and the cash surrender value.

NONFORFEITURE VALUES *see* NONFORFEITURE CASH SURRENDER BENEFIT; NONFORFEITURE EXTENDED TERM BENEFIT; NONFORFEITURE REDUCED PAID-UP BENEFIT.

NONHAZARDOUS describing a RISK whose PROBABILITY of loss is less than the norm or the standard EXPECTATION OF LOSS for that UNDERWRITING classification.

NONINVESTMENT GRADE BONDS bonds that are less than investment grade plus the bonds that are in or approaching default, which comprise part of the insurance company's investment bond portfolio.

NONINSURANCE RISK *see* UNINSURABLE RISK.

NONINSURANCE TRANSFER risk management technique for shifting a corporation's exposure from itself. A risk manager looks at many alternatives to insurance to limit the risks a business firm faces. One transfer method is by contract, such as HOLD-HARMLESS AGREEMENTS, or to insert in an existing contract an endorsement stating that the business firm will not be responsible for something that would normally fall within its responsibility.

NONINSURED DRIVER operator with no liability insurance. If a noninsured driver hits another car, the victim sometimes has no recourse against the driver. For this reason, many motorists carry UNINSURED MOTORIST COVERAGE, an endorsement to the PERSONAL AUTOMOBILE POLICY (PAP) that covers them if they are involved in a collision with a driver without liability insurance. Some states also maintain an UNSATISFIED JUDGMENT FUND to pay claims to innocent victims of automobile accidents.

NONLEDGER ASSETS assets of an INSURER that are due and payable in the current year but have yet to be received by the insurer.

NONLIQUID ASSETS assets that are not readily convertible into cash without a significant loss of principle, such as an automobile, a house, a television set, a radio, etc.

NONMEDICAL APPLICATION *see* NONMEDICAL LIFE INSURANCE.

NONMEDICAL LIFE INSURANCE coverage in which an applicant not required to take a medical examination, instead answers written questions to ascertain his current physical condition.

NONMEDICAL LIMIT dollar ceiling on a life insurance policy for applicants who are not given a medical examination. The insurer accepts a health questionnaire in the place of a physical examination. At one time, a medical examination was a requirement for anyone buying life insurance. In recent years, however, most companies write NONMEDICAL LIFE INSURANCE because the savings in expenses for the company have been found to offset the higher risk of underwriting insurance without the benefit of an examination. However, nonmedical policies are written only for a STANDARD RISK.

NONOCCUPATIONAL DISABILITY condition that results from injury or disease that is not job related. Workers compensation applies to employees disabled by on-the-job injuries or disease. In addition, five states require employers to pay income (not medical expense) benefits if a worker is disabled by illness or injury that did not occur at work: Rhode Island, California, New Jersey, New York, and Hawaii. Except for Rhode Island, employers may buy private coverage; in Rhode Island, they must get coverage from a state fund. Hawaii is the only state without an optional state fund.

NONOCCUPATIONAL HEALTH INSURANCE POLICY insurance coverage for accidents and sickness that are not job related.

NONOCCUPATIONAL POLICY health and medical insurance that excludes coverage for job-related injuries and illnesses. Most medical insurance policies do not provide benefits for job-related claims, which are covered by WORKERS COMPENSATION BENEFITS.

NONOWNERSHIP AIRCRAFT LIABILITY INSURANCE coverage in a separate policy or as an endorsement to the COMMERCIAL GENERAL LIABILITY (CGL) form, for insureds responsible for aircraft they do not own. If an aircraft is leased from another firm or owned by employees who operate it for a business owner, the insured's liability exposure is not covered by the CGL policy; a special endorsement is necessary.

NONOWNERSHIP AUTOMOBILE LIABILITY INSURANCE coverage in a separate policy or as an endorsement to the COMMERCIAL GENERAL LIABILITY (CGL) form, for liability exposures for an employee who drives a leased car or his or her own automobile for business purposes.

NONOWNERSHIP LIABILITY INSURANCE coverage for an employer against liability for property damage or physical injury caused by an employee operating a personally owned vehicle for the business firm. Employers can be held liable if an employee has an accident while driving a leased automobile or operating a motorboat that the employee owns, if it is done for the benefit of the employer. *See also* NONOWNERSHIP AIRCRAFT LIABILITY INSURANCE; NONOWNERSHIP AUTOMOBILE LIABILITY INSURANCE.

NONPARTICIPATING GUARANTEED INSURANCE CONTRACT (GIC) type of GUARANTEED INSURANCE CONTRACT in which the term is fixed, the rate is fixed, and the contract owner does not participate in the insurance company's earnings.

NONPARTICIPATING INSURANCE policy not designed to pay the policyowner a dividend. *See also* CURRENT ASSUMPTION; PARTICIPATING INSURANCE.

NONPARTICIPATING LIFE INSURANCE *see* NONPARTICIPATING INSURANCE.

NONPARTICIPATING POLICY *see* NONPARTICIPATING INSURANCE.

NONPROFIT INSURER company formed and operated without the profit motive as its normal business objective; normally sells and services health insurance policies. *See also* BLUE CROSS; BLUE SHIELD.

NONPROPORTIONAL AUTOMATIC REINSURANCE obligatory reinsurance contract in which a reinsurer agrees to pay for all or a large portion of losses up to a limit, when these losses exceed the retention level of the cedent. The reinsurance premium paid by the cedent is calculated independently of the premium charged to the insured. It is not expected that every treaty will pay for itself or that every loss will be recouped by the reinsurer. When a cedent reinsures on a nonproportional basis, it retains substantially more of its profits than reinsuring on a proportional basis. Nonproportional differs from proportional reinsurance in that it does not involve the sharing of risks.

NONPROPORTIONAL FACULTATIVE REINSURANCE coverage in which an insurer is not bound to CEDE and a reinsurer is not bound to accept a risk. A separate reinsurance contract covers each cession. The contract is automatically renewed if the original insurance is renewed. Casualty facultative reinsurance is usually written on excess of loss basis, and the reinsurer shares only in losses which exceed retention level of the cedent.

NONPROPORTIONAL REINSURANCE arrangement in which a reinsurer makes payments to an insurer whose losses exceed a predetermined retention level. Nonproportional reinsurance is either *facultative* or *automatic*. *See also* CATASTROPHE LOSS; EXCESS OF LOSS REINSURANCE; STOP LOSS REINSURANCE.

NONQUALIFIED DEFERRED COMPENSATION type of DEFERRED COMPENSATION PLAN in which income deferred and supplemental retirement benefits are provided to a KEY EMPLOYEE (KEY PERSON). To fund this plan, life insurance policies are often the vehicle.

NONQUALIFIED PLAN employee benefit plan that does not have the federal tax advantages of a *qualified pension plan*, in which employers receive a federal tax deduction for contributions paid into the plan on behalf of their employees. For an employer, not having a tax deduction can be a serious disadvantage, but a nonqualified plan has these advantages:
1. otherwise discriminatory coverage for some employees is allowed.
2. benefits can be allocated to certain employees whom the employer wishes to reward. The result could be that the total cost of the benefits for a particular group of employees may be less under a nonqualified plan than for all employees under a qualified plan.

NONRENEWAL CLAUSE provision in a policy that states the circumstances under which an insurer may elect not to renew the policy.

NONRESIDENT AGENT agent who is licensed and who markets and services insurance policies in a state in which he or she is not domiciled.

NONSMOKER health characteristic considered by an insurer underwriting an applicant for life or health insurance. Many insurance companies charge reduced premiums for nonsmokers.

NONSTANDARD RISK *see* IMPAIRED RISK.

NONSTOCK INSURANCE COMPANY INSURANCE COMPANY that has no outstanding shares of stock, such as a MUTUAL INSURANCE COMPANY.

NONTRADITIONAL REINSURANCE types of REINSURANCE instruments under which the amount of RISK transferred is more limited than under TRADITIONAL RISK REINSURANCE instruments. The limitations on risk transfer take the form of an aggregate dollar amount or loss ratio limits according to the reinsurance coverage in effect. Premiums for nontraditional reinsurance instruments are usually larger than those for traditional reinsurance instruments.

NONVALUED INSURANCE POLICY POLICY under which the INSURER will pay the actual cash value of the property at the time the property was damaged or destroyed provided the loss falls within the LIMITATIONS of the policy.

NONWAIVER AGREEMENT agreement by the insured that, simply because the INSURER investigates and determines a value for the CLAIM, the insurer does not admit liability for the claim.

NOON CLAUSE CLAUSE in the INSURANCE POLICY that stipulates the exact time the policy coverage begins and terminates.

NORMAL ANNUITY FORM cost computation form that assumes retirement and commencement of annuity payments on the first day of the month nearest the birthday when a retiree reaches normal retirement age. Most employee pension plans provide for a normal retirement age of 65, with pension or annuity payments to begin at that time. But many also provide an *optional annuity form* for those who wish to either retire before or continue working past the normal retirement age. These employees receive reduced benefits, in the case of the early retirees, or, possibly, enhanced benefits for those who work longer.

NORMAL LOSS particular type of loss which is expected by an organization and for which provision is usually made in the budgeting process of the organization. *See also* SELF INSURANCE; SELF-INSURED RETENTION (SIR).

NORMAL RETIREMENT AGE earliest age at which an employee can retire without a penalty reduction in pension benefits after having (1) reached a minimum age and (2) served a minimum number of years with an employer. Historically, this has been 65 years, but many private pension plans now envision earlier or later normal retirement ages.

NORTH AMERICAN FREE TRADE AGREEMENT (NAFTA) OF 1993 agreement that eliminates tariffs among the United States, Canada, and Mexico over a 15-year period. Approximately 65% of United States agricultural and industrial exports would be eligible for duty-free entry into Mexico and Canada, either on an immediate basis or within five years. This could very well expand insurance operations both south and north of the border.

NOTICE OF CANCELLATION CLAUSE provision in an insurance policy that permits an insured to cancel the policy and recoup the excess of the paid premiums above the customary *short rate* for the expired time. The clause also permits a company to cancel the policy at any time by sending the insured five days' written notice and repaying the excess of the paid premium above the *pro rata* premium for the expired time.

NOTICE TO COMPANY written notice, to be submitted by the CLAIMANT, required by the insurance company in the event of an INSURED PERIL. This notice is part of the standard PROPERTY AND CASUALTY INSURANCE PROVISIONS defining the insured's obligations after a loss.

NSC *see* NATIONAL SAFETY COUNCIL.

NUCLEAR ENERGY LIABILITY INSURANCE coverage for bodily injury and property damage liability resulting from the nuclear energy material (whether or not radioactive) on the insured business's premises or in transit. This insurance has become more significant since the Three Mile Island accident. In order to obtain a license for a nuclear facility, there must be evidence of financial responsibility such as insurance. Nuclear energy liability is excluded from nearly all other liability policies.

NUCLEAR REACTION EXCLUSION clause in most property insurance policies that excepts coverage for loss from a nuclear reaction or radiation, or radioactive contamination. (However, a fire resulting from one of these perils would be covered.) Because of this exclusion, insurer pools have been formed to write coverage for nuclear reactors.

In addition, the NUCLEAR REGULATORY COMMISSION is authorized to provide coverage under the PRICE-ANDERSON ACT.

NUCLEAR REGULATORY COMMISSION U.S. government agency (formerly the Atomic Energy Commission) responsible for regulating the nuclear energy industry. The commission also provides supplemental insurance for nuclear facilities to augment coverage by private insurance pools.

NUISANCE product or service that does more harm than good to society, or endangers life or health. Society would probably be better off without such a product or service. *See also* ATTRACTIVE NUISANCE.

NUMERICAL RATING SYSTEM underwriting method used in classifying applicants for life insurance according to certain demographic factors and assigning weights to these factors. Factors include physical condition, build, family history, personal history, habits, and morals. For example, if an applicant is 5 feet 8 inches and weighs 250 pounds, his mortality expectation based on this height-weight ratio may be 160% of a standard risk who weighs 150 pounds at that height. In this instance a debit of 60 percentage points would be listed next to the weight factor on the applicant's underwriting sheet. If the applicant has an excellent family history (no hereditary diseases such as diabetes), his mortality expectation based on this factor is 90% of the standard risk. Here a credit of 10 percentage points would be listed next to the family history factor. Upon completion of the debiting/crediting process, debits and credits would be totaled for a final rate, which would classify the applicant as *standard, substandard,* or an *uninsurable risk.*

O

OASDHI *see* OLD AGE, SURVIVORS, DISABILITY, AND HEALTH INSURANCE (OASDHI).

OBLIGATORY REINSURANCE *see* AUTOMATIC REINSURANCE.

OBLIGEE *see* FIDELITY BOND; LIABILITY, BUSINESS EXPOSURES; SURETY BOND.

OBLIGOR individual or other entity who has promised to perform a certain act. For example, an insurance company promises to pay a death benefit if a life insurance policy is in force at the time of the death of an insured.

OBSOLESCENCE decrease in value of property as the result of technological advancement and/or changing social mores. This factor is used to measure the amount of depreciation in determining the ACTUAL CASH VALUE of damaged or destroyed property protected by PROPERTY INSURANCE COVERAGE.

OCCUPANCY AND FIRE RATES direct relationship between the use to which a building is put and the likelihood that it will catch on fire. Occupancy is one of the most important factors in setting fire insurance rates. For example, a building that houses an explosives manufacturer is at much greater risk than one occupied by a jewelry boutique. Other factors that influence the risk of fire are geographical location, construction, nature of the neighborhood, and the adequacy of protective devices.

OCCUPATION *see* OCCUPATIONAL HAZARD.

OCCUPATIONAL ACCIDENT work-related accident. Occupational accidents that injure employees are the responsibility of the employer and are covered by WORKERS COMPENSATION INSURANCE. In recent years, the term occupational accident has been expanded to include job-related long-term exposure to hazardous substances that result in occupational diseases, and such emotional injuries as nervous breakdowns and even heart attacks.

OCCUPATIONAL CLASSIFICATION classification of occupations according to the DEGREE OF RISK inherent in that occupation. *See also* OCCUPATIONAL HAZARD; OCCUPATION, RISK.

OCCUPATIONAL DISEASE illness contracted as the result of employment-related exposures and conditions. Coverage for such diseases is found under WORKERS COMPENSATION INSURANCE.

OCCUPATIONAL HAZARD condition surrounding a work environment that increases the probability of death, disability, or illness to a worker. This class of hazard is considered when writing WORKERS

COMPENSATION INSURANCE or determining which underwriting classification to place an applicant for life or health insurance.

OCCUPATIONAL INJURY *see* OCCUPATIONAL ACCIDENT; OCCUPATIONAL HAZARD; OCCUPATION RISK.

OCCUPATIONAL SAFETY AND HEALTH ACT (OSHA) 1970 legislation that set federal standards for workplace safety and imposed fines for failure to meet them. A controversial law, it took much of the power from the states for regulating workplace safety. It authorized the U.S. Department of Labor to have federal compliance officers make surprise inspections of business firms. It set up the NATIONAL COMMISSION OF STATE WORKERS COMPENSATION LAWS to recommend upgrade of worker protection, including higher disability benefits, compulsory coverage, and unlimited medical care and rehabilitation. Most states adopted the recommendations, which incidentally led to increases in workers compensation insurance premiums.

OCCUPATIONAL SAFETY AND HEALTH ADMINISTRATION STANDARD ON BLOOD-BORNE PATHOGENS standard designed to reduce occupational exposure to blood-borne pathogens (microorganisms in human blood that can cause diseases in humans, such as HIV and hepatitis B). The standard emphasizes using a combination of personal protective clothing and equipment, vaccination, engineering controls, work practice controls, and training.

OCCUPATION, RISK relationship between occupation of an insured and degree of risk in such coverages as life, health, and workers compensation. Some occupations are more risky than others; for example, a high wire performer would have to pay more for life insurance than a banker. But the impact of occupation goes further. Claims resulting from exposure to toxic substances that result in occupational disease have been one of the most costly business insurance expenses of recent years. Life and health insurance underwriters also consider whether the occupation of a potential insured is likely to encourage a reckless lifestyle. For example, certain high-pressure occupations, like acting or Wall Street trading, might be considered to lead to overconsumption of alcohol or drug abuse. Occupation is one of many factors weighed by the underwriter in RISK SELECTION.

OCCURRENCE event that results in bodily injury and/or property damage to a THIRD PARTY. A CLAUSE that is common to most LIABILITY INSURANCE policies stipulates that all bodily injuries and/or property damages resulting from the same general conditions are interpreted as resulting from one occurrence and thus subject to the policy limits per occurrence.

OCCURRENCE BASIS coverage, in liability insurance, for harm suffered by others because of events occurring while a policy is in force, regardless of when a claim is actually made. *See also* CLAIMS MADE BASIS LIABILITY COVERAGE.

OCCURRENCE FORM *see* OCCURRENCE BASIS.

OCCURRENCE/INJURY THEORY viewpoint that an insurer whose liability policy is in force at the time of an accident or injury should pay a claim. *See also* LONG-TAIL LIABILITY; MANIFESTATION/INJURY THEORY.

OCCURRENCE LIMIT maximum amount that an insurance company is obligated to pay all injured parties seeking recourse as the result of the occurrence of an event covered under a LIABILITY INSURANCE policy. In order for the coverage to apply, the policy must have been written on an OCCURRENCE BASIS.

OCEAN ACCIDENT AND GUARANTEE CORPORATION major credit insurer of the early 20th century that merged into the London Guarantee and Accident Co. in 1931.

OCEAN MARINE EXPOSURE possibility of loss associated with water transportation, including hull damage or destruction, cargo damage or destruction, liability to others for bodily injury, and property damage or destruction.

OCEAN MARINE INSURANCE coverage in the event of a marine loss. Marine loss is damage or destruction of a ship's hull and the ship's cargo (freight) as the result of the occurrence of an insured peril. Perils insured against include collision of the ship with another ship or object; the ship sinking, capsizing, or being stranded; fire; piracy; jettisoning (throwing overboard of property to save other property); barratry (fraud or other illegal act by a ship's master or crew, resulting in damage or destruction of the ship and/or cargo), and various other liability exposures. To be covered, an act cannot involve prior knowledge by the owner of the ship or its cargo. Excluded are wear and tear, dampness, decay, mold, and war. *See also* OCEAN MARINE INSURANCE, WAR RISKS.

OCEAN MARINE INSURANCE, WAR RISKS coverage on cargo in overseas ships for war-caused liability excluded under standard OCEAN MARINE INSURANCE. Not covered is cargo awaiting shipment on a wharf, or on ships after 15 days of arrival at a port. Confiscation of the cargo by a government is covered. Most policies have an automatic termination clause that goes into effect within 60 days of the declaration of war between countries specified in the policy.

OCEAN MARINE PROTECTION AND INDEMNITY INSURANCE coverage for bodily injury and property damage liability excluded under standard OCEAN MARINE INSURANCE. Coverage includes protection of wharfs, docks, and harbors; bodily injury; cost of removing the wreck if ship is sunk; and the cost of disinfecting and quarantining a ship.

ODD LOT purchase of less than 100 shares of a stock.

ODDS probable number of times that a specified event is likely to occur. For example, if E is the event, then the odds for E occurring are X to Y according to the following relationship:

$$P(E) = \frac{X}{X + Y}$$

where P = probability. The odds against E occurring are Y to X. For example, if the probability of E occurring equals 0.6 [$P(E)$ = 0.6], then

$$P(E) = \frac{6}{6 + 4} = \frac{6}{10}$$

Therefore, the odds for E occurring are 6 to 4. The odds against E occurring are 4 to 6.

OFAC LIST (THE OFFICE OF FOREIGN ASSETS CONTROL OF THE U.S. TREASURY LIST) list of names of terrorists and terrorist organizations with whom financial institutions are prohibited from conducting transactions or any other business.

OFF-BALANCE-SHEET RISK risk associated with excessive rate of growth in premiums and contingencies such as affiliate company requirements.

OFFER application for a policy, in life insurance, accompanied by the first premium; in property and casualty insurance, the insurance application itself.

OFFER AND ACCEPTANCE submission of the APPLICATION and the first premium by the prospective INSURED—the "offer"—and the issuance of the INSURANCE POLICY by the insurance company—the "acceptance."

OFFEREE
1. in life insurance, receipt by a company of an insurance application accompanied by the first premium.
2. in property and casualty insurance, a company's receipt of an application.

OFFICE BURGLARY AND ROBBERY INSURANCE coverage for the office of a business, or an individual in a general office building or other structure. Includes burglary of a safe; damage caused by robbery and burglary, actual or attempted; theft of office furniture, equipment, supplies and fixtures within an office; robbery inside and outside an office; kidnapping so as to force managers of an office and/or their representatives to open the office from the outside; and theft of securities and monies from the home of a messenger of the office and/or from a night depository of a bank.

OFFICE CONTENTS FORM *see* OFFICE BURGLARY AND ROBBERY INSURANCE.

OFFICE PERSONAL PROPERTY FORM endorsement to many commercial property insurance policies that covers office equipment. Coverage includes all equipment, whether or not owned by an insured, improvements an insured has made to his or her office (if leased), and valuable documents such as manuscripts. This also applies to property that has been purchased for the office while in transit.

OFFICERS AND DIRECTORS LIABILITY INSURANCE *see* DIRECTORS AND OFFICERS LIABILITY INSURANCE.

OFFICERS PROTECTIVE MARINE INSURANCE type of insurance providing ALL RISKS coverage for personal property of the crew and passengers aboard a ship. Marine cargo insurance does not cover personal property of the crew and passengers, thus necessitating the purchase of an *Officers Protective Policy.*

OFFICIAL BONDS *see* PUBLIC EMPLOYEES BLANKET BOND; PUBLIC OFFICIAL BONDS.

OFF PREMISES location that is different from an insured's home or place of business. Under the standard HOMEOWNERS INSURANCE POLICY, the property of the insured is covered off premises; for example, if it is stolen from an airport. Likewise, an employer is liable for physical injury and property damage caused by an employee or by equipment, even if it does not occur at the place of business. If a truck spills chemicals on the highway or at another business site, or if a salesperson injures a client on a sales call, the employer is responsible. Business liability policies insure against such risks.

OFFSET APPROACH method of integrating an employee's Social Security or other retirement benefits with a qualified retirement plan. Some employers offset (reduce) retirement or disability income benefits from an employee's Social Security income, reasoning that since Social Security taxes are a business expense for them, they should reduce or offset employee pension benefits by a percentage of the Social Security money. An employer with a 100% offset would subtract the entire Social Security payment from the earned pension and pay only the difference as the employee pension. A 50% offset means the employer subtracts half of the Social Security benefit from the pension benefit and pays the difference.

OL&T *see* OWNERS, LANDLORDS, AND TENANTS LIABILITY POLICY.

OLD AGE, SURVIVORS, DISABILITY, AND HEALTH INSURANCE (OASDHI) federal social insurance program that provides monthly benefits to qualified retirees, their dependents, their survivors, and, in some cases, disabled workers. OASDHI was created by the Social Security Act of 1935. Federal taxes are withheld from the paychecks of all covered workers, which includes most workers with the exception of public employees and certain union employees. Self-employed persons are also required to pay the tax. Full benefits are paid to retired workers after age 65, if born prior to 1938, with a partial benefit for retirees at age 62. The full benefit retirement age continues to rise until age 67 is reached, if born after 1960, with a partial benefit remaining for retirees at age 62. Retirement may be delayed beyond the full benefit retirement age until age 70 with a percentage increase in benefits. Dependents and survivors of qualified workers also qualify for benefits, as do some categories of disabled workers and their dependents.

OLD LINE COMPANY imprecise term still occasionally used by commercial or PROPRIETARY INSURERS to differentiate them from *fraternal* insurers. "Old line" was apparently meant to make these companies sound more established and distinguished.

OLD LINE LEGAL RESERVE COMPANY commercial life insurers that operate on the LEGAL RESERVE system as opposed to FRATERNAL LIFE INSURANCE companies, many of which now operate on a legal reserve basis.

OMISSIONS wrongful inaction; failure to act; inactivity.

OMISSIONS CLAUSE provision of a *treaty reinsurance* contract stating that if an insurer fails to report a risk that would normally be covered, the reinsurer is still liable for the risk.

OMNIBUS CLAUSE provision in PERSONAL AUTOMOBILE POLICY (PAP) providing coverage to persons driving an automobile with permission of the NAMED INSURED.

ONE YEAR TERM OPTION *see* DIVIDEND OPTION.

OPEN CARGO FORM *see* SINGLE RISK CARGO INSURANCE.

OPEN CERTIFICATE *see* OPEN FORM (REPORTING FORM); OPEN POLICY.

OPEN COMPETITION LAW form of state rating legislation that allows each property/liability insurer to choose between using rates set by a bureau or its own rates. Individual states regulate insurers and approve their property insurance rates. There are three methods of rate approval in addition to open competition: PRIOR APPROVAL RATING, MODIFIED PRIOR APPROVAL RATING and *file and use*. At one time the insurance industry operated like a cartel, with rates set by bureaus and filed with the insurance commissioners of each state. Experts believed that competition would result in either unfairly high rates or unreasonably low rates that would lead to mass insurance company insolvencies. But open competition became widespread after New York State adopted it in 1969.

OPEN COMPETITION STATE *see* RATING BUREAU.

OPEN CONTRACT *see* OPEN POLICY.

OPEN DEBIT circumstance in which no agent is servicing a DEBIT. *See also* DEBIT INSURANCE (HOME SERVICE INSURANCE, INDUSTRIAL INSURANCE).

OPEN-END INVESTMENT COMPANY type of investment company that continues to buy and sell its own shares on the open market. There are an unlimited number of shares available. *See also* CLOSED-END INVESTMENT COMPANY.

OPEN END POLICY *see* OPEN FORM (REPORTING FORM); OPEN POLICY.

OPEN FORM (REPORTING FORM) single policy covering all insurable property of specified type(s) at all locations of an insured business. The form is appropriate for the business that has several locations. There are several different types of reporting forms: (1) *Form ML.1* insures businesses with substantial risk exposures on a multiple location basis; (2) *Form ML.2* insures businesses with a distilled spirits risk exposure; and (3) *Form A* insures businesses with relatively small risk exposures, at either a single or multiple locations. *See also* BLANKET INSURANCE.

OPEN PERILS AGREEMENT *see* ALL RISKS.

OPEN PERILS/OPEN COVERAGE insurance that covers each and every loss except for those specifically excluded. If the insurance company does not specifically exclude a particular loss, it is automatically covered. This is the broadest type of property policy that can be purchased. For example, if an insurance policy does not specifically exclude losses from wind damage, or from a meteor falling on the insured's house, the insured is covered for such losses. *See also* NAMED PERIL POLICY; SPECIFIED PERIL INSURANCE. Formerly referenced as ALL RISK INSURANCE.

OPEN POLICY coverage normally used on an indefinite basis under OCEAN MARINE INSURANCE and INLAND MARINE INSURANCE (TRANSPORTATION INSURANCE): BUSINESS RISKS for the damage or destruction of a shipper's goods in transit. While the policy is in force, the shipper is required each month to submit to the insurance company reports on goods being shipped to be covered by the policy; premiums are also submitted at that time.

OPEN STOCK BURGLARY POLICY *see* MERCANTILE OPEN-STOCK BURGLARY INSURANCE.

OPERATING CASH FLOW (OCF) indication of rate at which investment and underwriting operations generate cash that can then be used to fund various company activities such as dividend payments and new investments.

OPERATING INCOME total of NET INVESTMENT INCOME plus UNDERWRITING INCOME plus other miscellaneous income. This type of income is an indication of how the UNDERWRITING function and the INVESTMENT function of the insurance company are performing.

OPERATING LEVERAGE RATIO premium income divided by the SURPLUS ACCOUNT.

OPERATIONS LIABILITY business liability for bodily injury or property damage resulting from operations of the business. Business firms can buy insurance for this risk with a variety of liability policies, including the COMMERCIAL GENERAL LIABILITY INSURANCE (CGL).

OPIC *see* OVERSEAS PRIVATE INVESTMENT CORPORATION (OPIC).

OPPORTUNITY COST value of a foregone opportunity, one rejected in favor of a presumably better opportunity. For example, investment of a sum into a MUTUAL FUND instead of a *variable annuity* with a comparable equities portfolio, thereby foregoing the tax deferred advantages of the investment build-up under the variable annuity.

OPTION *see* OPTIONAL MODES OF SETTLEMENT.

OPTIONAL ANNUITY FORM *see* ANNUITY.

OPTIONAL BENEFITS choice of a lump sum payment for an injury incurred instead of a series of periodic payments, available under a health insurance policy.

OPTIONALLY RENEWABLE CONTRACT health insurance contract that is renewable at the option of the insurer. On the anniversary date of the contract, the insurer has the right to decide whether or not to renew.

OPTIONALLY RENEWABLE HEALTH INSURANCE *see* HEALTH INSURANCE.

OPTIONAL MODES OF SETTLEMENT choice of one of the following available to a life insurance policyowner (or beneficiary, if entitled to receive a death benefit in a lump sum at the death of an insured):
1. INTEREST OPTION—death benefit left on deposit at interest with the insurance company with earnings paid to the beneficiary annually. The beneficiary can withdraw part or all of the principal of the death proceeds, subject to any restrictions the policyowner may have placed on this option.
2. *fixed amount option*—death benefit paid in a series of fixed amount installments until the proceeds and interest earned terminate.
3. *fixed period option*—death benefit left on deposit with the insurance company with the death benefit plus interest thereon paid out in equal payments for the period of time selected.
4. *life income option*—death benefit plus interest paid through a life ANNUITY. Income continues under a *straight life income option,* for as long as the beneficiary lives; or whether or not the beneficiary lives, under a *life income with period certain* option.

OPTIONAL PERIL ENDORSEMENT provision in many property insurance policies that allows an insured to pick coverage for selected perils. The choices are (1) explosion; (2) explosion, riot and civil commotion; (3) explosion, riot and civil commotion, and vandalism and malicious mischief; and (4) aircraft and vehicle damage to property.

OPTIONS CONTRACT arrangement between the seller and the buyer in which the buyer has the right to buy (CALL OPTION) or sell (PUT OPTION) a security at some time in the future at a price stipulated at present.

ORDINARY AGENCY local life insurance office that sells and services *ordinary life insurance* as well as other forms of life insurance except DEBT INSURANCE.

ORDINARY LIFE INSURANCE policy that remains in full force and effect for the life of the insured, with premium payments being made for the same period. See also LIMITED PAYMENT LIFE INSURANCE; TERM LIFE INSURANCE.

ORDINARY LIFE—WHOLE LIFE—STRAIGHT LIFE three terms that are synonymous. *See also* ORDINARY LIFE INSURANCE.

ORDINARY PAYROLL *see* ORDINARY PAYROLL COVERAGE ENDORSEMENT.

ORDINARY PAYROLL COVERAGE ENDORSEMENT policy provision that provides coverage for continuing payroll expense of all employees of an insured business (except for officers and executives) for the first specified number of days of business interruption. Applies when the business's continuing operation is interrupted by damage or destruction by an insured peril.

ORDINARY PAYROLL EXCLUSION ENDORSEMENT provision in BUSINESS INTERRUPTION INSURANCE that excludes coverage for continuing the wages of rank and file employees. Business interruption insurance covers an employer for loss of earnings, including payroll expense, that occurs when a business must be shut down as a result of a direct insurable loss, such as a fire. However, in order to save on the premium, an employer may not want payroll coverage for ordinary workers because if the business were temporarily shut down, the workers could be replaced. In this case, the endorsement would be written to cover only officers and key employees.

ORDINARY REGISTER record of ordinary policies that a COMBINATION AGENT is responsible for servicing.

ORIGINAL AGE insured's age at the date a TERM LIFE INSURANCE policy is issued. An original age or *retroactive conversion* option permits the insured to convert the term policy to a cash value policy as of the original date of issue. Conversion is made without a physical examination, but a correction factor is charged to reflect the difference in premiums between the policies that would have been payable beginning at the original date of issue. This difference is accumulated at interest to reflect the time value of money. *See also* ATTAINED AGE.

ORIGINAL AGE CONVERSION *see* ORIGINAL AGE.

ORIGINAL COST actual price paid for property when it was acquired. The original cost might apply to a piece of jewelry, to a piece of equipment, or to a building. For insurance purposes, original cost is often different from *replacement cost* or ACTUAL CASH VALUE.

ORIGINAL COST LESS DEPRECIATION actual price paid for property when acquired, minus depreciation. Original cost less depreciation is used to compute ACTUAL CASH VALUE, which is often the insurable interest in a property.

OTHER INSURANCE presence of other contract(s) covering the same conditions. When more than one policy covers the exposure, each policy will pay an equal share of the loss.

OTHER INSURANCE CLAUSE provision in a property, liability, or health insurance policy stipulating the extent of coverage in the event that other insurance covers the same property. *See also* APPORTIONMENT; COORDINATION OF BENEFITS.

OTHER INSUREDS individuals or organizations covered by PROPERTY AND LIABILITY INSURANCE other than the named insured. For example, under the PERSONAL AUTOMOBILE POLICY (PAP), other insureds under Coverage A—Liability are the named insured's spouse, other relatives living with the insured, and any other person using the automobile with the permission of the insured or the insured's spouse. *See also* RIDERS, LIFE POLICIES.

OTHER STRUCTURES HOMEOWNERS COVERAGE B INSURANCE POLICY—SECTION I (PROPERTY COVERAGE) coverage for buildings on the insured's residence. The premises are distinctly separated from that residence by a clear space such as a detached workshop, garage, or photography shop.

OTHER-THAN-COLLISION LOSS option found in the PERSONAL AUTOMOBILE POLICY (PAP)—Coverage D—Comprehensive that pays for the physical damage to the insured's automobile except for COLLISION—Coverage E, and specific excluded losses.

OUTAGE INSURANCE *see* EXTRA EXPENSE INSURANCE.

OUTBOARD MOTOR BOAT INSURANCE coverage on an ALL RISKS basis for physical damage loss. Coverage applies to property damage to the insured boat or damage caused by the insured boat to a third party boat (property damage liability). Excluded perils are war damage, use of boat in a race or speed contest, nuclear loss, and so forth. Bodily injury liability coverage is excluded from this policy since the operator of the boat would be covered for this risk under a COMPREHENSIVE PERSONAL LIABILITY INSURANCE policy, HOMEOWNERS INSURANCE POLICY, or TENANTS INSURANCE.

OUT-OF-AREA EMERGENCY SERVICES *see* HEALTH MAINTENANCE ORGANIZATION (HMO).

OUTPATIENT individual receiving medical treatment who is not required to be hospitalized overnight.

OUTPATIENT HEALTH SERVICES AT HMO FACILITY *see* HEALTH MAINTENANCE ORGANIZATION (HMO).

OUTPATIENT HOSPITAL CARE, HMO *see* HEALTH MAINTENANCE ORGANIZATION (HMO).

OUTSTANDING PREMIUMS payments due to an insurance company but not yet paid.

OVERCHARGING charging the insured an amount that is above the actual PREMIUM required for placing and maintaining the POLICY in force.

OVERHEAD EXPENSE DISABILITY INCOME POLICY type of DISABILITY INCOME POLICY used to provide funds for the ongoing monthly business expenses (such as employee salaries, utility charges, rent, and equipment payment due) necessary to maintain continuing operations in the event an owner/key person becomes disabled. Generally, there is a 60-day ELIMINATION PERIOD after which monthly income payments commence until a stipulated aggregate limit has been reached.

OVERHEAD INSURANCE *see* BUSINESS INCOME COVERAGE FORM.

OVERINSURANCE situation in which insurance benefits exceed the actual loss of an insured. Overinsurance can be a problem for the insurer because it may tempt the insured to make a false claim in order to profit financially. Various safeguards are designed to prevent overinsurance. For example, in group health insurance, companies break down benefits paid by the primary carrier and the secondary carrier through COORDINATION OF BENEFITS. Still, some types of coverage, particularly disability income insurance, are subject to overinsurance abuse.

OVERLAPPING INSURANCE coverage by at least two insurance policies providing the same coverage for the same risk. *See also* APPORTIONMENT; CONCURRENCY; COORDINATION OF BENEFITS; NONCONCURRENCY; PRIMARY INSURANCE.

OVER LINE coverage that exceeds the normal insurance capacity of an insurer or reinsurer.

OVERRIDING COMMISSION payment to a broker, master general agent, general agent, or agent on any particular line of insurance written by other agents within a particular geographical area.

OVERSEAS PRIVATE INVESTMENT CORPORATION (OPIC) federal program to insure private U.S. investments in foreign countries, created by the Foreign Assistance Act of 1961. It is a joint government and private effort to encourage U.S. investments abroad by providing protection against three political risks: (1) inability to convert foreign currency; (2) expropriation of facilities by a foreign country; and (3) war or revolution. The program is guaranteed by the full faith and credit of the U.S. government.

OVER-THE-COUNTER SELLING OF INSURANCE method of selling insurance in which the INSURED purchases the product directly from the insurance company and not through an AGENT. *See also* SAVINGS BANK LIFE INSURANCE (SBLI).

OVERWRITING COMMISSION *see* OVERRIDING COMMISSION.

OWNERS AND CONTRACTORS PROTECTIVE LIABILITY INSURANCE endorsement to COMMERCIAL GENERAL LIABILITY FORM (CGL); OWNERS, LANDLORDS, AND TENANTS LIABILITY POLICY; MANUFACTURERS AND CONTRACTORS LIABILITY INSURANCE; or other liability policies for business firms that provides liability coverage for an insured who is sued because of negligent acts or omissions of an independent contractor or subcontractor resulting in bodily injury and/or property damage to a third party.

OWNER'S DESIGNATED BENEFICIARY designated individual who is to receive the POLICYHOLDER's interest in the policy should the policyholder die prior to the distribution of all of the policyholder's interest in the policy.

OWNERSHIP OF EXPIRATIONS retention of all files of policies sold by the agent of record who, according to written agreement with the insurance company, has the exclusive rights to solicit renewals. *See also* INDEPENDENT AGENCY SYSTEM INDEPENDENT AGENT.

OWNERSHIP OF LIFE INSURANCE *see* OWNERSHIP RIGHTS UNDER LIFE INSURANCE; POLICYHOLDER.

OWNERSHIP PROVISION *see* OWNERSHIP RIGHTS UNDER LIFE INSURANCE; POLICYHOLDER.

OWNERSHIP RIGHTS UNDER LIFE INSURANCE right of the *policyowner* as listed in a policy. An insured has the right to exercise all privileges and receive all benefits of the policy except when restricted by the right of an *irrevocable beneficiary* or an assignee of record. A policyowner can transfer ownership of the policy by making an *absolute assignment* (rights transferred to another individual without any conditions) or a COLLATERAL ASSIGNMENT (policy is security for a loan), transfer ownership by endorsement, change the plan of insurance (apply the cash value of present policy to purchase another type of policy with the original policy's date), *reinstate* the policy, select an OPTIONAL MODE OF SETTLEMENT, make a POLICY LOAN, select the DIVIDEND OPTION (if it is a *participating policy),* or select the NONFORFEITURE BENEFIT OPTION.

OWNERS, LANDLORDS, AND TENANTS LIABILITY POLICY coverage for bodily injury and property damage liability resulting from the ownership, use, and/or maintenance of an insured business's premises as well as operations by the business anywhere in the U.S. or Canada. Businesses that qualify for the Owners, Landlords, and Tenants Policy include mercantile establishments, apartment buildings, and office buildings. The only ineligible firms are those engaged in manufacturing. Excluded perils are: operation of an automobile, aircraft, contractual liability resulting from an agreement by the insured, war, nuclear disaster, and liquor liability.

OWN OCCUPATION *see* DISABILITY INCOME INSURANCE—DURATION OF BENEFITS.

P

PACKAGE INSURANCE *see* MULTIPLE LINE INSURANCE.

PACKAGE POLICY several basic property and/or liability policies combined to form a single policy. For example, the HOMEOWNERS INSURANCE POLICY is composed of such basic coverages as BROAD FORM PERSONAL THEFT INSURANCE, COMPREHENSIVE PERSONAL LIABILITY, and FIRE INSURANCE–STANDARD FIRE POLICY.

PAID BUSINESS life and health insurance business for which the prospective insured or insureds have signed the APPLICATION, completed the MEDICAL EXAMINATION, and paid the required PREMIUM.

PAID FOR insurance policy for which the required PREMIUM has been paid. *See also* PAID BUSINESS.

PAID-IN CAPITAL sum received by an insurance company at the sale of its stock. This capital represents the interest of the stockholders in the company.

PAID-IN SURPLUS excess of the value of an insurer's admitted assets over the total value of its liabilities and minimum capital requirements established by applicable statutes designed to assure the insurer's solvency.

PAID LOSSES actual amount of total losses paid by an insurance company during a specified time interval.

PAID-LOSS RETRO PLAN *see* RETROSPECTIVE RATING.

PAID-UP ADDITIONS option under a participating life insurance policy by which the policyowner can elect to have the dividends purchase paid-up increments of permanent insurance.

PAID-UP INSURANCE life insurance policy under which all premiums have already been paid, with no further premium payment due. *See also* LIMITED PAYMENT LIFE INSURANCE.

PAID-UP POLICY RESERVE present value of future benefits. This type of reserve would be applicable for SINGLE PREMIUM LIFE INSURANCE, PAID-UP INSURANCE, single premium ANNUITY, and a paid-up annuity.

PAIN AND SUFFERING DAMAGES see LIABILITY, CIVIL DAMAGES AWARDED.

PAIR CLAUSE *see* SET CLAUSE (PAIR OR SET CLAUSE).

PAIRED PLAN plan that combines a PROFIT SHARING PLAN with a MONEY PURCHASE PLAN. It permits the participant to maximize the flexible part of the combination (profit sharing plan) after satisfying the requirements for the annual contributions to the money purchase plan. Under this combination plan, the maximum annual contribution is

25% of the earned income subject to a maximum of $30,000. For example, if the participant desired to contribute annually the 25% maximum amount of earned income, the participant could commit to making a 15% annual contribution to the money purchase plan and then contribute the remainder to the profit sharing plan if business conditions permit. The only mandate contribution each year would be the 15% of earned income to the money purchase plan.

P&I *see* PROTECTION AND INDEMNITY INSURANCE (P&I).

PAR *see* PARTICIPATING INSURANCE.

PAR VALUE payment of principle of a bond at the end of the period of time.

PARAMEDICAL EXAMINATION medical check of an applicant for life or health insurance by a medical professional who is not a physician.

PARASOL POLICY *see* DIFFERENCE IN CONDITIONS INSURANCE.

PARCEL POST INSURANCE coverage for a shipper (owner/sender) for property damage or loss of goods in transit through the post office. A TRIP TRANSIT INSURANCE policy specifically excludes coverages on property sent through the post office since that agency is not a common carrier and does not incur the liability of a common carrier. This is why additional coverage must be purchased in the form of parcel post insurance, even if a business has a trip transit insurance policy. Parcel post insurance is sold by the post office in the form of a certificate, which covers property in its custody. It is issued on an ALL RISKS basis, subject to exclusions of spoilage, and financial instruments such as bills, currency, deeds, notes, and securities.

PARENT COMPANY insurer in a group of companies that act as subsidiaries. *See also* FLEET OF COMPANIES.

PARENT LIABILITY liability incurred by a parent by reason of a TORT committed by his or her minor child.

PAROL EVIDENCE RULE rule that prohibits the introduction into a court of law of any oral or written agreement that contradicts the final written agreement. For example, an insurance contract containing clauses and provisions is in writing, and as such this contract cannot be contradicted or modified by any oral statements or agreements that are inadmissible in a court of law.

PARTIAL DISABILITY *see* PERMANENT PARTIAL DISABILITY.

PARTIAL DISABILITY BENEFIT an amount usually expressed as 50% of the MONTHLY INDEMNITY for the TOTAL DISABILITY BENEFIT provided by a DISABILITY INCOME INSURANCE POLICY. This amount becomes payable when the insured wage earner's income has been interrupted or terminated because of illness, sickness, or accident. Payments continue up to the time and amount limitations as stipulated in the policy. This type of benefit has been replaced, in large part, by the RESIDUAL DISABILITY INCOME INSURANCE policy.

PARTIAL LOSS damage of property that is not total; average (in sense of partial) loss. *See also* SET CLAUSE.

PARTIAL PLAN TERMINATION scheme to recapture excess pension assets by splitting a qualified plan in two, and terminating one of them. In the mid-1980s, many pension plans became "overfunded" because their investments had performed so well. In order to recapture the "extra" money, some business firms split the pension plan into two plans, one for current employees and an overfunded one for retirees. The company buys annuities to pay the required benefits to retirees and reclaims the excess assets. The other plan is kept in place for current employees.

PARTICIPANT person covered under an EMPLOYEE BENEFIT INSURANCE PLAN.

PARTICIPATING *see* PARTICIPATING INSURANCE.

PARTICIPATING GUARANTEED INVESTMENTS CONTRACT (GIC) type of GUARANTEED INVESTMENTS CONTRACT in which the interest credited is adjusted on a periodic basis to reflect the investment earnings of the underlying assets of the contract.

PARTICIPATING INSURANCE policy that pays a dividend to its owner. *See also* PARTICIPATING POLICY DIVIDEND.

PARTICIPATING POLICY DIVIDEND life insurance contract that pays its owner dividends, which can be: (1) taken as cash; (2) applied to reduce a premium; (3) applied to purchase an increment of PAID-UP INSURANCE; (4) left on deposit with the insurance company to accumulate at interest; and (5) applied to purchase *term insurance* for one year.

PARTICIPATING POLICY DIVIDEND OPTION *see* PARTICIPATING POLICY DIVIDEND.

PARTICIPATING REINSURANCE *see* PROPORTIONAL REINSURANCE; QUOTA SHARE REINSURANCE; SURPLUS REINSURANCE.

PARTICIPATION *see* PARTICIPATING INSURANCE.

PARTICIPATION CLAUSE CLAUSE found in HEALTH INSURANCE CONTRACTS that requires the INSURED to pay a specified percentage of the covered health care expenses.

PARTICIPATION RATE percentage of the increase in the underlying index rate that will be credited to the ANNUITANT in an EQUITY INDEXED ANNUITY. For example, if the underlying index increases by 10% and the rate of participation is 60%, the annuitant will be credited with 6%.

PARTICULAR AVERAGE
1. expenses and damages incurred as the result of damage to a ship and its cargo, and/or of taking direct action to prevent initial or

further damage to the ship and its cargo. These expenses and damages are paid by the owner of the part of the ship and cargo which actually suffers a loss. Contrast with GENERAL AVERAGE.

2. partial loss of property resulting from an OCEAN MARINE EXPOSURE for which the owner of that property must bear the entire loss. *See also* FREE OF PARTICULAR AVERAGE (FPA).

PARTICULAR RISK type of RISK that affects relatively few individuals or units of capital in a given instance. It is thought that individuals can control their own particular circumstances concerning the occurrence or non-occurrence of an event.

PARTNERSHIP type of business organization structured such that two or more people are legally bound by a contractual relationship. *See also* GENERAL PARTNER, LIMITED PARTNERSHIP.

PARTNERSHIP ENTITY PLAN *see* PARTNERSHIP LIFE AND HEALTH INSURANCE.

PARTNERSHIP FOR LONG-TERM CARE combination of public and private LONG-TERM CARE (LTC) insurance plan adopted by many states including New York, California, Indiana, Connecticut, and Idaho. Under this plan a private long-term care policy has been approved for qualification by the particular state of residence. When the benefits are exhausted, the insured can make application for MEDICAID to cover the excess costs. The insured is allowed to retain assets for an amount equal to the received insurance benefits.

PARTNERSHIP INSURANCE *see* PARTNERSHIP LIFE AND HEALTH INSURANCE.

PARTNERSHIP LIFE AND HEALTH INSURANCE protection to maintain the value of a business in case of death or disability of a partner. Upon the death or long-term disability of a partner, insurance can provide for the transfer of a deceased or disabled partner's interest to the surviving partner according to a predetermined formula. Funding can be achieved through either of two plans:

1. *Cross Purchase Plan*—each partner buys insurance on the lives of the other partners. The beneficiaries are the surviving partners who use the proceeds to buy out the deceased's interest. This plan can become complicated when there are more than two partners. For example, if there are four partners, partner A will buy insurance on the lives of partners B, C, and D. The procedure would be repeated with partners B, C, and D. Total policies would be 12.

2. *Entity Plan*—because of the number of policies required, the entity plan is most often used for buy-and-sell agreements by larger partnerships. The partnership owns, is beneficiary of, and pays the premiums on the life insurance of each partner. When one of the partners dies, the partnership as a whole purchases the deceased partner's interest. Premiums are not tax deductible as a business expense. If whole life insurance is used, the cash values are listed

as assets on the balance sheet of the partnership and are available as collateral for loans.

Partners use insurance to fund other objectives. In personal service partnerships of doctors, lawyers, and accountants, when it is important to retain a deceased partner's name on the title of the firm, the heirs may agree to this for a share in subsequent partnership profits. An *income continuation insurance* plan funded through life insurance by the partnership, serves this purpose.

Disability of partner buy and sell insurance can be used by a partnership to provide income for the firm if a partner becomes disabled. The policy would pay a monthly income to the partnership for the duration of the partner's disability.

PARTY individual or entity who enters into a contract or other legal proceeding, such as a lawsuit.

PASSENGER BODILY INJURY LIABILITY INSURANCE coverage for automobile or aircraft operators if they are sued for negligently killing or injuring a passenger. The PERSONAL AUTOMOBILE POLICY (PAP) provides MEDICAL PAYMENTS INSURANCE for doctor and hospital bills for passengers of the insured, and BODILY INJURY liability insurance for anyone who is accidentally disabled, injured, or killed by the insured. Aviation policies split bodily injury liability into *general* and *passenger.* Passenger liability covers a passenger who is injured, killed, or disabled; general liability covers anyone else.

PASSIVE LOSS RULES rules passed as part of the TAX REFORM ACT OF 1986 that limit the amount of income investors can shelter from current tax. Losses can be deducted from passive activities only in the amount to which income results from passive activities. Furthermore, losses from one passive activity can be used only to offset the passive income earned from a similar passive activity. For example, losses from publicly traded partnerships can be applied only to offset passive income earned from publicly traded partnerships.

PASSIVE PORTFOLIO MANAGEMENT buying and selling of securities to reflect changes in a benchmark index. *See also* ACTIVE PORTFOLIO MANAGEMENT.

PASSIVE RETENTION practice in which no funds are set aside on a mathematical basis to pay for expected losses. This occurs when a risk manager is not aware of an exposure, when the cost of treating an exposure positively is prohibitive, or if the *severity* of a loss (should it occur) would be inconsequential. *See also* SELF INSURANCE.

PAST DUE ACCOUNTS funds receivable or payable that have not been paid in a timely manner. COMMERCIAL CREDIT INSURANCE protects an insured against declines in the value of receivables due to insolvency of a debtor. The insured may turn over to the insurer accounts that are up to 12 months past due or, by special endorsement, those that are 6 months overdue. For insurance purposes, these past due accounts will be treated as if they were accounts due from an insolvent company.

PAST SERVICE BENEFIT private pension plan credit given for an employee's past service with an employer prior to establishment of a pension plan. Usually, a lower percentage of compensation is credited for benefits for past service than for future service benefits.

PAST SERVICE CREDIT *see* PAST SERVICE BENEFIT.

PAST SERVICE LIABILITY employer's obligation to fund a pension plan for the time period when employees were qualified to participate but the plan was not yet established. For example, a pension plan is established at XYZ Co. in 1985. Because John Smith started at the firm in 1975, he would have a *past service credit* for his 10 years of service before the plan started. For funding purposes, annual contributions are broken down into FUTURE SERVICE BENEFITS and PAST SERVICE BENEFIT. Past service liability is not funded entirely in the initial year of a plan, primarily because it would be too expensive, and the IRS requires that deductions be spread over 10 years.

PAST SERVICE LIABILITY—INITIAL funding of an employee's benefits in a pension plan for his or her beginning past service of employment. This is a significant cost factor in pension planning and financing of future benefits.

PATENT AND COPYRIGHT INFRINGEMENT *see* UNFAIR TRADE PRACTICE.

PATENT INSURANCE coverage for a loss incurred by the INSURED resulting from an infringement of the insured's patent or coverage for a claim made against the insured resulting from infringement by the insured against another's patent.

PATTERSON v. SHUMATE legal case in which the United States Supreme Court held that pension assets are to be excluded from the bankruptcy estate of the plan participant.

PAUL v. VIRGINIA U.S. Supreme Court case in 1868 in which the decision (since overruled) was that an insurance policy was not an instrument of commerce, and thus did not involve interstate commerce transactions that would make it subject to federal regulation. *See also* MCCARRAN-FERGUSON ACT (PUBLIC LAW 15); SOUTH-EASTERN UNDERWRITERS ASSOCIATION (SEUA) CASE.

PAY abbreviation for premium payment. It usually applies to a limited number of annual premium payment policies such as a ten-day policy.

PAY-AS-YOU-GO PLAN *see* CURRENT DISBURSEMENT.

PAY-AT-THE-PUMP PLAN automobile insurance plan, debated for a number of years, that is financed through a surcharge of a given number of cents per gallon (estimates run from 30 to 40 cents) to be paid by the purchaser of the gasoline. The plan would operate on the NO-FAULT AUTOMOBILE INSURANCE basis. Claims would be paid from an insurance pool whose funds would be generated by the surcharge. Drivers would receive unlimited medical coverage, up to $25,000, for missed wages and collision damage. Drivers would be required to pay a $250 deductible. Those drivers desiring additional lost wages or damage coverage, could purchase it separately.

PAYEE
1. recipient.
2. insurance company that receives a premium payment from a payer.
3. insured or beneficiary who receives a loss or benefit payment from an insurer.

PAYEE CLAUSE CLAUSE in an INSURANCE POLICY that provides for the payment of a monetary sum to the individual(s) who incurred the loss.

PAYMASTER ROBBERY INSURANCE coverage for robbery of the payroll of a business. Coverage applies to money and checks from the time the payroll is withdrawn from the bank until it is distributed to the employees, whether inside or outside of the premises of the business. Employees are covered if robbed of their pay when the business itself is being robbed of the payroll. Excluded are manuscripts and records of accounts.

PAYMENT BOND bond guaranteeing that a contractor will pay fees owed for labor and materials necessary for construction of a project. If these fees are not paid, an owner who has paid the contractor might be confronted with subcontractor's or worker's liens filed against the completed project. If this happens, the owner could end up paying many times the value of the work done. *See also* PERFORMANCE BOND.

PAYMENT CERTAIN phrase used to describe a method of annuity payout that guarantees a specified number of years, regardless of whether an annuitant remains alive.

PAYMENT OF EXPOSURES INSURED BY COMPANY *see* CLAIM, OBLIGATION TO PAY; HOMEOWNERS INSURANCE POLICY; INTERINSURANCE COMPANY CLAIMS; INTERPLEADER; PERSONAL AUTOMOBILE POLICY (PAP); PROPERTY AND CASUALTY INSURANCE PROVISIONS.

PAYMENT OF PREMIUMS ON BONDS act that seals a contract and is noncancellable. SURETY BONDS and FIDELITY BONDS resemble insurance contracts in many ways. However, the surety, which is often an insurance company, cannot cancel a bond once the premium has been paid.

PAYOR CLAUSE provision found in JUVENILE INSURANCE that waives the premiums due on the insured child's policy provided that the payor of the premiums becomes totally disabled or dies before the child reaches a stipulated age.

PAYOUT PHASE period when the accumulated assets in an ANNUITY are returned to the annuitant. An annuity may be purchased either with a single payment or with many payments over the life of the contract. At some point, usually upon retirement, the annuitant elects to have the payments, plus earnings, returned. The 1982 Federal Tax Code declared that any money received during the payout phase is considered earnings first and is taxable.

PAYROLL AUDIT insurance company's examination of an insured business's payroll records in order to determine the final premium due on a WORKERS COMPENSATION INSURANCE policy.

PAYROLL BUYUP DISABILITY INSURANCE basic GROUP DISABILITY INSURANCE policy for all employees purchased by the employer. In addition, the employer usually purchases an individual disability policy for key executives. Employees purchase supplemental group disability insurance for themselves.

PAYROLL DEDUCTION INSURANCE plan under which an employee authorizes his or her employer to deduct from each paycheck premiums due on an insurance plan.

PAYROLL ENDORSEMENTS *see* ORDINARY PAYROLL EXCLUSION ENDORSEMENT.

PAYROLL SAVINGS INSURANCE *see* PAYROLL DEDUCTION INSURANCE.

PAYROLL STOCK OWNERSHIP PLANS (PAYSOP) EMPLOYEE STOCK OWNERSHIP PLAN (ESOP); TRUST (ESOP) under which an employer received tax credit instead of a tax deduction for contributions. Until passage of the TAX REFORM ACT OF 1986, the tax credit was limited to the lesser of the value of the stock contributed to the plan or .5% of the employer's payroll. The PAYSOP must have met all of the requirements of a qualified plan, and all participants must have had 100% immediate VESTING. The Tax Reform Act of 1986 repealed PAYSOP.

PEAK SEASON ENDORSEMENT endorsement attached to PROPERTY INSURANCE COVERAGE that provides additional limits of protection on a merchant's inventories during specific time intervals. The time intervals generally are the periods during the year when shopping is most intense.

PEL *see* PERMISSIBLE EXPOSURE LIMIT.

PENALTY liability limit on a FIDELITY BOND or SURETY BOND. A fixed-penalty bond is one with a fixed liability limit that the surety company will pay in the event of nonperformance.

PENSION ADMINISTRATION PLAN *see* IMMEDIATE PARTICIPATION GUARANTEE PLAN (IPG).

PENSION BENEFIT GUARANTY CORPORATION (PBGC) independent federal government organization authorized by the EMPLOYEE

RETIREMENT INCOME SECURITY ACT OF 1974 (ERISA) to administer the PENSION PLAN TERMINATION INSURANCE program. Its function is to ensure that *vested* benefits of employees, whose PENSION PLAN is being terminated, will be paid as they come due. The PBGC board of directors consists of the U.S. Secretaries of Labor, Commerce, and Treasury. Only qualified DEFINED BENEFIT PLANS are guaranteed; PROFIT SHARING PLANS, *stock bonus plans,* and MONEY PURCHASE PLANS are not. Plan termination insurance covers both voluntary termination and terminations ordered by the PBGC. Employers pay an annual premium rate per employee in their pension plans to the PBGC to finance the plan termination insurance program.

PENSION BENEFIT GUARANTY CORPORATION PARTICI-PANT NOTICE REQUIREMENT notice added to the EMPLOYEE RETIREMENT INCOME SECURITY ACT (ERISA) requiring the employer to disclose the following information concerning the PENSION PLAN to the employee:

1. the ratio of plan assets to current liability (value of the employer retirement benefits earned to date). This ratio is known as the funded percentage.
2. statement that the employer is responsible for paying all earned pension benefits, but such payment could be at risk should the employer have severe financial difficulties. A statement that, if the plan terminates, the PENSION BENEFIT GUARANTY CORPORATION (PBGC) becomes responsible for paying the employees their earned retirement benefits.
3. statements indicating any late funding of minimum contributions and the date the contributions were paid into the plan.
4. statement of any late quarterly contributions (more than 60 days late) and the actual date contributions were made.

A plan is subject to this notice requirement for a plan year if the plan paid to the PBGC is a variable premium during that plan year and the minimum funding requirement for the plan year is based on the DEFECIT REDUCTION CONTRIBUTION for the prior or the current plan year. Plans that are subject to this notice requirement for a plan year must notify all plan participants (current employees, VESTED employees who have terminated, retired employees, and beneficiaries of deceased employees).

PENSION EQUITY PLAN (PEP) modifications of the traditional DEFINED BENEFIT PLAN in which employees are credited with a specified percentage for each year of recognized service with the employer. Upon termination of service, the percentages are summed and multiplied times the final average pay. The resultant calculation is the employee's annual retirement benefit. These plans provide for an even accrual of the employee's retirement benefits and thus provide greater benefit for employees that have shorter periods of service.

PENSION FUND *see* PENSION PLAN.

PENSION MAXIMIZATION plan under which life insurance is substituted for retirement income. Under the plan, a married individual selects a SINGLE LIFE ANNUITY payout from the pension plan, which will generate the maximum monthly income benefit while that individual is alive, with nothing being paid to the surviving spouse after the death of that individual. The higher income generated from the single life annuity, compared with that from a JOINT LIFE AND SURVIVORSHIP ANNUITY, is used to buy a life insurance policy on the married individual's life. If this individual dies first, the proceeds of the policy will be used to purchase an ANNUITY for the lifetime of the spouse. Should the spouse die first, the married individual still has the higher income benefit from the single life annuity.

PENSION PLAN retirement program to provide employees (and often, spouses) with a monthly income payment for the rest of their lives. To qualify, an employee must have met minimum age and service requirements. Benefit formulas can be either the DEFINED CONTRIBUTION PENSION (MONEY PURCHASE PLAN) or the DEFINED BENEFIT PLAN. The EMPLOYEE RETIREMENT INCOME SECURITY ACT OF 1974 (ERISA) requires a pension plan to provide an income for the rest of a retired employee's life, and at least 50% of that amount to the surviving spouse of a retired employee for the rest of her life, unless the spouse waives this right in writing. Death and disability benefits are also provided by most pension plans. The TAX REFORM ACT OF 1986 has changed the VESTING requirements. With the passage of the PENSION PROTECTION ACT OF 2006, employer nonelective contributions as well as employer matching contributions, must vest according to the minimum three-year Cliff or six-year graded vesting schedule: year 1 = 0% vested; year 2 = 20% vested; year 3 = 40% vested; year 4 = 60% vested; year 5 = 80% vested; and year 6 = 100% vested. Funds for these plans can be generated under numerous PENSION PLAN FUNDING INSTRUMENTS.

PENSION PLAN: FUND COLLEGE EDUCATION group of plans (to include SECTION 401(k) PLANS and SECTION 403(b) PLANS) that permit in-service withdrawals to fund a college education if a HARDSHIP exists.

PENSION PLAN FUNDING: GROUP DEPOSIT ADMINISTRATION ANNUITY pension plan funding instrument in which contributions paid by an employer are deposited to accumulate at interest. (These plans are usually NONCONTRIBUTORY.) Upon retirement, an *immediate annuity* is purchased for the employee. The benefit is determined by a formula, and the investment earnings on funds left to accumulate at interest. Since the annuity is purchased at point of retirement, the deposit administration plan can be used with any benefit formula.

PENSION PLAN FUNDING: GROUP IMMEDIATE PARTICIPATION GUARANTEED (IPG) CONTRACT ANNUITY modification of the *group deposit administration annuity* under which an employer participates in the investment (which may prove to be adverse as well as favorable), mortality, and expense experience of the plan on an immediate basis. Under the IPG, contributions are paid into a fund to which interest is credited. At retirement, an IMMEDIATE ANNUITY is purchased for the employee. The size of the benefit will depend on the benefit formula used and the investment, mortality, and expense experience of the plan.

PENSION PLAN FUNDING: GROUP PERMANENT CONTRACT insurance policy under which the value equals the benefits to be paid to the plan participants (employees) at normal retirement age, assuming that (1) their rate of earnings remains the same until NORMAL RETIREMENT AGE, and (2) the contributions to the plan are sufficient to meet funding requirements for benefits under the plan. Adjustments to contributions are made as employee earnings increase. Retirement benefits depend on the benefit formula used, and the investment, mortality, and expense experience of the plan.

PENSION PLAN FUNDING: IMMEDIATE PARTICIPATION GUARANTEE CONTINGENT ANNUITY *see* PENSION PLAN FUNDING: GROUP IMMEDIATE PARTICIPATION GUARANTEED (IPG) CONTRACT ANNUITY.

PENSION PLAN FUNDING: INDIVIDUAL CONTRACT PENSION PLAN retirement plan for an individual based on a single contract with a benefit based on current earnings, as if they will remain static until NORMAL RETIREMENT AGE. As the earnings of the plan participant increase, additional contracts are purchased (with an increase in the contributions to the plan). The amount of retirement benefits depends on the benefit formula used and the investment experience of the company underwriting the plan.

PENSION PLAN FUNDING INSTRUMENTS means of paying the cost of benefits of pension plan participants including retirement, death, and disability. *See also* GROUP PERMANENT LIFE INSURANCE; PENSION PLAN; PENSION PLAN FUNDING: GROUP DEPOSIT ADMINISTRATION ANNUITY; PENSION PLAN FUNDING: GROUP IMMEDIATE PARTICIPATION GUARANTEED (IPG) CONTRACT ANNUITY.

PENSION PLAN FUNDING METHODS *see* PENSION PLAN FUNDING, GROUP DEPOSIT ADMINISTRATION ANNUITY; PENSION PLAN FUNDING: GROUP IMMEDIATE PARTICIPATION GUARANTEED (IPG) CONTRACT ANNUITY; PENSION PLAN FUNDING: GROUP PERMANENT CONTRACT; PENSION PLAN FUNDING: INDIVIDUAL CONTRACT PENSION PLAN.

PENSION PLAN INTEGRATION WITH SOCIAL SECURITY offset or subtraction of Social Security benefits from earned benefits in a qualified pension plan to reduce a pension benefit. Many business firms offset their pension payments by the amount of a retiree's Social Security benefit. For example, John Smith has earned a monthly pension benefit of $950. His monthly Social Security payment is $688. If his employer applies 100% integration, his pension is reduced by the entire Social Security benefit; he will receive $950 minus $688, or $262 monthly. More commonly, integration is based on a percentage of Social Security. With 50% integration, 50% of the Social Security benefit ($344) would be subtracted from the $950 pension for a monthly benefit of $606. Offsets were limited by the TAX REFORM ACT OF 1986.

PENSION PLAN LIMITS dollar limitations for 2007 under the Internal Revenue Service code as follows:

1. If participating in an employee-sponsored retirement plan, to include 401(K), PROFIT SHARING PLAN, DEFINED CONTRIBUTION PENSION PLAN (MONEY PURCHASE PLAN), and 403(b), the cumulative maximum contribution to all accounts is $45,000. This $45,000 limit includes salary-deferred contributions, employer matching contributions, and employer discretionary contributions. If the employee is at least age 50, a catch-up contribution of $5000 may be made.

2. If participating in a Salary Deferral Plan (401(k), 403(b), and 457), the contribution limit is $15,500 per plan. The aggregate limit for the 401(k) and 403(b) plans is $15,500. In addition, $15,500 can be contributed to a 457 Plan. A catch-up contribution of $5000 can be added to these totals for employees who are at least age 50.

3. If participating in a simple IRA or a simple 401(k) Plan (*see* SAVINGS INCENTIVE MATCH PLAN FOR EMPLOYEES (SIMPLE PLANS)), the salary amount that can be deferred is $10,500 with an additional catch-up contribution of $2500 for employees who are at least age 50.

4. If participating in employer-sponsored RETIREMENT PLANS, the maximum income of the employee that can be considered for contribution is $225,000.

5. If establishing a small business retirement plan (SEP plan), employees earning less than $1500 can be excluded from the plan.

6. If employee and spouse do not participate in an employer-sponsored retirement plan, contributions made to a Traditional IRA are tax deductible.

7. In order to contribute on a partial basis to a ROTH INDIVIDUAL RETIREMENT ACCOUNT (IRA), individuals filing a joint return must have combined income between $156,000 and $166,000 on an adjusted gross income basis. Individuals filing on a joint basis must have adjusted gross income of $156,000 or less to contribute the maximum amount. The individual filing on a single basis must have adjusted gross income of $114,000 or less to contribute the maximum amount.

PENSION PLANS: DISTRIBUTIONS prior to 1988, right to withdraw retirement assets before age 59½ without having to pay a 10% penalty under the following circumstances:

1. medical expenses are incurred.
2. the plan participant becomes disabled.

With the passage of the TECHNICAL AND MISCELLANEOUS REVENUE ACT OF 1988 (TAMRA): EMPLOYEE BENEFITS a third option is available to the plan participant:

3. distribution must be a part of a scheduled series of substantially equal periodic payments. The distributions must be made in such a manner that they will continue for the lifetime of the plan participant or the joint lifetime of the plan participant and his or her beneficiary.

PENSION PLANS: WITHDRAWAL BENEFITS rights of employees who leave an employer with a qualified plan to withdraw their accumulated benefits. With a CONTRIBUTORY plan, employees have immediate rights to their own contributions, plus earnings. If they leave the employer, the accumulated money belongs to them. But they are not entitled to employer contributions, unless vested. VESTING depends on the terms of the plan, but maximum time limits are set by law. A vested employee who withdraws accumulated benefits upon separation may either pay tax on the amount contributed by the employer and spend it, or roll it over into an INDIVIDUAL RETIREMENT ACCOUNT (IRA).

PENSION PLAN TERMINATION INSURANCE coverage provided by the PENSION BENEFIT GUARANTY CORPORATION (PBGC) that guarantees participants a certain level of pension benefits even if the plan terminates without assets. The PBGC was authorized under the EMPLOYEE RETIREMENT INCOME SECURITY ACT OF 1974 (ERISA). The insurance, paid for by employers, protects *vested interest* only.

PENSION PLAN VALUATION FACTORS present value computation of the accrued or projected benefits of a retirement plan. This computation is known as the *actuarial valuation* because it is based on (1) probability (retirement event will take place); (2) demographic changes (increase or decrease in employee's earnings); (3) interest rate (discount rate used to derive present value of future benefits).

PENSION PORTABILITY employee's right to transfer pension benefit credits from a former employer to a current employer.

PENSION PROTECTION ACT OF 2006 pension reform law designed to improve pension rights and contributions in the following areas:

1. INDIVIDUAL RETIREMENT ACCOUNT (IRA). Contribution limits for the traditional and ROTH IRAs are $4000 for tax years 2006 and 2007, $5000 for tax year 2008, and $5000 adjusted for inflation in $500 increments for tax year 2009 and beyond. The catch-up contribution is $1000 in addition to these limits for both the traditional and ROTH IRAs for people age 50 and older.

2. *401(k)s and 403(b)s.* In 2007 and beyond, contribution limits per tax year are $15,500 with a catch-up contribution of an additional $5000 per tax year for people age 50 or older.

3. *Rollovers Directly to Roth IRAs Beyond December 31, 2007.* Participants will be allowed to directly rollover distribution from

an employer-sponsored retirement plan. In the year of the rollover, any earning and pretax contributions are considered taxable income in the year of the rollover and conversion.

4. *Beneficiary.* Nonspouse beneficiary may transfer distributions from employer-sponsored plans directly into an inherited IRA. This direct transfer allows the beneficiary to withdraw sums from the inherited IRA on a life expectancy basis.

5. *IRA Charitable Donation:* If at least age 70½, distributions from an IRA may be sent directly to a qualified charity. The distributions may be $100,000 or less for each person, may be used to meet minimum distribution requirements, and do not have to be reported as income for tax purposes. Disallowed are gifts from retirement accounts that are IRAS, such as *401(k)* or *SEP* accounts.

6. *Tax Refund Directly to IRA.* An individual may have any tax refund directly deposited into an IRA by the Internal Revenue Service.

7. *College Savings Plan.* Each state can establish its own particular plan that allows the participant to be exempted from federal income tax on distribution from or contributions to the plan for education related expenses. In many instances, various states allow participants' contributions and distributions to be exempt from state income taxes.

8. *Favorable Tax Treatment for Long-Term Care (LTC) Contracts Included in Annuities.* Annuity sums applied to payment for premiums for qualified LONGTERM CARE (LTC) are not subject to tax. Benefit payments are received by the participant on a tax-free basis as well.

9. *Disappearance of Income Limits on Conversion of Traditional IRA to Roth IRA.* Beginning in 2010, a traditional IRA may be converted to a ROTH IRA regardless of the income level of the participant. Income taxes must be paid on the gains converted from a traditional nondeductible IRA.

10. CORPORATE-OWNED LIFE INSURANCE (COLI). Limits are placed on the scope of COLI and adds new notice and consent requirements. An employer who purchases COLI must file an annual return with the IRS if benefits from the policy are to be tax-free to the beneficiary.

11. *Vesting Schedules under Defined Contribution Plans by Statute.* One must select VESTING schedule that results in at least as favorable benefit to the employees as three-year Cliff Vesting or two through six-year GRADED VESTING. Under the three-year rule, after three years of service, the employee is entitled to full benefits that have accrued on his or her behalf (100% vested). If the employee leaves before three years of service, no benefits are paid (zero vesting). Under the two- through six-year rule, the employee is 20% vested after two years of service. The vesting increases by 20% a year thereafter until 100% vesting is reached. After six years of service, the employer may select a more favorable vesting schedule for the employee than that required by the statute.

12. *Vesting Schedules under Defined Benefit Plans.* By statute, one must select a VESTING schedule that results in at least as favorable benefit to the employee as five-year Cliff Vesting or three- through seven-year GRADED VESTING. Under the five-year rule, after five years of service, the employee is entitled to full benefits that have accrued on his or her behalf (100% vested). If the employee leaves before five years of service, no benefits are paid (zero vesting). Under the three- through seven-year rule the employee is 20% vested after three years of service. The vesting increases by 20% a year thereafter until 100% vesting is reached after seven years of service. The employer may select a more favorable vesting schedule for the employee than is required by the statute.

13. *Defined Benefit/401(k).* Combination of traditional DEFINED BENEFIT PLAN with a DEFINED CONTRIBUTION PLAN or SECTION 401(K) PLAN that becomes effective in 2010. This plan can provide benefits based on either a traditional defined benefit formula or a cash balance formula. Under the defined benefit formula, employees must have credited to their account at least 1% of their final average salary (subject to no more that the highest five years average earnings) for each year of service up to 20 years. Under the CASH BALANCE PLAN, employees must have credited to their account various percentages of compensation based on the employee's age at the beginning of each plan's year as follows: younger than age 30, 2% of earnings: ages 30–39, 4% of compensation; ages 40–49, 6% of compensation; ages 50 and older, 8% of compensation. For the 401(k) portion of the plan, if the employee does not select to be enrolled, that employee is automatically enrolled at a rate of 4% of compensation with a mandatory employer contribution of 2% of compensation. These contributions, both employer and employee, must be on a nonforfeitable basis. The FIDUCIARY for the 401(k) part of the plan is relieved from liability for default investments to include a third-party managed account, a balanced mutual fund, and a lifecycle mutual fund.

14. *Do-Over Provision.* Plan participants have the right to elect not to participate in the automatic enrollment and to receive amounts withheld from their earnings, provided request is made within 90 days of enrollment. The withdrawal amounts must be 100% of the earnings withheld plus any amount earned. There is no early withdrawal penalty paid. The withdrawal sums are included in the participant's earnings for the distribution year.

15. *Qualified Default Investment Alternative (QDIA).* Plan participants who do not make an investment decision will be placed into a default account. The default accounts include professionally managed accounts, balanced mutual funds, and lifecycle mutual funds. A minimum of 30 days notice must be given to the participant prior to the initial investment in the QDIA and for every year thereafter. The notice must include information concerning the directing of the participant's contribution to the QDIA. The participant has the right to elect out of the QDIA at any point in time and to select other investments.

PENSIONS *see* PENSION PLAN.

PENSION TRUST provision that funds a tax-qualified plan. Trust funds are the oldest, and still the most common, method of funding pensions. All contributions made by employer and employees are deposited into a trust fund, with a trustee responsible for investing the money, administering the plan, and paying benefits.

PER ACCIDENT LIMIT maximum amount that an insurance company will pay under a liability insurance policy for claims resulting from a particular accident. This maximum amount applies regardless of the amount of property damage or the number of persons injured in that accident.

PER CAPITA distribution of a deceased beneficiary's share of an estate among all of his or her living heirs. Contrast with PER STIRPES.

PER CAUSE DEDUCTIBLE requirement that the deductible must be met for each separate illness or accident before benefits are payable under major medical insurance.

PERCENTAGE DEDUCTIBLE calculation of DEDUCTIBLE based on a percentage of the value of the INSURED'S home. The range of the deductible is typically between 1 and 5%. This type of deductible is used in coverages for an ACT OF GOD such as hail, high winds, and hurricanes found in the HOMEOWNER INSURANCE POLICY—SECTION I (PROPERTY COVERAGE).

PERCENTAGE-OF-LOSS DEDUCTIBLE deductible, applied to every loss, expressed as a percentage of that loss. As the loss increases, the deductible amount increases.

PERCENTAGE PARTICIPATING DEDUCTIBLE *(stop loss)* amount over which a health insurance plan pays 100% of the costs in a PERCENTAGE PARTICIPATION plan. Here, an insured shares costs with the insurer according to some predetermined ratio. For example, an insured may pay 20% of covered costs and the insurer 80%. However, most group medical plans pick up all covered expenses over a certain deductible amount or specified dollar limit. For example, once the insured has paid a $2000 deductible amount, the plan may pay 100% of covered expenses for the remainder of the policy year.

PERCENTAGE PARTICIPATION (COINSURANCE) plan where a portion of medical expenses are paid by an insured. Some health insurance policies provide that the insured shares expenses with the insurer according to a predetermined ratio. For example, many group health plans provide that, after paying a deductible amount, the insured pays a portion (usually 20–25%) of covered medical expenses. For some types of services, such as psychiatry or dentistry, the percentage participation, which the insured pays, may go as high as 50% of covered services.

PER DIEM BUSINESS INTERRUPTION POLICY type of BUSINESS INTERRUPTION INSURANCE policy that provides a specific daily dollar amount benefit to the business owner for each day the business is unable to resume normal business operations because of property damage or destruction resulting from an INSURED PERIL.

PERFORMANCE BOND bond guaranteeing that a contractor will perform under the contract in accordance with all specifications of the bid submitted.

PERIL *see* ALL RISKS.

PERIOD *see* POLICY PERIOD.

PERIOD CERTAIN *see* ANNUITY.

PERIODIC LEVEL *see* LEVEL.

PERMANENT DISABILITY *see* DISABILITY.

PERMANENT LIFE INSURANCE *see* ORDINARY LIFE INSURANCE.

PERMANENT PARTIAL DISABILITY disability in which a wage earner is forever prevented from working at full physical capability because of injury or illness. *See also* DISABILITY INCOME INSURANCE.

PERMANENT TOTAL DISABILITY disability in which a wage earner is forever prevented from working because of injury or illness suffered. *See also* DISABILITY INCOME INSURANCE.

PERMISSIBLE EXPOSURE LIMIT (PEL) standard set under the OCCUPATIONAL SAFETY AND HEALTH ACT that sets allowable levels of worker exposure to such toxic substances as asbestos, certain chemicals, and radiation. In many cases workers must wear devices to determine their exposure to toxic workplace substances, and when the maximum is reached, they must be transferred to another workplace. Business firms that violate the standard can be fined.

PERMISSIBLE LOSS RATIO *see* EXPECTED LOSS RATIO.

PERMISSION GRANTED CLAUSE provision in most property insurance policies on *real property* that permits a policyholder to use an insured place for normal purposes related to occupancy. This might include storing remodeling materials or hobby equipment. This clause is important because a policy may be voided for fraud, concealment, or misrepresentation. A policy may also be suspended for increased hazard by an insured. The permission granted clause provides a defense against a charge that a policyholder has increased the hazard of covered property if the materials in question are a part of the insured's everyday lifestyle.

PERMISSIVE LAW *see* FILE-AND-USE RATING LAWS.

PERMISSIVE USER person who uses personal property such as an automobile with permission of an owner. For example, for insurance purposes, someone who uses an automobile with the owner's permission would be covered by the latter's PERSONAL AUTOMOBILE POLICY (PAP). On the other hand, the owner of property may not be responsible for a TRESPASSER.

PERMIT BOND contract guaranteeing that a person licensed by a city, county, or state agency will perform activities for which the bond was granted, according to the regulations governing the license.

PER PERSON LIMIT maximum amount that an insurance company will pay under a liability insurance policy for bodily injury incurred by any single person as a result of any one accident.

PERPETUAL INSURANCE coverage on *real property* written to have no time limit. A single deposit premium pays for insurance for the life of the risk. The insurer earns enough investment income on the deposit to cover losses and costs. Upon cancellation, the insured is entitled to return of the initial deposit premium. Perpetual insurance, first issued in the U.S. in Philadelphia in 1752, is still used for fire and homeowner's insurance.

PERPETUAL MUTUAL INSURANCE COMPANY type of MUTUAL INSURANCE COMPANY that requires a substantial initial premium payment. After the initial premium payment is made, future premium payments required will be paid from the investment earnings of the initial premium payment. *See also* PERPETUAL INSURANCE.

PERPETUITY ANNUITY type of ANNUITY in which income continues indefinitely.

PER RISK EXCESS INSURANCE *see* EXCESS OF LOSS REINSURANCE.

PERSISTENCY percentage of life insurance or other insurance policies remaining in force; percentage of policies that have not *lapsed*. The higher the percentage, the greater the persistency. Since it is an important measure of a company's retention of its life insurance business, most companies extend every effort to increase persistency. *See also* CONSERVATION.

PERSISTENCY BONUSES (ENHANCEMENTS) financial incentives credited to the policy to encourage the POLICYOWNER to keep the policy in force. The incentives may be utilized by: (1) applying them to the policy cash value after a stipulated time period that the policy has been in force has expired; (2) after a stipulated minimum number of premium payments has been paid into the policy; or (3) after the policy's cash value has attained a stipulated minimum value. These financial incentives may be added to the policy in the following manner:
1. Additional interest may be added to the policy's cash value.
2. Mortality credit may be added to the policy's cash value.
3. The policy's death benefit may be increased.

PERSONAL ACCIDENT CATASTROPHE REINSURANCE *see* AUTOMATIC NONPROPORTIONAL REINSURANCE; AUTOMATIC PROPORTIONAL REINSURANCE; AUTOMATIC REINSURANCE; EXCESS OF LOSS REINSURANCE; FACULATIVE REINSURANCE; NONPROPORTIONAL REINSURANCE; PROPORTIONAL REINSURANCE; QUOTA SHARE REINSURANCE; STOP LOSS REINSURANCE; SURPLUS REINSURANCE.

PERSONAL ARTICLES INSURANCE coverage for all kinds of personal property whether inside or outside an insured's (home) to include jewelry, musical instruments, cameras, fine arts, and precious stones. The insurance policy can be issued separately as an INLAND MARINE INSURANCE policy or as an endorsement to the HOMEOWNERS INSURANCE POLICY. Protection is on an ALL RISKS basis subject to exclusions of wear and tear, war, and nuclear disaster. Each piece of jewelry and other expensive items must be specifically listed in the policy. *See also* PERSONAL EFFECTS INSURANCE.

PERSONAL AUTOMOBILE POLICY (PAP) replacement for the earlier *Family Automobile Policy (FAP)* with these nine basic coverages:
   1. *Coverage A*—Liability. (a) The company pays damages for which an insured becomes legally obligated because negligent acts or omissions resulted in bodily injury and/or property damage to a third party; (b) the company defends the insured against liability suits for damages caused to the third party, paying various expenses in this connection; and (c) vehicles covered include the insured's own cars, a newly acquired car, and a temporary substitute car.
   2. *Coverage B*—Medical Payments. The company pays medical expenses for bodily injury incurred by the insured (including spouse and relatives) and any other person while they occupy the insured car.
   3. *Coverage C*—Uninsured Motorist Coverage. The company pays damages that the insured is legally entitled to collect from the owner or driver of an uninsured motor vehicle.
   4. *Coverage D*—Comprehensive. The company pays for loss to the insured's car for all damages, in excess of a deductible amount, except due to collision.
   5. *Coverage E*—Collision. The company pays for loss to the insured's car for all damages in excess of a deductible amount caused by collision.
   6. *Coverage F*—Car Rental Expense (optional). The company pays for car rental up to a daily dollar limit, when the insured's car cannot run due to a loss incurred.
   7. *Coverage G*—Death, Dismemberment, and Loss of Sight (optional). The company pays the insured or beneficiary for death or loss caused by an accident to the insured.
   8. *Coverage H*—Total Disability (optional). The company pays the insured a monthly disability income benefit because of bodily injury in an accident while occupying or being struck by a motor vehicle.

9. *Coverage I*—Loss of Earnings (optional). The company pays the insured a percentage of his or her loss of monthly earnings because of bodily injury as the result of an accident while occupying or being struck by a motor vehicle.

PERSONAL CATASTROPHE INSURANCE excess coverage over the first layer of medical insurance to provide for catastrophic medical payments. The first layer may be either group or individual medical insurance, or an individual may choose to pay for ordinary medical payments and buy insurance for those losses above a certain amount.

PERSONAL COMPREHENSIVE LIABILITY INSURANCE *see* COMPREHENSIVE PERSONAL LIABILITY INSURANCE.

PERSONAL CONTRACT agreement concerning an insured individual, not the insured's property. A *property and casualty insurance contract* cannot be assigned, since it follows the insured, not the property. For example, a HOMEOWNERS INSURANCE POLICY cannot be transferred with the home upon its sale because the insured no longer has an insurable interest (expectation of monetary loss) in the home. But a LIFE INSURANCE contract can be assigned (for example, to secure a line of credit for a business). Banks use the *American Bankers Form* for the assignment of life insurance policies pledged as security for a loan.

PERSONAL COVERAGES *see* PERSONAL INSURANCE.

PERSONAL EFFECTS INSURANCE coverage outside an insured's home for personal items usually carried or worn while traveling. Protection is for personal property (apparel and jewelry), not for real property or property not usually carried by the traveler (a piano, household furniture). Coverage applies anywhere in the world for the named insured and insured's spouse and unmarried children if residents of the household.

PERSONAL EXCESS LIABILITY INSURANCE *see* UMBRELLA LIABILITY INSURANCE.

PERSONAL FINANCIAL INVENTORY detailed descriptive list made available to the survivor(s) of the insured showing: attorney, accountant, insurance agent, and location of important documents such as wills, power of attorney, property deeds, insurance policies by account number, bank accounts by account number, investments by account number, loans by account number, credit cards by account number, and any other important financial papers. Safe deposit boxes and keys location should also be listed.

PERSONAL FLOATER POLICY *see* PERSONAL ARTICLES INSURANCE; PERSONAL EFFECTS INSURANCE.

PERSONAL FURS INSURANCE see FURRIERS BLOCK INSURANCE; FURS INSURANCE.

PERSONAL HAZARD *see* MORAL HAZARD.

PERSONAL HISTORY insurance applicant's life and health record, financial standing, driving record, general character, vocation, and habits. These factors are evaluated by a *home office underwriter* in classifying the applicant as insurable, preferred, extra-risk, or uninsurable. *See also* NUMERICAL RATING SYSTEM.

PERSONAL INCOME measurement of income received by households from employment, self-employment, or investment and transfer payments, as provided monthly by the United States Department of Commerce.

PERSONAL INJURY wrongful conduct causing false arrest, invasion of privacy, libel, slander, defamation of character, and bodily injury. The injury is against the person in contrast to property damage or destruction. *See also* BUSINESS LIABILITY INSURANCE (Insuring Agreements Section).

PERSONAL INJURY INSURANCE LIABILITY INSURANCE that provides coverage for the INSURED in the event the insured's negligent acts and/or omissions result in libel, slander, invasion of privacy, or false arrest suit.

PERSONAL INJURY PROTECTION (PIP) coverage to pay basic expenses for an insured and his or her family in states with NO FAULT AUTOMOBILE INSURANCE. No-fault laws generally require drivers to carry both LIABILITY INSURANCE and personal injury protection (PIP) coverage to pay for basic needs of the insured, such as medical expenses, in the event of an accident.

PERSONAL INSURANCE *see* ACCIDENTAL DEATH AND DISMEMBERMENT INSURANCE; ACCIDENT AND HEALTH INSURANCE; ADDITIONAL LIVING EXPENSE INSURANCE; ADJUSTABLE LIFE INSURANCE; ANNUITY; BROAD FORM PERSONAL THEFT INSURANCE; COMPREHENSIVE HEALTH INSURANCE; COMPREHENSIVE PERSONAL LIABILITY INSURANCE; DISABILITY INCOME INSURANCE; ENDOWMENT INSURANCE; FAMILY INCOME POLICY; FAMILY INCOME RIDER; FAMILY MAINTENANCE POLICY; FAMILY POLICY; FARMERS COMPREHENSIVE PERSONAL LIABILITY INSURANCE; HOMEOWNERS INSURANCE POLICY; LIFE INSURANCE; MINIMUM DEPOSIT WHOLE LIFE INSURANCE; PAID-UP INSURANCE; PERSONAL AUTOMOBILE POLICY (PAP); PERSONAL INJURY PROTECTION (PIP); PLEASURE BOAT COVERAGE; PURE ENDOWMENT.

PERSONAL INSURANCE NEEDS *see* NEEDS APPROACH.

PERSONAL JEWELRY INSURANCE coverage on jewelry and precious stones on an ALL RISKS basis at any location subject to exclusions of wear and tear, war, and nuclear disaster. Each item must be specifically listed in the policy. This coverage is of importance to insureds with valuable jewelry since most property insurance policies such as the HOMEOWNERS INSURANCE POLICY have relatively low limits of coverage for jewelry and precious stones.

PERSONAL LEGAL EXPENSE LIABILITY INSURANCE coverage for routine personal legal expenses, including probate, criminal defense, and divorce.

PERSONAL LIABILITY CLAIM INSURANCE *see* COMPREHENSIVE PERSONAL LIABILITY INSURANCE; HOMEOWNERS INSURANCE POLICY; PERSONAL AUTOMOBILE POLICY (PAP).

PERSONAL LIABILITY EXPOSURES *see* LIABILITY, PERSONAL EXPOSURES.

PERSONAL LIABILITY INSURANCE *see* COVERAGE E POLICY SECTION II HOMEOWNERS INSURANCE POLICY—SECTION II (LIABILITY COVERAGE).

PERSONAL LINES insurance written on the personal and real property of an individual (or individuals) to include such policies as the HOMEOWNERS INSURANCE POLICY and PERSONAL AUTOMOBILE POLICY (PAP).

PERSONAL LOSS *see* PROPERTY INSURANCE COVERAGE.

PERSONAL PRODUCING GENERAL AGENT (PPGA) individual appointed by the insurance company as an independent contractor. The agent receives various expense allowances for office-associated expenses and direct commissions on products sold as well as overriding commissions on products sold by other company agents. The PPGA usually has contracts to sell products from many different insurance companies. Insurance companies usually make available to the PPGA advanced sales technical support by supplying technicians and computer software and, in some instances, computer hardware.

PERSONAL PROPERTY *see* HOMEOWNERS INSURANCE POLICY; PERSONAL ARTICLES INSURANCE; PERSONAL EFFECTS INSURANCE; PERSONAL PROPERTY FLOATER.

PERSONAL PROPERTY FLOATER coverage for all personal property, regardless of location of an insured and household residents, including children away at school. Written on an ALL RISKS basis, subject to excluded perils such as war, wear and tear, mechanical breakdown, vermin, and nuclear disaster. "Personal property" includes clothing, television, musical instruments, cameras, jewelry, watches, furs, furniture, radios, and appliances. Coverage can be extended to damage of real property as the result of theft of personal property.

PERSONAL-RESIDENCE TRUST trust in which a home is transferred directly to the children while the parent(s) remain in the home for a fixed period of time, resulting in a substantially reduced estate tax cost. These trusts have a great flexibility in that the home in trust may be sold during the term of the trust, provided the proceeds from the sale is reinvested in another home within two years of the sale of the home. The primary drawbacks of this trust are that if the parent(s) die before the term of the trust expires, the home is included in the estate of the parent(s), and if the parent(s) outlive the term of the trust and has a desire to remain in the home, the parent(s) must rent that home from the children at its fair market value.

During the term of the trust, the parent(s) has the right to the income from the trust's property as well as the use of that property. As such, income and expenses associated with that property are reported on the income tax return of the parent(s). If the parent(s) is still alive at the time the term of the trust expires, the interest in the home that is transferred to the children is valued as a remainder interest. The tax advantage results from this remainder interest as the remainder interest in the home is valued at a substantially lower value for federal tax purposes than the full market value of the home.

PERSONAL THEFT INSURANCE *see* BROAD FORM PERSONAL THEFT INSURANCE; HOMEOWNERS INSURANCE POLICY.

PERSONAL UMBRELLA LIABILITY POLICY type of UMBRELLA LIABILITY INSURANCE that protects the INSURED in the event of lawsuits exceeding the basic limits of coverage in the HOMEOWNERS INSURANCE POLICY—SECTION II (LIABILITY COVERAGE); PERSONAL AUTOMOBILE POLICY (PAP)—*Coverage A—Liability*; and TENANTS INSURANCE. Coverage usually ranges from 1 million to 10 million in excess over these basic limits required in these primary policies before this umbrella policy goes into effect. The retained or basic limit eliminates the requirement for a deductible in the umbrella policy.

PER STIRPES distribution of a deceased beneficiary's share of an estate among that beneficiary's children. *Contrast with* PER CAPITA.

PET INSURANCE *see* LIVESTOCK FLOATER; LIVESTOCK INSURANCE; LIVESTOCK MORTALITY (LIFE) INSURANCE; LIVESTOCK TRANSIT INSURANCE.

PHANTOM STOCK *see* STOCK APPRECIATION RIGHTS.

PHANTOM STOCK PLANS plans that are similar to STOCK APPRECIATION RIGHTS (SARS) in that an employee is granted a contractual right by the employer to a stipulated number of units in the business, which is really a percentage of the business. As the value of the business increases, the value of these units increase. At the end of a stipulated period of time, the employee either can receive additional income based on the appreciation of the value of these units or can convert these units into an equity ownership in the business. Thus, the employee has a vested interest in the business increasing in value.

PHYSICAL CONDITION *see* APPLICATION; DISABILITY INCOME INSURANCE; INSPECTION REPORT; PREEXISTING CONDITION; PREFERRED RISK; UNDERWRITING; UNIQUE IMPAIRMENT.

PHYSICAL DAMAGE INSURANCE property damage coverage for a vehicle under the COLLISION INSURANCE and COMPREHENSIVE INSURANCE sections of the BUSINESS AUTOMOBILE POLICY (BAP) and the PERSONAL AUTOMOBILE POLICY (PAP).

PHYSICAL DAMAGE TO PROPERTY OF OTHERS *see* HOME-OWNERS INSURANCE POLICY—SECTION II (LIABILITY COVERAGE); PERSONAL AUTOMOBILE POLICY (PAP); PROPERTY AND LIABILITY INSURANCE.

PHYSICAL EXAMINATION PROVISION *see* APPLICATION; DISABILITY INCOME INSURANCE; REINSTATEMENT.

PHYSICAL HARM *see* HOMEOWNERS INSURANCE POLICY—SECTION II (LIABILITY COVERAGE); LIABILITY; PERSONAL AUTOMOBILE POLICY (PAP); PROPERTY AND LIABILITY INSURANCE.

PHYSICAL HAZARD *see* HAZARD; INCREASED HAZARD.

PHYSICALLY IMPAIRED RISK *see* IMPAIRED RISK (SUBSTANDARD RISK).

PHYSICIAN HOSPITAL ORGANIZATION (PHO) separate legal entity formed by one or more physicians and one or more hospitals whose objective it is to negotiate contracts with payer organizations. The PHO provides financial, marketing, and administrative services to its members.

PHYSICIANS AND SURGEONS EQUIPMENT INSURANCE coverage for equipment normally carried from location to location by a physician or surgeon; written on an ALL RISKS basis to include supplies and scientific books used in medical practice.

PHYSICIANS AND SURGEONS SERVICES IN HOSPITAL, HMO *see* HEALTH MAINTENANCE ORGANIZATION (HMO).

PHYSICIANS CARE *see* DISABILITY INCOME INSURANCE.

PHYSICIANS INSURANCE *see* PHYSICIANS AND SURGEONS EQUIPMENT INSURANCE; PHYSICIANS, SURGEONS, AND DENTISTS INSURANCE.

PHYSICIANS, SURGEONS, AND DENTISTS INSURANCE coverage for a practicing physician, surgeon, or dentist, when bodily injury, personal injury, and/or property damage is incurred by a patient and the patient sues for injuries and/or damages. The cost of defending the physician, surgeon, or dentist is in addition to the upper limits of the policy, and includes legal fees, court costs, and other general expenses. There is a crisis in this type of coverage, in that fewer companies are writing these policies. *See also* MALPRACTICE LIABILITY INSURANCE.

PIA *see* PRIMARY INSURANCE AMOUNT (PIA); PROFESSIONAL INSURANCE AGENTS (PIA).

PIERS, WHARVES, DOCKS, AND SLIPS INSURANCE coverage in the event of damage or destruction resulting from collision by a vessel or high waves. Excluded are fire, lightning, windstorm, earthquake, and explosion, since these perils are included under the *Standard Fire Policy* and the other business property policies. Piers, wharves, docks, and slips were the few properties that could be covered for flood damage under commercial insurance prior to passage of the Natural Disasters Act of 1968, of which the Federal Flood Insurance Program is a part.

PILFERAGE stealing small amounts of property. Insurance coverage is available under a number of policies. *See also* BLANKET CRIME POLICY; BROAD FORM PERSONAL THEFT INSURANCE; BURGLARY INSURANCE; BUSINESSOWNERS POLICY (BOP); DISHONESTY, DISAPPEARANCE, AND DESTRUCTION POLICY ("3-D" POLICY), HOMEOWNERS INSURANCE POLICY; PERSONAL AUTOMOBILE POLICY (PAP); COMMERCIAL PACKAGE POLICY.

PIP *see* PERSONAL INJURY PROTECTION (PIP).

PIPELINE INSURANCE type of INLAND MARINE insurance that covers pipelines. Although pipelines are stationary, the coverage is written on inland marine forms because they are considered part of the transportation system.

PITI abbreviation for Principal, Interest, Taxes, and Insurance. Generally, for the time period of the loan, the principal and interest amount remains fixed; however, tax and insurance amounts will vary according to changing economic conditions.

PLACED BUSINESS delivered insurance policy to the POLICYHOLDER in which the policy's first premium has been paid, the application has been reviewed, and all policy parts completed.

PLAINTIFF party who asserts a claim against another party in a legal proceeding.

PLAINTIFF'S REPLEVIN BOND *see* JUDICIAL BOND.

PLAN ADMINISTRATION *see* ADMINISTERING AGENCY; ADMINISTRATIVE CHARGE; ADVISORY COMMITTEE.

PLAN DOCUMENT formal, written, legal statement listing the provisions of an EMPLOYEE BENEFIT INSURANCE PLAN.

PLANNED PREMIUM PAYMENT/TARGET PREMIUM PAYMENT premium payment made by the POLICYOWNER under a UNIVERSAL LIFE INSURANCE policy, usually on an automatic monthly preauthorized bank draft basis. The amount of the payment is established according to how much the policyowner wants to save each month.

PLAN PARTICIPANTS employees participating in and covered under an EMPLOYEE BENEFIT INSURANCE PLAN.

PLANS COVERED, INSURANCE *see* BUSINESS INSURANCE; GROUP INSURANCE; INDIVIDUAL INSURANCE.

PLAN SPONSOR employer, association, labor union, or other group offering a qualified employee benefit plan such as a pension or profit sharing plan.

PLAN TERMINATION INSURANCE *see* PENSION PLAN TERMINATION INSURANCE.

PLATE GLASS INSURANCE *see* COMPREHENSIVE GLASS INSURANCE.

PLEASURE BOAT COVERAGE insurance for private pleasure boats. Coverage is not standard, but is generally broken down into insurance for (1) yachts, including sailboats; (2) boats with inboard motors under *marine* policies; and (3) outboard motor boats under INLAND MARINE policies.

Yacht insurance, which is written on an ALL RISKS or a *named peril* basis, is broken down into (1) hull insurance; (2) bodily injury and property damage liability insurance; (3) federal compensation insurance for crew members; and (4) medical payments insurance. Outboard coverage insures a boat on land or in the water on an ALL RISKS or named peril basis.

PLEDGE OF A LIFE INSURANCE POLICY transfer of the CASH VALUE of the policy from the POLICYOWNER to the policyowner's creditor as security for a loan.

PLUVIOUS INSURANCE *see* RAIN INSURANCE.

PML *see* MAXIMUM FORESEEABLE LOSS (MFL); MAXIMUM PROBABLE LOSS (MPL).

POINT 1% of the loan amount paid to the lender for making a loan.

POINT–OF-SERVICE (POS) device that enables the HEALTH MAINTENANCE ORGANIZATION (HMO) to present a premium quotation to the employer that would encourage the employer to replace the current health carrier. The POS offers three options for the delivery of health care:

1. *traditional gatekeeper (GK) option*—HMO network provides the care and there is a gatekeeper director.
2. *open access (OA) option*—HMO network provides the care but there is no gatekeeper director. At the time care is required, the member selects the provider.
3. *out-of-network option (OON)*—care is permitted outside the HMO network and there is no gatekeeper director. At the time care is required, the member selects the provider.

The member has increasing payments under the OA and OON options as compared with the GK option. For example, the GK option may have a $15 physician COPAYMENT and provide total hospital benefits. The OA option may have a $30 physician copayment with a 10% COINSURANCE requirement. The OON option may provide for a $500 DEDUCTIBLE, an 80/20 coinsurance requirement until the employee's out-of-pocket medical expenses reach $5000, and then the plan would pay all expenses up to a $750,000 lifetime maximum.

POINT-TO-POINT comparison of index values on specific dates used in calculating index increases in an EQUITY INDEXED ANNUITY.

POLICY written agreement that puts insurance coverage into effect. *See also* HEALTH INSURANCE CONTRACT; INSURANCE CONTRACT, GENERAL; INSURANCE CONTRACT, LIFE; INSURANCE CONTRACT, PROPERTY AND CASUALTY.

POLICY ANNIVERSARY 12-month period from the date of issue of a policy as stated in its DECLARATIONS SECTION.

POLICY CONDITION *see* CONDITION.

POLICY DATE *see* EFFECTIVE DATE.

POLICY DECLARATION *see* DECLARATION.

POLICY DEFINITIONS section of an insurance policy that provides definitions of terms referenced in the INSURING AGREEMENT, perils covered, EXCLUSIONS, and other parts of the policy.

POLICY DIVIDEND *see* PARTICIPATING POLICY DIVIDEND.

POLICY FACE *see* FACE AMOUNT (FACE OF POLICY).

POLICY FEE flat amount added to the basic premium rate to reflect the cost of issuing a policy, establishing the required records, sending premium notices, and other related expenses.

POLICY FEE SYSTEM flat dollar amount added to arrive (premium rate per $1000 of FACE AMOUNT × face amount) at the premium.

POLICYHOLDER individual or other entity who owns an insurance policy. Synonymous with *policyowner.*

POLICYHOLDER DIVIDEND *see* DIVIDEND.

POLICYHOLDER SURPLUS excess of an insurance company's assets above its legal obligations to meet the benefits (liabilities) payable to its policyholders. Also, the net worth in an insurance company adjusted for the overstatement of liabilities. *See also* SURPLUS ACCOUNT; SURPLUS LINES.

POLICY ILLUSTRATION financial projections of the values of an ANNUITY or LIFE INSURANCE policy (CASH SURRENDER VALUE; DEATH BENEFIT) if the actual investment, mortality, and expense experience is the same as the expected experience. These illustrations are not guaranteed and cannot be part of POLICY PROVISIONS.

POLICY JACKET *see* JACKET.

POLICY LIMIT *see* BUSINESS LIABILITY INSURANCE (Insuring Agreement Section); COORDINATION OF BENEFITS.

POLICY LOAN amount that the owner of a life insurance policy can borrow at interest from the insurer, up to the cash surrender value. If interest is not paid when due, it is deducted from any remaining cash value. When the cash value is exhausted, the insurance ceases. If the insured dies, any outstanding policy loan and interest due are subtracted from the death benefit.

The policyowner may repay the loan in whole or in part at any time; or may continue the loan, as long as the interest plus the principal of the loan do not equal or exceed the cash value (in essence only the interest on the loan must be serviced) or until the policy matures. Insurance companies reserve the right to delay payment of a policy loan for up to six months to protect their solvency, but this has rarely been done since the Depression of the 1930s. *See also* AUTOMATIC PREMIUM LOAN PROVISION.

POLICYOWNER *see* OWNERSHIP RIGHTS UNDER LIFE INSURANCE; POLICYHOLDER.

POLICYOWNERS EQUITY portion of a life insurance policy cash value after the deduction of all the policyowner's indebtedness.

POLICY PERIOD time interval during which policy is in force. *See also* CLAIMS MADE BASIS LIABILITY COVERAGE; CLAIMS OCCURRENCE BASIS LIABILITY COVERAGE.

POLICY PROVISIONS words, sentences, and paragraphs in an insurance policy. *See also* ANALYSIS OF PROPERTY AND CASUALTY POLICY; HEALTH INSURANCE CONTRACT; HOMEOWNERS INSURANCE POLICY; INSURANCE CONTRACT, GENERAL; INSURANCE CONTRACT, LIFE; INSURANCE CONTRACT, PROPERTY AND CASUALTY; PERSONAL AUTOMOBILE POLICY (PAP).

POLICY PROVISIONS, LIFE stipulations of the rights and obligations of an *insured* and an *insurer* under a policy. *See also* ACCIDENTAL DEATH CLAUSE; ASSIGNMENT CLAUSE, LIFE INSURANCE; BENEFICIARY CLAUSE; DISABILITY INCOME RIDER; DIVIDEND OPTION; GRACE PERIOD; INCONTESTABLE CLAUSE; LIFE INSURANCE, CREDITOR RIGHTS; MISSTATEMENT OF AGE; NONFORFEITURE PROVISION; OPTIONAL MODES OF SETTLEMENT; POLICY LOAN; REINSTATEMENT; SPENDTHRIFT TRUST CLAUSE; SUICIDE CLAUSE; WAR EXCLUSION CLAUSE.

POLICY PURCHASE OPTION *see* GUARANTEED INSURABILITY.

POLICY REPLACEMENT *see* CONSERVATION; REPLACEMENT, LIFE INSURANCE.

POLICY RESERVE *see* FULL PRELIMINARY TERM RESERVE PLAN; PROSPECTIVE RESERVE; RETROSPECTIVE METHOD RESERVE COMPUTATION.

POLICY STRUCTURE general arrangement of a contract between an insurer and an insured. The policy defines the insured and the type of coverage, lays out what the insurer must do, lists exceptions and limitations, and states the conditions for coverage. In a standard property and liability contract, the provisions are grouped into these four categories: DECLARATION, INSURING AGREEMENT, EXCLUSIONS, and CONDITIONS FOR QUALIFICATION.

POLICY SUMMARY policy report issued to the POLICYOWNER that must include at least the following: (1) first five years of premiums, cash values, death benefits, and dividends (if PARTICIPATING INSUR-

ANCE); (2) tenth year, twentieth year, and at least one year between the insured's age 60 and 65 and policy maturity year of premiums, cash values, death benefits, and dividends (if participating insurance); (3) effective interest rate at which POLICY LOANS may be made by the policyowner; (4) tenth and twentieth year cost surrender value; (5) the net premium payment cost indices; (6) insurance company name and address; (7) the insurance agent name and address; and (8) the type (generic) of life insurance policy.

POLICY TERM *see* POLICY PERIOD.

POLICY TERRITORY physical location and geographical description of the area where the policy meets the IN-FORCE REQUIREMENT for the insurance coverage to be in effect. For example, some insurance coverages apply only in the United States while others apply on a worldwide basis. In some instances, coverage applies only in the United States, its territories, and Canada.

POLICY YEAR *see* POLICY YEAR EXPERIENCE.

POLICY YEAR EXPERIENCE 12-month loss on a policy or line of business.

POLITICAL RISK investment risk associated with the changes in government policies that may have a dramatic effect on financial instruments. For example, if federal legislation is passed removing the tax-exempt status of tax-deferred buildup of the cash values in LIFE INSURANCE policies and ANNUITIES, one of the primary reasons for purchase of these products would be eliminated.

POLITICAL RISK INSURANCE coverage for business firms operating abroad to insure them against loss due to political upheavals including war, revolution, confiscation, incontrovertibility of currency, and other such losses. *See also* OVERSEAS PRIVATE INVESTMENT CORPORATION.

POLITICAL RISK INSURANCE: CONFISCATION, EXPROPRIATION AND NATIONALIZATION insurance coverage that protects a company's and/or individual's assets against financial loss resulting from acts of confiscation, expropriation, or nationalization by a foreign government. Asset protected may be mobile or permanent and include: structures, inventory, bank accounts, prepaid supplies, receivables, vacation homes owned by individuals, and personal belongings of employees on overseas assignment. The coverage may be purchased on a single asset basis or several asset basis worldwide, subject to limits per country and an aggregate policy limit.

POLITICAL RISK INSURANCE: CONTINGENCY INSURANCE insurance coverage that protects a contractor or other type of business providing a service for expenses incurred in the event a contract is not ratified by a foreign government. For example, if a contractor decides to start building a structure prior to the foreign government ratifying the agreement and the ratification fails, the contractor would be indemnified for expenses incurred.

POLITICAL RISK INSURANCE: CONTRACT FRUSTRATION insurance coverage that will INDEMNIFY the INSURED in the event a foreign government or company does not abide by the terms and conditions of the contract in such instances as:

1. *Exportation*—exporter incurs a loss because the buyer in a foreign country does not adhere to the contractual obligations.
2. *Deterioration and repudiation*—insured sells services to buyer who refuses to honor contractual obligations.
3. *Importation*—insured incurs a loss resulting from the nondelivery of products purchased and paid for in advance.

POLITICAL RISK INSURANCE: UNFAIR CALLING OF DEMAND BONDS insurance coverage that protects the exporter (even though the exporter may be in total compliance with the terms and conditions of the contract) in the event a foreign government calls the demand bonds. For example, after the Shah of Iran was overthrown, the new government called in the demand bonds posted by United States exporters and contractors to show its animosity toward the United States.

POLLUTION EXCLUSION liability insurance exception for pollution coverage that is not both sudden and accidental from the insured's standpoint. As a result of the damage suits from such incidents as the chemical pollution at Love Canal, insurance companies began to modify pollution coverage in their liability policies in the 1970s. First, companies changed coverage to apply only if pollution was "sudden and accidental," rather than "gradual." But some courts ruled that "sudden and accidental" could encompass several years of pollution problems. Consequently, the INSURANCE SERVICES OFFICE (ISO) introduced a new COMPREHENSIVE GENERAL LIABILITY INSURANCE (CGL) policy in 1985 (replaced today by the COMMERCIAL GENERAL LIABILITY form) that excluded coverage for nearly all types of pollution damage, leaving only limited liability coverage for pollution originating away from an insured's premises.

POLLUTION LIABILITY INSURANCE pollution coverage that is excluded under the COMPREHENSIVE GENERAL LIABILITY INSURANCE (CGL) policy. This coverage can be secured through an ENDORSEMENT to the CGL by adding the pollution liability extension endorsement. It negates the exclusion for BODILY INJURY and property damage under the CGL but keeps the clean-up costs exclusion.

POOL syndicate or association of insurance companies or REINSURANCE companies organized to underwrite a particular risk, usually with high limits of exposure. Each member shares in premiums, losses, and expenses according to a predetermined agreement.

POOLED INCOME FUNDS separate trust established by a charitable entity whose purpose is to receive contributions from numerous donors. All the donors' contributions are commingled. Each donor can retain a life-income interest in the donation. The donor's income payment is based on the number of units of participation calculated at the time the donation is made and the value of each unit. The value of each unit in turn is determined by the investment performance of the commingled funds.

POOLED INVESTMENT ACCOUNT combination of the funds of many POLICYHOLDERS held in a single account and invested as a single entity.

POOLING method by which each member of an insurance POOL shares in each and every risk written by the other members of the pool.

POOLING CHARGE amount that each member of a POOL contributes to that pool. *See also* POOLING.

POPULATION DECREMENTS reduction in a retirement plan's population resulting from the death, disability, and termination of its members.

POPULATION INCREMENTS additions of new entrants into an EMPLOYEE BENEFIT INSURANCE PLAN.

PORTABILITY *see* PENSION PORTABILITY.

PORTFOLIO insurance company's total investments in financial securities.

PORTFOLIO AVERAGE METHOD *see* PORTFOLIO RATE OF RETURN.

PORTFOLIO RATE FIXED ACCOUNT account in which the same interest rate is credited on all premiums regardless of the time period and amount contributed.

PORTFOLIO RATE OF RETURN weighted average of the returns earned on the insurance company's investments in stocks, bonds, real estate, etc., made at different times and earning different rates of return at these times. It has been argued that this rate of return does not reflect the true rate of return on investments being earned today. This led to the development of the CURRENT ASSUMPTIONS products.

PORTFOLIO REINSURANCE coverage in which an insurance company's portfolio is *ceded* to a *reinsurer* who reinsures a given percentage of a particular line of business.

PORTFOLIO RETURN process whereby a CEDING COMPANY resumes the insuring of a portfolio of insurance policies which it had previously CEDED to a REINSURER.

PORTFOLIO RUNOFF process of the continual REINSURANCE of a CEDING COMPANY'S portfolio of insurance policies. All premiums that have been CEDED become EARNED PREMIUMS.

PORT RISK INSURANCE coverage for ships in port for a lengthy stay and/or those that are under repair. Insures on an ALL RISKS basis to include the exposures associated with the ship moving from one dock to another.

POSITION SCHEDULE BOND *see* FIDELITY BOND.

POSSIBLE MAXIMUM LOSS *see* MAXIMUM FORESEEABLE LOSS (MFL).

POST-HOSPITAL RECOVERY INSURANCE short-term health care facility benefits designed to cover SUBACUTE CARE as well as assisted living care. The time period covered is typically 90 to 190 days.

POSTMORTEM DIVIDEND dividend in a *participating policy* paid after the death of an insured, representing dividends earned between the last dividend date and the insured's death.

POSTMORTEM PLANNING *see* ESTATE PLANNING; ESTATE PLANNING DISTRIBUTION; HUMAN LIFE VALUE APPROACH (ECONOMIC VALUE OF AN INDIVIDUAL LIFE) (EVOIL); NEEDS APPROACH.

POSTRETIREMENT FUNDING method of funding a pension plan after a worker retires. An employer purchases an annuity or sets aside a sum when an employee retires that will pay monthly lifetime benefits. Postretirement funding is no longer permitted under the EMPLOYEE RETIREMENT INCOME SECURITY ACT OF 1974 (ERISA), which requires current funding of future pension liabilities.

POSTSELECTION OF INSURED underwriting practice involving regular review of insurance contracts in force with the intent of either canceling a policy or not offering renewal for risks no longer deemed acceptable. *See also* CANCELLATION PROVISION CLAUSE; NONCANCELLABLE GUARANTEED RENEWABLE POLICY; NONRENEWAL CLAUSE; RENEWAL PROVISION.

POWER INTERRUPTION INSURANCE ENDORSEMENT addition to boiler and machinery insurance that covers loss to property or equipment caused by an interruption of power by a public utility. Coverage is available either on an hourly or daily basis for loss of use or for actual loss sustained.

POWER OF APPOINTMENT *see* ESTATE PLANNING DISTRIBUTION.

POWER OF ATTORNEY legal instrument whereby an individual is given the right to act on behalf of another individual. For example, the right to buy and sell stock and to sign all brokerage papers relating to buying and selling in a stockholder's account is given by the stockholder to another individual through power of attorney. Or the right to decide which settlement option is to be used under a life insurance policy may be given by a policyowner to another individual. Experts often advise extreme care in assigning a power of attorney since that person becomes free to make financial decisions that can enhance—or ruin—an individual represented.

POWER PLANT INSURANCE
1. form of BOILER AND MACHINERY INSURANCE that covers power generating plants.
2. form of BUSINESS INCOME COVERAGE FORM that covers a utility customer's losses resulting from interruption of power from a public utility.

PREAUTHORIZED CHECK PLAN plan for the automatic payment of premiums due through drafting by the insurer of the policyowner's preauthorized bank account. Usually, the insurer drafts this account on a monthly basis for the premium payment owed. Studies show that PERSISTENCY is highest when premium payments are made through bank draft plans.

PREAUTHORIZED CHECK SYSTEM (PAC) arrangement by which a policyowner authorizes an insurance company to draft his checking account for premiums due on an insurance policy. The drafting is usually monthly. PERSISTENCY of policies paid this way is substantially higher than when insureds pay them directly to an insurance company.

PREDICTABILITY *see* EXPECTED LOSS.

PREEXISTING CONDITION illnesses or disability for which the insured was treated or advised within a stipulated time period before making application for a life or health insurance policy. A preexisting condition can result in cancellation of the policy.

PREFERENCE BENEFICIARY CLAUSE *see* BENEFICIARY: BENEFICIARY CLAUSE.

PREFERRED BENEFICIARY *see* BENEFICIARY; BENEFICIARY CLAUSE.

PREFERRED PROVIDER ORGANIZATION (PPO) hospital, physician, or other provider of health care that an insurer recommends to insureds. A PPO allows insurance companies to negotiate directly with hospitals and physicians for health services at a lower price than would be normally charged. A PPO tries to combine the best elements of a fee-for-service and HEALTH MAINTENANCE ORGANIZATION (HMO) systems.

PREFERRED RISK insured, or an applicant for insurance, with lower expectation of incurring a loss than the *standard applicant.* For example, an applicant for life insurance who does not smoke can usually obtain a reduced premium rate to reflect his or her greater LIFE EXPECTANCY.

PRELIMINARY TERM life insurance accounting method that does not require any TERMINAL RESERVE for a policy at the end of the first year. First-year policy acquisition expenses, such as *agent commission,* MEDICAL EXAMINATION, and PREMIUM TAX, are often too large to leave enough of the end-of-the-year PREMIUM for addition to the premium reserve required under state FULL VALUATION RESERVE standards. In order to avoid taking the difference between the amount of the premium remaining and the required addition to reserves out of the insurance company's SURPLUS ACCOUNT, the FULL PRELIMINARY TERM RESERVE VALUATION method is sometimes used. This leaves more of the premium available to cover acquisition cost and first-year claims. *See also* MODIFIED RESERVE METHODS.

PREMATURE DISTRIBUTION PENALTY 10% surcharge paid by employees on benefits paid from a qualified RETIREMENT PLAN prior to age 59½.

PREMISES AND OPERATIONS LIABILITY INSURANCE part of a business liability policy that covers an insured for bodily injury or property damage liability to members of the public while they are on his premises. This coverage is available in basic business policies that include COMMERCIAL GENERAL LIABILITY INSURANCE (CGL); MANUFACTURERS AND CONTRACTORS LIABILITY INSURANCE; OWNERS, LANDLORDS, AND TENANTS LIABILITY POLICY; STOREKEEPERS LIABILITY INSURANCE.

PREMISES LIABILITY *see* LIABILITY, BUSINESS EXPOSURES; LIABILITY, PERSONAL EXPOSURES.

PREMISES MEDICAL PAYMENTS INSURANCE supplemental coverage written into or endorsed onto many business and personal liability policies. Covers medical costs and loss of income of persons injured on an insured's property, regardless of whether the insured was at fault in causing those injuries. This coverage enables the insured to volunteer to pay these medical costs and income losses when doing so serves the insured's business purposes or preserves personal relationships.

PREMISES SOLD EXCLUSION in a COMMERCIAL GENERAL LIABILITY (COMPREHENSIVE GENERAL LIABILITY) policy, exclusion of coverage for sold premises. The objective of this exclusion is to eliminate coverage for property damage and/or bodily injury due to inherently dangerous risks associated with property sold by the insured. For example, the insured may sell property that has defects that should have been repaired prior to the sale. These defects could then result in damage to the property, as well as bodily injury to a person or persons who came in contact with that property.

PREMIUM rate that an insured is charged, reflecting his or her expectation of loss or risk. The insurance company will assume the risks of the insured (length of life, state of health, property damage or destruction, or liability exposure) in exchange for a premium payment. Premiums are calculated by combining expectation of loss and expense and profit loadings. Usually, the periodic cost of insurance is computed by multiplying the premium rate per unit of insurance by the number of units purchased. The rate class in which the insured is placed includes large numbers of individuals with like characteristics who pose the same risk. Every individual in a given class will not incur the same loss; rather each has approximately the same *expecta-*

tion of loss (known as the *Principle of Equity*). *See also* EQUITY; GROSS PREMIUM; PURE PREMIUM RATING METHOD.

PREMIUM ADJUSTMENT ENDORSEMENT provision in an insurance policy allowing an INITIAL PREMIUM to be charged, but subject to adjustment during the period of coverage or at the end of coverage depending on the actual loss experience of the insured risk.

PREMIUM ADJUSTMENT FORM *see* PREMIUM ADJUSTMENT ENDORSEMENT.

PREMIUM ADVANCE *see* DEPOSIT PREMIUM.

PREMIUM, ANNUITY (consideration) cost of annuity based on expectation of life of the ANNUITANT and the expense and profit loadings of the insurance company. *See also* ANNUITY; CONSIDERATION.

PREMIUM AUDIT adjustment of estimated INITIAL PREMIUM (based on the LOSS FREQUENCY METHOD) to reflect the actual loss exposures for the POLICY PERIOD.

PREMIUM BASE *see* BASE PREMIUM.

PREMIUM CHARGE *see* PREMIUM.

PREMIUM COMPUTATION *see* PREMIUM; PURE PREMIUM RATING METHOD.

PREMIUM DEFAULT *see* DISCONTINUANCE OF CONTRIBUTIONS; LAPSE.

PREMIUM DEFICIENCY RESERVE supplementary life insurance reserve required by state regulators when the GROSS PREMIUM is lower than the VALUATION PREMIUM. Some life insurers are able to charge policyholders a premium that is lower than required by the reserve valuation system they use. This may be because mortality tables are outdated and their own experience reflects different loss statistics. But if the insurer charges a premium lower than that dictated in the calculation of policy reserves, it must set up a deficiency reserve for the difference.

PREMIUM DEPOSIT *see* DEPOSIT PREMIUM.

PREMIUM DEPOSIT RIDER RIDER attached to an ORDINARY LIFE INSURANCE policy that allows the POLICYOWNER to deposit excess premium payments into a separate account from which they can be withdrawn to meet premium payment requirements.

PREMIUM DISCOUNT reduction in rate reflecting the present value of a premium due on an annuity one year hence.

PREMIUM DISCOUNT PLAN plan whereby adjustments are made in the premium, as the premium increases to reflect the nonproportionate increases in expenses. Generally, the expenses of acquisition costs, administrative costs of placing the policy on the insurer's books, taxes, and claims do not increase in proportion to the increase in the premium. Thus, the GROSS PREMIUM should not reflect a proportionate increase in expenses as the NET SINGLE PREMIUM increases.

PREMIUM, EARNED *see* EARNED PREMIUM.

PREMIUM, GROSS *see* GROSS PREMIUM.

PREMIUM LOAN amount borrowed against the cash value of a life insurance policy to pay the premium due. *See also* AUTOMATIC PREMIUM LOAN PROVISION.

PREMIUM, MINIMUM *see* MINIMUM PREMIUM PLAN.

PREMIUM MODE frequency of premium payment, monthly, quarterly, or annually.

PREMIUM, NET *see* NET LEVEL PREMIUM.

PREMIUM NOTICE message from an insurance company or insurance agency informing a policyowner that a premium is due by a specified date.

PREMIUM, PURE *see* PURE PREMIUM RATING METHOD.

PREMIUM RATE *see* PREMIUM.

PREMIUM RATE EQUITY *see* EQUITY.

PREMIUM RECEIPT written evidence given to a policyowner by an insurance company or insurance agency that it has received a premium.

PREMIUM REFUND in some life insurance policies, provision that permits the beneficiary, upon the death of the insured, to receive not only the DEATH BENEFIT payable under the policy but also all premiums paid into the policy.

PREMIUM, RESTORATION *see* RESTORATION PREMIUM.

PREMIUM RETURN *see* RETURN OF PREMIUM.

PREMIUMS, ESTIMATED *see* ESTIMATED PREMIUM.

PREMIUMS IN-FORCE initial premiums on all insurance policies in force (those policies that have not been cancelled or expired). *See also* IN-FORCE BUSINESS.

PREMIUM, SINGLE *see* SINGLE PREMIUM.

PREMIUMS WRITTEN *see* WRITTEN PREMIUMS.

PREMIUM TAX payment to a state or municipality by an insurance company based on premiums paid by residents.

PREMIUM-TO-SURPLUS RATIO ratio commonly used by the property and casualty insurance industry as a measure of financial strength or to indicate to what degree a particular insurance company is leveraged. A low ratio can be a sign of financial strength, but it also may indicate insufficient loss reserves or premium growth.

PREMIUM, UNEARNED *see* UNEARNED PREMIUM RESERVE.

PRE-NEED FUNERAL INSURANCE SINGLE PREMIUM LIFE INSURANCE POLICY, from which the death benefit is used to pay the predetermined expenses of the insured's funeral. The funeral home agrees to provide the funeral in exchange for the life insurance policy proceeds.

PREPAID GROUP PRACTICE PACKAGE health insurance plan where a group of physicians and dentists provide medical services to a group of individuals for a predetermined fee. It is a basic type of HEALTH MAINTENANCE ORGANIZATION (HMO).

PREPAID INSURANCE EXPENSE expense listed on the Income and Expenditure accounting statement for the unexpired insurance policy owned.

PREPAID LEGAL INSURANCE *see* LEGAL EXPENSE INSURANCE.

PREPAYMENT *see* ADVANCE PAYMENTS.

PREPAYMENT OF PREMIUMS *see* ADVANCE PREMIUM.

PRESCRIPTION DRUG PLAN *see* COMMERCIAL HEALTH INSURANCE; COPAYMENT; COVERED EXPENSE; GROUP HEALTH INSURANCE; HEALTH MAINTENANCE ORGANIZATION (HMO).

PRESELECTION OF INSURED *see* INSPECTION REPORT; PREEXISTING CONDITION; PREFERRED RISK; UNDERWRITING; UNIQUE IMPAIRMENT.

PRESENT EXPECTED VALUE ACTUARIAL EQUIVALENT method of calculating the PREMIUM rate through the development of the following equation: PROBABILITY that the event insured against occurs × FACE AMOUNT of policy × PRESENT VALUE FACTOR.

PRESENT INTEREST (GIFT) *see* ESTATE PLANNING DISTRIBUTION; GIFT; GIFT TAX.

PRESENT VALUE *see* PRESENT VALUE FACTOR.

PRESENT VALUE FACTOR discount interest rate factor used to determine the present value of a sum in the future. The present value equation is:

$$P = R(1 + i)^{-N}$$

where:
P = present value of a sum in the future (discounted value of R)
R = sum of money in the future (accumulated value at the end of N periods)
N = number of periods a sum of money is to be discounted in the future
i = interest rate per period

For example, if one wished to determine a sum (P) that must be invested today in order for it to accumulate to $1000 (R) at the end of 20 years, (N) assuming an 8% interest rate (i), then the equation is:

$$P = \$1000 \ (1 + .08)^{-20}$$
$$= \$1000 \ (.2145482)$$
$$= \$214.55$$

PRESENT VALUE OF ANNUITY DUE *present value* of a series of payments such that the first payment is due immediately, the second payment one period from hence, the third payment two periods hence, and so forth. The continued payment is contingent upon the designated beneficiary (the ANNUITANT) continuing to live. *See also* PRESENT VALUE OF ANNUITY IMMEDIATE.

PRESENT VALUE OF ANNUITY IMMEDIATE *present value* of a series of payments such that the first payment is due one period hence, the second payment two periods hence, and so forth. The continued payment is contingent upon the designated beneficiary (the ANNUITANT) continuing to live. *See also* PRESENT VALUE OF ANNUITY DUE.

PRESENT VALUE OF FUTURE BENEFITS *see* PRESENT VALUE FACTOR.

PRESENT VALUE TABLES tables used to determine the present value of a sum in the future by taking into consideration the assumed interest rate and time period involved. *See also* PRESENT VALUE FACTOR.

PRESUMED NEGLIGENCE *see* RES IPSA LOQUITUR.

PRESUMPTIVE DISABILITY assumption of total disability when an insured loses sight, hearing, speech, or a limb. When such a loss occurs to an insured with disability income insurance, the insurer often assumes that the individual is disabled, even if he or she later returns to work. Here insurers may pay a lump sum in addition to monthly disability payments for the maximum benefit period set by the policy.

PRE-TAX INVESTMENT tax-sheltered investment such that funds are placed into an asset that has not been subject to tax. *See also* SECTION 401(K) PLAN (SALARY REDUCTION PLAN); SECTION 403(B) PLAN; and SECTION 457 DEFERRED COMPENSATION PLAN.

PREVENTION *see* LOSS PREVENTION AND REDUCTION.

PREVENTIVE CARE program of health care designed for the prevention and/or reduction of illnesses by providing such services as regular physical examinations. This care is in opposition to curative care, which goes into effect only after the occurrence of an illness. *See also* HEALTH MAINTENANCE ORGANIZATION (HMO).

PREVENTIVE HEALTH SERVICES *see* HEALTH MAINTENANCE ORGANIZATION (HMO).

PRICE-ANDERSON ACT 1957 federal law setting a limit on the liability of operators of nuclear facilities. The law, an amendment to the Atomic Energy Act of 1954, authorized establishment of private insurance pools to provide liability insurance for nuclear facilities, giving the Atomic Energy Commission (now the NUCLEAR REGULATORY COMMISSION) authority to sell additional insurance in excess of the amount of pool coverage available. *See also* MUTUAL ATOMIC ENERGY REINSURANCE POOL; NUCLEAR ENERGY LIABILITY INSURANCE.

PRICE/EARNINGS (P/E) RATIO price of a share of a common stock divided by the stock's annual earnings per share.

PRICING INADEQUACY RISK one of four types of risks affecting the life insurance company as identified by the SOCIETY OF ACTUARIES. This risk is associated with losses that the life insurance company may incur as the result of the premium rates charged not being sufficient to pay for the adverse changes in MORTALITY experience, MORBIDITY experience, inflation effects on health care claims, changes in social values and their general adverse effects on claims, etc. *See also* ASSET DEPRECIATION RISK; GENERAL BUSINESS RISK; INTEREST RATE CHANGE RISK.

PRIESTLY v. FOWLER 1837 British case that established that an employer was not responsible for injury to an employee if the injury was caused by another employee. Prior to this, English common law provided that an employer took responsibility for his employees; *Priestly v. Fowler* was the first crack in that relationship. Later, other exceptions to employer responsibility were established until finally the employee shouldered all responsibility for his own welfare because, it was argued, he or she had, after all, agreed to accept the job. Late in the 19th century in Great Britain, and early in the 20th century in the U.S., *workers compensation* laws were passed in which the employer accepts responsibility for on-the-job injuries and pays benefits according to an established schedule. In exchange, the employee accepts this as the exclusive remedy. However, in the past decade there have been many challenges to this system, including cases in which injured employees have been allowed to sue their employers.

PRIMA *see* PUBLIC RISK AND INSURANCE MANAGEMENT ASSOCIATION (PRIMA).

PRIMA BENEFICIARY *see* BENEFICIARY.

PRIMACY property, liability, or health coverage that takes precedence when more than one policy covers the same loss. In order to avoid OVERINSURANCE, or paying an insured more than the actual loss, the covering policies accept responsibility for insurance in an established order. For example, if a husband and wife cover each other as dependents in group medical insurance, the injured person's own policy assumes primacy. Therefore if the wife gave birth to a child, her policy would apply to obstetrical and hospital fees up to its limits. Only then would the husband's policy apply, covering the amount that had not been paid by his wife's policy up to the limits of his plan.

PRIMARY AND EXCESS INSURANCE coverage that requires PRIMARY INSURANCE to pay for a loss up to its policy limit and the excess insurance to pay above that limit up to the excess insurance's policy limit. *See also* PRIMARY INSURANCE; EXCESS INSURANCE.

PRIMARY BENEFICIARY *see* BENEFICIARY.

PRIMARY CARE PHYSICIAN physician responsible for routine, remedial, and referral care of the HEALTH MAINTENANCE ORGANIZATION (HMO) member. This physician must authorize treatment by a medical specialist.

PRIMARY INSURANCE first layer property or liability coverage carried by the insured that provides benefits (usually after a deductible has been paid by an insured) up to the limits of a policy, regardless of other insurance polices in effect. *See also* APPORTIONMENT; COORDINATION OF BENEFITS; EXCESS INSURANCE; GROUP HEALTH INSURANCE.

PRIMARY INSURANCE AMOUNT (PIA) monthly benefit payable to retired or disabled worker under Social Security. It is calculated by using the average monthly earnings of the covered person while working. Under this formula, lower-income workers receive a greater percent of the income they had earned while employed than do more highly paid workers. Benefits for spouse, other dependents, and survivors are figured as a percentage of the PIA. A worker who takes early retirement may receive a portion of the PIA at age 62. The PIA is used to calculate most other benefits.

PRIMARY INSURER *see* PRIMARY INSURANCE.

PRIMARY PLAN *see* COORDINATION OF BENEFITS.

PRIME RATE rate of interest charged by a bank for funds that are loaned to its most creditworthy borrowers.

PRINCIPAL insurance company that employs or contracts with an insurance AGENT to represent it. *See also* SURETY BOND.

PRINCIPAL SUM *accidental death benefit* option that can be added to a DISABILITY INCOME (DI) policy under which a lump sum is payable at the loss of life, dismemberment, or loss of sight.

PRINCIPLE OF DIVERSIFICATION *see* DIVERSIFICATION.

PRINCIPLE OF INDEMNITY *see* INDEMNITY.

PRINCIPLE OF INSURABLE INTEREST *see* INSURABLE INTEREST.

PRIOR ACTS COVERAGE liability insurance coverage for claims arising from acts that occurred before the beginning of the policy period. Policies written on a *claims made basis,* such as MALPRACTICE LIABILITY INSURANCE and ERRORS AND OMISSIONS LIABILITY INSURANCE, cover only claims during the policy period. Prior acts coverage is necessary for covering a claim made during a current policy period for an event that happened before a policy was in force.

PRIOR APPROVAL RATING requirement of state approval of property insurance rates and policy forms before they can be used. Individual states regulate insurers and approve their rates. There are three methods of rate approval, in addition to prior approval: *modified prior approval, open competition,* and *file and use.*

PRIOR-APPROVAL STATES those states requiring insurers to obtain PRIOR APPROVAL RATING of rates and policy forms before they use them. Although most states once fell into this category, many followed the lead of New York State in 1969 when it moved to a system of *open competition.*

PRIOR CONFINEMENT REQUIREMENT requirement that the insured must have stayed in a hospital or other health care facility for at least a specified period of time before being entitled to receive insurance benefits. This requirement is usually found in LONG-TERM CARE (LTC) insurance policies.

PRIOR INCOME average earned monthly income (AEMI) for the tax year in which the insured wage earner has income interrupted or terminated because of illness, sickness, or accident. This AEMI is important to the calculation of the MONTHLY INDEMNITY benefit and the LOSS OF INCOME amount provided under the DISABILITY INCOME INSURANCE policy.

PRIOR INSURANCE insurance in force previous to the present insurance policy.

PRIOR SERVICE BENEFIT PENSION PLAN participant's retirement benefit credited for prior years of recognized service with the employer prior to a specific date.

PRIVATE ANNUITY payment to the seller over the seller's LIFE EXPECTANCY for the sale of the seller's ASSETS. This procedure provides for the immediate removal of assets that have appreciated from the estate.

PRIVATE ANNUITY TRUST assets sold to a trust in exchange for a lifetime ANNUITY. Upon the death of the ANNUITANT, the trust's heirs receive any balance remaining in the trust on an estate tax-free basis. The seller is taxed on the full, fair market value of the annuity at the time of the exchange.

PRIVATE FAMILY FOUNDATION type of charitable giving through a qualified nonprofit organization that is controlled by an individual or family.

PRIVATE INSURANCE *see* SOCIAL INSURANCE.

PRIVATE MORTGAGE INSURANCE (PMI) insurance written by a COMMERCIAL INSURANCE COMPANY that indemnifies the mortgage lender in the event there is a default on the mortgage.

PRIVATE NONCOMMERCIAL HEALTH INSURANCE *see* HEALTH INSURANCE.

PRIVATE PENSION PLAN *see* PENSION PLAN; PENSION PLAN FUNDING, GROUP DEPOSIT ADMINISTRATION ANNUITY; PENSION PLAN FUNDING, GROUP IMMEDIATE PARTICIPATING GUARANTEED (IPG) CONTRACT ANNUITY; PENSION PLAN FUNDING, GROUP PERMANENT CONTRACT; PENSION PLAN FUNDING, INDIVIDUAL CONTRACT PENSION PLAN.

PRIVATE PLACEMENT technique used by insurance companies in the purchasing of debt obligations of corporations as a means to: (1) avoid the uncertainties of the market; (2) replace market negotiations with private negotiations; and (3) avoid Securities and Exchange Commission restrictions. *See also* DIRECT PLACEMENT.

PRIVATE REPLACEMENT VARIABLE LIFE (PPVL) life insurance policy in which the CASH VALUE and in some circumstances the DEATH BENEFIT will vary according to the investment performance of an underlying portfolio usually comprised of equities. Thus, this product is considered to be a VARIABLE LIFE INSURANCE policy. In order for a PPVL policy to be sold in any state, the insurance company must be approved to distribute that product in the state and the product must be approved for distribution. Section 817 of the Internal Revenue Code, which discusses the tax treatment of variable policies, and Regulation 1.817.5, which discusses the diversification requirements for life insurance policies, VARIABLE DOLLAR ANNUITIES, and ENDOWMENT INSURANCE POLICIES, pertain to the tax considerations for the PPVL. All variable life insurance policies are considered securities and are subject to federal securities law. One life insurance product currently being directed on a private placement basis is CORPORATE-OWNED VARIABLE LIFE INSURANCE.

PROBABILITY chance that an event will occur. The foundation of insurance is probability and STATISTICS. By pooling a large number of HOMOGENEOUS EXPOSURES an insurance company can predict with a given degree of accuracy the chance that a policyholder will incur a loss. The company reflects this expectation in the pure cost of insurance, known as the *pure premium*. The chance that an event will occur can be expressed as follows:

$$\frac{\text{Probability of}}{\text{Event Occurring}} = \frac{\text{Number of Successful Ways Event Can Occur}}{\text{Total Number of Ways Event Can Occur}}$$

For example, the probability of rolling a six on one die can be expressed as:

$$P(6) = \frac{1}{6}$$

PROBABILITY DISTRIBUTION outcomes of an experiment and their probabilities of occurrence. If the experiment were to be repeated any number of times, the same probabilities should also repeat. For example, the probability distribution for the possible number of heads from two tosses of a fair coin having both a head and a tail would be as follows:

Number of Heads	Tosses	Probability of Event
0	(tail, tail)	.25
1	(head, tail) + (tail, head)	.50
2	(head, head)	.25

PROBABILITY OF LOSS *see* PROBABILITY.

PROBABLE MAXIMUM LOSS (PML) *see* MAXIMUM PROBABLE LOSS (MPL).

PROBATE legal proceeding whereby the will of a deceased is tested for validity.

PROBATE BOND *see* JUDICIAL BOND.

PROBATE COURT court that presides over estate distribution settlements, documentation of wills, and the appointment of legal guardians.

PROBATIONARY PERIOD time, in health insurance, from the first day of a disability, illness, or accident during which no benefits are payable. The longer the probationary period, the lower the premium. *See also* ELIMINATION PERIOD.

PROCEEDS benefits payable under any insurance policy or annuity contract.

PRODUCER *see* AGENT.

PRODUCERS COOPERATIVE health plans established by associations of hospitals and physicians to provide hospital service and care, and medical and surgical care. *See also* BLUE CROSS; BLUE SHIELD.

PRODUCT DEVELOPMENT design, testing, packaging, and marketing of an insurance policy.

PRODUCT FAILURE EXCLUSION *see* BUSINESS RISK EXCLUSION.

PRODUCT LIABILITY CATASTROPHE REINSURANCE *see* AUTOMATIC NONPROPORTIONAL REINSURANCE; AUTOMATIC PROPORTIONAL REINSURANCE; AUTOMATIC REINSURANCE; EXCESS OF LOSS REINSURANCE; FACULTATIVE REINSURANCE; NONPROPORTIONAL REINSURANCE; PROPORTIONAL REINSURANCE; QUOTA SHARE REINSURANCE; STOP LOSS REINSURANCE; SURPLUS REINSURANCE.

PRODUCT LIABILITY INSURANCE coverage usually provided under the COMMERCIAL GENERAL LIABILITY INSURANCE (CGL); it can also be purchased separately. *See also* PRODUCTS AND COMPLETED OPERATIONS INSURANCE.

PRODUCT LIABILITY RISK RETENTION ACT act first passed by the United States Congress in 1981 and later amended in 1986 that provides for the establishment of RISK RETENTION GROUPS whose purpose is to sell PRODUCT LIABILITY INSURANCE to its membership.

PRODUCT RECALL EXCLUSION exception in general liability policies for all expenses associated with product recall. In recent years, there have been increasing instances of federal recalls. In addition, there have been many instances of deliberate tampering and of manufacturers issuing their own recalls. In either event, the cost of identifying the products, communicating with consumers, inspecting the returned products, and repairing or replacing them can be enormous. These costs are excluded from general liability policies, but PRODUCT RECALL INSURANCE can be purchased for this purpose.

PRODUCT RECALL INSURANCE coverage for the expenses incurred by a business resulting from the recall of products, whether defective or not. *See also* PRODUCT LIABILITY INSURANCE; PRODUCT AND COMPLETED OPERATIONS INSURANCE; PRODUCT RECALL EXCLUSION.

PRODUCTS AND COMPLETED OPERATIONS INSURANCE coverage for an insured manufacturer for claims after a manufactured product has been sold and/or a claim results from an operation which the manufacturer has completed. *See also* COMPLETED OPERATIONS INSURANCE.

PRODUCT VARIABILITY uneven quality of a product made by the same manufacturer. A manufacturer is responsible for producing products of similar quality, and can be held liable for those that deviate materially from a model, sample, or standard.

PROFESSIONAL *see* PROFESSIONAL LIABILITY INSURANCE.

PROFESSIONAL INSURANCE AGENTS (PIA) (NATIONAL ASSOCIATION OF PROFESSIONAL INSURANCE AGENTS). Independent agent membership group, originally mutual agents but today open to both mutual and stock agents. Association views are presented both nationally and locally on insurance legislation. There is an extensive education program for members.

PROFESSIONAL LIABILITY *see* LIABILITY, PROFESSIONAL.

PROFESSIONAL LIABILITY INSURANCE coverage for specialists in various professional fields. Since basic liability policies do not protect against situations arising out of business or professional pursuits, professional liability insurance is purchased by individuals who hold themselves out to the general public as having greater than average expertise in particular areas. *See also* ACCOUNTANTS PROFESSIONAL LIABILITY INSURANCE; DRUGGISTS LIABILITY INSURANCE; ERRORS AND OMISSIONS LIABILITY INSURANCE; INSURANCE AGENTS AND BROKERS LIABILITY INSURANCE; LAWYERS (ATTORNEYS PROFESSIONAL) LIABILITY INSURANCE; PHYSICIANS, SURGEONS, AND DENTISTS INSURANCE.

PROFESSIONAL REINSURER company formed to sell and service PROPORTIONAL REINSURANCE and NONPROPORTIONAL REINSURANCE with profit motive as the normal business objective.

PROFESSIONAL STANDARDS REVIEW ORGANIZATION (PSRO) group that monitors government health insurance programs. Authorized by the 1972 amendment to the Social Security Act, PSROs were set up to cut costs and minimize abuses by checking on the need of applicants for care and the cost and quality of care.

PROFITABILITY UNDERWRITING degree of UNDERWRITING profit that an insurance company's book of business shows. *See also* UNDERWRITING GAIN (LOSS).

PROFITS AND COMMISSIONS FORM coverage protecting future profits to be earned from a manufacturer's inventory. A manufacturer may lose all or part of an inventory of finished goods due to a peril such as fire and still be able to operate. But in the event that an inventory and other merchandise is destroyed by an insured peril, the insured is indemnified for the loss profit or commissions.

PROFITS AND COMMISSIONS INSURANCE *see* PROFITS AND COMMISSIONS FORM.

PROFIT SHARING/MONEY PURCHASE COMBINATION PLAN joint PROFIT SHARING and MONEY PURCHASE plan that is appropriate for businesses that desire the funding flexibility (25% of pay or $40,000 respectively). This combination of the two plans provides that the profit sharing contributions remain discretionary and the money purchase contributions remain mandatory.

PROFIT-SHARING PLAN arrangement by an employer in which employees share in profits of the business. To be a *qualified plan,* a predetermined formula must be used to determine contributions to the plan and benefits to be distributed, once a participant attains a specified age, becomes ill or disabled, severs employment, retires, or dies. When a profit-sharing plan is first installed, employees with considerable past service usually do not receive such credit. An advantage to an employer is that in low or no profit years, the business does not have to contribute to the plan, since contributions are voluntary and the Internal Revenue Code does not require a minimum contribution, as with a *deferred benefit plan* or a MONEY PURCHASE PLAN.

PROGRESSIVE IMPAIRMENT gradual or accelerated deterioration of the body resulting from a disease such as cancer.

PROGRESSIVE INCOME TAX structure under which tax rates increase with increases in income. One way to minimize such taxes is to purchase tax advantaged financial instruments. *See also* TAX DEFERRED ANNUITY; TAX BENEFITS OF LIFE INSURANCE.

PROGRESSIVELY DIMINISHING DEDUCTIBLE *see* DISAPPEARING DEDUCTIBLE.

PROHIBITED RISK uninsurable risk.

PROHIBITED TRANSACTIONS actions not allowed between a trust and a DISQUALIFIED PERSON under the EMPLOYEE RETIREMENT INCOME SECURITY ACT OF 1974 (ERISA). The disallowed actions are designed to prevent a conflict of interest between the trust plan and those who have a vested interest in that plan. The disallowed actions between the trust plan and the disqualified person include the sale, lending, exchange, and leasing of goods or services between the two parties.

PROJECTED DIVIDEND estimated future dividends to be paid by a PARTICIPATING INSURANCE POLICY. These dividend estimations cannot be part of the policy since they are not guaranteed. They are normally shown in a separate computer printout and are only as accurate as the basic interest rate assumptions made.

PROJECTION FACTORS expectations of investment return, mortality experience, and expenses used in projecting future cash values for life insurance and annuities. These projections cannot be part of the actual policy since they are not guaranteed. Rather, they take the form of separate computer printouts and are used in sales presentations.

PROOF OF DEATH *see* PROOF OF LOSS.

PROOF OF INTEREST *see* INSURABLE INTEREST; INSURABLE INTEREST, LIFE INSURANCE; INSURABLE INTEREST, PROPERTY AND CASUALTY INSURANCE.

PROOF OF LOSS documentation of loss required of a policyowner by an insurance company. For example, in the event of an insured's death, a death certificate (or copy) must be submitted to the company for a life insurance death benefit to be paid to the beneficiary.

PROPERTY *real* (land and attachments) and *personal* (movable effects not attached to land). Both classifications of property give rise to an insurable interest. *See also* INSURABLE INTEREST; PROPERTY AND CASUALTY INSURANCE PROVISIONS.

PROPERTY AND CASUALTY INSURANCE CONTRACT *see* INSURANCE CONTRACT, PROPERTY AND CASUALTY.

PROPERTY AND CASUALTY INSURANCE PROVISIONS specifications dealing with exclusions, policy requirements, cancellations and related matters.
1. *Perils*—Most policies exclude enemy attack, invasions, insurrection, rebellion, revolution, civil war, unsurped power, neglect of an insured to reasonably preserve damaged property from further loss, and explosion or riot unless caused by fire. Other exclusions may be specified in a policy. Among them are concealment and fraud by the insured; increased hazard by an insured's actions; and vacancy in an insured building for at least 60 consecutive days.
2. *Requirements*—In the event of a loss the insured must give immediate written notice to the insurance company; protect the insured property from further damage; separate damaged from undamaged

property; give the company a complete inventory of the damaged or destroyed property, with signed proof of loss within 60 days; and submit to the company's examination of damaged or destroyed property.

3. OTHER INSURANCE—If two or more separate policies over the same loss, each will pay no more than its pro rata share of the loss.

4. SUBROGATION—After the company pays the insured for a loss incurred as the result of actions of a third party, the company reserves the right to seek recovery for damages against that third party. (The insured has passed the right of suit against the third party to the insurance company.)

5. *Cancellation*—The insured and the insurance company can terminate the policy under specified circumstances. The insured can terminate the policy at any time, and will receive a return of part of the premium, less an amount for administrative expenses. The insurance company can cancel a property policy by sending the insured written notice at least 5 days before the intended date of cancellation. For a liability policy, after the policy has been renewed the first time, or has been in force for at least 60 days, the insurance company can cancel only for causes such as failure of an insured to pay a premium when due, if an insured is involved in illegal activities, drives while intoxicated, or is under the influence of drugs.

PROPERTY AND LIABILITY INSURANCE coverage for an insured whose property is damaged or destroyed by an insured peril, or whose negligent acts or omissions damage or destroy another party's property or cause bodily injury to another party. *See also* BUSINESS AUTO COVERAGE FORM; BUSINESS PROPERTY AND LIABILITY INSURANCE PACKAGE; BUSINESSOWNERS POLICY; CONDOMINIUM INSURANCE; HOMEOWNERS INSURANCE POLICY; PERSONAL AUTOMOBILE POLICY (PAP); COMMERCIAL PACKAGE POLICY; TENANTS INSURANCE.

PROPERTY AND LIABILITY INSURANCE PLANNING FOR BUSINESS *see* BUSINESS AUTO COVERAGE FORM; BUSINESS CRIME INSURANCE; BUSINESS INSURANCE; BUSINESS INCOME COVERAGE FORM; BUSINESS LIABILITY INSURANCE; BUSINESS PROPERTY AND LIABILITY INSURANCE PACKAGE; BUSINESSOWNERS POLICY.

PROPERTY AND LIABILITY INSURANCE PLANNING FOR INDIVIDUALS AND FAMILIES *see* COMPREHENSIVE PERSONAL LIABILITY INSURANCE; HOMEOWNERS INSURANCE POLICY; LIABILITY, PERSONAL EXPOSURES; LIABILITY, PROFESSIONAL; PERSONAL AUTOMOBILE POLICY (PAP); TENANTS INSURANCE.

PROPERTY CATASTROPHE *see* FIRE CATASTROPHE REINSURANCE. INSURANCE; REINSURANCE, PROPERTY AND CASUALTY-CASUALTY CATASTROPHE

PROPERTY DAMAGE *see* BUSINESS LIABILITY INSURANCE (Insuring Agreement Section); PERSONAL AUTOMOBILE POLICY (PAP).

PROPERTY DAMAGED OR DESTROYED *see* PROPERTY INSURANCE COVERAGE.

PROPERTY DAMAGE LIABILITY INSURANCE coverage in the event that the negligent acts or omissions of an insured result in damage or destruction to another's property. Coverage can be purchased with BODILY INJURY liability under various insurance policies. *See also* BUSINESS AUTO COVERAGE FORM; BUSINESS PROPERTY AND LIABILITY INSURANCE PACKAGE; HOMEOWNERS INSURANCE POLICY; PERSONAL AUTOMOBILE POLICY (PAP).

PROPERTY DEPRECIATION INSURANCE coverage that provides for replacement of damaged or destroyed property on a new replacement cost basis without any deduction for depreciation. This is equivalent to *replacement cost* property insurance.

PROPERTY INSURANCE indemnifies an insured whose property is stolen, damaged, or destroyed by a covered peril. The term property insurance encompasses numerous lines of available insurance.

PROPERTY INSURANCE COVERAGE coverage for direct or indirect property loss that can be analyzed under the following headings:

1. *Peril*—a particular peril may be included or excluded. For example, the *Standard Fire Policy* names specific perils such as fire and lightning; the ALL RISKS policy covers all entities unless specifically excluded.
2. Property—a policy may cover only specified or scheduled property such as an automobile; all of an insured's personal property up to a specified amount on each item regardless of its location (PERSONAL PROPERTY FLOATER); or all property of the insured with no specific limit (BLANKET POLICY).
3. Person—the person covered must be specifically identified as the *named insured* in a policy. Residents of that household also covered are the spouse, relatives of either, and anyone else below the age of 21 under the insured's care, custody, and control.
4. Duration—policies are usually written for one year; a personal automobile policy is usually for six months.
5. *Limits*—limits are stated as a face amount in a policy. The insurer will never pay more than the lesser of the following amounts: limits stated in a policy; actual cash value of destroyed or damaged property; or amount resulting from the coinsurance formula.
6. Location—a policy may cover perils that strike only the premises of the insured, or it may provide off-premises coverage subject to a geographic restriction. For example, the personal automobile policy covers only the U.S. and Canada.
7. HAZARD—the exclusions and suspension section states that if the insured increases a covered hazard the company can suspend or exclude the coverage. For example, the insured starts processing explosives at home.

8. LOSS—insurance contracts cover either direct or indirect (CONSE-QUENTIAL) loss. For example, a homeowners policy covers damage due to the direct loss by fire, lightning, and other perils. It does not cover consequential losses such as loss of income by an insured who is unable to go to work because of fatigue.

PROPORTIONAL REINSURANCE system whereby the reinsurer shares losses in the same proportion as it shares premium and policy amounts. Proportional reinsurance may be divided into the two basic forms: AUTOMATIC PROPORTIONAL REINSURANCE and *facultative proportional reinsurance. See also* REINSURANCE.

PROPOSAL *see* APPLICATION.

PROPOSAL BOND *see* BID BOND.

PROPRIETARY INSURER for-profit insurance company, such as a mutual or stock company or LLOYD'S OF LONDON association. Proprietary insurers contrast with cooperative insurers, or Blue Cross/Blue Shield plans, or FRATERNAL LIFE INSURANCE organizations.

PRO RATA *see* PRO RATA CANCELLATION; PRO RATA DISTRIBUTION CLAUSE; PRO RATA LIABILITY CLAUSE; PRO RATA REINSURANCE.

PRO RATA CANCELLATION revocation of a policy by an insurance company that returns to the policyholder the *unearned premium* (the portion of the premium for the remaining time period that the policy will not be in force). There is no reduction for expenses already paid by the insurer for that time period. *See also* SHORT RATE CANCELLATION.

PRO RATA CLAUSE CLAUSE in an INSURANCE POLICY that stipulates that the policy will pay for losses in proportion to the amount of insurance coverage that the policy has in force in relation to the total amount of insurance in force from all other policies.

PRO RATA DISTRIBUTION CLAUSE provision in many property insurance policies that automatically distributes coverage over insured property at various locations in proportion to their value. For example, if an insured buys a $100,000 policy to cover three properties worth $75,000, $30,000 and $20,000, the insurance (which would not be enough to cover a total loss) would be distributed in the same manner. If the $75,000 property were totally destroyed, the insured would receive 60% of the value of the insurance, or $60,000, because that property represents 60% of the covered property. If the insured buys adequate coverage, this clause is important because it can spread the insurance to different locations as inventories decrease or increase, rather than forcing the insured to constantly revise the coverage. *See also* DOUBLE RECOVERY.

PRO RATA LIABILITY CLAUSE provision in many property insurance policies that spreads the obligation to pay a claim among various insurers covering that claim in proportion to the insurance each has written on the property. For example, there are three different policies covering a $130,000 building. Co. A wrote a $60,000 policy, Co. B a $50,000 policy, and Co. C a $20,000 policy. A fire results in $25,000 damage. The loss would be spread in the same ratio as the coverage: Co. A's share would be $11,750, or 47%; Co. B would pay $9500, or 38%; and Co. C would pay $3750, or 15%. One purpose of this clause is to prevent an insured from capitalizing on a loss. In the case cited, the insured could collect the full amount ($25,000) twice from the first two insurers, and $20,000 from the third, giving him or her $70,000 to cover a $25,000 loss.

PRO RATA RATE premium rate charged for a particular time interval which is less than the normal time interval. For example, if the time interval of coverage is one month, the premium due each month would be one-twelfth of the annual premium payment.

PRO RATA REINSURANCE *see* PROPORTIONAL REINSURANCE; QUOTA SHARE REINSURANCE; SURPLUS REINSURANCE.

PRO RATA TREATY *see* PROPORTIONAL REINSURANCE; QUOTA SHARE REINSURANCE; SURPLUS REINSURANCE.

PRO RATA UNEARNED PREMIUM RESERVE *see* UNEARNED PREMIUM RESERVE.

PRORATION *see* PRO RATA CANCELLATION; PRO RATA LIABILITY CLAUSE.

PRORATION OF COVERAGE *see* OTHER INSURANCE CLAUSE.

PROSPECT individual or organization that is a potential purchaser of an insurance product.

PROSPECTING soliciting of customers for the purchasing of an insurance product. *See also* PROSPECT.

PROSPECTIVE AGGREGATE EXCESS OF LOSS REINSURANCE type of EXCESS OF LOSS REINSURANCE in which the insurance company (CEDENT) is guaranteed REINSURANCE for future covered losses once they exceed a specified amount on either a per loss, per risk, or aggregate basis. The cedent pays at the inception of the contract the excess of loss reinsurance contract.

PROSPECTIVE COMPUTATION *see* PROSPECTIVE RATING.

PROSPECTIVE EXPERIENCE RATING *see* PROSPECTIVE RATING.

PROSPECTIVE RATING determination of (1) a future property or liability insurance or reinsurance rate or (2) a premium for a specified future period of time. It is based on the loss experience of a specified past period of time.

PROSPECTIVE RESERVE amount designated as a future liability for life or health insurance to meet the difference between future benefits and future premiums. NET LEVEL PREMIUM is determined so that this basic relationship holds: the present value of a future premium equals the present value of a future benefit. This relationship, incidentally, exists in fact only at the point of issuance of a life insurance policy. After that, the value of future premiums is less than the value of future benefits because fewer premiums are left to be paid. Thus, a reserve must be maintained at all times to make up this difference.

PROSPECTIVE VALUATION calculations involving the MORTALITY RATE of a company's insureds and the rate of return on the company's investments. It is used in calculating the PROSPECTIVE RESERVE.

PROSPECTUS document showing the terms and conditions of an equity sale. This is a company's detailed discussion of the proposed debt or equity offering to potential investors in a binding legal form.

PROTECTED RISK property to be insured, or that is insured, which is located within the specific geographical region falling under the auspices of the fire department.

PROTECTION *see* COVERAGE.

PROTECTION AND INDEMNITY INSURANCE (P&I) broad type of marine legal liability coverage. HULL MARINE INSURANCE is limited to an insured ship. With the addition of a RUNNING DOWN CLAUSE, a policy can be extended to cover liability in case of collision with another ship. But many shipowners desire the much broader coverage offered by protection and indemnity insurance since it covers the ship operator for liability to crew members and other people on board, damage to fixed objects like docks, and other miscellaneous claims.

PROTECTIVE LIABILITY INSURANCE *see* OWNERS AND CONTRACTORS PROTECTIVE LIABILITY INSURANCE.

PROVISIONAL PREMIUM (RATE) *see* DEPOSIT PREMIUM.

PROXIMATE CAUSE *see* DIRECT LOSS.

PRUDENT MAN RULE *see* TORT, UNINTENTIONAL.

PS-58 COST METHOD OF THE SPLIT DOLLAR LIFE INSURANCE PLAN payment of that portion of the annual premium by the employee necessary to cover the PS-58 cost for that given year. Any unpaid premium balance for that particular year is paid by the employer. *See also* PS-58 RATE TABLE; SPLIT DOLLAR LIFE INSURANCE.

PS-58 RATE TABLE table used by the Internal Revenue Service (IRS) in evaluating SPLIT DOLLAR LIFE INSURANCE plans as to the extent of the economic benefit that is considered taxable ordinary income to the employee. The taxable ordinary income to the employee is the premium cost of one-year term insurance on the life of the employee minus that portion of the premium paid by the employee. If the employee pays that portion of the premium that is in excess of the economic benefit, the employee incurs no ordinary income tax liability.

The premium cost of one-year term insurance at each age is listed in this IRS table.

PUBLIC ADJUSTER representative of an insurance claimant in situations only where an adjuster can act for an insurance company or an insured. *See also* ADJUSTER, STAFF.

PUBLIC EMPLOYEE DEFERRED COMPENSATION PLAN qualified retirement plan under the INTERNAL REVENUE CODE Section 457 for employees of the states and political subdivisions within the states.

PUBLIC EMPLOYEES BLANKET BOND fidelity bond provided under a BLANKET POSITION BOND (in which each position is covered on an individual basis) or a COMMERCIAL BLANKET BOND (in which a loss is covered on a blanket basis regardless of the number of employees causing the loss) for employees of public institutions and agencies.

PUBLIC ENTITY RISK INSTITUTE (PERI) DATA EXCHANGE statistics used for the comparison of claims among various governmental agencies including universities, cities and towns, counties, housing authorities, public school districts, and public transit authorities. The emphasis is on statistical analysis of liability and workers compensation claims.

PUBLIC LAW 15 *see* MCCARRAN-FERGUSON ACT (PUBLIC LAW 15).

PUBLIC LAW 87-311 1961 federal legislation that allows the U.S. Export-Import Bank to set up insurance protection for U.S. exporters against credit risk and political risk in order to help make U.S. exports more competitive and bolster the U.S. trade balance. The *Foreign Credit Insurance Association* oversees the insurance program, which is written by private insurers.

PUBLIC LAW 91-156 1969 federal legislation requiring states to treat national banks, including those whose principal offices are out of state, the same way for tax purposes as they treat their own state-chartered banks.

PUBLIC LAW 92-500 amendments to the WATER QUALITY IMPROVEMENT ACT OF 1970 that extends liability of shipowners to any hazardous substances discharged by their ships. The 1970 act made shipowners responsible for cleanup of oil spills. Public Law 92-500 (the Federal Water Pollution Control Act Amendments of 1972) extended responsibility to other hazardous substances.

PUBLIC LIABILITY INSURANCE very broad term for insurance covering liability exposures for individuals and business owners. It provides broad coverage, generally including all exposures for property damage and bodily injury, except exposures that relate to ownership of airplanes and automobiles, and to employees. Liability insurance may be written to cover specified hazards, as a COMMERCIAL GENERAL LIABILITY INSURANCE (CGL) POLICY, PACKAGE POLICY, or SCHEDULED POLICY.

PUBLIC OFFICIAL BOND type of SURETY BOND that guarantees the performance of public officials. Public officials are responsible for a broad range of property including fees that they collect, money that they handle, and bank accounts that they oversee. They may also be held responsible for misdeeds that result in a loss of public funds by those they supervise. In some cases coverage is available for an entire group of employees under a PUBLIC EMPLOYEES BLANKET BOND.

PUBLIC RISK AND INSURANCE MANAGEMENT ASSOCIATION (PRIMA) organization based in Washington, D.C., that is composed of risk and insurance managers of various public entities, to include municipalities and school boards.

PUBLIC TRUCKMENS LEGAL LIABILITY FORM INLAND MARINE policy that covers truck drivers for loss or damage to merchandise they haul. The Interstate Commerce Commission requires this coverage for trucks engaged in interstate commerce.

PUNITIVE DAMAGES *see* LIABILITY, CIVIL DAMAGES AWARDED.

PUP COMPANY subsidiary, smaller company that is owned and controlled by a much larger company. In many instances pup companies are used to write SPECIAL RISK INSURANCE for which the larger company does not have UNDERWRITING facilities.

PURCHASE *see* OWNERSHIP RIGHTS UNDER LIFE INSURANCE; POLICY-HOLDER.

PURCHASE PAYMENT premium payment.

PURCHASE PRICE cost of an ANNUITY. Annuities are often paid for in a lump sum rather than annual or other periodic payments. This sum, which guarantees an income, usually for life, is called the *purchase price* rather than the PREMIUM, which is generally associated with payments for insurance.

PURCHASING GROUP *see* GROUP HEALTH INSURANCE; GROUP LIFE INSURANCE; MASS MERCHANDISING; MASS UNDERWRITING; MASTER POLICY.

PURCHASING POWER RISK investment risk associated with the relationship between the yield (interest, dividends, and capital) of financial instruments and the rate of inflation in the economy. For fixed income financial instruments such as a FIXED DOLLAR ANNUITY and fixed dollar LIFE INSURANCE, the financial security of the recipient is diminished in proportion to the rise of inflation.

PURE *see* PURE ANNUITY; PURE ENDOWMENT; PURE PREMIUM RATING METHOD; PURE RISK.

PURE AMOUNT OF PROTECTION *see* NET AMOUNT AT RISK.

PURE ANNUITY contract sold by insurance companies that pays a monthly (quarterly, semiannual, or annual) income benefit for the life of a person (the ANNUITANT). The annuitant can never outlive the income from the annuity. Upon the death of the annuitant all income payments cease. There are no beneficiary benefits under this type of annuity. Contrast with REFUND ANNUITY.

PURE ASSIGNMENT MUTUAL INSURANCE COMPANY *see* ASSESSABLE MUTUAL.

PURE ENDOWMENT life insurance policy under which its face value is payable only if the insured survives to the end of the stated endowment period; no benefit is paid if the insured dies during the endowment period. Few if any of these policies are sold today. Contrast with ENDOWMENT INSURANCE.

PURE LOSS COST RATIO *see* BURNING COST RATIO.

PURE NO-FAULT PLAN policy wherein the injured party foregoes the right to sue regardless of the seriousness of the injury suffered. Also under this plan, the injured party cannot sue for pain and suffering. *See also* NO-FAULT AUTOMOBILE INSURANCE.

PURE PREMIUM *see* PURE PREMIUM RATING METHOD.

PURE PREMIUM RATING METHOD approach that reflects losses expected. It is a calculation of the pure cost of property or liability insurance protection without loadings for the insurance company's expenses, premium taxes, contingencies, and profit margins. The pure premium is calculated according to the relationship:

$$\text{Pure Premium} = \frac{\text{Total Amount of Losses (and Loss Adjustment Expenses) Incurred per Year}}{\text{Number of Units of Exposure}}$$

PURE RISK situation involving a chance of a loss or no loss, but no chance of gain. For example, either one's home burns or it does not; this risk is insurable. *See also* STANDARD RISK.

PUT OPTION right to sell a given security at a stipulated price until a future expiration date. For example, assume the "None-Do-Well" company's stock has a market value of $20. Investor A sells Investor B an option (right) to buy Investor A's shares in the "None-Do-Well" company at a price of $25, good until 60 days hence. Investor B pays a premium of $4 per share for this right. If the stock's market value increases to a price greater than $29, Investor B will make a profit on the transaction. If, however, the stock falls below its original price of $20, Investor A will keep the stock as well as the $4 premium right per share it received from Investor B. If the 60-day limit expires without the right being executed, the option becomes void and worthless.

PYRAMIDING situation in which several liability insurance policies are in force to cover the same risk, thereby resulting in higher limits of coverage than is required to adequately insure the risk.

Q

Q SCHEDULE provision of the NEW YORK INSURANCE CODE and regulations under which (1) the life insurance company must file with the Insurance Commissioner all expenses associated with selling new life insurance policies; and (2) a limit is set on expenses to acquire new business.

The expense limitation serves to restrict agent commissions in New York State. This is one important reason why many national insurance companies do not sell life insurance in New York, or why some organize subsidiary companies for the sole purpose of conducting life insurance business only in New York. Many life insurance companies feel the expense limitation too restrictive to attract brokerage business.

QUADRUPLE INDEMNITY *see* ACCIDENTAL DEATH CLAUSE.

QUALIFIED DEFAULT INVESTMENT ALTERNATIVE (QDIA) alternative plan for participants who do not make an investment decision in a qualified PENSION PLAN. The default accounts include professionally managed accounts, balanced mutual funds, and lifecycle mutual funds. A minimum of 30 days notice must be given to the participant prior to the initial investment in the QDIA and for every year thereafter. The notice must include information concerning the directing of the participant's contribution to the QDIA. The participant has the right to elect out of the QDIA at any point in time and the right to select other investments.

QUALIFIED DOMESTIC TRUST type of TRUST established for the purpose of permitting the federal estate MARITAL DEDUCTION for ASSETS transferred from the decedent's estate to a surviving spouse who is not a citizen of the United States. The TRUSTEE for this trust must be a United States corporation or citizen, and if the assets are in excess of $2,000,000, the trustee must be a United States bank. Income from this trust can be distributed to the surviving spouse without incurring any estate tax consequences; however, any distributions of principal are subject to the federal estate tax. Upon the death of the surviving spouse and/or termination of the trust, the distributed principal of the trust is subject to federal estate tax.

QUALIFIED IMPAIRMENT INSURANCE waiver of an impairment of an applicant for health insurance by attaching an ENDORSEMENT to the health insurance policy stating that the policy will pay no benefits in connection with the impairment. This waiver enables an applicant, who otherwise would not qualify, to be insured. *See also* SUBSTANDARD HEALTH INSURANCE (QUALIFIED IMPAIRMENT INSURANCE).

QUALIFIED JOINT AND SURVIVOR ANNUITY *see* ANNUITY, JOINT-LIFE AND SURVIVORSHIP ANNUITY; PENSION PLAN.

QUALIFIED LONG-TERM CARE (Q-LTC) type of LONG-TERM CARE (LTC) insurance that receives advantageous tax treatment (amounts received are excluded from income tax but are subject to certain limitations) provided benefits are required by a CHRONICALLY ILL INDIVIDUAL. These benefits include personal care treatments, rehabilitation treatments, preventive and therapeutic treatments, diagnostic procedures, nursing home care, home health care, and assisted living care. The only benefits that can be provided are LTC services not provided under MEDICARE and the policy must be subject to RENEWAL.

QUALIFIED PENSION PLAN *see* PENSION PLAN.

QUALIFIED PERSONAL RESIDENCE TRUST (QPRT) TRUST instrument that permits the owner of a residence (grantor) to transfer ownership of that residence with the grantor still being allowed to stay in that residence for a stipulated period of time on a tax advantage basis. The procedure in establishing such a trust would be for: (1) the grantor to establish an irrevocable trust that would allow the grantor to stay in that residence for a given period of time (for example 15, 20, or 30 years); and (2) the grantor to contribute the residence to the trust. At the end of that given time period, the residence will then be transferred to the beneficiary(s) of the trust as selected by the grantor at the inception of the trust. The tax rules value the residence that transfers to the beneficiary(s) of the trust at a substantial discount from the actual value of the residence on the date the grantor contributed it to the trust. The disadvantages of the QPRT include the following: (1) at the end of the given period of time, the grantor can no longer stay in the residence and the beneficiary(s) own the residence outright; and (2) if the grantor dies before the expiration of the QPRT, the residence's actual value on the day it was contributed to the trust is included in the grantor's estate and thus becomes subject to FEDERAL ESTATE TAX. For example, a father retains, for a given time period, the right to use and possess the home. At the end of that time, the home's ownership reverts to the children but the father can continue to live in the home. If the father dies during the given time period, the home is taxed at full value as part of the father's estate. The life insurance policy previously purchased with the children as the beneficiary will override the lost estate tax savings because of the death of the father within that term period.

QUALIFIED PLAN INSURANCE PARTNERSHIP (QPIP) type of financial plan that establishes a LIMITED LIABILITY COMPANY (LLC) whose principal members are an IRREVOCABLE TRUST and a retirement account. The LLC purchases and is the BENEFICIARY of a life insurance policy on the life of the account owner and spouse. Cost of this purchase comes from contributions from the trust. The trust and the retirement account also make excess contributions into the LLC. The LLC invests these contributions and the earnings on the investments can be applied to the premiums due on the life insurance policy. The LLC then makes a gift of its interest in the life insurance policy to the trust.

QUALIFIED TERMINABLE INTEREST PROPERTY (Q TIP) TRUST strategy that provides that all income from assets in trust be paid at least annually for the life of the surviving spouse. This trust, which prohibits transfer of any assets to anyone else, can provide for the surviving spouse to will the property to one or more individuals among a group previously designated by the deceased spouse. For example, a husband establishes a Q TIP trust that gives his widow income for life. At the death of the wife, the corpus of the Q TIP trust will go the children, even though the corpus is part of the wife's estate. Since the husband elects how much of the estate is to be treated as Q TIP property, the estate tax strategy is to have only that portion of Q TIP property necessary to achieve zero estate death tax. *See also* ESTATE PLANNING, ESTATE PLANNING DISTRIBUTION.

QUALIFIED TRUST *see* PENSION PLAN.

QUALIFIED TUITION PLANS *see* SECTION 529 PLANS (QUALIFIED TUITION PLANS).

QUALITY INSURANCE CONGRESS (QIC) organization founded in 1993, the thesis of which is to apply quality management principles to insurance functions. To this end, the organization is involved in insurance industry-wide customer research and the needs and perceptions of the insurance buyer is studied. *See also* TOTAL QUALITY MANAGEMENT (TQM).

QUANTITY DISCOUNT *see* GROUP INSURANCE; MASS MERCHANDISING.

QUARTER OF COVERAGE quarter credited, for retirement benefits under Social Security, when the worker's earnings exceed a minimum amount in a given quarter. Credited quarters are extremely important for FULLY INSURED and CURRENTLY INSURED status to qualify for Social Security benefits. The minimum amount of earnings required for a quarter credited is subject to annual increases.

QUICK ASSETS liquid property that can be converted easily to cash. For example, a policyowner can borrow readily against the cash value of a life insurance policy. *See also* POLICY LOAN.

QUID PRO QUO exchange, in insurance, of an adequate *consideration* (premium paid by an insured) for the promise of an insurance company to pay benefits in the event the insured incurs a loss.

QUOTA SHARE REINSURANCE automatic reinsurance that requires the insurer to transfer, and the reinsurer to accept, a given percentage of every risk within a defined category of business written by the insurer. For example, in the case of a 20% quota share, the insurer transfers 20% of its liability and premiums on every risk to the reinsurer, who must pay 20% of any loss sustained, whether total or partial. The percentage is constant throughout and applies to premiums and losses alike. *See also* REINSURANCE.

QUOTA SHARE TREATY *see* QUOTA SHARE REINSURANCE.

R

RABBI TRUST TRUST named from a private-letter ruling by the IRS that involved a trust established by a Jewish congregation on behalf of its rabbi. The operation of the trust involves the employer's making contributions to the trust that are irrevocable. An independent trustee has control of the trust and must pay benefits from it if a stipulated event occurs, such as the death, disability, or retirement of the employee. If the employer becomes bankrupt or insolvent, the funds held in the trust are subject to the claims of the employer's creditors. The employer cannot take income tax deductions for its contributions to the trust until the funds in the trust are actually distributed to the employee.

RACKETEER INFLUENCED AND CORRUPT ORGANIZA-TIONS ACT OF 1970 (RICO) legislation that provides support for legal actions against individuals or organizations involved in systematic illegal activities. This act has been applied against insurance organizations when they were accused of bad-faith failure to pay claims or when there was a question of insolvency.

RADIOACTIVE CONTAMINATION INSURANCE form of INLAND MARINE INSURANCE under which an insured is indemnified for damage or destruction of his or her on-premises property if it is due to radioactive material stored or used within the premises. *See also* MOTOR TRUCK CARGO RADIOACTIVE CONTAMINATION INSURANCE; SHIPPERS RADIOACTIVE CONTAMINATION INSURANCE.

RADIO AND TELEVISION TRANSMITTING EQUIPMENT, TRANSMISSION LINES, PIPELINES, TRAFFIC LIGHTS INSURANCE coverage if transmission equipment is damaged or destroyed on an ALL RISKS basis excluding the perils of war, wear and tear, inherent defect, and nuclear damage. CONSEQUENTIAL LOSS (indirect loss) may be added by endorsement to include such eventualities as lost revenue because of damage to a radio-transmitting line. This endorsement can be of special importance to businesses, such as stock brokerages, that transmit buy and sell orders.

RADIUM FLOATER *see* RADIOACTIVE CONTAMINATION INSURANCE.

RADIX base upon which a MORTALITY TABLE is built by beginning with a randomly selected group of people who are alive at the earliest age for which statistics are available on the number of people alive at that age. From this data, the rates of mortality can be used to build "the number of people alive at a given age" and "the number of people who die at a given age" columns in the mortality table.

RAILROAD RETIREMENT ACT *see* RAILROAD RETIREMENT SYSTEM.

RAILROAD RETIREMENT SYSTEM insurance established under the federal Railroad Retirement Act for railroad employees, covering death, retirement, disability, and unemployment. Benefits are adjusted for cost of living increases according to the formula used for Social Security.

RAILROAD ROLLING STOCK INSURANCE coverage for railroad equipment, liability of a railroad for damaging another railroad's equipment, or the damage to goods under its care, custody, and control. Coverage is provided on an ALL RISKS basis subject to perils specifically excluded in the policy.

RAILROAD SIDETRACK AGREEMENT *see* SIDETRACK AGREEMENT.

RAILROAD TRAVEL POLICY *see* TRAVEL ACCIDENT INSURANCE.

RAIN INSURANCE business interruption insurance in which the insured is indemnified for loss of earnings and payment of expenses resulting from adverse weather conditions. For example, the raining out of a fair, horse race, or boxing match can cause a substantial loss of money for a promoter who may have spent huge sums in advance of the event for rental, advertising, and site conditioning. However, the policy does not cover damage to property because of rain.

RANCHOWNERS INSURANCE *see* FARMOWNERS AND RANCHOWNERS INSURANCE.

RANDOM INSURANCE coverage up to specific limits for payments demanded by kidnappers for the release of an insured held against his or her will. Most random insurance policies have a deductible and exclude abductions within certain geographical areas from coverage.

RANDOM SAMPLE sample of n elements selected from a population of N elements in such a way that the sample has essentially the same characteristics as the population. The random sample serves as the foundation of all PROBABILITY theory as it relates to probability in sampling. In theory, all subsets drawn from the same sample have an equal chance of being drawn. Sampling is extremely important to the calculation of premium rates. For example, if the INSURER wants to predict the probability that a wood-frame house will burn, the sample must be drawn from the population of wood-frame houses, not brick-frame houses.

RATE *see* RATE MAKING; RATE MANUAL; RATING; RATING BUREAU.

RATE, BLANKET AVERAGE RATE applied when two or more separate buildings are insured under one policy, and/or when two or more separate contents are insured under one policy.

RATE CARDS record prepared by the RATING BUREAU describing the particulars of an insured property and the applicable PREMIUM RATE.

RATE CREDIT OR DEFICIENCY annual contributions to a pension plan that exceed or are smaller than (1) the minimum required for future employee benefits currently being earned; and (2) any supplemental liability for past benefits earned but not previously funded.

RATED POLICY statement in which a life insurance applicant is charged a higher-than-standard premium to reflect a unique impairment, occupation, or hobby, such as a history of heart disease or a circus performer or sky diver.

RATED UP *see* RATED POLICY.

RATE FACTORS *see* RATE MAKING.

RATE MAKING process of calculating a PREMIUM so that it is (1) *adequate*—sufficient to pay losses according to expected FREQUENCY and *severity,* thereby safeguarding against the insurance company becoming insolvent; (2) *reasonable*—the insurance company should not be able to earn an excessive profit; and (3) *not unfairly discriminatory* or *inequitable.* Theoretically, it can be said that each insurance applicant should pay a unique premium to reflect a different expectation of loss, but this would be impractical. Instead, classifications are established for applicants to be grouped according to similar expectation of loss. Statistical studies of a large number of nearly homogeneous exposures in each underwriting classification enable the projection of losses after adjustments for future inflation and statistical irregularities. The adjusted statistics are used to calculate the *pure cost of protection,* or *pure premium,* to which the insurance company adds on loads for agent commissions, premium taxes, administrative expenses, contingency reserves, other acquisition costs, and profit margin. The result is the GROSS PREMIUM to be charged to the insured.

RATE MANUAL publication that lists premiums charged for products sold by an insurance company. A manual also has underwriting guidelines for agents. A life insurance rate manual includes minimum guaranteed NONFORFEITURE values; and if a *participating* policy, *dividend* scales.

RATE OF RETURN METHOD OF COST COMPARISON approach advocated by the Federal Trade Commission (FTC) in its 1979 LIFE INSURANCE COST disclosure report. It calculates the rate of return earned by the savings element of a life insurance policy in these steps:
1. determine *pure cost of protection* (mortality expectation).
2. determine amount of dividends paid (if it is a *participating policy*).
3. subtract the pure cost of protection plus dividends from the GROSS PREMIUMS paid into the policy. This is the savings element.
4. the rate of return equals the interest rate at which the savings element must be accumulated in order to equal the cash value of the policy at some future specified time period. *See also* INTEREST ADJUSTED COST.

RATE OF SURPLUS FORMATION RATIO insurance company's growth rate of ADJUSTED SURPLUS divided by its ADJUSTED LIABILITIES. The greater this ratio, the more financially sound the insurance company, as the surplus would be increasing at a faster rate than the liabilities.

RATES cost per unit of insurance. *See also* RATE MAKING.

RATES AND SELECTION *see* RATE MAKING.

RATIFICATION BY AGENCY sanction or affirmation by an insurance company of acts of its agents that become the acts of the company, with all the legal obligations these acts entail.

RATING a valuation of risk of an individual or organization.

RATING BUREAU cooperative organization among insurers that rates and prepares new policy forms according to guidelines and regulations of the state INSURANCE DEPARTMENT. Loss experience, collected according to the line of business in specific geographical areas, is used to suggest rates for use by the rating bureau member companies. They may either use these rates or file their own *deviated rates* for approval by the state insurance department if it is a *prior approval state.* In an *open competition state,* a company does not need approval for a deviated rate. In *a file-and-use state,* a company can use a deviated rate without approval, after having filed it with the state insurance department. In a *modified prior approval state,* a company can use a deviated rate after filing it with the state insurance department provided it is a modest deviation and not a new rate classification.

RATING CLASS *see* CLASS RATE.

RATING CLAUSE *see* RATE MAKING.

RATING DOWN *see* AGE SETBACK.

RATING, EXPERIENCE *see* EXPERIENCE RATING.

RATING, MERIT *see* MERIT RATING.

RATING ORGANIZATION *see* RATING BUREAU.

RATING, RETROSPECTIVE *see* RETROSPECTIVE RATING.

RATING, SCHEDULE *see* SCHEDULE RATING.

READJUSTMENT INCOME *see* ADJUSTMENT INCOME.

REAL ESTATE land and attached structures. Interest in real estate can be protected through various insurance policies. *See also* BUSINESS PROPERTY AND LIABILITY INSURANCE PACKAGE; BUSINESSOWNERS POLICY; HOMEOWNERS INSURANCE POLICY.

REAL ESTATE SWAP transaction in which the property owner (for example, a pension fund) agrees to pay the insurance company a rate of return tied to the fluctuations in real estate prices. In return, the insurance company stipulates that it will pay the property owner a rate of return that is more predictable, such as a floating interest rate, if the insurance company believes that the depressed real estate market has an attractive potential for capital gains but has no desire to own and/or manage property. Meanwhile a pension fund owns more property than it deems prudent. The solution, through the swap, would entail the pension fund passing on to the insurance company any gains or losses generated by the property in return for the insurance company paying the pension fund a floating interest rate. This floating interest rate to be paid would be tied to a stipulated index such as the U.S. Treasury Bill rate. The result would be that the pension fund lowers its real estate portfolio to a more acceptable level, and the insurance company has increasing capital gains expectations.

REAL INTEREST RATE NOMINAL INTEREST RATE minus the rate of inflation.

REALIZED CAPITAL GAINS (LOSSES) increases (decreases) in capital assets (such as stocks and bonds) between the date of purchase and the date of sale.

REAL PROPERTY *see* REAL ESTATE.

REAL RATE OF RETURN net gain on an investment after the deduction for inflation and taxes.

REASONABLE AND CUSTOMARY CHARGE fee that is most consistent with that of physicians, hospitals, or other health providers for a given procedure; usual fee for a procedure charged by the majority of physicians with similar training and experience within the same geographical area.

REASONABLE EXPENSES *see* EXCLUSIONS, MEDICAL BENEFITS.

REASONABLE MAN TEST *see* TORT, UNINTENTIONAL.

REASONABLENESS OF PREMIUM RATE *see* RATE MAKING.

REASSURED *see* CEDING COMPANY.

REBATING *see* ANTI-REBATE LAW.

RECAPTURE practice of a CEDING COMPANY whereby insurance previously CEDED to a REINSURER is returned to that ceding company. *See also* RECAPTURE OF PLAN ASSETS BY EMPLOYER.

RECAPTURE OF PLAN ASSETS BY EMPLOYER return of employer contributions to a pension if that plan is (1) newly established and is determined by the IRS not to be tax qualified; or (2) long established but the IRS disallows a portion or all of the employer contribution.

RECEIPT *see* PREMIUM RECEIPT.

RECEIVERSHIP/REHABILITATION case where an insurance company is placed by the state court under the control of the STATE INSURANCE DEPARTMENT. Claims are paid in the order filed until the insurance company's ability to pay is exhausted.

RECIPIENT PROPERTY insurance against interruption of supply of goods and services. If firm A depends on firm B for its supply of goods and services, an interruption caused by damage or destruction to B can jeopardize A. CONTINGENT BUSINESS INTERRUPTION FORM can be used by A to protect against this possibility.

RECIPROCAL EXCHANGE unincorporated association with each insured insuring the other insureds within the association. (Thus, each participant in this pool is both an insurer and an insured.) An attorney-in-fact administers the exchange to include paying losses experienced by the exchange, investing premium inflow into the exchange, recruiting new members, underwriting the inflow of new business, underwriting renewal business, receiving premiums, and exchanging reinsurance contracts. Members share profits and losses in the same proportion as the amount of insurance purchased from the exchange by that member.

RECIPROCAL INSURANCE EXCHANGE *see* RECIPROCAL EXCHANGE.

RECIPROCAL INSURER *see* RECIPROCAL EXCHANGE.

RECIPROCAL LEGISLATION law under which one state gives favorable tax treatment to an insurance company *domiciled* in a different state that is admitted to do business, provided the second state does the same for companies domiciled in the first state. *See also* RETALIATION LAWS.

RECIPROCITY *see* RECIPROCAL EXCHANGE; RECIPROCAL LEGISLATION.

RECISSION cancellation of a contract. Under the federal Truth in Lending Act, a person who signs a contract can nullify it within three business days of having signed it without penalty; funds paid into the contract by the signer must be returned. Also, fraud or misrepresentation provides legal grounds for cancellation of a contract. For example, life insurance contracts with minors are voidable (by minors but not by insurers) since they are under legal age for making a contract.

RECORDING AGENT see AGENT OF RECORD.

RECORDING METHOD *see* ACCIDENT-YEAR STATISTICS; CALENDAR YEAR EXPERIENCE.

RECORD KEEPING *see* DEBIT; DEBIT AGENT (HOME SERVICE AGENT); DEBIT INSURANCE (HOME SERVICE INSURANCE, INDUSTRIAL INSURANCE).

RECOVERY damaged insured property in receipt by the insurance company resulting from ABANDONMENT AND SALVAGE, SUBROGATION, and REINSURANCE.

RECRUITING search, attraction, interview, and employment of insurance agents. This is a primary function of the GENERAL AGENT (GA) or AGENCY MANAGER.

RECURRENT DISABILITY *see* DISABILITY INCOME INSURANCE.

RECURRING CLAUSE time period in health insurance that must elapse between a previous illness and a current one, if the current one is to be considered a separate illness eligible for a new set of benefits.

REDETERMINATION PROVISION PROVISION found in CURRENT ASSUMPTION WHOLE LIFE INSURANCE policies under which the insurance company retains the contractual right to recalculate the premium (after a minimum period of time that the policy has been in force). However, the company guarantees that, at the least, a minimum interest rate will be credited to the cash value and, at the most, a maximum mortality charge will be subtracted. The resultant new premium may be greater than or less than the original premium. If the new premium is greater than the original premium, the POLICYOWNER may pay this greater premium, thereby retaining the original death benefit under the policy, or the policyowner may still pay the original premium, but the new death benefit will be lower than it was originally. On the other hand, if the new premium is less than the original premium, the policyowner may pay this lesser premium, thereby retaining the original death benefit under the policy, or the policyowner may still pay the original premium with the death benefit becoming greater than it was originally, or the difference in the new premium and the original premium can be added to the policy's cash value.

REDLINING refusal by an insurance company to underwrite or to continue to underwrite questionable risks in a given geographical area. This is an important civil rights issue.

REDUCED PAID-UP INSURANCE *see* NONFORFEITURE REDUCED PAID-UP BENEFITS.

REDUCED RATE CONTRIBUTION CLAUSE *see* COINSURANCE; DOUBLE RECOVERY

RE-ENTRY TERM LIFE INSURANCE *yearly renewable term (YRT)* life insurance under which an insured can usually re-apply for term insurance every fifth year at a lower premium than the guaranteed renewal rate. If the insured's health is good (as documented by evidence of insurability), the guaranteed renewable term premium can be reduced. If not, the guaranteed rate must be continued to be paid on renewal.

RE-EQUITIZATION deleveraging of the insurance company's balance sheet.

REFORMED correction of a contract containing a mistake in order to prevent a party to that contract from gaining from that mistake. For example, if $1,000,000, instead of the correct amount of $100,000, is filled in the blank for property coverage, it will be corrected to the intended $100,000 amount.

REFUND ANNUITY form of annuity returning premiums plus interest to a beneficiary if the annuitant dies during the accumulation period. A refund annuity costs more than a pure annuity. If the annuitant dies during the liquidation period, benefits paid to any beneficiary depend on whether the refund annuity is in the form of a LIFE ANNUITY CERTAIN, INSTALLMENT REFUND ANNUITY, or CASH REFUND ANNUITY.

REFUND LIFE INCOME OPTION *see* ANNUITY.

REGIONAL OFFICE BRANCH OFFICE of an insurance company's home office that markets, underwrites, and services the company's lines of business within a specified geographical area.

REGISTER record of debit or industrial insurance policies. *See also* DEBIT INSURANCE (HOME SERVICE INSURANCE, INDUSTRIAL INSURANCE).

REGISTERED MAIL AND EXPRESS MAIL INSURANCE coverage for damage or destruction of property with relatively high monetary value, such as stock brokerage house and bank shipments, which involve the transfer of securities and monies to different locations and whose loss would result in great expense. Coverage is on an ALL RISKS basis excluding war, nuclear disaster, and illegal trade items.

REGISTERED MAIL INSURANCE *see* REGISTERED MAIL AND EXPRESS MAIL INSURANCE.

REGISTERED REPRESENTATIVE individual licensed to sell securities to the public. For example, to sell *variable annuities* and VARIABLE LIFE INSURANCE products and mutual funds, an insurance agent is required to pass examinations given by the National Association of Securities Dealers.

REGISTERED RETIREMENT SAVINGS PLAN (RRSP) Canadian retirement plan much like U.S. INDIVIDUAL RETIREMENT ACCOUNT (IRA). Here, an employee can contribute on a tax deductible basis as follows: 2007, $19,000; 2008, $20,000; 2009, $21,000; and 2010, $22,000. each year as a member of an employer pension plan. Earnings under this plan accumulate tax-deferred. RRSPs are issued by life insurance companies and trust companies.

REGRESSION process of comparing the relationship among variables and using this comparison to predict the PROBABILITY of a loss.

REGULAR MEDICAL EXPENSE INSURANCE INSURANCE providing coverage for physicians' fees, expenses associated with nonsurgical care whether in the insured's home, hospital, or the physician's office, and expenses connected with X-rays and laboratory tests. *See also* MEDICAL EXPENSE INSURANCE.

REGULAR MEDICAL INSURANCE health insurance that provides coverage for physicians' fees for all services, with the exception of surgeons' fees.

REGULATION OF INSURANCE COMPANIES *see* STATE SUPERVISION AND REGULATION.

REGULATION OF LIFE INSURANCE *see* STATE SUPERVISION AND REGULATION.

REGULATION Q the regulation that, prior to its repeal, limited the amount of interest a time deposit at a bank could pay.

REHABILITATION *see* REHABILITATION CLAUSE.

REHABILITATION BENEFIT sum provided by a DISABILITY INCOME INSURANCE that pays a multiple of the MONTHLY INDEMNITY to cover the costs associated with a retraining course attended by the insured wage earner when the wage earner's income is interrupted or terminated because of illness, sickness, or accident. This retraining course is designed to enable the disabled worker to be retrained to perform another economic function.

REHABILITATION CLAUSE provision in health insurance under which an insured disabled person is required to undertake (and is reimbursed for) expenses associated with vocational rehabilitation for retraining to perform another economic function.

REIMBURSE BENEFITS payment by the insurance company to the insured for the actual expenses incurred by the insured, such as medical expenses.

REIMBURSEMENT DISABILITY INCOME POLICY policy used to provide the funds for BUY AND SELL AGREEMENTS under which an income payment or a series of income payments is paid to the buyer of the disabled partner's interest contained in a PARTNERSHIP LIFE AND HEALTH INSURANCE PLAN or disabled stockholder's interest contained in a CLOSE CORPORATION PLAN to reimburse that buyer for the sum paid. If this sum to be paid the buyer by the insurance company exceeds the actual market value of the business at the time of the sale, that sum is reduced to the actual market value.

REIMBURSEMENT OF INSURED payment of benefits by an insurance policy to a POLICYOWNER (usually the insured) if a loss occurs.

REINSTATEMENT restoration of a policy that has lapsed because of nonpayment of premiums after the grace period has expired. In life insurance the reinstatement time period is three years from the premium due date. The company usually requires the insured to show evidence of continued insurability (for example, by taking a medical examination); to pay all past premiums plus interest due; and to either reinstate or repay any loans that are still outstanding. Because the insured is now older and a new policy would require a higher premium, it may be to the advantage of an insured to reinstate a policy.

REINSTATEMENT CLAUSE *see* REINSTATEMENT.

REINSTATEMENT OF POLICY *see* REINSTATEMENT.

REINSTATEMENT PREMIUM *see* REINSTATEMENT.

REINSTATEMENT PROVISION *see* REINSTATEMENT.

REINSURANCE form of insurance that insurance companies buy for their own protection, "a sharing of insurance." An insurer *(the reinsured)* reduces its possible maximum loss on either an individual risk

(FACULTATIVE REINSURANCE) or a large number of risks (AUTOMATIC REINSURANCE) by giving *(ceding)* a portion of its liability to another insurance company *(the reinsurer).*

Reinsurance enables an insurance company to (1) expand its capacity; (2) stabilize its underwriting results; (3) finance its expanding volume; (4) secure catastrophe protection against shock losses; (5) withdraw from a class or line of business, or a geographical area, within a relatively short time period; and (6) share large risks with other companies.

There are two broad forms of reinsurance: PROPORTIONAL REINSURANCE and NONPROPORTIONAL REINSURANCE.

REINSURANCE ASSOCIATION *see* REINSURANCE EXCHANGE.

REINSURANCE ASSUMED *see* CEDE.

REINSURANCE, AUTOMATIC *see* AUTOMATIC REINSURANCE.

REINSURANCE BROKER individual who represents a *ceding* insurance company in placing its business with a reinsurer. *See also* REINSURANCE.

REINSURANCE CAPACITY (1) largest amount of REINSURANCE available from a company or from the general market; (2) large amounts of reinsurance on one risk; or (3) maximum premium volume that can be written by a reinsurer.

REINSURANCE CAPTIVE fronted program by the insured acquires a licensed insurance company to issue insurance policies.

REINSURANCE, CARPENTER PLAN *see* CARPENTER PLAN (SPREAD LOSS COVER, SPREAD LOSS REINSURANCE).

REINSURANCE CEDED *see* CEDE.

REINSURANCE CLAUSE provision that covers a business to be protected under a reinsurance treaty. The class either can appear at the beginning of the agreement or may be included in the RETENTION AND LIMITS CLAUSE at a later stage of the contract.

REINSURANCE COMMISSIONS AND EXPENSES total amount of commissions and expense allowances paid by the REINSURER to its CEDING COMPANY minus the total amount of REINSURANCE commissions and expense allowances that, in turn, its ceding company paid on its assumption of reinsurance from another CEDENT. *See also* ADJUSTED SURPLUS; SURPLUS RELIEF.

REINSURANCE CREDIT credit reflected on a CEDING COMPANY'S ANNUAL STATEMENT, showing REINSURANCE PREMIUMS CEDED and losses recoverable from the REINSURER.

REINSURANCE, EXCESS *see* EXCESS OF LOSS REINSURANCE.

REINSURANCE, EXCESS OF LOSS RATIO *see* STOP LOSS REINSURANCE.

REINSURANCE EXCHANGE group in which subscribing members agree to (1) regulations governing their behavior, and (2) the qualifications that REINSURANCE contracts *ceded* to them must meet in order to be acceptable. The exchange is run by a manager who has the power of attorney to represent each member and the exchange in the conduct of the reinsurance business. However, today these exchanges are no longer a factor in the reinsurance market.

REINSURANCE FACILITY
1. pool that contains various reinsurance companies with each sharing reinsurance contracts on a pro rata basis as they are submitted to the pool.
2. market that operates much like the New York Stock Exchange in that reinsurance contracts are bought and sold on a bid and asked basis. *See also* REINSURANCE.

REINSURANCE, FACULTATIVE *see* FACULTATIVE REINSURANCE.

REINSURANCE, LIFE *see* LIFE REINSURANCE.

REINSURANCE, POOLING *see* POOL; REINSURANCE FACILITY.

REINSURANCE PREMIUM *see* AUTOMATIC REINSURANCE; BURNING COST RATIO (PURE LOSS COST); CARPENTER PLAN (SPREAD LOSS COVER, SPREAD LOSS REINSURANCE); EXCESS OF LOSS REINSURANCE; FACULTATIVE REINSURANCE; NONPROPORTIONAL REINSURANCE; PROPORTIONAL REINSURANCE; QUOTA SHARE REINSURANCE; STOP LOSS REINSURANCE; SURPLUS REINSURANCE.

REINSURANCE, PROPERTY AND CASUALTY—CASUALTY CATASTROPHE *see* AUTOMATIC NONPROPORTIONAL REINSURANCE; AUTOMATIC PROPORTIONAL REINSURANCE; AUTOMATIC REINSURANCE; EXCESS OF LOSS REINSURANCE; FACULTATIVE REINSURANCE; NONPROPORTIONAL REINSURANCE; PROPORTIONAL REINSURANCE; QUOTA SHARE REINSURANCE; STOP LOSS REINSURANCE; SURPLUS REINSURANCE.

REINSURANCE, QUOTA SHARE *see* QUOTA SHARE REINSURANCE.

REINSURANCE RESERVE (UNEARNED PREMIUM RESERVE) fund in a segregated account to provide for the return of unearned premiums on policies that are canceled. *See also* PRO RATA CANCELLATION; SHORT RATE CANCELLATION.

REINSURANCE, SPECIFIC EXCESS *see* SPECIFIC EXCESS REINSURANCE.

REINSURANCE, SPREAD LOSS *see* CARPENTER PLAN (SPREAD LOSS COVER, SPREAD LOSS REINSURANCE).

REINSURANCE, STOP LOSS *see* STOP LOSS REINSURANCE.

REINSURANCE, SURPLUS *see* SURPLUS REINSURANCE.

REINSURANCE TREATY contract between the REINSURER and the CEDING COMPANY stipulating the manner in which insurance written on various RISKS is to be shared.

REINSURED *see* CEDING COMPANY.

REINSURER insurance company that assumes all or part of an INSURANCE or REINSURANCE policy written by a primary insurance company (CEDING COMPANY). *See also* REINSURANCE; REINSURANCE BROKER; REINSURANCE EXCHANGE; REINSURANCE FACILITY.

REJECTION refusal by an insurance company to underwrite a risk. *See also* RISK CLASSIFICATION.

RELATIONSHIP BETWEEN RISK AND CHANCE *see* WAGERING V. INSURANCE.

RELATIVE VALUE SCHEDULE (RVS) list of the values of specific medical procedures in comparison with other medical procedures.

RELATIVE VALUE STUDY (RVS) SCHEDULE assignment of a unit value to each of various medical procedures for the purpose of cost comparisons.

RELEASE discharge of the insurance company from an obligation of having to make future payments under an INSURANCE POLICY.

REMAINDER INTERESTS IN A RESIDENCE OR FARM charitable planning strategy under which a donor transfers title to his or her residence or farm to the charity. Upon transfer of title, the donor reserves the right to occupy the property as well as enjoy all the other benefits of property ownership for life, for a specified number of years, or for the life of a given number of tenants. A partial donation of the property may be made; the property does not have to be donated as a whole unit.

REMOVAL insured peril in some property insurance policies that encompasses any accidental damage to insured property while being removed to safety from the immediate threat of damage by another peril covered by that policy. For example, if an insured removes a chair from a burning home, puts it on the lawn, and then rain damages the chair, the loss insured would be covered by fire insurance on the furnishings of the home.

REMOVAL BOND *see* JUDICIAL BOND.

RENEWABLE TERM HEALTH INSURANCE *see* COMMERCIAL HEALTH INSURANCE.

RENEWABLE TERM LIFE INSURANCE coverage that is renewable at the option of the insured, who is not required to take a medical examination. Regardless of physical condition, the insured must be allowed to renew the policy and the premium cannot be increased to reflect any adverse physical condition. However, the premium of each renewal increases to reflect the LIFE EXPECTANCY of the individual at that particular age.

RENEWAL automatic reestablishment of an insurance policy's in-force status, usually achieved through payment of the premium due. *See* *also* COMMERCIAL HEALTH INSURANCE RENEWAL CERTIFICATE; RENEWAL PREMIUM; RENEWAL PROVISION; RENEWABLE TERM LIFE INSURANCE.

RENEWAL CERTIFICATE form showing notification that an insurance policy has been renewed with the same provisions, clauses, and benefits of the previous policy.

RENEWAL COMMISSION commission paid to an AGENT after the FIRST YEAR COMMISSION has been paid to that agent. Renewal commissions generally form a substantial portion of an agent's income after four years in the business and serve as an important incentive for him or her to make every effort to keep the policies on an IN-FORCE BUSINESS status.

RENEWAL EXPENSES costs associated with renewal commissions as a percentage of the renewal premiums, and the servicing charges for previously issued insurance policies.

RENEWAL PREMIUM payment due on the renewal of an insurance policy. The premium may be adjusted up or down to reflect the loss experience of the UNDERWRITING classification to which the insured belongs. *See also* RENEWABLE TERM LIFE INSURANCE.

RENEWAL PROVISION clause in an insurance policy that permits an insured to renew without having to take a medical examination, regardless of his or her physical condition; the premium cannot be increased to reflect an adverse medical condition. *See also* RENEWABLE TERM LIFE INSURANCE.

RENEWALS *see* RENEWAL PREMIUM.

RENT *see* RENT INSURANCE.

RENTAL VALUE INSURANCE *see* RENT INSURANCE.

RENTERS INSURANCE *see* TENANTS INSURANCE.

RENT INSURANCE endorsement to an existing policy or a separate policy covering loss of rental income to the property owner, caused by the damage or destruction of a building, rendering it unrentable. The coverage applies whether or not the dwelling is rented at the time of loss. The insured can select a coinsurance requirement of 50%, 80%, or 100%. The higher the coinsurance amount, the lower the premium.

REPARATIONS payment made by a party causing harm to the party incurring that harm.

REPLACEMENT CAR automobile purchased or leased by the insured or the insured's spouse that takes the place of the insured or the insured spouse's present car as covered in the PERSONAL AUTOMOBILE POLICY (PAP). It will have the same coverage as the vehicle it replaced. The insurance company must be notified within 30 days of delivery of this car to the insured or the insured's spouse only if the insured wishes to add or continue physical damage coverage. *See also* ADDITIONAL CAR.

REPLACEMENT COST *see* REPLACEMENT COST LESS PHYSICAL DEPRE-
CIATION AND OBSOLESCENCE.

**REPLACEMENT COST LESS PHYSICAL DEPRECIATION AND
OBSOLESCENCE** sum it takes to replace an insured's damaged or
destroyed property with one of like kind and quality, equivalent to the
actual cash value, minus physical depreciation (fair wear and tear) and
obsolescence. The objective is to place the insured in the same financial position after a loss as prior to it; the insured should not profit or
lose by incurring a loss.

REPLACEMENT, LIFE INSURANCE exchange of a new policy for
one already in force. *See also* CONSERVATION.

REPLACEMENT RATIO measure showing how much life insurance
an agent has lost through replacement. It is expressed as a percentage
of number of policies, face amount, or premium volume.

**REPLACEMENT, RECONSTRUCTION, AND REPRODUCTION
COST** option to an insurance company to replace, reconstruct (repair),
or reproduce (rebuild) damaged or destroyed property covered by
property insurance rather than indemnify an insured in cash. This is
rarely done.

REPLEVIN BOND *see* JUDICIAL BOND.

REPORTABLE EVENT obligation of the insured to report losses from
a covered peril to the insurance company or its representative as soon
after its occurrence as possible.

REPORTING ENDORSEMENT *see* OPEN FORM (REPORTING FORM).

REPORTING FORM *see* OPEN FORM (REPORTING FORM).

REPORTING REQUIREMENTS *see* OPEN FORM (REPORTING FORM).

REPORT TO SOCIAL SECURITY ADMINISTRATION requirement
of an employer to report annually to the U.S. Treasury Department the
names of employees who terminated employment with vested benefits, and the amount of the benefits. The Treasury sends the Social
Security Administration a copy, which is available to an employee on
request. A statement on vested benefits is given by the Social Security
Administration to an applicant for Social Security benefits.

REPRESENTATIONS statements by an insurance applicant concerning
personal health history, family health history, occupation, and hobbies.
These statements are required to be substantially correct; that is, applicants must answer questions to the best of their knowledge.

REPRESENTATIVE *see* AGENT; BROKER-AGENT; CAPTIVE AGENT; INDE-
PENDENT AGENT.

REPRESENTATIVE SAMPLE sample in which the relative sizes of
the subpopulation samples are selected in such a manner as to be equal

to the relative sizes of the subpopulations. For example, when measuring the viewing audience of a particular television show, the audience is stratified into several subpopulations: income groups, age groups, vocational groups, and so on. Then random samples are drawn from the various strata in proportion to the relative sizes of the REPLACE-MENT, RECONSTRUCTION, AND REPRODUCTION COST.

REQUIRED BEGINNING DATE (RBD) specific rules under the tax code that regulates when distributions from retirement plans must begin. Also required is a minimum amount withdrawal each year after reaching the RBD.

REQUIRED INSURANCE *see* COMPULSORY INSURANCE.

REQUIRED MINIMUM DISTRIBUTION (RMD) requirement that an individual must withdraw a minimum sum annually from retirement savings that have accumulated on a tax-deferred basis. This withdrawal must begin by April 1 of the year one reaches age 70½. All deferred tax retirement savings plans (with the exception of the ROTH IRA) are subject to this rule to include the traditional INDIVIDUAL RETIREMENT ACCOUNT (IRA), SIMPLIFIED EMPLOYEE PENSION (SEP), SAVINGS INCENTIVE MATCH PLAN FOR EMPLOYEES (SIMPLE PLANS), SECTION 401 (K) PLAN (SALARY REDUCTION PLAN), SECTION 403 (B) PLAN, QUALIFIED PENSION PLAN, AND PROFIT-SHARING PLAN. Withdrawals may be made based on the individual's LIFE EXPECTANCY or the joint life expectancy of the individual and the individual's oldest PRIMARY BENEFICIARY. The steps for calculating the RMD are
1. determining the total market value of the retirement plan as of December 31 of the year prior to the retirement year.
2. determining the life expectancy factor according to the Internal Revenue Service tables.
3. dividing the value of the retirement plan by the life expectancy factor.

REQUIREMENTS *see* REQUIREMENTS OF INSURABLE RISK.

REQUIREMENTS OF INSURABLE RISK
1. a large number of homogeneous exposures (in order for the deviation of actual losses from expected losses to approach *zero,* and the creditability of the prediction to approach *one*).
2. loss must be definite in time and amount.
3. loss must be fortuitous. An insured cannot cause the loss to happen; it must be due to chance.
4. must not be an exposure to catastrophic loss; risks must be spread over a large geographical area to prevent their concentration. REINSURANCE often is used to spread potentially catastrophic risks.
5. premium must be reasonable in relation to the potential loss. In theory, one could even insure against a pencil point breaking, but the premium would be much greater than any possible loss.

RESERVE *see* RESERVES AND THEIR COMPUTATION.

RESERVE FACTORS *see* RESERVES AND THEIR COMPUTATION.

RESERVE, FULL PRELIMINARY TERM *see* FULL PRELIMINARY TERM RESERVE PLAN.

RESERVE, INCURRED BUT NOT REPORTED LOSSES *see* INCURRED BUT NOT REPORTED LOSSES (IBNR).

RESERVE LIABILITIES REGULATION
1. LIFE INSURANCE: specification by each state regarding (a) the minimum assumptions that must be used in reserve calculations as they pertain to the maximum interest rate that can be assumed; (b) the mortality table that can be used (the more conservative the table, the higher the death rates that will be shown that exceed the death rates actually expected); and (c) the reserve valuation that must be used (the minimum is established by the National Association of Insurance Commissioners' *Standard Valuation Law*).
2. PROPERTY AND LIABILITY INSURANCE specification by each state regarding the minimum assumptions that must be used in reserve calculations as they pertain to unpaid loss reserves and *unearned premium reserves*.

RESERVE, LOSS *see* LOSS RESERVES.

RESERVE, PROSPECTIVE *see* PROSPECTIVE RESERVE.

RESERVE, RETROSPECTIVE *see* RETROSPECTIVE METHOD RESERVE COMPUTATION.

RESERVES AND THEIR COMPUTATION *see* FULL PRELIMINARY TERM RESERVE PLAN; PROSPECTIVE RESERVE; RETROSPECTIVE METHOD RESERVE COMPUTATION.

RESERVE, UNEARNED PREMIUM *see* UNEARNED PREMIUM RESERVE.

RESIDENCE AND OUTSIDE THEFT INSURANCE coverage provided for the INSURED'S personal property in the event the insured incurs a loss resulting from theft, burglary, robbery, or malicious mischief, regardless of whether the loss occurred on or outside the insured's premises. *See also* HOMEOWNERS INSURANCE POLICY—SECTION I (PROPERTY COVERAGE).

RESIDENT AGENT salesperson who markets and services insurance policies in the state in which he or she is domiciled.

RESIDENTIAL CONSTRUCTION INSURANCE coverage in the event an insured's negligent acts and/or omissions involving the construction of a new one- or two-family residential structure result in bodily injury and/or property damage to a third party. The "insured" includes his or her employees and independent contractors. This coverage is normally part of the HOMEOWNERS' INSURANCE POLICY and extends coverage on an automatic basis for this exposure at no extra premium.

RESIDENTIAL FORM *see* RESIDENTIAL CONSTRUCTION INSURANCE.

RESIDUAL AUTOMOBILE INSURANCE MARKET *see* BUSINESS AUTO COVERAGE FORM; PERSONAL AUTOMOBILE POLICY.

RESIDUAL DISABILITY inability to perform one or more important daily business duties, or inability to perform the usual daily business duties for the time period usually required for the performance of such duties. *See also* RESIDUAL DISABILITY INCOME INSURANCE.

RESIDUAL DISABILITY INCOME INSURANCE coverage for an individual with a residual disability. Benefits are usually payable for the unused portion of the total disability benefit period up to age 65. If an individual is at least age 55 at the time of disablement, and total disability lasts less than a year, residual benefits are payable for the unused portion of the benefit period for up to 18 months, but not beyond age 65. If there is at least a 25% loss in current earnings, the residual benefits will equal the percentage of loss times the monthly benefit for total disability. The residual disability monthly benefit can be expressed in this equation:

$$\frac{\text{Loss of Monthly Income}}{\text{Prior Monthly Income}} \times \begin{array}{c}\text{Monthly Benefit for Total}\\ \text{Disability}\end{array}$$

See also RESIDUAL DISABILITY.

RESIDUAL MARKET *see* AUTOMOBILE ASSIGNED RISK INSURANCE PLAN; RESIDUAL DISABILITY; RESIDUAL DISABILITY INCOME INSURANCE.

RES IPSA LOQUITOR Latin phrase for "The facts speak for themselves." This is a rule of evidence under which an individual is deemed, under certain specific circumstances, to be negligent by the mere occurrence of an accident. These circumstances are defined as when the law presumes that an accident could not have occurred had the individual not been negligent.

RESPONDEAT SUPERIOR Latin for "Let the superior reply." That is, an employer is liable for the torts of employees that result from their employment. For example, an insurance company (the master) acts through its agent (servant); because of this master-servant relationship, any wrongs the agent commits are deemed to have been committed by the insurance company, which must accept responsibility.

REST CURE care in a sanitarium, nursing home, or other facility designed to provide CUSTODIAL CARE on behalf of the mental and physical well-being of the patient. The cost may or may not be provided by health insurance policies.

RESTORATION OF LIMITS reduction of policy limits after a property loss by the amount of the loss paid. After the property has been repaired or replaced, the original policy limits go into effect.

RESTORATION OF PLAN authority of the PENSION BENEFIT GUARANTY CORPORATION (PBGC) to stop the termination of a pension plan and restore it to its previous status by returning a portion or all of the plan's assets and liabilities. For example, such an action could be taken by the PBGC when a company whose pension plan is being terminated has experienced a reversal in the adverse conditions that originally caused the termination.

RESTORATION OF VESTED BENEFITS plan under the EMPLOYEE RETIREMENT INCOME SECURITY ACT OF 1974 (ERISA) for employees who are less than 50% *vested.* An employee must be permitted to buy back retirement benefits lost because of the withdrawal of his or her contributions. The employee pays back to the pension plan the withdrawal contributions, plus 5% interest compounded annually.

RESTORATION PREMIUM sum that an insurance company charges a business firm to restore a property or liability insurance policy, or a bond, to its initial face value after the insurance company has paid a claim either to the insured business or to a third party on behalf of the insured business.

RESTRICTIVE EXECUTIVE BONUS ARRANGEMENT nonqualified executive benefit plan that provides the employer an income tax deduction on contributions, selection of participating employees, unrestricted funding limitations on qualified plans, and ability to retain a KEY EMPLOYEE (KEY PERSON).

RESUMPTION OF OPERATIONS CLAUSE in a BUSINESS INTERRUPTION INSURANCE policy, clause that stipulates that if, by resuming operations, the business can reduce a loss, the business is obligated to so do. If the business refuses to resume operations, it will incur a portion of the loss.

RETAIL CREDIT REPORT report developed by or supplied by a credit agency to an insurer dealing with the financial standing and character of an insurance applicant. These factors are carefully weighted by the company's *underwriter* in deciding the INSURABILITY of the applicant. *See also* NUMERICAL RATING SYSTEM.

RETAINED ASSET SERVICES (RAS) insurance company program in which the beneficiary of an insurance policy is encouraged to leave the death proceeds in an account on deposit with the insurance company instead of receiving a LUMP SUM payment. If the beneficiary elects to participate in the RAS, a bank account is established in the beneficiary's name and the beneficiary will receive a personalized checkbook. The RAS provides the insurer with a vehicle to retain assets to invest as well as a means to cross-sell additional insurance products to the beneficiary.

RETAINED EARNINGS net profit of a business, less dividends. Reinvestment of retained earnings enables an insurance company to write more business from a stronger capital base. Contributions to retained earnings come from three sources: (1) excess interest from investment earnings; (2) loss savings (fewer and/or smaller losses than were loaded into premiums); and (3) expense savings (less expense costs than were loaded into premiums). *See also* SURPLUS ACCOUNT.

RETAINED LIFE ESTATE donation of home or other property to an organization, but retention of the right to live at that home or property until death.

RETAINER CLAUSE provision in a *nonproportional reinsurance contract* that the reinsurance will protect only the business retained by the *cedent* for its own account. In this connection, losses must be assumed by the cedent if it cannot enforce payment for any loss falling under its other *surplus* or QUOTA SHARE REINSURANCE contract.

RETALIATION LAWS legislation by a state that taxes out-of-state insurance companies operating in its jurisdiction in the same way that the state's own insurance companies are taxed in the second state. For example, state #1 charges a tax of 4% on its *domiciled* insurers. But if these insured are charged a higher tax when operating in state #2, then state #1 will charge the higher tax to insurers of state #2 who wish to do business in state #1.

RETALIATORY PREMIUM TAX *see* RETALIATION LAWS.

RETENTION *see* RETENTION AND LIMITS CLAUSE; RISK MANAGEMENT; SELF INSURANCE.

RETAINED LIFE ESTATE donation of home or other property to an organization, but retention of the right to live at that home or property until death.

RETENTION AND LIMITS CLAUSE provision in almost all EXCESS OF LOSS REINSURANCE contracts under which payment is made by a reinsurer of each and every loss incurred by the *cedent* in excess of a specified sum, up to a fixed limit. Under this clause, there is no restriction on the number of claims that may be recovered by the cedent under the contract for any one event. The only stipulation is that each claim must arise as a result of the event in question.

RETENTION DEDUCTIBLE in UMBRELLA LIABILITY INSURANCE clause that stipulates that in the event of a loss where there are no underlying policies providing coverage, the DEDUCTIBLE will apply.

RETENTION OF LOSS *see* RETENTION AND LIMITS CLAUSE; RISK MANAGEMENT; SELF INSURANCE.

RETIRED LIVES RESERVE EMPLOYEE BENEFIT INSURANCE PLAN whose objective is to provide the retired employee with life insurance. This group life insurance product is composed of two basic parts: (1) annually RENEWABLE TERM LIFE INSURANCE until age 100; and (2) accumulation of a reserve element while the employee is working from which premium payments will be made on the annually renewable term life insurance after the employee retires. Premium payments that the employer makes on behalf of the employee are a tax-deductible expense, not considered taxable income to the employee by the Internal Revenue Service. Should the employee terminate service prior to retirement, regardless of the reason, funds remaining in the employee's account are used to fund the benefits of the remaining employees.

RETIREMENT AGE age at which a pension plan participant is entitled to receive retirement benefits, or point at which retirement benefits are payable: (1) NORMAL RETIREMENT AGE is the earliest age permitted to retire and receive full benefits; (2) EARLY RETIREMENT is earlier-than-normal age permitted to retire provided attained minimum age and service requirement are met, but there is a proportionate reduction in benefits; (3) DEFERRED RETIREMENT age beyond automatic retirement age permitted to retire, usually with no increase in benefits; (4) *automatic retirement age* is age at which retirement is automatically effective.

RETIREMENT ANNUITY *see* ANNUITY; GROUP DEFERRED ANNUITY; GROUP DEPOSIT ADMINISTRATION ANNUITY: PENSION PLAN FUNDING; GROUP IMMEDIATE PARTICIPATION GUARANTEED (IPG) CONTRACT ANNUITY.

RETIREMENT BENEFITS *see* ALLOCATED FUNDING INSTRUMENT; DEFINED BENEFIT PLAN; DEFINED CONTRIBUTION PENSION (MONEY PURCHASE PLAN); GROUP IMMEDIATE PARTICIPATION GUARANTEED (IPG) CONTRACT ANNUITY; GROUP PERMANENT LIFE INSURANCE; PENSION PLAN FUNDING; GROUP DEPOSIT ADMINISTRATION ANNUITY; INDIVIDUAL CONTRACT PENSION PLAN; PENSION PLAN FUNDING INSTRUMENTS.

RETIREMENT EQUITY ACT OF 1984 act that makes it mandatory for employees with spouses to be in receipt of retirement income from a PENSION PLAN in the form of a JOINT LIFE AND SURVIVORSHIP ANNUITY, unless the employee's spouse waives that right in writing. This is to prevent the employee from writing the spouse out of the benefit income.

RETIREMENT INCOME ANNUITY LADDERING process of transferring funds from a retiree's retirement savings to purchase increments of an ANNUITY over a period of time.

RETIREMENT INCOME ENDOWMENT POLICY type of ENDOWMENT INSURANCE that matures at a stipulated retirement age and whose purpose is to provide retirement income to the INSURED.

RETIREMENT INCOME PAYMENTS *see* RETIREMENT BENEFITS.

RETIREMENT INCOME POLICY form of DEFERRED ANNUITY; a life insurance policy that usually guarantees from 120 to 180 monthly income payments to the annuitant at retirement. If the annuitant dies during the deferral (or guaranteed) period, a beneficiary receives a death payment of the face amount or the cash value, whichever is larger. During the deferred period, the policyowner can withdraw part or all of the annuity's cash value (the latter terminating the annuity). *See also* ANNUITY.

RETIREMENT INSURANCE NEEDS *see* RETIREMENT ANNUITY; RETIREMENT BENEFITS; RETIREMENT INCOME POLICY; RETIREMENT PLANNING.

RETIREMENT PLAN *see* ALLOCATED FUNDING INSTRUMENT; DEFINED BENEFIT PLAN; DEFINED CONTRIBUTION PENSION (MONEY PURCHASE PLAN); GROUP DEPOSIT ADMINISTRATION ANNUITY; PENSION PLAN FUNDING; PENSION PLAN FUNDING INSTRUMENTS; RETIREMENT BENEFITS; RETIREMENT INCOME POLICY, RETIREMENT PLANNING; UNALLOCATED FUNDING INSTRUMENT.

RETIREMENT PLANNING formal process of setting aside funds on a mathematical basis to provide deferred income benefits. *See also* RETIREMENT PLAN.

RETIREMENT PLAN OPTIONS choice among the following options made by retiree prior to retirement concerning the distribution of benefits:

1. Monthly payments for lifetime of retiree with no SURVIVORSHIP BENEFIT—income payments are the largest to the retiree under this option since all income payments cease upon the death of the retiree.

2. Monthly payments for lifetime of retiree with 100% survivorship benefit—income payments are paid during the time the retiree is alive and continue at the 100% level to a beneficiary after the death of the retiree. There is a significant reduction in the dollar amount of each monthly income payment to the retiree because beneficiary's number of payments are likely to continue for a long time.

3. Monthly payments for lifetime of retiree subject to a minimum number guaranteed to be paid—income payments are paid during the time the retiree is alive. Should the retiree die before receiving a minimum number of income payments, payments are made to a beneficiary until the minimum number has been paid, at which time all payments cease. The longer the minimum number of payments guaranteed, the greater the reduction in the dollar amounts of each monthly income payment to the retiree.

4. Monthly payments for lifetime of retiree with 50% survivorship benefit—income payments paid during the time the retiree is alive and continue at the 50% level to a beneficiary after the death of the retiree. There is a reduction in the dollar amount of each monthly income payment to the retiree because beneficiary's number of payments are likely to continue for a long time.

5. Monthly payments for a guaranteed number of years—income payments are made for a stipulated number of years (period certain), not for the life of the retiree. The stipulated number of years is usually 5 years, 10 years, 15 years, or 20 years. Should the retiree die before receiving income payments for the stipulated time period, the beneficiary would receive income payments until the time period expires.

6. Lump sum (cash refund)—accumulation in retiree's account distributed in one sum.

Once income payments commence under any of the above options, the retiree cannot change the option. The retiree cannot exclude the spouse from the survivorship benefit unless the spouse waives his or her right in writing.

RETIREMENT RATE ASSUMPTIONS *see* PENSION PLAN FUNDING INSTRUMENTS.

RETIREMENT TEST requirement that a retired worker can have annual earnings of no more than a stipulated amount in order to receive a full retirement income under Social Security if under the full benefit retirement age (67 if born after 1960). If less than the full retirement age, there is a reduction of one dollar in benefits for each two dollars in earnings above an annual limit. In the year of full benefit retirement age, there is a reduction of one dollar in benefits for every three dollars in earnings above the annual limit until the month of the full benefit retirement age. After that month, full benefits are paid regardless of earnings.

RETROACTIVE CONVERSION *see* ORIGINAL AGE.

RETROACTIVE DATE date after which losses may occur and be covered under a CLAIMS-MADE BASIS LIABILITY COVERAGE.

RETROACTIVE INSURANCE *see* ORIGINAL AGE.

RETROACTIVE LIABILITY INSURANCE coverage that is purchased to provide protection for a loss that has already occurred. The severity of the loss, however, is uncertain.

RETROACTIVE PERIOD *see* ORIGINAL AGE.

RETROACTIVE RATE REDUCTION *see* RETROSPECTIVE RATING.

RETROACTIVE RESTORATION REINSTATEMENT of an INSURANCE POLICY or BOND to its original FACE AMOUNT (FACE OF POLICY) after the payment by the INSURER of a loss. The purpose of this type of coverage is to INDEMNIFY the INSURED if, at a time period in the future, previous losses incurred by the insured are discovered.

RETROCESSION REINSURANCE of a reinsurer. *See also* RETROCESSION CATASTROPHE COVER.

RETROCESSIONAIRE REINSURER of a reinsurer. *See also* RETROCESSION.

RETROCESSION CATASTROPHE COVER REINSURANCE of a *reinsurer* such that the reinsurer protects itself from a catastrophe occurrence. Just as an insurer must decide to CEDE to the reinsurer a portion of a risk it has underwritten, the reinsurer must make the same decision as to which risks it can sustain within its resources, and what portion of the risks it must retrocede. Retrocession may be either *pro-*

portional or *nonproportional. See also* NONPROPORTIONAL REINSURANCE; PROPORTIONAL REINSURANCE.

RETRO-NOTE PLAN means of financing by which some large organizations pay their property or liability insurance premiums to reflect losses actually paid during the first year of coverage, plus claims expenses, administrative and servicing expenses, and a loading for the company's profit. The insured signs a promissory note to the company for the difference in the normal or standard premium that should have been charged.

RETROSPECTIVE AGGREGATE EXCESS OF LOSS REINSURANCE type of EXCESS OF LOSS REINSURANCE in which the insurance company (cedent) cedes its risk of loss on INCURRED BUT NOT REPORTED LOSSES (IBNR) and previously reported losses.

RETROSPECTIVE COMPUTATION *see* RETROSPECTIVE PREMIUM.

RETROSPECTIVE METHOD RESERVE COMPUTATION accumulated value of assumed past net life insurance premiums, minus the accumulated value of past benefits (claims paid).

RETROSPECTIVE PREMIUM *see* RETROSPECTIVE RATING.

RETROSPECTIVE RATING method of establishing rates in which the current year's premium is calculated to reflect the actual current year's loss experience. An initial premium is charged and then adjusted at the end of the policy year to reflect the actual loss experience of the business.

RETURN COMMISSION return of a *pro rata* portion of an agent's commission for a policy that is canceled prior to its expiration date. A commission is paid to an agent in the expectation that the premium will be earned over the life of a policy. If the policy is canceled, a portion of the unearned premium (either *pro rata* or *short rate)* also must be returned to the policyowner.

RETURN OF CASH VALUE CLAUSE provision in a life insurance policy that if an insured dies within a given period of time, the beneficiary receives the *face value* of the policy plus its *cash value. See also* CASH SURRENDER VALUE.

RETURN OF PREMIUM clause that is found in TERM LIFE INSURANCE, UNIVERSAL LIFE INSURANCE, UNIVERSAL VARIABLE LIFE INSURANCE, LONG-TERM CARE, and DISABILITY INCOME and that provides for the return of or a percentage of the paid-in premiums if coverage is not used within a specified time period. *See also* CANCELLATION PROVISION CLAUSE.

RETURN OF PREMIUM TERM LIFE INSURANCE modification of TERM LIFE INSURANCE such that the POLICYOWNER receives the return of the premiums paid in should the insured survive the term period. These policies cost approximately 25 to 50% more each year than a straight term policy.

RETURN ON ASSETS (ROA) net income expressed as a percentage of average total assets. This percentage measures profitability by expressing the efficiency of asset utilization.

RETURN ON EQUITY (ROE) net income expressed as a percentage of average total equity. This percentage measures profitability by expressing how efficiently invested capital or equity is being utilized.

RETURN ON EQUITY RATIO insurance company's NET GAIN FROM OPERATIONS divided by its ADJUSTED SURPLUS. This is the accounting rate of return on stockholder's equity since the ratio shows the rate of return the company is earning on its capital and surplus committed to conducting its insurance business and investments made. The greater this ratio, the greater the use the company is making of the funds invested in it by its stockholders.

RETURN ON NET WORTH (RONW) ratio of net income after taxes to total end of the year NET WORTH. This ratio indicates the return on stockholder's total equity.

RETURN PREMIUM amount received by the POLICYHOLDER if the policy is canceled, benefits are reduced, or the PREMIUM is reduced. *See also* PRO RATA CANCELLATION; SHORT RATE CANCELLATION.

REVENUE BULLETIN 1988-52 ruling issued in 1988 by the Internal Revenue Service that stipulates that, when computing the pension benefits of an employee still working after 1987, the years of service on the job after the employee reaches age 65 cannot be disregarded. The issuance of this revenue bulletin makes it mandatory that pension benefits reflect all years on the job, to include those years after age 65.

REVENUE RULING 59-60 ruling that is the most significant source for the valuation of closely held corporation capital stock critical to the CLOSE CORPORATION PLAN. This ruling defines the fair market value as "the price at which the property would change hands between a willing buyer and a willing seller when the former is not under any compulsion to buy and the latter is not under any compulsion to sell, both parties having reasonable knowledge of the relevant facts." The valuation of the shares of closely held corporations involves the comparison of "prices at which the stocks of companies engaged in the same or similar line of business are selling in a free and open market." This ruling stipulates that the following factors must be carefully considered in such an evaluation: (1) intangible values such as goodwill; (2) financial ability to generate an ongoing dividend stream; (3) earnings capability; (4) type of business and its financial and market history; (5) economic outlook for the industry in which the business resides; (6) financial condition of the corporation as well as the book value of its stock; (7) size of the block of stock requiring a valuation; and (8) market value of stocks actively traded on an exchange or over-the-counter market of similar corporations engaged in similar lines of business.

REVERSE-ANNUITY MORTGAGE (RAM) loan under which the owner of a home receives the equity in the form of a series of monthly income payments for life. Upon the owner's death, the lender institution (usually a bank) gains title to the home and is free to keep or sell it. The longer that monthly income payments are made, the greater the reduction in the owner's equity in his or her home. This type of mortgage is of value to older individuals who own their homes free and clear. Their large equity enables them to continue to live there and to receive a monthly income benefit.

REVERSE SPLIT DOLLAR LIFE INSURANCE policy that is the opposite of the traditional SPLIT DOLLAR LIFE INSURANCE policy in that: (1) the employee is the POLICYOWNER and as such can exercise all ownership rights inherit to that policy; (2) the employee owns the CASH VALUE of the policy; (3) the employees's beneficiary has the right to that portion of the death benefit equal to the cash value; (4) the employer retains the right to that portion of the death benefit equal to the pure protection element (death benefit minus the cash value); (5) the employer pays that portion of the premium charged for its economic benefit gained according to the PS 58 RATE TABLE; and (6) the employee pays that portion of the premium equal to the total premium minus that part of the premium paid by the employer in the above.

REVERSIONARY ANNUITY *see* SURVIVORSHIP ANNUITY.

REVERSIONARY INTEREST interest of a beneficiary in the proceeds of a SURVIVORSHIP ANNUITY. *See also* SURVIVORSHIP ANNUITY.

REVIVAL *see* REINSTATEMENT.

REVOCABLE *see* BENEFICIARY.

REVOCABLE BENEFICIARY *see* BENEFICIARY.

REVOCABLE LIVING TRUST TRUST in which rights to make any changes therein are retained by the GRANTOR. At the grantor's death all rights become irrevocable. This type of trust has several advantages: it can avoid PROBATE, it prevents public disclosure of the assets of the trust, it can easily be revised or terminated, and it promotes continuity for the transfer of the estate. However, since the grantor retains ownership rights under this trust, the trust loses all of the income and estate tax advantages available under an IRREVOCABLE LIVING TRUST.

RIDER endorsement to an insurance policy that modifies clauses and provisions of the policy, including or excluding coverage.

RIDERS, LIFE POLICIES endorsements to life insurance policies that provide additional benefits or limit an insurance company's liability for payment of benefits under certain conditions. These include:
1. *Waiver of Premium for Disability.* An insured with total disability that lasts for a specified period no longer has to pay premiums for the duration of the disability. In effect, the company pays the premiums.

   2. *Accidental Death Benefit.*

   3. GUARANTEED INSURABILITY.

   4. COST-OF-LIVING ADJUSTMENT (COLA).

   5. *Other Insured.* Term life insurance is added on a person other than the primary insured, with the rate based on the other person's age, sex, underwriting classification, and amount of coverage.

   6. *Children's Insurance.* Term insurance on each child is added, usually to the age of majority. Generally, a child cannot become insured before the age of 15 days or after his or her eighteenth birthday.

   7. *Additional Insurance.* Term insurance can be added to *ordinary life* policies as an additional layer of coverage for some specified time interval.

   8. *Transfer of Insureds.* In business situations, generally used to insure key persons with the cash value and the insurance coverage transferable from the initial insured person to another person.

RIGHT OF SURVIVORSHIP right of survivors to the interest in property of a deceased joint tenant as the result of property held in joint tenancy. *See also* SURVIVOR PURCHASE OPTION; SURVIVORSHIP BENEFIT; SURVIVORSHIP LIFE INSURANCE.

RIMS *see* RISK AND INSURANCE MANAGEMENT SOCIETY (RIMS).

RIOT AND CIVIL COMMOTION INSURANCE coverage for damage to property resulting from riot or civil commotion. Riot is defined by most state laws as a violent disturbance involving three or more (in some states two or more) persons. Civil commotion is a more serious and prolonged disturbance or violent uprising. Losses from riots in major cities during the 1960s caused insurers to stop writing this type of coverage in certain urban areas. In response, Congress enacted legislation creating the FEDERAL CRIME INSURANCE program and providing riot reinsurance in states that established acceptable pooling plans. *See also* FAIR ACCESS TO INSURANCE REQUIREMENTS (FAIR) PLAN.

RIOT COVERAGE *see* RIOT AND CIVIL COMMOTION INSURANCE.

RIOT EXCLUSION clause in the *Standard Fire Policy* and many other property insurance policies that excepts coverage for losses caused by riot or civil commotion. Coverage for riot and civil commotion can be added with the EXTENDED COVERAGE ENDORSEMENT.

RISK uncertainty of financial loss; term used to designate an insured or a peril insured against.

RISK AND CHANGE *see* RISK CLASSIFICATION.

RISK AND INSURANCE MANAGEMENT SOCIETY (RIMS) society dedicated to the advancement of professional standards of RISK MANAGEMENT. Its membership is composed of risk and insurance managers of business organizations, public organizations, and service organizations. Both profit and nonprofit organizations are represented. The goal of RIMS is to upgrade the management of risk and employee benefit plans in order to preserve the assets of the organization in question. Included in the activities of RIMS are research, conferences and seminars, and sponsorship of the INSURANCE INSTITUTE OF AMERI-CAS (IIA) ASSOCIATE IN RISK MANAGEMENT (ARM) program.

RISK AND OCCUPATION FREQUENCY and *severity* of accidents resulting from conditions and environment surrounding one's workplace. Occupation is an important underwriting factor when considering an applicant for insurance.

RISK APPRAISAL *see* RISK MANAGEMENT.

RISK ASSUMPTION *see* RETENTION AND LIMITS CLAUSE; RISK MANAGEMENT; SELF INSURANCE.

RISK AVOIDANCE *see* AVOIDANCE.

RISK-BASED CAPITAL amount of required capital that the insurance company must maintain based on the inherent risks in the insurer's operations. These risks include ASSET DEPRECIATION RISK, CREDIT RECEIVABLES RISK, UNDERWRITING RISK, and OFF-BALANCE-SHEET RISK.

RISK-BASED CAPITAL RATIO measurement of the amount of capital (assets minus liabilities) an insurance company has as a basis of support for the degree of risk associated with its company operations and investments. This ratio identifies the companies that are inadequately capitalized by dividing the company's capital by the minimum amount of capital that the regulatory authorities feel is necessary to support the insurance operations. A ratio of 1.00 or greater is deemed to be satisfactory. This standard can be used to identify inadequately capitalized life and health companies, thereby enabling regulatory authorities to intervene before a company becomes insolvent.

RISK-BASED CAPITAL STATISTIC (RBCS) ratio of AUTHORIZED CONTROL LEVEL RISK-BASED CAPITAL of an insurance company to its TOTAL ADJUSTED CAPITAL. This statistic determines regulatory action taken by the state's insurance commissioner. If the RBCS is greater than 200%, no regulatory action is required. If the RBCS is between 150 and 200%, the insurer must file a plan of corrective action with the insurance commissioner as well as provide an explanation of why the RBCS standards were not met. If the RBCS is between 100 and 150%, the insurer must file a plan of corrective action with the insurance commission and the insurance commissioner will examine the insurer. If the RBCS is between 70 and 150%, the insurance commissioner may seize the insurer. If the RBCS is below 70%, the insurance commissioner is required to liquidate or rehabilitate the insurer.

RISK BEARER *see* SELF INSURANCE.

RISK CLASSIFICATION analysis of uncertainty of financial loss. This classification can be according to whether a risk is FUNDAMENTAL, PARTICULAR, PURE, SPECULATIVE, DYNAMIC, or STATIC. In life insurance the process by which a company determines how much to charge for a policy according to an applicant's age, occupation, sex, and health. *See also* UNDERWRITING.

RISK CONTROL *see* RISK MANAGEMENT.

RISK, DEGREE OF *see* DEGREE OF RISK.

RISK EQUIVALENT *see* ACTUARIAL EQUIVALENT.

RISK EXPERIENCE LOSS RATIO *see* EXPERIENCE RATING; FREQUENCY AND DISTRIBUTION OF LOSSES; LOSS RATIO.

RISK FINANCING utilization of source(s) of funds to pay for losses. Source(s) of funds can be classified as:
1. *internal*—a RETENTION program is established to use funds from within the organization to pay for losses.
2. *external*—a transfer program (generally through the purchase of INSURANCE) is established to use funds from without the organization to pay for losses.

Usually, a RISK MANAGEMENT program combines retention and transfer to form a comprehensive program for loss protection.

RISK IDENTIFICATION *see* RISK MANAGEMENT.

RISK IDENTIFICATION IN LIABILITY EXPOSURES process of discovering sources of loss concerning the liability RISK faced by individuals and business firms. The first step in risk management is to identify the causes of a loss by analyzing possible negligent acts and/or omissions that could result in bodily injury and/or property damage. *See also* RISK MANAGEMENT.

RISK IDENTIFICATION IN PROPERTY EXPOSURES process of discovering sources of loss concerning the property RISK faced by individuals and business firms. The first step is to analyze possible *perils* that can damage or destroy both real and personal property. *See also* RISK MANAGEMENT.

RISK MANAGEMENT procedure to minimize the adverse effect of a possible financial loss by (1) identifying potential sources of loss; (2) measuring the financial consequences of a loss occurring; and (3) using controls to minimize actual losses or their financial consequences. *See also* BUSINESS PROPERTY AND LIABILITY INSURANCE PACKAGE; CONDOMINIUM INSURANCE; DISABILITY INCOME INSURANCE; HEALTH INSURANCE; HOMEOWNERS INSURANCE POLICY; HUMAN LIFE VALUE APPROACH (EVOIL); LIFE INSURANCE; LOSS PREVENTION AND REDUCTION; PENSION PLAN; PERSONAL AUTOMOBILE POLICY (PAP); RISK IDENTIFICATION, LIABILITY EXPOSURE; RISK IDENTIFICATION, PROPERTY EXPOSURES; SELF INSURANCE; TENANTS INSURANCE.

RISK MANAGER *see* RETENTION AND LIMITS CLAUSE; RISK MANAGEMENT; SELF INSURANCE.

RISK MAP graph that illustrates in grid format the FREQUENCY and SEVERITY RATE of possible and probable losses that may be incurred by the organization.

RISK MEASUREMENT *see* RISK MANAGEMENT.

RISK PHILOSOPHY personal view regarding how losses occur and the validity of loss prevention and reduction; also, whether an individual is a risk taker or a risk avoider. For example, if a driver takes the view that dying in a serious automobile accident is inevitable, then use of seat belts is unnecessary. On the other hand, a driver's philosophy may be that wearing a seat belt will minimize injury and reduce the chance of dying in an accident.

RISK POSITION REPORTS quantification of the risk inherit in the operation of an insurance company. These risks include 1) *asset risk,* refers to the positive or negative movement in the value of an asset; (2) *operational risk,* refers to the occurrence of a negative event; and (3) *liability risk*, which refers to the increasing costs of claims and expenses.

RISK PREMIUM INSURANCE *see* RENEWABLE TERM LIFE INSURANCE.

RISK RATING, INDIVIDUAL rating system under which a specific premium rate, rather than a manual or class rate, is assigned to each unit of exposure.

RISK REDUCTION *see* ENGINEERING APPROACH; HUMAN APPROACH; LOSS PREVENTION AND REDUCTION.

RISK RETENTION *see* SELF INSURANCE.

RISK RETENTION ACT OF 1986 federal act composed of amendments to the Product Liability Risk Retention Act of 1981 and enacted to make the procedures more efficient for creating RISK RETENTION GROUPS (capitalized, member-owned INSURANCE COMPANY) and PURCHASING GROUPS (INSURANCE buyers group formed to obtain coverage for homogeneous LIABILITY RISKS, in many instances hard to insure, from an insurance company).

RISK RETENTION GROUP *see* SELF INSURANCE.

RISK/REWARD BASIS investment theory that states, "The greater the RISK, the greater the financial reward; the lower the risk, the lower the financial reward."

RISK SECURITIZATION *see* SECURITIZATION.

RISK SELECTION methods by which a home office underwriter chooses applicants that an insurer will accept. The underwriter's job is to spread the costs equitably among members of the group to be insured. Therefore, the underwriter must determine which are normal risks, or STANDARD RISKS, to be charged the standard rate; which are *substandard risks,* to be charged a higher rate; and which are PRE-

FERRED RISKS, to receive a discount. This process is made more difficult by SELF-SELECTION and ADVERSE SELECTION. The underwriter must screen applicants who are looking for insurance, specifically because they have a greater-than-normal chance of loss, and set the correct PREMIUM *rate* for them.

RISK SOURCES, PERSONAL *see* HUMAN LIFE VALUE APPROACH (ECONOMIC VALUE OF AN INDIVIDUAL LIFE—EVOIL); RISK MANAGEMENT.

RISK SPREAD *see* POOLING.

RISK, SUBJECTIVE *see* SUBJECTIVE PROBABILITY.

RISK, SYSTEMATIC *see* STATIC RISK.

RISK TRANSFER shifting a PURE RISK by means of a two party contract such as INSURANCE.

RISK, UNSYSTEMATIC *see* DYNAMIC.

ROBBERY use of the threat of violence or actual violence in taking property from someone else's possession. This peril is covered on a personal basis through the purchase of a HOMEOWNERS INSURANCE POLICY or *renters insurance* or on a business basis through a SPECIAL MULTIPERIL INSURANCE (SMP) policy. Specialty items such as coin and stamp collections must be specifically scheduled on a property policy in order for the insured to receive full value for a loss.

ROBBERY INSURANCE *see* HOMEOWNERS INSURANCE POLICY; RENTERS INSURANCE; COMMERCIAL PACKAGE POLICY.

ROLLOUT method of terminating a SPLIT DOLLAR LIFE INSURANCE policy by the company transferring its interest in the policy (after the company has effected the largest POLICY LOAN permitted equal to the cash value) to the insured employee. The insured employee, by accepting this transfer, incurs the obligation to continue to service the interest on the policy loan made by the company.

ROLLOVER payment of an employee's EMPLOYEE BENEFIT INSURANCE PLAN benefits to the employee's INDIVIDUAL RETIREMENT ACCOUNT (IRA) or to another plan maintained by the employer.

ROLLOVER AND WITHHOLDING RULES FOR QUALIFIED PLAN DISTRIBUTIONS rules stating that every administrator of a QUALIFIED PENSION PLAN, PROFIT SHARING PLAN, SECTION 401(K) PLAN (SALARY REDUCTION PLAN), SECTION 403(B) PLAN, and stock bonus plan must provide the employee the option to directly roll over all or part of that employee's distribution to an INDIVIDUAL RETIREMENT ACCOUNT (IRA) or to another qualified plan. Any part of the distribution that has not been directly transferred to another qualified plan is subject to a mandatory 20% withholding subject to federal income taxes. Employees have 60 days within which to directly transfer their distribution to another qualified plan. The only distributions that may not be rolled over are the following: (1) periodic payments that continue for at least ten years; (2) minimum required distribution amounts paid to employees who are at least age 70½; and (3) periodic payments made at least annually and based upon the life or joint lives of the employee and the employee's designated beneficiary.

ROLLOVER AND WITHHOLDING RULES FOR QUALIFIED PLAN DISTRIBUTIONS: PAYMENT PAID TO EMPLOYEE

rules stating that, for any portion of the payment made to the employee from an ELIGIBLE ROLLOVER DISTRIBUTION, the plan administrator is required by federal law to withhold 20% of the distribution. The amount withheld is sent to the IRS as income tax withholding to be credited against the employee's tax obligations. If the employee is paid an eligible rollover distribution, the distribution can still be rolled over (in total or in part) into an eligible employer plan or an IRA, provided the rollover is accomplished within 60 days of the time the employee receives the payment. That portion of the distribution that is rolled over will not be subject to taxes until the employee withdraws it from the eligible employer plan or from the IRA. If the employer should receive a distribution before reaching age 59½ and does not roll it over, it will be taxed as ordinary income in the year received, plus an extra tax of 10% of the taxable portion of the distribution must be paid. This extra 10% penalty does not apply to the distribution under the following circumstances: (1) the employee separates from service with the employer during or after the year the employee attains age 55; (2) distribution is paid to the employee in equal payment over the life expectancy of the employee and/or that of the employee's beneficiary; and (3) distribution is paid due to the retirement on disability of the employee.

If the employee receives a lump sum distribution (payment within one year of the employee's total funds on deposit under the EMPLOYEE BENEFIT INSURANCE PLAN because the employee has attained age 59½, or has separated from the employer's service; or if self-employed, has reached age 59½ or has become disabled) after having participated in the plan for at least five years, the distribution is subject to special tax treatment as follows: (1) Five-Year Averaging; (2) Ten-Year Averaging if the employee was born before January 1, 1936; and (3) long-term capital gain treatment at a rate of 20 percent if the employee was born before January 1, 1936. If the employee desires to roll over 100% of the eligible rollover distribution to an employee benefit insurance plan or IRA, including the 20% withheld for income tax purposes, other funds must be contributed within the 60-day period to replace the 20% withheld (if only 80% of the distribution received is rolled over, the employee must pay ordinary income taxes on the 20% withheld).

ROLLOVER AND WITHHOLDING RULES FOR QUALIFIED PLAN DISTRIBUTIONS: PAYMENT PAID TO SURVIVING SPOUSES AND OTHER BENEFICIARIES

rules that apply to employee distributions (*see* ROLLOVER AND WITHHOLDING RULES FOR QUALIFIED PLAN DISTRIBUTIONS: PAYMENT PAID TO EMPLOYEE) and that also apply to distributions to surviving spouses of employees and other beneficiaries. The surviving spouse can elect to have an ELIGIBLE ROLLOVER DISTRIBUTION paid into a DIRECT ROLLOVER TO AN INDIVIDUAL RETIREMENT ACCOUNT (IRA) or to the surviving spouse. If the distribution is paid directly to the surviving spouse, that spouse may retain it or roll it over into an IRA. Beneficiaries other than the surviving spouse cannot elect a direct rollover, and cannot in turn roll over the distribution. Surviving spouse's and other beneficiaries' distributions are not subject to the additional 10% tax penalty, even if they are under the age of 59½.

ROLLOVER INDIVIDUAL RETIREMENT ACCOUNT individual retirement account (IRA) established to receive distribution of assets from a qualified pension or retirement plan. For example, if employees resign from their jobs and receive a lump sum distribution of $75,000, they may roll it over into an IRA without paying taxes. Rollover IRAs are governed by the same tax rules as other IRAs. They provide a way to maintain the tax-deferred status of distributions from pensions or other qualified plans until an age specified by law, when withdrawals must begin.

ROTH 401 (K) PLAN combination of a traditional SECTION 401(K) PLAN and ROTH INDIVIDUAL RETIREMENT ACCOUNT (IRA). Taxes are paid at the time of the employee's contribution. When the employee withdraws benefits, there is no tax on the principal or earnings if the employee is at least age 59½ and has contributed to the plan for at least five years or more. If the employee makes withdrawls prior to age 59½ or has not contributed to the plan for at least five years, the principal is not taxable, but the earnings on the principal are subject to ordinary income tax plus a 10% premature distribution penalty. Consolidation of a former employer's plan with a current employer's plan is permitted.

ROTH CONVERSION option, effective in 2010, that permits the conversion of a traditional INDIVIDUAL RETIREMENT ACCOUNT (IRA) into a ROTH INDIVIDUAL RETIREMENT ACCOUNT (IRA) regardless of income. Upon conversion to the ROTH IRA, only the earnings on the participant's nondeductible contributions would be subject to income tax. After the conversion, the ROTH IRA gains would accumulate on a tax-free basis, and distributions at retirement would also be on a tax-free basis.

ROTH INDIVIDUAL RETIREMENT ACCOUNT (IRA) separate account created by the Tax Relief Act of 1997 and named after Senator William Roth Jr. of Delaware. A working individual may contribute up to 100% of compensation or $4000. The lesser amount applies for each taxable year; and, the contribution must be made by April 15 (or the tax filing deadline) of the following year. A nonworking spouse can contribute up to $4000. These contributions are subject to compensation limits (not included as compensation is income received from pensions, annuities, or as deferred compensation) for the adjusted gross income (AGI) in the following manner: (1) single individuals with an AGI of less than $99,000 may contribute up to $4000; (2) married individuals filing a joint income tax return with an AGI less than $166,000 may contribute up to $4000; (3) partial contributions may be made by single individuals with an AGI between $99,000 and $114,000 and by married individuals with an AGI between $156,000 and $166,000; and, by married individuals filing separately with an AGI of less than $10,000. These contributions are not deductible for federal income tax purposes. The funds once contributed grow on a tax-free basis. Tax-free withdrawals from this IRA may be made after it has been in existence for at least five years and the individual has reached at least age 59½. If death or permanent disability occurs, tax-free withdrawals can also be made. Tax-free withdrawals up to $10,000 are also permitted for the purchase of a first home. Funds may be withdrawn for educational purposes subject to the payment of income tax, but there is no 10% penalty paid, as is the case with the traditional IRA. There is no maximum age by which the individual must start taking distributions as there is at the age of 70½ with the traditional IRA. Even though contributions are not tax-deductible, these contributions can be withdrawn tax-free at any time while the earnings accumulate on a tax-deferred basis after age 59, provided the funds have been in the account for at least five years. Conversions from a traditional IRA to a Roth IRA may be made provided the IRA owner has an AGI of $100,000 or less. Upon conversion to a Roth IRA, income tax is payable on the taxable portion of the amount converted from the traditional IRA (earnings and deductible contributions). The amount converted from a traditional IRA to a Roth IRA is subject to a 10% tax penalty if withdrawn within five years of the conversion.

RULE 72(t) *see* INTERNAL REVENUE CODE:RULE 72(t).

RULE AGAINST ACCUMULATIONS state laws that prohibit for an unreasonable period of time the accumulation of income under the OPTION MODES OF SETTLEMENT of a LIFE INSURANCE policy unless the BENEFICIARY of the policy is a minor; thus, if the INTEREST OPTION is selected under the optional modes of settlement, the beneficiary must be a minor.

RULE AGAINST PERPETUITIES time limit on the deferred ownership of property such that, 21 years after the property owner dies, the deferred ownership of that property terminates.

RUNNING DOWN CLAUSE coverage in liability insurance for a ship owner in the event of collision with another ship. A running down clause, when added to basic HULL MARINE INSURANCE, protects against liability for damage to the other vessel, its freight and cargo, and for lost income to the other vessel's owner during the time it cannot be used.

RUN-OFF liability of an insurance company for future claims that it expects to pay and for which a reserve has been established.

S

SAFE BURGLARY INSURANCE coverage against a loss resulting from the forcible entry of a safe. In order for this coverage to be applicable, there must be signs of forcible entry into the premises in which the safe is located. *See also* MERCANTILE SAFE BURGLARY INSURANCE.

SAFE DRIVER PLAN procedure for offering reduced auto insurance rates to drivers with good records, and imposing higher rates on bad drivers. Typically, premiums are weighted under a system that assigns points for traffic violations and accidents. The more points awarded during a certain rating period, the higher the premium. Most plans consider violations only during the past two or three years, giving bad drivers who improve their records a chance to reduce their premiums.

SAFETY important means of preventing accidents and injuries. Insurers take corporate safety programs into account when rating workers compensation and other business insurance policies. *See also* ENGINEERING APPROACH; HUMAN APPROACH; LOSS PREVENTION AND REDUCTION.

SAFETY OF ASSETS quality of investments of insurance companies. State insurance regulators establish rules for company investments. Authorized investments vary, depending on whether a company is a life insurer or property casualty company and, in some instances, on whether it is a mutual or stock company. Investments must meet standards for asset type, credit quality, and diversification. Generally, insurance company assets are limited to government securities, bonds, stocks, mortgages, and certain real estate holdings. *See also* ADMITTED ASSETS; LIQUIDITY OF ASSETS; SEPARATE ACCOUNT FUNDING.

SAFETY AUDIT study of an organization's operations, and real and personal property to discover existing and potential HAZARD and the actions needed to render these hazards harmless.

SAFETY MARGIN adjustment made to the statistics in a mortality table to provide an increase in the mortality rates above that expected for life insurance and a decrease in the mortality rates below that expected for annuities.

SAFETY RESPONSIBILITY LAW *see* FINANCIAL RESPONSIBILITY LAW.

SALARY CONTINUATION PLAN arrangement, often funded by life insurance, to continue an employee's salary in the form of payments to a beneficiary for a certain period after the employee's death. The employer itself may be the beneficiary, collecting the death benefit and making payments to the employee's beneficiary.

SALARY DEDUCTION GROUP INSURANCE *see* PAYROLL DEDUCTION INSURANCE; SECTION 401(K) PLAN (SALARY REDUCTION PLAN).

SALARY REDUCTION PLAN *see* SECTION 401(K) PLAN (SALARY REDUCTION PLAN).

SALARY SAVINGS INSURANCE (DEDUCTION OR ALLOTMENT) *see* SECTION 401(K) PLAN (SALARY REDUCTION PLAN).

SALARY SAVINGS PROGRAM *see* PAYROLL DEDUCTION INSURANCE.

SALARY SCALES system whereby benefits in an EMPLOYEE BENEFIT INSURANCE PLAN vary according to the employee's earnings. *See also* DEFINED BENEFIT PLAN; EMPLOYEE STOCK OWNERSHIP PLAN (ESOP) TRUST; GROUP LIFE INSURANCE; PENSION PLAN.

SALES CHARGE commission and expenses by the vendor of the product. *See also* FRONT LOADING; BACK LOAD.

SALESMAN'S SAMPLE FLOATER coverage for sample merchandise while in the custody of a salesperson.

SALES REPRESENTATIVE *see* AGENT; BROKER-AGENT; CAPTIVE AGENT; INDEPENDENT AGENT.

SALVAGE *see* ABANDONMENT AND SALVAGE.

SALVAGE CHARGES expense of recovering property by a salvor. Salvage charges are not provided for in insurance contracts. If the owner and the salvor cannot agree on salvage charges, a court makes a determination based on the value of the salvaged items and the salvor's expenses. Rules governing payment of salvage charges originated in marine insurance but are now used in other policies, such as personal automobile insurance.

SAMPLE item given or sold to a buyer that establishes a standard of quality by which later products will be judged. Since the UNIFORM COMMERCIAL CODE does not distinguish between a sample and a model, a sample may create an implied warranty that all goods will conform to this standard. If other goods shipped later do not meet this standard, the manufacturer may be held liable.

SAMPLE, RANDOM *see* RANDOM SAMPLE.

SAMPLE, REPRESENTATIVE *see* REPRESENTATIVE SAMPLE.

SAMPLING, STRATIFIED RANDOM *see* STRATIFIED RANDOM SAMPLING.

SARBANES-OXLEY ACT OF 2002 legislation whose main purpose is to protect investors by increasing the reliability and accuracy of corporate disclosures so that they are in compliance with both the letter and the spirit of the securities law. The Public Company Accounting Oversight Board is established by the act whose purpose it is to monitor the audit of publicly listed companies that are subject to the SECURITY AND EXCHANGE COMMISSION (SEC) regulations as well as require the companies to register with the oversight board. The act prohibits a registered public accounting firm from performing an audit of the organization (1) if the Chief Executive Office (CEO), Chief Financial Officer (CFO), Controller, or any other person serving in an equivalent position was an employee of the auditing firm for a period of time of one year preceding the audit or (2) if the auditing firm has provided non-audit services, such as management consulting, at the same time the audit is being conducted. Also required under the act, the CEO and the CFO must certify to the best of their knowledge that the annual and quarterly reports do not contain untrue and/or misleading statements and that they have reviewed all of these statements.

SAVINGS *see* SAVINGS ELEMENT, LIFE INSURANCE.

SAVINGS ARE VITAL TO EVERYONE RETIREMENT ACT OF 1997 act that requires the Department of Labor (DOL) to have a formal program to educate the public about the importance of saving for retirement. The DOL is also required to educate the public concerning the characteristics of the various PENSION PLANS. The act requires the President to conduct three national summits on retirement savings in the years 1998, 2001, and 2005.

SAVINGS BANK LIFE INSURANCE (SBLI) low-cost life insurance sold by savings banks in the states of Connecticut, Massachusetts, and New York. SBLI is a popular source of life insurance in these states for two reasons: it is offered in bank lobbies, which makes it convenient; and there are no commissions, as with commercial life insurance, which makes it cheaper. Although banks generally are barred from the insurance business, SBLI was allowed by these three states at the urging of consumer groups. Other states have refused to adopt similar legislation. Maximum policy amounts are limited by state law.

SAVINGS ELEMENT cash value of life insurance that accumulates according to a table in a policy. It reflects premiums in the early years that exceed the *pure cost of protection* during that period. If a policy is surrendered, the policyowner receives the cash surrender value and the insurance ends. This is why a cash value policy can be considered a savings or investment vehicle. Cash value is also the part of a life insurance product used as an investment for an INDIVIDUAL RETIREMENT ACCOUNT (IRA).

SAVINGS ELEMENT, LIFE INSURANCE buildup of policy cash value, as distinguished from the death benefit. A policyholder has a choice between surrendering the policy for its cash surrender value or keeping it in force for its death benefit. The rates of return on cash value policies, such as *whole life insurance*, *universal life,* or *variable life,* depend on schedules in the insurance contract or, in some types of policies, on prevailing interest rates or the performance of an investment portfolio. *See also* CASH SURRENDER VALUE.

SAVINGS INCENTIVE MATCH PLAN FOR EMPLOYEES (SIMPLE PLANS) small business retirement plans created by the

Small Business Job Protection Act of 1996. These plans permit small business owners who have fewer than 100 employees to establish an employee retirement plan. Because the required administration of these plans is much less than that required of traditional plans, the cost is low as compared to traditional plans.

There are two types of simple plans made available under the 1996 act: the simple IRA and the simple 401 (k). Under both simple plans, employers are required to contribute a 3% match for all plan participants' salaries or a 2% match for eligible employees, regardless of whether or not the employees participate in the plan. An exemption to this rule is that under the simple IRA, but not under the simple 401(k), the employer may lower the 3% match to 1% for every two years out of a five-year period of time. Under both simple plans, all employer matches are immediately VESTED in the employees, which is not the case with traditional retirement plans.

The simple IRA must be the only retirement plan provided by the employer and it must exclude any ROLLOVERS from any other non-simple IRA plans. All employees that earn at least $5000 annually must be eligible to participate on a SALARY REDUCTION PLAN basis if so elected by the employees. Contributions to this plan are not subject to federal income tax and are not subject to nondiscrimination or top-heavy rules applicable to qualified plans. Distributions made from the plan prior to age 59½ are subject to a 10% surcharge as a penalty, and, in addition, if that distribution is made during the first two years that the employee is participating in the plan, the surcharge becomes 25% of the amount distributed. Transfer from a simple IRA to a regular IRA is permitted only after the employee has participated in the simple IRA for at least two years. If a transfer is made earlier than the two-year requirement, it is subject to a 25% surcharge. Upon termination of employment, the simple plan becomes a regular IRA provided the two-year rule has expired. Simple IRAs do not allow loans. The HEALTH INSURANCE PORTABILITY AND ACCOUNTABILITY ACT OF 1996 (HIPA ACT) stipulates that the IRA owner is not subject to the 10% penalty for distributions prior to age 59½ if the distributions are used to pay medical expenses in excess of 7.5% of the adjusted gross income.

SAVINGS INCENTIVE MATCH PLAN FOR EMPLOYEES (SIMPLE PLANS) 401(k) PLANS type of SIMPLE RETIREMENT (PENSION) PLAN for employers with no more than 100 employees that can be made part of a SECTION 401 (K) PLAN (SALARY REDUCTION PLAN). The employer may make a tax-deductible contribution on behalf of the employee in an amount of the greater of 15% of employee's annual compensation or the required annual contribution to the SIMPLE RETIREMENT (PENSION) PLAN.

SAVINGS, NEED FOR LIFE INSURANCE *see* SAVINGS ELEMENT, LIFE INSURANCE.

SCHEDULE BOND *see* NAME POSITION BOND; NAME SCHEDULE BOND.

SCHEDULED COVERAGE *see* SCHEDULED POLICY.

SCHEDULED LIMIT specified limit on the dollar amount of coverage for a given loss.

SCHEDULED PERSONAL PROPERTY ENDORSEMENT addition to a HOMEOWNERS INSURANCE POLICY, or other personal or business property policies, to provide extra coverage for listed articles. The standard policy has dollar limits on certain items, such as jewelry, furs, art, or guns. This endorsement allows a policyholder to purchase additional coverage for specific items of property, with each item or group of items, and the amount of coverage, listed.

SCHEDULED POLICY policy permitting an insured to choose desired coverages. These policies are important for items with relatively low limits of coverage under standard property insurance forms. For example, an insured would have to specifically schedule expensive jewelry, furs, and paintings in order to receive full value for a loss.

SCHEDULE FLOATER *see* FLOATER.

SCHEDULE INJURY injury covered under WORKERS COMPENSATION INSURANCE. For every part of the body that may be injured, there is a listed financial sum that will be paid. For example, a right severed index finger in a particular state might be worth X dollars, whereas a right severed toe might be worth Y dollars. The injured employee is entitled to these benefits as a matter of right as established by statutory law.

SCHEDULE OF BENEFITS *see* GROUP HEALTH INSURANCE (Schedule of Benefits).

SCHEDULE OF INSURANCE *see* SCHEDULED POLICY.

SCHEDULE P RESERVE statutory reserve for automobile liability, representing specific dollar estimates for future claims. The NATIONAL ASSOCIATION OF INSURANCE COMMISSIONERS (NAIC) established formulas to project the amount that liability insurers must put aside for unpaid claims. These formulas are based on the assumption that future claims will approximate those paid out in recent years. The name comes from the NAIC convention ANNUAL STATEMENT blank, where it is designated as Schedule P.

SCHEDULE PROPERTY FLOATER *see* FLOATER; PERSONAL ARTICLES INSURANCE; PERSONAL PROPERTY FLOATER.

SCHEDULE Q *see* Q SCHEDULE.

SCHEDULE RATING method of pricing property and liability insurance. It uses charges and credits to modify a class rate based on the special characteristics of the risk. Insurers have been able to develop a schedule of rates because experience has shown a direct relationship between certain physical characteristics and the possibility of loss. For example, for fire insurance, the underwriter might make an additional charge above the standard rate for the class if a building contains a flammable liquid. A credit may be given if it has a sprinkler system. In automobile insurance, a credit might be given for driver education. In life insurance, credit is usually given for a nonsmoker. Schedule rating is commonly used for fire, automobile and workers compensation insurance. *See also* EXPERIENCE RATING; PREMIUM DISCOUNT; RETRO-SPECTIVE RATING.

SCLP *see* SIMPLIFIED COMMERCIAL LINES PORTFOLIO (SCLP).

"S" CORPORATIONS corporations that have elected to be taxed according to the provisions of Subchapter S of the Internal Revenue Code. In order to qualify under these provisions, the corporation can have only one class of stock. By so qualifying, tax is eliminated at the corporate level and the shareholders are taxed on their proportionate share of the corporation's profit. This is important because currently the highest individual income tax rate is lower than the highest corporate income tax rate.

SCREENS system established for checking claims to determine whether they should be paid immediately or checked further for validity.

SEASONAL RISK exposure present only at certain times of the year. For example, resort property faces a business interruption risk only from damage that cannot be repaired in time for the resort season.

SEAWORTHINESS ADMITTED CLAUSE part of a marine cargo policy that exempts the policyholder from vouching for the seaworthiness of the vessel. For example, while a purchaser of HULL MARINE INSURANCE warrants that a ship is in proper condition for a voyage, the purchaser of CARGO INSURANCE, who has no control over the ship's condition, is not expected to vouch for it.

SECONDARY BENEFICIARY *see* BENEFICIARY.

SECONDARY PLAN *see* COORDINATION OF BENEFITS.

SECOND DEATH INSURANCE life insurance policy with a death benefit that is paid only when the second of two insureds dies. No benefits are paid as long as both live or if just one lives.

SECOND-INJURY FUND insurance fund set up by most states to encourage employers to hire handicapped workers. Where workers with existing handicaps suffer further work-related injuries or diseases that result in *total* disability, the employer is responsible for the WORKERS COMPENSATION BENEFIT only for the second injury or disease. The fund makes up the difference between the benefit for total disability and the benefit for the second injury. Second-injury funds are financed through general state revenues or assessments on workers compensation insurers.

SECOND MORTGAGE mortgage loan secured by real estate that already has a first mortgage. In case of default, the claim of the second mortgage holder is subordinate to that of the first mortgage holder. Generally, insurance companies are not permitted by state laws to offer or invest in second mortgages.

SECOND SURPLUS REINSURANCE amount of REINSURANCE accepted by a second REINSURER which is in excess of the original insurer's retention limit and the first reinsurer's first surplus treaty's limit. *See also* RETENTION AND LIMITS CLAUSE, SURPLUS REINSURANCE.

SECOND-TO-DIE *see* SECOND DEATH INSURANCE.

SECTION 79 PLAN group *whole life* insurance policy designed to reduce an employee's exposure to income tax on the value of life insurance provided by the employer. The policy separates the term element from the cash value element, and apportions part of the premium to each. The plan takes advantage of the tax exemption to employees on a specified amount of group term insurance plans and the special tax rate on the premium for the amount of insurance over that amount.

SECTION 101 (a) (1) OF THE INTERNAL REVENUE CODE section of the code that qualifies that the death benefit paid under a life insurance policy is received by the BENEFICIARY income-tax free. These tax consequences apply regardless of the size of the CASH VALUE of the policy, total premiums paid, who the POLICYOWNER may be, who the INSURED may be, who the premium payor may be, or who the beneficiary may be.

SECTION 105 OF THE INTERNAL REVENUE CODE federal statute that permits the self-employed a 100% tax deduction for the family health care expenses to include HEALTH INSURANCE premiums, DISABILITY INCOME insurance premiums, and LONG-TERM CARE insurance premiums. Also deductible on a 100% basis are noninsured medical, dental, and vision care expenses.

SECTION 105 MEDICAL REIMBURSEMENT PLAN eligible employees reimbursed from the employer for family health care expenses paid by those employees to include HEALTH INSURANCE premiums, DISABILITY INCOME insurance premiums, and LONG-TERM CARE insurance premiums. Also reimbursable to the employees from the employer are non-insured medical expenses. The employer receives a 100% tax deduction for this reimbursement.

SECTION 125 PLANS (CAFETERIA PLANS) additions made by Congress in 1978 to the Internal Revenue Code that provide an employee benefit plan under which the employee makes an irrevocable decision to forego a portion of future income in exchange for receiving future benefits not subject to income tax at reception date. The employer deducts the cost of the employee's future benefits from present income as a business expense. These plans usually provide three options:

1. *Premium Conversion*—Employee contributes a proportionate share of the family health care costs with pre-tax dollars.
2. *Medical Reimbursement Account*—Employee is able to use a SALARY REDUCTION PLAN to pay with dollars on a pre-tax basis for medical expenses not covered by insurance; a separate medical reimbursement account is established for each employee.

3. *Dependent Care Reimbursement Account*—Employee is able to use a salary reduction plan to pay with dollars on a pre-tax basis for dependent care expenses.

An additional option sometimes provided for employees only (family members are excluded) is TERM LIFE INSURANCE for an amount up to $50,000 and DISABILITY INCOME INSURANCE. All employees must have equal access to the plans whether they are highly compensated or nonhighly compensated employees. Any monies left in the employee's account not used by the end of the year revert back to the company; this is known as the *Use It or Lose It* rule. As the employee incurs expenses, that employee applies for reimbursement through a form attached to the bill. When the administrator of the plan issues a check to the employee for the expenses, a statement is also provided that shows the amount remaining in the employee's account.

SECTION 401 (a) PLAN retirement plan offered by school systems to select teachers (such as science and mathematics who are hard to recruit). These plans are on an employer match basis on the amounts the employees have deferred to the SECTION 403 (b) PLAN.

SECTION 401 (h) PENSION PLAN TRUST trust established under the auspices of the Internal Revenue Code that permits the maintenance of a separate account within the employer's DEFINED BENEFIT PENSION PLAN from which to pay the employee's life insurance and medical expense costs. Contributions to this account are tax deductible, and the investment's earnings accumulate on a tax deferred basis.

SECTION 401 (k) PLAN (SALARY REDUCTION PLAN) employer sponsored retirement savings program named for the section of the Internal Revenue Code that permits it. These plans allow employees to invest pre-tax dollars that are often matched in some portion by employers. Because of their flexibility, 401 (k)s became a popular employee benefit during the 1980s. But the TAX REFORM ACT OF 1986 limited their use as short-term savings plans by imposing a 10% penalty on all money withdrawn before retirement. It also reduced the maximum annual contribution from $30,000 to $7000 and tightened nondiscrimination rules. Employees may still borrow the money, however, and pay themselves interest.

SECTION 401(K) PLAN (SELF-EMPLOYED ONE PERSON) type of plan that has the ability to contribute more than twice the maximum on traditional self-employed retirement plans and allows an extra contribution if self-employed is at least age 50. Self-employed who borrow from the plan must pay back this amount within five years. A person may roll over other retirement plan balances into this plan. This plan is covered by the EMPLOYEE RETIREMENT INCOME SECURITY ACT OF 1974, and thus its assets are protected from claims of bankruptcy and creditors.

SECTION 401(k) PLAN SWITCHBACKS (KSOPs) device that allows plan participants in EMPLOYEE STOCK OWNERSHIP PLAN (ESOP) TRUST to reinvest the dividends into their SECTION 401(K) PLAN. Under the switchback approach, plan participants are permitted to select whether they wish to reinvest their dividends paid on the company's stock into the KSOP on a tax-deferred basis or take the dividends in cash and be subject to ordinary income tax. If the plan participant elects to reinvest the dividends into the KSOP, the participant's contribution to the Section 401(k) is reduced by the amount of the dividend. The KSOP concept allows dividends to be retained in the retirement plan and permits the plan participant to increase the amount of his or her contribution into the plan by the amount of dividends reinvested.

SECTION 403 (b) PLAN retirement plan offered by public employers and tax-exempt organizations. Under Section 403(b) of the Internal Revenue Code, certain tax-exempt organizations such as public school systems can make payments for retirement annuity policies for their employees and have the payments excluded from the employees' gross income for tax purposes, subject to certain limitations.

SECTION 404 (c) OF THE EMPLOYEE RETIREMENT INCOME SECURITY ACT OF 1974 section of the act stating that regulation requires employers to offer plan participants at least three diversified investment choices. Each choice must have materially different risk and return characteristics. Participants must be given the opportunity to switch from one fund to another on at least a quarterly basis. Also, employers must provide sufficient information for participants to make informed investment decisions.

SECTION 408 (k) PLAN section of the Internal Revenue Code that provides for SIMPLIFIED EMPLOYEE PENSIONS (SEP).

SECTION 412 (I) PLAN type of qualified retirement plan (DEFINED BENEFIT PLAN) that is entirely funded by a GUARANTEED INVESTMENT CONTRACT (GIC); ANNUITY; LIFE INSURANCE policy; or a combination thereof. The retirement benefit is specified in advance and funded by the guaranteed rates in the GIC, annuity, or life insurance policy.

SECTION 457 DEFERRED COMPENSATION PLAN plan in which a public employer (such as a university, state, county, or municipality) sponsors a retirement savings program, named for the section of the Internal Revenue Code that permits it. This plan allows the employer, upon agreement with the employee, to reduce the employee's salary by a specific amount and invest this amount, with pre-tax dollars, in various financial instruments. Upon termination of employment, the principal amount invested and any investment earnings are distributed to the terminating employee or the employee's estate. A deferred FIXED DOLLAR ANNUITY or VARIABLE DOLLAR ANNUITY are among the financial instruments that can be used to fund this plan.

SECTION 501 (c) (9) VOLUNTARY EMPLOYEES BENEFICIARY ASSOCIATION (VEBA) trust established under the Internal Revenue Service code that is used to provide accident and sickness benefits to member employees.

SECTION 529 PLANS (QUALIFIED TUITION PLANS) state-sponsored tax advantaged deferred plans that have as their objective to help families pay for higher education expenses. A parent, grandparent, relative, or any other person who desires to contribute funds for the future higher education expenses of a beneficiary may establish these accounts. Although contributions are not federally tax deductible, these accounts grow on a tax-deferred basis. The student withdraws the account's earnings on a tax-free basis as established by the Pension Protection Act when used to pay for the qualified higher education expenses (tuition, room, board, books, fees, supplies, and equipment). The instate plans (state residents contribute to a plan sponsored by their state of residence) provide numerous benefits to include: withdrawals on a state tax-free basis, contributions made on a state tax deduction basis, protection of the plan's assets from creditors, and in some cases, matching scholarships. There are two types of these tuition plans: (1) prepaid plan that typically provides fixed returns correlated to increases in higher education expenses where future tuition, based on current costs, is stipulated; and (2) savings plans that typically provide market returns based on the underlying portfolio of the plan. For nonqualified withdrawals, ordinary income tax plus 10% federal penalty on earnings goes into effect. Each contributor to the plan can contribute up to $60,000 ($120,000 for a married couple) on behalf of each beneficiary's plan in one year without triggering a federal gift tax by electing to treat the entire contribution as a series of five annual gifts and filing a gift tax return for the year in which this contribution is made. There are no income-based limits on participation in these plans. If the child for whom the plan has been established does not go to an institution of higher leaning, the account balance can be transferred to other family member siblings and/or cousins. Contributors can invest in any state's plan regardless of the state of residence. Beneficiary of the plan can attend any U.S. institution of higher learning.

SECTION 1035 EXCHANGE section of the Internal Revenue Code that provides for the taking of the proceeds from one LIFE INSURANCE policy or ANNUITY and the reinvesting of these proceeds immediately in another life insurance policy or annuity of the same type without being required to pay a tax on any gain. This exchange should be handled by the seller of the REPLACEMENT, LIFE INSURANCE policy or annuity.

SECTION 2503 (c) OF THE INTERNAL REVENUE CODE section of the code that qualifies the establishment of a trust for minors under which income can be accumulated until the minor reaches age 21. At that point, the accumulated income can be disbursed and the $10,000 annual GIFT TAX EXCLUSION for each beneficiary can be utilized.

SECTION 4958 OF THE INTERNAL REVENUE CODE portion of a
federal law that imposes a penalty excise tax on an EXCESS BENEFIT
TRANSACTION of 25% of the excess benefit on the person from inside
the organization (DISQUALIFIED PERSON) receiving the benefit. Also
imposed is a penalty excise tax of 10% of the excess benefit on the
manager within the organization awarding the excess benefit. If this
excess amount is not repaid to the tax-exempt organization within a
reasonable period of time, the disqualified person incurs an additional
tax penalty of 200% of the excess benefit received.

SECTION 7702 OF THE INTERNAL REVENUE CODE restrictions
on the investment feature of life insurance by mandating minimum
death benefits and/or limiting the permitable premiums paid into the
policy. This section uses two tests in determining whether a life insurance policy qualifies, in fact, as a life insurance policy under the INTER-
NAL REVENUE CODE. Both tests have a maximum limit on the size of the
premiums paid and/or cash value in order for the policy to qualify as
life insurance and thus be subject to the advantageous tax benefits.

SECULAR TRUST [402(b)] (NONEXEMPT TRUST) NONQUALIFIED
PLAN of DEFERRED COMPENSATION whose goal is to compensate KEY
EMPLOYEES without having to provide similar benefits to rank and file
employees. The TRUST is irrevocable, and funds placed in it are protected against claims made by the company's creditors. Even though
funds in this trust are not in the employee's possession, they are
deemed by the Internal Revenue Service to have been constructively
received by the employee. The company is allowed to take an income
tax deduction for the funds it contributed to the trust, even though
these funds have not been distributed to the employee while he or she
has current taxable income. At the time funds from the trust are actually distributed, the employee is taxed only to the extent that these distributions are from earnings of the trust or from current trust income,
which will allow the employee to pay taxes owed as the result of the
company's contributions to the trust. The employer is not taxed on the
trust income: the employee pays all taxes on this income. For example,
assume that the company is in the 34% tax bracket and contributed
$40,000 to the trust on behalf of John Employee, who is in the 28%
tax bracket. The result is that John Employee will have an $11,200 tax
liability ($40,000 × 28%) and the company will incur a $13,600 tax
deduction ($40,000 × 34%). In order that John Employee will have the
necessary funds to pay the taxes owed, the company usually will
bonus him the $11,200 required, which of course is tax deductible as
a business expense for the company.

SECURED CREDITOR creditor with a documented claim on a specific
asset of a *debtor. See also* COLLATERAL BORROWER; COLLATERAL CRED-
ITOR (ASSIGNEE).

SECURED LIEN *see* COLLATERAL BORROWER; COLLATERAL CREDITOR
(ASSIGNEE); SECURED CREDITOR.

SECURE MONEY ANNUITY OR RETIREMENT TRUST (SMART) proposed new small business pension plan advocated in President Clinton's administration's fiscal year 1999 budget. This plan would be made available to small businesses with 100 or fewer employees that do not currently provide employees with a DEFINED BENEFIT PLAN or a DEFINED CONTRIBUTION PLAN (MONEY PURCHASE PLAN). In order to qualify for this new pension plan, neither a defined benefit plan nor a defined contribution plan could have been offered by the business to its employees during the previous five years.

SECURITIES *see* SECURITIES AND EXCHANGE COMMISSION (SEC); SECURITIES BOND; SECURITIES INVESTOR PROTECTION CORPORATION (SIPC).

SECURITIES ACT OF 1933 landmark legislation passed by Congress providing the first regulation of the securities markets. The law, enforced by the SECURITIES AND EXCHANGE COMMISSION (SEC), requires registration of securities issues and disclosure of material information about the financial condition of the issuers. *Variable annuity* and VARIABLE LIFE INSURANCE policies have been determined to be securities under the terms of this law and thus are subject to regulation both by the SEC and by state insurance departments.

SECURITIES AND EXCHANGE COMMISSION (SEC) federal agency that regulates the securities markets. The independent, five-member commission was created under the Securities Exchange Act of 1934 to enforce the SECURITIES ACT OF 1933. Members are appointed by the president and serve five-year terms. The SEC has responsibility to regulate securities exchanges and markets, to set disclosure and accounting rules for most issuers of corporate securities, and to oversee securities firms, investment companies, and investment advisers.

SECURITIES AND EXCHANGE COMMISSION (SEC) DIVISION OF CORPORATION FINANCE one of four SEC divisions that administers the procedure through which public companies must disclose all relevant material in order that a potential investor might make an informed decision.

SECURITIES AND EXCHANGE COMMISSION (SEC) DIVISION OF ENFORCEMENT one of four SEC divisions that enforces the federal securities laws in federal courts and before SEC's administrative law judges by bringing actions for violations.

SECURITIES AND EXCHANGE COMMISSION (SEC) DIVISION OF INVESTMENT MANAGEMENT one of four SEC divisions charged with regulating investment companies, investment advisors, and variable insurance products. The SEC requires variable insurance products to register with the SEC by filing a registration statement. This statement must include a prospectus, financial statement, exhibits, and a statement of any additional relevant information. This division is permitted to provide interpretive advice for laws and rulings that may seem to be unclear. This division also has the authority to grant exemptions from the SEC laws and rules if the insurance product does not fit within the regulatory parameters that it administers.

SECURITIES AND EXCHANGE COMMISSION (SEC) DIVISION OF MARKET REGULATION one of four SEC divisions that regulates the securities markets and the participants within these markets.

SECURITIES AND EXCHANGE COMMISSION (SEC) RULE 2821 rule that requires a suitability obligation by the seller on behalf of the purchaser of a VARIABLE DOLLAR ANNUITY. This obligation mandates that the seller sign documentation verifying that he or she has accomplished the following:

1. Has informed the purchaser of the principles of the variable annuity.

2. Believes that the purchaser would benefit from the unique characteristics of the variable annuity such as tax-deferred growth of the investment and life income.

3. Believes that the purchaser understands the principles of the subaccounts and would benefit from the investments in the subaccount.

4. Believes that any exchanges of an existing ANNUITY for this variable annuity would benefit the purchaser. The purchaser would not be adversely affected by a SURRENDER CHARGE or loss of current annuity benefits, incur increased charges and fees, and enter a new subscriber period.

5. Believes that the purchaser would benefit from the variable annuity's new features not present on a currently owned annuity.

6. Believes that the purchaser has not exchanged other variable annuities within 36 months of the current purchase.

SECURITIES AND EXCHANGE COMMISSION (SEC) STAFF ACCOUNTING BULLETIN NO. 92 (SAB92) bulletin issued June, 1993, with disclosure requirements that strongly suggest that insurance companies establish reserves or add to current reserves for asbestos and environmental risks to the insured.

SECURITIES BOND forgery insurance covering securities issues such as stocks and bonds. They protect the issuer of securities against forgery of the securities.

SECURITIES INVESTOR PROTECTION CORPORATION (SIPC) federal insurance fund that protects assets in client accounts held by registered securities broker-dealers. The SIPC is a nonprofit corporation created by Congress in 1970 under the Securities Investor Protection Act. Membership in SIPC is mandatory for all broker-dealers registered with the SECURITIES AND EXCHANGE COMMISSION and with the national stock exchanges. When the SIPC is unsuccessful in finding a healthy firm to acquire a failed brokerage, it pays off account holders of the failed brokerage for losses up to the coverage limit. Maximum coverage for cash and securities in a customer's account is $500,000, with a limit of $100,000 on the amount of cash that is insured.

SECURITIES VALUATION RESERVE *see* VALUATION RESERVE (SECURITIES VALUATION RESERVE).

SECURITIZATION process of converting assets into securities. Typically, a financial institution will convert illiquid assets such as receivables into liquid assets such as bonds by pooling or packaging the illiquid asset class. This converted liquid asset class is then sold to investors. Investors will purchase this liquid asset because of interest and principal payments.

SECURITIZED BOND TRANSACTIONS (SECURITIZING CATASTROPHE RISK/SECURITIZING INSURANCE RISK) method of accessing capital by the insurance industry in order to hedge against a future catastrophic occurrence. The mechanism works as follows: Primary insurance company AJAX pays a premium to purchase a CATASTROPHE REINSURANCE contract from REINSURANCE company BJAX. Reinsurance company BJAX then sells its bonds in an amount equal to the catastrophe reinsurance contract issued to insurance company AJAX. The proceeds from the bonds sold by BJAX are then placed in a trust to securitize the reinsurance contract. Interest is earned on the proceeds placed in the trust; the proceeds are usually invested in United States Treasury issues. If AJAX does not have any reinsurance claims, the purchasers of the bonds receive the return of the amount they have invested (safely on deposit in the trust) plus interest earned. If AJAX does have a reinsurance claim, the claim is paid out of the trust with the payment coming from the initial amount invested in the bonds plus interest earned. The investors in the bonds incur a bond default. The rating of these bonds uses the same criteria as used for all types of bonds, whether corporate or government, that is the probability of default. Just like any other type of bond, whether corporate or government, the price of the bond and thus the yield increases or decreases subject to market conditions.

SECURITY VALUATION rules used by state regulators to value securities on the books of insurance companies. Bonds with acceptable credit quality are carried at *amortized value,* which is the face value plus or minus the amount of any purchase discount or premium, as amortized over the life of the bond. Preferred stock is valued at cost and COMMON STOCK INVESTMENTS at year-end market price. Valuations for impaired securities such as bonds in default are determined by the Committee on Valuation of Securities of the NATIONAL ASSOCIATION OF INSURANCE COMMISSIONERS (NAIC). *See also* MANDATORY SECURITIES VALUATION RESERVE.

SEGREGATION OF EXPOSURE UNITS risk management practice designed to control losses by physically separating assets or operations (on separating a single exposure unit into various parts) to reduce maximum potential loss. The objective of such a separation is to reduce the risk of loss to the whole exposure unit through dispersion. For example, two related chemical processing operations, both subject to loss from explosion or fire, would be built a sufficient distance apart—perhaps even on separate premises—so that the explosion of one would not damage the other.

SELECTION *see* SELECTION OF RISK.

SELECTION, ADVERSE *see* ADVERSE SELECTION.

SELECTION OF RISK *see* RISK SELECTION; UNDERWRITING.

SELECT MORTALITY TABLE MORTALITY TABLE that includes data only on people who have recently purchased life insurance. Experience shows that such people have a lower mortality rate in the years immediately following their purchase of insurance than those who have been insured for some time, probably because they have recently passed medical and other tests, and because they are younger. For example, a select mortality table would show the number of deaths per 1000 of individuals age 30 who have been insured for one year. An ULTIMATE MORTALITY TABLE shows the rate of the group, exclusive of the initial period after the purchase of insurance. An AGGREGATE MORTALITY TABLE includes all data.

SELF-ADMINISTERED PLAN qualified pension or other employee benefit where responsibility rests with an employer rather than an insurer. A TRUST FUND plan, where assets are deposited with and invested by a trustee, is the most common self-administered plan. A TRUST AGREEMENT governs the plan administration and retirees are paid benefits from the trust or the *trustee* buys annuities for them. The self-administered, or trust fund plan, contrasts with the insured (insurance company) pension plan.

SELF-DIRECTED ACCOUNT type of INDIVIDUAL RETIREMENT ACCOUNT (IRA) allowed by the EMPLOYEES RETIREMENT INCOME SECURITY ACT OF 1974 (ERISA) in which contributions are paid into a custodial account sponsored by a bank or stockbroker. The owner of the account selects the types of investments into which the contributions are made.

SELF FUNDING *see* SELF INSURANCE.

SELF-INFLICTED INJURY intentional injury caused by the person injured. For life and health insurance purposes, self-inflicted injury typically is not covered by accident policies, because it is intentional, not an accident. This applies for WORKERS COMPENSATION INSURANCE purposes as well. However, for life insurance purposes, suicide is covered after the policy has been in force for two years.

SELF INSURANCE protecting against loss by setting aside one's own money. This can be done on a mathematical basis by establishing a separate fund into which funds are deposited on a periodic basis. Through self insurance it is possible to protect against high-FREQUENCY, low-*severity* losses. To do this through an insurance company would mean having to pay a premium that includes loadings for the company's general expenses, cost of putting the policy on the books, acquisition expenses, premium taxes, and contingencies.

SELF-INSURED EXCESS PLAN plan for excess layer(s) of insurance coverage over the primary coverage, for example, if a corporation buys $8 million as excess above a $2 million SELF INSURANCE retention level. Excess coverage can be purchased from either a PRIMARY INSURER or a REINSURER. Before deciding on a self-insurance plan, the corporation should review its past loss experience according to pattern, timing, and types, as well as its current financial position.

SELF-INSURED RETENTION (SIR) portion of a property or liability loss retained by a policyholder. Most policyholders do not purchase insurance to cover their entire exposure. Rather, they elect to take a deductible, or portion that they will cover themselves. For example, a homeowner may purchase $150,000 worth of insurance with a $500 deductible for certain losses, such as roof damage by hail. The $500 deductible is one form of self insurance. It means the homeowner will cover all losses for that amount or less. *See also* SELF INSURANCE.

SELF-INSURER *see* SELF INSURANCE; SELF-INSURED RETENTION (SIR).

SELF-PROCURED INSURANCE policy purchased by the insured from a NONADMITTED INSURER. This policy can be purchased directly from the insurer by the insured.

SELF-REGULATION action by insurance companies and agents to voluntarily refrain from business conduct that is misleading, fraudulent, and in general would have adverse consequences for the purchaser of the insurance product.

SELF RETAINED LIMIT provision in an UMBRELLA LIABILITY INSURANCE policy that requires the INSURED to pay a DEDUCTIBLE before policy makes a claim payment on behalf of the insured.

SELF-SELECTION effort of a poor risk to seek insurance coverage. The onset of a health problem such as heart disease, for example, may prompt a person to apply for life insurance before seeking medical treatment. Such applicants, if not screened out, would weight the insured pool toward bad risks. The UNDERWRITING process is intended to counter the natural tendency toward self-selection among insurance applicants, either by requiring higher rates for poorer risks or by denying them coverage. *See also* ADVERSE SELECTION.

SELF-TRUSTEED TRUST arrangement in which individuals serve as trustees of their own LIVING TRUST and name another party (successor trustee) to manage the assets if they should become incapacitated. In this type of trust, individuals are assured that their assets will continue to be managed as desired without interruption.

SELLING AGENTS' COMMISSION INSURANCE coverage that provides for the indemnification of a salesperson for the amount of his or her lost commission on a product to be sold that cannot be produced because of damage incurred by the manufacturer or that, once produced, cannot be delivered by the manufacturer because of damage incurred. *See also* CONTINGENT BUSINESS INTERRUPTION FORM.

SELLING PRICE CLAUSE property insurance coverage available to businesses that pays the established market (sales) value of products that are damaged rather than simply their lower (production) cost. This fills the gap between ACTUAL CASH VALUE, which provides coverage only for the cost to the insured, and BUSINESS INTERRUPTION INSURANCE. For manufacturers, it covers the cost of all finished goods; for mercantile firms, it applies only to goods that have been sold but are not yet delivered.

SEMIENDOWMENT INSURANCE modified ENDOWMENT INSURANCE policy under which the insured receives one-half the DEATH BENEFIT as the MATURITY VALUE of the policy.

SENIOR CITIZENS' FREEDOM TO WORK ACT OF 2000 legislation that enables working beyond the NORMAL RETIREMENT AGE without losing retirement income from Social Security for each dollar earned. When the employee continues to work beyond the normal retirement age while receiving social security benefits, the Social Security Administration will review the employee's record to determine any change in retirement income.

SEPARATE ACCOUNT *see* SPLIT FUNDED PLAN.

SEPARATE ACCOUNT FUNDING *see* SPLIT FUNDED PLAN.

SEPARATE ACCOUNT GUARANTEED INVESTMENT CONTRACT (GIC) type of GUARANTEED INVESTMENT CONTRACT in which funds for the contract are placed in the insurance company's separate account.

SEPARATE PROPERTY property acquired before marriage—by gift, by inheritance, or bought with separate monies.

SERIES EE SAVINGS BONDS bonds sold at a discount from their face value; accumulated interest paid at maturity, as in the case of ZERO COUPON BONDS. Interest rate minimum is guaranteed with the prevailing interest rate adjusted semiannually. As with all U.S. Treasury issues, interest earned on these bonds is exempt from state and local taxes. Federal income tax on the interest earned does not have to be prepaid until the bonds reach maturity.

SERIES OF CATASTROPHES hazard covered under *catastrophe reinsurance*. This form of EXCESS OF LOSS REINSURANCE protects the CEDING COMPANY for loss above the *retention* limit caused by multiple catastrophic events. *See also* CATASTROPHE HAZARD; CATASTROPHE LOSS.

SERIOUS INJURY FREQUENCY RATE number of serious injuries per 1,000,000 employee-hours worked. *See also* FREQUENCY.

SERVICE ADJUSTMENT change in YEARS OF SERVICE credited to employee in calculating pension benefits and other employee benefits.

SERVICE BENEFIT *see* SERVICE PLANS.

SERVICE INSURER AGREEMENT arrangement whereby an insurance company agrees to pay specified health care service vendors a predetermined sum for providing such services to the covered individuals. *See also* BLUE CROSS; BLUE SHIELD.

SERVICEMEN'S GROUP LIFE INSURANCE (SGLI) U.S. government group term life insurance for male and female members of the federal uniformed forces on active duty, underwritten by private insurance companies. Premiums reflect peacetime mortality rates for this group, with any additional costs of military risks (such as wartime exposure) being borne by the federal government. Upon discharge, SGLI policies can be converted either to five-year nonrenewable term VETERANS GROUP LIFE INSURANCE (VGLI) or to a permanent policy at the veteran's attained age (at higher cost) with one of the commercial insurance companies participating in the servicemen's plan.

SERVICE PLANS types of insurance coverage under which health care benefits are provided to the covered individuals instead of monetary reimbursement for health care expenses. *See also* BLUE CROSS; BLUE SHIELD.

SERVICES OFFERED POLICYHOLDERS range of administrative and risk management services that can be purchased by an insured. Increasingly, insurance can be purchased UNBUNDLED so that policyholders may pay for straight coverage without available services. However, some policyholders may want to purchase from the insurer additional services such as loss control, claims adjustment, captive management, or other services.

SETBACK *see* AGE SETBACK.

SET CLAUSE (PAIR OR SET CLAUSE) provision in many business and personal policies that loss or damage to one of a pair or set of individual items does not represent the loss of the pair or set. For example, the loss of one diamond earring would not entitle an insured to be reimbursed for a pair of earrings, but for only the resulting decrease in the overall pre-loss value of the pair.

SETTLEMENT disposition of a claim or policy benefit. Policies may specify time limits for payment of claims or benefits and designate various methods of settlement at the option of the insurer or the insured. *See also* OPTIONAL MODES OF SETTLEMENT; SETTLEMENT OPTIONS; PROPERTY AND CASUALTY INSURANCE.

SETTLEMENT AGREEMENT *see* OPTIONAL MODES OF SETTLEMENT; PROPERTY AND CASUALTY INSURANCE; SETTLEMENT OPTIONS.

SETTLEMENT ARRANGEMENT *see* LIFE INSURANCE; OPTIONAL MODES OF SETTLEMENT; PROPERTY AND CASUALTY INSURANCE; SETTLEMENT OPTIONS.

SETTLEMENT OPTIONS, LIFE INSURANCE *see* OPTIONAL MODES OF SETTLEMENT.

SETTLEMENT OPTIONS, PROPERTY AND CASUALTY INSURANCE methods for payment of the value of a policy. An insurance company can select one of three options in settlement of a loss: (1) make a cash payment; (2) take possession of damaged or destroyed property and replace it with property of like kind and quality; or (3) repair the property so that it is restored to its structural condition prior to the loss, and return the repaired property to the insured. Usually insurance companies settle losses by a cash payment to the insured.

SEUA *see* SOUTH-EASTERN UNDERWRITERS ASSOCIATION (SEUA) CASE.

SEVEN-YEAR VESTING (GRADED VESTING) type of VESTING schedule in a RETIREMENT PLAN that provides 20% vesting after three years of recognized service with the employer, 40% after four years, 60% after five years, 80% after six years, then 100% after seven years. With the passage of the PENSION PROTECTION ACT OF 2006, employer nonelective contributions as well as employer matching contributions vest according to either the minimum three-year Cliff or six-year graded vesting schedule: year 1 = 0% vesting, year 2 = 20% vested, year 3 = 40% vested, year 4 = 60% vested, year 5 = 80% vested, year 6 = 100% vested.

SEVERABILITY OF INSURANCE application of coverage on a separate individual basis to each INSURED covered under the POLICY.

SEVERITY *see* SEVERITY RATE.

SEVERITY RATE size of the losses used as a factor in calculating *premium rates*. For example, the U.S. Bureau of Labor Statistics studies the number of days lost by injured employees per million person-hours worked. *See also* FREQUENCY AND DISTRIBUTION OF LOSSES.

SEX demographic designation used in life insurance to calculate *premium rates* for life and health insurance and annuity contracts. Since females have a longer LIFE EXPECTANCY than males of the same age, life insurance premiums for females are lower than for males of the same age. Annuity income for females, by the same token, is lower than for males of the same age. These differences are being contested.

SEX DISCRIMINATION classification of insured life and health risks based on the sex of the proposed insured. Gender has long been one of many factors in classifying, accepting, and rating risks. For example, because experience shows that women live longer than men, life insurance rates for women are lower. By the same token, annuity payments are lower for women because it is expected that they will be paid out for more years. On the other hand, women have sometimes paid lower rates for auto insurance. Insurance rating by sex became an issue in the early 1980s when many women charged that it was discriminatory. They demanded through UNISEX LEGISLATION to be rated no differently. Although insurers have resisted it, individual states have passed laws prohibiting the use of sex in risk classification. *See also* RISK CLASSIFICATION.

SFP *see* FIRE INSURANCE—STANDARD FIRE POLICY.

SHARED MARKET *see* AUTOMOBILE ASSIGNED RISK INSURANCE PLAN; RESIDUAL DISABILITY; RESIDUAL DISABILITY INCOME INSURANCE.

SHARE REINSURANCE *see* PROPORTIONAL REINSURANCE; QUOTA SHARE REINSURANCE; SURPLUS REINSURANCE.

SHERMAN ANTITRUST ACT 1890 law prohibiting monopolies and restraint of trade in interstate commerce. The Sherman Act was strengthened in 1914 with amendments known as the Clayton Act that added further prohibitions against price-fixing conspiracies. These federal antitrust laws at first were not applied to the insurance industry because of the 1869 Supreme Court ruling in PAUL V. VIRGINIA that insurance was not commerce and thus not subject to federal regulation. After the SOUTH-EASTERN UNDERWRITERS ASSOCIATION (SEUA) CASE in 1944 and passage of the MCCARRAN-FERGUSON ACT (PUBLIC LAW 15) in 1945, Congress made it clear that states would retain the power to regulate insurance but price-fixing and restraint of trade not sanctioned by state laws and regulations would be subject to federal antitrust prosecution.

SHIP INSURANCE, PLEASURE CRAFT AND COMMERCIAL *see* MARINE INSURANCE.

SHIPPERS RADIOACTIVE CONTAMINATION INSURANCE coverage for shippers of certain radioactive materials, such as medical or commercial isotopes, for direct loss or damage by radioactive contamination; does not cover transport of radioactive waste or nuclear reactor fuel. Coverage has two forms: one for transport on common carriers and the other for transport on vehicles operated by or for an insured. *See also* MOTOR TRUCK CARGO RADIOACTIVE CONTAMINATION INSURANCE; NUCLEAR ENERGY LIABILITY INSURANCE; RADIOACTIVE CONTAMINATION INSURANCE.

SHIPPING INSURANCE *see* INLAND MARINE INSURANCE (TRANSPORTATION INSURANCE): BUSINESS RISKS.

SHOCK LOSS loss so catastrophic in nature that the insurance company will experience a significant UNDERWRITING LOSS. Protection against such an event can be purchased through various REINSURANCE instruments. *See also* REINSURANCE, PROPERTY AND CASUALTY—CASUALTY CATASTROPHE.

SHORE CLAUSE provision in MARINE INSURANCE listing onshore perils covered. In the case of marine cargo, these may include such occurrences as damage from flooding, sprinklers, collapse of docks, and wharf or warehouse fires. It may also cover damage from accidents during ground transportation.

SHORT PERIOD INSURANCE coverage for less than one year in duration.

SHORT RATE CANCELLATION cancellation by the insured of a property or disability insurance policy for which the returned unearned premium is diminished by administration costs incurred when the insurance company placed the policy on its books.

SHORT RATE PREMIUM premium charge for a policy that is going to be in force for less than the normal period of time.

SHORT RATE, SHORT TERM INSURANCE coverage for less than one year. Insurers generally charge higher rates for short-term policies than for longer term insurance, such as an ANNUAL POLICY, because of (1) the need to recoup relatively fixed administrative and processing costs over a shorter policy life; and (2) the likelihood of ADVERSE SELECTION, with buyers seeking insurance only at times of the year when they know they face greatest likelihood of loss.

SHORT RATE TABLE display of percentage of earned premiums as a function of the time in days for term property insurance policies originally written for one year or longer. These tables are used to compute the refund or the excess of the paid premium above the customary short rate for the expired term in the event the INSURED cancels the policy (makes a SHORT RATE CANCELLATION).

SHORT TERM DISABILITY INCOME INSURANCE *see* DISABILITY INCOME INSURANCE.

SHORT TERM INSURANCE *see* SHORT PERIOD INSURANCE.

SHORT TERM POLICY *see* SHORT RATE, SHORT TERM INSURANCE.

SHORT TERM REVERSIONARY TRUST financial instrument established irrevocably for a minimum of 10 years, after which the principal reverts to the grantor upon termination of the trust. A key feature is that earnings from the principal traditionally have been taxed at the beneficiary's tax rate instead of the presumably higher tax rate of the grantor. An example is the CLIFFORD TRUST commonly used to save for a child's college expenses. Another example is the funded irrevocable LIFE INSURANCE TRUST. Under a typical arrangement, a grandparent might establish such a trust to fund premiums for permanent insurance on the life of a son or daughter, with the grandchildren as beneficiaries. At termination of the trust, the grandchildren would have a fully paid policy on their parent's life, and the trust assets would revert to the grandparent. Congress curtailed the tax advantages of short-term reversionary trusts in the *Tax Reform Act of 1969* and again in the TAX REFORM ACT OF 1986.

SICK BUILDING SYNDROME condition in which buildings are built with sealed windows resulting in poor ventilation causing occupants to experience dizziness, nausea, respiratory problems, headaches, fatigue, sinus congestion, and/or respiratory problems. This health concern has the potential for substantially increasing health and WORKERS COMPENSATION claims.

SICKNESS COVERAGE *see* HEALTH INSURANCE.

SICKNESS INSURANCE *see* HEALTH INSURANCE.

SIDETRACK AGREEMENT type of *hold-harmless agreement* made by a property owner as a condition for being served by a railroad spur. If the owner wants a special sidetrack, the railroad requires the owner to assume responsibility for certain losses for property damage or injury arising from use of the track, even if the railroad is at fault. Most common in these agreements is responsibility for loss due to fire.

SIDETRACK INSURANCE *see* SIDETRACK AGREEMENT.

SIGN FLOATER INSURANCE endorsement to a business property floater policy that covers neon signs for all perils, both while they are being moved and once they are in place. Signs that are attached to a building can be covered under the underlying property insurance. The sign floater policy provides broader coverage for each sign that is listed on the policy.

SIMPLE INTEREST sum of money paid on the principal amount of money invested or loaned. *See also* INTEREST.

SIMPLE PROBABILITY *see* PROBABILITY.

SIMPLE RETIREMENT (PENSION) PLAN *see* SAVINGS INCENTIVE MATCH PLAN FOR EMPLOYEES (SIMPLE PLANS).

SIMPLIFIED COMMERCIAL LINES PORTFOLIO POLICY (SCLP) policy that provides coverage through four parts:
1. *Commercial property*—coverage is provided under the BUILDING AND PERSONAL PROPERTY COVERAGE FORM (BPPCF), divided into three major categories: owned buildings, owned business personal property, and nonowned business personal property.
2. *Crime*—coverage is provided under the commercial crime program, which includes the following coverages: forgery; theft, disappearance, and destruction; employee dishonesty; safe robbery and burglary; burglary of the premises; computer fraud; extortion; and liability for the property of guests.
3. *Boiler and machinery*—coverage is provided according to four items of classification: electrical, turbine, mechanical, and pressure and refrigeration. Property covered in these four groups is that which is owned by the insured or is under the care, custody, or control of the insured.

4. *Liability*—coverage is provided for general liability, products and completed operations liability, medical payments, advertising and personal liability, and fire legal liability. Each of these categories has a separate limit of liability that is applicable. However, an annual AGGREGATE LIMIT of liability is applicable to the total of these categories except for the products and completed operations liability, which has a separate annual aggregate limit.

SIMPLIFIED EARNINGS FORM addition to a business property insurance policy to cover loss of earnings, subject to a monthly limit, in the event that property of an insured is destroyed and a business cannot continue. The property insurance policy pays only in the event that property of an insured is destroyed and a business cannot continue. The property insurance policy pays only for DIRECT LOSS of income-producing property. A building destroyed by fire represents a direct loss. Lost income resulting from the shutdown of a manufacturing facility housed in the burned building represents an INDIRECT LOSS that would be covered by BUSINESS INTERRUPTION INSURANCE, which is written on a number of separate forms.

SIMPLIFIED EMPLOYEE PENSION (SEP) employee INDIVIDUAL RETIREMENT ACCOUNT funded by an employer or a self-employed person. (Also known as SEP-IRA.) Differs from a pension plan in that contributions are immediately vested and employees have control of the investment of the SEP-IRA. IRS rules require that SEP-IRA contributions be made according to a written allocation formula. The maximum contribution is 15% of compensation or $30,000, whichever is less. Employees may elect to take cash instead of their SEP-IRA contribution but must pay income taxes on it. The TAX REFORM ACT OF 1986 also allows a SEP-IRA to be used as an alternative to a SECTION 401 (K) PLAN (SALARY REDUCTION PLAN) for an employer with 25 or fewer employees. The maximum annual contribution limit per employee for such salary-reduction SEP-IRAs is $10,000. In 2006 and thereafter, this limit increases in $500 increments as required by inflation adjustments. For example, in 2007, the limit is $10,500.

SINE QUA NON RULE Latin phrase meaning "without which not," signifying a legal rule in TORT and NEGLIGENCE cases. Under this rule, a plaintiff trying to prove that an injury was a direct result of a negligent act by the defendant would have to establish that the injury would not have occurred without the negligent act.

SINGLE ANNUITANT (SINGLE LIFE ANNUITY) ANNUITY that continues income payments as long as the annuitant lives, ceasing upon the individual's death.

SINGLE INTEREST POLICY property insurance coverage for only one of the parties having an INSURABLE INTEREST in that property.

SINGLE LIFE ANNUITY *see* SINGLE ANNUITANT (SINGLE LIFE ANNUITY).

SINGLE LIMIT *see* COMBINED SINGLE LIMIT.

SINGLE PREMIUM ANNUITY *see* SINGLE PREMIUM DEFERRED ANNUITY; SINGLE PREMIUM IMMEDIATE ANNUITY.

SINGLE PREMIUM DEFERRED ANNUITY DEFERRED ANNUITY under which one premium payment is made and the annuity is paid up (no further premium payments are required).

SINGLE PREMIUM GROUP ANNUITY one premium payment made to fund the future benefits of a group of employees.

SINGLE PREMIUM IMMEDIATE ANNUITY IMMEDIATE ANNUITY under which one premium payment is made and the annuity is paid up (no further premium payments are required).

SINGLE PREMIUM LIFE INSURANCE coverage in which one premium payment is made and the policy is fully paid up with no further premiums required. *See also* LIMITED PAYMENT LIFE INSURANCE.

SINGLE PREMIUM VARIABLE UNIVERSAL LIFE INSURANCE type of UNIVERSAL VARIABLE LIFE INSURANCE policy that provides guideline premiums to be paid usually by the POLICYOWNER. Charges on a monthly basis usually include the COST OF INSURANCE, administrative expenses, premium tax, and in some instances, a contract fee. The policyowner may execute POLICY LOANS and in many instances on a zero cost basis if the policy loans come from the policy's gains. The policyowner may also make a partial CASH SURRENDER VALUE of policy at no SURRENDER CHARGE for that portion of the premium not previously surrendered. When surrender charges are levied, they usually apply for the first 10 years that the policy is in force and range from 6 to 15% in the first year decreasing to zero by the end of the tenth year. Within the policy, the policyowner can effect tax-free transfers of funds among the sub-accounts in order to try to optimize the return.

SINGLE RISK CARGO INSURANCE marine cargo coverage for a single shipment of goods. Also known as SPECIAL RISK INSURANCE and *trip cargo insurance*. Contrasts with *open policy cargo insurance* that covers all of a shipper's goods in transit.

SINKING FUND money set aside to pay for losses. Rather than buy insurance coverage for all potential losses, some businesses and individuals choose this form of SELF INSURANCE to cover all or a portion of certain losses.

SIR *see* SELF-INSURED RETENTION (SIR).

SISTERSHIP CLAUSE *see* SISTERSHIP EXCLUSION.

SISTERSHIP EXCLUSION part of the BUSINESS RISK EXCLUSION in GENERAL LIABILITY INSURANCE that denies coverage for subsequent claims if a defective product is not recalled by an insured. For example, if a consumer filed a damage suit against XYZ Co. claiming that he or she became sick while eating a can of soup from a particular lot that was contaminated, the insurer would not pay later claims filed by other consumers if the XYZ Co. did not recall that lot of the soup. The general liability insurance policy for businesses also excludes costs associated with the withdrawal of a product from the market whether it is ordered by a government agency or by company management. A business that wants coverage for product recall would need to buy PRODUCT RECALL INSURANCE to include the extra wages and other costs of identifying the faulty product, notifying consumers, correcting or repairing the product, and redistributing it.

SIZE *see* FACE AMOUNT (FACE OF POLICY).

SKIP PERSON person (the transferee to whom the property is transferred) who is at least two generations younger than the person (the transferor) who is transferring the property. This type of property transfer prompts the generation-skipping transfer tax.

SLANDER *see* TORT, INTENTIONAL.

SLIDING SCALE COMMISSION percentage that has an inverse relationship to the loss experience on the business brought in. For example, if a CEDING COMPANY laid off better risks that resulted in better and more profitable business for the reinsurer, it would get a higher commission.

SMALL BUSINESS EQUIPMENT BREAKDOWN INSURANCE type of BOILER AND MACHINERY INSURANCE designed for the small business. Coverage is limited to heating and cooling equipment and air compressors. No coverage is provided for processing equipment.

SMALL BUSINESS PROTECTION ACT act passed in 1996 that includes
1. an increase in the amount a nonworking spouse can contribute to an INDIVIDUAL RETIREMENT ACCOUNT (IRA) increased from $250 to $2000.
2. creation of the SAVINGS INCENTIVE MATCH PLAN FOR EMPLOYEES (SIMPLE PLANS).
3. the stipulation that, for the person covered under a QUALIFIED PENSION PLAN who is age 70½ and has not retired, that person is not required to begin minimum distributions from that plan until April 1 of the year following the year in which he or she retires.

SMALL LOSS PRINCIPLE statement regarding an insured's retention of low-severity risks because they are not catastrophic, and can be absorbed without having a dramatic effect on the financial structure of a business or individual. Insurance purchased for small-loss coverage is, in effect, swapping dollars with the insurance company, since the premium charged reflects the individual's expected losses plus loadings for the insurance company's expenses, profit margin, and contingencies. *See also* LARGE LOSS PRINCIPLE.

SMOKE CLAUSE provision in the EXTENDED COVERAGE ENDORSEMENT stating that smoke damage is covered when it results from the sudden, unusual, and faulty operation of an on-premises cooking or heating unit, provided that it has been connected to the chimney by means of a vent.

SMOKE DAMAGE *see* SMOKE CLAUSE.

SMP *see* SPECIAL MULTIPERIL INSURANCE (SMP).

SNOWMOBILE COVERAGE *see* SNOWMOBILE FLOATER.

SNOWMOBILE FLOATER endorsement to a HOMEOWNERS INSURANCE POLICY or a PERSONAL AUTOMOBILE POLICY (PAP) that covers physical damage to a snowmobile wherever it happens to be. Coverage can be on *named peril* or ALL RISKS basis.

SNOWMOBILE INSURANCE *see* SNOWMOBILE FLOATER.

SOCIAL INSURANCE compulsory employee benefit plan under which participants are entitled to a series of benefits as a matter of right. The plan is administered by a federal or state government agency and has as its objective the provision of a minimum standard of living for those in lower and middle wage groups. *See also* SOCIAL SECURITY ACT OF 1935.

SOCIAL INSURANCE SUPPLEMENT additional coverage designed to provide protection against economic losses incurred by insured wage earners when their income is interrupted or terminated because of illness, sickness, or accident, and these losses are not covered under WORKERS COMPENSATION INSURANCE disability income benefits or the disability income benefits of Social Security.

SOCIAL SECURITY ACT OF 1935 federal legislation that established the OLD AGE SURVIVORS, DISABILITY, AND HEALTH INSURANCE (OASDHI).

SOCIAL SECURITY ACT, TITLE XIX 1965 federal law that provides for medical assistance to those who cannot afford to pay for it. Four categories of the needy can qualify: aged, blind, disabled, and families with dependent children. The MEDICAID program was enacted at the same time as MEDICARE.

SOCIAL SECURITY ADJUSTMENT OPTION choice an employee can make of receiving higher private pension benefits prior to eligibility for Social Security, and lower pension benefits thereafter. For example, employees taking early retirement may wish to receive higher-than-normal benefits in the months or years before their Social Security benefits begin. In exchange, they would have to accept reduced pension benefits once the Social Security payments started.

SOCIAL SECURITY FREEZE maintenance of Social Security benefits at current dollar or percentage levels. Social Security benefits are indexed to the Consumer Price Index and rise in tandem with the Index. A benefit freeze is one solution that legislators and regulators have proposed to cope with a troubled Social Security system, but many powerful lobbying groups oppose such a remedy.

SOCIAL SECURITY NORMAL RETIREMENT AGE earliest age at which a person covered under Social Security can retire without a penalty reduction in income benefits. This age will ultimately increase from 65 to 67 by the year 2027.

SOCIAL SECURITY OFFSET reduction of private pension benefits to avoid "duplication" of Social Security benefits, according to a formula. Many pension plans "offset," or reduce, monthly pension benefits by a percentage of the employee's monthly Social Security benefit. *See also* PENSION PLAN INTEGRATION WITH SOCIAL SECURITY.

SOCIAL SECURITY RIDER option found in DISABILITY INCOME INSURANCE that provides additional income, at an additional cost, if a DISABILITY does not qualify for benefits under Social Security.

SOCIETY OF ACTUARIES (SA) membership organization of individuals especially trained in the application of ACTUARIAL mathematics, including compound interest, annuities, life contingencies, measurement of mortality probability, and statistics. The organization holds a series of actuarial examinations for prospective members seeking the designation of Fellow or Associate of the Society of Actuaries (FSA, ASA).

SOCIETY OF CHARTERED PROPERTY AND CASUALTY UNDERWRITERS membership organization of individuals especially trained in the application of property and casualty insurance to personal and business situations. Membership is achieved by passing a series of examinations administered by the American Institute for Property and Liability Underwriters, plus three years of industry experience. Successful completion of the examinations results in the designation of Chartered Property Casualty Underwriter (CPCU).

SOCIETY OF INSURANCE RESEARCH organization formed to encourage research in insurance and to foster an exchange of ideas and research methodology among the society members.

SOFT INSURANCE MARKET *see* UNDERWRITING CYCLE.

SOLE PROPRIETOR type of business where individual proprietor and business of proprietor are considered the same for debt, liability, and tax considerations. The business is owned directly by one individual.

SOLE PROPRIETOR LIFE AND HEALTH INSURANCE coverage for the owner of a business. When a proprietor dies, debts of the business become the debts of the estate since in this circumstance the law recognizes business and personal assets as one. The executor is required to dispose of the business as quickly as possible. Life insurance can fund the disposition in several ways:
1. If the business is transferred through a will, the life insurance's death benefit can be applied to the deceased proprietor's personal and business debts and estate taxes.
2. If the executor conducts a forced sale or liquidation, a death benefit can be used to reduce or eliminate any debts. The death benefit

can also be used as a source of working capital for interim financing to operate the business in the short run.

3. If the business is to be transferred to a child or employee, the death benefit can provide funds to effect the transfer.

4. If the business is to be sold to a key employee(s) through a buy-and-sell agreement, the key employee(s) usually has previously bought a life insurance policy on the sole proprietor and made all premium payments. The buy-and-sell agreement stipulates the formula to be used in valuing the business as well as other conditions of the sale. Upon the death of the proprietor and the sale of the business to the key employee(s), the proprietor's estate receives the cash amount according to the buy-and-sell agreement, and the key employee(s) receives the deceased proprietor's business.

SOLICITING AGENT *see* SOLICITOR (SOLICITING AGENT).

SOLICITING OFFER *see* SOLICITOR (SOLICITING AGENT).

SOLICITOR (SOLICITING AGENT) insurance salesperson who contacts potential customers and handles clerical responsibilities but has no authority to make insurance contracts. *See also* BINDER; GENERAL AGENT (GA).

SOLIDITY SURPLUS additional amount of SURPLUS generated by an additional amount of capital to be included in the surplus above that required by the STATUTORY REQUIREMENTS. This additional surplus is necessary in the event unforeseen contingencies occur. Such contingencies could impair the insurance company's ability to make future benefit payments for which it has received the premiums as well as to fund the growth of new sales.

SOLVENCY minimum standard of financial health for an insurance company, where assets exceed liabilities. State laws require insurance regulators to step in when solvency of an insurer is threatened and proceed with *rehabilitation* or *liquidation.*

SOLVENCY SURPLUS additional amount of SURPLUS generated by an additional amount of CAPITAL to be included in book value surplus. This additional surplus is necessary to act as a supplement to the STATUTORY RESERVES in the event unforeseen contingencies occur. Such contingencies could impair the insurance company's ability to make future benefit payments for which it has received the premiums.

SONIC BOOM LOSSES property damage resulting from aircraft traveling faster than the speed of sound. Although the vibrations caused by such high speed can cause damage, it is excluded on most property forms.

SOUND EQUIPMENT INSURANCE special endorsement to PERSONAL AUTOMOBILE POLICY (PAP) covering loss of records, tapes, and other sound equipment caused by an insured peril in an insured automobile.

SOURCES OF INCOME in insurance, company revenues from underwriting and investment. Insurance companies make money first, by underwriting good risks so that their premium dollars cover claims losses and expenses (the money left over being called underwriting income), and second, by investing premium dollars until claims have to be paid (called investment income), sometimes many years later. In the late 1970s, for example, casualty insurers lost money on underwriting but made up for the loss with a gain in investment income.

SOURCES OF SURPLUS cash carried forward from the previous year, plus gains from operations for the current year, plus any capital gains.

SOUTH-EASTERN UNDERWRITERS ASSOCIATION (SEUA) CASE important 1944 U.S. Supreme Court ruling that the insurance business constituted interstate commerce and was thus subject to the SHERMAN ANTITRUST ACT. This decision came in *U.S.* v. *South-Eastern Underwriters Association,* a price-fixing case, brought against a fire insurance rate-making group by the U.S. Attorney General, at the urging of the state of Missouri. SEUA relied for its defense on the 1869 PAUL V. VIRGINIA decision by the Supreme Court that insurance activities were not commerce and the Sherman Act did not apply. The high court subsequently accepted the argument that the industry was subject to the antitrust law. In response, Congress passed the MCCARRAN-FERGUSON ACT (PUBLIC LAW 15) in 1945, in effect overruling the court by stating affirmatively that regulation of insurance was the job of the states, not the federal government. The law exempted insurance from federal antitrust rules if it was covered by state regulation.

SPECIAL ACCEPTANCE extension of a REINSURANCE treaty to include a risk that was not originally in its terms.

SPECIAL AGENT individual who sells and services life insurance in an exclusive territory; in property and casualty insurance, an individual who represents a property and casualty insurance company as a marketing representative.

SPECIAL BUILDING FORM endorsement to the SPECIAL MULTIPERIL INSURANCE (SMP) policy that provides ALL RISKS damage coverage for real property. This special form provides only minimum cover, leaving the option for adding forms to the policyholder. The policyholder has a choice of the general building form, which provides named peril coverage, or the special building form for the broader all-risks coverage.

SPECIAL CHARGE any fee imposed on insurance companies by a state. Insurers pay special taxes, including premium taxes and franchise taxes. In addition, various states have their own special charges to cover costs of such things as maintaining fire departments, licensing agents, or filing reports.

SPECIAL CLASS RISK waiver of payment for specific health claims related to the preexisting condition(s) at the time the health insurance application is made.

SPECIAL DAMAGES *see* LIABILITY, CIVIL DAMAGES AWARDED.

SPECIAL EXTENDED COVERAGE endorsement to a property insurance policy providing ALL RISKS coverage for insured property. Excluded properties include residences, farms, and manufacturing properties. This endorsement is generally used for property that does not qualify for a packaged form such as the standard multiperil policy.

SPECIAL FEATURES *see* OPTIONAL BENEFITS.

SPECIAL FORM *see* SPECIAL PERSONAL PROPERTY FORM.

SPECIAL INSURANCE POLICIES *see* SPECIAL RISK INSURANCE.

SPECIAL MORTALITY TABLE one used to determine the life expectancy of ANNUITANTS. Annuity buyers are not representative of the population as a whole, or of life insurance buyers. Because annuities pay an income for life, only those in good health, and who expect to live a long time, will spend their money for an annuity contract. Recognizing this, life insurers, who sell annuity contracts, use special mortality tables, which chiefly consider age and sex, to predict their deaths. For example, if a 50-year-old applicant purchases an IMMEDIATE ANNUITY for life with $100,000, the income would be less than that for a 70-year-old. Likewise, because women have longer life expectancies, their monthly income payments would be lower than men of the same age.

SPECIAL MULTIPERIL INSURANCE (SMP) coverage usually provided for large businesses in four areas:

1. *Section I (Property)*—The building(s) and contents are covered against either any peril (ALL RISKS basis) or only perils listed in Section I. It is to the advantage of the business to have coverage written on an ALL RISKS basis. Endorsements can be added for sprinkler leakage, business interruption, extra expense, water damage, rental loss, valuable records and papers, mercantile robbery and safe burglary, mercantile open stock burglary, glass and fine arts, or these items can be covered separately.

2. *Section II (Liability)*—The insured is covered for actions or nonactions that result in liability exposure arising out of ownership, use, possession and/or maintenance of the covered locations and structures. Also covered are the business's activities conducted by the insured whether at or from the covered locations and structures. Endorsements can be added to cover for medical payments, liability arising out of products and completed operations, and liability arising out of operation of a nonowned automobile. Additional endorsements can be added to this section to broaden liability coverage.

3. *Section III (Crime)*—Coverage for employee dishonesty, premises loss both inside and outside of the structure, forgery by depositions, paper currency that proves to be counterfeit, and money orders. The comprehensive DISHONESTY, DISAPPEARANCE, AND DESTRUCTION POLICY (3-D POLICY) and the BLANKET CRIME POLICY provide these coverages.

4. *Section IV (Boiler and Machinery)*—Coverage for explosion of a boiler, engine, turbines, and/or pipes owned or under the control of the insured. Endorsements can be added to cover indirect and consequential losses resulting from accidents associated with the boiler and machinery expenses. The SMP has generally been replaced by the COMMERCIAL PACKAGE POLICY.

SPECIAL NEEDS TRUST type of TRUST established usually for family members who are unable to provide for their own requirements. Typically a trustee who has the responsibility to manage the trust's assets is appointed.

SPECIAL PERSONAL PROPERTY FORM endorsement to the SPECIAL MULTIPERIL INSURANCE (SMP) policy that provides ALL RISKS damage coverage for personal property. There are special limitations on amounts of coverage for furs, jewelry, precious stones and metals, patterns and dies, and stamps, tickets, and letters of credit. Certain electronic equipment and fragile materials are only covered for specific perils.

SPECIAL PURPOSE REINSURER type of REINSURER whose purpose is to issue insurance linked securities as the funding instrument for a REINSURANCE TREATY.

SPECIAL RISK INSURANCE transfer of highly individualized loss exposures that is not based on the usual pooling principles of insurance such as *risk identification* and *classification selection.* Rather than setting up an insurance pool of standard risks, the underwriter accepts responsibility for a unique or special risk. Some examples would be insurance by LLOYD'S OF LONDON underwriters for athletes, artists, and entertainers; insurance on Betty Grable's legs; or insurance for dangerous scientific experiments or moon travel.

SPECIFIC COVERAGE *see* SPECIFIC INSURANCE.

SPECIFIC DOLLAR LIMITS *see* SPECIFIC LIMIT.

SPECIFIC EXCESS CONTRACT policy in which an insurer agrees to pay property or liability losses in excess of a specific amount per occurrence. For example, this type of coverage typically is used by an employer that self insures its workers compensation but wants to limit the loss per accident to, say, $40,000. Contrasts with *stop loss aggregate contract* that pays for total losses above a certain amount during the year.

SPECIFIC EXCESS REINSURANCE EXCESS OF LOSS REINSURANCE written on a FACULTATIVE REINSURANCE basis to provide cover for a particular PRIMARY INSURANCE policy.

SPECIFIC INSURANCE single insurance policy for only one kind of property at only one location of an insured. For example, property insurance on a rare piano in the insured's home would cover only that piano, not any other property of the insured.

SPECIFIC LIMIT maximum limit of LIABILITY of an insurance company for a particular claim or kind of loss that is applicable in general to all such claims or losses. This maximum limit of liability is usually less than the POLICY LIMIT of liability.

SPECIFIC RATE property insurance premium rate that is applicable to a single, particular piece of property.

SPECIFIC REINSURANCE *see* FACULTATIVE REINSURANCE.

SPECIFIC STOP LOSS INSURANCE coverage that goes into effect when an individual's claim reaches a specific threshold selected by the employer who has SELF-INSURANCE. After this threshold is reached, the policy pays claims up to the health insurance's lifetime limit per employee.

SPECIFIED DISEASE POLICY *see* DREAD DISEASE INSURANCE.

SPECIFIED PERIL INSURANCE policy covering loss only for a named peril in the policy. For example, the *Standard Fire Policy* covers only the two named perils of fire and lightning. Other perils can be added by endorsement, such as theft, vandalism, malicious mischief, and burglary.

SPECULATIVE *see* SPECULATIVE RISK.

SPECULATIVE RISK uncertain prospect of financial gain or loss. A business investment that could either return a profit or sustain a loss, such as the purchase of a common stock, is an example of a speculative risk. In most instances, speculative risks are not insurable. *See also* PURE RISK; STANDARD RISK.

SPELL OF ILLNESS period of time an insured is sick and entitled to receive health insurance benefits. *See also* DISABILITY INCOME INSURANCE, GROUP HEALTH INSURANCE.

SPENDTHRIFT TRUST *see* SPENDTHRIFT TRUST CLAUSE.

SPENDTHRIFT TRUST CLAUSE provision in a life insurance policy that protects its proceeds from the beneficiary's creditors. On payment, the beneficiary loses the protection of the spendthrift trust clause and the beneficiary's creditors can then bring suit to attach the proceeds.

SPINOUT method of terminating a SPLIT DOLLAR LIFE INSURANCE policy in which the company transfers its interest in the life insurance policy to the insured employee. Through such a transfer, the insured employee incurs a tax liability on the policy's transferred value.

SPLIT ANNUITY division of a sum of money between a DEFERRED ANNUITY and an immediate LIFE ANNUITY CERTAIN.

SPLIT DEDUCTIBLE deductible applicable to each loss so that the amount of each loss retained by the insured varies according to the PERIL that caused the loss. For example, the split deductible in a policy may specify that the insured must retain the first $300 of any fire loss and $100 of any vandalism and malicious mischief loss.

SPLIT DOLLAR LIFE INSURANCE policy in which premiums, ownership rights, and death proceeds are split between an employer and an employee, or between a parent and a child. The employer pays the part of each year's premium that at least equals the increase in the *cash value.* The employee may pay the remainder of the premium, or the employer may pay the entire premium. When the increase in cash value equals or exceeds the yearly premium, the employer pays the entire premium. If the employee dies while in the service of the employer, a beneficiary chosen by the employee receives the difference between the face value and the amount paid to the employer (the cash value or the total of all premiums paid by the employer—whichever is greater). Thus, during employment, the employee's share of the death benefit decreases. If the employee leaves the employer, the latter has the option of surrendering the policy in exchange for return of all premiums, or selling the policy to the employee for the amount of its cash value. There are two types of split dollar life insurance policies: (1) *Endorsement*—the employer owns all policy privileges; the employee's only rights are to choose beneficiaries and to select the manner in which the death benefit is paid. (2) *Collateral*—the employee owns the policy. The employer's contributions toward the premiums are viewed as a series of interest-free loans, which equal the yearly increase in the cash value of the policy. The employee *assigns* the policy to the employer as collateral for these loans. When the employee dies, the loans are paid from the face value of the policy. Any remaining proceeds are paid to the beneficiary.

SPLIT FUNDED PLAN retirement arrangement in which contributions are divided between *allocated* (insured) and *unallocated funding instruments* (an uninsured plan). It seeks to combine the advantages of guarantees-of-income of the allocated funding instrument with the investment flexibility (and possible higher *yields)* of an unallocated funding instrument. For example, 60% of contributions could be placed in a RETIREMENT INCOME POLICY (or other permanent life insurance policy) and 40% in a DEPOSIT ADMINISTRATION PLAN (or other fund held and invested by a trustee).

SPLIT FUNDING *see* SPLIT FUNDED PLAN.

SPLIT LIFE INSURANCE combination life insurance policy composed of TERM LIFE INSURANCE and an INSTALLMENT REFUND ANNUITY.

SPLIT LIMIT *see* SPLIT LIMITS COVERAGE.

SPLIT LIMITS COVERAGE technique for expressing limits of liability coverage under a particular insurance policy, stating separate limits for different types of claims growing out of a single event or combination of events. Coverage may be split (limited) per person, per occurrence, between bodily injury and property damage, or in other ways. Property damage liability is listed with a limit per accident. For example, a policy with split limits quoted as $100,000/$300,000/

$25,000 would provide a maximum of $100,000 bodily injury coverage per person, $300,000 total bodily injury coverage per accident, and $25,000 total property damage liability coverage per accident.

SPOUSAL INDIVIDUAL RETIREMENT ACCOUNT (IRA) INDIVIDUAL RETIREMENT ACCOUNT established under the TAX REFORM ACT OF 1986, for a spouse who has unearned income. The maximum annual combined contribution into the worker's and spouse's IRA is $4000 ($5000 if at least age 50) per spouse for a total of $10,000 if both spouses are at least age 50. The contributions can be apportioned between the two accounts in any manner desired.

SPOUSE'S BENEFIT insured sum paid regularly to a married partner (usually a wife but sometimes a husband) of a retired worker. There are several forms:
1. The Federal Retirement Equity Act mandates a spouse's benefit payable out of a husband's pension, unless cancelled under specified conditions.
2. Under Social Security, a spouse receives a benefit upon reaching the normal retirement age, whether or not that person has earned Social Security credits.
3. Some business firms provide for a spouse's benefit at the death of a retired worker, usually a percentage of the deceased worker's last highest salary, funded out of the deceased's pension.
4. A joint and survivor annuity can provide a spouse's benefit. For example, a joint and two-thirds annuity gives the couple an income for as long as both are alive, and when one dies the survivor receives two-thirds of the amount they had been getting.

SPREAD percentage subtracted from the underlying index increase in an EQUITY INDEXED ANNUITY. For example, if the underlying index increases by 12% and the spread is 4%, the ANNUITANT will be credited with 8%.

SPREAD LOSS *see* CARPENTER PLAN (SPREAD LOSS COVER, SPREAD LOSS REINSURANCE).

SPREAD LOSS COVER *see* CARPENTER PLAN (SPREAD LOSS COVER, SPREAD LOSS REINSURANCE).

SPREAD LOSS REINSURANCE *see* CARPENTER PLAN (SPREAD LOSS COVER, SPREAD LOSS REINSURANCE).

SPREAD ON INTEREST-BEARING FUNDS difference between the yield on earning assets and the cost of interest-bearing liabilities.

SPREADSHEET risk management tool to determine risk exposure and to help spread the risk. A risk manager considers a business firm's individual exposures separately. As the number of exposures increases, the threat that all units will suffer loss decreases, and the manager is able to spread the risk.

SPRINKLER DAMAGE INSURANCE *see* SPRINKLER LEAKAGE INSURANCE; SPRINKLER LEAKAGE LEGAL LIABILITY INSURANCE.

SPRINKLER LEAKAGE INSURANCE coverage for property damage caused by untimely discharge from an automatic sprinkler system. This coverage, available through an endorsement to the *Standard Fire Policy,* typically excludes losses from fire, lightning, windstorm, earthquake, explosion, rupture of steam boiler, riot, civil commotion, and order of civil authority.

SPRINKLER LEAKAGE LEGAL LIABILITY INSURANCE coverage for liability for damage to property of others from untimely discharge of fire-fighting sprinkler systems. This coverage is available as an endorsement to broad-form COMPREHENSIVE GENERAL LIABILITY INSURANCE (CGL).

SPRINKLING TRUST trust in which the TRUSTEE distributes capital and income to the beneficiaries of the trust according to their economic needs.

STABLE VALUE FUNDS combination of a GUARANTEED INVESTMENT CONTRACT (GIC) and bonds. Usually these funds have a low yield.

STACKING circumstance under which the insured maintains that, if an insurance policy covers at least two scheduled items of real or personal property, in the event of a loss applicable coverage should be twice the stated limit in the policy. In an effort to avoid the stacking issue, automobile policies include a stipulation that the limit of liability stated in the DECLARATIONS SECTION is the maximum amount the INSURER will pay for all damages resulting from one accident, regardless of the number of insureds, claims made, vehicles, or premiums stated in the declarations section, or vehicles involved in an accident.

STAFF ADJUSTER *see* ADJUSTER.

STAFF (GROUP) HEALTH MAINTENANCE ORGANIZATION (HMO) traditional HMO made up of physicians who are salaried by the HMO. These physicians treat solely HMO members who are covered only if they use HMO physicians and hospitals.

STAFF UNDERWRITER *see* UNDERWRITER, LAY.

STAMP AND COIN COLLECTIONS INSURANCE coverage on an ALL RISKS basis at any location for stamp and coin collections, excluding wear and tear, war, nuclear disaster, and mysterious disappearance. Usually each item is specifically listed and valued in the policy. This insurance is of particular importance for insureds with valuable stamp and coin collections. Standard property insurance policies such as the HOMEOWNERS INSURANCE POLICY have a relatively low limit of coverage of specialty items such as stamp and coin collections.

STAMP AND COIN DEALERS INSURANCE coverage on an ALL RISKS basis, subject to exclusions of war, wear and tear, loss resulting from delay, loss of market, infidelity of the insured's employee, loss due to rain, sleet, snow, or flood, except while the stamps or coins are in transit. This is a special INLAND MARINE insurance coverage designed specifically for dealers.

STANDARD method of UNDERWRITING insurance in which the INSURANCE COMPANY utilizes regular MORTALITY TABLES without additions for abnormalities.

STANDARD & POOR'S 500 STOCK PRICE INDEX (S&P 500) index of the most widely traded 500 stocks on the New York Stock Exchange (NYSE). The index is generally used by the investment community as the BENCHMARKING device for the state of the common stock market.

STANDARD ANNUITY TABLE, 1937 historical MORTALITY TABLE used for individual ANNUITY contracts subsequently replaced by the ANNUITY TABLE, 1949.

STANDARD AVERAGE CLAUSE see COINSURANCE.

STANDARD DEVIATION OR VARIATION statistic indicating the degree of dispersion in a set of outcomes, computed as the *arithmetic mean* of the differences between each outcome and the average of all outcomes in the set.

STANDARD FIRE POLICY *see* FIRE INSURANCE—STANDARD FIRE POLICY.

STANDARD FIRE POLICY ANALYSIS method of rating that compares property to be insured to a standard and adjusts the rate for deviations from the standard. A standard building is situated in a standard city of specific construction with specified fire protection. Other risks are compared to the standard and given credits or debits if they are a better or worse risk.

STANDARD FORM approved or accepted policy for a particular type of risk. The only type of risk covered by a standard form mandated by law is the fire policy. In 1886, New York adopted a standard fire form that has since been revised and adopted by every other state. In other types of coverage, states may prescribe mandatory or optional minimums or may forbid certain provisions. Therefore, while life and health benefits may vary widely, for example, policyholders are given certain uniform rights like grace periods for paying premiums. In other areas, insurers have voluntarily adopted standard forms. One example is the standard automobile policy. Other types of coverage are offered on standard forms developed by rating bureaus such as the INSURANCE SERVICES OFFICE (ISO). Although insurers may use these forms, they are not obligated to do so, and many develop their own forms.

STANDARD GROUP *see* STANDARD RISK.

STANDARD INSURANCE CONTRACT PROVISION *see* STANDARD PROVISIONS, LIFE INSURANCE; STANDARD PROVISIONS, PROPERTY AND CASUALTY INSURANCE.

STANDARD LIMIT *see* BASIC LIMITS OF LIABILITY.

STANDARD MORTGAGE CLAUSE *see* MORTGAGEE CLAUSE.

STANDARD NONFORFEITURE LAWS *see* NONFORFEITURE BENEFIT (OPTION); NONFORFEITURE CASH SURRENDER BENEFIT; NONFORFEITURE EXTENDED TERM BENEFIT; NONFORFEITURE PROVISION; NONFORFEITURE REDUCED PAID-UP BENEFIT.

STANDARD POLICY *see* STANDARD FORM; STANDARD PROVISIONS, LIFE INSURANCE; STANDARD PROVISIONS, PROPERTY AND CASUALTY INSURANCE.

STANDARD PREMIUM *see* BASIC PREMIUM.

STANDARD PROVISIONS, LIFE INSURANCE elements common to all life insurance policies. While state insurance laws do not prescribe the exact words that must be in a life insurance policy, certain standard provisions must be included to provide specified basic benefits for an insured, who cannot be charged extra for them. Additional benefits can be provided, if the insurance company desires. Standard provisions include the BENEFICIARY; GRACE PERIOD; INCONTESTABLE CLAUSE; NONFORFEITURE (CASH SURRENDER BENEFIT, REDUCED PAID-UP BENEFIT, EXTENDED TERM BENEFIT); POLICY LOAN; REINSTATEMENT; SUICIDE CLAUSE; WAR EXCLUSION CLAUSE.

STANDARD PROVISIONS, PROPERTY AND CASUALTY INSURANCE sections with standard wording common to all property and casualty insurance contracts: CONDITIONS, DECLARATIONS, EXCLUSIONS, INSURING AGREEMENT. *See also* PROPERTY AND CASUALTY INSURANCE PROVISIONS.

STANDARD RISK one that is regarded by underwriters as normal and insurable at standard rates. Other classifications of risks are given credits or debits based on their deviation from the standard.

STANDARD VALUATION LAW legislation that requires that life insurance reserves be equal to the present value of future guaranteed benefits minus the present value of future modified net premiums. *See also* MODIFIED RESERVE METHODS.

STANDARD WORKERS COMPENSATION INSURANCE *see* WORKERS COMPENSATION INSURANCE.

STANDBY TRUSTS trusts in which individuals manage their own assets and only if a predetermined event occurs, such as incapacity, will another party take over the management of these assets. Upon recovering from the incapacity, the individual may resume the management of the assets.

STANDING TIMBER INSURANCE coverage against only two perils, fire and lightning. The amount of coverage is per acre of standing timber for either merchantable trees (living trees with no decay, and minimum diameter), or for trees used in reforestation. This coverage is commonly purchased by tree farmers and investors. Historically, because of tax write-offs, investing in tree farms has been particularly popular among certain investors. With the passage of the TAX REFORM ACT OF 1986 such a tax shelter is no longer possible, but the reason for purchasing timber insurance for protection remains unchanged.

STARE DECISIS Latin phrase meaning "to stand by the decisions." This legal doctrine under common law requires courts to rely on precedents, or previous decisions, when deciding disputes unless there is a compelling reason to reject those precedents. In most instances, this doctrine means that courts will decide disputes over insurance contracts the same way they have decided cases with similar facts and legal issues in the past.

STATE AGENT insurance salesperson who markets and services policies in one or more states and holds a supervisory position. *See also* SPECIAL AGENT.

STATE ASSOCIATIONS OF INSURANCE AGENTS see INDEPENDENT INSURANCE AGENTS OF AMERICA (IIAA); NATIONAL ASSOCIATION OF LIFE UNDERWRITERS (NALU); PROFESSIONAL INSURANCE AGENTS (PIA).

STATE CHILDREN'S HEALTH INSURANCE PROGRAM (SCHIP) government program that provides HEALTH INSURANCE to children from families who do not qualify for MEDICAID.

STATED AMOUNT ENDORSEMENT addition to a property policy providing coverage for a specified amount. This endorsement is typically used for an unusual or valuable piece of property that does not fit standard descriptions and, instead of declining, retains its value. For example, a classic Austin Healey 3000 Mark IV might be covered by this type of endorsement to a PERSONAL AUTOMOBILE POLICY (PAP).

STATE DISABILITY PLAN account established and administered by a state agency to finance a mandatory state insurance program for job-related injuries or to finance a non-job-related injuries insurance program on a statewide basis. *See also* WORKERS COMPENSATION INSURANCE.

STATE EXEMPTION STATUTE laws in most cases protecting life insurance policies from an insured's creditors. These laws typically exempt death benefit proceeds and policy cash values from attachment by creditors, particularly if the beneficiary is a spouse or child of the insured. Many exemption laws have limits, with all insurance proceeds over a certain amount, say $20,000, available to the insured's creditors. In some states, ENDOWMENT INSURANCE and ANNUITY policies are granted less protection from creditors than ORDINARY LIFE INSURANCE because such policies are often used as investment vehicles. *See also* LIFE INSURANCE, CREDITOR RIGHTS.

STATE FUND account established and administered by a state agency to finance a mandatory insurance program, for example, WORKERS COMPENSATION INSURANCE.

STATE GOVERNMENT INSURANCE health insurance coverage offered by some states for medical expenses and loss of income from nonoccupational disability. The merits of federal health insurance have been debated for some time. In the meantime, several states have passed plans that may be used as a testing ground for a more comprehensive plan. For example, Rhode Island pays for out-of-pocket expenses that total more than $5000 or a certain percentage of income. Other states have passed similar laws, including Georgia, Maine, Minnesota, and Connecticut.

STATE HIGH RISK POOLS FOR THE MEDICALLY UNINSURABLE state plans that provide health insurance coverage for those who are unable to purchase medical insurance. Coverage is provided by a specially formed nonprofit-making pool comprised of all the health insurance companies doing business in that particular state. The pool offers the insurance coverage to those residents of the state who: (1) have been rejected for health insurance coverage by at least one insurance company; and/or (2) have higher premium payments for a currently insured plan than that required by the pool; and/or (3) have insurance under a rated health insurance policy or have a restrictive rider attached to that policy. The typical lifetime maximum benefits in most states is $500,000 with a $500 DEDUCTIBLE. The waiting period in most states is usually six months if the applicant has been treated for a medical problem within six months of the application. Generally, in most states the premium paid by the insured ranges from 125% to 150% of the standard premium rate for that of an individual health insurance policy purchased through a standard carrier.

STATE INSURANCE DEPARTMENT *see* INSURANCE DEPARTMENT.

STATE LIFE FUND *see* WISCONSIN STATE LIFE FUND.

STATEMENT BLANK *see* ANNUAL STATEMENT.

STATEMENT (INSURANCE COMPANY TO INSURED) annual report to policyholders of certain CASH VALUE LIFE INSURANCE products and annuities to inform them of the value of the investment portion of their contracts. Buyers of whole life insurance can be said to purchase both an insurance product and a tax-deferred savings vehicle. If the insurance is terminated, the policyholder is entitled to the cash value buildup. In addition, newer forms of these policies, such as UNIVERSAL LIFE INSURANCE, *variable annuities,* and VARIABLE LIFE INSURANCE, offer policyholders a choice of investments rather than a guaranteed return. A statement informs the insured of the annual cash buildup and the performance of the investment portion.

STATEMENT OF OPINION (ACCOUNTANTS REPORT, AUDITORS REPORT) statement by an auditor or certified public accountant indicating if a company's financial statements fairly present its true financial condition. A statement of opinion may be unqualified, qualified, or adverse. An unqualified, or "clean," opinion indicates no exceptions or qualifications were found by the auditor. A qualified report means the statement makes a fair presentation of a firm's financial condition except for some important uncertainties with effects that cannot be determined by the auditor. In the case of an insurance company, an example of an important uncertainty that might lead to a qualified opinion would be the outcome of litigation over a major disputed claim. An adverse opinion means the auditor is unwilling to vouch for the financial statements presented by the company.

STATE MUTUAL assessment mutual company that operates on a state-wide basis or in more than one state. *See also* ASSESSABLE MUTUAL.

STATE-OF-THE-ART DEFENSE provision established either by state statute or court order that permits the defendant to establish that at the time of the injury incurred by the plaintiff, the defendant provided goods and services in accordance with the state of technological and scientific knowledge as of the date and/or was in compliance with industry or government standards at that time.

STATE RATE standard property/casualty insurance premium set by a state rating bureau. States have responsibility for regulating insurers and making certain that rates are reasonable. To this end, experience information is gathered by rating bureaus, and standard (or advisory) rates are set for various lines of insurance in that state. The rates are simply for guidance and individual companies may charge more or less as long as their rates are approved by the state commissioner. The bureau may represent the companies that write a particular line of insurance in that state, such as *workers compensation,* and may request rate increases from the state commissioner on behalf of its members.

STATE RATE SHEET *see* STATE RATE.

STATE SAVINGS GUARANTEE CORPORATION state-sponsored insurance fund that was intended to guarantee deposits at state-chartered savings institutions. A handful of these funds existed in the early 1980s, but after a string of savings and loan failures in Maryland and Ohio in 1985, these funds were phased out and the member savings institutions converted to Federal Deposit Insurance.

STATE SUPERVISION AND REGULATION primary responsibility for overseeing the insurance industry that has rested with individual states since 1945, after Congress passed the MCCARRAN-FERGUSON ACT (PUBLIC LAW 15). In addition to supervision and regulation, states receive taxes and fees paid by the industry that amount to several billion dollars a year. State insurance laws are administered by state insurance departments that are responsible for making certain that (1) rates are adequate, not unfairly discriminatory, and not unreasonably high, and (2) insurance companies in the state are financially sound and able to pay future claims.

To this end, states set requirements for company reserves, require annual financial statements, and examine company books. Each state has an insurance commissioner or superintendent who is either elected or appointed by the governor, with responsibility for investigating company practices, approving rates and policy forms, and ordering liquidation of insolvent insurers. The NATIONAL ASSOCIATION OF INSURANCE COMMISSIONERS (NAIC) has drafted model legislation and worked for policy uniformity, but regulations vary widely from state to state.

Whether insurers should be regulated by the states or the federal government remains at issue, but so far insurers and the NAIC lobbying have been effective in resisting federal regulation. Nevertheless, the federal government has a profound effect on the insurance industry through its taxes and a variety of regulations. *See also* STATE TAXATION OF INSURANCE.

STATE TAXATION OF INSURANCE authority of states to tax the insurance companies they regulate. States levy income taxes, real and personal property taxes, and special levies, the most important of which is a premium tax—in effect, a sales tax on premiums. Although it is generally 2% of premiums, some states tax as much as 4%. Insurers also pay franchise taxes, licensing fees, and SPECIAL CHARGES. Insurance taxes are an important source of revenue for the states, amounting to several billion dollars a year. *See also* FEDERAL TAXATION.

STATE UNEMPLOYMENT INSURANCE *see* UNEMPLOYMENT COMPENSATION.

STATIC TABLE MORTALITY TABLE, MORBIDITY TABLE that does not include current statistical experience.

STATIC RISK damage or destruction of property and/or property that is illegally transferred as the result of misconduct of individuals. The risk is insurable.

STATISTICS collection of numbers to record and analyze data such as occurrences of events and particular characteristics. Statistics are absolutely vital to all elements of insurance. In life and health insurance, they are used to tabulate age, sex, disability, cause of death, occupation, and other data needed to construct a MORBIDITY TABLE and MORTALITY TABLE, which in turn figure importantly in calculating premiums. Similarly, in property and casualty insurance statistics are used to record losses and injuries to help predict their future occurrence in order to calculate premiums.

STATUTE OF LIMITATIONS period, set by law, after which a damage claim cannot be made. Limits are set by individual states and usually range from one to seven years.

STATUTORY ACCOUNTING rules that insurance companies must follow in filing an annual financial statement known as the *convention blank,* with state insurance departments. The reported financial condition of an insurance company can differ markedly depending on whether statutory accounting rules or GENERALLY ACCEPTED ACCOUNTING PRINCIPLES (GAAP) are used in preparing financial statements. In general, statutory accounting is more conservative than GAAP because it tends to overstate expenses and liabilities while understating income and assets.

STATUTORY BONDS any of a number of types of SURETY BONDS that the law requires of government contractors, licensed businesses, litigants, fiduciaries, government officials, and others whose performance of some duty or obligation must be assured in the public interest. *See also* APPEAL BOND; BAIL BOND; BID BOND; COMPLETION BOND; CONTRACT BOND; FEDERAL OFFICIALS BOND; JUDICIAL BOND; LICENSE BOND; LOST INSTRUMENT BOND; PENSION PLANS PERFORMANCE BOND; PERMIT BOND; SECURITIES BOND; TRUSTEE ROLE.

STATUTORY EARNINGS revenue based on conservative reserve requirements of various states. Statutory earnings do not meet GENERALLY ACCEPTED ACCOUNTING PRINCIPLES (GAAP). A role of state regulation is to make certain that insurers have enough money set aside in STATUTORY RESERVES to pay all future claims and that the company will remain solvent. For this reason, regulators take a conservative approach to setting reserve requirements. But because an increase in reserves translates into lower earnings for a stock insurer, investors, and securities analysts argue that they are not helpful in gauging the health of a company for investment purposes. Therefore, insurers calculate statutory earnings for regulators and another set of earnings, based on natural reserves, for investors.

STATUTORY LAW *see* STATUTORY LIABILITY.

STATUTORY LIABILITY *see* ANNUAL STATEMENT; FULL PRELIMINARY TERM RESERVE PLAN; LIABILITIES: LIFE INSURANCE COMPANIES; PROSPECTIVE RESERVE; RETROSPECTIVE METHOD RESERVE COMPUTATION; STATUTORY ACCOUNTING; STATUTORY REQUIREMENTS; STATUTORY RESERVES.

STATUTORY PROVISIONS *see* STANDARD PROVISIONS, PROPERTY AND CASUALTY INSURANCE.

STATUTORY PROFIT total EARNED PREMIUMS minus total EXPENSES and LOSSES PAID of the INSURANCE COMPANY.

STATUTORY REQUIREMENTS standards set by the various state regulatory authorities that determine how financial statements must be prepared for regulators. The states are responsible for making certain that insurers will remain solvent and have enough set aside in reserves to pay future claims. To this end, they have devised STATUTORY ACCOUNTING principles that govern insurance company reporting. These requirements differ from GENERALLY ACCEPTED ACCOUNTING PRINCIPLES (GAAP). Among other things, statutory requirements include the setting of STATUTORY RESERVES, and the immediate expensing of the cost of acquiring new business, rather than allowing insurers to spread the exposure over the life of the policy. *See also* STATE SUPERVISION AND REGULATION.

STATUTORY RESERVES reserves required by state regulators. Because regulators must assure that an insurance company remains solvent and that it can pay future claims, they set conservative standards for insurer reserves. Regulators have various formulas for valuing reserves, such as the LOSS FREQUENCY METHOD and the *Commissioners Reserve Valuation Method.*

STATUTORY RESTRICTION limitation imposed on insurance companies by state law. States oversee the insurance industry, being responsible for making certain that the rates are fair, reasonable, and adequate, and that among other things, the companies that write insurance in the state are financially sound and able to pay future claims. To this end, the states restrict the types of investments insurance companies can make with their premium dollars, and they control insurers' relationships with insureds by guaranteeing certain minimum rights to insureds.

STATUTORY STATEMENT OF ACCOUNTING PRINCIPLE (SSAP) 16—EDP EQUIPMENT state law that limits the admitted value of an insurance company's EDP equipment to 3% of the company's ADJUSTED SURPLUS.

STATUTORY STATEMENT OF ACCOUNTING PRINCIPLE (SSAP) 52—DEPOSIT-TYPE CONTRACTS state law that stipulates accounting rules for products sold by insurance companies that have no contingent benefits such as GUARANTEED INVESTMENT CONTRACTS.

STATUTORY STATEMENT OF ACCOUNTING PRINCIPLE (SSAP) 65—PROPERTY AND CASUALTY CONTRACTS state law that stipulates the establishment of required reserves for CLAIMS MADE BASIS LIABILITY COVERAGE contracts, removes the excess STATUTORY RESERVES, and directs that all amounts that represent contractual reimbursements to the insurance company be reflected as a reduction in PAID LOSSES.

STATUTORY STATEMENT OF ACCOUNTING PRINCIPLE (SSAP) 68—BUSINESS COMBINATIONS AND GOODWILL state law that stipulates that GOODWILL as an ADMITTED ASSET cannot be greater than 10% of ADJUSTED SURPLUS.

STATUTORY STATEMENT OF ACCOUNTING PRINCIPLE (SSAP) 83—FEDERAL INCOME TAXES state law by which insurance companies are permitted to establish deferred tax assets and liabilities subject to maximum limitations.

STATUTORY STATEMENT OF ACCOUNTING PRINCIPLE (SSAP) 89—SEPARATE ACCOUNTS state law that stipulates that the worth of separate accounts must be valued at current market with the exception of those separate accounts established and maintained for GUARANTEED INVESTMENT CONTRACTS (GICS).

STATUTORY SURPLUS excess funds above the amount required to establish LEGAL RESERVES for the policies in force. These excess funds are generated as the result of mortality savings, excess interest earned on investments (an amount above that expected), and expense savings.

STATUTORY UNDERWRITING PROFIT OR LOSS difference between the EARNED PREMIUMS and the losses and expenses of an insurance company. *See also* STATUTORY EARNINGS; STATUTORY REQUIREMENTS; STATUTORY RESERVES.

STEAM BOILER INSURANCE *see* BOILER AND MACHINERY INSURANCE.

STEVEDORES LEGAL LIABILITY INSURANCE liability coverage for dockworkers for damage to property in transit while in their care.

STIGMA DAMAGE environmental contamination claims resulting from a loss in ECONOMIC OR USE VALUE of property. Claims may result from property owners as well as surrounding property owners who feel they have suffered a loss in property value because of actual contamination or perceived loss due to public fear.

STIPULATED PREMIUM COMPANY *see* STIPULATED PREMIUM INSURANCE.

STIPULATED PREMIUM INSURANCE a form of ASSESSMENT INSURANCE for which a regular premium is charged. In addition to paying the regular stipulated premium, an insured and other members of a mutual ASSESSMENT COMPANY may be subject to an additional assessment premium to make up for underwriting losses.

STOCK *see* STOCK INSURANCE COMPANY.

STOCK APPRECIATION RIGHTS (SARs) contractual rights to a stipulated percentage of the increase in the value of an insurance agency over a given future period of time. They are used to convey a percentage of the increase in the agency's value to a key employee without resulting in the owner(s) of the agency owning less than 50%. The advantages of such a stock transfer for the agency owner include the following:
1. Noncompete agreements not further reinforced since the key employee does not receive benefits if an agreement is violated.
2. The key employee is tied to the agency because that employee can become an equity owner without actually committing his or her own funds.

These SARs are really long-term deferred compensation plans for the employee(s) whose ultimate value is tied to the increase in the value of the agency's book of business over the value at the time the right was granted to the employee(s). This circumstance should increase the commitment of the employee(s) to increase the economic value of the agency.

STOCK BONUS PLAN type of DEFERRED PROFIT-SHARING plan that invests in the stock of the employer and/or stocks in other companies.

STOCK COMPANY INSURANCE insurance sold by a stock insurance company that is usually in the form of NONPARTICIPATING INSURANCE.

STOCKHOLDER owner of at least one share of stock of a business entity.

STOCKING A MUTUAL *see* DEMUTUALIZATION (STOCKING A MUTUAL).

STOCK INSURANCE COMPANY business owned by stockholders, as contrasted to a MUTUAL INSURANCE COMPANY, which is owned by its policyholders. Many major life insurers are mutual companies whereas some leading *property/casualty* and *multiline* insurers are stock insurance companies. *See also* DEMUTUALIZATION (STOCKING A MUTUAL).

STOCK INSURER *see* STOCK INSURANCE COMPANY.

STOCK PROCESSING INSURANCE coverage in the event that stock sent to others for processing is damaged or destroyed en route or at their premises except those perils specifically excluded. For example, this coverage can be used when processing milk into cheese since the farmer would lose everything if the milk were damaged or destroyed en route or at the processor's premises.

STOCK PURCHASE PLAN plan that permits purchase of shares by a company's employees.

STOCK REDEMPTION PLAN *see* CLOSE CORPORATION PLAN.

STOCK SPLIT increase in the number of shares of a COMMON STOCK INVESTMENT and a corresponding decrease in the price of the stock by the amount of the split. This is an exchange of additional shares or a percentage of shares for each share owned by a stockholder. This does not result in a change in the equity position of the stockholder. For example, a 2-for-1 split of a stock whose price is $100 would result in the STOCKHOLDER owning two shares for each share originally owned, but at a stock price of $50 a share. Stockholders are in the same financial position immediately after the split as they were prior to the split.

STOCK SWAP trading of stock to enhance portfolio performance and reduce taxes. This practice is followed when the investor has accumulated losses on stocks and sells these stocks in order to use the losses to offset capital gains on other investments, thereby reducing taxable income. Losses incurred in this manner can be used to offset capital gains dollar-for-dollar. For any additional losses, they can be used to offset ordinary income of up to $3000. All excess losses can be carried forward to future years.

STOCK TRANSFER reregistration of existing shares when there is any change in the name of the owner(s). Such a circumstance may occur when the owner(s) of the shares gives these shares to another person, establishes a trust, marries and changes the name, or adds or removes a name as owner. The transfer is executed through a letter of instruction with the signature of all owners guaranteed by a bank or a broker and sent to the transfer agent.

STOP LOSS *see* STOP LOSS REINSURANCE.

STOP LOSS AGGREGATE CONTRACT *see* STOP LOSS REINSURANCE.

STOP LOSS INSURANCE coverage purchased by employers in order to limit their exposure under SELF INSURANCE medical plans. This coverage is available in two types:

1. *Specific stop loss*—Coverage is initiated when a claim reaches the threshold selected by the employer. After the threshold is reached, the stop-loss policy would pay claims up to the lifetime limit per employee for the self insurance medical plan.

2. *Aggregate stop loss*—Coverage is initiated when the employer's self insurance total group health claims reach a stipulated threshold selected by the employer. Typically, this threshold is 125% of the self insurer's annual estimated group health claims cost.

STOP LOSS LIMIT type of COINSURANCE REQUIREMENT found in MAJOR MEDICAL INSURANCE that stipulates the maximum dollar amount required by the INSURED.

STOP LOSS PROVISION *see* STOP LOSS REINSURANCE.

STOP LOSS REINSURANCE protects a *cedent* against an aggregate amount of claims over a period, in excess of a specified percentage of the earned premium income. Stop loss reinsurance does not cover individual claims. The *reinsurer's* liability is limited to a stipulated percentage of the loss and/or a maximum dollar amount. The stop loss method protects the cedent against the possibility that the aggregate value of an accumulation of small losses will exceed a specified percentage of earned premium income of a particular class. Stop loss reinsurance is the exact opposite of the QUOTA SHARE REINSURANCE and SURPLUS REINSURANCE, and differs considerably from other forms of EXCESS OF LOSS REINSURANCE. For example, a reinsurer can provide a cedent with 50% of the amount by which aggregate incurred losses of the cedent in any year exceed 70% of the cedent's earned premium income during that year.

STOREKEEPERS BURGLARY AND ROBBERY INSURANCE coverage for small mercantile establishments on a package basis. Combines six layers of protection: burglary of a safe; damage caused by robbery and burglary, whether actual or attempted; robbery of a guard and burglary of the business's merchandise; robbery inside or outside the premises of the business; kidnapping to physically force a businessowner and/or his or her representative(s) to open the premises of the business from the outside; and theft of securities and monies either from the home of a messenger of the business and/or from a night depository of a bank.

STOREKEEPERS LIABILITY INSURANCE coverage for bodily injury and property damage liability resulting from ownership, use, and/or maintenance of the insured business's premises, completed operations, and products. Covers medical payment expenses associated with bodily injury to another party when an accident causes hazardous conditions on the business's premises or within the business's operation. Also covers costs in defending the insured against liability suits, even if the suits are without foundation.

STORM INSURANCE (WINDSTORM INSURANCE) additional coverage to a property policy. Windstorms are not one of the standard covered perils. If an insured desires coverage for windstorms and hail, an endorsement is required.

STRAIGHT DEDUCTIBLE CLAUSE section of a policy that specifies the dollar amount or percentage of any loss that the insurance does not pay. Most property and medical policies specify that the first portion of any loss is absorbed by the insured. A straight deductible clause, which is common in auto and homeowners insurance, might provide for a deductible stated in a dollar amount, such as $500. For example, the Smiths have a homeowners policy with a $500 straight deductible clause. Fire damage to the home amounts to $1500. Under the terms of the policy, the Smiths would pay the first $500 and the insurance company would reimburse them for $1000. Some straight deductibles are expressed as a specific percentage of value rather than a dollar amount. For example, the insured might absorb the loss for 5% of the value of property that is totally destroyed. *See also* DISAPPEARING DEDUCTIBLE.

STRAIGHT LIFE ANNUITY *see* ANNUITY; ANNUITY DUE; LIFE ANNUITY CERTAIN; PURE ANNUITY; REFUND ANNUITY.

STRAIGHT LIFE INSURANCE see ORDINARY LIFE INSURANCE.

STRAIGHT LINE RULE method of depreciating an asset in which its useful life is divided into an appropriate number of years (or other periods), the final salvage value is deducted, and the asset is written off in an equal portion for each period. Depreciation is a business expense for tax purposes. Straight line depreciation is the simplest method, but is not as advantageous to an owner as ACCELERATED DEPRECIATION, which allows a company to recover its costs more quickly.

STRAIGHT TERM *see* TERM.

STRATEGIC RISK FINANCING elimination of unnecessary financing costs and the redirection of those sums to activities that are more profitable. The concept is for the company to have a long-term view of its risk exposure as opposed to concentrating on the availability of insurance at any time. For example, in a soft market, companies tend to buy more insurance than they need because premiums are low. In a hard market, companies tend to retain their insurance coverage regardless of price. The methodology involves a cost/benefit analysis of the numerous risk retention options to discern the difference in the cost of a retention option and that of full/partial insurance for that option. In the analysis of each option, the company's past loss experience is examined and maximum possible loss scenarios in the future are projected. After the statistical studies are completed, a program is designed to provide an effective plan of risk coverage at an efficient price.

STRATIFICATION OF LOSSES technique of breaking down the various losses as a whole into useful components called *subsets (strata)* so that no subset is overrepresented. The result is the classification of losses according to dollar amount in order to predict the probabilities of various degrees of loss severity so that the organization can adopt the proper RISK MANAGEMENT techniques. *See also* RATE MAKING.

STRATIFIED RANDOM SAMPLING selection of restricted random samples in order to obtain a more accurate estimate of the EXPECTED LOSS (mean) than could be obtained by the selection of completely RANDOM SAMPLES. For example, assume it is the desire to obtain an accurate estimate of the average number of automobile accidents experienced by juniors in the Louisiana State University System. By selecting the proper size of random samples among the various colleges within the system, a more accurate estimate of the number of automobile accidents experienced by juniors system-wide can be obtained than by selecting the same total random sample from the system as a whole.

STREET CLOCK FLOATER endorsement to a *scheduled property floater* that provides ALL RISKS protection for street clocks. Clocks and signs attached to business property can be covered under the *Standard Fire Policy*. But a street clock floater provides broader coverage and protects the owner of the clock both in transit and wherever it is located. Each clock and its value must be listed on the schedule.

STRICT LIABILITY tort liability, which is defined by law, requiring an injured party to prove only that he or she was harmed in a specified way in order to collect damages. For example, the law provides that an employer is responsible if a worker is injured on the job. All the worker must do to collect WORKERS COMPENSATION BENEFITS is to prove that the injury took place at work. *See also* ABSOLUTE LIABILITY.

STRIKE INSURANCE coverage to protect employers from losses due to labor disruptions. The *ocean marine policy* exempts losses caused by strikes, riots, and civil commotion. Special coverage is necessary.

STRIKES, RIOTS, AND CIVIL COMMOTION CLAUSE exemption in *ocean marine policy* for losses caused by strikes, riots, and civil commotion. *See also* RIOT AND CIVIL COMMOTION INSURANCE, RIOT EXCLUSION; STRIKE INSURANCE.

STRIKE-THROUGH CLAUSE (CUT-THROUGH CLAUSE) provision that holds a reinsurer liable for its share of losses even if the CEDING COMPANY becomes insolvent before paying these losses. For example, XYZ Insurance Co. writes a fire policy for Acme Manufacturing and then reinsures 80% of the risk with ABC Reinsurance. XYZ is declared insolvent. Then Acme Manufacturing burns to the ground. ABC Reinsurance would be responsible for the 80% of the risk it reinsured and would pay the claim directly to Acme.

STRUCTURED SETTLEMENT periodic payments to an injured person or survivor for a determinable number of years or for life typically in settlement of a claim under a liability policy. Terms may include immediate reimbursement for medical and legal expenses and rehabilitation, and long-term payments for loss of income or as compensation for other injuries. A structured settlement can be expected to be less costly to the insurance carrier than a LUMP SUM settlement, especially if it enables costly litigation to be avoided.

STRUCTURED SETTLEMENT ANNUITY SINGLE PREMIUM IMMEDIATE ANNUITY purchased to fund a STRUCTURED SETTLEMENT. This product is purchased when the injured party (the plaintiff) wishes to have a monthly income payment for life and the insurance company (the liability insurance company providing coverage for the defendant) wishes to minimize the sum required to be paid to the plaintiff.

SUBACUTE CARE care for the interval of time between the MEDICARE patient's hospital departure and the stay at home, in a chronic long-term care facility or hospice.

SUBJECTIVE PROBABILITY projections of losses based on qualitative (emotional) rather than quantitative reasoning.

SUBJECTIVE RISK *see* SUBJECTIVE PROBABILITY.

SUBJECT PREMIUM *see* BASE PREMIUM.

SUBLIMITS *see* BROAD FORM PERSONAL THEFT INSURANCE; HOMEOWNERS INSURANCE POLICY—SECTION I (PROPERTY COVERAGE).

SUBMITTED BUSINESS applications for insurance coverage that have been forwarded to an insurer but not yet processed.

SUBORDINATED DEBT payment of interest and principal on the debt by the debtor only after having paid claims to assets of other higher priority creditors.

SUBROGATION *see* SUBROGATION CLAUSE.

SUBROGATION CLAUSE section of PROPERTY INSURANCE and LIABILITY INSURANCE policies giving an insurer the right to take legal action against a third party responsible for a loss to an insured for which a claim has been paid. For example, an insurance company pays a claim for $40,000 in damages to an insured storekeeper for losses caused by a negligent contractor working next door. The policy's subrogation clause gives the insurer the right to be subrogated to, or take on as its own, the storekeeper's claim and to sue the contractor for damages.

SUBROGATION PRINCIPLE surrender of rights by an insured against the third party to an insurance company that has paid a claim.

SUBROGATION, PROPERTY AND CASUALTY INSURANCE circumstance where an insurance company takes the place of an insured in bringing a liability suit against a third party who caused injury to the insured. For example, if a third party, through negligence, damages an insured's car and the insured's insurance company pays to restore the car, the insurance company has recourse against the third party for the costs involved. The insured cannot sue the third party for damage, since if successful, the insured could collect twice for the same damage.

SUBROGATION RELEASE *see* SUBROGATION CLAUSE.

SUBROGATION, WAIVER OF *see* WAIVER OF SUBROGATION RIGHTS CLAUSE.

SUBROSEE insurance company that becomes subrogated to the rights of another party. *See also* SUBROGATION CLAUSE; SUBROGATION PRINCIPLE; SUBROGATION, PROPERTY AND CASUALTY INSURANCE.

SUBROSOR insured whose rights against a third party are transferred to an insurance company (the SUBROSEE) according to the process required by the SUBROGATION CLAUSE in the policy.

SUBSCRIBER, BLUE CROSS, BLUE SHIELD person insured under a BLUE CROSS hospitalization or BLUE SHIELD medical health insurance plan.

SUBSCRIPTION DATE OF THE POLICY *see* DATE OF SUBSCRIPTION OF THE POLICY.

SUBSEQUENT NEGLIGENCE *see* LAST CLEAR CHANCE.

SUBSIDIZATION difference between the ACTUARIAL EQUIVALENT (rate) and the often lower rate actually charged to insure a risk.

SUBSTANDARD *see* SUBSTANDARD HEALTH INSURANCE (QUALIFIED IMPAIRMENT INSURANCE); SUBSTANDARD LIFE INSURANCE.

SUBSTANDARD GROUP *see* SUBSTANDARD HEALTH INSURANCE (QUALIFIED IMPAIRMENT INSURANCE); SUBSTANDARD LIFE INSURANCE.

SUBSTANDARD HEALTH INSURANCE (QUALIFIED IMPAIRMENT INSURANCE) coverage for persons whose medical history includes serious illness such as heart disease or whose physical condition is such that they are rated below standard. A policy may specifically deny coverage for recurrence of a particular illness or medical condition through an *impairment exemption rider,* or may provide only partial benefits. *See also* RATED POLICY.

SUBSTANDARD LIFE INSURANCE coverage for risks deemed uninsurable at standard rates by normal standards (persons whose medical histories include serious illness such as heart disease or whose physical conditions are such that they are rated below standard.) A policy may specifically deny benefits for death caused by a specific illness or medical condition or may provide only partial benefits. Many risks that would have been rejected as uninsurable under earlier underwriting standards, either because of their hazardous occupations or physical impairment, now can be insured under an extra-risk policy at an extra premium; even applicants who have survived cancer may be acceptable. The premium may include an extra flat fee per thousand dollars of coverage, or is one that would normally be charged to an older person. *See also* RATED POLICY.

SUBSTANDARD RISK *see* IMPAIRED RISK (SUBSTANDARD RISK); SUBSTANDARD HEALTH INSURANCE (QUALIFIED IMPAIRMENT INSURANCE); SUBSTANDARD LIFE INSURANCE.

SUBSTANTIAL EMPLOYER *see* SUBSTANTIAL OWNER BENEFIT LIMITATION.

SUBSTANTIAL OWNER effective proprietor of a business. Under the TAX REFORM ACT OF 1986, a uniform accrual rule prevents a qualified PENSION PLAN from being weighted in favor of the substantial owner of the business. The owner can select the accrual method to be applied provided the same method is used for all qualified employees of the business.

SUBSTANTIAL OWNER BENEFIT LIMITATION restriction on the benefit that owners and other highly compensated individuals may receive from a qualified pension or other employee benefits. The U.S. Tax Code requires that benefits under a qualified plan, and some other benefits, do not unduly favor a business firm's top hierarchy. The TAX REFORM ACT OF 1986 provides a uniform definition of "highly compensated" as an employee who either owned more than 5% interest in the business, received more than $75,000 in compensation, received more than $50,000 in compensation and was in the top 20% of employees as ranked by salary, or was an officer and received compensation greater than 150% of Section 415 defined contribution dollar amount. *See also* SUBSTANTIAL OWNER.

SUCCESSION BENEFICIARY CLAUSE section of a LIFE INSURANCE policy setting the procedure for revoking a current beneficiary and designating a successor beneficiary. Insurers require written notice of a beneficiary change, usually on a form designated for that purpose. Some may require return of the policy for the beneficiary change to be added. *See also* BENEFICIARY; BENEFICIARY CLAUSE.

SUCCESSOR BENEFICIARY *see* SUCCESSION BENEFICIARY CLAUSE.

SUCCESSOR PAYEE *see* SUCCESSION BENEFICIARY CLAUSE.

SUE AND LABOR CLAUSE section of *ocean marine policy* making it an obligation of the insured to take specific measures to limit losses to ship or cargo when a mishap occurs. Expenses incurred to limit physical damages, or to take legal action to protect the ship and its cargo, are reimbursed by the insurer to the extent they reduce the loss otherwise payable by the insurer, according to policy terms.

SUE, LABOR, AND TRAVEL CLAUSE *see* SUE AND LABOR CLAUSE.

SUICIDE CLAUSE limitation in all life insurance policies to the effect that no death payment will be made if an insured commits suicide within the first two years that the policy is in force. This clause protects the company against ADVERSE SELECTION—that is, purchase of a policy in contemplation of planned death in order for a beneficiary to collect the proceeds.

SUMMARY ANNUAL REPORT synopsis of the key financial figures concerning the PENSION PLAN that is contained in the FORM 5500 that must be filed annually with the Internal Revenue Service. This report must be given to the plan participants but does not have to be filed with any government agency.

SUMMARY PLAN DESCRIPTION layman description of the key features and benefits of a PENSION PLAN that must be filed with the Department of Labor. Periodic updates of this summary must also be provided to the Department of Labor as well as the employees to reflect any substantial changes in the plan or regulatory laws.

SUPERFUND AMENDMENTS AND REAUTHORIZATION ACT OF 1986 (SARA) act that provides retroactive LIABILITY for environmental claims by mandating that those who polluted the environment must pay to clean up the pollution, regardless of how long ago their actions harmed the environment.

SUPERGRIT type of GRANTOR-RETAINED INCOME TRUST (GRIT) in which the grantor retains the right to the assets of the trust should he or she die before the term of the trust expires.

SUPERINTENDENT OF INSURANCE *see* COMMISSIONER OF INSURANCE (INSURANCE COMMISSIONER, SUPERINTENDENT OF INSURANCE).

SUPERIOR GOOD condition in which life insurance sales increase at a rate greater than the general rate of growth of the economy. As a society moves from an agriculture-based economy to an industry-based economy, the transferring of the PURE RISK from the family to the insurance company becomes more expedient.

SUPERSEDED SURETYSHIP RIDER endorsement to a FIDELITY BOND or SURETY BOND to cover losses that occurred after lapse of the DISCOVERY PERIOD of the previous bond. Coverage is limited to the amount provided by the previous bond.

SUPPLEMENTAL ACCIDENT EXPENSE *see* GROUP HEALTH INSURANCE.

SUPPLEMENTAL BENEFIT FORMULA procedure in Social Security that sets the benefit level for a dependent of a retired or disabled person who is receiving Social Security benefits. For example, if a retired or disabled worker has a spouse over age 65, the spouse is entitled to a benefit that is 50% of that paid to the primary recipient.

This benefit is also available to dependent children. Further, the spouse can elect to take a reduced benefit if he or she is between ages 62 and 65.

SUPPLEMENTAL CONTRACT *see* SUPPLEMENTARY CONTRACT.

SUPPLEMENTAL EXECUTIVE RETIREMENT PLAN combination of two categories of plans: DEFINED BENEFIT PLAN and ACCOUNT BALANCE PLAN. This plan is generally more appropriate for upper-level executives whose employers contribute to each executive's account balance plan on a performance basis.

SUPPLEMENTAL EXECUTIVE RETIREMENT PLAN (SERP) SWAP election by a company executive to exchange a NONQUALIFIED PLAN for a SPLIT DOLLAR LIFE INSURANCE plan. This is a post retirement salary continuation plan that is an additional benefit to the employee's customary retirement plan. Usually these plans are made available to a select group of highly compensated employees.

SUPPLEMENTAL EXTENDED REPORTING PERIOD period of time after the expiration of a CLAIMS MADE BASIS LIABILITY COVERAGE policy during which claims may be made. *See also* MAXI TAIL (FULL TAIL); MIDI TAIL; MINI TAIL.

SUPPLEMENTAL LIABILITY INSURANCE broad excess protection for liability over the level of primary coverage or self insurance. Umbrella policies are written for both business and personal liability. For example, a personal umbrella policy might add $1 million in liability coverage for an insured's negligent use of a car, boat, and all other property, over and above regular coverage. For a business, its applications would be even broader, including workers compensation, general liability, and all other coverage. Policyholders must have a certain minimum level of primary insurance before they can buy this supplemental coverage. For a personal policy the minimum might be $100,000 in homeowners liability insurance and $500,000 per accident for bodily injury in an auto policy. *See also* UMBRELLA LIABILITY INSURANCE.

SUPPLEMENTAL MAJOR MEDICAL INSURANCE *see* SUPPLEMENTARY MEDICAL INSURANCE.

SUPPLEMENTAL MEDICAL INSURANCE *see* SUPPLEMENTARY MEDICAL INSURANCE.

SUPPLEMENTAL SECURITY INCOME (SSI) income supplement program under Social Security to provide a minimum monthly income to aged, blind, and disabled persons. The SSI payments, which were introduced in January 1974, make up the difference between family income and a guaranteed minimum amount for families who have only a specified amount of other resources such as savings accounts.

SUPPLEMENTAL TAIL *see* TAIL COVERAGE.

SUPPLEMENTAL TERM LIFE INSURANCE extra life insurance benefit found in the FAMILY INCOME POLICY, FAMILY INCOME RIDER, FAMILY MAINTENANCE POLICY, and FAMILY POLICY payable to the BENEFICIARY should the INSURED die within a stipulated time period.

SUPPLEMENTARY CONTRACT terms of a settlement of a life insurance or annuity contract under which monies are currently payable or used at least in part by the beneficiary to fund a new insurance policy. Supplementary contracts are a balance sheet liability for a life company. They represent money held for policyholders that will eventually be paid out. But because the contract no longer involves insurance on a life, it is not included in the company's policy reserves.

SUPPLEMENTARY COVERAGE in property insurance, percentages of basic coverages which may be applied to provide coverage for other real and personal property. For example, under the HOMEOWNERS INSURANCE POLICY—SECTION I (PROPERTY COVERAGE) *Coverage B,* structures not attached to or part of the home (garage or appurtenant private structures) can be covered up to 10% of the basic home structure as found under *Coverage A.*

SUPPLEMENTARY MEDICAL INSURANCE part of the federal Medicare program for additional coverage on a voluntary basis. The Medicare program is divided into two parts: (1) *Hospital Insurance* provides hospital benefits to persons over 65 who qualify for Social Security, and to disabled persons who have been receiving Social Security benefits for at least two years; and (2) SUPPLEMENTARY MEDICAL INSURANCE provides physician services to those over 65, and their dependents, who have enrolled in the program. Those enrolled in the program pay half the cost, and the U.S. government pays the other half.

SUPPLEMENTARY PAYMENTS in a LIABILITY INSURANCE policy, provision for the payment of the insured's expenses as stated in the policy in three areas above the policy limit of liability: legal fees resulting from defending the insured, expenses incurred by the insured as the result of legal actions taken against him or her as the result of requests by the insurance company, and premium payments for bonds required by the insured.

SUPPLIES AND TRANSPORTERS FORMS *see* INLAND MARINE INSURANCE (TRANSPORTATION INSURANCE): BUSINESS RISKS.

SURETY *see* FIDELITY BOND; LIABILITY, BUSINESS EXPOSURES; OBLIGOR; SURETY BOND.

SURETY ASSOCIATION OF AMERICA (SAA) association whose membership is composed of surety bonding companies. The association's primary purpose is to act as a rating bureau for member companies by collecting statistics and developing rating tables.

SURETY BOND contract by which one party agrees to make good the default or debt of another. Actually, three parties are involved: the *principal,* who has primary responsibility to perform the obligation (after which the bond becomes void); the *surety,* the individual with the secondary responsibility of performing the obligation if the principal fails to perform. (After the surety performs, recourse is against the principal for reimbursement of expenses incurred by the surety in the performance of the obligation, known as *surety's right of exoneration*); and the *obligee,* to whom the right of performance *(obligation)* is owed.

SURETY BOND GUARANTEE PROGRAM program instituted by the Small Business Administration (SBA) that guarantees a construction contract bond in the event the issuing surety company suffers a loss. This is an effort by the SBA to encourage the awarding of more construction bids to minority contractors. *See also* SURETY BOND.

SURETYSHIP *see* FIDELITY BOND; SURETY BOND.

SURETY'S RIGHT OF EXONERATION *see* SURETY BOND.

SURGICAL EXPENSE INSURANCE policy providing benefits to pay for surgery.

SURGICAL INSURANCE BENEFITS *see* SURGICAL EXPENSE INSURANCE.

SURGICAL SCHEDULE list of cash allowances for various types of surgeries. *See also* SURGICAL EXPENSE INSURANCE.

SURPLUS *see* SURPLUS ACCOUNT; SURPLUS LINES.

SURPLUS ACCOUNT assets minus liabilities of the insurance company. *See also* STATUTORY LIABILITY.

SURPLUS ADEQUACY RATIO insurance company's ADJUSTED SURPLUS divided by its ADJUSTED LIABILITIES. The greater this ratio, the greater the financial strength of the company that can be used for writing new business and covering benefit payments.

SURPLUS LINES
Reinsurance: SURPLUS REINSURANCE contracts under which the agreement between an insurer and a reinsurer is based on the *ceding* company's line guide, such that the amount reinsured is expressed in terms of the multiples of the retention and is referred to as a number of lines. *See also* SURPLUS REINSURANCE.
Regular market: insurance coverage not available from an ADMITTED COMPANY in the regular market; thus a surplus lines broker agent representing an applicant seeks coverage in the surplus lines market from a NONADMITTED INSURER according to the insurance regulations of a particular state.

SURPLUS LINES BROKER *see* EXCESS LINE BROKER (SURPLUS LINE BROKER).

SURPLUS LINES (EXCESS-SURPLUS LINES) specialized property or liability coverage provided by a NONADMITTED INSURER in instances where it is unavailable from insurers licensed by the state. Examples of surplus lines are coverage for some environmental impairment liability risks, or liability coverage for directors and officers of certain companies. *See also* EXCESS LINE BROKER (SURPLUS LINE BROKER).

SURPLUS RATIO percentage of total assets set aside by an insurance company to provide for unexpected losses. In general, a minimum of a 5% surplus ratio (5 cents in reserve for each $1 of assets) is advocated for determining whether the company has an adequate reserve against unexpected losses.

SURPLUS REINSURANCE automatic REINSURANCE that requires an insurer to transfer (CEDE) and the reinsurer to accept the part of every risk that exceeds the insurer's predetermined retention limit. The reinsurer shares in premiums and losses in the same proportion as it shares in the total policy limits of the risk. The *surplus method* permits the insurer to keep for its own account small policies, and to transfer the amount of risk on large policies above its retention limit. For example, assume an insurer issues a policy for $20,000. The insurer keeps $5000 ($\frac{1}{4}$) and transfers the remaining $15,000 ($\frac{3}{4}$) to its reinsurer. This is called a *three line surplus* because the amount transferred equals three times the retained line of the insurer. The insurer keeps $\frac{1}{4}$ and transfers $\frac{3}{4}$ of the premium to the reinsurer. In the event of total loss, the settlements between the insurer and the reinsurer would be effected on the identical $\frac{1}{4}$–$\frac{3}{4}$ basis. The same principle applies if there is a partial loss, in that the reinsurer must reimburse the insurer in the same proportion as the reinsurance premium received.

SURPLUS RELIEF insurance company's REINSURANCE COMMISSIONS AND EXPENSE ALLOWANCES divided by its ADJUSTED SURPLUS account. The smaller this ratio, the more financially sound the insurance company, since this ratio shows the extent to which the insurance company relies on reinsurance to maintain its surplus strength.

SURPLUS RELEASE method of using REINSURANCE to counteract the unexpected impact of business on the POLICYHOLDER SURPLUS. *See also* PORTFOLIO REINSURANCE; REINSURANCE.

SURPLUS SHARE *see* SURPLUS REINSURANCE.

SURPLUS TO POLICYHOLDERS *see* POLICYHOLDER SURPLUS.

SURPLUS TREATY REINSURANCE *see* SURPLUS REINSURANCE.

SURRENDER CHARGE fee charged to a policyowner when a life insurance policy or annuity is surrendered for its cash value. This fee reflects insurance company expenses incurred by placing the policy on its books, and subsequent administrative expenses. *See also* BACK LOAD.

SURRENDER COST INDEX method of comparing the costs of a set of CASH VALUE LIFE INSURANCE policies that takes into account the TIME VALUE OF MONEY. The true costs of alternative cash value policies with the same death benefit depend on a number of factors—amount and timing of premiums paid, amount and timing of dividends (in the case of *participating* policies), time period involved, and the CASH SURRENDER VALUE. In evaluating a particular group of policies, a surrender cost index can be calculated using INTEREST ADJUSTED COST comparison. The index ranks the policies for the same period of time, say the first 20 years of the policy life, by cost per $1000 of FACE AMOUNT, showing the cheapest through the most expensive. In effect, the index illustrates the relative cost of acquiring a dollar's worth of each policy's cash surrender value after 20 years. Contrast with the NET PAYMENTS INDEX, a ranking of policy costs using the traditional *net cost method* of comparison that ignores the time value of money and thus gives a less accurate picture of relative policy costs.

SURRENDER COST METHOD *see* SURRENDER COST INDEX.

SURRENDER, LIFE INSURANCE action by the owner of a cash value policy to relinquish it for its CASH SURRENDER VALUE. Since the depression of the 1930s, companies have reserved the right to delay payment of a cash surrender value up to six months; however, payments have been prompt.

SURRENDER PERIOD length of time one must stay invested in an annuity in order to avoid paying early withdrawal penalties.

SURRENDER VALUE *see* SURRENDER, LIFE POLICY.

SURVEY *see* SURVEY APPROACH.

SURVEY APPROACH study of buying habits of consumers to determine their insurance needs.

SURVIVAL STATUTE *see* UNIFORM SIMULTANEOUS DEATH ACT.

SURVIVOR PURCHASE OPTION provision applied as a RIDER attached to an ORDINARY LIFE INSURANCE POLICY for the purpose of meeting ESTATE PLANNING requirements. When the INSURED dies, the BENEFICIARY is entitled to receive the DEATH BENEFIT in cash or to use the death benefit to purchase a new ordinary life insurance policy. This new policy is not subject to additional underwriting requirements and has, as the date of issue, the same time as the original policy. The initial premium due is automatically subtracted from the original policy's death benefit.

SURVIVORSHIP ANNUITY agreement under which an annuitant receives a predetermined monthly income benefit for life upon the death of the insured. Should the annuitant predecease the insured, the contract is terminated and no benefits are ever paid. The life expectancy of both the insured and annuitant must be taken into consideration in determining the premium, and such, the annuitant cannot be changed once selected. This is also called a *revisionary annuity* (a life insurance policy combined with an annuity agreement).

SURVIVORSHIP BENEFIT retirement income benefit of a survivor (or survivors) of an insured individual, according to a particular formula. For example, if a retired male worker dies, all or a portion of his monthly pension (perhaps one half or two-thirds) may continue to go to his wife if he has elected the JOINT AND SURVIVOR OPTION. Survivors of a person entitled to Social Security benefits may also be entitled to receive a survivorship benefit. For example, a widower may get as much as 100% of his wife's benefits, if claimed at age 65 or over.

SURVIVORSHIP CLAUSE *see* COMMON DISASTER CLAUSE (SURVIVORSHIP CLAUSE).

SURVIVORSHIP INCOME PAYMENTS *see* SURVIVORSHIP BENEFIT.

SURVIVORSHIP LIFE INSURANCE coverage on more than one person that pays a benefit after all of the insureds die. This type of *joint life policy* is significantly cheaper than a regular policy. Survivorship life insurance might be used to help fund estate taxes after the deaths of a husband and wife or as a form of *business continuation insurance*. *See also* TONTINE.

SURVIVORSHIP SPLIT DOLLAR INSURANCE modification of SPLIT DOLLAR LIFE INSURANCE policy in that the death benefit becomes payable upon the second death. This type of policy is ideal in those circumstances when ESTATE TAXES must be paid, which is usually the case upon the death of the second spouse. Since this is a second-to-die policy, the premiums are substantially lower than those for a single life insurance policy. The procedure is for two individuals (usually spouses) to form a LIFE INSURANCE TRUST and then to enter into a SPLIT DOLLAR LIFE INSURANCE agreement with the trust. The individual(s) pay(s) that portion of the premium equal to the CASH VALUE of the policy and the trust pays the term cost of the premium. The individual is reimbursed for the premiums paid when the death benefit is paid or when the policy is surrendered for its CASH SURRENDER VALUE. The remainder of the death proceeds is paid to the LIFE INSURANCE TRUST.

SURVIVOR'S RIGHT TO SUE legal recourse available to survivors of a person who suffers a wrongful death. Under COMMON LAW, only an injured person had the right to sue for damages. If a wrongfully injured person died of those injuries, there was no one with a legal right to sue to recover damages for the death. State laws now provide for the right of the survivor to sue, not just for the wrongful death but for loss of income and other losses.

SUSPENSION OF COVERAGE interruption of insurance provided for in most property insurance policies under circumstances where a substantial increase in hazard has arisen with the knowledge or control of the insured. The policy's WORK AND MATERIALS CLAUSE gives the insured the right to use materials and processes needed in his or her business without facing suspension from increased hazard. But major changes in the characteristics of the risk will trigger suspension of coverage. For example, a building used to warehouse dry goods when fire insurance first is written on it may be converted by the insured to store paint. The substantial increase in hazard results in suspension of coverage. Vacancy for more than 60 days and riot or explosion also result in suspension. Coverage is reinstated automatically for the remainder of the policy term when the condition that triggered suspension is corrected.

SUSPENSION PROVISION *see* SUSPENSION OF COVERAGE.

SYMMETRIC RISK EXPOSURE gain that occurs when the move in the underlying asset in one direction is similar to the loss when the underlying asset moves in the opposite direction. For example, if a stock goes up by X dollars, there is an X dollar gain. On the other hand, if a stock goes down by X dollars, there is an X dollar loss.

SYNDICATE group of insurers or reinsurers involved in joint underwriting. Members typically take predetermined shares of premiums, losses, expenses, and profits. Syndicates, more common in REINSURANCE than in PRIMARY INSURANCE, are formed to cover major risks that are beyond the CAPACITY of a single underwriter. *See also* POOL; POOLING.

SYNDICATE POLICY INSURANCE POLICY underwritten and issued by a SYNDICATE listing each RISK insured by each syndicate member.

SYNTHETIC GUARANTEED INVESTMENT CONTRACT modified GUARANTEED INVESTMENT CONTRACT (GIC) in which the underlying assets of the synthetic contract are owned by the plan itself rather than the insurance company as is the case with the GIC. This ownership right is of particular importance if there is a concern about the long-term financial soundness of an insurance company. The synthetic plan segregates the plan's assets from the assets of the insurance company.

SYNTHETIC PRODUCTS type of GUARANTEED INVESTMENTS CONTRACT that enables the sponsor of the plan to own the title of the underwriting assets. In addition, benefit payments at BOOK VALUE are made for qualified plan withdrawals.

SYSTEM SAFETY method of accident prevention whose objective is to detect system-component deficiencies that have the potential for causing accidents.

SYSTEMS SAFETY ENGINEERING risk management technique for identifying risks and taking steps to minimize losses.

T

TABLE OF MORBIDITY see MORBIDITY TABLE.

TABLE OF MORTALITY *see* MORTALITY TABLE.

TABULAR COST OF INSURANCE *see* TABULAR PLANS.

TABULAR INTEREST RATE *see* TABULAR PLANS.

TABULAR MORTALITY rate exhibited in a MORTALITY TABLE; EXPECTED MORTALITY. *See also* TABULAR PLANS.

TABULAR PLANS RETROSPECTIVE RATING system with basic, minimum, and maximum premium rates listed in manual tables. Calculation of an individual premium involves adjusting the basic premium for appropriate discounts, losses, and a tax multiplier. The rate is then set between the minimum and the maximum, based on the loss experience, the size of the risk, and the underwriter's judgment.

TABULAR-VALUE RESERVE METHOD means of setting life insurance reserves based on expected mortality rates as reflected in a MORTALITY TABLE. *See also* RETROSPECTIVE METHOD RESERVE COMPUTATION.

TAFT-HARTLEY ACT provision of federal legislation that prohibits an employer from making contributions (premium payments) directly to a union for the purchase of employee benefits; instead the contributions can be paid into a trust fund established for these purposes.

TAFT-HARTLEY PENSION PLAN PENSION PLAN under which both the contribution (employer and employee if a contributory plan) and the benefit structure are fixed. In order to properly maintain the ACTUARIAL EQUIVALENT, the benefit structure and the contribution schedule are modified.

TAIL COVERAGE liability insurance that extends beyond the end of the policy period of a liability insurance policy written on a *claims-made* basis. Liability claims are often made long after the accident or event that caused the injury. Many liability policies are written on a claims-made basis, which means the insurer pays only claims that are received during the policy period. In that case, an insured needs tail coverage to protect against claims not known about at the end of the policy period. For example, a doctor retires, allows her insurance policy to lapse, and a claim comes in six months later. In order to protect herself, the doctor purchases tail coverage.

TAILORED LIFE INSURANCE type of policy that establishes a schedule of net insurance amounts (the amount of the DEATH BENEFIT that exceed the CASH SURRENDER VALUE instead of just the FACE AMOUNT).

TAPES INSURANCE *see* DATA PROCESSING INSURANCE.

TARGET BENEFIT PLAN type of pension in which benefits may vary depending on the investment performance of the pension plan assets. Contributions are made to fund a target benefit, such as 35% of compensation, using acceptable mortality and interest rate assumptions. Funds are invested wholly or partially in such vehicles as variable annuities or mutual funds, and benefits may exceed or fall below target levels depending on investment performance. Target plans are subject to the same annual contribution limits for individual participants as a MONEY PURCHASE PLAN. *See also* VARIABLE DOLLAR ANNUITY.

TARGET RISK
  1. prospective buyers of insurance classified according to various demographics such as age, sex, and insurance.
  2. risk so hazardous that it is difficult to obtain insurance coverage.

TARIFF *see* TARIFF RATE.

TARIFF RATE standard property-liability insurance premium set by a rating bureau for a particular class of risk.

TAXABLE-EQUIVALENT YIELD tax-free yield ÷ (1 − individual's combined federal and state income tax bracket). The calculation is made according to the following steps:
  1. Determine individual's effective state tax rate (percentage that individual pays in state taxes after deduction of these state taxes from his or her federal tax).

  where: effective state tax rate = (state tax rate + local tax rate) × (1 − federal income tax rate).

  Assume that the individual's taxable income is $60,000. The individual is in the 33% federal marginal income tax bracket, and his or her state tax rate on dividend income is 7.9%. Then the effective state tax rate = 0.079(1 − 0.33) = 0.05293.

  2. Determine individual's combined federal and state income tax bracket (federal marginal tax rate + effective state tax rate). For the above example, this relationship equals 0.33 + 0.05293 = 0.38293.
  3. Determine taxable-equivalent yield. Assume, for the above example, that an individual is considering an investment that has a tax-free yield of 8%. Then

  tax-equivalent yield = tax-free yield. (1 − individual's
        combined federal and state income
        tax bracket)

  $$= \frac{0.08}{0.61707} = 12.96\%$$

TAXABLE INCOME earned and unearned income on which current taxes must be paid. Tax avoidance is one of the goals of investment, and various tax-free or tax-deferred investments have been devised for this purpose. In the past, real estate and oil and gas limited partnerships have been a method of avoiding tax on current income, but changing tax legislation frequently alters the nature of taxable income and the taxes that must be paid on it. For example, the TAX REFORM ACT OF 1986 eliminated contributions to INDIVIDUAL RETIREMENT ACCOUNTS as a deduction for many taxpayers.

Insurance products have long enjoyed special tax benefits because of the belief in the importance of protecting one's family. For example, the interest buildup in annuities is allowed to accumulate, tax deferred. Taxes are paid on the earnings only when the money is withdrawn. Because the 1986 federal tax law eliminated so many other forms of tax shelters, insurance products became even more attractive for these properties.

TAX ADVANTAGES OF QUALIFIED PLAN *see* PENSION PLAN.

TAX-APPRAISED VALUE estimate of an asset that is used to determine tax obligations. It is usually in the interest of the owner to have a low value put on a piece of property for tax purposes. However, the owner sometimes wants the same property to carry a higher appraisal value for insurance purposes so that losses can be easily recovered if the property is lost or damaged.

TAXATION, INTEREST ON DIVIDENDS interest earned on dividends from a *participating life insurance policy* left on deposit with the insurance company and subject to taxation.

TAXATION, PARTICIPATING DIVIDENDS dividends of a *participating life insurance policy* deemed by the Internal Revenue Service to be a return of a portion of premiums and thus not subject to taxation.

TAXATION, PROCEEDS *see* AUTHORITY TO TERMINATE PLAN; GIFT TAX; TAXABLE INCOME; TAXATION, INTEREST ON DIVIDENDS; TAXATION, PARTICIPATING DIVIDENDS; TAX DEFERRAL; TAX DEFERRED ANNUITY (TDA).

TAX BENEFITS OF ANNUITY *see* ANNUITY.

TAX BENEFITS OF LIFE INSURANCE tax advantages of investing in life insurance fall into two main areas: (1) TAX DEFERRAL on untaxed buildup of earnings in such *cash value* policies as whole life insurance and annuities, and (2) exclusion from federal income tax of the proceeds of a death benefit of an insurance policy. *See also* TAX REFORM ACT OF 1986.

TAX BRACKET SHIFTING arrangement of financial affairs such that a family member who is in a lower income tax bracket receives income that another family member would otherwise have received (thereby reducing the taxes paid by the family unit).

TAX DEFERRAL postponement of taxes on investment or other earnings until the investor begins to consume them and anticipates being in a lower tax bracket. One example of a tax-deferred investment is an INDIVIDUAL RETIREMENT ACCOUNT (IRA). Earnings accumulate tax free until the account holder retires after age 59½. At that time, taxes must be paid on the earnings as money is withdrawn from the account. Other examples of tax deferred investments are insurance products such as *annuities* and various types of *whole life insurance* such as VARIABLE LIFE and UNIVERSAL LIFE. The TAX REFORM ACT OF 1986 limited the use of IRAs, making insurance products one of the few tax-deferred investments still available.

TAX DEFERRED ANNUITY (TDA) retirement vehicle permitted under SECTION 403 (B) PLAN of the U.S. Internal Revenue Code for employees of a public school system or a qualified charitable organization. Under such an agreement, the maximum annual contribution is $4500. Cash values and dividends accrue but are not taxed until the annuitant actually receives benefits. At that time, the annuitant is taxed only on the amount that exceeds the investment in the annuity. Should the annuitant receive a monthly benefit under one of the various *annuities,* the percentage of each payment that would not be subject to taxation is determined by the *exclusion ratio*:

$$\text{Exclusion Ratio} = \frac{\text{Amount Invested in Annuity}}{\text{Expected Return under Annuity}}$$

where the expected return under the annuity equals the life expectancy of the annuitant × the annual income payment.

For example, if an annuitant invested $40,000 in an annuity, and at age 60 has a 14-year life expectancy, and receives an annual income of $5000, then 57.14% of each income payment would not be subject to taxation.

TAX-EQUIVALENT INCOME tax-exempt income that, for comparative purposes, has been increased by an amount equal to the taxes that would be paid if this income were fully taxable at statutory rates. See *also* TAXABLE-EQUIVALENT YIELD.

TAX (FEDERAL), INCOME OF PENSION PLAN see PENSION PLAN.

TAX-FREE EXCHANGE OF INSURANCE PRODUCTS under Section 1035 of the Internal Revenue Code, stipulation that the exchange of one life insurance policy for another life insurance policy will generally not result in a recognized gain for the purpose of federal income tax purposes to the policyowner who exchanges the policy. The insured must be the same person under both policies. If the policy owner should surrender the second policy in a taxable transaction, the untaxed gain is then recognized. The types of policy exchanges that can be made on a tax-free basis are as follows: (1) a life insurance policy for another life insurance policy; (2) a life insurance policy for an annuity contract; and (3) an annuity contract for another annuity contract. An annuity contract cannot be exchanged on a tax-free basis for a life insurance policy. The ANNUITANT must be the same person under both annuity contracts in order to maintain the tax-free basis. *See also* MINIMUM DEPOSIT RESCUE.

TAX-FREE INCOME *see* TAXATION, PARTICIPATING DIVIDENDS; TAX BENEFITS OF LIFE INSURANCE; TAX DEFERRAL; TAX DEFERRED ANNUITY (TDA); TAX FREE ROLLOVER; TAX PLANNING.

TAX-FREE MONEY MUTUAL FUNDS investments restricted to short-term financial instruments issued by state, city, and county governments and agencies. Interest paid by those instruments are not subject to federal income tax, thus their attraction for high income tax bracket investors.

TAX-FREE ROLLOVER
1. transfer of money from or an employer-sponsored pension or other qualified plan into an INDIVIDUAL RETIREMENT ACCOUNT (IRA) without paying tax on the distribution.
2. transfer of money from one individual retirement account to another without paying tax.

    In both cases, the law allows the account holder 60 days to place the money in a new IRA account. Transfer from one account to another can be accomplished either by withholding the money from one account and depositing it in another within 60 days, or by instructing one institution to transfer it to a second. As long as the new deposit is made within 60 days, there is no current tax liability.

TAX LIEN claim against property for payment of taxes. Life insurance proceeds and annuity benefits are protected against certain creditors of the insured, but the federal government is not one of them. Thus life insurance and annuity benefits can be held liable if the federal government has a tax lien against the insured.

TAX MULTIPLIER factor applied in RETROSPECTIVE RATING in order to increase the BASIC PREMIUM to cover state premium taxes for liability and workers compensation insurance. For example, if a state premium tax is 2%, the tax multiplier used in the formula to determine the *retrospective premium* would be 1.02.

TAX PLANNING arrangement of discretionary income, expenses, and investments in a way that enhances after-tax wealth. Insurance policies can be used to increase after-tax income through the tax-deferral features of CASH VALUE LIFE INSURANCE and to reduce estate taxes through the preferential tax treatment of the life insurance DEATH BENEFIT. *See also* ESTATE PLANNING.

TAX-QUALIFIED PLAN tax advantaged DEFINED BENEFIT PLAN or DEFINED CONTRIBUTION PENSION PLAN (MONEY PURCHASE PLAN). These plans include INDIVIDUAL RETIREMENT ACCOUNT (IRA); ROTH INDIVIDUAL RETIREMENT ACCOUNT (IRA); SIMPLIFIED EMPLOYEE PENSION (SEP);

KEOGH PLAN (HR-10); TAX-DEFERRED ANNUITY (TDA); SECTION 403(b) PLAN; SECTION 457 DEFERRED COMPENSATION PLAN; SECTION 401(k) PLAN (SALARY REDUCTION PLAN); and SAVINGS INCENTIVE MATCH PLAN FOR EMPLOYEES (SIMPLE PLANS).

TELEGRAM PROPOSAL OF INSURANCE binding contract for insurance completed by telegraph. The law has recognized the date an insurance agreement is made as the date that coverage commences, rather than the date stated on the insurance policy. Acceptance of a proposal by telegram, like a letter or an oral agreement, represents a binding contract.

TELE-UNDERWRITING procedure in which a home office interviewer (who may or may not have UNDERWRITING experience) interviews APPLICANTS on the telephone. The questions asked the applicant are automated and scripted. The applicant's response to a particular question triggers the interviewer to either ask more details about the response or to ask another question. This procedure lists among its benefits: reduction in the time required to process applications; delivery of policies in a shorter period of time; nonduplication of the same question asked by agents, medical examiners, and underwriters; reduction in the number of omitted answers to questions on the application; and the reduction of paperwork required by an agent.

TEMPERATURE EXTREMES EXCLUSION provision in an ALL RISKS INLAND MARINE policy that denies coverage for exposure to dampness and extremes of temperature. Some property, like living plants, might be particularly vulnerable to extremes of temperature and is not considered as insurable risk.

TEMPORARY DISABILITY BENEFITS income paid to a worker who is temporarily disabled by an injury or sickness that is not work related. Compare with WORKERS COMPENSATION BENEFITS, which are available only to workers injured on the job. And unemployment benefits are available only to those who are able to work. Temporary disability benefits fill in for those who cannot work because of illness and who were not injured on the job. After a waiting period that is typically about a week, the disabled worker is paid a weekly income. Temporary disability benefits may come from a group benefit plan, from a union medical plan, or, in some cases, from a state insurance fund. Five states have temporary disability plans: California, Hawaii, New Jersey, New York, and Rhode Island.

TEMPORARY LIFE ANNUITY ANNUITY that provides income payments for a number of years provided the ANNUITANT is alive to receive them. All income payments cease upon the death of the annuitant.

TEMPORARY LIFE ANNUITY DUE limited number of payments, the first of which is due immediately, and payments thereafter are contingent upon the designated beneficiary (the ANNUITANT) continuing to live. After the limit has been reached all payments cease even if the annuitant is still alive.

TEMPORARY LIFE INSURANCE *see* TERM LIFE INSURANCE.

TEMPORARY MAJOR MEDICAL INSURANCE modification of the MAJOR MEDICAL INSURANCE policy that provides coverage for the terminating employee who otherwise would not be covered by a health insurance policy. Usually, this coverage is for no more than six months and cannot be renewed.

TEMPORARY NONOCCUPATIONAL DISABILITY PLAN social insurance that provides benefits to temporarily disabled workers in a few states. Five states require employers to pay cash benefits if workers are disabled. They are Rhode Island, California, New Jersey, New York, and Hawaii.

TEMPORARY PARTIAL, TOTAL DISABILITY *see* DISABILITY INCOME INSURANCE; TEMPORARY DISABILITY BENEFITS.

TENANCY *see* ESTATE PLANNING DISTRIBUTION: JOINT TENANTS; TENANCY BY THE ENTIRETY.

TENANCY BY THE ENTIRETY ownership of property by a husband and wife together; the law views the couple as one person. This can have a bearing on insurance claims. For example, if the wife willfully destroys property, her husband's claim may be denied by an insurer on the grounds that he is not separate from his wife for insurance purposes, and this constitutes destruction by the insured. Contrasts with TENANTS IN COMMON.

TENANTS IMPROVEMENTS AND BETTERMENTS improvements or renovations to a leased business or residential property made by a tenant to meet its particular needs. Loss of use of these improvements as a result of damage is covered by an endorsement to the *Standard Fire Policy.*

TENANTS IN COMMON ownership of property by two or more persons who do not have rights of survivorship. The share of a deceased tenant passes to that person's heirs and not to the other tenants. Because insurance is a personal contract, all parties with an interest in the property must be listed. When filing an insurance claim, the policyholder must prove there was a loss and that the property damaged belonged to the policy holder. For example, four tenants in common own a resort condominium. Only one is listed on the insurance policy. A fire destroys the condo. The insurer probably could argue successfully that the interests of the other three are not covered.

TENANTS INSURANCE coverage for the contents of a renter's home or apartment and for liability. Tenant policies are similar to homeowners insurance, except that they do not cover the structure. They do, however, cover changes made to the inside structure, such as carpeting, kitchen appliances, and built-in bookshelves.

TENDER OFFER offer by one business entity to purchase shares of another business entity at a stipulated price per share. *See* TENDER OFFER DEFENSE EXPENSE INSURANCE.

TENDER OFFER DEFENSE EXPENSE INSURANCE coverage for defense costs incurred in defending a company from an unfriendly takeover attempt. Hostile takeovers have been one of the hottest business topics in recent years. Vulnerable companies have responded in a variety of ways including changing the corporate bylaws, selling off their most attractive assets, and, in the last resort, voting themselves huge severance packages or "golden parachutes." When a company or individual makes a tender offer for the stock of its takeover target, the latter company usually hires legal experts and mounts a costly defense. This insurance is an example of a specialized coverage that grew to meet a specific need.

TENDER OF UNEARNED PREMIUM return of a pro rata portion of premium after a policy is canceled by the insurer. Under most property and liability insurance policies, the insurer can cancel at any time but must return to the insured the portion of the premium that has not been used. Although some courts have held that a policy has not been cancelled until the insurer returns the unearned premium, others allow the insurer to cancel the policy and inform the insured that the unearned premium will be refunded on demand.

TEN-PAY LIFE INSURANCE POLICY *see* LIMITED PAYMENT LIFE INSURANCE.

TEN-YEAR AVERAGING accounting method used to reduce income taxes on distributions from qualified pension or retirement plans. Ten-year averaging was repealed by the TAX REFORM ACT OF 1986 but is still available to persons who reached age 50 before January 1, 1986. They are allowed at any future date to make a one-time use of 10-year averaging at 1986 income tax and capital gains rates. Everyone else is limited to *5-year forward averaging*. For those still eligible, 10-year averaging provides the opportunity to pay tax on a lump sum distribution as if it were the only income received over a 10-year period. For example, a lump sum distribution of $50,000 would be taxed at $5874.

TEN-YEAR-CERTAIN PERIOD *see* OPTIONAL MODES OF SETTLEMENT.

TEN-YEAR PERIOD—CERTAIN LIFE ANNUITY *see* LIFE ANNUITY CERTAIN.

TEN-YEAR VESTING (CLIFF VESTING) method of vesting under the EMPLOYEE RETIREMENT INCOME SECURITY ACT OF 1974 (ERISA) that requires an employee to have 10 years of service with an employer to be vested. An employee who leaves an employer prior to that time does not receive retirement benefits from that job. Under the TAX REFORM ACT OF 1986, after December 31, 1988, the 10-year vesting rule is reduced to 5 years. Under the Pension Protection Act of 2006, employer nonelective contributions vest according to either the minimum three-year cliff or six-year graded vesting schedule: year 1 = 0% vesting, year 2 = 20% vested, year 3 = 40% vested, year 4 = 60% vested, year 5 = 80% vested, year 6 = 100% vested. *See also* VESTING.

TERM period of time of insurance coverage. If a loss occurs during this time, insurance benefits are paid. If a loss occurs after this time period has expired, no insurance benefits are paid.

TERM CONTRACT *see* COMMERCIAL HEALTH INSURANCE.

TERMINAL DIVIDEND additional policy dividend paid to a life insurance policyholder when a policy terminates. A MUTUAL INSURANCE COMPANY is owned by its policyholders and writes participating policies, which pay annual policy dividends to policyholders. (Some *stock insurance* companies pay dividends on some policies as well.) In addition to the annual dividend, many policies pay a terminal dividend when the policy terminates after a minimum period in force—usually 10 to 20 years. This represents a realm to the policyholder of an equitable portion of the overall increase in the insurer's surplus over this period. Some companies pay this dividend no matter how a policy is terminated; others pay it only under certain conditions.

TERMINAL FUNDING former method of funding a pension plan. When employees retire, the employer sets aside a lump sum that will pay them lifetime monthly benefits. When determining the amount, these factors are considered life expectancy, the promised monthly benefit, and expected earnings on the sum set aside. The lump sum can either be placed in a trust fund or used to buy an annuity. Terminal funding, along with the current disbursement method, are no longer permitted for qualified pension plans under the EMPLOYEE RETIREMENT INCOME SECURITY ACT of 1974 (ERISA). ERISA requires current funding of future pension liabilities.

TERMINAL ILLNESS BENEFIT portion of the DEATH BENEFIT in a life insurance policy paid upon the insured being diagnosed as having a terminal illness that will result in death within a year.

TERMINAL RESERVE life insurance reserve at the end of any policy year. Insurers are required by state regulatory authorities to set up reserves to pay for future claims. The INITIAL RESERVE is the reserve at the beginning of the policy year; the MEAN RESERVE is the average of the initial reserve and the terminal reserve for that year. The terminal reserve is used for dividend distributions and to set NONFORFEITURE VALUES for CASH VALUE LIFE INSURANCE. The terminal reserve for one policy year is the initial reserve for the next policy year.

TERMINATION cancellation of a policy by an insurance company. *See also* PENSION BENEFIT GUARANTY CORPORATION (PBGC); TERMINATION INSURANCE.

TERMINATION DATE *see* EXPIRATION; EXPIRATION NOTICE.

TERMINATION INSURANCE *see* PENSION PLAN TERMINATION INSURANCE.

TERMINATION RATE measure of the rate at which policies are cancelled or allowed to lapse. The termination rate is a factor in setting premiums for group life and health policies.

TERM INSURANCE *see* TERM LIFE INSURANCE.

TERM INSURANCE COST low-cost life insurance providing coverage only for a limited time, such as one year, five years, or to age 65. Term insurance costs less at younger ages than a comparable amount of CASH VALUE LIFE INSURANCE, or permanent insurance, which covers the remaining life of the insured. Term insurance has become increasingly popular; it costs less because there is less likelihood that an insured will die during the term, whereas with cash value insurance, a policy must pay off whenever a policyholder dies. However, the premium for term insurance increases dramatically as an insured grows older, but the premium for permanent insurance usually remains level throughout an insured's lifetime.

TERM LIFE INSURANCE life insurance that stays in effect for only a specified, limited period. If an insured dies within that period, the BENEFICIARY receives the death payments. If the insured survives, the policy ends and the beneficiary receives nothing. For example, if an insured with a five year term policy dies within that period, the beneficiary receives the face amount of the policy. If the insured survives the five year period, the policy ends, with no benefit payable. *See also* ORDINARY LIFE INSURANCE; RENEWABLE TERM LIFE INSURANCE.

TERM OF THE POLICY length of time INSURANCE POLICY is in force.

TERRITORIAL GROUPING OF RISKS method of classifying risks to establish equitable rates. In many property and liability insurance lines, the location of an insured has a significant impact on the loss experience. For example, in automobile insurance the chance of a policyholder sustaining a loss is much greater in New York City than in rural Iowa. In lines like workers compensation, insurers may consider the attitude of the state courts and its impact on the cost of claims in that state. The insurer's task is to define a territorial grouping that has an exposure that is either smaller or greater than the standard, yet the group must be large enough to provide significant loss experience for rate making.

TERRITORIAL LIMITS condition for INLAND MARINE liability insurance coverage that states a loss or claim must occur in the policy territory. Policy territory for a liability policy includes the U.S., its territories, and Canada; international water or air space (except for when the injured person is traveling to another country); and injuries sustained anywhere in the world if a product is produced in the U.S. and the suit is brought in the U.S.

TERRITORIAL LIMITS LIABILITY INSURANCE *see* TERRITORIAL LIMITS.

TERRORISM RISK INSURANCE ACT legislation that created a federal government REINSURANCE program in which there is a sharing of losses between private insurance companies and the federal government in the event of future terrorist attacks. In the event of claims resulting from terrorism, the insurance company would pay an amount within a deductible equal to an increasing percentage each year of its WRITTEN PREMIUMS for the previous calendar year. After this deductible has been satisfied, the federal government on an EXCESS OF LOSS REINSURANCE basis would pay 90% of the insured claims basis. Under this act, insurance companies that participate in this federal government reinsurance program must provide coverage for losses resulting from terrorism on the same basis as coverage for losses resulting from other perils.

TERTIARY BENEFICIARY third-in-line BENEFICIARY to receive benefits from an insurance policy should the primary and secondary beneficiaries not survive.

TESTAMENTARY TRUST *see* ESTATE PLANNING DISTRIBUTION; TESTAMENTARY DISPOSITION.

TESTAMENTARY DISPOSITION disposition or transfer of property at time of death. Although the law provides that property may be transferred at death only by means of a will that meets the requirements of state statutes, life insurance proceeds are exempt from this requirement. They pass to the stated beneficiary without regard to the state requirements for wills.

TESTATE having in force a valid WILL.

TESTATOR/TESTATRIX individual who institutes a valid WILL.

TESTATE DISTRIBUTION *see* ESTATE PLANNING DISTRIBUTION.

THEATRICAL FLOATER endorsement to a *scheduled property floater* that provides named perils coverages for props, costumes, and other materials that might be used by a theatrical company. Coverage is provided for these perils: fire, lightning, windstorm, explosion, collapse of bridges, flood, theft, smoke, and transportation perils.

THEFT act of stealing. Coverage can be purchased under most property insurance policies such as the HOMEOWNERS INSURANCE POLICY.

THEFT, CHARACTERISTICS *see* BURGLARY INSURANCE; HOMEOWNERS INSURANCE POLICY; PERSONAL AUTOMOBILE POLICY (PAP); SPECIAL MULTIPERIL INSURANCE (SMP).

THEFT, DISAPPEARANCE, AND DESTRUCTION POLICY (FORM C) COMBINATION POLICY PLAN of FIDELITY INSURANCE and CRIME INSURANCE under five standard agreements:

1. *Insuring Agreement I*—dishonesty of employees on either a COMMERCIAL BLANKET BOND or BLANKET POSITION BOND basis.
2. *Insuring Agreement II*—coverage inside an insured's premises or a bank premises if money and securities are lost due to dishonesty, disappearance, or destruction.
3. *Insuring Agreement III*—coverage of money and securities being transported by an insured's messenger outside an insured's premises if they are lost due to dishonesty, disappearance, or destruction.
4. *Insuring Agreement IV*—coverage if an insured accepts counterfeit U.S. or Canadian paper currency or money orders of no value.
5. *Insuring Agreement V*—coverage for depositor forgery if an insured's own commercial paper is forged or altered. Additional coverages can be added through endorsement, including check forgery, paymaster robbery, *broad form* payroll robbery coverage both inside and outside an insured's premises, broad form payroll robbery coverage inside premises only, burglary and theft of merchandise, forgery of warehouse receipts, wrongful obstruction of securities or losses from safe deposit boxes, burglary of office equipment, theft of office equipment, paymaster robbery inside premises only, and forgery in use of credit cards.

THEFT, EXCLUSION *see* BURGLARY INSURANCE; HOMEOWNERS INSURANCE POLICY; PERSONAL AUTOMOBILE POLICY (PAP); SPECIAL MULTIPERIL INSURANCE (SMP).

THEFT, HOMEOWNERS INSURANCE POLICY *see* HOMEOWNERS INSURANCE POLICY.

THEORY OF PROBABILITY *see* LAW OF LARGE NUMBERS; PROBABILITY; PROBABILITY DISTRIBUTION.

THIEF *see* BURGLARY INSURANCE; HOMEOWNERS INSURANCE POLICY; PERSONAL AUTOMOBILE POLICY (PAP); SPECIAL MULTIPERIL INSURANCE (SMP).

THIRD PARTY individual other than the insured or insurer who has incurred a loss or is entitled to receive a benefit payment as the result of the acts or omissions of the insured.

THIRD PARTY: ADMINISTRATION performance of managerial and clerical functions related to an EMPLOYEE BENEFIT INSURANCE PLAN by an individual or committee that is not an original party to the benefit plan. In selecting a Third Party Administration (TPA), the following factors should be taken into consideration: (1) Has the TPA been operating on a profitable basis? (2) Does the TPA have a long operating record? (3) What percentage of the TPA's total business will your company's business comprise? (4) Does the TPA have the technical capacity (for example, sophisticated computer operations) to adequately service its acquired business? (5) Are current and former clients of the TPA positive about that TPA? (6) Are the employees of the TPA technically competent and committed to providing effective and efficient services? *See also* ADMINISTERING AGENCY; ADMINISTRATIVE CHARGE; ADVISORY COMMITTEE.

THIRD PARTY: BENEFICIARY individual who has a legally enforceable right to receive all benefits allocated to him or her under the insurance policy or employee benefit plan even though this person was not an original party to the insurance policy contract or employee benefit contract.

THIRD PARTY: INSURANCE liability insurance purchased by the insured (first party) from an insurance company (second party) for protection against possible suits brought by another (third party). See *also* LIABILITY INSURANCE.

"3-D" POLICY *see* DISHONESTY, DISAPPEARANCE, AND DESTRUCTION POLICY (3-D POLICY).

THREE-FACTOR CONTRIBUTION METHOD principle of SURPLUS distribution as the result of excess funds above the amount required to establish LEGAL RESERVES. These excess funds are generated from three sources: (1) MORTALITY SAVINGS; (2) excess interest earned on investments; and (3) expense savings.

THREE-FOURTHS LOSS CLAUSE provision requiring insurance company to pay no more than three-fourths of the actual cash value of the damaged or destroyed property. Historically, this clause was found in property insurance policies and marine insurance policies. Today, this clause is no longer used.

THREE-FOURTHS VALUE CLAUSE *see* THREE-FOURTHS LOSS CLAUSE.

THREE STEPS INVOLVED *see* RISK MANAGEMENT.

THRESHOLD LEVEL minimum degree of injury or loss for which an injured party can sue, even though covered by NO FAULT AUTOMOBILE INSURANCE. Traditionally, an accident victim had to prove the other driver was at fault in order to collect damages from that driver's insurance company. Today, more than 20 states have some type of automobile no-fault law designed to eliminate long and costly legal action, and to assure quick payment for medical and hospital costs, loss of income, and other unavoidable costs stemming from automobile accidents. An injured person can collect from his or her insurance company up to the threshold level, or specified limit, no matter who is at fault. For expenses above these limits, the injured person is still allowed to sue. There are three types of thresholds: a *specific dollar amount,* a *specific period of disability,* or *specified injuries* such as loss of a leg.

THRIFT PLAN type of employee savings plan under which an employee may contribute up to a specified percentage of the salary on an after-tax basis and the employer matches the employee's contribution up to a specified percentage. Investment earnings on the sums contributed accrue on a tax-deferred basis until distributed.

TICKET POLICY *see* TRANSPORTATION TICKET INSURANCE.

TIE-INS placement of insurance policies by a BROKER with a particular insurance company with that company, in turn, agreeing to use the broker for its reinsurance requirements.

TIME AND DISTANCE REINSURANCE type of EXCESS OF LOSS REINSURANCE in which the insurance company (CEDENT) receives payments from its REINSURER in a specific pattern of payments.

TIME ELEMENT (TIME POLICY) COVERAGE insurance that covers an INDIRECT LOSS stemming from a DIRECT LOSS by a covered peril to income-producing property. A building destroyed by fire represents a direct loss. Lost income resulting from the shutdown of a manufacturing facility housed in the burned building represents an indirect time element loss and would be covered by BUSINESS INTERRUPTION INSURANCE, a form of time element insurance.

TIME FOR NOTIFICATION OF LOSS period allowed an insured to notify an insurer of loss. Many policies require immediate written notice, or notice as soon as practicable. Different types of policies have their own time periods. For example, health insurance policies require notice within 20 days, windstorm insurance policies within 10 days, and hail insurance policies within 48 hours. The purpose of a time period is to allow the insurer to investigate the loss and protect the property from further damage.

TIME LIMIT
  1. part of the *Model Uniform Life and Health Insurance Policy Provisions Law* giving an insurer a time limit on contesting coverage for preexisting conditions or misrepresentation. This law, developed in 1950 as model legislation by the NATIONAL ASSOCIATION OF INSURANCE COMMISSIONERS (NAIC), has been adopted by all states. While the model law gave insurers three years for certain defenses, such as misrepresentation of facts by an insured or nondisclosure of a preexisting condition, many states have lowered it to two years.
  2. period of time that proof of loss or claim must be filed with an insurance company.

TIME LIMITS period of time during which notice of claim and proof of loss must be submitted by the INSURED or his or her legal representatives.

TIME POLICY *see* TIME ELEMENT (TIME POLICY) COVERAGE; VOYAGE POLICY.

TIME VALUE OF MONEY relationship determined by the mathematics of COMPOUND INTEREST between the value of a sum of money at one point in time and its value at another point in time. Time value of money can be illustrated by the fact that a dollar received today is worth more than a dollar received a year from now because today's dollar can be invested and earn interest as the year elapses. Implicit in any consideration of time value of money are the rate of interest and the period of compounding. For example, the *present value* of $1 million received 10 years from now is only $386,000 today, assuming a 10% rate of interest and annual compounding. Insurance companies make use of time value of money by earning investment income on premiums between the time of receipt and the time of payment of claims or benefits. *See also* STRUCTURED SETTLEMENT.

TITLE INSURANCE coverage for losses if a land title is not free and clear of defects that were unknown when the title insurance was written. Title insurance protects a purchaser if there is a defect in the title, such as a lien against the property, that is not discovered at the time of purchase. Although a title search is a routine part of a property transaction, it is possible that a search may overlook some encumbrance. Title insurance is written by title insurance companies that generally operate in a specific geographic area because of the need to examine local records. The TORRENS SYSTEM is a form of title insurance used in some states.

TITLE XIX INSURANCE *see* MEDICAID.

TLO *see* TOTAL LOSS ONLY (TLO) INSURANCE.

TONTINE early life insurance that provided benefits only to survivors who lived to the end of a certain period of time. In the mid-17th century, Lorenzo Tonti, an Italian, devised a scheme to raise money for the French government of Louis XIV. It involved a state lottery in which the oldest survivor would collect the pot. One woman, age 96, hit the jackpot shortly before her death. Tontine policies were introduced in the U.S. in the 1860s, but condemned in the ARMSTRONG INVESTIGATION in 1905 in New York State and subsequently outlawed everywhere 45 years later.

TOP HAT PLAN NONQUALIFIED DEFERRED COMPENSATION PLAN for highly compensated employees or select group of personnel. The reporting and disclosure requirements of the EMPLOYEE RETIREMENT INCOME SECURITY ACT OF 1974 (ERISA) and the INTERNAL REVENUE CODE require only the following information: name of the employer, number of employees in the plan, and a statement from the employer that the plan is maintained and funded strictly to provide nonqualified deferred compensation to select number of personnel.

TOP-HEAVY PLAN pension or other employee benefit plan that favors highly compensated employees or top executives or owners of a company. Prior to the TAX REFORM ACT OF 1986, there was no uniform definition of a "highly compensated" employee, but that law provided a specific definition that was used for *qualified pension plans, 401(k) plans,* and some other employee benefits. Under that act, an employee was considered highly compensated if he or she: (1) directly or indirectly owned more than a 5% interest in the company; (2) received compensation from the company of more that $75,000; (3) was paid more than $50,000 *and* was among the top 20% of employees ranked by compensation; or (4) was at any time an officer and received compensation that was more than 150% of the Section 415 defined-contribution dollar amount.

Under the PENSION REFORM ACT OF 2006, the top-heavy definition has been amended for DEFINED CONTRIBUTION PENSION PLANS to mean at the point when the aggregate value of the key employees' plan accounts exceed 60% of the aggregate value of all employees' plan accounts. In DEFINED BENEFIT PLANS, it is at the point when the present value of the accrued benefits of the key employees' plan accounts exceed 60% of the present value of all employees' plan accounts. The key employee is defined as owning more than 5% of a company and/or is part of the top 1% employee group that has income in excess of $150,000 from that company. The key employee can also be an officer of the company with an income in excess of $140,000 indexed according to inflation rates.

TORRENS SYSTEM means of land title registration used in some states that in effect, provides a government sponsored form of TITLE INSURANCE. Under this system, a government official, such as county recorder or county clerk, maintains Torrens System deed records and guarantees clear title when property is transferred. Fees charged for registration and transfer of title are used in part to finance a Torrens insurance fund in each jurisdiction to compensate claimants for damages resulting from errors.

TORT in general, a civil wrong, other than breach of contract, for which a court will provide a remedy in the form of a suit for damages. Torts include negligent acts or omissions on the part of a defendant. Liability insurance is designed to cover an insured (defendant) for *unintentional tort acts. See also* NEGLIGENCE.

TORT, DEFENSE AGAINST UNINTENTIONAL excuses raised by a defendant in a negligent suit (unintentional tort). There are three basic defenses to unintentional torts or negligence.
1. ASSUMPTION OF RISK—an individual (plaintiff), by not objecting to the negligent conduct of another, acknowledges awareness of the present danger and consents to it.
2. CONTRIBUTORY NEGLIGENCE—both individuals have contributed to an injury or property damage sustained by one or both individuals. Under this circumstance neither should be allowed to collect from the other.

3. COMPARATIVE NEGLIGENCE—where both plaintiff and defendant contributed to plaintiff's injury, the apportionment of some fault to the plaintiff reduces the liability of the defendant.

TORT FEASOR person who commits a TORT, a type of wrongful act, that causes injury or damage.

TORT, INTENTIONAL deliberate act or omission. These torts include *trespass*—an individual enters property owned or in the possession of another without permission; *conversion*—an individual exerts control and subverts another's property to his or her own benefit; *assault*—an individual's conduct causes another to fear for his or her life or the damage to his or her property; *battery*—an individual physically strikes another without permission; *false imprisonment*—an individual confines another illegally; *libel*—dissemination of written injurious and false information about another's character; and *slander*—oral dissemination of injurious and false information about another's character.

TORT LAW legislation governing wrongful acts, other than breaches of contract by one person against another or his or her property, for which civil action can be brought. Tort law and contract law define civil liability exposures. The four areas of torts are negligence, intentional interference, absolute liability, and strict liability. For example, the owner of a decrepit boat dock that collapses while people are standing on it might be liable under negligence. Assault and battery are an example of intentional interference. The owner of a poisonous snake that bit someone could be liable for injury under absolute liability, even if he or she did not intend to harm anyone. The maker of a defective product that harms the buyer might be held liable under strict liability. *See also* TORT LIABILITY.

TORT LIABILITY *see* TORT; TORT, DEFENSE AGAINST UNINTENTIONAL; TORT, INTENTIONAL; TORT, UNINTENTIONAL.

TORT, UNINTENTIONAL individual action or failure to act as a reasonably prudent person would under similar circumstances, resulting in harm to another. Also called NEGLIGENCE. A reasonably prudent person is defined by the standards of the profession that are followed, and the level of expertise expected of a person with like training. An example is a CPA who fails to complete tax returns on behalf of a client according to GENERALLY ACCEPTED ACCOUNTING PRINCIPLES.

TOTAL DISABILITY *see* DISABILITY.

TOTAL DISABILITY BENEFIT monthly income payment from a DISABILITY INCOME INSURANCE policy made to the insured wage earner when income has been interrupted or terminated because of illness, sickness, or accident provided the following stipulations by the wage earner have been met: (1) total disability for the duration that the policy is in force and beyond the ELIMINATION PERIOD; and (2) while remaining totally disabled, income payment made at the end of each month until the limits on the maximum amount of benefit are reached, at which time payments will cease.

TOTAL LOSS condition of real or personal property when it is damaged or destroyed to such an extent that it cannot be rebuilt or repaired to equal its condition prior to the loss.

TOTAL OPERATING INCOME insurance company's total premium income plus investment income.

TOTAL LOSS ONLY (TLO) INSURANCE ocean marine policy that pays an insured only if a ship or cargo is a total loss. Because total loss is rare, these policies are much less expensive than regular hull insurance. Therefore, it is used by shipowners who cannot afford more complete coverage or who cannot get it for some other reason.

TOTAL QUALITY MANAGEMENT (TQM) management philosophy developed by W. Edwards Deming, the thesis of which is the continuous improvement in quality through research in customer satisfaction and the empowerment of employees. To that end, a range of team-building and work flow-analysis techniques are emphasized. This management technique is useful in its application to insurance company operations since these operations involve transactions between the company and customers to include policy sales, distribution, and claims. *See also* QUALITY INSURANCE CONGRESS (QIC).

TOTAL RETURN comprehensive gain or loss on a security over a stipulated period of time comprised of capital appreciation plus dividend/interest received.

TOTAL RETURN UNITRUST (TRU) modification of the CHARITABLE REMAINDER UNITRUST through which the BENEFICIARIES receive a specified percentage of the assets' value in the TRUST usually paid out on a quarterly basis. If the trust's assets earn a greater return than the amount being received by the beneficiaries, the excess amount earned remains in the trust to further accumulate. As the assets grow in this trust, the income to the beneficiaries will also become larger.

TOURIST BAGGAGE INSURANCE coverage for personal effects of a tourist, including apparel, books, toilet articles, watches, jewelry, luggage, portable typewriters, photographs and photography equipment and supplies. This is a SPECIFIED PERIL INSURANCE policy that specifically includes fire, lightning, damage due to automobile accident, theft of items in the care, custody, and control of a common carrier, and theft of items from the hotel room in which the insured tourist is registered. Excluded are baggage theft from checkrooms, baggage theft from hotel lobbies unless checked, items at the permanent premises of the insured tourist, and items that cannot be found but have not been stolen.

TOWING INSURANCE endorsement to an automobile policy that pays specified amount for towing and related labor costs.

TOWNHOUSE MULTIPLE LINE INSURANCE homeowners policy to cover the owner of a townhouse. *See also* HOMEOWNERS INSURANCE POLICY.

TRACKING STOCK a series or separate class of a company's COMMON STOCK INVESTMENTS. The stock reflects the separate performance of a select group of assets.

TRADITIONAL INDIVIDUAL RETIREMENT ACCOUNT (IRA) *see* INDIVIDUAL RETIREMENT ACCOUNT (IRA).

TRADITIONAL NET COST METHOD OF COMPARING COSTS *see* INTEREST ADJUSTED COST; LIFE INSURANCE COST.

TRADITIONAL RISK REINSURANCE application of conventional terms and conditions to the REINSURANCE of a RISK. Contrast with NON-TRADITIONAL REINSURANCE.

TRAILER INSURANCE liability and physical damage coverage for trailers under business or personal auto policies. Most *automobile insurance* policies offer liability coverage for common types of trailers owned by an insured, including house trailers, boat trailers, and campers. For COLLISION INSURANCE coverage, personally owned trailers must be scheduled on a personal policy. The BUSINESS AUTOMOBILE POLICY (BAP) offers only limited insurance without scheduled coverage for both liability and collision.

TRANCHE type of bond that is class specific as part of a larger securities offering.

TRANSFERABILITY *see* ASSIGNMENT; ASSIGNMENT CLAUSE, LIFE INSURANCE; COLLATERAL ASSIGNMENT.

TRANSFER ABSOLUTE *see* LIFE INSURANCE, ASSIGNMENT CLAUSE.

TRANSFER BY ASSIGNMENT *see* ASSIGNMENT CLAUSE, LIFE INSURANCE.

TRANSFER BY ENDORSEMENT *see* ASSIGNMENT; COLLATERAL ASSIGNMENT; LIFE INSURANCE, ASSIGNMENT CLAUSE.

TRANSFER FOR VALUE RULE an exception to SECTION 101 (A) (1) OF THE INTERNAL REVENUE CODE tax-exempt status of the DEATH BENE-FIT in a life insurance policy where the transfer of the interest in the policy by the policyowner to another party in exchange for a valuable consideration results in the death benefit losing its tax-exempt status. However, the death benefit will not lose its tax-exempt status when the policy is transferred to the insured, to a partner of the insured, to a partnership in which the insured is a full partner, or to a company, provided the insured is a stockholder and/or an officer in that company.

TRANSFER OF INSUREDS provision in corporate life insurance policies that allows coverage to be transferred to a new individual with proof of insurability, for a premium appropriate to the age of the new individual. These policies are designed to cover key executives of a corporation and to provide continuous insurance in force without the necessity of obtaining a new policy. For example, if a corporation buys insurance to cover the chief executive officer who later retires, the policy could be transferred to the new CEO. *See also* RIDERS, LIFE INSURANCE.

TRANSFER OF RISK *see* RISK TRANSFER.

TRANSFER ON DEATH (TOD) form of stock ownership that permits the stockholder to select a BENEFICIARY to receive the stock upon the death of the stockholder. The stockholder retains all rights of stock ownership during his or her lifetime. At the death of the stockholder, the stock is transferred to the beneficiary not subject to PROBATE. The beneficiary can be a corporation, TRUST, or individual. The stockholder may nullify the TOD and change the beneficiary at will.

TRANSFER PAYMENTS redistribution of wealth by taking money from one group of individuals and allocating that sum to another group of individuals. SOCIAL INSURANCE is such a mechanism, since the high-income group of individuals will pay proportionately more in Social Security taxes and receive proportionately less in retirement income benefits than the low-income group of individuals.

TRANSIT INSURANCE INLAND MARINE policy that protects an insured against loss for property that is shipped. One policy may be written for a single shipment, as for a family moving household goods, or it may be an open policy written for a manufacturer who continuously ships products. The basic inland transit policy is written on one of two policy forms, the ANNUAL POLICY or the OPEN POLICY. TRIP TRANSIT INSURANCE is available for single shipments.

TRANSPLANT BENEFIT TOTAL DISABILITY BENEFIT in the form of a monthly income payment found in a disability income insurance policy to insured wage earners when their income has been interrupted or terminated due to total disability resulting from an organ transplant from the insured's body to the body of another individual.

TRANSPORTATION INSURANCE *see* INLAND MARINE INSURANCE (TRANSPORTATION INSURANCE): BUSINESS RISKS.

TRANSPORTATION INSURANCE RATING BUREAU (TIRB) one of two bureaus that writes forms and files standard rates for inland marine insurance. The other is the INLAND MARINE INSURANCE BUREAU.

TRANSPORTATION TICKET INSURANCE accident policy that covers a traveler for a single trip on an airplane or other common carrier. The name comes from its origin as part of the ticket or ticket stub, but these policies are no longer sold with the ticket. They are commonly sold in airports, often from vending machines.

TRAUMATIC INJURY bodily or emotional injury resulting from physical or mental wound or shock. A traumatic injury is caused by something outside the person's body as opposed to a sickness or a disease. An example would be injury to a hand that is smashed in a machine, or a nervous breakdown caused by stress on the job.

TRAVEL ACCIDENT INSURANCE special-purpose health insurance policy that covers an insured for accidents while traveling. The policy may cover the insured for one specific trip or one particular type of travel, or it may cover all trips taken in a year. This type of insurance can be purchased in airport vending machines or from an agent.

TRAVEL INSURANCE insurance coverage for pitfalls associated with travel. The coverage can be classified as follows:
1. *Trip Cancellation*—the traveler(s) must cancel the trip because of unforeseen circumstances such as an illness;
2. *Trip Interruption*—coverage in the event a trip is terminated because of illness or hotel ceases to continue to operate;
3. *Lost Luggage*—valuables are lost and expenses are incurred because of the inconvenience;
4. *Default Protection*—a trip is cancelled because a carrier or tour operator is no longer in business.

TREASURY INFLATION PROTECTION BONDS (TIPs) bonds issued by the United States Treasury that pay a semiannual interest rate tied to the Treasury auction plus an additional interest rate tied to the rate of inflation during this semiannual period. The rate of inflation is measured by the increases or decreases in the Consumer Price Index for Urban Consumers (CPI-U). The TIPs are issued in minimum denominations of $1000 with varying maturities. The additional rate of inflation interest adjustment is paid on the principal of the bond at maturity. Taxes are paid annually on both the interest earned on the TIP as well as the additional rate of inflation interest adjustment.

TREATMENT OF DEATH BENEFITS *see* (1) ESTATE PLANNING; (2) ESTATE PLANNING DISTRIBUTION; (3) GROUP LIFE INSURANCE; (4) PENSION PLAN; (5) TAX BENEFITS OF LIFE INSURANCE; (6) TAX PLANNING.

TREATMENT OF EMPLOYEE WITHDRAWALS *see* PENSION PLANS: WITHDRAWAL BENEFITS.

TREATY FACILITY facility used to gain access to the REINSURANCE markets by the CAPTIVE INSURANCE COMPANIES for their large property exposures. The facility reinsures a relatively small percentage of its captive company members' property exposure and uses a RETROCESSION to transfer the remainder of the property exposure on a TREATY REINSURANCE basis. The facility institutes all renewals of reinsurance for its captive company members at the same instance and arranges FACULTATIVE REINSURANCE for those members that cannot meet the UNDERWRITING requirements of the facility.

TREATY REINSURANCE *see* AUTOMATIC NONPROPORTIONAL REINSURANCE; AUTOMATIC PROPORTIONAL REINSURANCE; AUTOMATIC REINSURANCE.

TRENDED describing the process of developing the ultimate losses and then adjusting them to the cost levels projected for the period of time to be forecasted.

TRESPASS *see* TORT, INTENTIONAL; TRESPASSER.

TRESPASSER person who enters property without the right to do so. For liability purposes, it has been held that property owners are not responsible for trespassers as long as they do not intentionally trap or injure them. On the other hand, a property owner can be liable for injury to a person who has been invited onto his or her property, including messengers, delivery people, and service people, as well as guests. However, trespassers are very narrowly defined. No one in a public place is considered a trespasser. Likewise, owners of an ATTRACTIVE NUISANCE have been held liable for injuries to trespassing children. Further, recent interpretations by the courts have sometimes made owners liable for injury to trespassers if the owner was negligent.

TRICARE Department of Defense TRIPLE OPTION managed health care program consisting of three options: Tricare Prime (HEALTH MAINTENANCE ORGANIZATION), Tricare Extra (PREFERRED PROVIDER ORGANIZATION), and Tricare Standard (non-network provider system). This program is designed to coordinate health care between the military and civilian systems for members of the military. Included is a program for resource sharing in order to increase the availability of health care services and to facilitate referral to the proper health providers.

TRIGGERING EVENT activity that must occur before payment can be paid to an ANNUITANT from a TAX DEFERRED ANNUITY (TDA) without having to pay a tax penalty on the income (for example, an annuitant becoming disabled.)

TRIP CARGO INSURANCE *see* CARGO INSURANCE.

TRIPLE INDEMNITY *see* ACCIDENTAL DEATH CLAUSE.

TRIPLE OPTION PLAN plan that permits the insurance company to administer health care plans that permit the patient to choose from three benefit options at the time of need: INDEMNITY (insurance), HEALTH MAINTENANCE ORGANIZATION (HMO), and PREFERRED PROVIDER ORGANIZATION (PPO). The indemnity plan, even though more costly, would provide the patient with the greatest number of choices among physicians and hospitals. The PPO would allow the patient to have more choices among physicians and hospitals than the HMO and would not require the patient to go through the primary care physician or gatekeeper, as the HMO requires. The HMO would be the lowest cost option (no deductible) but the most restrictive as to the patient's choice.

TRIPLE PROTECTION combination life insurance policy consisting of ORDINARY LIFE and double the amount of TERM LIFE. Should the insured die within a stipulated time period, the double term amount and ordinary life amount are paid to the beneficiary. If the insured dies beyond the stipulated time period, only the ordinary amount is paid to the beneficiary. This policy may be applicable in situations where the family is young and extra amounts of protection are required until the children reach the age of majority.

TRIPLE-X model regulation for the valuation of insurance policies. This regulation makes it mandatory for the advanced funding of the future liabilities of a TERM LIFE INSURANCE policy over the length of time policy is in force. RESERVES AND THEIR COMPUTATION must be on an individual basis for each LEVEL PREMIUM segment and calculated for the total policy period.

TRIP TRANSIT INSURANCE coverage on a single shipment of property while in temporary storage or in transit. This policy is most commonly used in moving of household goods, which are covered from the time they are picked up, put in temporary storage, shipped to another location and put in temporary storage, and then delivered to the insured's new address. Protection is on an ALL RISKS basis subject to exclusions such as war, wear and tear, and nuclear disaster.

TRUCKERS INSURANCE limited special purposes policy that provides liability and physical damage insurance for owners and operators of trucks while engaged in business. This insurance is often purchased by a business that employs owner-operators.

TRUE GROUP PLAN insurance arrangement in which all employees of a given business firm are accepted into a plan regardless of their physical condition. The employee cannot be required to take a physical examination in order to qualify. The employees are covered under a *Master Contract. See also* GROUP HEALTH INSURANCE; GROUP LIFE INSURANCE.

TRUE NO-FAULT AUTOMOBILE INSURANCE *see* NO-FAULT AUTOMOBILE INSURANCE.

TRUST legal entity that provides for ownership of property by one person for the benefit of another. The TRUSTEE receives title to the property, but does not have the right to benefit personally from that property. The trustee has a legal obligation to manage the property and invest its assets solely for the BENEFICIARY OF TRUST. Since the trustee is required to manage the property and its assets in a prudent manner, if the trustee fails to perform in accordance with the PRUDENT MAN RULE the trustee becomes personally responsible for any lost funds or profits incurred by the trust. There are basically two types of trusts: LIVING TRUST (established during the life of the GRANTOR) and TESTAMENTARY TRUST. For example, a trust may be established by a parent to hold assets for the benefit of a child. *See also* BENEFICIARY OF TRUST; ESTATE PLANNING DISTRIBUTION.

TRUST AGREEMENT legal document setting out the rules to be followed by a TRUSTEE in administering assets of a TRUST. The trust agreement may limit investment of trust assets to specified types of securities, for example, or provide for distribution of the trust principal or earnings to a BENEFICIARY OF TRUST only under certain circumstances.

TRUSTEE *see* ESTATE PLANNING DISTRIBUTION.

TRUSTEE, BOND *see* TRUSTEE ROLE, PENSION PLANS.

TRUSTEED INDIVIDUAL RETIREMENT ACCOUNT establishment of an INDIVIDUAL RETIREMENT ACCOUNT (IRA) through which the account owner is able to provide income distributions to a surviving spouse for life. Upon the death of the surviving spouse, designated beneficiaries will receive the remaining assets.

TRUSTEE LIABILITY INSURANCE coverage provided for the fiduciaries of a retirement plan as well as for the plan itself in the event negligence of the fiduciaries results in losses to the plan and/or liability suits filed against the plan and/or the fiduciaries.

TRUSTEE, NEGLIGENCE *see* TRUSTEE LIABILITY INSURANCE.

TRUSTEE ROLE, PENSION PLANS *see* PENSION PLAN; PENSION PLAN FUNDING INSTRUMENTS; PENSION PLAN FUNDING, GROUP DEPOSIT ADMINISTRATION ANNUITY; PENSION PLAN FUNDING, GROUP IMMEDIATE PARTICIPATION GUARANTEED (IPG) CONTRACT ANNUITY; PENSION PLAN FUNDING, GROUP PERMANENT CONTRACT; PENSION PLAN FUNDING, INDIVIDUAL CONTRACT PENSION PLAN.

TRUSTEE, TERMINATED PLAN one named under provisions of the EMPLOYEE RETIREMENT INCOME SECURITY ACT OF 1974 (ERISA) for a terminated pension plan with an unfunded liability for its benefits.

TRUST FUND PLAN one of two basic types of funding instruments for pensions or employee benefits, in which responsibility for plan assets is vested in a trustee. The other type is known as an *insured plan,* whose assets are held by a life insurance company, typically under a group annuity contract that guarantees payment of benefits. A COMBINATION PLAN makes use of both approaches, with some contributions going to a trustee and the remainder to an insurance company. *See also* SELF-ADMINISTERED PLAN.

TRUST FUND PLAN ANALYSIS *see* TRUST FUND PLAN.

TRUST INDENTURE document setting out the responsibilities of a borrower, such as a corporation issuing bonds, and the powers of a trustee who will be looking after the interests of the bondholders.

TRUSTOR *see* ESTATE PLANNING DISTRIBUTION.

TRUTH-IN-SAVINGS ACT act passed by Congress in 1991, the purpose of which is to make it easier for consumers to compare deposit accounts among savings institutions (SI). Some of the act's more important provisions include: (1) SI must pay interest on the full amount of a depositor's balance; (2) SI must use a standardized formula for computing the annual percentage yield (APY). The APY is based on the interest rate and the method of compounding that interest; (3) SI must disclose all fees imposed on checking, savings, money market, or Super NOW accounts as well as any other terms or restrictions. These disclosures are required before the account is opened, before automatic renewals, or upon the request of the savings customer. The savings institution must inform current savings account customers of the availability of the disclosures and include these disclosures with the savings customer's regular account statement; and (4) SI must be in compliance with standardized rules concerning their promotional activities for advertising. All solicitations (whether in print, TV, radio, etc.) for savings deposits must state in a clear and conspicuous manner: (1) annual percentage yield; (2) period of time that the yield is in effect; (3) minimum account balance required to earn the yield; (4) minimum time period required to earn the yield; (5) minimum amount required to open the account; (6) interest penalty is required for early withdrawals; (7) and the fact that fees may result in the reduction of the Annual Percentage Yield.

TUITION FEES INSURANCE indemnification of a school for the loss of tuition, and room and board fees when it is forced to suspend classes because of the occurrence of a peril. *See also* TUITION FORM.

TUITION FORM coverage in the event a school, summer camp, or similar operation suffers loss of tuition because a peril destroys a building. The tuition form reimburses the institution for loss of tuition and rental income from room and board. *See also* TUITION FEES INSURANCE.

TUNNEL INSURANCE coverage in the event a tunnel is damaged or destroyed. Written on an ALL RISKS basis, excluding perils of war, wear and tear, inherent defect, and nuclear damage. For example, this coverage would be important to businesses that have underground tunnels connecting different locations.

TURNKEY INSURANCE Contractor's and Architect's Errors and Omissions Insurance, which also serves as a general liability policy for these professionals.

TURNOVER RATE frequency with which employees resign, are fired, or retire from a company, usually computed as the percentage of an organization's employees at the beginning of a calendar year. The turnover rate is one of the factors affecting the cost of a pension plan. Employees who leave a company before they have a *vested interest* in the plan represent a cost saving to plan administrators, because they will not receive benefits when they retire. For this reason, most actuaries make assumptions about the turnover rate of a particular company when calculating how much money must be contributed to a retirement plan to pay future benefits.

TWENTY-PAY LIFE INSURANCE POLICY *see* LIMITED PAYMENT LIFE INSURANCE.

TWISTING UNFAIR TRADE PRACTICE, in insurance, whereby an agent or broker attempts to persuade a life insurance policyholder through misrepresentation to cancel one policy and buy a new one. Some states have laws requiring full disclosure of relevant comparative information about existing and proposed policies by an agent trying to convince a customer to switch policies. These laws may provide for notification of the insurance company that issued the existing policy to give it an opportunity to respond to the agent's proposal.

TWO/TWENTY YEAR VESTING SCHEDULE type of GRADED VESTING schedule that has a maximum term of six years as follows: Year 1 = 0% vested; Year 2 = 20% vested; Year 3 = 40% vested; Year 4 = 60% vested; Year 5 = 80% vested; Year 6 = 100% vested. *See also* PENSION PLAN PROTECTION ACT OF 2006.

TYPE A UNIVERSAL LIFE *see* UNIVERSAL LIFE INSURANCE.

TYPE B UNIVERSAL LIFE *see* UNIVERSAL LIFE INSURANCE.

U

U&O *see* USE AND OCCUPANCY INSURANCE.

UBERRIMAE FIDEI CONTRACT agreement "of utmost good faith." Under law, it is assumed that insurance contracts are entered into by all parties in good faith, meaning that they have disclosed all relevant facts and intend to carry out their obligations. Where lack of good faith can be proved, such as in a fraudulent application to obtain insurance, the contract may be nullified.

UJF *see* UNSATISFIED JUDGMENT FUND.

UL *see* UNDERWRITERS LABORATORIES, INC. (UL).

ULTIMATE MORTALITY TABLE presentation of data that excludes the first 5 to 10 years of experience of those who purchase life insurance. A MORTALITY TABLE shows the number of deaths per 1000 of a group of people. Experience shows that people have a lower mortality rate in the first years after they have purchased insurance, probably because they have recently passed a medical and other tests. A SELECT MORTALITY TABLE includes data only on people who have recently purchased insurance. An AGGREGATE MORTALITY TABLE includes all data.

ULTIMATE NET LOSS insurer's total payments resulting from a claim, including all related expenses, less any recoveries from salvage, reinsurance, and the exercise of *subrogation* rights or other rights against third parties. *See also* LOSS DEVELOPMENT.

ULTRA VIRES Latin phrase meaning "beyond power or authority" describing an act by a corporation that exceeds its legal powers. For example, corporations do not have the authority to engage in the insurance business without a charter. A corporation offering insurance without authority would be acting ultra vires. Similarly, an insurance company chartered to engage in a single line of business would be operating ultra vires by offering some other line.

UMBRELLA LIABILITY INSURANCE excess liability coverage above the limits of a basic business liability insurance policy such as the OWNERS, LANDLORDS AND TENANTS LIABILITY POLICY. For example, if a basic policy has a limit of $500,000, and it is exhausted by claims, the umbrella will pay the excess above $500,000 up to the limit of the umbrella policy, which may be as high as $10,000,000, $25,000,000 or more. The umbrella policy also fills gaps in coverage under basic liability policies.

UMBRELLA REINSURANCE protection for all classes of business including automobile, fire, general liability, homeowners, multiple peril, burglary, and glass, by combining the contracts for these classes of business into one reinsurance contract. This enables the *cedant* to obtain reinsurance more cheaply, with greater capacity, and with greater spread of risk. An umbrella reinsurance contract is offered to one set of reinsurers who all take a fixed percentage of every treaty in the contract. One reinsurer may take 5% across the board, another may take 10%, and so on, until the umbrella contract is totally placed. All the treaties that compose the umbrella contract are written as one block of business; hence, the reinsurers are prohibited from choosing which treaty they want to reinsure. By combining all the reinsurance treaties into one contract, if a catastrophe loss results, each reinsurer will assume only a percentage of the loss instead of assuming the entire loss by itself.

UMPIRE arbitrator who settles disputes over the amount of loss when an insurer and an insured do not agree.

UMPIRE CLAUSE *see* ARBITRATION CLAUSE.

UNALLOCATED BENEFIT *see* UNALLOCATED FUNDING INSTRUMENT.

UNALLOCATED FUNDING INSTRUMENT pension funding agreement under which funds paid into a retirement plan are not currently allocated to purchase retirement benefits. The funds of one plan cannot be commingled with funds of another plan, and the plan trustee guarantees neither principal nor interest of the funds deposited. At retirement the trustee can either purchase an *immediate retirement annuity* for the retiring employee or pay the benefits directly from the fund as they become due. *See also* PENSION PLAN FUNDING: GROUP DEPOSIT ADMINISTRATION ANNUITY; PENSION PLAN FUNDING: GROUP IMMEDIATE PARTICIPATION GUARANTEED (IPG) CONTRACT ANNUITY; PENSION PLAN FUNDING INSTRUMENTS; TRUST FUND PLAN.

UNAFFILIATED INVESTMENTS insurance company's investments in assets other than in companies it controls and/or companies with which it shares common ownership, stocks, and bonds.

UNAUTHORIZED INSURANCE insurance policy sold by NONADMITTED INSURER.

UNAUTHORIZED INSURER *see* NONADMITTED INSURER.

UNAUTHORIZED PRACTICE OF LAW act of practicing law or providing legal advice without a license.

UNAUTHORIZED REINSURANCE REINSURANCE ceded to an insurance company that is a NONADMITTED INSURER.

UNBUNDLED term that describes commercial insurance with no administrative services attached, or alternatively, administrative services from an insurer without insurance coverage. Years ago, insureds bought a package that included coverage for exposures as well as claims paying, loss control, and other risk management services. With the increasing sophistication of risk management in the past decade, and to reduce their costs, many corporations elect to perform some of these duties themselves and to purchase insurance and other services on an unbundled basis.

UNBUNDLED LIFE INSURANCE POLICY coverage in which the investment features, mortality element, and cost factors of a LIFE INSURANCE policy are separated, permitting each part to be independently analyzed. The SAVINGS ELEMENT of the policy then becomes interest-sensitive (rate of return paid to the POLICYHOLDER is more consistent with the rate of returns earned by the life insurance company over a period of time than is the rate of return paid to the holder of a traditional life insurance policy). *See also* UNIVERSAL LIFE INSURANCE.

UNCONDITIONAL VESTING no limitation under a CONTRIBUTORY pension plan of an employee's right to receive vested benefits, regardless of whether or not the employer withdraws contributions. *See also* VESTING; VESTING, CONDITIONAL.

UNDERGROUND STORAGE INSURANCE type of insurance policy that provides coverage through an ENDORSEMENT to the COMPREHENSIVE GENERAL LIABILITY (CGL) policy for BODILY INJURY and property damage resulting from an underground storage tank accident.

UNDERINSURANCE
1. failure to maintain adequate coverage for a specific loss or damage.
2. failure to meet a COINSURANCE requirement.

UNDERINSURED MOTORIST COVERAGE LIMITS TRIGGER mechanism for providing coverage when the insured's underinsured motorist coverage limit is more than the TORT FEASOR's limit of liability.

UNDERINSURED MOTORIST COVERAGE MODIFIED LIMITS TRIGGER mechanism for providing coverage when the insured's underinsured motorist coverage limit is more than the TORT FEASOR's limit of liability that has been previously reduced by claim payments to other CLAIMANTS.

UNDERINSURED MOTORIST ENDORSEMENT addition to a PERSONAL AUTOMOBILE POLICY (PAP) that covers an insured who is involved in a collision with a driver who does not have sufficient liability insurance to pay for the damages. *See also* UNINSURED MOTORIST INSURANCE.

UNDERLYING MORTALITY ASSUMPTION see MORTALITY ASSUMPTION.

UNDERLYING RETENTION *see* RETENTION AND LIMITS CLAUSE; RISK MANAGEMENT; SELF INSURANCE.

UNDERWRITER, LAY individual who works in the home office of an insurance company and performs the function of UNDERWRITING to determine if an applicant is insurable at standard rates, substandard rates, insurable at preferred rates, or is uninsurable.

UNDERWRITER, LIFE *see* AGENT.

UNDERWRITERS ASSOCIATION *see* POOL; PRODUCERS COOPERATIVE.

UNDERWRITERS LABORATORIES, INC. (UL) independent agency supported by the insurance industry that tests a variety of materials, products, and devices, such as appliances and electrical equipment, to assure that they meet safety standards.

UNDERWRITER SYNDICATE *see* LLOYD'S OF LONDON.

UNDERWRITING process of examining, accepting, or rejecting insurance risks, and classifying those selected, in order to charge the proper premium for each. The purpose of underwriting is to spread the risk among a pool of insureds in a manner that is equitable for the insureds and profitable for the insurer. *See also* RISK MANAGEMENT; RISK SELECTION.

UNDERWRITING CYCLE tendency of property and liability insurance premiums, insurers' profits, and availability of coverage to rise and fall with some regularity over time. A cycle can be said to begin when insurers tighten their underwriting standards and sharply raise premiums after a period of severe underwriting losses. Stricter standards and higher premium rates often bring dramatic increases in profits, attracting more capital to the insurance industry and raising underwriting capacity. On the other hand, as insurers strive to write more premiums at higher levels of profitability, premium rates may be driven down and underwriting standards relaxed in the competition for new business. Profits may erode and then turn into losses if more tax underwriting standards generate mounting claims. The stage would then be set for the cycle to begin again.

UNDERWRITING EXPENSES salaries plus commissions plus overhead expenses plus office rent plus fees charged for memberships in industry associations and bureaus plus guaranty association assessments plus taxes (not including federal income taxes, foreign income taxes, and real estate taxes).

UNDERWRITING FACTORS: HEALTH INSURANCE factors on the APPLICATION that must be evaluated in order to complete the UNDERWRITING PROCESS: age; sex; physical condition; personal health history; family health history; financial condition; use of alcohol, drugs, or tobacco; occupation; avocation; and if in the military.

UNDERWRITING FACTORS: LIFE INSURANCE factors on the APPLICATION that must be evaluated in order to complete the UNDERWRITING process: (1) age; (2) sex; (3) physical condition; (4) personal health history; (5) family health history; (6) financial condition; (7) use of alcohol, drugs, or tobacco; (8) occupation; (9) avocation; (10) and if in the military.

UNDERWRITING GAIN (LOSS) profit (deficit) that remains after paying claims and expenses. Insurers generate profits from underwriting and from investment income. Their chief business is insuring against risks for a profit, and one measure of success is whether there is money left after paying claims and expenses. This amount, if any, is their underwriting gain. *See also* COMBINED RATIO.

UNDERWRITING INCOME EARNED PREMIUM minus INCURRED LOSSES plus LOSS ADJUSTMENT EXPENSE plus other incurred UNDERWRITING expenses plus policyowner DIVIDENDS. This income is generated from the insurance business—that of insuring people and property.

UNDERWRITING PROFIT (LOSS) see UNDERWRITING GAIN (LOSS).

UNDERWRITING RISK risk that premiums will not be sufficient to cover future INCURRED LOSSES and that losses and loss adjustment expenses' current reserves are not sufficient.

UNEARNED PREMIUM *see* UNEARNED PREMIUM INSURANCE; UNEARNED PREMIUM RESERVE; UNEARNED REINSURANCE PREMIUM.

UNEARNED PREMIUM INSURANCE coverage for loss of unearned premium if insured property is destroyed before the end of a policy period. The policyholder pays in advance for insurance, but the insurer does not earn the premium until coverage is provided. For example, if a policy period is one year, one-twelfth of the premium is earned each month. After six months, one-half of the premium is still unearned and belongs to the policyholder if the policy is canceled. If the property is destroyed in the second month and the insurer pays the claim, the policyholder would have nothing left to insure. Unearned premium insurance reimburses the insured for the part of the premium paid up front that is no longer needed for insurance coverage.

UNEARNED PREMIUM RESERVE fund that contains the portion of the premium that has been paid in advance for insurance that has not yet been provided. For example, if a business pays an annual premium of $1000 on January 1, the money is not earned by the insurer until the insurance coverage has been provided. On July 1, $500 would have been earned and $500 would remain as unearned premium, belonging to the policyholder. If either party cancels the contract, the insurer must have the unearned premium ready to refund. For this reason, insurance regulators require that insurers maintain an unearned premium reserve so that, in the event an insurer must be liquidated, there is enough money to pay claims and refund the unearned premium. Because computations for individual policies would be cumbersome, regulators have devised formulas for figuring unearned premium reserves. *See also* REINSURANCE RESERVE (UNEARNED PREMIUM RESERVE).

UNEARNED REINSURANCE PREMIUM portion of reinsurance premium received by the reinsurer that relates to the unexpired part of the reinsured policy. *See also* AUTOMATIC PROPORTIONAL REINSURANCE; FACULTATIVE REINSURANCE; NONPROPORTIONAL REINSURANCE; PROPORTIONAL REINSURANCE; REINSURANCE.

UNEMPLOYMENT COMPENSATION money paid through state and federal programs to workers who are temporarily unemployed. The program, which was created by the SOCIAL SECURITY ACT OF 1935, is managed by the individual states, which decide the level of benefits that will be paid and assess a payroll tax on employers to pay for the program. Employers may pay more or less tax depending on the stability of their workforces. Weekly benefits vary widely among the states.

UNEMPLOYMENT COMPENSATION AMENDMENT OF 1992 amendment to the law that requires companies that manage retirement plans to permit terminating participants to directly transfer any plan distribution to the INDIVIDUAL RETIREMENT ACCOUNT (IRA) or QUALIFIED PENSION PLAN of the participant's choice. If the participant receives the distribution directly, the plan administrator is required to remit a 20% withholding penalty directly to the Internal Revenue Service. *See also* ROLLOVER AND WITHHOLDING RULES FOR QUALIFIED PLAN DISTRIBUTIONS; ROLLOVER AND WITHHOLDING RULES FOR QUALIFIED PLAN DISTRIBUTIONS: PAYMENT PAID TO EMPLOYEE.

UNFAIR CLAIMS PRACTICE abuse by an insurer in an effort to avoid paying a claim filed by an insured, or to reduce the size of the payment. The NATIONAL ASSOCIATION OF INSURANCE COMMISSIONERS (NAIC) has developed model legislation requiring that claims be handled fairly and that there be free communication between policyholder and insurer. Many states have adopted unfair claims practice laws.

UNFAIR TRADE PRACTICE in insurance, fraudulent or unethical practice that is illegal under state law. States may fine or revoke the licenses of agents and brokers for unfair trade practices, including misrepresentation, false advertising, misappropriation of policyholder's money, and TWISTING.

UNFRIENDLY FIRE *see* HOSTILE FIRE.

UNFUNDED *see* UNALLOCATED FUNDING INSTRUMENT.

UNIFORM COMMERCIAL CODE standardized set of business laws that has been adopted by most states. The Uniform Commercial Code governs a wide range of transactions including borrowing, contracts, and many other everyday business practices. It is useful because it standardizes practices from state to state.

UNIFORM COMPUTER INFORMATION TRANSACTIONS ACT legislation that limits the LIABILITY of a software seller for defects. The seller is obligated to return only the purchase price. The seller is not responsible for CONSEQUENTIAL LOSS, THIRD-PARTY liability, and/or BUSINESS INTERRUPTION. Although the buyer of the software is liable to third parties because of the damage resulting from the operation of the software, this liability cannot be transferred back to the seller. For example, INSURANCE COMPANY (INSURER) uses a software package to pay health claims, and a defect in the software results in the underpayment or no payment of the claims. The results are numerous LIABILITY suits by the CLAIMANTS against the insurer and not the software seller.

UNIFORM FORMS widely accepted standard policy forms that have been developed by various RATING BUREAUS or insurance companies. Some forms are required by state law, and some are used by custom. In some cases provisions are mandated, but a form is not. Even so, many companies use the same forms, which become widely recognized as the standard for certain types of risk.

UNIFORM GIFTS TO MINORS ACT act in which an irrevocable gift is made by the parent to the child. As of 2007, for children younger than age 18, the first $850 of annual investment earnings is tax free and the next $850 is taxed at the child's 15% tax rate. The remainder of the funds is taxed at the parents' marginal tax rate (top bracket tax rate). If the child is at least age 18, all income is taxed at the child's rate. Once the child reaches the age of majority, which in most states is 18 or 21, the child can use the money in that account as desired.

UNIFORM INDIVIDUAL ACCIDENT AND SICKNESS POLICY PROVISIONS ACT regulations of the NATIONAL ASSOCIATION OF INSURANCE COMMISSIONERS (NAIC) that dictate provisions that all individual health insurance policies must contain. All states now require these provisions, which include the circumstances under which changes can be made to the policy; how the BENEFICIARY can be changed; submission of PROOF OF LOSS; REINSTATEMENT of the policy; and GRACE PERIOD.

UNIFORM POLICY PROVISIONS, HEALTH INSURANCE basic contract language in individual health and accident insurance policies. These provisions are required under a model state law known as the UNIFORM INDIVIDUAL ACCIDENT AND SICKNESS POLICY PROVISIONS ACT. The uniform provisions, some mandatory and some optional under the model act, deal with such questions as proof of loss, medical examination, claims notice, claims forms, policy renewal, and premium grace period. The act does not require companies to adopt exact wording in their policies but to substantially follow the provision guidelines.

UNIFORM PROVISIONS language adopted by the NATIONAL ASSOCIATION OF INSURANCE COMMISSIONERS (NAIC) and recommended or required by state law. While they rarely dictate the language of policies, states often prescribe mandatory or optional policy minimums, or may forbid certain provisions. Therefore, while life and health benefits may vary widely, for example, policyholders are given certain uniform rights, like grace periods for paying premiums and loan and surrender values.

UNIFORM RECIPROCAL LICENSING ACT law by which many states attempt to regulate insurers who are unlicensed in those states. With a few notable exceptions, such as reinsurers, insurance companies must be licensed in the states where they do business. If a U.S. insurer sells insurance in a state where it is unauthorized, the insurer's home state may revoke its license under the Uniform Reciprocal Licensing Act.

UNIFORMED SERVICES EMPLOYMENT AND RE-EMPLOY-MENT RIGHTS ACT (USERRA) provision of federal statute prohibiting discrimination against members of the military on leave from civilian jobs by protecting their civilian rights and benefits by requiring: (1) the re-employment of the members up to five years after reporting for military duty; (2) the re-employment of the members in the same or similar jobs with the same rank, pay, and benefits as they would have been entitled to if not for being recalled to military duty.

UNIFORM SIMULTANEOUS DEATH ACT statute in most states under which, if no evidence exists in a *common disaster* (when an insured and beneficiary die within a short time of each other in an accident for which determination cannot be made as to who died first), the presumption is that the insured survived the beneficiary and the life insurance proceeds will either be paid to a secondary beneficiary (if named in a policy) or, if not named, then to the insured's estate.

UNIFORM TRANSFER TAX combination of the FEDERAL ESTATE TAX and the federal GIFT TAX.

UNIFORM TRANSFERS TO MINORS ACT (UTMA) act in which a life insurance company is permitted to transfer the DEATH BENEFIT from the policy to the custodian of a minor BENEFICIARY provided the beneficiary designation has specifically nominated the custodian to receive the death benefit on behalf of the minor.

UNILATERAL CONTRACT legal agreement in which only one of the two parties makes legally enforceable promises. An insurance contract is a unilateral contract because only the insurer has made a promise of future performance and only the insurer can be charged with breach of contract. In contrast, in a bilateral contract, both parties promise future performance.

UNINSURABLE PROPERTY *see* UNINSURABLE RISK.

UNINSURABLE RISK risk that substantially fails to meet the REQUIREMENTS OF INSURABLE RISK.

UNINSURED MOTORIST COVERAGE coverage C under the PERSONAL AUTOMOBILE POLICY (PAP) that covers an insured involved in a collision with a driver who does not have liability insurance. The insured includes named insured and relatives who are residents of the insured's household while they are driving or are passengers in an owned automobile covered under the PAP. The insured is also covered while driving or is a passenger in a non-owned automobile or while a pedestrian. Any other person is covered when occupying an insured automobile under the PAP.

UNINTENTIONAL TORT *see* NEGLIGENCE; TORT, UNINTENTIONAL.

UNIQUE IMPAIRMENT physical, moral, or financial circumstance of a life insurance applicant that sets him or her apart from a physically, morally, and financially sound standard applicant. The underwriting weight attached to this impairment (such as a history of bankruptcy or a serious health condition) could result in the applicant being classified as substandard or uninsurable.

UNISEX LEGISLATION regulations affecting the right of insurance companies to use sex as one of the factors in the actuarial determination of premium rates. The precedent case for such legislation is *Arizona Governing Committee* v. *Norris* in which the decision was that a municipal retirement plan could not provide retirement benefits based on sex.

UNIT BENEFIT *see* DEFINED BENEFIT PLAN; UNIT BENEFIT PLAN.

UNIT BENEFIT APPROACH *see* DEFINED BENEFIT PLAN.

UNIT BENEFIT PLAN retirement plan under which a discrete increment of periodic retirement income is credited to an employee for each year of service with an employer. This increment is either a flat dollar amount or, more often, a percentage of compensation. If percentage of compensation is credited, it generally is $1\frac{1}{4}$–$2\frac{1}{2}\%$. At retirement, years of service are multiplied by percentage of compensation. The resulting percentage is applied to the employee's final average or career average of earnings. For example, if an employee has 30 years of service, a final average earnings of $100,000, and the percentage of compensation is $1\frac{1}{2}\%$, the employee's annual retirement benefit would be $45,000 ($30 × $100,000 × .015). *See also* DEFINED BENEFIT PLAN.

UNITED STATES AIRCRAFT INSURANCE GROUP one of the major underwriting organizations for insurance company pools insuring commercial aircraft liability exposure.

UNITED STATES GOVERNMENT LIFE INSURANCE (USGLI) *see* GOVERNMENT LIFE INSURANCE.

UNITED STATES LONGSHOREMEN AND HARBOR WORK-ERS ACT OF 1927 *see* LONGSHOREMEN AND HARBOR WORKERS ACT LIABILITY.

UNITED STATES TREASURY MONEY MUTUAL FUNDS investments restricted to short-term Treasury bills (T-bills) and repurchase agreements secured by Treasury bills. These T-bills are secured by the full faith and credit of the Unites States Treasury and thus are considered to be the most RISK free of any financial instrument. T-bills are said to be the "standard" for safety worldwide since the United States has a long history of economic, political, and social stability.

UNITED STATES V. THE SOUTH-EASTERN UNDERWRITERS ASSOCIATION *see* SOUTH-EASTERN UNDERWRITERS ASSOCIATION (SEUA) CASE.

UNITING AND STRENGTHENING AMERICA BY PROVIDING APPROPRIATE TOOLS REQUIRED TO INTERCEPT AND OBSTRUCT TERRORISM (USA PATRIOT ACT) ACT OF 2001 legislation that requires the Secretary of the Treasury to regulate financial institutions such that the institution must consult lists of known or suspected terrorists or terrorist organizations before allowing them to establish an account. The financial institution is prohibited from conducting business with anyone or any organization on those lists. These prohibited lists are referred to as the OFAC LIST.

UNIVERSAL ACCESS stipulation that every participant in health care has the right according to law to purchase health insurance from a private insurance entity. The participant's purchase is voluntary and must not be eligible for a public health insurance program.

UNIVERSAL COVERAGE provision for every citizen of the United States to be guaranteed by law the right to purchase health insurance and is required by law to make such a purchase.

UNIVERSAL LIFE II *see* UNIVERSAL VARIABLE LIFE INSURANCE.

UNIVERSAL LIFE INSURANCE ADJUSTABLE LIFE INSURANCE under which (1) premiums are flexible, not fixed; (2) protection is adjustable, not fixed; and (3) insurance company expenses and other charges are specifically disclosed to a purchaser. This policy is referred to as UNBUNDLED *life insurance* because its three basic elements (investment earnings, *pure cost of protection,* and company expenses) are separately identified both in the policy and in an annual report to the policyowner. After the first premium, additional premiums can be paid at any time. (There usually are limits on the dollar amount of each additional payment.) A specified percentage expense charge is deducted from each premium before the balance is credited to the cash value, along with interest. The pure cost of protection is subtracted from the cash value monthly. As selected by the insured, the death benefit can be a specified amount plus the cash value or the specified amount that includes the cash value. After payment of the minimal initial premium required, there are no contractually scheduled premium payments (provided the cash value account balance is sufficient to pay the pure cost of protection each month and any other expenses and charges. Expenses and charges may take the form of a flat dollar amount for the first policy year, a sales charge for each premium received, and a monthly expense charge for each policy year). An annual report is provided the policy owner that shows the status of the policy (death benefit option selected, specified amount of insurance in force, cash value, surrender value, and the transactions made each month under the policy during the year—premiums received, expenses charged, guaranteed and excess interest credited to the cash value account, pure cost of insurance deducted, and cash value balance). *See also* UNIVERSAL VARIABLE LIFE INSURANCE.

UNIVERSAL VARIABLE *see* UNIVERSAL VARIABLE LIFE INSURANCE.

UNIVERSAL VARIABLE LIFE INSURANCE policy combining features of UNIVERSAL LIFE INSURANCE and VARIABLE LIFE INSURANCE in that excess interest credited to the cash value account depends on investment results of separate accounts (equities, bonds, real estate, etc.). The policyowner selects the accounts into which the premium payments are to be made. However, since this is an EQUITY product, filing with the SECURITIES AND EXCHANGE COMMISSION (SEC), an annual prospectus, an audit of separate accounts, and agent registration with the NATIONAL ASSOCIATION OF SECURITIES DEALERS (NASD) are required. This policy can be considered a replacement for universal life insurance when interest rates of U.S. Treasury issues and other money market instruments are low. Contrast with UNIVERSAL LIFE INSURANCE.

UNLIMITED MARITAL DEDUCTION deduction allowed for gifts and bequests to a spouse for federal estate and gift tax purposes. Under the Economic Recovery Tax Act of 1981 (ERTA), the deduction became unlimited. Prior to this, there was a dollar and percentage limitation for the marital deduction.

UNOCCUPANCY absence of people for at least 60 consecutive days from a given property. Many property insurance policies suspend coverage after a structure has been unoccupied for 60 consecutive days because the probability of loss increases dramatically from such perils as vandalism and malicious mischief. Premiums for these policies were based on statements of an insured that the structure would be occupied. Unoccupancy results in an increase in hazards within the control of an insured, which gives the insurance company the right to suspend the policy. *See also* VACANCY.

UNREALIZED CAPITAL GAINS (LOSSES) appreciation in the unsold assets' value. When assets are sold, their capital gain (loss) is shown on the insurance company's income statement; any unrealized gain or loss is not included within the income statement.

UNREPORTED CLAIMS *see* INCURRED BUT NOT REPORTED LOSSES (IBNR).

UNSATISFIED JUDGMENT FUND money set aside in some states to pay otherwise uncompensated bodily injury claims to innocent victims of automobile accidents. The claimants must prove that they were not at fault and that they cannot collect damages from the drivers who hit them. The responsible drivers then lose their licenses until they reimburse the fund.

UNSCHEDULED PROPERTY FLOATER insurance that offers blanket coverage up to a certain dollar amount on all property of the classification covered by the policy. Floater policies, which cover property wherever it happens to be and while it is in transit, can also be purchased as a SCHEDULED POLICY where each individual item is listed.

UNSOLICITED APPLICATION request for life insurance coverage by an individual, not through an agent or broker. It is given extra scrutiny by an insurance company because of the possibility of SELF-SELECTION, which is the likelihood that poorer risks will seek insurance on their own initiative. *See also* ADVERSE SELECTION; RISK SELECTION.

UNVALUED MARINE POLICY coverage that does not put a dollar value on a hull or cargo that is insured. A *valued marine policy* puts a specific value on the insured property. With unvalued property, the value is determined at the time of loss.

UPSTREAM HOLDING COMPANY holding company formed by at least one stock insurance company. This holding company is owned by its stockholders and is usually listed on the New York Stock Exchange or the NASDAQ. In turn, the holding company owns 100% of the stock of the subsidiary insurance companies.

URBAN DEVELOPMENT ACT OF 1970 law that provided for federal crime insurance. Because private insurance is not available for business owners and residents of certain high-crime areas, the act provides that the FEDERAL INSURANCE ADMINISTRATION write the coverage. Private insurers service the program.

USA PATRIOT ACT *see* UNITING AND STRENGTHENING AMERICA BY PROVIDING APPROPRIATE TOOLS REQUIRED TO INTERCEPT AND OBSTRUCT TERRORISM (USA PATRIOT ACT) ACT OF 2001.

USE AND OCCUPANCY INSURANCE type of BUSINESS INTERRUPTION INSURANCE that provides indirect loss coverage by endorsement to BOILER AND MACHINERY INSURANCE. The latter, sometimes called POWER PLANT INSURANCE, provides for both direct and indirect loss coverage. Direct loss would indemnify an insured for damage to property. Use and occupancy insurance covers an insured for loss of use of the equipment due to damage from a named peril.

USGLI *see* GOVERNMENT LIFE INSURANCE.

USUAL AND CUSTOMARY CHARGE
1. fee that is the most consistently charged by the physician for a particular procedure.
2. fee that is usual for a particular procedure charged by the majority of physicians with similar training and experience within the same geographic area.

USUAL, CUSTOMARY, AND REASONABLE CHARGES (UCR) limits on reimbursement by an insurance company. Health insurance plans pay a doctor's full charge for service if it does not exceed the usual charge; that is, if it does not exceed the charge for the same service by other physicians in the area or if it is reasonable.

USUFRUCT right that has a limited time in duration for an individual to receive the income generated by assets owned by another individual.

USUFRUCTUARY individual who has the right to the use of assets while the USUFRUCT is in force.

UTILIZATION measurement of the use of health insurance by employees of an insured employer, stated in terms of the average number of claims per employee.

UTILITY quality of being useful. Risk diminishes maximum utility in society because resources gravitate to activities, businesses, and investments that are least risky. By absorbing or protecting against some risks, insurance increases utility. When individuals know they will have some cushion against loss, their assets can be spread out over a greater range of activities and enterprises.

UTILIZATION REVIEW (UTILIZATION MANAGEMENT) integral part of MANAGED CARE health plans designed to control and limit medical expenses. This review includes: (1) requirement of certification for admission to a health care facility; (2) continuous analysis of the reasons for the patient to remain in the health care facility; (3) projected date for release of the patient; and (4) cost-effective ways of handling patients with catastrophic illnesses. *See also* HEALTH MAINTENANCE ORGANIZATION (HMO); PREFERRED PROVIDER ORGANIZATION (PPO).

UTMOST GOOD FAITH *see* UBERRIMAE FIDEI CONTRACT.

V

VACANCY circumstance where no people or contents occupy or are kept in a building for at least 60 consecutive days. The same stipulations apply to property coverages as found in unoccupancy. *See also* UNOCCUPANCY.

VALIDATION PERIOD length of time required to amortize the excess expenses of acquiring a given group of life insurance policies. In acquiring a policy, a life insurance company may incur expenses (such as the costs of sales commissions, paperwork, and medical examinations) that are greater than the amount allocated for LOADING in the first year's premium. In effect, this means new policies are acquired at a loss, forcing insurers to dip into *surplus* to add the new business. After the first year, because expenses are lower, premiums and their invested earnings begin to generate a contribution to surplus, gradually making up for the excess expense of the first year. The length of the validation period depends on many factors, including the levels of GROSS PREMIUMS and expenses, but in some companies validation periods can extend for 10 years or more.

VALID CONTRACT agreement signed by both parties that meets the requirements of state law and is therefore in force.

VALUABLE PAPERS (RECORDS) INSURANCE coverage in the event that papers of intrinsic value are damaged or destroyed. Coverage is on an ALL RISKS basis. Limits of coverage can be quite high; but the insurance company will not pay an amount in excess of the actual cash value of the loss, or the amount necessary to repair or replace the damaged papers. Also, the papers must be kept under lock and key.

VALUATION
   1. method of determining the worth of property to be insured, or of property that has been lost or damaged.
   2. method of setting insurance company reserves to pay future claims.

VALUATION CLAUSE provision in a MARINE INSURANCE policy in which agreement has been reached between the insured and the insurance company concerning the worth of the property that is to be covered under the policy.

VALUATION FACTORS, PENSION PLANS *see* PENSION PLAN VALUATION FACTORS.

VALUATION METHOD means of determining that a loss has occurred and setting an economic value on it so that a claim can be paid. When an insured suffers a loss, an adjuster must determine that it actually occurred, that it was covered by insurance, and the value of the lost or damaged property. The adjuster, with the help of the insured, determines the cost to repair or replace the covered property. The adjuster computes actual cash value, or replacement cost, minus depreciation. For indirect losses, such as BUSINESS INTERRUPTION, the adjuster must make rough estimates, and then must consider COINSURANCE and adjust claims payments for it.

VALUATION MORTALITY TABLE   MORTALITY TABLE used to calculate the LEGAL RESERVE and life insurance policy CASH SURRENDER VALUES.

VALUATION OF ASSETS rules by state insurance regulators for valuing ADMITTED ASSETS on the books of insurance companies. Part of the STATE SUPERVISION AND REGULATION of insurers is the determination of which assets—"admitted assets"—are allowed to back STATUTORY RESERVES. Admitted assets include real estate, mortgages, securities, cash, and bank deposits. Mortgage loans, cash, and bank deposits are recognized at face value. Real estate is allowed at book value. Securities are carried according to SECURITY VALUATION rules. *Bonds* with acceptable credit quality are carried at *amortized value,* which is the face value plus or minus the amount of any purchase discount or premium, as amortized over the life of the bond. Preferred stock is valued at cost and COMMON STOCK INVESTMENTS at year-end market price. Valuations for impaired securities such as bonds in default are determined by the Committee on Valuation of Securities of the NATIONAL ASSOCIATION OF INSURANCE COMMISSIONERS (NAIC). *See also* MANDATORY SECURITIES VALUATION RESERVE.

VALUATION OF LOSS method of setting a dollar value on loss suffered by an insured. In some cases, a loss is straightforward, such as the cost of gallbladder surgery. But with burglary of a home or a traffic accident that damages a car, the amount of loss is open to interpretation. In many cases, the insured needs receipts, appraisal documents, or other evidence of value. In other cases, a claim adjuster values the loss and determines how much the insurer will pay.

VALUATION OF POTENTIAL PROPERTY LOSS risk management technique that evaluates property exposures preparatory to managing the risk. Although risk managers consider the ORIGINAL COST, DEPRECIATION, *market value,* and TAX-APPRAISED VALUE of property, *replacement cost* is the most helpful in determining the value of the property, giving the truest indication of the degree of the exposure to be insured or otherwise financed.

VALUATION PERIOD for a VARIABLE ANNUITY, the period of time from the close of business on the first BUSINESS DAY to the close of business on the second business day.

VALUATION PREMIUM life insurance rate determined by the valuation of company policy reserves. State regulators set strict standards for policy reserves to make certain that life insurers will have enough assets to make good on their policies. Once the reserves are valued, the company works backward to set a valuation premium that will cover all of its liabilities. However, some companies determine that they can justify setting a GROSS PREMIUM that is lower than the valuation premium because their experience, based on updated mortality tables, is better than that used to determine the valuation premium. If they do charge a premium that is lower, they are required to deposit the difference in a DEFICIENCY RESERVE.

VALUATION RESERVE (SECURITIES VALUATION RESERVE) amount set up as a cushion against fluctuations in securities prices. *See also* MANDATORY VALUATION SECURITIES RESERVE.

VALUE *see* ACTUAL CASH VALUE; MARKET VALUE V. ACTUAL CASH VALUE; MARKET VALUE CLAUSE; REPLACEMENT COST LESS PHYSICAL DEPRECIATION AND OBSOLESCENCE.

VALUED agreement by an insurance company to pay a predetermined amount, as indicated in an insurance policy, should a loss occur.

VALUED BASIS INDEMNIFICATION benefit found in a DISABILITY INCOME INSURANCE policy that endeavors to replace the insured wage earner's income with a monetary sum equal to the actual lost income terminated because of illness, sickness, or accident.

VALUED CLAUSE provision in an insurance policy that states the monetary value of each piece of property to be insured.

VALUED CONTRACT *see* VALUED POLICY.

VALUED FORM *see* VALUED POLICY.

VALUED MARINE POLICY *see* VALUED POLICY.

VALUED POLICY policy that pays a specified sum not related in any way to the extent of the loss. The term applies to a life insurance policy rather than to a contract of indemnity because the former does not purport to restore an insured (or beneficiary) to the same financial position after a loss as prior to the loss. The sum of money that a life insurance policy pays as a death benefit is a definite amount that may or may not have any relation to the quantitative value of the death. Thus, the life insurance policy is deemed to be a valued policy.

VALUED POLICY LAW legislation in a number of states requiring insurers to pay the FACE AMOUNT of a fire insurance policy in case of total loss to a dwelling (or sometimes another specified type of building), rather than the ACTUAL CASH VALUE of the loss. Such laws in effect override the principle of INDEMNITY that normally governs property and liability insurance contracts.

VALUE REPORTING FORM form that provides coverage for a business whose inventory has fluctuating values during the year. The amount of insurance coverage is adjusted monthly, quarterly, or annually to reflect the changing monetary value of the inventory. The use of this FORM should eliminate the problem of overinsurance as well as underinsurance.

VALUES *see* NONFORFEITABILITY; NONFORFEITURE BENEFIT (OPTION); NONFORFEITURE PROVISION.

VANDALISM AND MALICIOUS MISCHIEF INSURANCE coverage usually written as an endorsement to property policies such as the *Standard Fire Policy.* A loss must be by the intentional acts of vandals. This peril is of particular importance to owners of structures that are not occupied during particular periods during the day, such as schools and churches. Vandals have little risk of being caught during these periods, when they are most likely to strike. Because of high frequency, a high deductible is usually required when insuring churches and schools.

VANDALISM ENDORSEMENT *see* VANDALISM AND MALICIOUS MISCHIEF INSURANCE.

VANISHING PREMIUM (PREMIUM OFFSET) life insurance policy under which there is rapid buildup of cash values due to high initial premiums such that after a given point in time no further premium payments are required (future premium payments are borrowed from the cash value).

VANISHING PREMIUM OPTION *see* VANISHING PREMIUM PROVISION.

VANISHING PREMIUM PROVISION CLAUSE in a life insurance policy that states that once the CASH VALUE exceeds the NET SINGLE PREMIUM (based on current interest and mortality rates) required for the policy to become PAID-UP INSURANCE, the POLICYOWNER may elect not to make further premium payments. If the CASH VALUE falls below the amount necessary to fund the net single premium, additional premium payments are required. *See also* VANISHING PREMIUM.

VARIABLE ANNUITIES see VARIABLE DOLLAR ANNUITY.

VARIABLE ANNUITY GUARANTEED MINIMUM DEATH BENEFIT (GMDB) attached provision to a VARIABLE DOLLAR ANNUITY that will pay the BENEFICIARY the greater of the interest on the accumulated premiums or account value on the policy anniversary. *See also* EARNINGS ENHANCEMENT BENEFIT (EEB).

VARIABLE BENEFIT PLAN *see* VARIABLE DOLLAR ANNUITY; VARIABLE LIFE INSURANCE.

VARIABLE DOLLAR ANNUITY annuity in which premium payments are used to purchase *accumulation units,* their number depending on the value of each unit. The value of a unit is determined by the value of the portfolio of stocks in which the insurance company invests the premiums.

At the time of the payment of benefits to the annuitant, the accumulation units are converted to a monthly fixed number of units. The variable element is the dollar value of each unit. For example, assume that the annuitant pays a monthly premium of $100. If the accumulation unit value during one month is $50, two units are purchased. In another month, if the value of the accumulation unit is $25, four units are purchased. In a third month, the value of the unit is $10, resulting in the purchase of 10 units. This allows the market use of the investment strategy of dollar cost averaging. Accumulation units are credited to the annuitant's account, a procedure that is similar to purchasing shares in a mutual fund.

When income benefits are scheduled to begin, total accumulation units are converted to assume 100 income benefit units per month. The value of the income unit will vary according to the company's stock investments; in one month the annuitant's income might be $1000, in another month $500, in another month $1200. Changes in the investment experience by the insurance company are passed on to the annuitant, but the company absorbs fluctuations in expenses and mortality experience. *See also* ANNUITY.

VARIABLE DOLLAR INVESTMENTS financial instruments whose principal and income are not established in advance according to contractual terms set forth in the financial instruments document. Both the principal and income can fluctuate according to the up and down swings in the value of an underlying portfolio. Examples of such investments include stocks, mutual funds, real estate, VARIABLE ANNUITIES, VARIABLE LIFE INSURANCE, and UNIVERSAL VARIABLE LIFE INSURANCE.

VARIABLE LIFE INSURANCE investment-oriented *whole life insurance* policy that provides a return linked to an underlying portfolio of securities. The portfolio typically is a group of mutual funds established by the insurer as a *separate account,* with the policyholder given some investment discretion in choosing the mix of assets among, say, a common stock fund, a bond fund, and a money market fund. Variable life insurance offers fixed premiums and a minimum death benefit. The better the total return on the investment portfolio, the higher the death benefit or surrender value of the variable life policy. *See also* INDEXED LIFE INSURANCE.

VARIABLE LIMIT in property insurance coverages, provision whereby the limit of the policy automatically increases at each policy anniversary date, subject to the insured's rejection of such an increase. The objective of the variable limit is to increase the amount of coverage in tandem with the annual increase in the inflation rate so as to prevent less than adequate coverage in the event of a loss. *See also* UNDERINSURANCE.

VARIABLE PAY LIFE INSURANCE *see* VARIABLE PREMIUM LIFE INSURANCE.

VARIABLE PREMIUM LIFE INSURANCE policy that allows premium payments to vary, within certain limits, at the option of the policyholder. In return, the death benefit and rate of cash value accumulation vary with the premium payments. UNIVERSAL LIFE INSURANCE is the most common type of policy offering variable premiums. *See also* FLEXIBLE PREMIUM LIFE INSURANCE.

VARIABLE RATE MORTGAGE *see* ADJUSTABLE RATE MORTGAGE (ARM).

VARIABLE SURVIVORSHIP LIFE INSURANCE policy that combines life insurance coverage on two lives and pays policy proceeds on the second person's death with the accumulation potential of an underlying variable investment portfolio. This variable portfolio will allow the policy proceeds to rise and fall just as in the single-life VARIABLE LIFE POLICY.

VARIABLE UNIVERSAL LIFE *see* UNIVERSAL VARIABLE LIFE INSURANCE.

VARIANCE *see* STANDARD DEVIATION OR VARIATION.

VARIANCE FROM PRESCRIBED STANDARDS *see* STANDARD DEVIATION OR VARIATION.

VEHICLE COVERAGE *see* BUSINESS AUTO COVERAGE FORM; INLAND MARINE INSURANCE (TRANSPORTATION INSURANCE): BUSINESS RISKS; INSTRUMENTALITIES OF TRANSPORTATION INSURANCE; OCEAN MARINE INSURANCE; PERSONAL AUTOMOBILE POLICY (PAP).

VENDING MACHINE MARKETING sale of life insurance policies through vending machines. This method of distribution is generally limited to TRAVEL ACCIDENT INSURANCE, supplemental health or disability policies, or life insurance policies with a small face amount.

VENDOR'S ENDORSEMENT type of ENDORSEMENT in which the seller of a product is added to the MANUFACTURERS AND CONTRACTORS LIABILITY INSURANCE policy as an additional INSURED.

VERMIN EXCLUSION section of some INLAND MARINE insurance *(transportation insurance)* and many other property insurance policies excluding coverage for damage to shipped goods by vermin such as rats. *See also* INSECT EXCLUSION.

VESSEL *see* HULL MARINE INSURANCE.

VESTED ACCOUNT *see* VESTING.

VESTED BENEFIT entitlement of a PARTICIPANT in an EMPLOYEE BENEFIT INSURANCE PLAN to receive benefits regardless of his or her employment status. *See also* VESTING.

VESTED INTEREST *see* VESTING.

VESTING entitlement of a pension plan participant (employee) to receive full benefits at NORMAL RETIREMENT AGE, or a reduced benefit upon EARLY RETIREMENT, whether or not the participant still works for the same employer. The EMPLOYEE RETIREMENT INCOME SECURITY ACT OF 1974 (ERISA) mandates vesting under one of these rules:

1. FORTY-FIVE YEAR RULE
2. FIVE TO FIFTEEN YEAR RULE
3. TEN YEAR RULE

On January 1, 1989, under the TAX REFORM ACT OF 1986, the above vesting requirements were replaced with the following:

1. full vesting (100%) after a participant completes five years of service with an employer; or
2. vesting of 20% after completion of three years of service with an employer, increasing by 20% for each year of service thereafter, until 100% vesting is achieved at the end of seven years of service.

With the passage of the PENSION PROTECTION ACT OF 2006, employer nonselective contributions as well as employer matching contributions must VEST on either the minimum three-year Cliff or six-year GRADED VESTING schedule (Year 1 = 0% vested; Year 2 = 20% vested; Year 3 = 40% vested; Year 4 = 60% vested; Year 5 = 80% vested; Year 6 = 100% vested).

VESTING, CONDITIONAL limitation under a contributory pension plan of an employee's right to receive vested benefits. The employee can withdraw contributions to the pension plan only according to stated conditions. *See also* VESTING.

VESTING, DEFERRED specified requirements of minimum age and years of service to be met by an employee before the individual's benefits are vested. For example, under the TEN YEAR VESTING rule, an employee must work ten years for the particular employer before benefits vest. *See also* VESTING, IMMEDIATE.

VESTING, FULL *see* FULL VESTING.

VESTING, IMMEDIATE employee's full entitlement, with no waiting period, to benefits under a pension or retirement plan. In the case of a CONTRIBUTORY plan, there is immediate vesting of the employee's own contributions, plus the earnings attributable to those contributions. As to employer contributions in contributory and NONCONTRIBUTORY plans, VESTING depends on the terms of the plans, although maximum time limits for full vesting are set by law. Some plans provide immediate vesting of employer contributions in the case of death or disability. SIMPLIFIED EMPLOYEE PENSION (SEP) plans require immediate vesting of employer contributions. *See also* VESTING.

VETERANS ADMINISTRATION (VA) U.S. government agency that administers life insurance, health insurance, welfare, mortgage loans, education, pension benefits, and other programs for veterans of the U.S. armed forces.

VETERANS GROUP LIFE INSURANCE (VGLI) five-year nonrenewable TERM LIFE INSURANCE policy for veterans who were covered by SERVICEMENS GROUP LIFE INSURANCE (SEGLI) while on active duty in the U.S. uniformed forces. At the end of the five-year term, the insured may convert the policy to individual *permanent life insurance* with any company that participates in the VGLI program.

VIATICAL SETTLEMENT act by a person who is terminally ill of cashing in a life insurance policy to pay for the necessary associated illness, medical expenses, and final wishes. This terminally ill person contacts a viatical agent who bids the life insurance policy on the terminally ill person to the many VIATICAL SETTLEMENT COMPANIES.

The package that is sent out for bids includes the terms of the life insurance policy as well as the medical prognosis of the terminally ill person. The viatical settlement company that is awarded the bid agrees to pay 50% to 80% of the FACE AMOUNT of the policy, varying according to the gravity of the terminally ill person's condition and LIFE EXPECTANCY. In turn, the viatical settlement company sells the terminally ill person's life insurance policy to an investor who then becomes the POLICYHOLDER as well as the BENEFICIARY and assumes payment of the premiums of the policy. Upon the death of the terminally ill person, the investor will receive 100% of the life insurance policy's face amount from the insurance company. The sooner the terminally ill patient dies, the higher the investor's return. While returns of 15% to 20% are typical for investors, the policies can pay off a substantially higher return if death occurs early.

VIATICAL SETTLEMENT COMPANY company that buys life insurance policies from policyowners on the lives of insureds who are terminally ill. This type of company pays cash for the life insurance policies, usually in the range of 50% to 80% of the FACE AMOUNT. It also pays the premiums due and receives the DEATH BENEFIT when that person dies. Policies are purchased when the terminally ill person has 24 months or less to live.

VIATICATION process under which terminally ill people sell their life insurance policy for value thereby excluding the policy from being subject to the transfer for value under the three-year rule.

VICARIOUS LIABILITY *see* CONTINGENT LIABILITY (VICARIOUS LIABILITY).

VICTIM COMPENSATION payment under a state-sponsored program for victims of crimes. *See also* FEDERAL CRIME INSURANCE.

VISION CARE INSURANCE health insurance coverage for eye examinations, and eyeglass or contact lens prescriptions.

VIS MAJOR Latin phrase meaning "overpowering force"; an unavoidable accident or calamity; an accident for which no one is responsible; an ACT OF GOD.

VOIDABLE CONTRACT VALID CONTRACT that can be canceled for cause by one or more parties to the contract. An insurance contract can be voided by the insurer if the insured has used fraudulent means to obtain it or has intentionally concealed information or misrepresented the risk.

VOID CONTRACT apparent agreement that is not a valid contract.

VOLUNTARY ACCIDENTAL DEATH AND DISMEMBERMENT (AD&D) INSURANCE additional amount of ACCIDENTAL DEATH AND DISMEMBERMENT INSURANCE not provided by the employee benefit plan (standard group life plan) that may be chosen by the employee. Generally, the employee pays the entire premium that is deducted through the employer's payroll deduction accounting system used for other employee benefit plans.

VOLUNTARY COMPENSATION ENDORSEMENT addition to a WORKERS COMPENSATION INSURANCE policy to cover payments to injured employees who are not covered by a state's workers compensation law. This endorsement provides employees who are not covered by the state law a choice of receiving WORKERS COMPENSATION BENEFITS or suing the employer. Under workers compensation laws, employers agree to supply, according to a formula, income lost by workers accidentally injured on the job, as well as medical and rehabilitation benefits and death and survivor benefits. In exchange, these benefits are to be the final obligation of the employer to compensate workers, or the exclusive remedy. However, there has been considerable erosion of the exclusive remedy concept since the early 1970s. Workers have been allowed to sue their employers for various types of on-the-job injuries. Each state has its own workers compensation law.

VOLUNTARY DEDUCTIBLE EMPLOYEE CONTRIBUTION PLAN pension plan that allows an employee to contribute by electing to have money deducted from each paycheck. Some qualified plans such as 401 (k) allow employees to contribute pre-tax dollars, while others require employees to put in after-tax dollars.

VOLUNTARY DEFERRAL PLAN vehicle for the deferring of unneeded current income for a later date, such as retirement, providing the following benefits:
1. There is no tax on earnings of the plan until distributed.
2. Employee is able to defer compensation in excess of the amount subject to the limitations of qualified plans since the voluntary plan is a nonqualified plan.
3. The amount the employee defers can be matched by the employer.
4. The employer and employee have flexibility in designing BENEFITS and VESTING requirements.
5. The employer can select employees to participate in the plan since it is a nonqualified plan and does not have to comply with the antidiscrimination provisions of qualified plans found under the EMPLOYMENT RETIREMENT INCOME SECURITY ACT (ERISA).
6. Life insurance can be used as the funding instrument and, as such, the employer can receive the death benefit, thereby recovering its matching contribution to the plan.

VOLUNTARY EMPLOYEES BENEFICIARY ASSOCIATION (VEBA) tax-exempt entity as qualified under Section 501 (c)(9) of the Internal Revenue Code. The VEBA usually provides its members and their dependents and beneficiaries with paid life insurance, health insurance, and accident insurance. The VEBA can be established by any employer for employees even if they already have a retirement plan. Employers are permitted to make tax-deductible contributions to the VEBA that is usually established as a trust with the bank acting as a trustee. Earnings build within the trust on a tax-deferred basis. If the VEBA should terminate, all of the VEBA's assets are distributed to the active participants in the VEBA as of the date of termination. Distributions to a VEBA participant are not required to begin by age 70½, nor is a penalty charged if the distributions begin prior to age 59½. Survivor benefits are received on an income and estate tax-free basis. Assets of the VEBA are exempt from creditors' claims. The IRS code requires that the VEBA must have at least two participants (one of the participants can be a spouse); benefits must be based on annual compensation as well as age; and all full-time employees who are at least age 21 and have at least three years of full-time service must be allowed to participate. The employer can terminate the plan at any time.

VOLUNTARY GOVERNMENT INSURANCE see SOCIAL INSURANCE.

VOLUNTARY INSURANCE see SOCIAL INSURANCE.

VOLUNTARY LIFE INSURANCE additional amount of life insurance above that provided by the employee benefit plan (standard group life plan) that may be chosen by the employee. A limit is usually placed on this maximum and is expressed as a multiple of the employee's earnings.

VOLUNTARY PAYROLL DEDUCTION PLAN program through which employees purchase individual LIFE INSURANCE and DISABILITY INCOME INSURANCE by having the employer reduce their income by the required insurance PREMIUM. Since the policies are individual policies, paid for totally by the employees, the policies are portable and not a function of employment.

VOLUNTARY PLAN TERMINATION ending a pension plan at the election of an employer or sponsor. The employer has the unilateral right to change or terminate a pension plan at any time. However, the termination must meet requirements set out by the EMPLOYEE RETIREMENT INCOME SECURITY ACT OF 1974 (ERISA). Assets must be distributed to participants according to federal guidelines.

VOLUNTARY RESERVE amount established by an insurance company, but not required by state law, for any of a number of reasons, such as a reserve for payment of future dividends. A voluntary reserve is likely to appear as a LIABILITY on the company's balance sheet. Contrast with STATUTORY RESERVES. See also BALANCE SHEET RESERVES; POLICY RESERVE.

VOLUNTEER PROTECTION ACT OF 1997 act in which volunteers of nonprofit organizations and government entities do not incur liability if they are acting within the scope of their volunteer activities, their actions do not result in reckless misconduct, gross negligence, and/or willful or criminal misconduct, and they have the proper license, if required. Protection is only for individual volunteers; there is no protection for organizations or paid members of organizations.

VOLUNTEER PROTECTION LAWS laws enacted by all of the 50 states whose purpose it is to reduce or eliminate the volunteer's CIVIL LIABILITY exposure. An ideal law would exclude the volunteer from civil liability resulting from actions taken within the volunteer's official capacity unless the damage and/or injury caused was the result of a willful act by the volunteer.

VOYAGE POLICY OCEAN MARINE INSURANCE covering one trip. Ocean marine insurance is written either for a specific time period or per trip. A voyage policy is usually written for cargo, whereas a *time policy* covers a ship.

W

WAGE INDEX table used, among other purposes, to determine monthly Social Security benefit for a retired or disabled worker and his or her dependents. The AVERAGE MONTHLY WAGE (AMW) of the worker is computed, disregarding certain periods of low earnings. The AMW is used to determine the PRIMARY INSURANCE AMOUNT (PIA). Then, benefits are figured from the table depending on how old the worker is upon retirement, whether there are dependents or survivors, and when they will retire.

WAGERING V. INSURANCE common misunderstanding about insurance. In gambling a RISK is created that did not exist prior to placing a bet. Under insurance, a risk exists whether or not an insurance policy is purchased. For example, the uncertainty of one's home burning exists independent of the purchase of insurance; the purchase of insurance should not affect the probability of loss.

WAIT AND SEE SURVIVORSHIP UNIVERSAL LIFE type of single premium UNIVERSAL LIFE INSURANCE policy insuring two lives with the death benefit payable on the LAST SURVIVOR INSURANCE basis. The policyowner may receive the return of the initial premium at the end of 10 or 20 years. If the policyowner elects not to have the initial premium returned, the policy would continue in force at current mortality, expense, and interest rates. Typically there is no surrender charge.

WAITING PERIOD *see* DISABILITY INCOME INSURANCE (ELIMINATION PERIOD).

WAIVE *see* WAIVER; WAIVER OF INVENTORY CLAUSE; WAIVER OF PREMIUM (WP); WAIVER OF PREMIUM FOR PAYER BENEFIT; WAIVER OF RESTORATION PREMIUM; WAIVER OF SUBROGATION RIGHTS CLAUSE.

WAIVER relinquishment of a legal right to act. For example, an insured relies on statements of an agent of an insurance company concerning coverages under an insurance policy. Agents by their actions may have waived certain provisions the insurance company has written in the insurance policy, with the company's authority. Another example would be the provision in the HOMEOWNERS INSURANCE POLICY that suspends coverage if a hazard is increased by the actions of an insured. An insured who stores explosives near the family home notifies the insurance company; the company grants permission to do so, thereby waiving its defense of the increase in hazard clause.

WAIVER OF COINSURANCE CLAUSE provision in property insurance that stipulates that the COINSURANCE REQUIREMENT will not be in effect.

WAIVER OF INVENTORY CLAUSE provision in property insurance that waives, under specified circumstances, the requirement for an inventory of undamaged property when a damage claim is filed. A COINSURANCE clause in a fire insurance policy typically requires such an inventory or appraisal at the time of a claim. The waiver avoids the expense of an inventory when the claim is small. Under one common formula, the inventory requirement is waived when the claim is for less than $10,000 and is also for less than 5% of the limit of all insurance coverage applicable to the property.

WAIVER OF PREMIUM FOR DISABILITY *see* RIDERS, LIFE POLICIES.

WAIVER OF PREMIUM FOR PAYER BENEFIT clause added to an insurance policy providing WAIVER OF PREMIUM (WP) if the premium payer dies or becomes disabled. For example, this option is available on insurance policies on a child's life where the premium is paid by an adult, or on life and health policies for adults.

WAIVER OF PREMIUM RIDER *see* WAIVER OF PREMIUM (WP).

WAIVER OF PREMIUM (WP) in life insurance, action by an insurance company canceling premium payments by an insured who has been disabled for at least six months. The policy remains in force and continues to build cash values and pay dividends (if it is a participating policy), just as if the insured was still making premium payments. Experts suggest that this clause should be considered in a life insurance policy since the probability of becoming disabled is 7 to 10 times greater than death at younger or middle ages.

WAIVER OF RESTORATION PREMIUM clause in a SURETY BOND contract providing for restoration of coverage after a loss without requirement of a RESTORATION PREMIUM.

WAIVER OF SUBROGATION RIGHTS CLAUSE endorsement to a property liability policy whereby an insurer gives up the right to take action against a third party for a loss suffered by an insured. Typically, under terms of the SUBROGATION CLAUSE, the insurer, having paid an insured for a loss, takes over any rights possessed by the insured who has suffered the loss. For example, an insured, John Smith, is hit by another car while he is driving. His insurance company pays his claim and then may sue or attempt to recover damages from the other driver. In certain instances, the insured might want to get a waiver of subrogation rights from the insurer. For example, if a landlord assured a tenant that the tenant was not responsible for damage to the landlord's property, the landlord could make good on that promise only by getting the insurer to waive its subrogation rights. Otherwise, if the landlord's property was damaged by the tenant, the insurer would have to pay the claim and could then try to collect damages from the tenant.

WANTON DISREGARD legal phrase used in NEGLIGENCE cases to describe one person's overwhelming lack of care for the rights or well-being of another. Wanton disregard of another's rights is evidence of GROSS NEGLIGENCE.

WAR DAMAGE INSURANCE CORPORATION government reinsurance program that provided coverage for U.S. properties during World War II. Private insurers shared the first layer of coverage, with the government providing catastrophic loss coverage. This is one of several government insurance programs for exposures that private insurers cannot cover because techniques of spreading the risk do not apply.

WAREHOUSE BOND type of surety bond that guarantees that goods stored in a warehouse will be delivered upon presentation of a receipt.

WAREHOUSERS LIABILITY FORM special insurance that covers warehousers liability to customers whose property is damaged by an insured peril while in the custody of an insured warehouser. Policy deductibles may range from $50 to $10,000. Typical exclusions are war risks, money, securities, and spoilage of perishable goods.

WAREHOUSE-TO-WAREHOUSE CLAUSE part of an *ocean marine* policy that provides coverage of goods through all of the stages of a journey. Coverage begins when goods leave the warehouse of a shipper, and continues until they reach the customer's warehouse.

WAR EXCLUSION CLAUSE provision in a life insurance policy that death benefits will not be paid in the event an insured dies from war-related causes; or in lieu of a death benefit there is a return of premiums plus interest, or a refund equal to the reserve portion (cash value) of the policy. For example, during the Vietnam War, if a whole life policy with a war exclusion clause had a face amount of $10,000 and an insured died as the result of war-related injuries, the beneficiary would receive the cash value of the policy. This clause cannot be added to a policy that had none originally. If it is included in a policy bought in time of war, it is typically removed by life insurance companies at the end of the war and, once removed, can never be restored.

WARN *see* WORKER ADJUSTMENT AND RETRAINING NOTIFICATION ACT (WARN).

WAR PERIL *see* WAR RISK INSURANCE.

WARRANT document that gives bearer the right to purchase common stock at a specified price for a limited time period.

WARRANTY pledge by an insured in writing, and a part of the actual contract, that a particular condition exists or does not exist. For example, an insured warrants that a sprinkler system works. In exchange, the insurance company charges a reduced premium for fire coverage. Statements by an insured in an application for property insurance are deemed to be warranties, not representations, as is generally the case in life insurance policy applications. *See also* REPRESENTATIONS.

WAR RISKS exposures usually excluded from life and health insurance, or subject to a maximum limit if covered. For property coverage, *see* WAR RISK INSURANCE.

WAR RISK INSURANCE coverage for damage due to peril of war, usually written as part of an OCEAN MARINE INSURANCE policy.

WASHINGTON, D.C. V. GREATER WASHINGTON BOARD OF TRADE legal decision in which the Supreme Court of the United States ruled that states cannot require employers to provide disabled employees the same health insurance with which they provide active employees. Regulation by states of EMPLOYEE BENEFIT INSURANCE PLANS is precluded when it relates in any way to employee benefit plans governed by the federal statute on pensions and benefits (EMPLOYEE RETIREMENT INCOME SECURITY ACT OF 1974—ERISA). The issue in this case was the relationship between WORKERS COMPENSATION INSURANCE (as required by the states for job-related illness or injuries incurred by the employee) and federally regulated health insurance provided by the company for actively at work employees. The Greater Washington Board of Trade challenged the Washington, D.C. law that required employers who provide health insurance for actively at-work employees to continue to offer equivalent health insurance coverage to disabled employees who are eligible for workers compensation insurance.

WASH SALE RULE rule concerning stock sold and then repurchased or a similar security repurchased (warrants or options) within 30 full days before or after the day of the sale. Losses established from such a sale cannot be used to offset capital gains for tax purposes; however, this disallowed loss is not lost forever, as it can be added to the cost basis of the repurchased security for tax purposes.

WATER BACKUP AND SUMP OVERFLOW coverage for the backup of water through sewers and drains and the overflow from a sump by an ENDORSEMENT to the HOMEOWNERS INSURANCE POLICY— SECTION I (PROPERTY COVERAGE). Without such an endorsement, these perils would be excluded from the homeowner's insurance policy.

WATERCRAFT ENDORSEMENT addition to the HOMEOWNERS INSURANCE POLICY AND COMMERCIAL PACKAGE POLICY that provides liability and medical coverage for damages resulting from the operation of motor boats too large to qualify for insurance under homeowners and commercial package policies.

WATERCRAFT NONOWNED INSURANCE endorsement to COMMERCIAL GENERAL LIABILITY INSURANCE (CGL) for a business responsible for boats it does not own. Whether the boats are leased from another firm or owned by employees who operate them for the benefit of the business owner, a business has a liability exposure that is not covered by a CGL policy; the special endorsement is needed for this coverage.

WATER DAMAGE INSURANCE protection in the event of accidental discharge, leakage, or overflow of water from plumbing systems, heating, air conditioning, and refrigerating systems, and rain or snow through broken doors, open doors, windows, and skylights resulting in damage or destruction of the property scheduled in the policy. This type of water damage coverage can also be acquired through an endorsement of a standard property insurance policy.

WATER DAMAGE LEGAL LIABILITY INSURANCE coverage for an insured's liability for damage to another's property from leakage or overflow of water. Some liability policies specifically exclude water damage, including that caused by rain or snow. Therefore, a special policy was necessary to cover this exposure. However, most liability policies today have dropped this exclusion, and coverage for water damage liability is part of the regular liability policy.

WATER EXCLUSION CLAUSE provision in many property insurance policies that excludes coverage for floods and backup from sewers or drains and underground water. Because floods and hurricanes are generally confined to certain areas, only policyholders in those areas need flood insurance. Therefore, it is impossible for underwriters to spread the risk, which is the basis of underwriting. But because homeowners in the endangered areas need insurance, the U.S. government developed a special FEDERAL FLOOD INSURANCE program.

WATER POLLUTION LIABILITY obligations of shipowners for water polluted by spills from their ships. If a ship discharges oil or other polluting or hazardous substances into the water, the shipowner is responsible either for removing them, paying for their removal, or, if the substances cannot be removed, paying a fine. Following passage of the WATER QUALITY IMPROVEMENT ACT OF 1970 establishing the liability of shipowners, marine underwriters formed the WATER QUALITY INSURANCE SYNDICATE to provide insurance.

WATER QUALITY IMPROVEMENT ACT OF 1970 federal law that requires shipowners to clean up or pay for the cleanup of waters polluted by discharges from their ships. Shipowners may be refused navigation privileges if they cannot demonstrate that they have the financial resources to pay for cleanups.

WATER QUALITY INSURANCE SYNDICATE group of marine underwriters formed in 1971 to provide coverage for shipowners for WATER POLLUTION LIABILITY. The federal WATER QUALITY IMPROVEMENT ACT OF 1970 made shipowners responsible for hazardous substances discharged by their ships into the water. This led to the Water Quality Insurance Syndicate. Coverage extends to liabilities imposed by states. The syndicate vouches for the financial responsibility of those it insures.

WEAR AND TEAR EXCLUSION denial of coverage for damage, in INLAND MARINE insurance, stemming from routine use of the property. Property can be expected to deteriorate somewhat over time from normal use. This is not considered an insurable loss.

WEATHER INSURANCE *see* RAIN INSURANCE.

WEDDING PRESENTS FLOATER personal property insurance that provides ALL-RISKS coverage for wedding presents, wherever they may be in the world, until they are permanently located. Because the new owners of wedding presents may not yet have a home or a HOMEOWNERS INSURANCE POLICY, and because their gifts may be moved from place to place until they are settled, this policy fills a gap in coverage, but it can be purchased only for as long as 90 days following the wedding.

WEEKLY PREMIUM INSURANCE *see* DEBIT INSURANCE (HOME SERVICE INSURANCE, INDUSTRIAL INSURANCE).

WEIGHT OF ICE, SNOW, OR SLEET INSURANCE coverage for damage to a building or its contents due to the weight of these elements. Outdoor property such as patios, swimming pools, and sidewalks are usually excluded.

WELFARE AND PENSION PLANS DISCLOSURE ACT federal law that requires administrators of pension plans with more than 25 participants to file a plan description with the U.S. Department of Labor. A plan description includes schedules of benefits, type of administration, and copies of the plan. If the plan has more than 100 participants, the administrator must also file an annual financial report. This information must be made available to plan participants upon request, and the person responsible for handling the funds must be bonded.

WELLNESS PROGRAM employee benefit program that emphasizes the pursuit of a lifestyle that minimizes the occurrence of sickness through an organized program of preventive medicine. Such a program includes screening for high blood pressure, obesity, breast cancer, and stress; a smoke-free workplace; a systematized exercise and fitness approach for general health; and training and education programs for employees concerning proper nutrition, stress management, weight control, cardiopulmonary resuscitation, and prenatal care.

WHITE COLLAR CRIME *see* BLANKET POSITION BOND; BOND; FIDELITY BOND; JUDICIAL BOND; SURETY BOND.

WHITE LIST STATES states that allow the placement of SURPLUS LINES only with insurance companies that the states have approved.

WHOLE LIFE ANNUITY *see* ANNUITY; ANNUITY DUE; LIFE ANNUITY CERTAIN; PURE ANNUITY; REFUND ANNUITY.

WHOLE LIFE ANNUITY DUE *see* ANNUITY DUE.

WHOLE LIFE INSURANCE *see* ORDINARY LIFE INSURANCE.

WHOLESALE INSURANCE *see* FRANCHISE INSURANCE (WHOLESALE INSURANCE).

WHOLESALE LIFE INSURANCE variation of GROUP LIFE INSURANCE that covers a small group of persons who work for the same employer. With group life insurance, the employer owns the policy; with wholesale insurance, each employee applies for and owns his or her own policy. However, the employer must agree to pay at least part of wholesale life insurance premiums for the group to qualify for wholesale insurance. Wholesale insurance was devised for groups as small as 10 persons when group insurance was limited by law to a minimum of 50 members. Today, group insurance is sold to smaller groups and wholesale insurance is written for groups as small as five persons. *See also* FRANCHISE INSURANCE (WHOLESALE INSURANCE).

WHOLESALING action in which an insurance company develops an insurance product and sells that product to a third party (usually financial advisors such as accountants, lawyers, and/or bankers) who add their own commissions and/or fees to that product, and resell that product to their clients.

WILL usually a written document stipulating the disposition of one's assets at death. If this document does not exist at death, the assets are distributed according to state law. This document should include the following central points: (1) name of individual who is to be responsible for carrying out the wishes of the deceased; (2) name of guardian for any minor children; (3) two notarized signatures of two witnesses; (4) requirements for the disposition of property; and (5) establishment of state of residence. This is of particular importance if there is ownership of property in different states.

WINDOW GUARANTEED INVESTMENT CONTRACT (GIC) type of GUARANTEED INVESTMENT CONTRACT (GIC) under which a series of payments are made into an account (usually monthly to reflect the frequency of the employee's salary) of an insurance company where it will remain for a stipulated number of years. Both the principal of the account and the interest rate are guaranteed by the insurance company. At an agreed upon future date, both principal and interest are returned to the payor (usually a DEFINED CONTRIBUTION PLAN).

WINDSTORM HAZARD *see* STORM INSURANCE (WINDSTORM INSURANCE).

WINDSTORM INSURANCE additional coverage available on most property insurance policies through the EXTENDED COVERAGE ENDORSEMENT. Windstorms, including hurricanes, cyclones, and high winds, are not among the covered perils under most property insurance policies. *See also* STORM INSURANCE (WINDSTORM INSURANCE).

WISCONSIN STATE LIFE FUND life insurance distribution system under which the state underwrites and sells life insurance to any resident of Wisconsin who makes application.

WINTER RANGE FORM type of livestock insurance that covers for cattle and sheep on the range from October 1 to May 1 in the Western states. Perils insured against are the weather, including freezing; most natural disasters; riot and civil commotion; collision with vehicles; and theft.

WITH BENEFIT OF SURVIVORSHIP phrase describing a form of joint tenancy ownership where property passes to the survivors when one party dies.

WITHDRAWAL BENEFITS, PENSION PLAN *see* PENSION PLANS: WITHDRAWAL BENEFITS.

WITHDRAWAL CREDITS, PENSION PLAN *see* PENSION PLANS: WITHDRAWAL BENEFITS.

WITHOUT EVIDENCE OF INSURABILITY *see* EVIDENCE OF INSURABILITY.

WOMEN LEADERS ROUND TABLE group of women life insurance agents who sell sufficient insurance to qualify for membership. The round table is sponsored by the NATIONAL ASSOCIATION OF LIFE UNDERWRITERS (NALU).

WOOL GROWERS FLOATER INLAND MARINE policy addition that provides coverage to owners of sheep, and to warehouseowners who store wool as well as wool in transit.

WORK AND MATERIALS CLAUSE provision in most property insurance policies that permits a policyholder to use the insured premises to store materials and handle them in the manner needed to pursue his or her line of business. Without this clause, a policy may be voided for fraud, concealment, or misrepresentation of an undisclosed INCREASED HAZARD. The clause provides a defense for a policyholder against a charge of increasing the hazard of a workplace if the materials in question are necessary to the business.

WORKER ADJUSTMENT AND RETRAINING NOTIFICATION ACT (WARN) federal law, effective February 4, 1989, that requires company notification of employees prior to laying them off or closing a plant or an office. Workers covered under WARN are to include office workers, field representatives, agents, managers, and any other employees of insurance companies. To be affected by WARN, the company must employ at least 100 full-time employees. Part-time employees are not included in the 100 full-time employees count unless the total hours worked per week by all employees is at least 4000 hours. WARN requires the company to notify its employees of impending layoffs when one or more of the following circumstances occur:

1. At least 500 employees are terminated or laid off during a 30-day period.
2. At least 50 employees are terminated or laid off, comprising at least 33% of the total employment force, during a 30-day period.
3. A plant or an office is closed, whether on a temporary or permanent basis.

WORKERS COMPENSATION *see* WORKERS COMPENSATION INSURANCE.

WORKERS COMPENSATION BENEFITS income, medical, rehabilitation, death, and survivor payments to workers injured on the job. State workers compensation laws, which date from early in the twentieth century, provide that employers take responsibility for on-the-job injuries. Each state defines the benefit level for employers in that state. Although these benefits were designed to be the final obligation of employers to their employees, there has been considerable erosion of this concept since the early 1970s; workers have been allowed by the courts to sue employers for various on-the-job injuries in addition to workers compensation benefits. Because workers compensation benefits are a routine and fairly predictable risk, many employers use SELF INSURANCE. Some states mandate that employers buy workers compensation insurance from a state fund, but some offer a choice of a state fund, self insurance, or commercial insurance.

WORKERS COMPENSATION CATASTROPHE COVER excess coverage for employers who use SELF INSURANCE for routine workers compensation risks. Many employers consider workers compensation exposure to be routine and predictable and set up a fund to pay these losses themselves rather than trade premium and claims dollars with an insurance company. To supplement a self-insurance program, an employer may buy insurance for catastrophic loss above a certain limit. A *stop loss aggregate contract* will pay all losses in one year over a specified dollar limit. A SPECIFIC EXCESS CONTRACT pays losses over a stated limit per accident.

WORKERS COMPENSATION, COVERAGE A agreement under which an insurance company promises to pay all compensation and all benefits required of an insured employer under the workers compensation act of the state or states listed in the policy.

WORKERS COMPENSATION, COVERAGE B coverage under a commercial *workers compensation policy* for situations in which an employee not covered under workers compensation laws could sue for injuries suffered under common law liability.

WORKERS COMPENSATION INSURANCE coverage providing four types of benefits (medical care, death, disability, rehabilitation) for employee job-related injuries or diseases as a matter of right (without regard to fault). This insurance is usually purchased by the employer from an insurance company, although in a few states there are monopolistic state funds through which the insurance must be purchased. The premium rate is based on a percentage of the employer's payroll and varies according to the employee's occupation. *See also* WORKERS COMPENSATION BENEFITS.

WORLD INSURANCE *see* WORLDWIDE COVERAGE.

WORLDWIDE COVERAGE endorsement to the COMMERCIAL GENERAL LIABILITY INSURANCE (CGL) policy that provides liability coverage to an insured business for damages anywhere in the world. Policies typically have territorial limits for liability coverage, but this endorsement extends coverage worldwide, so long as a damage suit is brought in the U.S. or Canada.

WORLD WIDE WEB interconnection of computers that contain pages classified into groups called web sites that can be accessed over the INTERNET. The only requirement for visiting a web site is to have access to the Internet through the software of a BROWSER.

WORRY state of anxiety and distress. One goal of adequate insurance is to eliminate, or alleviate, worry on the part of a policyholder. Many people, for example, are concerned that they would not be able to handle the financial burden if they became ill, or that their spouse would be impoverished if they died. Insurance is designed to eliminate these concerns by assuring that benefits will be provided.

WRAP-AROUND INSURANCE PROGRAM program designed as protection for political risk (action taken by a foreign government resulting in financial loss to companies trading or investing overseas). Coverage is provided for deprivation, acts of government, embargo, sanction, partial loss, and forced abandonment.

WRAP-UP INSURANCE liability policy that covers all liability exposures for a large group that has something in common. For example, wrap-up insurance can be written for all the various businesses working together on a special project, to provide coverage for losses arising out of that work only.

WRIGHT, ELIZUR Massachusetts commissioner of insurance responsible for the passage of legislation (1861) that guaranteed policyowners of that state equity in the cash value of their life insurance. The nonforfeiture legislation stipulated that four-fifths of the cash value of a life insurance policy be applied to the purchase of extended term life insurance.

WRITE to sell a specific amount of insurance.

WRITTEN BUSINESS insurance for which (1) an application has been filed but the first premium has not yet been paid or (2) a life insurance policy that has not yet been delivered to an insured.

WRITTEN PREMIUMS total premiums generated from all policies written by an insurance company within a given period of time. *See also* EARNED PREMIUM.

WRONGFUL ACT error, misstatement, or breach of duty by an officer or director of a company that results in a lawsuit against the company. DIRECTORS AND OFFICERS LIABILITY INSURANCE covers claims arising from wrongful acts by directors or officers of a company while in that capacity. Wrongful acts specifically exclude dishonesty, theft, libel, and slander. During the liability insurance crisis of the 1980s, this type of coverage became unavailable in many industries as wrongful acts received an increasingly liberal interpretation by the courts and many expensive lawsuits were filed against business firms. *See also* TORT; TORT, DEFENSE AGAINST UNINTENTIONAL; TORT, INTENTIONAL; TORT, UNINTENTIONAL.

WRONGFUL DEATH death caused by a person without legal justification. Wrongful death may be the result of negligence, such as when a drunken driver hits and kills someone; or it may be intentional, as when someone kills another person with a gun. In most states, suits can be filed for damages caused by wrongful death. Much work has been done in an attempt to put a value on human life and, therefore, to determine the compensation allowable to the family of an individual who has been killed. *See also* HUMAN LIFE VALUE APPROACH (ECONOMIC VALUE OF AN INDIVIDUAL LIFE—EVOIL).

WRONGFUL TERMINATION CLAIM under a general liability policy, a claim by an employer arising when an employee terminated by a supervisor without authority or just cause brings suit against the employer. Such a claim is covered under most general liability policies provided that the following elements are in evidence:
1. the insurance policy is in force on the date of loss.
2. there has been no willful misinterpretation of any material facts.
3. the POLICYHOLDER did not have a willful (preconceived) intent to harm or injure the employee who was terminated.

X Y Z

XCU *see* EXPLOSION, COLLAPSE, AND UNDERGROUND EXCLUSION.

YACHT INSURANCE coverage for fire and explosion, against fire and any damage caused by explosion whether or not fire ensues, and whether or not an explosion occurs on- or off-board; sinking from floating debris, sunken hulks, and reefs; stranding against sand bars and filled channels resulting in salvage costs, material and labor expenses to refloat and repair a yacht; collision causing legal liability for damage to another vessel; assailing thieves (theft by forcible entry); and jettison and barratry of mariners or masters. Coverage for liability for bodily injury and loss of life is available through OCEAN MARINE PROTECTION AND INDEMNITY INSURANCE.

YEARLY PRICE OF PROTECTION METHOD ACTUARIAL procedure used to determine the cost of protection of a CASH VALUE LIFE INSURANCE policy on an annual basis. This cost of protection is developed by the following steps:
1. Cash value at the beginning of the year plus the premiums paid in for that year are summed up, and the total is multiplied by an assumed interest rate factor of (1+i), resulting in the theoretical end of the year CASH SURRENDER VALUE;
2. From the theoretical end of the year cash surrender value, the actual cash surrender value at the end of year and the dividends during that year are subtracted. The resultant figure is the sum allocated for MORTALITY CHARGES for that year;
3. The sum allocated for mortality charges for that year is then divided by the AMOUNT OF RISK (face value—end of the year cash surrender value) per $1000 of FACE AMOUNT.

YEARLY PROBABILITY OF DYING figure in a MORTALITY TABLE derived by dividing the number of people dying during a given year by the number of people alive at the beginning of that same year.

YEARLY PROBABILITY OF LIVING figure in a MORTALITY TABLE derived by dividing the number of people alive at the end of a given year by the number of people alive at the beginning of that same year.

YEARLY RATE OF RETURN METHOD ACTUARIAL procedure used to determine the annual rate of return at which annual benefits would have to be gained from the CASH VALUE LIFE INSURANCE policy in order to equal the annual investment made in the policy. The benefits under the policy are the CASH VALUE, dividends (if PARTICIPATING INSURANCE), and the DEATH BENEFIT for the year under discussion. The investment made in the policy is the amount of the premiums paid into the policy that year and the cash value at the beginning of that year. The equation then becomes:

$$\text{Yearly Rate of Return} = \frac{\text{Sum of Policy Benefits}}{\text{Sum of Policy Investments}} - 1$$

This method was developed by Dr. Joseph Belth, a professor at Indiana University.

YEARLY RENEWABLE GROUP TERM INSURANCE *see* GROUP TERM LIFE INSURANCE.

YEARLY RENEWABLE TERM (YRT) *see* RENEWABLE TERM LIFE INSURANCE.

YEARLY RENEWABLE TERM PLAN OF REINSURANCE type of PROPORTIONAL REINSURANCE under which the CEDING COMPANY (PRIMARY INSURER) cedes to a REINSURER its NET AMOUNT AT RISK for the amount above its retention limit on a life insurance policy. In the event the insured dies, the reinsurer is obligated to pay that part of the death benefit which is equivalent to the net amount at risk.

YEARS CERTAIN ANNUITY *see* LIFE ANNUITY CERTAIN.

YEARS OF SERVICE length of employment as measured to determine eligibility, VESTING, and benefit levels for employee participants in tax *qualified pension* plans. There is often a requirement that years of service be continuous (without unexcused breaks).

YIELD, CURRENT rate of return computed by dividing the current annual dividend (if a stock) or annual coupon amount (if a bond) by the amount paid for that financial instrument.

YIELD OF ASSETS *see* YIELD ON ASSETS.

YIELD ON ASSETS annual or other periodic rate of return on investments. Because life insurance companies act as custodians of premiums for many years, until money must be paid out in death benefits or other types of claims, they invest it to achieve a yield adequate to meet these obligations. Yield is also important to the policyowner of life policies that include a specific investment element. For example, some *annuities* and CASH VALUE LIFE INSURANCE policies pay a yield that approximates the market rate the policyholder could get elsewhere. While other contracts, such as a *variable annuity* and VARIABLE LIFE INSURANCE do not guarantee a specified yield, they pay one based on the performance of the underlying investments.

YIELD ON INVESTMENTS RATIO insurance company's net investment income divided by its invested assets. The greater the yield, the better the investments that are being made.

YIELD RATE *see* YIELD ON ASSETS.

YIELD TO MATURITY (YTM) sum total of the annual effective rate of return earned by an owner of a bond if that bond is held until its maturity date. This effective return includes the current income generated by the bond as well as any difference in the face value of the bond and the bond's purchase price. The relationship of YTM and the bond's coupon rate is as follows: (1) if the purchase price of the bond is greater than the face value of the bond (purchase made at a premium), the YTM is lower than the coupon rate (rate printed on bond certificate); (2) if the purchase price of the bond is less than the face value of the bond (purchase made at a discount), the YTM is higher than the coupon rate; and (3) if the purchase price of the bond is equal to the face value of the bond, the YTM is equal to the coupon rate. The equation for the computation of the YTM is as follows:

$$YTM = \frac{I + \dfrac{(FVOB - CVOB)}{n}}{\dfrac{(FVOB + CVOB)}{2}}$$

I = Interest rate paid annually (in dollars) by the bond (coupon rate of the bond)

where: FVOB = face value of bond (amount printed on bond certificate)

CVOB = current value of bond (market value of bond)

n = number of years until bond reaches maturity date.

For example, assume the following:

I = 8% coupon rate of the bond (rate printed on bond certificate)

FVOB = $1000 printed on bond certificate

CVOB = $980 market value

n = 30

then:

$$YTM = \frac{\$80 + \dfrac{(\$1000 - \$980)}{30}}{\dfrac{(\$1000 + \$980)}{2}} = 8.15\%$$

YORK ANTWERP RULES treaty adopted by most major countries to determine adjustment for GENERAL AVERAGE in OCEAN MARINE INSURANCE.

YRT *see* YEARLY RENEWABLE TERM (YRT).

ZERO COUPON BONDS bonds that are sold at discount from their maturity value with the interest compounding and paid at the bond's maturity date. Even though these bonds do not pay interest until maturity, the interest that accrues each year becomes taxable income in that year. These bonds can be purchased to provide a specific sum of money at a specific date.

ZONE SYSTEM method for triennial examination of insurance companies as established by the NATIONAL ASSOCIATION OF INSURANCE COMMISSIONERS (NAIC). Teams are composed of representatives from several state insurance commissioners' offices. Their findings are acceptable by all the states in which the examined insurance companies are licensed to conduct business.

ABBREVIATIONS AND ACRONYMS

A

AAI Alliance of American Insurers

AAM Associate in Automation Management

AD&D Accidental Death and Dismemberment

ADEA Age Discrimination in Employment Act

AGRIP Association of Government Risk Pools

AIA American Insurance Association

AICPA American Institute of Certified Public Accountants

AIME Average Indexed Monthly Earnings

AIR Assumed Interest Rate/Assumed Investment Return

AIRMIC Association of Insurance and Risk Managers in Industry and Commerce

AMW Average Monthly Wage

APR Annual Percentage Rate

ASO Administrative Services Only

AVR Asset Valuation Reserve

B

BAP Business Automobile Policy. Replaced by BUSINESS AUTO COVERAGE FORM

BOP Businessowners Policy

BPPCF Business and Personal Property Coverage Form

C

CAPM Capital Asset Pricing Model

CAS Casualty Actuarial Society

CBOT Chicago Board of Trade

CEBS Certified Employee Benefit Specialist

CERCLA Comprehensive Environmental Response, Compensation, and Liability Act

CFP Certified Financial Planner

CGL Comprehensive General Liability Insurance. Replaced by COMMERCIAL GENERAL LIABILITY INSURANCE

CHAMPUS Civilian Health and Medical Program of the Uniformed Service

ChFC Chartered Financial Consultant

CLU Chartered Life Underwriter

COB Coordination of Benefits

COBRA Consolidated Omnibus Budget Reconciliation Act

COLA Cost of Living Adjustment

COLI Corporate-Owned Life Insurance

COR Cost of Risk

CPCU Chartered Property and Casualty Underwriter

CPI Consumer Price Index

CPP Commercial Package Policy

CRM Customer Relationship Management

CRT Charitable Remainder Trust

CRUSAP Critical Review of the U.S. Actuarial Profession

CSI Commissioners Standard Industrial Mortality Table

CSO Commissioners Standard Ordinary Mortality Table

D

DB&C Dwelling, Buildings, and Contents Insurance
DCAP Dental Care Assistance Plans
DI Disability Income
DICLP Difference in Conditions Liability Policy
DOC Drive Other Car Insurance
DWI Driving While Intoxicated

E

EAPs Employee Assistance Programs
EEB Earnings Enhancement Benefit
EEL Emergency Exposure Limit
EGTRRA Economic Growth and Tax Relief Reconciliation Act
ERISA Employee Retirement Income Security Act of 1974
ESOP Employee Stock Ownership Plan
EVOIL Economic Value of an Individual Life

F

FACA Federal Insurance Contributions Act
FAIR Fair Access to Insurance Requirements Plan
FAP Family Automobile Policy
FASB Financial Accounting Standards Board
FCAS Fellow, Casualty Actuarial Society
FDIC Federal Deposit Insurance Corporation
FEGLI Federal Employee Group Life Insurance
FELA Federal Employers Liability Act

FIRREA Financial Institutions Reform, Recovery, and Enforcement Act
FLMI Fellow, Life Management Institute
FMLA Family Medical Leave Act
FPA Free of Particular Average
FSA Fellow, Society of Actuaries
FSLIC Federal Savings and Loan Insurance Corporation
FTC Federal Trade Commission

G

GA General Agent
GAAP Generally Accepted Accounting Principles
GAB General Adjustment Bureau
GAMC General Agents and Managers Conference
GDP Gross Domestic Product
GIC Guaranteed Investment Contract
GLBA Gramm-Leach Bliley Financial Services Modernization Act
GMDB Guaranteed Minimum Death Benefit
GMIB Guaranteed Minimum Income Benefit
GMWB Guaranteed Minimum Withdrawal Benefit
GNP Gross National Product

H

HIAA Health Insurance Association of America
HMO Health Maintenance Organization
HOLUA Home Office Life Underwriters Association

HRA Health Reimbursement Arrangement
HSA Health Savings Account

I

IBNR Incurred But Not Reported Losses
ICC Interstate Commerce Commission
IIA Insurance Institute of America
IIAA Independent Insurance Agents of America
IPG Immediate Participation Guarantee Plan
IPO Initial Public Offering
IRA Individual Retirement Account
IRD Income in Respect of a Decedent
IRIS Insurance Regulatory Information System
ISO Insurance Services Office

L

LANs Loca Area Networks
LBO Leveraged Buyout
LGEAN Local Government Environmental Assistance Network
LIC Life Insurers Conference
LIMRA Life Insurance Marketing and Research Association
LOMA Life Office Management Association
LTC Long-Term Care
LUPAC Life Underwriter Political Action Committee
LUTC Life Underwriting Training Council

M

MAPs Market Assistance Plans

MCO Managed Care Organization
MDO Monthly Debit Ordinary Insurance
MDRT Million Dollar Round Table
MFL Maximum Forseeable Loss
MIB Medical Information Bureau
MPL Maximum Probable Loss
MSVR Mandatory Securities Valuation Reserve
MVA Market Value Adjustment

N

NAFTA North American Free Trade Agreement
NAIC National Association of Insurance Commissioners
NAII National Association of Independent Insurance Adjusters
NALC National Association of Life Companies
NALU National Association of Life Underwriting
NASD National Association of Securities Dealers
NATB National Automobile Theft Bureau
NAV Net Asset Value
NFIA National Flood Insurers Association
NFPA National Fire Protection Association
NIMCRUT Net Income with Make-up Provision Charitable Remainder Unitrust
NSLI National Service Life Insurance

O

OASDHI Old Age, Survivors, Disability, and Health Insurance

OCF Operating Cash Flow

OFAC Office of Foreign Assets Control of the U.S. Treasury

OPIC Overseas Private Investment Corporation

OSHA Occupational Safety and Health Act

P

PAC Preauthorized Check System

P&I Protection and Indemnity Insurance

PAP Personal Automobile Policy

PAYSOP Payroll Stock Ownership Plans

PBGC Pension Benefit Guaranty Corporation

P/E Price/Earnings Ratio

PEL Permissible Exposure Limit

PERI Public Entity Risk Institute

PHO Physician Hospital Organization

PIA Primary Insurance Amount

PIA Professional Insurance Agents

PIP Personal Injury Protection

PMI Private Mortgage Insurance

PML Probable Maximum Loss

POS Point-of-Service

PPGA Personal Producing General Agent

PPO Preferred Provider Organization

PSRO Professional Standards Review Organization

Q

QDIA Qualified Default Investment Alternative

QIC Quality Insurance Congress

Q-LTC Qualified Long-Term Care

QPIP Qualified Plan Insurance Partnership

QPRT Qualified Personal Residence Trust

QTIP Qualified Terminable Interest Property Trust

QRP Qualified Retirement Planner

R

RAM Reverse-Annuity Mortgage

RBCS Risk-Based Capital Statistic

RBD Required Beginning Date

RICO Racketeer Influenced and Corrupt Organizations Act of 1970

RIMS Risk and Insurance Management Society

RMD Required Minimum Distribution

RONW Return on Net Worth

RRSP Registered Retirement Savings Plan

S

SA Society of Actuaries

SAA Surety Association of America

S&P500 Standard & Poor's 500 Stock Price Index

SBLI Savings Bank Life Insurance

SCHIP Standard Children's Health Insurance Program

SCLP Simplified Commercial Lines Portfolio Policy

SEC Securities and Exchange Commission

SEP Simplified Employee Pension

SERP Supplemental Executive Retirement Plan

SEUA South-Eastern Under-writers Association Case

SGLI Servicemen's Group Life Insurance

SIPC Securities Investor Protection Corporation

SIR Self-Insured Retention

SMP Special Multiperil Insurance. Replaced by COMMERCIAL PACKAGE POLICY

SSAP Statutory Statement of Accounting Principle

SSI Supplemental Security Income

T

TAMRA Technical and Miscellaneous Revenue Act of 1988

TDA Tax Deferred Annuity

TEFRA Tax Equity and Financial Responsibility Acts of 1982 and 1983

TIAA-CREF Teachers Insurance and Annuity Association—College Retirement Equities Fund

TIRB Transportation Insurance Rating Bureau

TLO Total Loss Only Insurance

TOD Transfer on Death

TSA Tax-Sheltered Annuity

U

UCR Uusual, Customary and Reasonable Charges

UL Underwriters Laboratories, Inc.

USSERA Uniform Service Employment and Re-employ-ment Rights Act

UTMA Uniform Transfers to Minors Act

V

VA Veterans Administration

VGLI Veterans Group Life Insurance

VUL Variable Universal Life

W

WP Waiver of Premium

Y

YRT Yearly Renewable Term

YTM Yield to Maturity

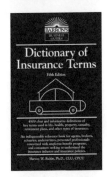